ISBN 978-0-428-34367-5
PIBN 10526040

LIBRARY OF CONGRESS

A LIST OF GEOGRAPHICAL ATLASES IN THE LIBRARY OF CONGRESS

WITH BIBLIOGRAPHICAL NOTES

COMPILED UNDER THE DIRECTION OF

PHILIP LEE PHILLIPS

CHIEF DIVISION OF MAPS

VOLUME IV

TITLES 4088–5324

WASHINGTON
GOVERNMENT PRINTING OFFICE
1920

L. C. card, 9—35009

For sale by the
Superintendent of Documents
Government Printing Office
Washington, D. C.

Price, $1.25

PREFATORY NOTE.

This volume contains a description of all the atlases received in the Library of Congress, from 1914 to the present date.

The titles are all numbered and the sequence is followed throughout each volume. Volume one, published in 1909, contains titles 1–3265; volume two, author list and index; volume three, titles 3266–4087; volume four, titles 4088–5324.

No attempt has been made to make any changes in the descriptive plan of the work. The usefulness of the copious indexes of the previous volumes and the ease with which they may be consulted sufficiently justify the continuance of them as a model. The present volume numbers 1237 titles. The former author lists have been combined in one general alphabet, making a complete index of all the authors whose works are contained in the collection. The prefaces to volumes one and three should be consulted for information as to the method pursued in the compilation of the complete work.

The county atlases of the states of the United States, which make up a considerable portion of this volume, are the atlases in the Division most consulted, especially by the various departments of the Government in their reference work.

The following are some of the rare items, especially to be noted:

Blaeu, Joan.
    Atlas maior. [1662–1672]
    Atlas mayor. [1659–1672]
Blaeu, William Janszoon.
    The light of navigation. 1622.
Burr, David H.
    American atlas. [1839]
English, The, pilot. The third book. 1716.
Goos, Pieter.
    The lighting colomne. 1660–[1661]
Jansson, Jan.
    Des nieuwen atlantis aenhang ofte des nieuwen wereld-beschrijvinghe. 1644.
Loon, Joannes van, and Voogt, C. J.
    Die nieuwe groote lichtende zee-fackel. [1699–1702]
Mercator, Gerard.
    Atlas minor. [1608]
    Italiae, Sclavoniæ, et Graeciæ tabule geographice. [1589]
Norman, John.
    The american pilot. 1794.
Norman, William.
    The american pilot. 1803.
Ortelius, Abraham.
    Theatro del mondo. [1655]

Ottens, Reiner.
Atlas maior. [1641–1729]

Rueda, Manuel de.
Atlas americano, desde la isla de Puerto-Rico, hasta el puerto de Vera-Cruz. [1766]

Sanson, Nicolas, d'Abbeville.
Cartes générales de tovtes les parties dv monde. 1658.

Seller, John.
Atlas maritimus. Editions of 1670? 1671? 1672? 1675.

Tavernier, Melchior.
Théâtre géographiqve dv royavme de France. 1638.

Waghenaer, Luc Janszoon.
Spieghel der zeevaerdt. 1585.

Wit, Frederik de.
Atlas minor. [1634–1708]

Wytfliet, Corneille.
Histoire vniverselle des Indes Occidentales et Orientales. 1611.

P. LEE PHILLIPS,
Chief, Division of Maps.

HERBERT PUTNAM,
Librarian of Congress,
Washington, 1920.

CONTENTS

Numbers refer to titles

VOLUME IV

AUTHOR LIST

Numbers refer to main entries

*Refers to works received too late to be entered under subjects.

Alaskan boundary tribunal.
Appendix to the case of his majesty's government. v. 2. Atlas. 1903.... 1192
British case. Atlas. 1903.... 1261
Case of the United States. Atlas. 1903.... 1193, 1259
Counter case of the United States. Atlas. 1903.... 1194, 1260
Proceedings. Atlas. 1904.... 1452

Alden, John B.
Home atlas. 1887.... 936

Alden, Ogle & co.
Plat book of Fayette county, Ill. 1891.... 1531
Plat book of Macon county, Ill. 1891.... 1549
Plat book of Marshall and Putnam counties, Ill. 1890.... 1553, 1561

Alden publishing co.
Standard atlas of Barnes county, N. Dak. 1910.... 3855
Standard atlas of Fillmore county, Nebr. 1905.... 2110
Standard atlas of Lyon county, Iowa. 1911.... 3748
Standard atlas of Norman county, Minn. 1910.... 3813
Standard atlas of Richland county, N. Dak. 1910.... 3863
Standard atlas of Walsh county, N. Dak. 1910.... 3867

Allard, Carolus.
Atlas minor. [1696?].... 523
Magnum theatrum belli. [1702].... 538

Allen, C. R.
Illustrated atlas of Harrison county, Iowa. 1884.... 1668
Illustrated atlas of Pottawattamie county, Iowa. 1885.... 1692

Allen, Fawcett, 1876–
Atlas of commercial geography. 1913.... 4107

Allodi, Pietro, *and* **Naymiller, F.**
Atlante di geografia universale. [1867].... 851

Alphen, Pieter van.
Nieuwe zee-atlas. 1682.... 491

Alting, Menso, 1637–1713, *and* **Schotanus à Sterringa, B.**
Uitbeelding der heerlijkeit Friesland zoo in't algemeen, als in haare xxx bijzondere grietenijen. 1718.... 3088

American atlas co.
Atlas and directory of Madison county, Ind. 1901.... 1617
Plat book of Coles county, Ill. 1893.... 1525
Plat book of Fulton county, Ill. 1895.... 1533
Plat book of Hillsdale county, Mich. 1894.... 1972
Plat book of Morgan county, Ill. 1894.... 1555

American baptist missionary union.
Missionary atlas. 1908.... 3337

American exporter.
Concise atlas of the world. [1912].... 4382

American express co.
Note book and atlas. 1889.... 948
Tourist's pocket atlas. 1881.... 893

American hotel register co.
Leahy's hotel guide and railway distance maps of America. 1916.... 4467

American tract society.
Bible atlas and gazetteer. [1862].... 79

Ancelin, ——— *and* Le Grand, ———

Atlas général et élémentaire de l'empire de toutes les Russies. 1795...... 4061

Anderson & Goodwin co.

Standard historical atlas of Plymouth county, Iowa. 1907................ 1690
Standard historical atlas of Sioux county, Iowa. 1908.................. 1695
Standard historical atlas of Winneshiek county, Iowa. 1905............. 1708

Anderson publishing co.

Atlas of Adams county, Nebr. 1919............................ *
Atlas of Allamakee county, Iowa. 1917......................... 4621
Atlas of Benton county, Iowa. 1917............................ 4623
Atlas of Boone county, Iowa. 1918............................. 4624
Atlas of Buffalo county, Nebr. 1919........................... *
Atlas of Butler and Polk counties, Nebr. 1918..................4878, 4901
Atlas of Butler county, Iowa. 1917............................ 4626
Atlas of Cass county, Iowa. 1917.............................. 4627
Atlas of Cass county, Nebr. 1918.............................. 4879
Atlas of Cedar county, Iowa. 1916............................. 4628
Atlas of Cerro Gordo county, Iowa. [1912]..................... 3744a
Atlas of Clay county, Iowa. 1919.............................. 4630a
Atlas of Cuming county, Nebr. 1918............................ 4883
Atlas of Dallas county, Iowa. 1916............................ 4632
Atlas of Dawson county, Nebr. 1919............................ *
Atlas of Dodge county, Nebr. 1918............................. 4885
Atlas of Fillmore county, Nebr. 1918.......................... 4887
Atlas of Floyd county, Iowa. 1913............................. 4637
Atlas of Hancock county, Iowa. 1914........................... 4641
Atlas of Iowa county, Iowa. 1917.............................. 4643
Atlas of Kossuth county, Iowa. 1913........................... 4646
Atlas of Monona county, Iowa. 1919............................ 4651
Atlas of Muscatine county, Iowa. 1916......................... 4652
Atlas of Pocahontas county, Iowa. 1918........................ 4654
Atlas of Pottawattamie county, Iowa. 1919..................... *
Atlas of Saline county, Nebr. 1918............................ 4903
Atlas of Saunders county, Nebr. 1916.......................... 4905
Atlas of Sioux county, Iowa. 1913............................. 4659
Atlas of Tama county, Iowa. 1916.............................. 4660
Atlas of Winnebago county, Iowa. 1913......................... 4664
Atlas of Woodbury county, Iowa. 1917.......................... 4666
Standard historical atlas of Chickasaw county, Iowa. 1915..... 4629
Standard historical atlas of Mills and Fremont counties, Iowa. 1910.. 3746, 3749
Standard historical atlas of Mitchell county, Iowa. 1911...... 3750
Standard historical atlas of Nodaway county, Mo. 1911......... 3819
Standard historical atlas of Worth county, Iowa. 1913......... 4667

Andreas, Albert T.

Atlas map of Richland county, Ohio. 1873...................... 2411
Atlas map of Vigo county, Ind. 1874........................... 3740
Historical atlas of Dakota. 1884.............................. 2339, 2572
Illustrated historical atlas of the state of Iowa. 1875....... 1639
Illustrated historical atlas of the state of Minnesota. 1874.. 2007

Andreas, Lyter & co.

Atlas map of Morgan county, Ill. 1872......................... 1554
Atlas map of Pike county, Ill. 1872........................... 1559
Atlas map of Scott county, Ill. 1873.......................... 1565
Atlas map of Tazewell county, Ill. 1873....................... 1571

Badeslade, Thomas.
Chorographia Britanniæ. 1742.......... 2916
—— 2d ed. 1745.......... *

Bæck, Elias, 1679–1747.
Atlas geographicus. [1710].......... 555

Bär, Johann Christian, *and* **Stülpnagel, F. von.**
Eisenbahn-atlas von Deutschland, Belgien, Elsass und dem nördlichsten theile von Italien. 1856.......... 2798

Bailly-Baillière & hijos.
Atlas de las cinco partes. [1900?].......... 1046
Mapas de las cuarenta y nueve provincias de España. 1904.......... 3139

Baist, George William.
Atlas of Camden, N. J. 1886.......... 2175
Atlas of Long Branch, N. J. 1886.......... 2186
Atlas of Philadelphia. 1888.......... 2535
Atlas of properties along the Schuylkill valley from Philadelphia to Norristown. 1886.......... 2447
Atlas of the city of Lancaster, Pa. 1886.......... 5022
Atlas of the city of Richmond, Va. 1889.......... 5071
Atlas of Wilmington, Del. 1887.......... 1494
Plat book of the city of Detroit and suburbs, Mich. 1916.......... 4771
Property atlas of Birmingham, Ala. 1902.......... 1450
Property atlas of Camden, N. J. 1902.......... 2176
Property atlas of Milwaukee and vicinity, Wis. 1898.......... 2676
Real estate atlas of surveys of Columbus and vicinity, Ohio. 1910.......... 3881
Real estate atlas of surveys of Denver, Col. 1905.......... 3708
Real estate atlas of surveys of Detroit, Mich. 1906.......... 2004
Real estate atlas of surveys of Detroit and Highland Park, Mich. 1911.......... 3809
Real estate atlas of surveys of Detroit and suburbs, Mich. 1915.......... 4770
—— 1918.......... 4772
Real estate atlas of surveys of Indianapolis and vicinity, Ind. 1908.......... 1638
—— 1916.......... 4619
Real estate atlas of surveys of Los Angeles, Cal. 1905.......... 3706
—— 1910.......... 3707
—— 1914.......... 4540
Real estate atlas of surveys of Omaha, Nebr. 1910.......... 3831
—— 1918.......... 4913
Real estate atlas of surveys of Seattle, Wash. 1905.......... 2626
—— 1908.......... 2626a
—— 1912.......... 3929
Real estate altas of surveys of Washington, D. C. 1903.......... 1505
—— 1907.......... 1506
—— 1909–1911.......... 3716
—— 1913–1915.......... 4550
—— v. 1. 1919.......... 4552

Baker, Marion M.
Historical geography maps of the United States. [1914].......... 4504

Baker, Oliver Edwin, 1883–, *and* **Finch, V. C.**
Geography of the world's agriculture. 1917.......... 4088

Baker & Tilden.
Atlas of Hartford city and county. 1869.......... 1478, 1487

Baldwin, M. C.
Popular atlas. 1885.......... 4362

Beers, Frederick W.

Bellue, Pierre.
Atlas ou Neptune des cartes de la mer Méditerranée. 1830–[1834]........ 189

Belmas, Jacques Vital, 1792–1864.
Journaux des sièges faits ou soutenus par les français dans la péninsule de 1807 à 1814. 1836........ 2964

Benazech, Peter, *engraver.*
See Pownall, Thomas. Six remarkable views in the provinces of New-York, New-Jersey, and Pennsylvania, in North America. [1761]

Benians, E. A., *and* **Knight, T. H.**
Historical atlas. 1908........ 2880a

Bennet, John, *and* **Sayer, R.**
American military pocket atlas. [1776]........ 1206, 1343

Bennet, Roelof Gabriel, 1774–1829, *and* **Wijk Roelandszoon, J. van.**
Verhandeling over de nederlandsche ontdekkingen in Amerika, Australië, de Indiën en de Poollanden. Atlas. 1827........ 1134, 3072a, 3252

Bennett, L. G., *and* **Smith, A. C.**
Map of Winona county, Minn. 1867........ 2046

Berecz, Antal, 1836–, **Brózik, K.,** *and* **Erödi, B.**
Nagy magyar atlasz. 1906........ 2865

Berghaus, Heinrich Karl Wilhelm, 1797–1884.
Atlas von Asia. 1832–1843........ 3175
Physikalischer atlas. 1850–1851........ 215
—— 2. aufl. 1852........ 216
—— 3. ausg. 1892........ 217
Physikalischer schul-atlas. 1850........ 214

Berghaus, Hermann, 1828–1890.
Schul-atlas der österreichischen monarchie. 1855........ 2861

Berlandier, Luis, *d.* 1851, *& others.*
Voyage au Mexique. Vues diverses. 1827–1831. *ms*........ 5117

Bernard, Guillaume.
See Barendsz, Willem, 1560?–1597.

Berry, William.
[Collection of maps of the world. 1680–1689]........ 3442

Bertius, Petrus, 1565–1629.
Geographischer eyn oder zusammengezogener tabeln. 1612........ 3413
P. Bertii tabvlarvm geographicvm. Editio secvnda. 1602........ 414
—— 1606........ 3409

Bettencourt, Emiliano Augusto de.
Atlas pecuario de Portugal. [1870]........ 3095

Bevan, George Phillips, *d.* 1889.
Royal relief atlas. 3d ed. 1885........ 245
Sonnenschein & Allen's royal relief atlas. [1880]........ 3352
Statistical atlas of England, Scotland and Ireland. 1882........ 2890

Beyer, Carlos.
Atlas general de la república Argentina. 6. ed. 1893........ 5135

Beyer, Carlos, *and* **Biedma, J. J.**
Atlas histórico de la república Argentina. 1909........ 3955

Bianco, Andrea, *15th century.*
[Fac-simile dell' atlante di Andrea Bianco dell' anno 1436. 1869]........ 3356
—— 1879........ 247

Brown, Milton R.
Continental atlas. 1889 .... 949, 1428

Brown, W. S., *and* **Foote, C. M.**
Plat book of Brown county, Wis. 1889 2636
Plat book of Dunn county, Wis. 1888 2644
Plat book of Waupaca county, Wis. 1889 2670

Browne, C. H.
Atlas adapted for the eighth, seventh, sixth, and fifth grammar grades. 1883 270
Butler's atlas. 1883 269

Brózik, Károly, 1849–, **Erödi, B.,** *and* **Berecz, A.**
Nágy magyar atlasz. 1906 2865

Brué, Adrien Hubert, 1786–1832.
Atlas. [1826] 3546
Atlas classique de géographie. 2. éd. 1830–[1832] 6
Atlas universel. 2. éd. 1830–[1834] 758
—— 2. éd. 1838–[1839] 4321
Grand atlas universel. 1816 726

Bruhns, Karl Christian, 1830–1881, **Kiepert, H., Gräf, C.,** *and* **Gräf, A.**
Hand atlas. [1874?] 871

Brunamonti, G., Danesi, C., *and* **Gibelli, G.**
Desegni e descrittioni delle fortezze . . . e fanteria dello stato ecclesiastico. [1888] 3056

Brunner, A., *and* **Voigt, L.**
Deutscher handelsschul-atlas. 3. aufl. [1913] 4189

Bryant literary union.
Panorama of the Hudson. 1888 3838

Bryce, James, 1838–, **Collier, W. F.,** *and* **Schmitz, L.**
International atlas. [1880?] 891

Buache, Philippe, 1700–1773.
Considérations géographiques . . . sur les nouvelles découvertes au nord de la Grande mer. 1753–[1754] 3342

Buache, Philippe, *and* **Delisle, G.**
Atlas géographique des quatre parties du monde. [1769–1799] 3512
—— [1789?] 671
—— [1831?] 759
[Atlas géographique et universel. 1700–1762] 3456
Atlas géographique et universel. 1781–[1784] 655
Cartes et tables de la géographie physique. 1754–[1757] 220

Buchon, Jean Alexandre C., 1789–1846.
Atlas géographique . . . des Amériques. 1825 1176

Buchon, Jean Alexandre C., *and* **Tastu, J.**
[Atlas catalan, 1375] 4251

Buck, Thaddeus E.
Atlas of Morrow county, Ohio. 1901 2404

Bulifon, Antoine.
Accuratissima e nuova delineazione del regno di Napoli. [1692] 3067

Bullard co.
Red road book for all New England and eastern New York. 1914 4516

Bulleit, F. A.
Illustrated atlas of Harrison county, Ind. 1906 1610

114882°—19——III

Cram, George F., co.
Descriptive review . . . of Pennsylvania. 1916........ 5012
—— 1917........ 5013
European historical atlas. 1918........ *
Historical war atlas of Europe. 1917........ 4220
History-atlas. "Story of the great war." 1919........ 4220a
Ideal reference atlas of the world. 1916........ 4425
Modern reference atlas. 1917........ 4435
United States at war. 1918........ 4222
Unrivaled atlas of the world. 1916........ 4132
—— 1917........ 4436

Cram, George F., & co.
Atlas of the war in Europe. 1914........ 4218
Historical atlas of Europe. 1916........ 5156
United States at war—American war atlas. 1917........ 4221

Cram atlas company.
New commercial atlas of the United States. [1875]........ 1275

Cramer, Louis H., *and* **Beers, F. W.**
Combination atlas of Saratoga and Ballston. 1876........ 2270, 2324

Cramer, Zadok, 1773–1813.
Navigator. 1806........ 1312
—— 1808........ 1313
—— 1811........ 1314
—— 1814........ 1315
—— 1817........ 1316
—— 1818........ 1317

Cramp, K. R., *and* **Bartholomew, J. G.**
Australasian school atlas. 1915........ 5317

Crawford, D. C.
Atlas of Ionia county, Mich. 1891........ 1975

Crawford, James Ludovic Lindsay, *26th earl of,* 1847–
Bibliotheca Lindesiana. Atlas. 1898........ 248

Crevaux, Jules Nicolas, 1847–1882.
Fleuves de l'Amérique du Sud, 1877–1879. 1883........ 2725

Croes, John James Robertson, 1834–1906.
Additions to, and revisions of the West Side atlas. [New York. 1879].... 2297

Croes & Van Winkle.
West side of the city of New York. [1873]........ 2294

Croscup, George Edward, 1851–
History made visible; a synchronic chart and statistical tables of United States history. 1910........ 4505
History made visible; United States history with synchronic charts. National ed. 1911........ 4506

Crowell & Kirkpatrick co.
New people's atlas. 1901........ 1062
New popular atlas. 1900........ 1048
Twentieth century peerless atlas. 1901........ 1063
Twentieth century pictorial atlas. 1901........ 1064
Twentieth century popular atlas. 1901........ 1065

Crowell publishing co.
Twentieth century peerless atlas. 1902........ 1076
—— 1903........ 1084
—— 1905........ 1099

Delamarche, Charles François, 1740–1817.
Atlas de géographie ancienne, du moyen-âge, et moderne. 1850 ... 3554
Atlas élémentaire. 1816 ... 727

Delamarche, Felix.
Atlas de la géographie ancienne et moderne. [1829?] ... 4317

Delesse, Achille Ernest Oscar Joseph, 1817–1881.
Lithologie du fond des mers . . . Atlas. 1872 ... 4161

Delisle, Guillaume, 1675–1726.
Atlante novissimo. 1740–1750 ... 594
Atlas de géographie. 1700–1712 ... 533
Atlas nouveau. 1730 ... 3486
—— 1733 ... 580, 581, 3487
—— [1741?] ... 596
Collection of maps of the world. 1722–1774 ... 565

Delisle, Guillaume, *and* **Buache, P.**
Atlas géographique des quatre parties du monde. [1769–1799] ... 3512
—— [1789?] ... 671
—— [1831?] ... 759
[Atlas géographique et universel. 1700–1762] ... 535, 636, 3456
Atlas géographique et universel. 1781–[1784] ... 655
Cartes et tables de la géographie physique. 1754–[1757] ... 220

Delisle, Guillaume, *& others.*
Atlas géographique et universel. 1789–[1790] ... 3525

Delisle, Joseph Nicolas, 1688–1768, *& others.*
Atlas rvssicvs. 1745 ... 4060
Атласъ россійской—Russian atlas. 1745 ... 4059
Russischer atlas. 1745 ... 3109

Delphi journal *and* **Hoosier democrat.**
Atlas and plat book of Carroll county, Ind. 1919 ... ..

Denaix, Maxime Auguste, *d.* 1844.
Atlas physique, politique et historique de la France. 1855 ... 4019
Atlas physique, politique et historique de l'Europe. 1855 ... 3965
—— 1860 ... 3966

Denis, Louis, *fl.* 1785.
Atlas géographique. [1764?] ... 3299
Empire des Solipses. 1764 ... 81

Denis, Louis, *and* **Pasquier, J. J.**
Plan topographique et raisonné de Paris. 1758 ... 3012

Denver weekly post.
Atlas containing . . . maps [of] Colorado, Utah, Wyoming . . . 1914 ... 4531
Atlas of the Rocky mountains and national forests. [1911] ... 3697

De Puy, William Harrison, 1821–1901.
People's atlas. [1885] ... 925
Universal guide and gazetteer. 1887 ... 940

Derok, D. J.
Атлас краљевина србије.—Atlas of Servia. 1911 ... 4063a

Desbuissons, L. E., 1827–, *& others.*
Nouvel atlas illustré. 1891 ... 964

[Descripcion de plazas, prendos y fuertes de las Filipinas. 1777?] ... 5304

Desmarest, Nicolas, 1725–1805, *and* **Bonne, R.**
Atlas encyclopédique. 1787–1788 ... 666, 667

Dow, Earle Wilbur, 1868–
Atlas of european history. 1907 2788

Dower, John.
New general atlas. 1831 3549
—— 1835 772
—— [1854] 812

Doyle, Joseph B., Barthel, O., Halfpenny, H. E., *and* **Hasson, T. W.**
Atlas of the city of Wheeling, W. Va. 1901 2630

Drioux, Claude Joseph, 1820–, *and* **Leroy, C.**
Atlas universel et classique. 1867 3562
—— 1879 889
—— 1882 3567
—— 1887 .... 940a

Dripps, Matthew.
Atlas of New Utrecht, Kings county, N. Y. [1887] 4940
Map of the city of Brooklyn, N. Y. 1869 2273
Plan of New York city from the battery to Spuyten Duyvil creek. 1867 2291

Droysen, Gustav, 1838–1908.
Allgemeiner historischer handatlas. 1886 105

Drury, Luke, *d.* 1845.
Geography for schools. 1822 279

Dubail, Augustin von Edmond, 1851–
Atlas de l'Europe militaire. 1880 2817

Dubois, Edmond Marcel, 1856–1916, *and* **Sieurin, E.**
Cartes d'étude pour servir à l'enseignement de la géographie. 7. éd. 1905 2857
Cartes d'étude pour servir à l'enseignement de la géographie . . . Amérique. 9. éd. 1905 281
Cartes d'étude pour servir à l'enseignement de la géographie . . . Asie, Insulinde, Afrique. 9. éd. 1905 280
Cartes d'étude pour servir à l'enseignement de la géographie. France et colonies. 9. éd. 1905 3009

Du Caille, Louis Alexandre.
Étrennes géographiques. 1760 .... 3505, 3506
—— 1760–1761 626

Dudley, *Sir* **Robert,** *styled duke of Northumberland and earl of Warwick,* 1573–1649.
Arcano del mare. 1661 3428
Dell' arcano del mare. 1646–1647 .... 457, 458

Duflot de Mofras, Eugène, 1810–1884.
Exploration du territoire de l'Orégon, des Californies et de la mer Vermeille . . . 1844 .... 1457, 2437

Dufour, Adolphe Hippolyte, 1798–1865.
Atlas géographique dressé pour l'histoire . . . de l'église catholique. 1861 3300
Atlas universel. 1860–[1861] 833
—— [1868] 852
Grand atlas univérsel. [1881] 894

Dufour, Adolphe Hippolyte, *and* **Duvotenay, T.**
France. Atlas des 86 départements et des colonies françaises. [1860?] 5227
Globo. Atlas historico universal de geografia. 1852 4331

English pilot.
Part I. 1715 ... 5179
—— 1718 ... 2837
—— 1747 ... 3496
Second part. 1716 ... 2836
—— 1723 ... 2838
Part III. Describing the . . . Mediterranean sea. 1736 ... 190, 2805
—— 1786 ... 191
Third book. 1716 ... 4278
—— 1748 ... 606
Fourth book. 1706 ... 1155
—— 1737 ... 1157
—— 1745 ... 3650
—— 1749 ... 3651
—— 1755 ... 3652
—— 1758 ... 1158
—— 1760 ... 1160
—— 1767 ... 1162, 1163
—— 1773 ... 3653
—— 1775 ... 1164
—— 1780 ... 1168
—— 1784 ... 1171
Part V. 1766 ... 3230
Describing the sea-coasts. 1775 ... 2844
Describing the West India navigation. 1789 ... 4460
For the southern navigation. 1758 ... 2842
—— 1764 ... 2843
—— 1790 ... 2846
—— 1792 ... 2847

Ensign, D. W., & co.
Atlas of Kane county, Ill. 1892 ... 1540
Plat book of Cass county, N. Dak. 1893 ... 2341
Plat book of DeKalb county, Ill. 1892 ... 1527
Plat book of Grand Forks, Walsh and Pembina counties, N. Dak. 1893 ... 2343

Erckert, Rodrich von, 1821–1900.
Wanderungen und siedelungen der germanischen stämme in Mittel-Europa. 1901 ... 2786

Erödi, Béla, 1846–, **Berecz, A.,** *and* **Brózik, K.**
Nagy magyar atlasz. 1906 ... 2865

Erskine, R.
To the right honorable s[r] Charles Wager . . . these views, plans and remarks are most humbly inscribed. *ms.* [1727–1734] ... 2804

Escudé y Bartolí, Manuel, 1856–
Atlas geográfico ibero-americano. [1900–1903] ... 5288

Espinosa y Tello, José, 1763–1815.
Relacion del viage hecho por las goletas Sutil y Mexicana . . . 1792 Atlas. 1802 ... 1221

Espinoza, Enrique, 1848–
Atlas de Chile. [1897] ... 2758

Estévanez, Nicolas.
Atlas geográfico de América. [1896] ... 4458

Estrada, Angel, & cia.
Atlas general de la república Argentina. 9. ed. 1910 5136
Atlas general de las dos Américas. 1907 4465

Euler, Leonhard, 1707–1783.
Atlas geographicus. 1753 3500
Geographischer atlas. 1760 625

Evans, *Rev.* **John,** 1767–1827.
New royal atlas. [1810] 717

Evening post co.
Atlas of american cities. [1910–1911] 3674
Louisville Evening post's atlas of the world. 1910–1911 3616

Everts, L. H.
Combination atlas map of Fairfield county, Ohio. 1875 2375
Combination atlas map of Licking county, Ohio. 1875 2394
New historical atlas of Butler county, Ohio. 1875 2357

Everts, L. H., & co.
Illustrated historical atlas of Miami county, Ohio. 1875 4986
Official state atlas of Kansas. 1887 1710

Everts, Baskin & Stewart.
Combination atlas map of McHenry county, Ill. 1872 4577
Combination atlas map of Rock county, Wis. 1873 2660
Combination atlas map of Walworth county, Wis. 1873 2665

Everts, Ensign & Everts.
Combination atlas map of Genesee county, New York. 1876 .... 3839c
Combination atlas map of Yates county, N. Y. 1876 4935

Everts & Kirk.
Official state atlas of Nebraska. 1885 2107

Everts & Richards.
New topographical atlas of surveys, Bristol county, Mass. 1895 1811
New topographical atlas of surveys, Providence county, R. I. 1895 2563

Everts & Stewart.
Combination atlas map of Dauphin county, Pa. 1875 2473
Combination atlas map of Jackson county, Mich. 1874 1977
Combination atlas map of Lenawee county, Mich. 1874 1984
Combination atlas map of Middlesex county, N. J. 1876 2165
Combination atlas map of St. Clair county, Mich. 1876 3807
Combination atlas map of Salem & Gloucester counties, N. J. 1876 ... 2159, 2169
Combination atlas map of Washtenaw county, Mich. 1874 2000

Everts publishing co.
New century atlas of counties of the state of New York. 1911 .... 3839a
—— 1912 .... 3839b

Faden, William, 1750–1836.
Atlas minimus universalis. 1798 690
Atlas of battles of the american revolution. [1845?] 1337
North American atlas. 1777 .... 1207, 1208
See also Petit, Le, neptune français.

Faehtz, Ernest F. M., *and* **Pratt, F. W.**
Real estate directory of the city of Washington, D. C. 1874 .... 1498, 3714
—— [1874] 3715

Gurrey, Alfred R.
Honolulu. [1906] 3263
Map of Honolulu. 1900 3262

Guthe, Hermann.
Bibelatlas . . . 1911 4080

Guthrie, William, 1708–1770.
Atlas universel. 1802 698
General atlas. 1820 738

Haack, Hermann, 1872- , *and* **Hertzberg, H.**
Grosser historischer wandatlas. [1912–1916?] 4134a

Haack, Hermann, *and* **Lüddecke, R.**
Deutscher schulatlas. 3. aufl. 1901 299
—— 7. aufl. 1914 4200

Habenicht, Hermann, 1844–1917, *and* **Sydow, E. von**
Methodischer wand-atlas. [1906–1915] 4176

Hacke, William.
Description of the sea coasts rivers &a. of Monomotapa . . . *ms.* [1690?] 3162

Hagelgans, Johann Georg, *d.* 1765.
Atlas historicus. 1751 3308

Hagnauer, Robert, Dickson, G. K., *and* **Riniker, H.**
New atlas of Madison county, Ill. 1892 1551

Hague, Arnold, 1840–1917.
Atlas to accompany monograph XXXII on the geology of the Yellowstone national park. 1904 5115
Atlas to accompany the monograph on the geology of the Eureka district, Nevada. 1883 2131

Hales, John Groves, 1785–1832.
Plans and records of the streets, lanes, courts, places, &c. in the town of Boston. 1894 4718

Halfeld, Henrique Guilherme Fernando, 1797–1873.
Atlas e relatorio concernente a exploração do rio de S. Francisco desde Cachoévia da Pirapóra até ao oceano Atlantico. 1860 2745

Halfpenny, H. E., *and* **Caldwell, J. W.**
Atlas of Oxford county, Me. 1880 3763

Halfpenny, H. E., Hasson, T. W., Doyle, J. B., *and* **Barthel, O.**
Atlas of the city of Wheeling, W. Va. 1901 2630

Hall, Basil, 1788–1844.
Forty etchings, from sketches made . . . in North America, in 1827 and 1828. 1829 4469

Hall, Sidney.
Black's general atlas. 1840 777
—— 1841 779
New general atlas. 1830 756
—— [1857] 821
Travelling county atlas [of England, 1846] 2928
See also Black, Adam, 1784–1874, *and* Black, Charles.

Hall, Sidney, Hughes, W., *& others.*
Black's general atlas. 1844 793
—— 1851 4328
—— 1852 4330
—— 1854 4333
See also Black, Adam, 1784–1874, *and* Black, Charles.

Hammond, C. S., & co.—Continued.
Pocket atlas of the United States. 1918........ 4535
Pocket atlas of the world. 1910........ 3606
Popular atlas of the world. 1911........ 3620
—— 1916[1915]........ 4427
Ready reference atlas. [1906]........ 1111
—— [1910]........ 3607
Record atlas of the world war. 1918........ 4226
Standard atlas of the world. 1st ed. 1914........ 4412
—— 1917........ 4439
Telegram & times concise atlas of the world. 1913........ 4397
United States army and navy pictorial. [1917]........ 4226a
War atlas. 1914........ 4227

Hammond publishing co.
Plat book of Greene and Jersey counties, Ill. 1893........ 1534, 1538

Hancock, C. F., *and* **Weston, W. J.**
Plat book of Houghton county, Mich. 1911........ 3803

Handtke, Friedrich H., 1815–1879.
Special-karte der europäischen Turkei. [1876]........ 3159

Hannak, Emanuel, 1841–1899, *and* **Umlauft, F.**
Historischer schulatlas. 1908........ 2789a

Hannum, E. S.
Atlas of Fairfield county, Ohio. 1866........ 4985

Hansteen, Christopher, 1784–1873.
Magnetischer atlas. 1819........ 224

Hantzsch, Viktor, *i. e.* **Karl Viktor Gustav,** 1868–
Die ältesten gedruckten karten der Sächsisch-Thüringischen länder. [1905]........ 3042

Hantzsch, Viktor, *i. e.* **Karl Viktor Gustav,** *and* **Schmidt, L.**
Kartographische denkmäler zur entdeckungsgeschichte von Amerika, Asien, Australien und Afrika. 1903........ 250

Hardesty, Hiram H.
Historical and geographical encyclopedia. 1883........ 1287, 2350
—— 1884........ 1288, 2351

Hardesty, L. Q.
Illustrated historical atlas of Ottawa county, Ohio. 1874........ 3877

Harms, Heinrich.
Vaterländischer reform-schulatlas. [1911]........ 3371

Harmsworth atlas and gazetteer. [1908]........ 1132

Harrisburg title co.
Atlas of the city of Harrisburg, Dauphin county, Penn. 1901........ 2512

Harrison, R. H.
Illustrated historical atlas of Scotland county, Mo. 1876........ 4873

Harrison, R. H., *& others.*
Atlas of Hamilton county, Ohio. 1869........ 2381, 2422

Harrison, Sutton & Hare.
Atlas of Marion county, Ohio. 1878........ 2398
Atlas of Union county, Ohio. 1877........ 4990

Harrison & Warner.
Atlas of Benton county, Iowa. 1872 1644
Atlas of Cedar county, Iowa. 1872 1651
Atlas of Clinton county, Iowa. 1874 1655
Atlas of Columbia county, Wis. 1873 2638
Atlas of Dane county, Wis. 1873 2641
Atlas of Dodge county, Wis. 1873 2642
Atlas of Dubuque county, Iowa. 1874 1657
Atlas of Green county, Wis. 1873 2647
Atlas of Hardin county, Iowa. 1875 1667
Atlas of Iowa county, Iowa. 1874 1673
Atlas of Keokuk county, Iowa. 1874 1679
Atlas of Madison county, Iowa. 1875 1682
Atlas of Marion county, Iowa. 1875 1684
Atlas of Marshall county, Iowa. 1871 1685
Atlas of Muscatine county, Iowa. 1874 1688
Atlas of Tama county, Iowa. 1875 1697
Atlas of Warren county, Iowa. 1872 1702
Atlas of Washington county, Iowa. 1874 1704
Atlas of Waukesha county, Wis. 1873 2668
Illustrated historical atlas of Adair county, Mo. 1876 .... 1395, 2064, 2066

Harrower, Henry Draper, *and* **Mecutchen, S.**
Pocket atlas. [1887] 941

Harrower, Henry Draper, *and* **Swinton, W.**
Descriptive atlas of the United States. [1884] 1419

Hart, Albert Bushnell, 1854–
Epoch maps illustrating american history. 1891 .... 1188, 1289
—— 1893 4466
—— 1899 .... 1189, 1290
—— 1904 .... 1190, 1291
—— 1910 3662

Hart, Joseph C., *d.* 1855.
Modern atlas. 5th ed. 1828 290
—— 7th ed. 1830 .... 291, 757

Hartleben, Alors, 1859–
Volks-atlas. [1910?] 3608

Hartley, F. G.
Atlas of business district of Des Moines, Iowa. 1913 4669

Haskell, W. W.
Atlas of Valley county, Nebr. 1904 3829

Hassenstein, Bruno, 1839–1902.
Atlas von Japan. 1885–1887 3210

Hasson, Thomas W., Doyle, J. B., Barthel, O., *and* **Halfpenny, H. E.**
Atlas of the city of Wheeling, W. Va. 1901 2630

Hastain, E.
Township plats of the Creek nation. [1910] 3883
Township plats of the Seminole nation. 1913 5006

Havenga, W. J.
Atlas van nederlandsch Oost-Indië. 1885 ....

Hawes, J. B.
[Maps showing the consular and diplomatic offices of the United States. 189-?] ... 4498

Hawkesworth, John, 1715?-1773.
Account of the voyages. Atlas. [1773] ... 642, 3241

Hayden, Ferdinand Vandiveer, 1829-1887.
Geological and geographical atlas of Colorado. 1877 ... 1473
—— 1881 ... 3707a

Hayes, E. L.
Atlas of Grand Traverse county, Mich. 1881 ... 1969
Atlas of Isabella county, Mich. 1879 ... 1976
Atlas of Leelanau county, Mich. 1881 ... 1983
Atlas of Mecosta county, Mich. 1879 ... 1987
Atlas of Newaygo county, Mich. 1880 ... 1992
Atlas of Osceola county, Mich. 1878 ... 1995
Atlas of Sebastain county, Ark. [1887] ... 1455
Illustrated atlas of the upper Ohio river. 1877 ... 2348, 2442

Haynes, M. B.
Atlas of Renville county, Minn. 1888 ... 2037

Hayward & Howard.
Atlas of the city of Brockton, Mass. 1898 ... 1866

He mau palapala aina a me na niele e pili ana. 1840 ... 778, 3259
—— 1842 ... 4087

He ninau no ka palapala honau. [1860?] ... 830, 3260

Heather, William.
Marine atlas. [1804] ... 704
—— [1808?] ... 713
New Mediterranean harbour pilot. New ed. 1814 ... 193
New Mediterranean pilot. 1802 ... 192
North sea and Baltic pilot. 1807 ... 2850

Heermans, Anna A.
Hieroglyphic geography of the United States. 1875 ... 1284

Hellert, J. J.
Nouvel atlas, physique, politique et historique de l'empire ottoman. 1843. 3158

Helms, J. C.
Plat book of Hancock county by townships. 1908 ... 1536

Henion, J. W., *and* **Foote, C. M.**
Plat book of Columbia county, Wis. 1890 ... 2639
Plat book of Dodge county, Wis. 1890 ... 2643
Plat book of Fond du Lac county, Wis. 1893 ... 2645
Plat book of Goodhue county, Minn. 1894 ... 2018
Plat book of Lafayette county, Wis. 1895 ... 2651
Plat book of Manitowoc and Calumet counties, Wis. 1893 ... 2637, 2652
Plat book of Rock county, Wis. 1891 ... 2661
Plat book of Washington and Ozaukee counties, Wis. 1892 ... 2654, 2667
Plat book of Waukesha county, Wis. 1891 ... 2669
Plat book of Winona county, Minn. 1894 ... 2047

Herbertson, Andrew John, 1865-1915, *and* **Bartholomew, J. G.**
Atlas of meteorology. 1899 ... 213

Hérisson, Eustache, 1759-
Atlas du dictionnaire de géographie universelle. 1806 ... 710

Homans, J. E.
See Collier, P. F. & son.

Homem de Mello, Barão, *and* **Homem de Mello, Francisco Ignacio Marcondes,** 1837–
Atlas do Brazil. 1909 3959
Geographia-atlas do Brazil. 1a ed. 1912 5142

Hondius, Henricus, 1587–1638.
Nouveau théâtre dv monde. 1639 452

Hondius, Henricus, *and* **Jansson, J.**
Nouveau théâtre dv monde. 1639–1640 3422

Hondius, Jodocus, 1563–1611.
Nova et accvrata Italiæ hodiernæ descriptio. 1627 4041

Hondius, Jodocus, *and* **Mercator, G.**
Atlas ofte afbeeldinghe vande gantsche weerldt. Dutch edition. [1634] ... 447

Hood, Edwin C.
Plat book of Richland county, Wis. 1895 2659
Plat book of Vernon county, Wis. 1896 2664

Hood, Edwin C., *and* **Foote, C. M.**
Plat book of Barron county, Wis. 1888 2635
Plat book of Chisago county, Minn. 1888 2013
Plat book of Isabella county, Mich. 1899 4748
Plat book of Jefferson county, Wis. 1899 2648
Plat book of Juneau county, Wis. 1898 2649
Plat book of Keokuk county, Iowa. 1887 4645
Plat book of Polk county, Wis. 1887 2656

Hooghe, Romein de, 1646?–1708.
Zee atlas tot het gebruik van de vlooten des konings van Groot Britanje. 1694 2835

Hoover, H. S.
Atlas of Bremer county, Iowa. 1875 1646

Hopkins, Griffith Morgan.
Atlas of Allegheny. 1890–1891 2505
Atlas of Baltimore county, Md. 1877 1783
Atlas of Beverly, Mass. 1880 1852
Atlas of Binghamton, N. Y. 1885 2271
Atlas of Bridgeport, Conn. 1888 1484
Atlas of Brookline, Mass. 1874 1869
—— 1884 1870
Atlas of Bryn Mawr and vicinity. 1881 .... 2443, 2508
Atlas of Buffalo, N. Y. 1884 2280
—— 1891 2281
Atlas of Cambridge, Mass. 1873 1871
—— 1886 1872
Atlas of Chattanooga, Tenn. 1889 2585
Atlas of county of Allegheny, Pa. 1876 2459
Atlas of county of Suffolk, Mass. 1874–1875 1857
Atlas of Danbury, Conn. 1880 1486
Atlas of Delaware county, Pa. 1870 2474
Atlas of East Orange, N. J. 1879 2179
Atlas of fifteen miles around Baltimore, including Anne Arundel county, Md. 1878 1728

Hopkins, G. M., co.

Atlas of greater Pittsburgh, Pa. 1910 3894
Atlas of Hudson county, N. J. 1908–1909 .... 2162a, 2183a, 3833
Atlas of Nashville, Tenn. 1908 2589
Atlas of . . . Syracuse, N. Y. 1908 .... 2329a, 3854
Atlas of the city of Rochester, N. Y. 1910 3853
Atlas of the county of Fayette and the state of Pennsylvania. 1872 .... 2452, 2476
Atlas of the county of Montgomery and the state of Pennsylvania. 1871 .... 2451, 2487
Atlas of the vicinity of Camden, N. J. 1907 2177
Plat book of Cuyahoga county, Ohio. 1914 4984
Plat book of Jersey City and Bayonne . . . N. J. v. I. 1919 .... *
Plat book of the city of Akron, Ohio. 1915 4992
Plat book of the city of Chattanooga, Tenn. 1914 5065
Plat-book of the city of Cleveland, Ohio. 1912 .... 3880, 4994
Plat book of the city of Providence, R. I. 1918 5056
Plat book of the city of Rochester, N. Y. 1918 4955
Plat book of the city of Saint Paul, Minn. 1916 4827
Plat-book of the city of Toledo, Ohio, and suburbs. 1913 4997
Real estate plat-book of Allegheny. 1907 2507
Real estate plat-book of Chattanooga. 1904 2586
Real estate plat-book of Pittsburgh. 1903 2550
—— 1904–1906 2551
—— 1914–1917 5052
Real estate plat-book of the city of Pittsburgh, Pa. 1904–1906 3893
Real estate plat-book of the city of Pittsburgh, Pa. 1911 3895
Real estate plat-book of the eastern vicinity of Pittsburgh, Pa. 1903 2549
Real estate plat-book of the northern vicinity of Pittsburgh, Pa. 1906 2553
Real estate plat-book of the southern vicinity of Pittsburgh, Pa. 1905 2552

Hopkins, G. M., & co.

Atlas of Buffalo, N. Y. 1872 2279
Atlas of Salem, Mass. 1874 1935
Atlas of Somerville, Mass. 1874 1937
Atlas of the county of Suffolk, Mass. 1874–1875 1825
Combination atlas of the county of Butler and the state of Pennsylvania. 1874 .... 2455, 2465
Combination atlas of the county of Mercer and the state of Pennsylvania. 1873 .... 2454, 2484

Hopkins, Henry W.

Real estate plat book of Allegheny. 1901–[1902] 2506

Hopley printing co.

Crawford county, [Ohio] 1912 .... 3873a

Horn, Georg, 1620–1670.

Accuratissima orbis antiqui delineatio. 1654 16
Accuratissima orbis delineatio. 1660 3278
—— 1740 17
Compleat body of ancient geography. 1741 3279

Horsburgh, James, 1762–1836.

Atlas of the East Indies and China sea. 1806–1821 3171

Horsburgh, James, *and* **Steel, P.**

New and complete East-India pilot. 1817 4312

House, W. M.

North Dakota and Richland county chart. 1897 4959

Instituto geográfico argentino. *Buenos Aires.*
Atlas de la república Argentina. 1886 2732
—— 1898 2735

Instituut voor taal-, land-, en volkenkunde van Nederlandsch Indië, *The Hague.*
Atlas van karten over Nieuw Guinea. 1862 3264

International boundary commission. *United States and Mexico.* 1882–1896.
Boundary between the United States and Mexico . . . 1882. [Atlas] Revived . . . 1889. [1899] 1262, 2680
Linea divisoria entre México y los Estados Unidos . . . 1882, renovada . . . 1889. [Atlas] [1901] 1263, 2681

—— *United States and Mexico,* 1893–
Proceedings . . . 1903 4492

International geological congress, *12th. Toronto,* 1913.
Coal resources of the world. 1913 .... 4104b

International joint commission (U. S. and Canada) 1909–
Atlas to accompany report to International joint commission relating to official reference re Lake of the Woods levels. 1915 4487

Interstate publishing co.
Plat book of Clay county, Iowa. 1887 1652
Plat book of Rock county, Minn. 1886 2040

Iowa publishing co.
Atlas of Black Hawk county, Iowa. 1910 3743
Atlas of Carroll county, Iowa. 1906 1650
Atlas of Dubuque county, Iowa. 1906 1659
Atlas of Grundy county, Iowa. 1911 3747
Atlas of Linn county, Iowa. 1907 1681
Atlas of Rock Island county, Ill. 1905 1563
Atlas of Scott county, Iowa. 1905 1694
Atlas of Washington county, Iowa. 1906 1706

Istituto geografico de Agostini, *Novara.*
Atlante della nostra guerra. 1916 4228
Calendario-atlante de Agostini. [1914] 4413
—— [1915] 4420
—— [1916] 4428
Europe ethnique et linguistique. [1917] 5155, 5162a

Istituto italo-britannico.
Atlante della guerra mondiale. 1918 4229

Italy. *Direzione generale della statistica.*
Carte topografiche, idrografighe e geologiche annesse alle monografia statistica della città di Roma. 1883 3070

—— *Istituto topografico militare.*
Carte delle province Napolitane. [1874] 5264

—— *Ministero dei lavori pubblici.*
Album dei porti i, ii e iii classe. [1873] 3057

—— *Ministero della guerra.*
Genio nella campagna d'Ancona e della bassa Italia. Atlante. [1864] 5256

—— *Ministero della marina.*
Portolano della Liguria. 1855 .... 3066, 5263
Portolano della Sardegna. [1842] 3071

Italy. *Ufficio idrografico.*
[Carte delle provincie meridionali. 1876–1884] 5262
Vedute delle coste d'Italia. 1884 4040
—— 1897 5255
Vedute di costa dell'isola di Sardegna. 1882 4044
—— *Ufficio tecnico del corpo di stato maggiore.*
Quadro d' unione della carta della Sicilia. 1872 5265

Ivison, Blakeman, Taylor & co.
Handy atlas of the world. [1883] 4360
—— [1884] 917
Standard classic atlas. [1885] 20

Jackson map co.
Twentieth century plat book of Grayson county, Tex. 1908 .... 3922, 3582

Jacobsz, Theunis, *or* **Anthonie,** *called* **Loots-man.**
Fifth part of the new great sea-mirrour. 1717 3648
Lighting colom of the Midland-sea. 1692 194
Lightningh columne. 1692 .... 510, 2834
Nieuw groot straets-boeck, inhoudende d'Middellantse zee. 1648 3341
Nieuwe groote geoctroyeerde verbeterde en vermeerderde Loots-man zee-spiegel. 1707 3467

Jacobsz, Theunis, *or* **Anthonie,** *called* **Loots-man, Doncker, H.,** *and* **Goos, H.**
Lightning columne. 1689–[1692] 504, 2832

Jacquemart, Alfred, *i. e.* **Eugène Alfred,** 1836–, *and* **Mager, H.**
Atlas colonial. 1890 2952

Jaeger, Julius, 1848–
Atlas van het koningrijk der Nederlanden. [1883] 3085

Jaillot, Charles Hubert Alexis, 1640–1712.
Atlas françois. 1695 520
—— 1695–[1696] 519

Jaillot, Charles Hubert Alexis, *& others.*
Atlas françois. 1700–[1724] 534

James, George Wharton, 1858–, *& others.*
New pictorial atlas of the world. [1919] .... *

Janson, William.
Atlas of Richland county, Mont. 1917 4876
Atlas of Roosevelt and Sheridan counties, Mont. 1919 .... *
[McKenzie county, North Dakota. In township form. 1916] 4969

Jansson, Jan, *d.* 1666.
Atlantis majoris. Editio secunda. 1657 465
Atlas minor. 1651 3426
Guerre d'Italie. 1702 3060
Illustriorum Hispaniæ urbium tabulæ. [1652?] 3294
Illvstriorvm principumque urbium septentrionalium Evropæ tabulæ. [1657?] 5153
Ioannis Ianssonii novus atlas. 1646–1649 459
Joannis Jansonii atlas contractus. 1666 475
Nieuwen atlantis aenhang. 1644 4258
Nieuwen atlas, ofte werelt-beschrijbinge. 1652–1653 3427
Novus atlas. 1646 2894
Nuevo atlas. 1653 463

Jansson, Jan, *and* **Hondius, H.**
Nouveau théâtre dv monde. 1639–1640 3422

Kitchin, Thomas, *& others.*
General atlas. [1768-1788] ... 668
—— [1768-1793] ... 4295
—— [1770?] ... 643
—— 1773 ... 3514
—— 1777 ... 4296
—— 1780 ... 653
—— 1782 ... 3521
—— 1782-[1787] ... 3522
—— [1790] ... 4300
—— 1795 ... 3529
—— 1801 ... 3533
—— 1804 ... 4305a
New universal atlas. [1789]-1796 ... 685
—— 1795 ... 682
—— 1799 ... 3531
—— 1801 ... 3534
—— 6th ed. 1802 ... 699
—— 7th ed. 1805 ... 709

Kitchin, Thomas, Bowen, E., *& others.*
Royal english atlas. [1778] ... 2920, 2921

Klinckowström, Axel Leonhard, *friherre,* 1775-1837.
Atlas . . . om de Förente Staterne. [1824] ... 1375

Klint, Gustaf, 1771-1840.
Sveriges sjö atlas. [1832-1845] ... 2854

Knapp, Charles, 1855-, *and* **Michel, G.**
Documents cartographiques de géographie économique. 1913-1915 ... 4125

Knapton, John, *d.* 1770, *and* **Knapton, Paul,** *d.* 1755.
Geographia classica. 8th ed. 1747 ... 29

Knight, Thomas Harold, *and* **Benians, E. A.**
Historical atlas. 1908 ... 2880a

Koch, Christophe Guillaume, 1737-1813.
Maps and tables of chronology and genealogy. 1831 ... 2791

Koch, Wilhelm, 1823-1902.
Verkehrs-atlas von Europa. 1906 ... 2783

Koch, Wilhelm, *and* **Opitz, C. A.**
Eisenbahn- und verkehrsatlas von Russland. [1900] ... 3115
—— 3. verb. aufl. 1912 ... 5278

Koch & Shigley.
Atlas and directory of Buckeye lake. 1911 ... 3869

Kochersperger, H. L., *and* **Kochersperger, D. H.**
People's illustrated and descriptive family atlas. 1884 ... 919
—— [1886] ... 930

Köhler, Johann David, 1684-1755.
Atlas manualis. [1724?] ... 567, 568, 569
Bequemer schul- und reisen-atlas. [1734?] ... 582
[Descriptio orbis antiqvi. 1720?] ... 30, 31

Köllner, August.
Views of cities . . . in the United States and Canada. [1848-1851] ... 1267

Kohl, Johann Georg, 1808-1878.
Die beiden ältesten general-karten von Amerika. 1860 ... 1135

Laet, Joannes de, 1593–1649.
Beschrijvinghe van West-Indien. 1630 1148
L'histoire dv Nouveau Monde. 1640 1150
Historie ofte Iaerlijck verhael van de verrichtinghen der geoctroyeerde West-Indische compagnie. 1644 3647
Nieuvve wereldt. 1625 1147
Novvs orbis; seu descriptionis Indiæ Occidentalis. 1633 1149

La Feuille, Daniel de.
Atlas portatif. 1706–[1708] 2820

La Feuille, Paul de.
Geographisch-toneel. 1732 3970
Millitary [!] tablettes. 1707 5167
Tablettes guerrières. 1708 5168
—— 1717 3971

Lafréry, Antoine, 1512–1577.
Geografia tavole moderne di geografia. [1575?] 3392

La Guilbaudière, Jouhan de.
Description des principaux endroits de la Mer du Sud. *ms.* [1696] 1154

La Harpe, Jean François de, 1739–1803.
[Abrégé de l'histoire générale des voyages. Atlas. 1820] 591

Laird & Lee.
Handy reference atlas and gazetteer of the world. [1911] 3621

Lake, D. J.
Atlas of Athens county, Ohio. 1875 2355
Atlas of Columbiana county, Ohio. 1870 2364
Atlas of Cuyahoga county, Ohio. 1874 2367
Atlas of Guernsey county, Ohio. 1870 2380
Atlas of Hocking county, Ohio. 1876 2386
Atlas of Jackson county, Ohio. 1875 2388
Atlas of Lake and Geauga counties, Ohio. 1874 .... 2379, 2392
Atlas of Lorain county, Ohio. 1874 2395
Atlas of Mahoning county, Ohio. 1874 3875
Atlas of Vinton county, Ohio. 1876 2416

Lake, D. J., *and* **Griffing, B. N.**
Atlas of Brown county, Ohio. 1876 2356

Lake, D. J., Sanford, G. P., *and* **Gould, F. A.**
Atlas of Randolph county, Ind. 1874 1624
Atlas of Wayne county, Ind. 1874 3741

Lake, D. J., *& others.*
Atlas of Allegan county, Mich. 1873 1961
Atlas of Ashtabula county, Ohio. 1874 2353
Atlas of Branch county, Mich. 1872 1964
Atlas of Cass county, Mich. 1872 1966
Atlas of Clarke county, Ohio. 1870 2358
Atlas of Clermont county, Ohio. 1870 2360
—— 1891 2361
Atlas of Coshocton county, Ohio. 1872 2365
Atlas of Frederick county, Md. 1873 1788
Atlas of Highland county, Ohio. 1871 2384
Atlas of Morrow county, Ohio. 1871 2403
Atlas of Pickaway county, Ohio. 1871 2408
Atlas of Preble county, Ohio. 1871 2410
Atlas of Washington county, Ohio. 1875 2420

Lake, D. J., & co.
Atlas of Bath & Fleming counties, Ky. 1884........ 1746, 1754
Atlas of Boone, Kenton, and Campbell counties, Ky. 1883..... 1747, 1750, 1760
Atlas of Bracken and Pendleton counties, Ky. 1884........ 1749, 1764
Atlas of Carroll and Gallatin counties, Ky. 1883........ 1751, 1755
Atlas of Clay county, Ill. 1881........ 1523
Atlas of Gibson and Pike counties, Ind. 1881........ 1606, 1621
Atlas of Greene county, Ind. 1879........ 1607
Atlas of Harrison county, Ind. 1882........ 1609
Atlas of Henry and Shelby cos., Ky. 1882........ 1757, 1765
Atlas of Jennings county, Ind. 1884........ 1615
Atlas of Nelson & Spencer cos., Ky. 1882........ 1761, 1766
Atlas of Owen county, Ky. 1883........ 1763
Atlas of Ripley county, Ind. 1883........ 1625
Atlas of Rockingham county, Va. 1885........ 2614
Atlas of Switzerland and Ohio counties, Ind. 1883........ 1620, 1629
Atlas of Union county, Ill. 1881........ 1572
Illustrated historical atlas of Henderson and Union counties, Ky. 1880........ 1756, 1767
Illustrated historical atlas of Spencer county, Ind. 1879........ 1628
Illustrated historical atlas of Warrick county, Ind. 1880........ 1634

Lake, Griffing & Stevenson.
Atlas of Wicomico, Somerset & Worcester counties, Md. 1877.. 1792, 1794, 1795
Illustrated atlas of Carroll county, Md. 1877........ 1786
Illustrated atlas of Talbot & Dorchester counties, Md. 1877........ 1787
Illustrated historical atlas of Clinton county, Ohio. 1876........ 2362

Lalande, Joseph Jérome Le Français de, 1732–1807.
Voyage en Italie. [Atlas] 1786........ 4042

Lanagan, J., *and* **Beers, D. G.**
Atlas of Jefferson and Oldham counties, Ky. 1879........ 1758, 1762

Lanciani, Rodolfo Amadeo, 1847–
Forma vrbis Romae. [1901]........ 3068

Lane, Michael, Cook, J., *& others,*
Collection of charts of the coasts of Newfoundland and Labradore. [1765–1768]........ 1254
Pilote de Terre-Neuve. 1784........ 4490

Lange, Henry, 1821–1893.
Atlas von Nord-Amerika. 1854........ 1230
Atlas von Sachsen. 1860........ 3045
Kartenwerk zu dr. Karl Andree's Nord-Amerika. 1854........ 1231
Volksschul-atlas. [1892]........ 3573

Lange, Henry, *and* **Liechtenstern, T. von.**
Schul-atlas zum unterricht in der erdkunde. 50. aufl. 1880........ 4198

Langenes, Barent.
Caert-thresoor. 1599........ 410
Hand-boeck. 1609........ 424
Thrésor de chartes. [1602]........ 415
—— [1610?]........ 428

Langeren, Jacob van.
Direction for the english traviller. 1643........ 5203a

Langhans, Paul, 1867–
Deutscher kolonial-atlas. 1897........ 5243
Justus Perthes' deutscher marine-atlas. 2. aufl. 1898........ 173, 3025

Langlois, Hyacinthe.
Atlas portatif et itinéraire de l'Europe. 1817 2809
Grand atlas français départemental. 1856 4028

Lapérouse, Jean François de Galaup, *comte* **de,** 1741–1788.
Voyage de La Pérouse. Atlas. 1797 688
Voyage round the world. Atlas. 1799 693

Lapie, Alexandre Émile, *fils, and* **Lapie, P.**
Atlas universel. 1829–[1833] 754, 765
—— 1829–[1842] 123
—— 1841–[1842] 123a, 787

Lapie, Pierre, 1779–1850.
Atlas classique et universel. 1824 744

Laplace, Cyrille Pierre Théodore, 1793–1875
Voyage autour du monde. Atlas hydrographique. 1833–1839 .... 202, 3174

Laporte, Joseph de, 1713–1779.
Atlas moderne portatif. 1781 654
Atlas . . . pour l'intelligence du voyageur françois. 1787 662

Larousse, Librairie.
Atlas de poche du théâtre de la guerre. 2. éd. [1916] 4231, 5184
Atlas départemental Larousse. [1914] 5230
Atlas Larousse illustré. [1899] 1035
—— [1917?] .... *

Las Cases, Emmanuel, *i. e.* **Marie Joseph Auguste Emmanuel Dieudonné,** *comte* **de,** 1766–1842.
Atlante storico. 1813–[1814] 3540
—— 1826 126
—— Veneta ed. 1826–[1840] 127
Atlas historico. 1826 3312
Atlas historique. [1803] 124
—— [1807] 125
—— [1829] 3313
—— Ed. populaire. [1835] 128
—— 1853 129
Historisch-genealogisch-geographischer atlas. [1831] 3550
LeSage's [*pseud.*] historical . . . atlas. 2d ed. 1818 130
Mappe geografiche storiche. [1835?] 3314

Lasor a Varea, Alphonsus, *pseud.*
See Savonarola, Raffaello.

Lat, Jan de.
Atlas portatif. 1747 4287

Latham, E. B., *and* **Baylor, H. B.**
Atlas of Atlanta, Ga. 1893 1508

Lathrop, J. M.
Atlas of the city of Trenton and borough of Princeton, Mercer county, N. J. 1905 .... 2195, 2199

Lathrop, J. M., *and* **Dayton, A. W.**
Atlas of Frederick county, Va. 1885 2612

Lathrop, J. M., *and* **Flynn, T.**
Atlas of the Oranges . . . N. J. 1911 3837

Lathrop, J. M., *and* **Kiser, E.**
Atlas of Atlantic City . . . New Jersey. 1908 .... 2172a

Leard, John, *& others.*
[Charts and plans of Jamaica] 1793 5129

Leavenworth, A., Warner, G. E., Beers, F. W., *& others.*
Atlas of Delaware county, Ohio. 1866 2372

Le Boucher, Odet Julien, 1744–1826.
Atlas pour servir à l'intelligence . . . de la guerre de l'indépendance des États-Unis. [1830] 1340

Le Clerc, Jean, 1657–1736.
Atlas antiquus. [1705] 3283

Lecuna, Vicente.
Atlas de Venezuela. 1916 5151

Lee, R. H.
Farm atlas of Carroll county, Ohio. 1915. [1916] 4983

Leer, Genrikh Antonovich, 1829–
Карты къ стратегіи— Strategical maps. 1885–1887 2821

Leete, Charles Henry, 1857–, *and* **Chisholm, G. G.**
Longman's new school atlas. New ed. 1901 271
—— New ed. 1912 4190

Lefévre, I. A.
Atlas of Manhattan island, N. Y. 1895–1896 2311
Atlas of Staten Island, Richmond county, N. Y. 1894 2205
Index to atlas of Manhattan island, N. Y. 1896 2312
Yearly index to atlas of Manhattan island, N. Y. 1896 2313

Legendre, Pierre, *and* **Malleterre, G.**
Livre-atlas des colonies françaises. [1900] 2953

Le Grand, —— *and* **Ancelin,** ——.
Atlas général et élémentaire de l'empire de toutes les Russies. 1795 4061

Lehmann, Richard, 1845–, *and* **Petzold, W.**
Atlas für mittel- und oberklassen höherer lehranstalten. 3. aufl. 1904 297

Lehmann, Richard, *and* **Scobel, A.**
Atlas für höhere lehranstalten. 1903 .... 74, 298

Leidel, Edward F., *and* **Poetsch, C. J.**
Official quarter sectional atlas of the city of Milwaukee. 1907 2677

Lelewel, Joachim, 1786–1861.
Atlas do J. Lelewela. 1818 133
Géographie du moyen âge. Atlas. 1850 252

Le Mars sentinel.
Atlas and farm directory . . . of Plymouth county, Iowa. 1914 4653

Le Masson du Parc, ——
[Collection of maps. 1717?] 560
Vües, plans et perspectiues de diuers lieux et places considérables. [1713]. 2781

Lemau de la Jaisse, Pierre.
Plans des principales places de guerre et villes maritimes frontières du royaume de France. 1736 2974

Lenglet Dufresnoy, Nicolas, 1674–1755.
Kurzverfassete kinder geographie. 5. aufl. 1764 4197

Lenormant, François, *i. e.* **Charles François,** 1837–1883.
Atlas d'histoire ancienne de l'Orient. [1868] 31a

Leonard-Stuart, Charles.
Standard atlas and chronological history of the world. 1912 3637

Luffman, John.
Geographical & topographical atlas. 1815–1816 725
[Geographical principles. Maps. 1803] 4461
Select plans of the principalc ities . . . &c. in the world. 1801–[1802] .. 62
—— 1801–[1803] 63

Luncan, I., *and* **Gorjan, A.**
Atlas-geografie. 1895 1000
Atlas-geografie România. 1895 3097

Luyts, Jan, 1655–1721.
Introductio ad geographiam novam et veterem. 1692 511

Lyde, Lionel William, 1863–
Home-work atlas of maps. 1910 3374

Lyman, Azel. S.
Lyman's historical chart. 1874 135

McClure, Edmund.
Historical church atlas. 1897 86

McComiskey, Alexander H.
Maps of parish of Orleans, city, districts, wards, precincts, and boundaries of same. 1904 3760

MacCoun, Townsend, 1845–
Early New York [1609–1783] [1909] 3839
Historical geography of the United States. 1889 1293
—— 1890 1294
—— [1901] 1295

McCulloch, John Ramsay, 1789–1864.
Dictionary . . . of commerce . . . Atlas. 1859 76

Macdonald, D.
Illustrated atlas of the dominion of Canada. 1881 4482

McDougall's educational co. *ltd.*
Contour atlas of the British Isles. [1919?] 5189

McGlumphy, W. H. S.
Atlas of Caldwell county, Mo. 1907 3818

McKenzie, Murdoch, *the elder, d.* 1797.
Aanwyzing voor de zeelieden, door de Orcadische eylanden. [1753] 2943

Mackey, Dick.
Plat book of Clark county, Kans. 1909 3757

McKinley publishing co.
Historical notebook for ancient history. [1915] 4097
Outline atlases . . . Ancient history. 2d. rev. ed. [1915] 4098
Outline atlases . . . European history. [1915] 5158

McLean, Robert.
New atlas of Australia. [1886] 3253

Maclot, Jean Charles, 1728–1805.
Atlas général méthodique et élémentaire. 1770 645
—— 1786 658

Macpherson, D., *and* **Macpherson, Alexander.**
[Atlas of ancient geography. 1806] 4099, 4100

Macullar, Parker & co.
Atlas sample book. [1879] 1404

Mathews & Leigh.
Scripture atlas. 1812 87

Matson, Nehemiah.
Map of Bureau county, Ill. 1867 1519

Matthews, J. N., co.
War atlas of Europe. [1914] 4234

Matthews, John, R. N.
Twenty-one plans . . . of different actions in the West Indies. 1784 2700

Matthews-Northrop co.
Adequate travel-atlas of the United States. [1893] 1435
Complete handy atlas. [1898] 1024
Handy atlas of the world. 1916 4429
Up-to-date handy atlas. [1898–1899] 1030

Maurette, Fernand, 1878–
Petit atlas de la guerre et de la paix. 1918 4235

Maverick, Peter, 1780–1831.
[General atlas. 1816] 728

Mawson, Christopher Orlando Sylvester, 1870–
Geographical manual and new atlas. 1917 4440
—— 1918 .... 4447a

May, B., & co.
Album pintoresco de la isla de Cuba. [1860?] 3948

Mayo, Robert, 1784–1864.
Atlas of ten select maps of ancient geography. 1814 4101
—— 1815 4102
[Atlas to accompany . . . ancient geography. 1813] 33

Meacham, J. H., & co.
Illustrated historical atlas of the counties of Frontenac, Lennox, and Addington, Ont. 1878 .... 3671a

Mecutchen, Samuel, 1827–, *and* **Harrower, H. D.**
Pocket atlas. [1887] 941

Mees, Gregorius, *jr.*, 1802–1883.
Historische atlas van Noord-Nederland. 1865 3073

Meisner, Daniel, *d.* 1684.
Thesavrvs philo-politicvs. 1625–1627 64

Mekeel, Charles Haviland.
Stamp collector's maps of the world. 1895 345

Mela, Pomponius, *fl.* A. D. 50.
Pomponii Melæ de situ orbis. 1739 3284

Meleney, C. E., *and* **Griffin, W. M.**
Primary geography of the state of New Jersey. 1884 2147

Melish, John, 1771–1822.
Military and topographical atlas of the United States. 1813 1346
—— 1815 1347
New juvenile atlas, 1814. *See* Laurie, R., and Whittle, J.

Melvill van Carnbée, Pieter, *baron,* 1816–1856, *and* **Versteeg, W. F.**
Algemeene atlas van nederlandsch Indië. [1875] 3214

Mendel, P. J.
Album voor de aardrijkskunde . . . 1841 .... 4050a

Mendes de Almeida, Candido, 1818–1881.
Atlas do imperio do Brazil. 1868 2749

Meyer, Hermann Julius, 1826–1909.
Atlas der Östlichen hemisphäre. 1851 .... *
Geographischer hand-atlas. 1905 .... 1103a
Hand-atlas. 1900 1053
Historischer handatlas. 1911 .... 4137a

Meyer, Joseph, 1796–1856.
Neuester grosser schulatlas. [1838?] 4202

Michel, ——
L'indicateur fidèle. 1765 2991

Michel, Gaston, *and* **Knapp, C.**
Documents cartographiques de géographie économique. 1913–1915 4125

Michigan. *Geological survey.*
Atlas accompanying reports on upper peninsula. [1874?] 3800

Mickleburgh, *Rev.* **James,** *of Ashill.*
Index to the principal places in the world. 1844 .... 794a

Middendorff, Aleksandr Theodor von, 1815–1894.
Karten-atlas zu dr. A. v. Middendorff's reise in den aussersten norden und osten Sibiriens. 1859 3125

Middle-west publishing co.
20th century atlas of Du Page county, Ill. 1904 1529
20th century atlas of Kane county, Ill. 1904 1541

Midland map co.
Atlas of Appanoose county, Iowa. 1915 4622
Atlas of Greene county, Iowa. 1909 4638
Atlas of Mahaska county, Iowa. 1913 4649
Atlas of Sac county, Iowa. 1912 4657
Atlas of Warren county, Iowa. 1915 4663

Miger, Pierre Auguste Marie, 1771–1837.
Ports de France, peints par Joseph Vernet et Huë. 1812 5219

Miguel, Gregorio.
Estudio sobre las islas Carolinas. [1887] 3258

Mikîeshin, Konstantin Osipovich, *d.* 1868.
Географическій атласъ—Geographical atlas. 1864 3560

Milan. *Istituto geographico militare. See* **Austria.** *Militärgeographisches institut.*

Milbert, Jacques Gérard, 1766–1840.
Itinéraire pittoresque du fleuve Hudson. [1828–1829] 4957

Miles & co.
Illustrated historical atlas of the county of York. 1878 1253

Miller, D. L.
Atlas of Chemung county, N. Y. 1904 .... 4923, 4938
Atlas of Harrison and Kearny and the borough of East Newark . . . N. J. 1903 .... 2178, 2181, 2184
Atlas of Leominster, Worcester county, Mass. 1895 1897
Atlas of North Adams, Adams, Williamstown, and Cheshire, Berkshire county, Mass. 1894 .... 1808, 1849, 1874, 1916, 1951
Atlas of Pittsfield, Berkshire county, Mass. 1893 1923
Atlas of Schenectady, N. Y., embracing maps of the village of Scotia. 1905 .... 2327, 2328
Atlas of Utica, N. Y. 1896 2333

Miller, D. L., *& others.*
Atlas of Fitchburg, Worcester county, Mass. 1895........................ 1883
Atlas of New Britain, Hartford county, Conn. 1902........................ 1489
Atlas of Northampton and town of Easthampton, Hampshire county, Mass. 1895........................ 1878, 1918

Miller, Herman P.
Outline maps of the counties of Allegheny, Berks, Bucks, Cambria, Dauphin, Fayette . . . Pa. 1901........................ 2458

Miller, James Martin.
Twentieth century atlas. [1899]........................ 1037
—— [1909]........................ 3593
World up-to-date. [1899]........................ 1038

Miller, Konrad, 1864–
Itineraria romana. 1916........................ *
Mappaemundi: die ältesten weltkarten. 1895–1898........................ 255

Mills, Robert, 1781–1855.
Atlas of the state of South Carolina. [1825]........................ 2570

Milner, Thomas, *d.* 1882, *and* **Petermann, D. H.**
Descriptive atlas of astronomy, and of physical and political geography. 1850........................ 231
Library atlas of physical and political geography. 1855........................ 232

Miniscalchi, Erizzo F., *conte.*
Scoperte artiche atlante. [1855]........................ 3641

Minneapolis tribune.
Unrivaled atlas. 1899........................ 1039

Missouri. *Geological survey.*
Report on the iron ores and coal fields. Atlas. 1873........................ 2059

Missouri publishing co.
Plat book of Barton county, Mo. 1903........................ 2069

Mitchell, Samuel Augustus, 1792–1868.
Ancient atlas. [1844]........................ 35
—— 1859........................ 36
Atlas of outline maps. 1839........................ 300
Maps of New Jersey, Pennsylvania, Maryland & Delaware, Philadelphia city and Washington city. 1846........................ 3692
New atlas of America. 1874........................ 1183
New atlas of North and South America. 1851........................ 1179
New general atlas. 1860........................ 831
—— 1862........................ 3558
—— 1865........................ 846
—— 1866........................ 848
—— 1867........................ 850
—— 1868........................ 3563
—— 1870........................ 859
—— 1873........................ 870
—— 1876........................ 880
—— 1878........................ 888
—— 1879........................ 890
—— 1880........................ 892
—— 1881........................ 895
—— 1882........................ 906
—— 1884........................ 920
—— 1893........................ 983

Mortier, David.
Nouveau théâtre de la Grande Bretagne. 1715–1728 4002
Mortier, Pieter, *d.* 1724.
Atlas nouveau des cartes géographiques choisies. 1703 2823
Forces de l'Europe, Asie, Afrique et Amérique. [1702?] 537, 2781a
Moule, Thomas, 1784–1851.
English counties delineated. 1838 2926
Mount, Richard, *and* **Page, T.**
Atlas maritimus novus. 1702 3334
Mudie, Robert, 1777–1842.
Gilbert's modern atlas. [1841?] 780
Mueller, A. H.
Atlas of Absecon island, N. J. 1914 .... 4915, 4916, 4917, 4919, 4920
Atlas of Delaware county [Pa.] 1909–1913 .... 3888, 5016
Atlas of Lower Merion, Montgomery co. [Pa.] 1896 2514
Atlas of part of Morris county, N. J. 1910 3834
Atlas of properties on main line Pennsylvania railroad from Devon to Downingtown and West Chester [Pa.] 1912 .... 3887a
Atlas of properties on main line Pennsylvania railroad from Overbrook to Paoli [Pa.] 1908 2450
—— 1913 5011
Atlas of properties on the Reading railroad. 1909 .... 3890, 3891, 3897
Atlas of the North Penn section of Montgomery county, Pa. 1916 5018
Atlas of the city of Erie, Pa. 1917 5021
Atlas of the city of Paterson, N. J. 1915 4918
Atlas of Yonkers, N. Y. 1907 2337
Mueller, A. H., & co.
Atlas of Cheltenham, Abington, and Springfield townships and vicinity of Montgomery county, Pa. 1897 .... 2490, 2501, 2509, 2557
Atlas of Essex county, New Jersey. [1901]–1906 2157
Atlas of properties on line of Pennsylvania r. r. from Rosemont to Westchester [Pa.] 1897 .... 2449, 2555, 2558
Atlas of surveys of Mahoning county, Ohio. 1899–1900 2397
Müller, Johann Christoph, 1673–1721.
Schweizerischer atlas. [1712?] 3150
Müller, Johann Ulrich.
Kurtz-bündige abbild- und vorstellung der gantzen welt. 1692 512
Muir, Ramsay, *i. e.* **John Ramsay Bryce,** 1872–
Hammond's new historical atlas for students. 2d ed. [1914?] 4138
New school atlas of modern history. 1911 3316
Mulert, Hermann, *and* **Heussi, K.**
Atlas zur kirchengeschichte. 1905 .... 82, 2784
Munn, A. M.
Atlas of Otoe county, Nebr. 1902 2122
Murray, Paul R.
Atlas of Morgan county, Ohio. 1902 3876
Murray-Aaron, Eugene, 1852–
Home and library map-atlas of the United States. 1914 4532
Nabert, Heinrich, 1818–1890.
Karte der verbreitung der deutschen in Europa. [1890] ....
Naeff, M. A.
Property atlas of Montgomery county, Pa. 1893 2489

Nolin, Jean Baptiste, *sr.*, 1648–1708.
Nouvelle édition du théâtre de la guerre en Italie. 1718................ 5258

Nolin, Jean Baptiste, *jr.*, 1686–1762.
Atlas général à l'usage des collèges et maisons d'éducation. 1783........ 4297

Noll, E. P., & co.
Property atlas of St. Joseph county, Mich. 1893........................ 1997

Nordenskiöld, Nils Adolf Erik, *freiherre*, 1832–1901.
Bidrag till Nordens äldsta kartografi. [1892]........................ 256, 3091
Facsimile atlas. 1889.. 257
Periplus. 1897.. 258

Norie, John William, 1772–1843.
Complete East India pilot. 1816.. 3173

Noriega, Eduardo.
Atlas miniatura de la república Mexicana. 1899........................ 3938

Norman, John, 1748–1817.
American pilot. 1792.. 4474a
—— 1794.. 4475

Norman, William.
American pilot. 1798.. 1217
—— 1803.. 4477

Norris, John, 1660?–1749.
Compleat sett of new charts, containing the North-sea, Cattegatt, and Baltick. 1723.. 2839

Norris, Robert, *& others.*
African pilot. [1794]–1804.. 4082

North American pilot. 1777.. 1209
—— First part. New ed. 1799.. 4476
—— —— —— 1806.. 1236
—— Second part. New ed. 1795.. 3668
—— —— —— 1800.. 1220

Northern trust company bank.
Complete atlas. 1904.. 1091

Northwest publishing co.
Plat book of Anderson county, Kans. 1901........................ 1712
Plat book of Appanoose county, Iowa. 1896........................ 1643
Plat book of Audrain county, Mo. 1898........................ 2068
Plat book of Barton county, Kans. 1902........................ 1713
Plat book of Bates county, Mo. 1895........................ 2070
Plat book of Boone county, Iowa. 1896........................ 1645
Plat book of Boone county, Mo. 1898........................ 2071
Plat book of Boone county, Nebr. 1899........................ 2109
Plat book of Brown county, Kans. 1904........................ 1715
Plat book of Cass county, Mo. 1895........................ 2074
Plat book of Chariton county, Mo. 1897........................ 2075
Plat book of Chippewa county, Minn. 1900........................ 2012
Plat book of Coffey county, Kans. 1901........................ 1718
Plat book of Dallas county, Iowa. 1901........................ 1656
Plat book of De Kalb county, Mo. 1897........................ 2077
Plat book of Des Moines county, Iowa. 1897........................ 4634
Plat book of Dubuque county, Iowa. 1892........................ 1658
Plat book of Franklin county, Kans. 1903........................ 1720
Plat book of Fremont county, Iowa. 1891........................ 1664
Plat book of Greene county, Iowa. 1896........................ 1665

Northwest publishing co.—Continued.

Plat book of Greenwood county, Kans. 1903 1721
Plat book of Hamilton county, Iowa. 1896 1666
Plat book of Henry county, Mo. 1895 2078
Plat book of Howard county, Nebr. 1900 2114
Plat book of Humboldt county, Iowa. 1896 1672
Plat book of Jackson county, Kans. 1893 1675
—— 1903 1722
Plat book of Jasper county, Mo. 1895 2079
Plat book of Jefferson county, Nebr. 1900 2115
Plat book of Jo Daviess county, Ill. 1893 1539
Plat book of Jones county, Iowa. 1893 1678
Plat book of Kandiyohi county, Minn. 1886 2023
Plat book of Kingman county, Kans. 1903 1723
Plat book of Lafayette county, Mo. 1897 2080
Plat book of Lesueur county, Minn. 1898 2024
Plat book of Lincoln county, Kans. 1901 1725
Plat book of Lyon county, Minn. 1902 2025
Plat book of McLean county, Ill. 1895 1547
Plat book of McPherson county, Kans. 1903 1727
Plat book of Madison county, Iowa. 1901 1683
Plat book of Madison county, Nebr. 1899 2118
Plat book of Marathon county, Wis. 1901 2653
Plat book of Merrick county, Nebr. 1899 2119
Plat book of Nance county, Nebr. 1899 2120
Plat book of Nicollet county, Minn. 1899 2029
Plat book of Nodaway county, Mo. 1893 2086
Plat book of Norton county, Kans. 1900 1730
Plat book of Nuckolls county, Nebr. 1900 2121
Plat book of Osborne county, Kans. 1900 1732
Plat book of Page county, Iowa. 1902 1689
Plat book of Pettis county, Mo. 1896 2087
Plat book of Platte county, Nebr. 1899 2123
Plat book of Polk county, Minn. 1902 2034
Plat book of Portage county, Wis. 1895 2657
Plat book of Reno county, Kans. 1902 1733
Plat book of Renville county, Minn. 1900 2038
Plat book of Rice county, Kans. 1902 1735
Plat book of Rice county, Minn. 1900 2039
Plat book of Rush county, Kans. 1901 1736
Plat book of Russell county, Kans. 1901 1737
Plat book of St. Louis county, Mo. 1909 3821
Plat book of Saline county, Kans. 1903 1738
Plat book of Saline county, Mo. 1896 2093
Plat book of Saline county, Nebr. 1900 2124
Plat book of Schuyler county, Mo. 1898 2095
Plat book of Scotland county, Mo. 1898 2096
Plat book of Sherburne county, Minn. 1903 2041
Plat book of Stanton county, Nebr. 1899 2125
Plat book of Stephenson county, Ill. 1894 1570
Plat book of Tama county, Iowa. 1892 1698
Plat book of Taylor county, Iowa. 1894 1699
Plat book of Thayer county, Nebr. 1900 2126
Plat book of Union county, Iowa. 1894 1700

Ogle, George A. & co.—Continued.

Standard atlas of Lenawee county, Mich. 1916 4751
Standard atlas of Lewis county, Mo. 1916 4856
Standard atlas of Lincoln county, Kans. 1918 4685
Standard atlas of Lincoln county, Mo. 1899 2085
Standard atlas of Lincoln county, S. Dak. 1910 3911
Standard atlas of Lincoln county, Wash. 1911 3926
Standard atlas of Lincoln county, Wis. 1914 5096
Standard atlas of Livingston county, Ill. 1911 3723
Standard atlas of Livingston county, Mich. 1915 4752
Standard atlas of Livingston county, Mo. 1917 4859
Standard atlas of Logan county, Colo. 1917 4544
Standard atlas of Logan county, Ill. 1910 3724
Standard atlas of Logan county, N. Dak. 1916 4968
Standard atlas of Louisa county, Iowa. 1917 4648
Standard atlas of Lyman county, S. Dak. 1911 3912
Standard atlas of Lyon county, Kans. 1918 4687
Standard atlas of McCook county, S. Dak. 1911 3913
Standard atlas of McDonald county, Mo. 1909 4860
Standard atlas of McDonough county, Ill. 1913 4576
Standard atlas of McHenry county, N. Dak. 1910 3859
Standard atlas of McIntosh county, N. Dak. 1911 3860
Standard atlas of McLean county, Ill. 1914 4578
Standard atlas of McLean county, N. Dak. 1914 4970
Standard atlas of McLeod county, Minn. 1898 2026
Standard atlas of Macomb county, Mich. 1916 4753
Standard atlas of Macon county, Mo. 1918 4861
Standard atlas of McPherson county, S. Dak. 1911 3914
Standard atlas of Madison county, Nebr. 1918 4893
Standard atlas of Marinette county, Wis. 1912 .... 3932a
Standard atlas of Marion county, Ill. 1915 4580
Standard atlas of Marion county, Mo. 1913 4862
Standard atlas of Marquette county, Wis. 1919 .... *
Standard atlas of Marshall and Putnam counties, Ill. 1911 .... 3725, 3727
Standard atlas of Martin county, Minn. 1911 3812
Standard atlas of Mason county, Mich. 1904 4754
Standard atlas of Menominee county, Mich. 1912 .... 3805a
Standard atlas of Mercer county, N. Dak. 1918 4971
Standard atlas of Merrick county, Nebr. 1917 4894
Standard atlas of Midland county, Mich. 1914 4757
Standard atlas of Minnehaha county, S. Dak. 1903 3915
Standard atlas of Missaukee county, Mich. 1906 4758
Standard atlas of Mitchell county, Kans. 1917 4688
Standard atlas of Monroe county, Mich. 1896 1989
Standard atlas of Monroe county, Mo. 1917 4864
Standard atlas of Monroe county, Wis. 1915 5097
Standard atlas of Montgomery county, Ill. 1912 4583
Standard atlas of Montgomery county, Ind. 1917 4612
Standard atlas of Montgomery county, Mo. 1918 4865
Standard atlas of Morgan county, Colo. 1913 4545
Standard atlas of Morrill county, Nebr. 1913 4895
Standard atlas of Morton county, N. Dak. 1917 4972
Standard atlas of Moultrie county, Ill. 1913 4584
Standard atlas of Mountrail county, N. Dak. 1917 4973

Standard atlas of Richardson county, Nebr. 1913 4902
Standard atlas of Richland county, Ill. 1901 1562
Standard atlas of Richland county, Wis. 1919 .... 5100a
Standard atlas of Ringgold county, Iowa. 1915 4656
Standard atlas of Roberts county, S. Dak. 1910 3917
Standard atlas of Rock county, Minn. 1914 4809
Standard atlas of Rock county, Nebr. 1912 3828
Standard atlas of Rolette county, N. Dak. 1910 3864
Standard atlas of Roseau county, Minn. 1913 4810
Standard atlas of Rusk county, Wis. 1914 5101
Standard atlas of Saginaw county, Mich. 1916 4762
Standard atlas of St. Clair county, Mich. 1897 1996
—— 1916 4763
Standard atlas of St. Joseph county, Ind. 1895 1626
—— 1911 3739
Standard atlas of Saline county, Mo. 1916 4871
Standard atlas of Sanborn county, S. Dak. 1912 .... 3917a
Standard atlas of Sanilac county, Mich. 1906 4764
Standard atlas of Schuyler county, Ill. 1913 4589
Standard atlas of Schuyler county, Mo. 1916 4872
Standard atlas of Shawano county, Wis. 1911 3934
Standard atlas of Shawnee county, Kans. 1898 1740
Standard atlas of Shelby county, Ill. 1914 4590
Standard atlas of Shelby county, Iowa. 1911 3753
Standard atlas of Sheridan county, Kans. 1906–1907 4700
Standard atlas of Sheridan county, Nebr. 1914 4906
Standard atlas of Sheridan county, N. Dak. 1914 4976
Standard atlas of Sherman county, Oreg. 1913 5008
Standard atlas of Shiawassee county, Mich. 1915 4766
Standard atlas of Sioux county, Nebr. 1916 4907
Standard atlas of Smith county, Kans. 1917 4701
Standard atlas of Spokane county, Wash. 1912 3927
Standard atlas of Stafford county, Kans. 1904 4702
Standard atlas of Stanton county, Nebr. 1919 4908
Standard atlas of Stark county, N. Dak. 1914 4977
Standard atlas of Steele county, N. Dak. 1911 3865
Standard atlas of Stephenson county, Ill. 1913 4591
Standard atlas of Stutsman county, N. Dak. 1911 3866
Standard atlas of Sully county, S. Dak. 1916 5063
Standard atlas of Sumner county, Kans. 1902 1742
—— 1918 4703
Standard atlas of Taylor county, Wis. 1913 5105
Standard atlas of Tazewell county, Ill. 1910 3728
Standard atlas of Thayer county, Nebr. 1916 4909
Standard atlas of Tripp county, S. Dak. 1915 5064
Standard atlas of Turner county, S. Dak. 1911 3918
Standard atlas of Umatilla county, Oreg. 1914 5009
Standard atlas of Union county, Ill. 1908 4592
Standard atlas of Union county, Iowa. 1916 4661
Standard atlas of Union county, S. Dak. 1910 3919
Standard atlas of Van Buren county, Iowa. 1918 4662
Standard atlas of Van Buren county, Mich. 1912 .... 3808a
Standard atlas of Vermilion county, Ill. 1915 4593

Ortelius, Abraham—Continued.
Theatrvm orbis terrarvm. Dutch edition. 1598.......... 407
—— Latin edition. 1601.......... 412
—— —— 1603.......... 419
—— English edition. 1606.......... 3410
—— Latin edition. 1609.......... 427
Vierdte zusatzs des Theatri . . . der gantzen welt. 1591.......... 3399

Osceola sentinel.
Complete atlas of Clarke county, Iowa. 1909.......... 4630

Ottens, Reiner.
Atlas maior. [1641–1729].......... 4257

Ottens, Reiner, *and* **Ottens, J.**
Atlas. [1756?].......... 617
Atlas minor. [1695–1756?].......... 522
—— [1703–1756?].......... 542
—— [1745?].......... 3495
—— 1756?.......... 616

Ottens heirs.
Atlas. [1740?].......... 3490

Oxenham, Edward Lavington, 1843–1896.
Historical atlas of the Chinese empire. 1898.......... 3182

Oxford historical society.
Old plans of Oxford. [1899].......... 2936, 5212a

Ozanne, Nicolas-Marie, 1728–1811.
Nouvelles vues perspectives des ports de France . . . [1783–1791?].......... 4017a

Paddock, H. G.
Plat book, Moline and East Moline, Ill. 1904.......... 1591, 1595

Page, H. R., & co.
Atlas of Chicago. 1879.......... 1581
Illustrated atlas of Winnebago and Boone counties, Ill. 1886.......... 1517, 1579
Illustrated historical atlas of Wisconsin. 1881.......... 5079

Page, Thomas, *and* **Mount, R.**
Atlas maritimus novus. 1702.......... 3334

Page & Smith.
Illustrated historical atlas of the county of Brant, Ontario. 1875.......... 3672

Pajol, Charles Pierre Victor, *comte,* 1812–1891.
Atlas des guerres sous Louis xv. 1886.......... 2977
Atlas des itinéraires, campagnes, opérations militaires de Pajol. 1874.......... 2978

Palairet, Jean, 1697–1774.
Atlas méthodique. 1755.......... 3502

Palairet, Jean, *& others.*
Bowles's universal atlas. [1794–1798].......... 681
[Collection of maps. 1755–1771].......... 4290

Palmer, Loomis T.
Gaskell's new and complete family atlas. 1886.......... 932
Unique album atlas. 1894.......... 988

Palmer, *Sir* **Thomas,** *and* **Covert, W.**
Survey of the coast of Sussex, made in 1587. 1870.......... 2891

Papen, Augustus.
Topographischer atlas des königreichs Hannover und herzogthums Braunschweig. 1832–1847.......... 3039

New handy atlas of the world. [1908] 3584
—— [1911] 3626
New handy census gazetteer and atlas. [1894] 996
New ideal state and county survey and atlas. 1908 1132b, 1600
—— 1909 3596
New ideal state and county survey and atlas containing a large county and railway map of Ohio. 1909 3873
New ideal state and county survey and atlas containing a . . . map of Connecticut. 1911 3709
New ideal state and county survey and atlas, containing a . . . map of Illinois. 1911 3718
New imperial atlas. 1905 1107
—— 1911 3629
—— 1917 4445
New indexed atlas. 1886 934
—— 1894 1440
New indexed atlas of the northwest. [1880] 1407
New indexed business atlas. 1881 1408, 1409, 1410
—— 1883 1413
—— 1884 1417, 1418
New international indexed atlas. 1898 1027
New pictorial atlas. [1896] 1010
New pocket atlas . . . of all states and territories in the United States. 1892 1434
—— 1893 1437
New popular atlas. 1896 1012
New reference atlas of the world and the war. [1918] 4449
New standard atlas. [1890] 960
—— [1892] 976, 977
—— 1897 4375
—— [1899] 1043
On the battle lines. [1915] 4244, 5183
Pocket atlas. 1886 935
—— [1900] 1057
—— 1911 3627
—— 1915 4424
—— 1917 4446
Standard war atlas. [1898] 3689
Toronto mail and empire atlas of Canada. [1904] 1247
Twentieth century atlas. 1896 1013
Universal atlas. 1892 978
—— 1893 986
—— 1895 1004, 1005
—— 1896 1014
—— [1899] 1044
—— 1901 1067
—— 1916 4433
Unrivaled atlas. 1911 3630
War atlas. 1898 4521
War map of Europe. 1914 4245

Randall, G. A., & co.
Illustrated historical atlas of Sheboygan county, Wis. 1875 3935

Robinson, Earl J., & co.
Illustrated review showing commercial, industrial, agricultural, historical development of the state of Iowa. [1915] ... 4620

Robinson, Elisha.
Atlas of Chicago, Ill. 1886 ... 1583
Atlas of Essex county, N. J. 1890 ... 2155
Atlas of Jefferson county, N. Y. 1888 ... 2232
Atlas of Kings county, N. Y. 1890 ... 2233
Atlas of Morris county, N. J. 1887 ... 2168
Atlas of Norfolk county, Mass. 1888 ... 1822
Atlas of Rochester, Monroe county, N. Y. 1888 ... 2323
Altas of the Oranges, Essex county, N. J. 1904 ... 2180, 2191, 2196, 2200
Atlas of the 29th, 30th, 31st, and 32d wards . . . city of New York. 1898 ... 2278
Certified copies of important maps appertaining to the 23rd and 24th wards, city of New York. 1888–1890 ... 2035
Certified copies of important maps of wards 8, 17, 18, 22, 23, 24, and 25, city of Brooklyn, N. Y. 1889 ... 2277

Robinson, Elisha, *and* **Pidgeon, R. H.**
Atlas of Brooklyn, N. Y. 1886 ... 2276
Atlas of Cincinnati, Ohio. 1883–1884 ... 2423
Atlas of Detroit and suburbs. 1885 ... 2003
Atlas of Mansfield, Ohio. 1882 ... 2433
Atlas of New Orleans, La. 1883 ... 1771
Atlas of New York. 1883–1887 ... 2302
—— 1884 ... 2303
—— 1885 ... 2304
—— 1890–1893 ... 2308
Atlas of Paterson, N. J. 1884 ... 2193
Atlas of Richmond, city of New York. 1907 ... 2316
Atlas of Springfield, Ohio. 1882 ... 2435
Real estate atlas of the city of New York. 1889–1890 ... 2306

Robinson, Elisha, *and* **Tenney, L. E.**
Atlas of the city of Newark, N. J. 1901 ... 2189

Robinson, Elisha, *& others.*
Atlas of Denver, Colo. 1887 ... 1475
Atlas of Passaic and Acquackanonk township, Passaic county, N. J. 1901. 2192
Atlas of Summit, N. J. 1900 ... 2107

Robinson, Elisha, & co.
Certified copies of maps of the annexed district . . . city of New York. 1897 ... 2314

Robiquet, ——
Atlas hydrographique. [1844–1851] ... 795
—— 1882 ... 909

Rochambeau, Jean Baptiste Donatien de Vimeur, *comte* **de,** 1725–1807.
Amérique campagne, 1782. *ms.* [1782] ... 1335

Rockwood, C. H.
Atlas of Cheshire county, N. H. 1877 ... 2138

Rocque, John, *d.* 1762.
Set of plans and forts in America. 1763 ... 1186
Small british atlas. 1764 ... 5205

Russia. *Mezhevoĭ korpus voennago vi͡edomstva.*
Атласъ Тверской губерніи—Topographical survey atlas of the Tver province. 1853 3126

—— *Ministerstvo Morskoe.*
Атласъ Чернаго моря—Atlas of the Black sea. 1841 3118
Атласъ Каспійскаго моря—Atlas of the Caspian sea. 1826 3181

—— *Otdi͡el statistiki i kartografīi ministerstva puteĭ soobschenīi͡a.*
Статистическій атласъ путей сообщенія Россіи—Statistical atlas of the commerce and traffic of Russia. 1902 3101

I. Russkoe geograficheskoe obshchestvo.
Атласъ къ x книжкѣ записокъ кавказскаго отдѣла—Atlas to accompany the 10th volume of Zapinski's works. 1879 5280

Rychkov, Petr Ivanovich, 1712–1777, *and* **Krasil'nikov, A. D.**
Оренбургская губернія—Province of Orenburg. 1880 3122

Sällskapet för Finlands geografi.
Atlas de Finlande. 1899 3121
—— 1910. 1911 4063
Suomen kartasto, 1910. 1911 5281

St. Louis plat and record co.
Atlas of St. Louis county, [Mo.] 1909 3822
Atlas of the city of St. Louis. 1905 2106

St. Peterburg. *Gornoe uchilishche.*
Новый атласъ земнаго шара—New atlas . . . of the globe. [1793] 679

Sampaio, Theodoro Fernandes.
Atlas dos estados unidos do Brazil. 1911 5141
Exploração dos rios Itapetininga e Paranapanema. 1889 2747

Sandby, Paul, 1725–1809.
See Pownall, Thomas. Six remarkable views in the provinces of New-York, New-Jersey, and Pennsylvania, in North America.

Sánchez, Alexandro.
Mapa general de les almas . . . 1845 5305

Sanctis, Gabriello de.
Atlante corografico del regno delle due Sicilie. 1843 4043

Sandler, Christian, 1859–1912.
Reformation der kartographie um 1700. Atlas. 1905 261

Sanford, G. P., Beers, F. W., *& others.*
Atals of Bennington co., Vt. 1869 2595
Atlas of Bradford county, Pa. 1869 2463
Atlas of Chemung county, N. Y. 1869 2218
Atals of Chittenden county, Vt. 1869 2597
Atlas of Clinton county, N. Y. 1869 2219
Atlas of Stark county, Ohio. 1870 2415
Atlas of Tioga county, N. Y. 1869 2257
Atlas of Windsor county, Vt. 1869 2604

Sanford, G. P., Gould, F. A., *and* **Lake, D. J.**
Atlas of Randolph county, Ind. 1874 1624
Atlas of Wayne county, Ind. 1874 3741

Sanford & Everts.
Atlas of Stafford county, N. H. 1871 2130

Sanford, Everts & co.
Atlas and history of Androscoggin county, Me. 1873 3761
Atlas of York co., Me. 1872 3766

Sangamon county abstract co.
Plat book of Sangamon county, Ill. 1914 4588

Sanson, Nicolas, *d'Abbeville,* 1600–1667.
Afriqve en plvsievrs cartes novvelles. 1656 5310
Amérique en plusieurs cartes. 1657 1151
Amérique en plusieurs cartes nouvelles. 1662 1152
—— [1667?] 1153
Asie en plusieurs cartes novvelles. 1652–[1653] 4068
Atlas nouveau. 1689–[1690] 503
—— 1692–1696 .... 514, 3452
—— 1696 524
Cartes générales de tovtes les parties dv monde. 1658 4260
Cartes particulières de la France. 1676 4017

Sanson, Nicolas, *d'Abbeville, and* **Sanson, Nicolas,** *fils,* 1626–1648.
Description de tout l'univers. 1700 528
Europe [l'Asie, l'Afrique, l'Amérique] en plusieurs cartes. 1683 494
Geographische en historische beschryvingh der vier bekende werelds-deelen. 1683 495

Sanson, Nicolas, *d'Abbeville,* **Sanson, Guillaume,** *d.* 1703, *and* **Sanson, N.,** *fils.*
Cartes générales de la géographie. 1675 486
Cartes générales de tovtes lae parties dv monde. 1670 3436
[Géographie universelle. 1675?] 484, 4264

Santarem, Manuel Francisco de Barros e Sousa, de Mesquita de Macedo Leitão e Carvalhosa, *2d visconde de,* 1791–1856.
Essai sur l'histoire de la cosmographie et de la cartographie pendant le moyen-âge. Atlas. 1849–1852 262

Santini, P.
Atlas portatif d'Italie. 1783 3059
Atlas universel. 1776–[1784] 647

Sardinia. *Corpo reale dello stato maggiore.*
Carta topografica degli stati in terraferma di s. m. il re di Sardegna. [1854–1875] 5261

Sargent, Charles Sprague, 1841–
Report on the forests of North America. Atlas. 1884 1278
Sixteen maps accompanying report on forest trees of North America. [1884] 1187

Sauer, William C.
Detailed official atlas of Wayne county, Mich. [1905] 2002

Sauer, bros.
Detailed official atlas of Wayne county, Mich. 1915 4768

Saunders, Trelawney.
Atlas of twelve maps of India. 1889 5300

Sauvage, Maxime Joseph Marie, 1869–
Guerre Sino-Japonaise. 1897 3185

Savage, Robert Ferguson.
Atlas of commercial geography. 1905 .... ’

Savonarola, Raffaelo.
Universus terrarum orbis. 1713 3475

Saxton, Christopher, *fl.* 1570–1596.
Maps of England and Wales. 1574–1579 2913
[Maps of England and Wales, amended by P. Lea. 1659–1689] .... *

Schwann, L.
Schwann'scher schul-atlas. [1914?] *See* Bludau, A. Schwann'scher schul-atlas. [1914?]

Scobel, Albert, 1851-1912.
Handels-atlas zur verkehrs- und wirtschafts-geographie. 1902............ 78
Velhagen & Klasings kleiner handatlas. 1912............................ 3640

Scobel, Albert, *and* **Lehmann, R.**
Atlas für höhere lehranstalten. 1903.................................. 74, 298

Scofield, Horace G.
Atlas of the city of Bridgeport, Conn. 1876............................ 1483

Scott, A.
Republica de Chile. Puerto de Valparaíso. 1910......................... 5147

Scott, J. D.
Atlas of the 24th & 27th wards, West Philadelphia. 1878................ 2525
Combination atlas map of Bucks county, Pa. 1876........................ 2464
Combination atlas map of Burlington county, N. J. 1876................. 2153
Combination atlas map of Montgomery county, Pa. 1877................... 2488

Scott, Joseph.
Atlas of the United States. 1796....................................... 4521a

Scribner's, Charles, sons.
Scribner-Black atlas. 1890... 961

Seaman, J. W.
Map of city of Long Branch, N. J. 1906................................. 2185

Sears, J. H.
Historical atlas of Kearney county, Nebr. 1894......................... 2117

Ségur, Louis Philippe, *comte* **de,** 1753-1830.
Atlas pour l'histoire universelle. 1822................................. 146
—— 1840.. 4143
Atlas pour servir à l'histoire ancienne, romaine et du Bas-Empire 1827... 3287

Seine. *Direction des travaux de Paris.*
Atlas administratif des 20 arrondissements de la ville de Paris. 1868...... 5235
Atlas municipal des vingts arrondissements de la ville de Paris. 1878..... 5236

Selander, Nils, *and* **Hildebrand, E.,** *i. e.* **H. R. T. E.**
Atlas till allmänna och svenska historien. [1883]....................... 109, 2790, 3141

Seller, John, *fl.* 1667-1700.
Atlas maritimus. [Copy A. 1670?].. 4150
—— [Copy B. 1670?]... 4151
—— [1671?]... 4152
—— [1672?]... 4153
—— 1675.. 487, 4154
Atlas minimus. [1678]... 490
Atlas terrestris. [1700?]... 529
Coasting pilot. [1672].. 2915, 3077
English pilot. First book. 1671... 3985
—— —— 1690... 2833
Hydrographia universalis. [1695].. 505
New systeme of geography. [1685].. 3450
—— 1690.. 4267

Senex, John, *d.* 1740.
Itinéraire de toutes les routes de l'Angleterre. 1766.................... 2911
Modern geography. [1708-1725]... 550
New general atlas. 1721... 563

Silvestre, Israel, 1621–1691.
Recueil des vues de villes. 1751 3963

Simpson, William, 1823–1899.
Seat of the war in the east. 1855–1856 5279

Sipman, Friedrich.
Ergänzungsheft für haus- und schulatlanten. 1907 .... 1126b

Skelton, Gordon V.
Atlas map of Washington county, Ark. [1894] 1456

Smedley, Samuel L.
Atlas of the city of Philadelphia. [1862] 2519

Smiley, Thomas T.
Improved atlas. 1824 313
New atlas. 7th ed. [1830] 314
—— 14th ed. [1832] 315
—— [22d ed. 1834] 316
—— [1838] 317

Smith, A. C., *and* **Bennett, L. G.**
Map of Winona county, Minn. 1867 2046

Smith, Benjamin Eli, *editor.*
Century atlas. [1897] 1020
—— [1899] 1045
—— [1901] 1070
—— [1902] 1080
—— [1903] 3577
—— [1904] 1093
—— [1906] 1112a
—— [1911] 3633

Smith, Benjamin H.
Atlas of Delaware county, Pa. 1880 5015

Smith, Charles, *map seller.*
New english atlas. 1804 5200
New general atlas. 1816 729

Smith, Elvino V.
Atlas of the 24th, 34th & 44th wards of the city of Philadelphia. 1911 3892

Smith, George Adam, 1856–
Atlas of the historical geography of the Holy Land. 1915 5302

Smith, J. L.
Atlas of properties along the Philadelphia, Wilmington and Baltimore r. r. 1889 2448

Smith, J. Mott.
Geography of the Hawaiian islands. [1889] 3261

Smith, Lucien Herbert.
Historical and chronological atlas of the United States. 1881 1296

Smith, Roswell C.
Atlas. 1835 318
—— [1839] 319
—— Improved ed. 1839 320
—— Improved ed. 1850 321
—— 1853 322
—— 1854 3380
—— 1866 4347
—— 1868 323

Stanford's geographical establishment.
Atlas of the world war. [1917?] 4246

Starkweather, George A.
Sunday school geography. 1872 89

Starling, Thomas.
Geographical annual. 1833 4319

Starr, J. W., Caldwell, J. A., *& others.*
Atlas of Knox county, Ohio. 1871 2390

Staunton, *Sir* **George Leonard,** 1737–1801.
Authentic account of an embassy from the king of Great Britain to the emperor of China. Atlas. [1798] 3190, 4070

Steel, Penelope, *and* **Horsburgh, J.**
New and complete East-India pilot. 1817 4312

Stein, Christian Gottfried Daniel, 1771–1830.
Neuer atlas der ganzen erde. 12. aufl. 1833–[1834] 766
—— 28. aufl. 1856 4337

Steinwehr, Adolph Wilhelm August Friedrich von, 1822–1877.
[Atlas. 1869?] 854

Stemfoort, J. W., *and* **Siethoff, J. J.**
Atlas der nederlandsche bezittingen in Oost-Indië. 1883–1885 3215

Stephenson, John, *and* **Burn, G.**
Laurie & Whittle's channel pilot. [1794]–1803 3986

Sternegg, Johann Khoss von.
Schlachten-atlas. [1907–1914] 177a, 3336, 4158

Stevenson, Edward Luther, 1860–
Maps illustrating early discovery and exploration in America. 1903 1139
—— Text and key maps. 1906 1139

Stewart, Charles W., *and* **Ockerson, J. A.**
Mississippi river from St. Louis to the sea. 1892 1324

Stewart & Page.
Combination atlas map of Erie county, Ohio. 1874 2373

Stieler, Adolf, 1775–1836.
Atlante scolastico. 1855 325
Atlas of modern geography. [1909] 3597
Atlas von Deutschland. [1853] 2855
Grande atlante geografico. 1914 .... *
Hand-atlas. [1853] 4333
—— [1856] 819
—— [1865] 3561
—— [1868] 4351
—— [10. aufl. 1868] 4350
—— [1871–1875] 4352
—— Specialkarte von Australien. 1875 5322
—— [1876] 881
—— [1877] 3566
—— [7th ed. 1879–1882] 4356
—— [1882] 910
—— [1896] 1015
—— 1905 .... 1071, 1108
—— 1918 .... *
Kleiner atlas der deutschen bundesstaaten. 1852 3028
Schul-atlas. 1841 3381
—— 1856 326
—— 1910 3382

Tornau, Nikolaĭ Nikolaevich, *baron,* 1848–
Учебный историческій атласъ—Historical school atlas. 1893........ 3324

Treat bros.
Pocket atlas of Lenawee county, [Mich.] 1906........................ 1985

Trolley press.
Travelers' atlas-guide. 1910.. 3696
—— Series 2. 1911... 3698
Travelers' atlas-guide to New England. 1913......................... 4530
Trondhjems historiske forening. *See* Koren Kristian Brinch. Karter og topografiske 'tegninger vedkommende Trondhjem og Trøndelagen. 1899.

T' Sersteuens, ——
Cartes descriptions générales et particulières. *ms.* [1726]........... 570

Türke, Juan.
Atlas de Chile. 1895.. 2757

Tunison, Henry Cuthbert.
Atlas. 1901... 1072

Tunnicliff, William.
Topographical survey of the counties of Hants, Wilts, Dorset, Somerset, Devon, and Cornwall. 1791... 2923

Turner, Charles Heber.
Dollar atlas. [1890]... 962
Peerless atlas. [1889]... 955
Twentieth century peerless atlas. [1903]............................ 1089

Turney, O. H.
Salt River valley. 1908... 3702

Tuttle, Frank W., *and* **Pike, D. W.**
Atlas of Kansas City and vicinity. 1908............................. 2103

Tuttle & Pike.
Atlas of Chariton county, Mo. 1915.................................. 4838
Atlas of Lafayette county, Mo. [1914]............................... 4855
Atlas of Linn county, Mo. 1915...................................... 4857

Tyson, J. Washington.
Atlas of ancient and modern history. 1845............................ 156

Uetrecht, Erich, 1879– *and* **Krauss, P.**
Meyers deutscher städteatlas. 1913.................................. 5240

Uhl, John B.
Official atlas of Lucas county, Ohio. 1900.......................... 2396

Ullitz, Hugo, *& others.*
Atlas of Suffolk county, Long Island, N. Y. 1902–1909.............. 2255, 3842

Umlauft, Friedrich, 1844–, *and* **Hannak, E.**
Historischer schulatlas. 1908...................................... 2789a

Union publishing co.
Plat book of Bremer county, Iowa. 1894.............................. 1647
Plat book of Butler county, Iowa. 1895.............................. 1649
Plat book of Fayette county, Iowa. 1896............................. 1662
Plat book of Floyd county, Iowa. 1895............................... 1663
Plat book of Freeborn county, Minn. 1895............................ 2017

United States. *Adjutant general's office.*
Atlas of ports, cities, and localities of the island of Cuba. 1898........... 2714

—— *Census office, 9th census, 1870.*
Statistical atlas of the United States. 1874........................ 1330

—— *Census office, 11th census, 1890.*
Statistical atlas of the United States. 1898........................ 1333

United States. *Office of farm management.*
Atlas of american agriculture. 1918 ... 4491
— *Treasury department. Bureau of statistics.*
Territorial development of the United States. [1901] ... 4508
— *War department.*
Atlas containing maps of Chicago river. [1900] ... 1510
Atlas of battlefields of Chickamauga, Chattanooga, and vicinity. 1900–1901 ... 1355
Atlas of the battlefield of Antietam. 1904 ... 1354
Atlas to accompany the official records of the Union and Confederate armies. 1891–1895 ... 1353
Internal improvements. [1825–1843] ... 1377
Military maps illustrating the operations of the armies of the Potomac & James. [1869] ... 3688
Reconnoissance of the Mississippi & Ohio rivers. [1875] ... 1325
— *Weather bureau.*
Climatic charts of the United States. 1904 ... 4493
Rainfall and snow of the United States. 1894 ... 1360
Summary of international meteorological observations. 1893 ... 1359

United States express co.
Express and railway guide. [1895] ... 4512

Universal history. Maps and charts to the modern part of the Universal history. 1766 ... 639

Universal reference co.
Reference atlas of Manhattan. 1910 ... 385

Unwin, William Jordan.
Homerton college atlas. 1863 ... 330

Unz & co.
Atlas of New York city and the metropolitan district. 1916 ... 4951

Ustrīalov, Nikolaĭ Gerasimovich, 1805–1870.
Карты, планы и снимки къ первымъ тремъ томамъ Исторіи царствованія Петра Великаго—Maps, plans, and reproductions in connection with the first 3 volumes of the History of Peter the great. 1858–1863. 4056

Vacani, Camillo, 1784–1862.
Atlante topografico-militare per servire alla storia delle campagne e degl' Italiani in Ispagna al MDCCCVIII al MDCCCXIII. 1823 ... 3130

Valck, Gerard, 1626–1720.
Nova totius geographica telluris projectio. [1720?] ... 562
— [1748?] ... 605

Valck, Gerard, *and* **Schenk, P.**
Atlantis sylloge compendiosa. 1709 ... 4276
Atlas anglois. 1715 ... 4001

Vallardi, Francesco, 1809–1895.
Atlante corografico, orografico, idrografico e storico dell' Italia. [1867–1897] ... 3063, 3064

Van Antwerp, Bragg & co.
Eclectic atlas . . . of the United States. [1881] ... 1411

Van Horne, Thomas Budd.
History of the army of the Cumberland. 1875 ... 4519

Vancouver, George, 1758–1798.
Voyage de découvertes à l'océan Pacifique du nord. Atlas. [1799] ... 198, 1219
Voyage of discovery to the North Pacific ocean. Atlas. 1798 ... 197, 1218

Walker & Miles.
New standard atlas of the dominion of Canada. 1875.................... 1237

Walker lithograph & publishing co.
Atlas of Barnstable county, Mass. [1910]................................ 3769, 3772, 3773, 3776–3778, 3780, 3782, 3784, 3786, 3790–3792, 3794, 3795, 3799
Atlas of the towns of Braintree and Weymouth, Norfolk county, Mass. 1909.. 3774, 3798
Atlas of the towns of Needham, Dover, Westwood, Millis, and Medfield, Norfolk county, Mass. 1909............................ 3779, 3787–3789, 3797
Atlas of the towns of Topsfield, Ipswich, Essex, Hamilton and Wenham, Essex county, Mass. 1910......................... 3781, 3783, 3785, 3793, 3796

Wall, W. G.
[Hudson river portfolio. 1828]... 4958

Wall, Mann & Hall.
Illustrated atlas of Noble county, Ohio. 1879.......................... 2406

Wallace, J. B., *and* **Shillington, T.**
Empire city lot book, being a complete atlas of Manhattan island north of forty-second street. [1873].. 2295

Walling, Henry F.
Atlas of Canada. 1875.. 1238
Atlas of Michigan. [1873]... 1960
Atlas of Ohio. 1868... 1389, 2346
Atlas of Wisconsin. [1876]... 2633
Tackabury's atlas of the dominion of Canada. 1876..................... 4481

Walling, Henry F., *and* **Campbell, R. A.**
New atlas of Illinois. 1870... 1511

Walling, Henry F., *and* **Gray, O. W.**
New topographical atlas of Ohio. 1872.................................. 2347
New topographical atlas of Pennsylvania. 1872.......................... 2453
Official topographical atlas of Massachusetts. 1871.................... 1800

Walling, Henry F., *and* **Hitchcock, C. H.**
Atlas of the state of New Hampshire. [1877]............................ 2136

Walling, Henry F., Gray, O. W., *and* **Martenet, S. J.**
New topographical atlas of the state of Maryland and the District of Columbia. 1873... 1497, 1780

Walser, Gabriel, 1695–1776.
Schweitzer-geographie. 1770... 4067

Walter, Thomas U.
Quadrangle, Birmingham, map book of business district. 1914............ 4536

Ward, *lady* **Emily Elizabeth Swinburne.**
Six views of the most important towns . . . of Mexico. 1829............. 5116

Ward & co.
Miniature atlas. 1857... 825

Ward, Lock & co.
Handy atlas and world gazetteer. 1908................................... 3586

Warne, Frederick, & co.
Junior atlas. New ed. 1868.. 332

Warner, George E.
Plat book of Clayton county, Iowa. 1886................................. 1653
Plat book of Howard county, Iowa. 1886.................................. 1671

Warner, George E., Beers, F. W., *& others.*
Atlas of Greene county, N. Y. 1867 2229
Atlas of Jefferson county, Ohio. 1871 2389
Atlas of New York and vicinity. 1867 2290

Warner, George E., Beers, F. W., Leavenworth, A., *& others.*
Atlas of Delaware county, Ohio. 1866 2372

Warner, George E., *and* **Foote, C. M.**
Atlas of Grant county, Wis. 1877 2646
Plat book of Allamakee county, Iowa. 1886 1642
Plat book of Buchanan county, Iowa. 1886 1648
Plat book of Fayette county, Iowa. 1879 1661
Platt book of Houston county, Minn. 1878 2021
Plat book of Iowa county, Iowa. 1886 1674
Plat book of Marshall county, Iowa. 1885 1686
Plat book of Olmstead county, Minn. 1878 2031
Plat book of Otter Tail county, Minn. 1884 2033
Platt book of Winneshiek county, Iowa. 1886 1707

Warner & Beers.
Atlas of Bond county and the state of Illinois. 1875 1516
Atlas of Bureau county and the state of Illinois. 1875 1520
Atlas of De Witt county and the state of Illinois. 1875 1528
Atlas of Grundy county and the state of Illinois. 1874 1535
Atlas of Henry county and the state of Illinois. 1875 1537
Atlas of Illinois. 1876 1513
Atlas of La Salle county and the state of Illinois. 1876 1544
Atlas of McLean county and the state of Illinois. 1874 1546
Atlas of Macon county and the state of Illinois. 1874 1548
Atlas of Macoupin county and the state of Illinois. 1875 1550
Atlas of Moultrie county and the state of Illinois. 1875 1556
Atlas of Piatt county and the state of Illinois. 1875 .... 1560, 4586
Atlas of Shelby county and the state of Illinois. 1875 1566
Atlas of Stark county and the state of Illinois. 1873 1568
Atlas of Whiteside county and the state of Illinois. 1872 1576
Atlas of Woodford county and the state of Illinois. 1873 1580

Warner & Higgins.
Atlas of Edgar county and the state of Illinois 1870 1530

Warner, Higgins & Beers,
Atlas of the state of Illinois. 1871 1512
Atlas of Warren county and the state of Illinois. 1872 1574

Warre, *Sir* **Henry James,** 1819–1898.
Sketches in North America and the Oregon territory. [1848] 4470, 4471

Warren, William, 1806–1879.
Atlas to Warren's system of geography. 1843 333

Wartmann, Hermann.
Atlas über die entwicklung von industrie und handel der Schweiz. 1873. 3146

Washington Post.
Standard war atlas with marginal index. [1898] 4217

Watering, The, places of Great Britian. 1831 5196

Watson, Gaylord.
New and complete illustrated atlas. [1885] 929
New commercial . . . atlas of the United States and british provinces. [1875] 1392
New indexed family atlas of the United States. 1883 .... 915, 1414

Waupaca abstract & loan co.

Plat book of Waupaca county, Wis. 1912....3935a

Webb publishing co.

Atlas and farm directory . . . Barron county, Wis. 1914.... 5081
Atlas and farm directory . . . Benton county, Minn. [1914].... 4775
Atlas and farm directory . . . Buffalo county, Wis. 1914.... 5082
Atlas and farm directory . . . Chippewa county, Minn. 1914.... 4778
Atlas and farm directory . . . Crawford county, Wis. 1914.... 5085
Atlas and farm directory . . . Dakota county, Minn. 1916.... 4780
Atlas and farm directory . . . Dodge county, Minn. 1914.... 4781
Atlas and farm directory . . . Grant county, Minn. 1914.... 4786
Atlas and farm directory . . . Green Lake county, Wis. [1914].... 5088
Atlas and farm directory . . . Jackson county, Wis. [1914].... 5090
Atlas and farm directory . . . Juneau county, Wis. 1914.... 5092
Atlas and farm directory . . . Kandiyohi county, Minn. 1915.... 4791
Atlas and farm directory . . . Lincoln county, Minn. 1915.... 4795
Atlas and farm directory . . . Mille Lacs county, Minn. [1914].... 4799
Atlas and farm directory . . . of Clayton county, Iowa. 1914.... 4631
Atlas and farm directory . . . of Fillmore county, Minn. 1915.... 4783
Atlas and farm directory . . . of Lyon county, Minn. 1914.... 4796
Atlas and farm directory . . . of Redwood county, Minn. 1914.... 4806
Atlas and farm directory . . . of Trempealeau county, Wis. 1914.... 5106
Atlas and farm directory . . . of Vernon county, Wis. [1915].... 5107
Atlas and farm directory . . . of Winneshiek county, Iowa. 1915.... 4665
Atlas and farm directory . . . Pipestone county, Minn. [1914].... 4804
Atlas and farm directory . . . Renville county, Minn. 1913.... 4807
Atlas and farm directory . . . Rice county, Minn. 1915.... 4808
Atlas and farm directory . . . Sherburne county, Minn. 1914.... 4812
Atlas and farm directory . . . Steele county, Minn. 1914.... 4814
Atlas and farm directory . . . Traverse county, Minn. [1915].... 4816
Atlas and farm directory . . . Wabasha county, Minn. [1915].... 4817
Atlas and farm directory . . . Waseca county, Minn. [1914].... 4818
Atlas and farm directory . . . Watonwan county, Minn. 1915.... 4820
Atlas and farm directory . . . Waushara county, Wis. [1914].... 5110
Atlas and farm directory . . . Wright county, Minn. 1915.... 4823
Atlas and farm directory of Nicollet county, Minn. 1913.... 4801
Atlas and farm directory of Todd county, Minn. [1914].... 4815
Atlas and farmers' directory . . . of Kanabec county, Minn. 1915.... 4790
Atlas and farmers' directory . . . of Mower county, Minn. 1915.... 4800
Atlas and farmers' directory . . . of Polk county, Minn. 1915.... 4805
Atlas and farmers' directory . . . of Wilkin county, Minn. 1915.... 4821
Atlas and farmers' directory of Anoka county, and the eleven northern townships of Hennepin county, Minn. 1914.... 4774, 4787
Atlas and farmers' directory of Brown county, Minn. 1914.... 4777
Atlas and farmers' directory of Faribault county, Minn. 1913.... 4782
Atlas and farmers' directory of Goodhue county, Minn. 1914.... 4785
Atlas and farmers' directory of Isanti county, Minn. 1914.... 4788
Atlas and farmers' directory of Lac qui Parle county, Minn. 1913.... 4793
Atlas and farmers' directory of McLeod county, Minn. 1914.... 4797
Atlas and farmers' directory of Meeker county, Minn. 1913.... 4798
Atlas and farmers' directory of Olmstead county, Minn. 1914.... 4803
Atlas and farmers' directory of St. Croix county, Wis. 1914.... 5103
Atlas and farmers' directory of Scott county, Minn. 1913.... 4811
Atlas and farmers' directory of Sibley county, Minn. 1914.... 4813

Wolff, Carl, 1838–
Historischer atlas. 1877 .... 158, 2796

Wolff, Carl, *and* **Kiepert, H.,** *i. e.* **J. S. H.**
Historischer schul-atlas. [7. aufl. 1897] 116

Wolfgang, Abraham.
Atlas minor. [1689] 502

Wolverton, Chester, *and* **Breou, F.**
Atlas of Monmouth county, N. J. 1889 4914

Woodbridge, William Channing, 1794–1854.
Larger atlas. [1822] 336
Modern atlas. [1824] 337
—— 4th ed. 1831 340
—— New ed. [1831] 339
—— [1843] 343
School atlas. 5th ed. [1821] 335
—— 14th ed. 1831 338
—— Improved ed. 1833 341
—— [16th ed.] 1835 342

Woodman, Prentiss M.
Minnetonka map-directory. 1908 .... 2006a

Woodward, Horace Bolingbroke, 1848–
Stanford's geological atlas of Great Britain. 1904 2879
Stanford's geological atlas of Great Britain and Ireland. 1907 2880
—— 3d ed. 1914 5190
—— Photographic supplement. 1913 5191

Woolman, H. C., Price, T. T., *and* **Rose, T. F.**
Historical and biographical atlas of the New Jersey coast. 1878 2141

Worcester, Joseph Emerson, 1784–1865.
Historical atlas. New ed. 1827 159
—— 3d ed. 1828 4144
Worcester's outline map. [1829?] 210

World missionary conference. *Edinburgh.*
Statistical atlas of christian missions. 1910 3340

Wright, Harry Andrew.
Early maps of the Connecticut valley in Massachusetts. 1911 3767

Württemberg. *Statistisches landesamt.*
Topographischer atlas des koenigreichs Württemberg. [1826–1851] 3048

Wyld, James, 1812–1887.
Emigrant's atlas. [1848] 3304
Maps & plans showing the principal movements . . . in which the british army was engaged . . . 1808 to 1814. [1840] 2893, 3131
New general atlas. [1840?] .... *
—— [1852] 808

Wyss, Johann Rudolf, 1781–1830.
Hand atlas für reisende in das Berner oberland. 1816 3153

Wytfliet, Corneille.
Descriptionis Ptolemaicæ avgmentvm. 1597 .... 1140, 3644
—— 1598 3645
—— 1603 1142
Histoire vniverselle des Indes Orientales et Occidentales. 1605 1143
—— 1611 4459

[illegible]
Map of the north shore, Beverly to Magnolia, Essex Co., Mass. 1848. [illegible]

[illegible]
[illegible] 1869 [illegible]

[illegible], Pohl, 1809-1883, and [illegible], J. M.
Atlas containing ... Poland. 1879 [illegible]

[illegible], 1811-1896.
[illegible]—School atlas [illegible]
1877 [illegible]

Rizzi-Zannoni, Giovanni Antonio Bartolomeo, 1736-1814.
Atlante marittimo delle due Sicilie. 1792 [illegible]
Atlas géographique. 1762 [illegible]
Atlas géographique et militaire ou théâtre de la guerre présente en Allemagne. [1763] [illegible]
Atlas historique de la France ancienne et moderne. 1764 [illegible]
Petit Neptune françois. 1765 [illegible]

[illegible], Antonio.
Atlante novissimo. 1778-[1784] [illegible]
1779-[1785] [illegible]

[illegible], Antonio and [illegible]
[illegible]

[illegible], 1787-[illegible]
[illegible]
Topographia Helvetiae [illegible]
Topographia Italiae [illegible]

[illegible]
[illegible]
[illegible]

[illegible]
[illegible]

[illegible]
[illegible]
[illegible]
[illegible]

WORLD.

AGRICULTURAL.

Finch, V. C., *and* **Baker, O. E.**

Geography of the world's agriculture . . . 149 pp. incl. 180 maps, diagrs. obl. 4°. Washington, government printing office, 1917. 4088

Note.—At head of title: U. S. Department of agriculture. Office of the secretary. Contribution from office of farm management.

ANCIENT.

Butler, S.

An atlas of antient geography . . . 3 p. l., 3–34 pp., 21 maps. 8°. Philadelphia, Carey & Lea, 1831. 4089

Note.—Contains plans of ancient Rome, Athens, Syracuse, and Jerusalem. Maps engraved by P. E. Hamm and J. Yeager.

An atlas of antient geography . . . 4 p. l., 3–34 pp., 21 maps. 8°. Philadelphia, Carey, Lea & Blanchard, 1834. 4090

Note.—Contains plans of ancient Rome, Athens, Syracuse, and Jerusalem.

An atlas of antient geography . . . 3 p. l., 34 pp., 21 maps. 8°. Philadelphia, Lea & Blanchard, 1843. 4091

Note.—Contains maps of ancient Rome, Athens, Syracuse, and Jerusalem. Maps engraved by P. E. Hamm and J. Yeager.
Stereotyped by J. Howe.

An atlas of antient geography . . . 3 p. l., 3–34 pp., 21 maps. 8°. Philadelphia, Blanchard & Lea, 1855. 4092

Note.—Contains plans of ancient Rome, Athens, Syracuse, and Jerusalem. Maps engraved by P. E. Hamm and J. Yeager.

Hughes, W.

An atlas of classical geography. Edited by George Long. With a sketch of ancient geography, and other additions, by the american editor . . . With an index of places. 75, 4 pp., 26 maps. 8°. Philadelphia, Blanchard & Lea, 1856. 4093

Kampen, J. A. van.

Justus Perthes' atlas antiquus.—Atlas portátil de geografia antigua. 24 mapas coloridos grabados en cobre y una nomenclatura que consta de 7000 nombres. 2 p. l., 60 pp., 24 col. maps. 16°. Gotha, J. Perthes [1915?] 4094

Note.—Contains a reduced edition of the Tabula Peutingeriana.
Contains maps of ancient Athens, Rome, Mycena, Olympia, Carthage, Syracuse, Alexandria, Tyre, Troy, and Pergamum.

Kampen, J. A. van.—Continued.

In 1914, Maurice Besnier published, at Paris, his *Lexique de géographie ancienne*. As a basis for this work he used an earlier edition of Kampen's atlas, as stated in the "Avant-propos." In this *Lexique*, the place names have reference numbers to the maps of the above noted atlas, which may be considered as a necessary supplement to Besnier's work.

Kiepert, H., [*i. e.*, **J. S. H.**]

Atlas antiquus. Zwölf karten zur alten geschichte. 6. neu bearbeitete aufl. . . . 1 p. l., 12 maps. 4°. Berlin, D. Reimer, [1876] 4095

Atlas antiquus. Twelve maps of the ancient world for schools and colleges . . . With list of names. [12. ed. impr., cor. and enl.] 1 p. l., [2] 27 pp., 12 maps. sm. fol. Berlin, D. Reimer (E. Vohsen) [1903] 4096

NOTE.—Same as german edition, 1898? See v. 1, title 26.

McKinley publishing co.

McKinley historical notebook for ancient history. [Outline] 2 p. l., 25 maps. obl. 12°. Philadelphia, Pa., McKinley publishing co. [©1915] 4097

NOTE.—Blank leaf between maps.

McKinley's outline atlases for history classes containing 25 outline maps to be filled in by pupils with ink or colors. Atlas no. 3. Ancient history. 2d rev. ed. 2 p. l., 25 maps. obl. 12°. Philadelphia, Pa., McKinley publishing co., [©1915] 4098

Macpherson, D., *and* **A.**

[Atlas of ancient geography] 21 maps. 8°. [Philadelphia, 1806] 4099

NOTE.—Title-page wanting.

Maps taken from A. Rees. The Cyclopædia. Philadelphia, 1806. Plates. v. 6.

For complete descriptions of the american 1806 and english 1820 editions see entries under general atlases of the world for these years, titles 711 and 4312a.

Maps engraved by Young & Delleker, W. Harrison, S. Harrison, Kneass, Jones, and Hewitt.

Map entitled, Italiae regio Alpina, marked, W. H. Macpherson del[t].

[Atlas of ancient geography] 22 maps. 4°. [Philadelphia, 1806] 4100

NOTE.—Title-page wanting.

See note, title 4099.

All maps except the first, which is marked "Plate 1," have extra title, "Geographiæ antiquæ tab. I–XXII.

CONTENTS.

Plate 1. Imperium Car. Magn. ad finem saec. post Christ. VIII.

no. 1. Orbis veteribus cognitus. Young & Delleker sc.

" 2. Populi, urbes, &c., in Græcia, Thracia, et Asia, quorum meminit Homerus,. exceptis iis quorum situs ignoratur; cura et studio D. Macpherson. Insets: Ilium et theatrum Iliados.—Genles orientales.

no. 3. Britannia romana cum Hibernia et insulis adjacentibus.
" 5. Hellas sive Græcia propria, Thesalia et Epirus, antequam Romanæ ditionis fuerunt.
" 6. Macedonia et Thracia, antequam romanæ ditionis fuerunt.
" 7. Asia peninsularis cum insulis adjacentibus.
" 8. Ægyptus, provincia romana imperialis. Inset: Ægypti pars meridionalis.
" 9. Libyæ, vel Africæ, ora borealis.
" 10. Italiæ regio alpina, quæ vulgo, sed minus recte, dicitur Gallia cisalpina. Harrison sculp.
" 11. Italia media, vel Italiæ propriae pars borealis.
" 12. Italia ulterior, eujus pars australis Magna Græcia.
" 13. Sicilia, provincia romanorum, cum insulis adjacentibus. Kneass sc.
" 14. Italia in regiones undecim ab Augusto descripta, cum insulis Corsica et Sardinia.
" 15-16. Imperium romanum.
" 17. Hispania romana.
" 18. Galliæ, sicut ab Augusto divisæ, pars meridionalis. Inset: Gallia, qualis fuit antequam, J. Cæsar eam invasit.
" 19. Galliæ, sicut ab Augusto divisæ pars septentrionalis. Inset: Gallia qualis fuit ineunte seculo quinto æræ christianæ, in 17 provincias dispertita.
" 20. Rhætia et Noricum.
" 21. Germania magna. Inset: Gentes Rheno et Albi vicinae. Jones sc.
" 22. Terra filiorum Israelis. Inset: Judæa. Hewitt sculp.

Mayo, R.

An atlas of ten select maps of ancient geography, both sacred and profane; with a chronological chart of universal history and biography. Being intended as an accompaniment to Mayo's ancient geography and history. Calculated for the use of seminaries, &c. 2 p. l., 9 col. maps. sm. fol. Philadelphia, J. F. Watson, 1814. 4101

CONTENTS.

no. 1. Terra veteribus nota.
" 2. Romanum imperium.
" 3. Orientis tabula.
" 4. Græcia antiqua.
" 5. Italia antiqua.
" 6. Places recorded in the five books of Moses.
" 7. The land of Moriah or Jerusalem and the adjacent country.
" 8. State of nations at the Christian æra.
" 9. Historical chart representing in a chronological series the rise & fall of the principal empires of the world.

An atlas of ten select maps of ancient geography, both sacred and profane; with a chronological table of universal history & biography. Being intended as an accompaniment to Mayo's ancient geography and history. Calculated for the use of seminairies, &c. 2 p. l., 8 col. maps, 1 tab. 4°. Philadelphia, J. Melish, 1815. 4102

NOTE.—Maps engraved by J. Thackara, J. Vallance, and H. S. Tanner. The Library of Congress has two other copies of this atlas published by J. F. Watson in 1813 and 1814, see v. 1, title 33 and title 4101.

BIBLICAL.

Peloubet, F. N.

New biblical atlas with index. 4 pp., 12 col. maps. 8°. [Philadelphia, A. J. Holman co., ©1914] 4103

CITIES.

Avity, P. d'.

Newe archontologia cosmica, das ist / beschreibung aller kaÿserthumben / kônigreichen vnd republicken der gantzen welt . . . wie dieselbe in ihren grântzen vnd anmarckungen begrieffen . . . wie auch von der alten vnd newen innwohnern gebrâuchen . . . Alles auss vnverwerfflichen grûnden vnnd zeugnussen / vom anfang biss auff vnsere zeit / das jahr Christi 1646. zusammen gelesen / vnnd in eine richtige begreiffliche ordnung verfasset durch Johann Ludwig Gottfried. Mit . . . summarien vnd . . . registern versehen: auch mit den vornehmsten in kupffer gestochenen land-taffeln vnd stâtten gezieret / vnd verlegt von Matthæo Merian. 21 p. l., 760, [22] pp., 1 l. fold. plates, double maps, fold. plans. sm. fol. Franckfurt am Mayn / W. Hoffmans buchtruckerey, 1646. 4104

NOTE.—Translated from Pierre d'Avity's *Les empires, royaumes, estats . . . et principautez du monde, St. Omer, 1614,* by J. L. Gottfried (not a pseud. of Johann Philipp Abelin) See F. Gallati, *Der königlich schwedische in Teutschland geführte krieg (inaug.-diss.) Zürich, 1902.*

CONTENTS.

1. buch. Von den monarchen vnd freyen republicken in Europa.
2. " Von den monarchen / kônigen vnd fûrsten / in Asia vnd Africa.
3. " Von den Johanniter-rittern / ihrem vrsprung / auffnehmen / vnd zuståndigen insul Malta.

A set of most of the maps taken from this edition and bound is given in v. 1, title 58. This entry gives the list of all the maps and plates with those wanting in that set which appear in this perfect edition.

Braun, G.

Théâtre des cités dv monde . . . 6 v. in 2. fol. [Bruxelles, 1564–1620] 4105

NOTE.—Titles vary as follows: v. 1, Théâtre des cités dv monde. Premier volume. Addition to Privilege is dated "Bruxella xxii Nouemb. MDLXXIIII," and the Index, 1575; v. 2, Théâtre des principales villes de tovt l'vnivers. Second volvme. Addition to privilege dated 1574, preface 1575; v. 3, Livre troisième des villes principales dv monde, Libre tertivs. Addition to Privilege dated 1574, preface, 1580; v. 4, Liber qvartvs. Vrbivm præcipvarvm totivs mvndi. Addition to Privilege dated 1574; v. 5, Vrbivm praeciparvm mundi theatrvm qvintvm. Avctore Georgio Bravnio Agrippinate; v. 6, Théâtre des principales villes de tovt l'vnivers. Dedication, dated 1618.

For extensive note and list of maps in the latin edition see v. 3, no. 3292. The maps in the french edition are the same as those in the latin. Map no. 33 in v. 2, which comprises plans of "Novesium," "Verona," "Brvla," and "Sontina," shows slight changes of title, the date being omitted in the title

of "Novesivm" and "Brula" and changed from 1575 to 1620 in the other two. The maps which are wanting in the latin edition are found in this one. They are as follows:
v. 3, no. 37. Soest.—Warborch.
" 5, " 60. Avgvsti apvd Venetvs templi d: Marci accratissima effigvratio. Depinxit Georgius Houfnaglius.—Palatii Senatorii apvd Venetos conflagratio, anno MDLXXVII. Anno 1578.
" 5, " 65. Elegantissimus ad mare Tyrrhemm ex monte Pausilipo Neapolis montisque Vesuuỹ prospectus. Depinxit Georgius Houfnaglius. Anno 1578.
" 6, " 35. Pappa, inferioris Hungariæ oppidvm. Communicauit G. Houfnaglius, 1617.
" 6, " 52. Premislia celebris Rvssiae civitas.
Brunet and Grasse give a french edition with the title *Le grand théâtre des différentes cités du monde. Bruxelles, 1572, 6 v. in 3.* This edition is not mentioned.
Maps are dated from 1564–1620.
Volume 5 lacks index found in latin edition.

Ferreira de Loureiro, A.

Estudos sobre alguns portos commerciaes da Europa, Asia, Africa e Oceania e sobre diversos concernentes à engenheria civil . . . Atlas. 2 p. l., 30 pp. 8°. & 66 maps in portfolio. sm. fol. Coimbra, imprensa da universidade, 1886. 4106

NOTE.—Plans of Boulogne-sur-Mer.—Calais.—Dunkerque.—Rouen.—Havre.—Saint-Nazaire. — Marseilles. — Cette. — Toulon. — Bordeaux. —Antwerp. — Flushing. — Amsterdam. — Muiden. — Helder. — Rotterdam. — Hamburg.— Genoa. — Venice. — Naples. — Messina. — Trieste. — London. — Glasgow .— Greenock. — Liverpool. — Birkenhead. — Southampton. — Port Said. — Saigon. — Hong Kong. — Singapore. — Colombo. — Bombay. — Madras.— Calcutta.

COAL.

Gruner, É. *and* **Bousquet, J. G.**

Atlas général des houillères. Bassins houillers de France, Allemagne, Autriche-Hongrie, Belgique, États-Unis, Grand-Bretagne, Pays-Bas, Russie, par É. Gruner . . . G. Bousquet . . . 2 v. plates (part double) maps (part double) diagrs. fol. Paris, comité central des houillères de France, 1909–1911. 4106a

International geological congress. *12th Toronto, 1913.*

The coal resources of the world. Atlas. Edited by William McInnes . . . D. B. Dowling . . . and W. W. Leach . . . of the Geological survey of Canada. 2 p. l., 48 maps, pl. fol. Toronto, Can., Morang & co., [1913] 4106b

NOTE.—To accompany work entitled: *The coal resources of the world; an inquiry made upon the initiative of the Executive committee of the xii International geological congress, Canada, 1913, with the assistance of geological surveys and mining geologists of different countries. 3 v. illus., maps (part fold.) diagrs. 8°. Toronto, Can., Morang & co., limited, 1913.*
The following maps relate to America:
no. 1. Western hemisphere.
" 21. Coal areas of Canada. By D. B. Dowling.

International geological congress—Continued.

no. 22. Coal fields of Nova Scotia and New Brunswick.
" 23. Sydney coal field.
" 24. Coal fields of Manitoba and Saskatchewan.
" 25. Coal fields of Alberta and British Columbia.
" 26. Geological and topographical map of Crows nest coal-fields.—Blairmore—Frank coal-fields.
" 27. Southern Vancouver island.
" 28. Coal fields of the United States by Marius R. Campbell.

COMMERCIAL.

Allen, F.

An atlas of commercial geography. With an introduction by D. A. Jones . . . ix [1] 48, 24 pp. incl. 39 col. maps. 4°. Cambridge, University press, 1913. 4107

Philip, G., & son, *ltd.*

Philips' chamber of commerce atlas: a graphic survey of the world's trade, with a commercial compendium and gazetteer index. 2d ed. 2 p. l., v–viii, 128, 144 pp. incl. 84 col. maps, col. tables, col. diagrs. sm. fol. London, G. Philip & son, ltd., 1914. 4108

Rand, McNally & co.

The Rand McNally commercial atlas of America. Special edition with foreign supplement. Containing large-scale maps of all states in the United States and its outlying possessions, the provinces of the Dominion of Canada, Newfoundland, the republic of Mexico, Central America, Panama, Bermuda, the West Indies, Cuba, Austria-Hungary, the Balkan States, Belgium, Denmark, England and Wales, France, the German empire, Ireland, Italy, Luxemburg, Netherlands, Norway, Palestine, Portugal, Russia, Scotland, Spain, Sweden, Switzerland, Turkey in Asia, and various other useful maps; also large continental maps of North America, South America, Europe, Africa, Asia, and Oceania, and a new map of South America in four sections including complete and revised indices with latest population figures for each country . . . 1 p. l., XLII, 484 pp. incl. 137 col. maps, diagr. fol. Chicago, Rand, McNally & co., 1919. 4109

NOTE.—List of railroads, steamship lines, postal information, travel distance tables, in the United States, and diagram showing american tariff from 1791 to 1917.

Large maps of the following cities: Boston.—New York, Brooklyn, and Jersey City.—Buffalo.—Philadelphia.—Pittsburgh.—Baltimore.—Washington.—Louisville.—Cincinnati.—Cleveland.—Toledo.—Detroit.—Indianapolis.—Chicago.—Milwaukee.—Minneapolis.—St. Paul.—St. Louis.—Kansas City.—New Orleans.—San Francisco.—Montreal.—Toronto. Small maps of the following: Havana.—London.—Berlin.—Amsterdam.—Liverpool.—Paris.—Brussels.—Hamburg.—Petrograd.—Copenhagen.—Venice.—Budapest.—Vienna.—Moscow.—Stockholm.—Lisbon.—Odessa.—Madrid.—Jerusalem.

COMPARATIVE.

Arrowsmith, A. jr., *and* S.

Arrowsmith's comparative atlas. Part 1. Ancient geography. Part 2. Modern geography. 34, 31 pp., col. maps. 4°. [London, A. & S. Arrowsmith, 1829] 4110

NOTE.—Title-page wanting. Some of the maps are published by Saml. Arrowsmith, some by A. & S. Arrowsmith. Few are dated jany. 2, 1829. Many maps are similar to those in Aaron Arrowsmith, *jr., Orbis terrarum . . . 1828.* Maps 28 and 29 wanting. Index calls for no. 31.

CONTOUR-RELIEF.

Bacon, G. W., & co.

Bacon's excelsior contour-relief atlas. 36 [7] pp. incl. 43 col. maps. sm. 4°. London, G. W. Bacon & co., ltd., [1913–14] 4111

Philip, G.

Philips' visual contour atlas . . . 36 [12] pp. incl. 38 col. maps. sm. 4°. London, G. Philip & son, ltd., Liverpool, Philip, son & nephew, ltd. [1914] 4112

NOTE.—Consult also titles under subject "Relief."

ECCLESIASTICAL.

Arrowsmith, S.

The bible atlas, with ancient and modern names: being a delineation of the geography, and a chronological arrangement of the history of the holy bible, as also of the apocryphal books and Josephus. 17 (*i. e.* 30) l., [22] pp. incl. 13 maps, 6 tables, 1 diagr. sm. fol. London, the author, 1835. 4113

NOTE.—Contains index of the chronology and names of places. Plan of the city of Jerusalem and its environs, also, of the Temple and its court.

CONTENTS.

no. 1. The antediluvian world and the conquests of Nimrod.
" 2. The countries of the ancient world exhibiting the probable settlement of the descendants of Noah.
" 3. Canaan and the surrounding countries, illustrating the history of the patriarchs. Supplement of Canaan. Supplement of the countries on the south east.
" 4. Canaan, or the Land of Promise, in the time of the patriarchs.
" 5. The journeyings of the Hebrews or children of Israel, from Egypt to the Land of Promise. Supplement of the country beyond Jordan, illustrating its conquest by the Israelites under Moses.
" 6. Canaan, or the Land of Promise in the time of Joshua.
" 7. Canaan, or the Land of Promise during the time of the Judges.
" 8. The land of Judah, or the land of Israel during the time of the kings and governors. The land of Israel or Syria-Palæstina, illustrating the three captivities.
" 9. The dominions of David and Solomon. Supplement of the empires of the east of Israel.
" 10. Chronological and historical table of the kings and prophets of Judah and Israel.

Arrowsmith, S.—Continued.

no. 11. The land of Judea, or the land of Sion, from the time of the Babylonian captivity to the final destruction of the temple. Supplement, illustrating the partition of Judea, after the death of Herod the great, by the emperor Augustus.
" 12. Chronological table of the chief events connected with the Jews, from the close of the canon of the Old, to the opening of that of the New Testament.
" 13. Ministerial journeys of our Lord and Saviour Jesus Christ.
" 14. The travels of the apostle Paul, and the places recorded in the New Testament.
" 15. The temple, or house of God.
" 16. Jerusalem, or the city of the Lord.
" 17. Comparative table of sacred and profane history.

Case, O. D., & co.

Case's bible atlas, to illustrate the old and new testament. Designed to aid sunday school teachers and scholars in the study of the International series of sunday school lessons. 1 p. l., 16, 6 [2] pp., 16 (*i. e.* 15) col. maps, 1 pl. 4°. Hartford, O. D. Case & co., 1878. 4114

Colton, G. W., & C. B., & co.

Colton's strand atlas of bible geography designed for the use of families, sunday schools, and bible classes. cover-title, 7 col. maps. large fol. New York, G. W. & C. B. Colton & co., 1891. 4115

NOTE.—Contains map of the city of Jerusalem.

Darbishire, B. V.

A school bible atlas . . . 16 [6] pp. incl. 14 col. maps. sm. 4°. [Oxford, Oxford university press, 1914] 4116

Philip, G., & son, ***ltd.***

Philips' scripture atlas . . . cover-title, 16 col. maps. sm. 4°. Liverpool, G. Philip & son, ltd. [1915] 4117

NOTE.—Text on inside of covers.

Philips' scripture atlas, a series of 16 coloured plates, containing over 52 maps and plans, with introductory notes and an index of scriptural names and their modern identifications . . . 2 p. l., 7 pp., 16 col. maps. sm. 4°. London, G. Philip & son, ltd.; Liverpool, Philip, son & nephew, ltd. [1916?] 4118

NOTE.—Maps of ancient and modern Jerusalem.

Robertson, E.

The bible atlas. New edition. index-title, 1 p. l., xvi, 4 pp. incl. 16 col. maps. 4°. Edinburgh, W. & A. K. Johnston, ltd. [1915?] 4119

NOTE.—Plans of the Tabernacle, and Solomon's temple.

Streit, K.

Atlas hierarchicus. Descriptio geographica et statistica s. romanæ ecclesia tum occidentis tum orientis juxta statum præsentem accedunt etiam nonnullæ notæ historicæ necnon ethnographicæ . . . 4 p. l., 128 (*i. e.*, 207) 35, [3] pp., 37 col. maps. fol. Paderbornæ . . . sumptibus typographiæ Bonifacianæ; Friburgi Brisgoviæ, B. Herder, 1913. 4120

Note.—Text in german, italian, spanish, french, and english. Contains map of the city of Rome showing all catholic churches. Pp. 99–102 are two double fold. sheets.

ECONOMIC.

Bartholomew, J. G.

An atlas of economic geography . . . With introduction by L. W. Lyde . . . lxvi pp., 1 l., 64 (*i. e.* 82) col. maps, tables, diagrs. 4°. London, Oxford university press, 1914. 4121

A school economic atlas . . . With introduction by L. W. Lyde . . . Revised ed. xii, 64 pp. incl. 51 col. maps, diagrs. 8°. Oxford, Clarendon press, 1912. 4122

A school economic atlas . . . With introduction by L. W. Lyde . . . 3d ed. xii, 64 pp. incl. 44 col. maps, 1 pl. 4°. London, Oxford university press, 1915. 4123

Note.—Same maps are found in his *An atlas of economic geography.*

Hammond, C. S., & co.

Hammond's business atlas of economic geography, a new series of maps showing: relief of the land, temperature, rainfall, natural vegetation, productive and nonproductive regions, mineral products, agricultural products, distribution of population . . . 2 p. l., 51 col. maps. 8°. New York, C. S. Hammond & co., inc., 1919. 4124

Michel, G., *and* **Knapp, C.**

Documents cartographiques de géographie économique—Cartographic documents of economic geography—Kartographische beiträge zur wirtschaftsgeographie. Publiés avec le concours de nombreux collaborateurs. Sous le patronage de la Société internationale pour le développement de l'enseignement commercial et de l'Association suisse pour l'enseignement commercial. 1913–1915. no. 1–4. fol. Paris, Bern [etc.] geographischer kartenverlag Bern, [1914] 4125

EXPLORATIONS.

Plon, E., Nourrit & cie.

Atlas général des grandes explorations et découvertes géographiques comprenant: le tracé complet et distinct de tous les itinéraires suivis par les grands explorateurs et voyageurs depuis

Plon, E., Nourritt & cie.—Continued.
la plus haute antiquité jusqu' à la fin du XIXe siècle. 2 p. l., 32, xvi pp. incl. 32 maps. 8°. Paris, E. Plon, Nourrit & c^ie, 1899. 4126

NOTE.—At head of title: Collection des atlas Plon.

GAMES.

Gaultier, A. E. C., *l'abbé.*
Atlas de géographie, contenant sept cartes . . . Plus, une feuille d'étiquettes à coller sur de petites cartes ou sur des boules de loto, pour servir au jeu de géographie. Voyez les Leçons de géographie auxquelles cet atlas rapporte. . . . 1 p. l., 7 maps, 1 pl. sm. fol. Paris, J. Renouard, [1810?] 4127

NOTE.—List of the works of l'abbé Gaultier on reverse of title-page.

HISTORICAL.

Baquol, J., *and* **Schnitzler, J. H.**
Atlas historique et pittoresque, ou, histoire universelle disposée en tableaux synoptiques embrassant à la fois les faits politiques, religieux, littéraires et artistiques et illustrée de cartes et de planches. Ouvrage fondé par J. Baquol, continué sur le même plan depuis l'an 1000 et augmenté d'introductions, de répertoires, etc., par m. J. H. Schnitzler . . . 3 v. fol. Strasbourg, E. Simon, 1884–85. 4128

NOTE.—Volumes paged continuously.
Vol. 1 has engraved title.
For contents see v. 1, title 99.
Also contains the following, not mentioned in title 99:
Plate no. 27, v. 2, Plan of Rome.
" " 45, v. 3, Plan of the city of London.

Cambridge, The, modern history atlas, edited by A. W. Ward, G. W. Prothero, Stanley Leathes, assisted by E. A. Benians. xxii, 142 pp., 145–229 pp. 141 col. maps. 8°. New York, Macmillan co., 1912. 4129

NOTE.—To accompany *The Cambridge modern history* in 13 volumes, 1902–1912. In the introduction to this atlas, written by E. A. Benians, there is a descriptive text relating to the maps following. The end of the preface reads: "The maps in this Atlas have been executed by messrs. Stanford, to whom, as well as to mr. John Bolton, the editors desire to express their obligation for the care and attention given to the work at its successive stages."

Clay, H., *and* **Greenwood, A.**
An introductory atlas of international relations. Maps by H. S. Hattin. 74 pp., 47 maps. 8° London, Headley bros. 1916. 4130

Colbeck, C.
The public schools historical atlas . . . 8th impression. 6, 35 pp., 101 col. maps. 8°. London, New York, [etc.] Longmans, Green & co. 1907. 4131

NOTE.—For 2nd ed., see v. 1, title 104.

Cram, G. F.

Cram's unrivaled atlas of the world. New historical edition. Newly engraved maps and charts of each state in the United States, each grand division, and detailed maps of every country, state, and kingdom in the world. Historical maps, graphically showing the rise and fall of the various kingdoms, states, and empires, from the first great empires, B. C. 3000 to A. D. 500, roman empire A. D. 200–300, and Europe A. D. 500 to Europe A. D. 1878, accompanied by historical description of every state and country, comprising a descriptive gazetteer of the world, and a wealth of special feature maps and latest statistical diagrams, tables, etc. All carefully edited and brought up to the latest date, fully indexed. 494 pp. incl. 199 maps, front., illus. tables. fol. New York, Chicago, G. F. Cram co., 1916. 4132

NOTE.—On cover, new census edition.
Frontispiece is view of the east or main front of the United States capitol.
Atlas copyrighted in 1915.

Dittmar, H.

Historicher atlas . . . 4e. aufl. Revidirt, neu bearb. und ergänzt von D. Völter . . . 2 pt. in 1 v., cover-title, 2 p. l., 17 (i. e. 18) maps on 18 sheets, 6 pl. 8°. Heidelberg, C. Winter, [1856?] 4133

NOTE.—Supplement zu Dittmar's *Geschichte der welt.*
The date 1856 is found in several maps.

CONTENTS.

no. 1. Die welt der alten. Insets: Homerische welt-tafel.—Das ruinenfeld von Theben.
" 2. Phönicien, Palaestina, Petraeisches (!) Arabien, Aegypten und Cypern. Insets: Jerusalem 70 nach Christo.—Palaestina mit den 12 stämen.
" 3. Griechenland, die griechischen inseln und die westküste Kleinasiens 431 bis 404 vor Christo. Insets: Troja.—Athen.—Corinthus.—Acropolis von Athen.—Sparta.
" 4. Hellas und der Peloponnes.—Kleinasien und Syrien. Inset: Plan von Athen.
" 5. Die reiche der nachfolger Alexanders des grossen. 190 v. Chr.—Das reich Alexanders des grossen. Von 336 bis 323 v. Chr.
" 6a. Roemisches reich, 100 n. Chr.—Italien bis 450 v. Chr. Insets: Latium antiquum.—Roma vetus.
" 6b. Italia als republik. Insets: Plan von Rom.—Campania.
" 7. Das alte Gallien Britannien und Germanien mit den Oberdonauländern.
" 8. Der occident im anfang des sechsten jahrhunderts nach Christo.—Das westroemische reich bis zu seinem untergang im fünften jahrh. n. Christo.
" 9. Das Byzantinische reich und das reich der chalifen im Orient zur zeit Karl des grossen.—Das reich Karl des grossen.
" 10. Das zeitalter der Hohenstaufen.—Die zeit der kreuzzüge. Inset: Das lateinische kaiserthum.
" 11. Deutschland und Frankreich, 1275–1493. Insets: Constantinopel, 1453.—Das Osmanische reich, 1389–1403.

Dittmar, H.—Continued.

no. 12. Die Schweiz von 1218 bis 1331.—Das land der eidgenossen seit dem 14 jahrhundert. Inset: Das Mongolen—reich unter Dschingis—Chan und seinen nachfolgen.

" 13. Deutschland im dreissigjahrigen kriege.—Deutschland nach der kreiseintheilung durch Maximilian I. Inset: Deutschland nach seinen chemaligen erzbisthümern und bisthümern.

" 14. Europa zeit Friedrich dem grossen bis zur französ. revolution.—Die zeit der ersten franz. republik.—Europa zur zeit Napoleons.

" 15. Die laenderentdeckungen im 15 und 16 jahrhundert.

" 16. Die deutschen bundesstaaten, das kaiserthum Oesterreich, das königreich Preussen, die Schweiz, das kgr. Belgien, das kgr. der Niederlande u. die angrenzenden Länder.

" 17. Das europæische Russland nach seiner allmähligen vergrösserung seit 1462. Inset: Das russische reich nach seiner allmähligen vergrösserung seit 1462.

Foncin, P.

Géographie historique: (Leçons en regard des cartes) résumant l'histoire de la formation territoriale des pays civilisés et l'histoire de la civilisition. Antiquité—moyen-age—temps modernes—période contemporaine. 48 leçons,—48 cartes coloriées, 50 figures, lexique, table alphabétique . . . 136 pp. incl. 48 col. maps, illus. sm. 4°. Paris, A. Colin & c[ie]., 1888. 4134

Haack, H., *and* **Hertzberg, H.**

Haack-Hertzberg: grosser historischer wandatlas. abt. II–V. 11 col. maps. large fol. Gotha, J. Perthes, [1912–1916?] 4134a

NOTE.—In progress.

CONTENTS.

Abt. II. Karten zur staatengeschichte von Deutschland.

nr. 2. Deutschland und Italien im zeitalter der sächsischen und salischen kaiser. Von dr. B. Bohnenstaedt. 4 sheets.

" " " 3. Deutschland und Italien im zeitalter der Hohenstaufen. Von dr. B. Bohnenstaedt.

" III. Karten zur staatengeschichte Europas.

nr. 2. Europa im VI jahrhundert. Von dr. Max Georg Schmidt. 4 sheets.

" " " 3. Europa im VIII jahrhundert. Von dr. Max Georg Schmidt. 4 sheets.

" " " 4. Europa, mitte des X jahrhunderts. Von prof. dr. Max Georg Schmidt. 4 sheets.

" IV. Karten zur kulturgeschichte der welt.

nr. 5. Das zeitalter der entdeckungen. Von dr. Heinrich Hertzberg. 4 sheets.

" " " 6. Die koloniale expansion des 17. u. 18. jahrhunderts. Von dr. Heinrich Hertzberg. 4 sheets.

" V. Karten zur kriegsgeschichte.

a) Strategische karten.

" " nr. 10. Der krieg von 1806–07. Von dr. B. Bohnenstaedt. 2 sheets.

" " " 13. Der dänische krieg. 1864. Von dr. B. Bohnenstaedt. 2 sheets.

" " " 14. Der krieg von 1866. Von dr. B. Bohnenstaedt. 2 sheets.

" " b) Sclachtenpläne.

" " nr. 2. Die schlacht um La Belle Alliance. 18 juni 1815. Von prof. dr. Max Georg. Schmidt. 2 sheets.

Johnston, W. & A. K., *ltd.*

Historical atlas. Twenty-four plates printed in colours, containing forty maps and plans, together with historical notes and a chronological table of national history. Index to place-names. 3 p. l., 16 [2] pp., 40 col. maps. sm. 4°. Edinburgh, W. & A. K. Johnston; London, Macmillan & co., ltd, 1917. 4135

Jones, C. H., *and* **Hamilton, T. F.**

Historical atlas of the world illustrated. Giving histories and maps of all the countries in their geographical, statistical, and commercial aspects, together with a complete history of the original surveys of the United States, with a special map showing lands surveyed by government. Constructed by A. Keith Johnston . . . H. D. Rogers . . . Edw. Weller . . . and other eminent geographers. [199] pp. incl. 49 col. maps, 4. pl., illus. fol. Chicago, H. H. Hardesty & co., 1875. 4136

NOTE.—Various pagination.

Kiepert, Heinrich, *i. e.,* **J. S. H.**

Formae orbis antiqui. 36 karten im format von 52:64 cm mit kritischem text und quellenangabe zu jeder karte. 24 pts. fol. Berlin, D. Reimer (E. Vohsen) 1894–1913. 4137

NOTE.—In progress. For preceding parts see v. 1, title 27, and v. 3, title 3311.

CONTENTS.

no. 25. Gallia (provinciae ab Augusto constitutae)
" 34. Imperium Romanum cum provinciis a Diocletiano constitutis.
" 35. Europa et orae maris interni secundum Ptolemae.

Meyer, H. J.

Meyers historischer handatlas. Mit 62 hauptkarten, vielen nebenkarten, einem geschichtsabriss in tabellarischer form und 10 registerblättern. [250] pp. incl. 62 (*i. e.* 64) maps. 8°. Liepzig und Wien, bibliographisches institut, 1911. 4137a

NOTE.—Various paging.

Muir, R.

Hammond's new historical atlas for students; a series of 65 plates, containing 154 coloured maps and diagrams, with an introduction illustrated by 43 maps and plans in black and white. . . . 2d ed. xiv pp., 1 l., 62 p., 1 l., 31 p. illus. (maps, plans) 65 double maps. 4°. New York, C. S. Hammond & co., [1914?] 4138

Quin, E.

An historical atlas; in a series of maps of the world as known at different periods; constructed upon an uniform scale and coloured according to the political changes of each period: accompanied by a narrative of the leading events exhibited in the maps: forming

Quin, E.—Continued.

together a general view of universal history, from the creation to the present time . . . The maps engraved by Sidney Hall. 2d ed. 1 p. l., vi, 2 l., 186 pp. 21 col. maps. 4°. London, R. B. Seeley & W. Burnside, 1836. 4139

NOTE.—The Library of Congress has an edition of 1846, with maps and text bound separately. See v. 1, title 141.

The following maps show America:

no. 16. 1498. The discovery of America.
" 17. 1551. At the death of Charles v.
" 18. 1660. At the restoration of the Stuarts.
" 19. 1783. Independence of the United States
" 20. 1811. Empire of Napoleon Bonaparte.
" 21. 1828. End of the general peace.

Rhode, C. E.

Historischer schul-atlas zur alten, mittleren und neueren geschichte . . . 84 karten auf 28 blättern nebst erläuterndem text. 8te auflage. 1 p. l., 29 pp., 84 col. maps. obl. 4°. Glogau, C. Flemming, 1871. 4140

Historischer schul-atlas zur alten, mittleren und neueren geschichte . . . 89 karten auf 30 blättern nebst erläuterndem text. 11e aufl. 1 p. l., 30 pp., 28 (*i. e.* 30) col. maps. obl. 4°. Glogau, C. Flemming, [187-?] 4141

NOTE.—Maps nos. 21 and 22 wanting.

Rinaudo, C.

Atlante storico per le scuole secondarie . . . 3 pts. 67 maps. 8°. Torino-Roma, etc., G. B. Paravia & co. [1911] 4142

NOTE.—Among the maps is a plan of the city of Rome entitled: "Roma repubblicana e imperiale."

The following maps relate to America:

Pt. 2, no. 20. Le grandi scoperte geografiche del secolo XV e in principio del secolo XVI.
" 3, " 10. Formazione degli stati Uniti d' America.
" " " 12. Colonizzazione Europea verso il 1789.
" " " 28. Gli stati contemporanei (1904) con speciale riguardo alla colonizzazione europea.

CONTENTS.

Pt. 1. Il mondo antico.
" 2. Il medio evo.
" 3. I tempi moderni.

Ségur, L. P., *comte* **de.**

Atlas pour l'histoire universelle. Contenant vingt cartes ou plans, dessinés et gravés par Ambroise Tardieu . . . 2 p. l., 24 maps on 20 sheets. obl. 8°. Paris, Furne & cie., 1840. 4143

CONTENTS.

no. 1. Monde connu des anciens.
" 2. Egypte ancienne.
" 3. Grèce.
" 4. Athènes et ses environs.
" 5. Ruines de Sparte.—Carthage et ses environs.
" 6. Empire d'Alexandre.
" 7. Asia Mineure.
" 8. Italie ancienne.
" 9. Afrique propre, Numidie et Mauritanie.
" 10. Palestine ou Judée.
" 11. Royaume des Israélites sous les rois David et Salomon.—Les douze tribus d'Israël.
" 12. Jérusalem.—Syracuse.
" 13. Rome.—Constantinople.
" 14. Ibérie ou Espagne ancienne.
" 15. Les Gaules.
" 16. Germanie, Pannonie, Dacie et Sarmatie.
" 17. Empire romain, partie occidentale.
" 18. " " partie orientale.
" 19. Empire grec ou d'Orient, partie occidentale.
" 20. " " " " partie orientale.

Worcester, J. E.

An historical atlas . . . 3d ed. 1 p. l., 10 tab. fol. Boston, Hilliard, Gray, Little, & Wilkins; Cambridge, Hilliard, Metcalf, & co., 1828. 4144

NOTE.—For contents, see v. 1, title 159.

ISLANDS.

[Collection of col. maps mostly in manuscript of various islands of the world by the same author. anon.] [5] 63 (i. e. 65) pp. incl. 78 maps, 6 pl., 1 port. fol. [1810?] 4145

NOTE.—Maps are accompanied by descriptive text in english. In the text accompanying the map of Guadeloupe island, it is stated that it "is subject to the king of France . . . In 1703 it was taken by the english, but since deserted."—The island was delivered to the french in 1810 after having been occupied by the english.

The latest date found in the ms. text is 1741: "Païta was taken by commodore Anson nov[r] 10th. 1741."

Contains numerous plans of cities and forts. Also a col. ms. portrait of "Arnoldo Roggeveen. 1680."—The plates show colored ms. pictures of ships of various size and kinds, including "Admiral Drake's ship the Pellican."

Various printed maps taken from London magazine and the Gentleman's magazine have been inserted in the atlas. The latest date found on these is 1766: "Map of Bridge Town in the island of Barbadoes." no. 54.

[Collection of col. maps]—Continued.

CONTENTS.

no. [1] A chart of the english channel. By Thos Kitchin.
" [2] A new and accurate map of the northern coast of Choromandel in the East Indies. By T. Kitchin.
" [3] A plan of Quebec metropolis of Canada.
" [4] A plan of Dunkirk since the treaty of Utrecht 1714.
" [5] An accurate map of the West Indies with the adjacent coast. J. Gibson sculp.
" [6] [Callifornia] ms.
" [7] [Great Britain] ms.
" [8] Nova Terra or New-Found land. ms.
" [9] A description of Arica. ms.
" [10] The island of Sta Catalina or New Providence. ms.
" [11] A description of Golfo Dulce. ms.
" [12] Ilha Bastimentoes. ms.
" [13] Coquimbo bay described. ms.
" [14] Gulf of Nicoya described. ms.
" [15] I. de la Trinidad. ms.
" [16] Laguna or the gulf of Battona. ms.
" [17] Hispaniola isle. ms.
" [18] A description of ẏ english gulfe lying a little to the northward of Magellan's Straights. ms.
" [19] Jamaica.
" [20] A description of his royal highnesses isles. ms.
" [21] A description of Guasco. ms.
" [22] A description of Hilo. ms.
" [23] Bachian isle. ms.
" [24] Summer or Barmudas isles. ms.
" [25] Isla de Iuan Fernandez. ms.
" [26] A description of Paita & Colan. ms.
" [27] Long island. ms.
" [28] The bay of Panama & gulf of Battona.
" [29] La isle de Verragua.—En esta isla esta sepultado Francisco Drake. ms.
" [30] Isla de la Gorgona or capt Sharpes isle. ms.
" [31] Sr Fran. Drakes isle or isla de la Plata. ms.
" [32] Hibernia. ms.
" [33] 't fort Amsterdam en tinkomen van baia St Anna opt eÿlant Curacao—Fort Amsterdam en t eÿlandt Curacao [ms. view]
" [34] Isle of Thanet.—Isle of Sheppey. ms.
" [35] The isle of Man.—Anglesey. ms.
" [36] Desde la ysla Trinidad [with plan of fort]—Tobago. ms.
" [37] [Shetland.—Iseland]. ms.
" [38] [Portland.—I. of Wight.—Guernsee.—Alderny] ms.
" [39] The island of Cuba. ms.
" [40] The isle of Borneo. ms.
" [41] Sumatra. ms.
" [42] Insulæ Canariæ alias Fortunate dictæ. ms.
" [43] Insula Canariæ. ms.
" [44] Insula Canariæ. ms.
" [45] Insula Madera. ms.
" [46] The isle of St Iuan de Ulva, del peraje y de la ciudad de la Nouva Vera Cruz.—The isle of Vera Cruz. ms.
" [47] Sta Crus. ms.

no. [48] A map of the isle of Legoa & Porto Rico. ms.
" [49] Isle of St Iuan or Puerto Rico. ms.
" [50] Virgins islands. ms.
" [51] The isle of Margarita. ms.
" [52] Grada or Granada. ms.
" [53] S[t] Vincent. ms.
" [54] A plan of Bridge Town in the island of Barbadoes.—The part unshaded was destroy'd by fire May 14th 1766.
" [55] A map of Fort Royal bay in the island of Martinico.
" [56] Barbados. ms.
" [57] Martineco. ms.
" [58] [Puerto y ciudad de Santo Domingo] ms.
" [59] Deseada. ms.
" [60] Dominica. ms.
" [61] Antigua. ms.
" [62] Guardaloup. ms.
" [63] St Christophers. ms.
" [64] Nevis. ms.
" [65] Monseratte.—St Bartholemew. ms.
" [66] Boraquem.—Sombreroe. ms.
" [67] St Eustaciæ.—I. Aves. Granadillos. ms.
" [68] Islas de Cabo Verde. ms.
" [69] " " " " "
" [70] " " " " "
" [71] Islas de Azores. ms.
" [72] " " " "
" [73] " " " "
" [74] Sylly or I. Sorlingues. ms.
" [75] Bahama iles or Lucayes. ms.
" [76] Gulf of St Lawrence. ms.
" [77] The circle of the Upper Rhine. By T. Kitchin.
" [78] A map of the kingdom of Portugal. J. Gibson sculp.

MARITIME.

Brouckner, I.

Der erste preussische seeatlas 1749.—"Nouvel atlas de marine. Composé d'une carte générale, et de XII cartes particulières, qui représentent le globe terrestre jusqu'au 82°. degré du côté du nord, et jusqu'au 60°. du côté du sud. Le tout dressé sur les observations les plus nouvelles et les plus approuvées. Dédié à son excellence mgr. le comte de Schmettau . . . Approuvé par l'Académie royale des sciences à Berlin l'année 1749."—Herausgegeben von dr. M. Groll. 1 p. l., [3] pp., 14 maps. fol. Berlin, D. Reimer (E. Vohsen) 1912. 4146

NOTE.—"Avertissement sur l'atlas de marine, publié à Berlin 1749." p. [3]

Has accompanying facs. map entitled, "Carte pour résoudre les six problèmes. 1749."

For original atlas see v 1, title 612. Reprint of original title in cartouche.

Title of original atlas, also on map no. 3.

This is a photo-lithographic reproduction of the sheets of the *Nouvel atlas de marine* prepared by the geographer Isaac Brouckner, by order of field-marshall

Brouckner, I.—Continued.

count Samuel von Schmettau, who did so much in Prussia to raise the level of the scientific undertakings, not only theoretical but practical, of the Berlin Royal academy of sciences during the eighteenth century. In order that this atlas might be as complete as possible, Count von Schmettau placed at Brouckner's disposal all the sheets and memoirs that were available, which were dealt with in a masterly way by the geographer, with the result that a most creditable marine atlas for the time was prepared, which certainly deserves to be designated as the first Prussian marine atlas.

This atlas has now been reproduced under the editorship of Dr. M. Groll, who has also written an interesting note to accompany it, to which he has appended a list of the other cartographical works undertaken by the academy about the same period. Dr. Groll states that only three copies of the original atlas are known to him to be in existence, one of which is in the Congress Library at Washington, the second at the Nordenskiöld library at Helsingfors, and the third in the library of the Grand duke at Weimar; and it is from the last of these that his facsimile has been taken." See *Geographical journal, December, 1912. London, Royal geographical society, 1912. v. 40, no. 6.*

CONTENTS.

no. [a] Carte générale du globe terrestre. 1749.
" 1. Carte mar^{ne}. de Suède, Norwège, Nouv^{le} Zemble et de Spitsberge. 1749.
" 2. Carte marine de la mer glaciale, et la Sibérie septentrionale. 1749.
" 3. Carte marine de la mer glaciale avec une partie de la province de Jrkucki. 1749.
" 4. Carte marine de la B. de Baffin et une partie d'Hudson, d'Island et Groenland. 1749.
" . Carte mar^{ne}. d'une partie de l'Europe, de l'Asie et de l'Afrique. 1749.
" 6. Carte mar^{e}. d'une partie de l'Asie, ou des Indes Orient^{es}. et des Isl^{es} au dessus de l'équat^{r}. 1749.
" 7. Carte marine entre Californie et une partie de l'Asie la plus orientale. 1749.
" 8. Carte marine de l'Amérique septentrionale et une partie de la B^{e} d'Hudson. 1749.
" 9. Carte marine de l'Afrique méridionale. 1749.
" 10. Carte marine des iles mérid^{le}. Indes orient^{les}. et de la nouv^{e}. Hollande. 1749.
" 11. Carte mar^{e}. de la Nouv^{lle}. Zélande des iles Salomon et de plusieurs autres isles mérid^{es}. 1749.
" 12. Carte marine de l'Amérique méridionale, 1749.

Philip, G.

Philips' mercantile marine atlas. A series of 35 plates containing over 200 charts & plans, with tables of 10,000 distances between ports, national & commercial flags, lists of British & United States consulates, and complete index of 20,000 ports. Specially designed for merchant shippers, exporters & ocean travellers and for general use. 4th ed. viii, 28 pp. 33 col. maps, 2 pl. fol. London, G. Philip & son, ltd.; [etc., etc., 1913] 4147

New mercantile marine atlas. A series of 35 plates containing over 200 charts & plans, with tables of 10,000 distances between ports, national and commercial flags, cable & wireless telegraphy charts with list of wireless stations, lists of United States & British consulates, and complete index of 20,000 ports, &c. Specially designed for merchant shippers, exporters & ocean travellers and for general use. 6th ed. VIII, 28 pp. incl. 1 col. map, 32 col. map, 2 pl. fol. New York, C. S. Hammond & co.; London, G. Philip & son ltd. 1916. 4148

NOTE.—Contains also, "Statistical summary: Merchant shipping of the world.—Tables of distances between ports.—List of British consulates.—List of American consulates.—Speed table.—Foreign money, with english and american values.—Foreign measures of length.—Lloyd's signal stations, etc."

Philips' mercantile marine atlas. A series of 35 plates containing over 200 charts & plans, with tables of 10,000 distances between ports, national & commercial flags, cable & wireless telegraphy charts with list of wireless stations, list of british & United States consulates, and complete index of 20,000 ports, &c. Specially designed for merchant shippers, exporters & ocean travellers and for general use. 5th ed. viii, 28 pp. 33 col. maps, 2 pl. fol. London, G. Philip & son, ltd.; [etc.] 1915. 4149

NOTE.—"In preparing the fifth edition . . . the plates and letterpress have been exhaustively revised and carefully brought up-to-date . . . and several new features have been introduced, including a new chart of the North sea, extended to include the ports of Western Ireland and Northern Scotland."—*Preface, p. iv.*

Contains also "Statistical summary: Merchant shipping of the world.—Tables of distances between ports.—List of british consulates.—List of American consulates.—Foreign money.—Foreign measures of length.—Great circle sailing, the sea horizon, Lloyd's signal stations, etc." and a series of physical charts showing depth of the oceans.

Seller, J.

Atlas maritimus or a book of charts: describing the sea-coasts, capes, headlands, sands, shoals, rocks & dangers; the bayes, roads, harbors, rivers, and ports in most of the known parts of the world. With the true courses & distances from one place to another, gathered from the latest & best discoveries that have been made, by divers able & experienced navigators of our english nation: accommodated with an hydrographical description of the whole world. Sold by James Atkinson at Cherry-garden-staires on Rotherhith wall. 1 p. l., 10 pp., 26 maps. fol. [London, 1670?] 4150

NOTE.—Copy A. All copies of Seller's *Atlas maritimus* differ in contents. The Dictionary of national biography, says that Seller published a folio volume of charts and sailing directions under the title of the '*English pilot*' in 1671, and another called the '*Sea atlas*' the same year, but the present edition without Seller's name on the title-page and marked "Sold by James Atkinson at Cherry-garden staires on Rotherhith wall," judging by the plates is earlier than the undated edition to which the date 1671? has been given, so the date 1670? which has been added in ink on the title-page of copy B, evidently at some early date, is approximately the date. The title-page is a rather crude, early impression

Seller, J.—Continued.

from the plate which is much improved in the later editions. The view of London below the cartouche being a different one showing that the more finished one must have been substituted for it later. In copy A, the title is engraved on a slip and pasted in the center of the cartouche, which in this copy is blank. In copy B (title 4151) the title is engraved directly on the page. The maps of this issue which appear in later editions are here shown in a less finished state. Many of the maps contain the names not only of John Seller, but of John Thornton, William Fisher, James Atkinson, and John Colson, also. John Thornton, who published his *Atlas maritimus, 1702–1703,* is accused by Dalrymple of copying Seller almost verbatim. See v. 3, title 3455.

Copy A contains 26 maps and copy B 19. Of these, nine maps are the same. No. 17 in copy A and no. 11 in copy B, "A chart of the western part of the East-Indies with the adjacent islands from Cape Bona Esperanca to Cape Comorin," the first "By J. Seller, J. Colson, W. Fisher, J. Atkinson, & J. Thornton. F. Lamb sculp.," and the second, "By John Thornton, John Seller, William Fisher, James Atkinson, John Colson," and without Lamb's name as engraver, though very similar, are from different plates.

The fly leaf bears the date "july ye 10, 1699," and the name, "James Day."

CONTENTS.

no. [1] Novissima totius terrarum orbis tabula.

" [2] A generall chart of the Northern seas. By I. Thornton. F. Lamb sculp.

" [3] A chart of the sea coasts of Russia, Lapland, Finmarke, Nova Zembla and Greenland. Described by John Seller, John Colson, William Fisher, Iames Atkinson, John Thornton. Steph. Board sculp.

" [4] A large description of the two chanells in the river Dwina goeing up to the citty of Archangel.

" [5] A chart of the North sea. By John Seller, John Colson, Willm Fisher, James Atkinson, John Thornton. James Clark engra.

" [6] A chart of the East sea. Ia. Clerk sculp. Inset: A prospect of the city of Stockholm, the metropolis of Sweden.

" [7] A chart of the sea coasts from the Landsend of England to Cape Bona Esperanca. By J. Seller, W. Fisher, J. Colson, J. Atkinson, J. Thornton.

" [8] A chart of England, Scotland, France, and Ireland. By John Thornton.

" [9] A draught of the sands, channels, buoyes, beacons and sea-marks upon the coast of England. Made and sold by John Seller, John Colson, William Fisher, James Atkinson, John Thornton. F. Lamb sculp. Inset: The river of Thames from London Bridge to Tilburyhope.

" [10] A new mapp of the sea coasts of England, France & Holland. Described by John Seller, John Colson, William Fisher, James Atkinson and John Thornton. F. Lamb sculp.

" [11] A draught of the harbor of Brest. By John Thornton.

" [12] A sea chart describing the British chanel, bay of Biscaia, Galissia, Portugal, Spain, and the straits mouth. F. Lamb sculp.

" [13] A chart of the westermost part of the Mediterranean sea. By William Fisher & Richard Mount.

" [14] A chart of the eastermost part of the Mediterranean sea. By John Thornton, Iohn Seller, William Fisher, Iames Atkinson, Iohn Colson.

" [15] The coast of Barbaria, Gualata, Arguin and Guinea from the Borlings to Cape Verde. By John Thornton, John Seller, William Fisher, James Atkinson, John Colson.

" [16] A chart of Gvinea. By Iohn Thornton.

no. [17] A chart of the western part of the East Indies with all the adjacent islands from Cape Bona Esperanca to Cape Comorin. By J. Seller, J. Colson, W. Fisher, J. Atkinson, & J. Thornton. F. Lamb sculp.
" [18] A chart of the eastermost part of the East Indies with all the adjacent islands from Cape Comorin to Japan. By J. Seller, J. Colson, W. Fisher, J. Atkinson, and J. Thornton. F. Lamb sculp.
" [19] A general chart of the West Indias. By John Seller, John Colson, William Fisher, James Atkinson, John Thornton.
" [20] A chart of the West-Indies. By John Thornton, John Seller, William Fisher, James Atkinson, John Colson.
" [21] A chart of the Western ocean according to Mercators projection.
" [22] A chart of ye north part of America. For Hudsons bay coñonly called ye North West Passage. By Iohn Thornton.
" [23] A chart of the coast of America from New found Land to Cape Cod. By John Seller, John Colson, William Fisher, James Atkinson, and John Thornton.
" [24] A chart of the Caribe islands. By J. Seller, J. Colson, W. Fisher, and J. Atkinson, J. Thornton.
" [25] Novissima et accuratissima Insulæ Jamaicæ. Descriptio per Johannem Seller, Johannē Colson, Gulielmu Fisher Jacobū Atkinson, Johannem [que] Thornton.
" [26] A chart of the South-sea. By J. Seller, J. Colson, W. Fisher, J. Atkinson, & J. Thornton. Dundee sculp

Atlas maritimus or a book of charts: describing the sea-coasts, capes, headlands, sands, shoals, rocks & dangers; the bayes, roads, harbors, rivers, and ports in most of the known parts of the world. With the true courses & distances from one place to another, gathered from the latest best discoveries that have been made, by divers able & experienced navigators of our english nation: accommodated with an hydrographical description of the whole world. Sold by James Atkinson at Cherry-garden staires on Rotherhith wall. 1 pl., 10 pp., 19 maps. fol. [London, 1670?] 4151

NOTE.—Copy B. See copy A title 4150, for full note, also titles 4152, 4153, 4154.

CONTENTS.

no. [1] Novissima totius terrarum orbis tabula.
" [2] A generall chart of the Northern seas. By I. Thornton. F. Lamb sculp.
" [3] A chart of the North sea. By John Seller, John Colson, Willm Fisher, James Atkinson, John Thornton. James Clark engra.
" [4] A plat of the channel discovering the sea coasts of England, Scotland, Ireland and part of France. F. Lamb sculp.
" [5] A chart of France, Spain, Portugal and the straits mouth. By William Fisher and Richard Mount. F. Lamb sculp.
" [6] A chart of the Baltick-sea. By John Thornton, John Seller, William Fisher, James Atkinson, John Colson.
" [7] A chart of the sea coasts from Landsend of England to Cape Bona Esperanca. By J. Seller, W. Fisher, J. Colson, J. Atkinson, J. Thornton.
" [8] A chart of Gvinea. By Iohn Thornton.
" [9] The coast of Barbaria, Gualata, Arguin and Guinea from Borlings to Cape Verde. By John Thornton, John Seller, William Fisher, James Atkinson, John Colson.

Seller, J.—Continued.

no. [10] A chart of ye North part of America for Hudsons bay comonly called ye North West Passage. By Iohn Thornton.

" [11] A chart of the western part of the East-Indies. With all the aejacent islands from Cape Bona Esperanca to Cape Comorin. By John Thornton, John Seller, William Fisher, James Atkinson, John Colson.

" [12] A chart of the Mediterranean sea.

" [13] A general chart of the West Indies. By John Seller, John Colson, William Fisher, James Atkinson & John Thornton.

" [14] A chart of the tradeing part of the East Indies and China with the adjacent islands from Surrat to Iapan. By John Thornton.

" [15] A new mapp of Magellan straights. By John Thornton, Iohn Seller, William Fisher, James Atkinson, Iohn Colson.

" [16] A chart of the sea coast of Brazil. By John Seller, John Colson, William Fisher, James Atkinson, and John Thornton. To s^r. John Narborough, who passed and repased the streights of Magellan, 1670. [The only date in the atlas]

" [17] A chart of the South-sea. By J. Sellers, J. Colson, W. Fisher, J. Atkinson, & J. Thornton. Dundee sculp.

" [18] A chart of the Western ocean according to Mercators projection . . .

" [19] A chart of the West-Indies. By John Thornton John Seller William Fisher James Atkinson John Colson.

Atlas maritimus, or a book of charts, describeing the sea coasts capes headlands sands shoals rocks and dangers the bayes roads harbors rivers and ports, in most of the knowne parts of the world. With the true courses and distances, from one place to another, gathered from the latest and best discoveryes, that have bin made by divers able and experienced navigators, of our english nation, accomodated with an hydrographicall description of the whole world . . . 1 p. l., 12 pp., 43 maps on 28 sheets. fol. London, J. Seller, [1671?] 4152

NOTE.—The Library of Congress has a copy of Seller's *Atlas maritimus*, dated 1675 and four undated editions. The title-page of the 1675 edition and of the undated editions as given above differ. For title and half title of 1675 edition, see v. 4, title 4154.

In the *Dictionary of national biography*, under Seller, the first edition of this atlas is referred to as "*the Sea Atlas*," which is the half title of the edition of 1675, also the title of the text in all editions. This states, "In 1671 he [Seller] published a folio volume of sailing directions, under the title of 'The English Pilot,' and another called 'The Sea Atlas,' to which were prefixed letters patent from the king, setting forth that as he (Seller) had been for several years collecting and composing these works it was forbidden 'to copy, epitomise, or reprint' the treatises of navigation; 'to counterfeit any of the maps, plans or charts' in them, or to import them or any part of them from beyond the seas, 'either under the name of Dutch Waggoners or any other name whatsoever,' within the term of thirty years."

Though the half title, "*A sea atlas*," does not appear in this copy, the date 1671? has been assigned to it as the probable date. Many of the same maps appear in the later editions, and a number of them in Seller's *The english pilot. The first book. 1671.*

The title-page is the engraved title-page called "Englands famous discoverers," which shows sketches of "S^r. Fran. Drake, m^r. Tho. Candish, cap. Davies, s^r. Walter Raleigh, s^r. Hugh Willoughby, cap. Smith. A view of London appears below the cartouche containing the title. This is the same engraved title-page with a different title in the cartouche which is used in the English pilot. The first book. 1671, in Seller's *Coasting pilot*, [*1672*] and in the editions of the *Atlas maritimus*, "sold by James Atkinson," though in the latter case the view of London is quite different, evidently an earlier unfinished impression of the plate, and showing that another plate of the view of London must have been substituted later. Some of the maps also in the editions sold by Atkinson are earlier impressions of the plates.

There are 10 pages of text in the Atkinson editions and 12 pages in the 1671? and 1672? editions only 1 page of which is new, the other being made by the difference in the print. There are some small differences in the text, the editions of 1671?, 1672? and 1675 being the same impression, and the two editions sold by Atkinson of 1670? being alike. In this edition, the map no. [9] Comitatus Zelandiae . . . 1657, is inserted.

The engravers as far as stated are given in the contents.

CONTENTS.

no. [1] A general chart of the northerne navigation. Francis Lamb sculp.
" [2] A chart of the North sea. James Clark engra.
" [3] A draught of the sands, channels, buoyes, beacons and sea marks upon the coast of England. F. Lamb sculp. Inset: The river of Thames from London bridge to Tilburyhope.
" [4] The river of Humber.—The river of Tyne. Ia. Clarke sculpsit.
" [5] A chart of the north coast of England, from Yarmouth to Cocket island.—A description of the east coast of Scotland.
" [6] A chart of the islands of Shotland [Shetland]—A chart of the islands of Farre.—A chart of the Hebrides.
" [7] A chart of Holland Zealand and Flanders.—A chart of the road and harbor of Medenblick.
" [8] A chart of Flanders between Calis and Walcheren.
" [9] Comitatus Zelandiæ nova descriptio, anno 1657. Insets: Middelburgum orbs comitatus Zelandiæ primia, mercatura et navigatione emporium celeberrimum.—Zircikzee.—Vlissingen.
" [10] Chart of the Maes and Wielingen.—The coast of Holland between the Maes and the Texel.
" [11] A chart of the South sea, Texel and Fly-streame.—A chart of the Eemes.—A chart of the Fly and Amelander gat.
" [12] A chart of the Eemes Elve.
" [13] A chart of the coast of Iutland.—A chart shewing the sea coasts of the Bellt, Wedersound, Melversound with all the adjacent islands.
" [14] A chart of the Baltick sea with the North Bodom & Lading.
" [15] A chart of the sea coasts of Russia, Lapland, Finmarke, Nova Zembla and Greenland. Steph. Board sculp.
" [16] A chart of ye Narrow seas.
" [17] A discription of the sea coast of England, from the North foreland to Dover, and from Dover to Portland.—A chart of the west part of England from Portland to Silly.
" [18] A chart of the chanell of Bristoll, from Silly to St Davids head in Wales.—A draught of the Landsend of England and islands of Silly.
" [19] A chart of the east side of Ireland, from Waterford, to Carlingford.—A discription of the west side of Ireland, from Cape Clere, to the river of Waterford.

Seller, J.—Continued.

no. [20] A description of the north coast of Ireland, between Ban haven, and Cabo Moye.—A chart of the west coast of Ireland, between Cabo Moye and the river Shannon.—A chart of the southwest side of Ireland, from Cape Cleare to the river Shannon.
" [21] A discription of the east side of Ireland, betwene Carlingford and Banhaven, with the coast of Scotland lying right against the same.
" [22] A chart of Spaine.
" [23] A description of the sea coasts of England and France.
" [24] A description of the sea coasts of Normandie and Bretaigne.—The coast of Bretaigne and Poictou.
" [25] A description of the sea coast of France from Olone to Bayone in Biscay.—Inset: The river of Bourdeaux.
" [26] A chart of the sea coast of Portugall, between the Burlings and Cape de St Vincent.—A chart of part of the sea coasts of Gallisia and Portugall between Cape de Finisterre and the Burlings.
" [27] A chart of the sea coast of Biscay.—A chart of the sea coasts of Galisia betwen Cape de Pinas and Cape Finister.
" [28] A description of the sea coast of Elcondoda & Andalusia between Cape St Vincent and the strait of Gibralter with part of ye coast of Barbary. Inset: The new mole and haven of Tanger.

Atlas maritimus, or a book of charts, describeing the sea coasts capes headlands sands shoals rocks and dangers the bayes roads harbors rivers and ports, in most of the knowne parts of the world. With the true courses and distances, from one place to another, gathered from the latest and best discoveryes, that have bin made by divers able and experienced navigators, of our English nation, accomodated with an hydrographicall description of the whole world . . . 1 p. l., 12 pp., 75 col. maps on 51 sheets. fol. London, J. Seller, [1672?] 4153

NOTE.—The date 1672? has been assigned to this atlas as the *Term catalogues 1668–1709*, give map no. 4, A chart of the sea coasts of England Flanders & Holland, as published in 1672.

Where more than one map appears on a sheet they are sometimes arranged differently from the earlier editions.

Title-page and maps hand colored.

The calf binding bears on both sides an elaborately ornamented crest of three anchors, which design was the official stamp or seal of the Navy Office.

Original spelling in titles preserved.

For full note on the various editions of Seller's *Atlas maritimus*, see titles 4150, 4151.

CONTENTS.

no. [1] Novissima totius terrarum orbis tabula.
" [2] A chart of the North sea. James Clark engra.
" [3] A draught of the sands, channels buoyes beacons and sea marks upon the coast of England. F. Lamb sculp. Inset: The river of Thames from London Bridge to Tilburyhope.
" [4] A chart of the sea coasts of England Flanders and Holland. Ja. Clark sculpsit. [1672]
" [5] The river of Humber.—The river of Tyne. Ia. Clarke sculpsit.
" [6] A chart of the north coast of England, from Yarmouth to Cocket Island.—A description of the east coast of Scotland.

no. [7] A chart of the islands of Shotland [Shetland]—A chart of the islands of Farre.—A chart of the Hebrides.

" [8] A chart of the South sea, Texel and Fly-stream.—A chart of the Eemes.—A chart of the Fly and Amerlander gat.

" [9] A chart of the Eemes Elve.—A chart of the coast of Iutland.

" [10] A chart of the Maes and Wielingen.—The coast of Holland between the Maes and Texel.

" [11] A chart of Flanders between Calis and Walcheren.

" [12] A chart of the coast of Norway between Naze and Bergen.—A description of the coast of Norway between Bergen and Stemnesheft.

" [13] A chart of the sea coasts of Russia, Lapland, Finmarke, Nova Zembla and Greenland.

" [14] A chart of Norway between Stemnes-heft and the citty of Dronten.—A chart of the Northermost part of Norway, from the citty of Dronten to the North Cape.

" [15] A chart of part of Norway and Lapland. Insets: A description of the island Kilduin.—A description of Kegro and Lous.—A descriptiõ of the island Wardhouse.—A chart of the White sea from Knock John to the coast of Corelia.

" [16] A large description of the two chanells in the river Dwina goeing up to the citty of Archangel.

" [17] A chart of the Baltick sea with the North Bodom & Lading.

" [18] A description of the sea coasts of Coerland and Lyfland.—[Gulf of Finland]

" [19] A chart of the coast of Sweden, Bornholm, Oeland, Gotland.—A chart of the gat of Abbo or Uttoy.

" [20] A chart of the Narrow seas.

" [21] A chart of the Brittish chanel.

" [22] A chart of the west part of England, from Portland to Silly.—A draught of the Landsend of England and islands of Silly.

" [23] A chart of the east side of Ireland, from Waterford to Carlingford.—A discription of the west side of Ireland, from Cape Clere to the river of Waterford.

" [24] A description of the north coast of Ireland, between Ban haven, and Cabo Moye.—A chart of the west coast of Ireland between Cabo Moye and the river Shannon.—A chart of the southwest side of Ireland, from Cape Cleare to the river Shannon.

" [25] A discription of the eastside of Ireland, betwene Carlingford and Banhaven with the coast of Scotland lying right against the same.

" [26] A description of the sea coasts of England and France.

" [27] A description of the sea coasts of Normandie and Bretaigne.—The coast of Bretaigne and Poictou.

" [28] A chart of the bay of Biscaia. Ia. Clerk sculpsit.

" [29] A chart of Spaine.

" [30] A description of the sea coast of France from Olone to Bayone in Biscay. Inset: The river of Bourdeaux.

" [31] A chart of the sea-coast of Biscay. A chart of the sea-coasts of Galisia betwen Cape de Pinas and Cape Finister.

" [32] A chart of the sea coast of Portugall, between the Burlings and Cape de St Vincent.—A chart of part of the sea coasts of Gallisia and Portugall betweene Cape de Finisterre and the Burlings.

" [33] A description of the sea-coast of Elcondoda & Andalusia between Cape St Vincent and the strait of Gibralter. Inset: The new mole and haven of Tanger.

Seller, J.—Continued.

no. [34] A description of the coast of Barbarie from Cape Spartell to Cape Cantin.—A chart and description of the Canary islands.
" [35] A description of the coast of Barbarie between Cape de Cantin, and Cape de Geer.—A description of the road before the citty Angra in the island Tercera.—Sanct Michiels.—A chart of the islands of Madera and Porto Santo.—Inset: South point of the island of Fayal.
" [36] A chart of the westermost part of the Mediterranean sea.
" [37] A chart of the Levant or eastermost part of the Mediterranean sea.
" [38] A chart of the coasts of Barbarie, Gualata, Arguyn & Genehoa from C Vincent to C Verd.
" [39] A chart of Gvinea describeing the sea coast from Cape de Verde to Cape Bona Esperanca.
" [40] A chart of the western part of the East Indies, with all the aejacent islands from Cape Bona Esperanca to Cape Comorin. F. Lamb sculp.
" [41] A chart of the eastermost part of the East Indies with all the adjacent islands from Cape Comorin to Iapan. F. Lamb, sculp.
" [42] A chart of the Tartarian sea from Nova Zemla to Iapan.
" [43] A generall chart of the northerne navigation. Francis Lamb sculp.
" [44] A chart of the north part of America. Inset: A polar projection describing ye northermost parts of the world.
" [45] A chart of the western ocean.
" [46] A chart of the West Indies from Cape Cod to the river Oronoque.
" [47] A chart of the Caribe islands.
" [48] The Windward passage from Jamaica, betwene the east end of Cuba, and the west end of Hispaniola.
" [49] A chart of the sea coast of Brazil from Cape St Augustine to the straights of Magellan.
" [50] A chart of the South-sea. Dundee sculp.
" [51] A new mapp of Magellans straights.

Atlas maritimus, or the sea-atlas; being a book of maritime charts. Describing the sea-coasts, capes, headlands, sands, shoals, rocks and dangers. The bays, roads, harbors, rivers and ports, in most of the known parts of the world. Collected from the latest and best discoveries that have been made by divers able and experienced navigators of our english nation. Accommodated with a hydrographical description of the whole world; shewing the chief cities, towns, and places of trade and commerce; with the nature of the commodities and merchandizes of each country; very useful for merchants, and all other persons concerned in maritime affairs . . . 3 p. l., 12 [2] pp., 42 col. maps, 7 col. pl. fol. London, by J. Darby, for the author, 1675. 4154

NOTE.—Corrected title, see v. 1, no. 487.

Colored engraved half title reads: *A sea atlas describing the sea coasts in all the known parts of the world* . . . It contains portraits of sir Francis Drake and mr. Tho. Candish.

The main title-page differs from those of 1671? and 1672? and from the editions of 1670?, sold by James Atkinson, which do not carry Seller's name on the title-pages, and which are undoubtedly the works mentioned in the Privilege to this one in the following manner: "We are informed that endeavours are made by some of our subjects, secretly to copy and reprint the same, [the Sea-atlas] under another title, to the great prejudice and discouragement of the said John Seller."

Of this 1675 edition of the *Sea atlas*, Seller says in his preface that it was "the first essay of this nature that hath been compleated in England."

The [2] pp. mentioned in the collation, give "A catalogue of mathematical instruments, made and sold by John Seller", and "A catalogue of mathematical books, maritime charts, draughts, etc."

In the London Stationer's company. *A transcript of the registers of the worshipful company of stationers, from 1640–1708. A. D. London, 1914*, the following entry appears in connection with an edition of this work: "30 November 1679. Entred . . . by vertue of a licence from his Matie whereunto the hand of Master Warden Vere is subscribed one book or coppy entituled Atlas Maritimus, or Sea Atlas, being a book of martime charts, describeing the sea coasts, capes, headlands, sands, shoals, rocks, &c. By John Seller, hydrographer to the king. And alsoe one other book entituled, The English Pilot, the second book containeing the sea coasts, capes, headlands, soundings, sands, shoals, rocks, &c, by the same author."

The following maps and plates bear dates later than 1675:

no. 3. Schema solis ad ingressum mercurÿ Stæ Helenæ, anno 1677 octob 28 9h. 26'. 40'' A.M.

" 9. A mapp of the regions & countreyes vnder and about the North Pole. 1676.

" 26. A map containing the island & kingdome of Sicily. London, a°. 1676.

Maps engraved by James Clark, Sa. Moore, Ia. Bennett, Francis Lamb, W. Hollar, Io. Oliver.

Plan of Tangier, Messina, Naples, Tripoli and view of New York city are insets to various charts.

no. [32] A new map of the island of Saint Hellena.

CONTENTS.

no. [1] Novissima totius terrarum orbis tabula.

" [2–3] The right ascensions and declinations of the principal fixed starrs in both hemisphears to ye year 1678.

" [4] Zodiacus stellatus cujus limitibus planetarium omnium visibles viæ comprehenduntur.

" [5] A mapp of the hemispheres of the heavens.

" [6] Schema corporis solaris prout a P. P. Kerchero et Scheinero Romæ anno 1635 observatum suit. [Title also in english]

" [7] Nativa lvnæ plenæ facies cum disci librationis minimæ et maximæ termino utroque (ut antehac nunquam) accurate observata adumbrata ærique incisa. 1645. [Title also in english]

" [8] Tabvla selenographica. 1645. [Title also in english]

" [9] A mapp of the regions & countreyes vnder and a bout the North Pole.

" [10] A generall chart of the northerne navigation. Francis Lamb sculp.

" [11] A chart of the North sea. James Clarke engra.

" [12] The river of Humber.—The river of Tyne. Ia. Clarke sculpsit.

" [13] A chart of the sea coasts of England Flanders & Holland. Ja. Clark sculpsit.

" [14] A chart of the Baltick sea with the North Bodom & Lading.

" [15] A chart of the two channels goeing into the Baltique sea one through Catte Gat and the Sound and the other through the Belt.

Seller, J.—Continued.

no. [16] A chart of the sea coasts of Russia Lapland Finmarke Nova Zemla and Greenland. Steph Board sculp.
" [17] A large description of the two chanells in the river Dwina goeing up to the citty of Archangel.
" [18] A chart of the seacoasts from the Landsend of England to Cape Bona Esperanca.
" [19] A chart of ye Narrow seas.
" [20] A chart of the Brittish chanel.
" [21] A chart of the sea-coasts of England and Ireland.
" [22] A chart of the bay of Biscaia. Ia. Clerk sculpsit.
" [23] A chart of Spaine.
" [24] The royall citty of Tangier in Africa. Io. Oliver fecit.
" [25] A chart of the westermost part of the Mediterranean sea.
" [26] A mapp containing the island & kingdome of Sicily with a part of Naples, & other adiacent coasts inclvding the Tyrrhenean sea, where most of things betwixt Spaine & France & their alyes are acted. 1676. W. Hollar fecit. Inset: Prospect of the straights of Sicily vulgarly calld Faro di Messina from the north.—Messina.—Faro di Messina.
" [27] A mapp of the citie and port of Tripoli in Barbary. W. Hollar fecit. 1675. Inset: A prospect of the city of Tripoli in Barbary.
" [28] A chart of the levant or eastermost part of the Mediterranean sea.
" [29] A chart of the coasts of Barbarie, Gualata, Arguyn & Genehoa from C Vincent to C Verd.
" [30] A chart of Gvinea describeing the seacoast from Cape de Verde to Cape Bona Esperanca.
" [31] [Views of St. Helena and Ascension]—This showeth Cape Bona Esperanca.—The Pike mountaine upon the island of Teneriff.
" [32] A new mapp of the island of Saint Hellena. Io. Oliver fe.
" [33] A draught of Cape Bona Esperanca.
" [34] A chart of the western part of the East Indies with all the aejacent islands from Cape Bona Esperanca to Cape Comorin. F. Lamb sculp.
" [35] A chart of the eastermost part of the East Indies with all the adjacent islands from Cape Comorin to Iapan. F. Lamb sculp.
" [36] A chart of the Tartarian sea from Nova Zemla to Japan.
" [37] A chart of the north part of America. Inset: A polar projection describing ye northermost parts of the world.
" [38] A general chart of the West Indias.
" [39] A chart of the western ocean.
" [40] A chart of the West Indies from Cape Cod to the river Oronoque.
" [41] A chart of the coast of America from New found Land to Cape Cod.
" [42] A mapp of New England.
" [43] A chart of the sea coasts of New England, New Jarsey, Virginia, Maryland and Carolina from C. Cod to C. Hatteras. Iames Clerk sculpsit.
" [44] A mapp of New Jarsey. Ja. Clerk sculp. Inset: New York.
" [45] A chart of the Caribe islands.
" [46] Novissima et accuratissima insulæ Jamaicæ.
" [47] The Windward pasage from Jamaica, betwene the east end of Cuba, and the west end of Hispaniola.
" [48] A chart of the sea coast of Brazil from Cape S^t^. Augustine to the straights of Magellan, & in the South sea from the lattitud of eight degrees to the said straights.
" [49] A chart of the South sea. Dundee sculp.

Spain. *Dirección de hidrografia.*

Atlas maritimo español . . . 1 p. l. 53 maps (partly fold.) fol. Madrid, 1789-[1814] 4155

NOTE.—The following maps relate to America:

no. 11. Carta general del oceano Atlantico septentrional. 1813.
" 12. Carta esferica de las islas Antillas. 1802.
" 13. Carta esferica del mar de las Antillas y de s costas de Tierra Firme. 1805. Corregida en 1809. Insets: Plano de la boca del golfo de Cariaco y del fondeadero de Cumaná. 1793.—Plano del fondeadero de Truxillo.
" 14. Carta esferica de las islas Caribes de Sotavento. 1804.
" 15. Carta esferica de los canales que forma la isla San Martin, con las de San Bartolomé y Anguila. 1811.
" 16. Carta esferica que comprehende una parte de las islas Antillas, las de Puerto Rico, Santo Domingo, Jamayca y Cuba. 1799.
" 17. Carta esferica que comprehende los desemboques al norte de la isla de S^{to}. Domingo y la parte oriental del canal viejo de Bahama. 1802.
" 18. Carta esferica de una parte del canal viejo de Bahama. 1799. Insets: Plano del fondeadero que forman los cayos de Piedras, Mono, Monillo.—Plano del fondeadero que forman los cayos Verde y Confites.
" 19. Carta esferica que comprehende desde el rio Guaurabo hasta Boca-Grande en la parte meridional de la isla de Cuba. 1805.
" 20. Carta esferica que comprehende todas las costas del seno mexicano, golfo de Honduras, islas de Cuba, Sto. Domingo, Jamaica y Lucayas. 1813 y 1814. Insets: Plano de la Aguadilla.—Plano del baxo del Alacran. 1803.
" 21. Carta esferica que comprehende las costas del seno mexicano. 1799.
" 22. Nueva carta del canal de Bahama que comprehende tambien los de Providencia y Santaren con los bajos, islas y sondas de la Florida. 1805. Corregida en 1807.
" 23. Carta particular de las costas setentrionales del seno mexicano, que comprehende las de la Florída ocidental, las margenes de la Luisiana. 1807.
" 24. Carta particular de la parte sur del seno mexicano que comprehende las costas de Yucatan y sonda de Campeche. 1808. Corregida y aumentada en 1814.
" 25. Plano geometrico del Puerto, capital de la isla de Puerto Rico. 1794.
" 26. Plano del puerto y ciudad de la Havana. 1798.
" 27. Plano del puerto del Vera Cruz. 1798.
" 28. Plano del Puerto Cabello. 1804. Insets: Plano de la ensenada de Barcelona en la costa de Tierra Firme.—Plano del fondeadero de La Guayra.
" 29. Carta esferica del oceano meridional desde el cabo de Hornos hasta el canal de Mozambique. 1800.
" 30. Carta general del oceano Atlantico meridional. 1810. Inset: Carta particular de la entrada del Rio de la Plata.
" 31. Carta esferica del Rio de la Plata desde su embocadura hasta Buenos Ayres. 1812. Insets: Plano del pto. de Maldonado.—Plano del puerto de Montevideo.

Spain. *Dirección de hidrografia*—Continued.

no. 32. Carta esferica de las costas de la America Meridional desde el paralelo de 36°. 30′. hasta el cabo de Hornos. 1798. Inset: Carta esferica de la parte norte del golfo de S[n]. Jorge.

" 33. Carta esferica de las costas del reyno de Chile. 1799.

" 34. Carta esferica de una parte de la costa del Peru. 1798.

" 35. Carta esferica que comprehende la costa ocidentalde America. 1791 presentada. 1800.

" 36. Carta esferica de los reconocimientos hechos en 1792 en la costa n. o. de America para examinar la entrada de Juan de Fuca. 1795.

" 37. Carta esferica de los reconocimientos hechos en la costa no. de America desde los canales de la entrada de Juan de Fuca hasta la salida de las goletas sutil y mexicana. 1795.

" 38. Plano del puerto de S[ta]. Elena en la costa patagonica. 1794.—Plano del puerto de Melo en el golfo de S[n]. Jorge. 1795.

" 39. Plano del puerto de S[n]. Carlos situado en la isla de Chiloe. 1790.

" 40. Plano del puerto de Valdivia. 1788.—Plano de la rada de S[n]. Juan Bautista en la isla de Juan Fernandez.

" 41. Carta esferica de la parte interior de la America meridional desde Valparaiso a Buenos Ayres. 1810. Inset: Plano del paso de los Andes.

" 42. Plano del fondeadero del Callao de Lima. 1811. Insets: Plano del puerto de Concepcion. 1790.—Plano del puerto de Valparaiso. 1790.

" 50–53. Carta de la provincia de Quito y de sus adjacentes. 1750.

METEOROLOGY.

Freybe, O.

Wetterkartenatlas, ein methodisch geordnete sammlung von wetterkarten mit erläuterndem text . . . 2. aufl. cover-title, 20 pp. 20 maps. 4°. Berlin, Gea [1913 ?] 4156

MILITARY.

Schirmer, F.

Kriegsgeschichtlicher atlas zum studium der feldzüge der neuesten zeit . . . 2. aufl. 2 p. l. 58 maps. fol. Wien, L. W. Seidel & sohn, 1912. 4157

Sternegg, J. K. von.

Schlachten-atlas des neunzehnten jahrhunderts. Zeitraum: 1820 bis zur gegenwart. Pläne der wichtigsten schlachten, gefechte und belagerungen mit begleitendem texte, nebst uebersichts-karten mit compendiösen darstellungen des verlaufes der feldzüge in Europa, Asien, und Amerika. Lief. 1–72 (in 40 pts) fol. Iglau, P. Bäuerle [1907–14] 4158

NOTE.—In progress.

MISSIONARY.

Society for the propagation of the gospel in foreign parts. *London.*

The colonial church atlas, arranged in dioceses: with geographical and statistical tables . . . Printed for the Society for the propagation of the gospel and sold at the depository of the Society for promoting christian knowledge . . . 6 p. l., [4] pp., 19 maps. sm. fol. London, Rivington [R. Clay, printer] 1842. 4159

NOTE.—Maps drawn and engraved by J. Archer. The following maps relate to America:

no. [1a] A colonial and missionary church map of the world.
" 1. Diocese of Nova Scotia.
" 2. " " Quebec.
" 3. " " Toronto.
" 4. " " New Brunswick.
" 5. " " Newfoundland.
" 6. " " Jamaica.
" 7. " " Barbados.
" 8. " " Antigua.
" 9. " " Guiana.

Student volunteer movement for foreign missions.

World atlas of christian missions; containing a directory of missionary societies, a classified summary of statistics, an index of mission stations, and maps showing the location of mission stations throughout the world, ed. by James S. Dennis, Harlan P. Beach, Charles H. Fahs. Maps by John G. Bartholomew . . . 172 pp. 24 double maps (incl. front.) fol. New York, Student volunteer movement for foreign missions, 1911. 4160

OCEANS.

Delesse, A. E. O. J.

Lithologie du fond des mers . . . Atlas. cover-title, 3 maps. sm. fol. [Paris, E. Lacroix, 1872] 4161

NOTE.—In portfolio.
To accompany his *Lithologie des mers de France et des mers principales du globe.*
"Carte des mers anciennes et actuelles de la France", and "Carte des iles Britanniques donnant la distribution de la pluie", are wanting.

Spain. *Dirección de hidrografia.*

[Atlas of Mediterranean countries] 19 maps, 4 fold. plates. fol. [Madrid? 1810?] 4162

Indian.

Hamburg. *Deutsche seewarte.*

Indischer ozean. Ein atlas von 35 karten, die physikalischen verhältnisse und die verkehrs-strassen darstellend, mit einer erläuternden einleitung und als beilage zum segelhandbuch für den Indischen ozean. Hrsg. von der direktion. 16 pp. 35 col. maps. fol. Hamburg, L. Friederichsen & co. 1891. 4163

NOTE.—The Hamburg, Deutsche seewarte was founded in 1867 as the Norddeutsche seewarte, by W. J. A. Freeden and directed by him until 1875 when it was reorganized & passed under the control of the Reichs-Marine amt at Berlin.

Atlas der stromversetzungen auf den wichtigsten dampferwegen im Indischen ozean und in den Ostasiatischen gewässern. 8 pp. 52 maps. fol. Hamburg, L. Friederichsen & co. 1905. 4164

NOTE.—At head of title: Kaiserliche marine. Deusche seewarte.
For note on the Deutsche seewarte see title 4163.

Atlas der meeresströmungen in dem Indischen ozean auf grund der beobachtungen deutscher und Holländischer schiffe. 2 p. l., 24 maps. large obl. fol. Hamburg, L. Friederichsen & co. 1913. 4165

NOTE.—At head of title: Kaiserliche marine. Deutsche seewarte.
For note on the Deutsche seewarte, see title 4163.

North sea.

Hamburg. *Deutsche seewarte.*

Atlas der gezeiten und gezeitenströme für das gebiet der Nordsee und der britischen gewässer. 2 p. l., 12 col. maps. fol. Hamburg, L. Friederichsen & co. 1905. 4166

NOTE.—At head of title: Kaiserliche marine. Deutsche seewarte.
For note on the Deutsche seewarte, see title 4163.

OROGRAPHICAL.

Johnston, W. & A. K.

W. & A. K. Johnston's orographical atlas. iii, [21] pp. 32 col. maps, diagrs. 4°. Edinburgh & London, W. & A. K. Johnston, ltd. [1914] 4167

NOTE.—Scales, projections, etc., and a general index.

W. & A. K. Johnston's orographical atlas. 32 col. maps. 8°. Edinburgh & London, W. & A. K. Johnston ltd. [1914] 4168

NOTE.—Without index.

OUTLINE.

Parkinson, T. W. F.

Atlas of practical geography. pt. 1–11. 8°. London and Glasgow, Collins clear-type press [1914?]
[Collins' modern geographical series] 4169

CONTENTS.

pt. 1. The British Isles.
" 2. India.
" 3. Europe.
" 4. Australia.
" 5. Canada.
" 6. North America.
" 7. South America.
" 8. Asia.
" 9. Africa.
" 10. England and Wales.
" 11. Scotland.

PHYSICAL.

Atlas photographique des formes du relief terrestre. Album of landforms. Atlante geomorfologico. Morphologischer bilderatlas. Pub. sous les auspices d'une commission internationale, par Jean Brunhes, Émile Chaix, Emm. de Martonne . . . Sér. 1., livr. 1. 1 pt. illus., plates. sm. fol. Genève, F. Boissonnas & c[ie], 1914– 4170

NOTE.—Text in french, english, and german.

Bartholomew, J. G.

The advanced atlas of physical and political geography, a new series of maps specially designed for schools and private students . . . 2 p. l., 96, 31 pp. incl. 68 col. maps, 3 col. pl. sm. fol. London, New York, etc., Oxford university press, H. Milford, 1917. 4171

NOTE.—Contains small maps of the following cities: Paris, Madrid, Vienna, Buda-Pest, Hamburg, Berlin, Christiana, Copenhagen, Stockholm, Petrograd, Moscow, Odessa.
Contains maps showing volcanoes, earthquakes, vegetation, temperature, rainfall, climate, population, commerce, geology, industries, also an ethnographic map of Europe.

The physical & political school atlas. xvi, 32 pp., illus. 33 col. maps. 4°. London, Oxford university press [1914?] 4172

Johnston, A. K.

The physical atlas. A series of maps & notes illustrating the geographical distribution of natural phenomena . . . Based on the Physikalischer atlas of professor H. Berghaus, with the co-operation in their several departments of sir David Brewster . . .

Johnston, A. K.—Continued.

professors J. D. Forbes, Edward Forbes . . . 5 p. l., [94] pp., 30 maps. fol. Edinburgh, W. & A. K. Johnston, Cowan & co.; London, T. W. Saunders, 1848. 4172a

Note.—Expository text follows each map.
Maps same as contained in the edition published by Blackwood & sons, 1848, but do not follow in the same order.

The physical atlas: a series of maps & notes illustrating the geographical distribution of natural phenomena . . . Based on the Physikalischer atlas of professor H. Berghaus, with the co-operation in their several departments of sir David Brewster . . . professors J. D. Forbes, Edward Forbes . . . Divisions: geology, hydrography, meteorology, natural history. 3 p. l., [4] 34, 16, 10, 34 pp., 30 maps. fol. Edinburgh, W. Blackwood & sons, 1848. 4173

Note.—Maps same as contained in the edition published by W. & A. K. Johnston & Cowan & co., 1848, but not in same order.

CONTENTS.

Geological division:
no. 1. Mountain systems of Europe.
" 2. Geological structure of the globe.
" 3. Mountain chains in Asia and Europe.
" 4. Mountain chains in North America.
" 5. Mountain chains of South America.
" 6. Glacier regions.
" 7. Phenomena of volcanic action.
" 8. Comparative views of geological phenomena.
" 9–10. Palæontology of the British Islands.

Hydrographical division:
no. 1. Physical chart of the Atlantic ocean.
" 2. Physical chart of the Indian ocean.
" 3. Physical chart of the Pacific ocean.
" 4. Tidal chart of the British seas.
" 5. River systems of Asia and Europe.
" 6. River systems of America.

Meteorological division:
no. 1. Humboldt's system of isothermal lines.
" 2. Geographical distribution of currents of air.
" 3. Hyetographic or rain map of the world.
" 4. Hyetographic or rain map of Europe.
" 5. Projection of lines of equal polarization.

Phytological and zoological division:
no. 1. Geographical distribution of plants.
" 2. Geographical distribution & cultivation of food plants.
" 3. Distribution &c., of mammalia.
" 4. Distribution &c., of carnivora.
" 5. Distribution &c., of rodentia and ruminantia.
" 6. Distribution &c., of birds.
" 7. Distribution &c., of reptiles.
" 8. Ethnographic map of Europe.
" 9. Ethnographic map of British Isles.

Philip, G., & son, *ltd.*

Philips' comparative wall atlas of world-relations. Edited by J. F. Unstead . . . & E. G. R. Taylor. Scale on equator 1:40,000,000. Scale on 45th parallels 1:28,000,000. 8 col. fold. maps, 31½ x 40¾ each. London, G. Philip & son, ltd.; New York. C. S. Hammond & co. [1916?] 4174

CONTENTS.

no. 1. Natural vegetation.
" 2. Temperature.
" 3. Climate, may 1–oct. 31.
" 4. Climate, nov. 1–april 30.
" 5. Relief of land.
" 6. Annual rainfall & range of temperature with july currents.
" 7. Density of population.
" 8. Political divisions & communications.

Stanford, W.

The map and its story: a physical atlas . . . cover-title, 1 p. l., 44 pp. incl. 44 col. maps. 4°. London, G. W. Bacon & co., ltd. [1915?] 4175

Sydow, E. von, *and* **Habenicht, H.**

Sydow-Habenicht: Metodischer wand-atlas . . . Oro-hydrographischer schul-wandkarte nach E. v. Sydows plan . . . 15 maps. fol. Gotha, J. Perthes, [1906?–15] 4176

NOTE.—In progress. Issued in parts.

CONTENTS.

no. 1. Erdkarten.
" 2. Europa.
" 3. Asien.
" 5. Africa.
" 6. Nord-Amerika.
" 7. Sud-Amerika.
" 8. Deutches reich.
" 9. Osterreich-Ungarn.
" 10. Balkan-halbinsel.
" 11. Italien.
" 12. Spanische halbinsel.
" 13. Frankreich.
" 14. Britische inseln.
" 15. Skandinavien.
" 16. Russland.

Vilanova y Piera, J.

Atlas geográfico universal . . . 228 [1] pp., title. 31 col. maps, 4 col. pl., illus. fol. Madrid, Astort hermanos, 1877. 4177

NOTE.—A separate illustrated title to the atlas reads, *Atlas geográfico universal texto redactado bajo la direccion de dr. Juan Vilanova. Parte artistica, Otto Neussel.*

Maps have border text and each map of a separate country has a large illustration at the top of the plate.

The following maps relate to America:

no. [1] Mapa mundi.
" [6] Mapa geológico del globo.
" [12] América Central y las Antillas.
" [13] Planisferio hipsométrico.
" [14] Mapa etnográfico general.
" [16] América del Sur.
" [17] Mapas físicos del globo.
" [19] Mapas físicos del globo.
" [20] América del Norte.
" [23] Distribucion de las principales religiones.
" [26] Densidad de la poblacion terrestre.
" [30] Distribucion geográfica de las plantas.
" [31] Geografia zoológica.

PORTOLANI.

Hispanic society of America.

Facsimiles of portolan charts belonging to the Hispanic society of America, with an introduction by Edward Luther Stevenson. 2 p. l., 4 pp. 16 facsim. fol. New York, 1916. 4178

[Hispanic Society of America. Publication no. 104]

NOTE.—In portfolio.

A numbered edition of which this is no. 14.

CONTENTS.

no. 1. Giacomo Giroldi. Early fifteenth century.
" 2. Petrus Roselli. 1468.
" 3. Vesconte de Maiolo. 1512.
" 4. Conte Hoctomanno Freducci. 1524.
" 5. Anonymous. Early sixteenth century.
" 6. Anonymous. Early sixteenth century.
" 7. Bartolome Olivo. ca. 1550.
" 8. Hieronymo Giriva [?] After 1550.
" 9. Bartolome Olives. 1552.
" 10. Jaume Olives. 1566.
" 11. Anonymous. Late sixteenth century.
" 12. Anonymous. Late sixteenth century.
" 13. Vincentius Demetrei Volcius. 1600.
" 14. Maiolo e Visconte. 1605.
" 15. Placitus Caloiro et Olivo. Early seventeenth century.
" 16. Jouan Battista Cavallini. 1637.

Martines, J.

Portolan atlas. Joan Martines en Messina añy 1582. Facsimile. With an introduction by Edward Luther Stevenson. 4 p. l., 5 col. maps. fol. New York, [the Hispanic society of America] 1915. [Hispanic society of America. Publication no. 88] 4179

NOTE.—Contents taken from explanation of charts in the introduction.

CONTENTS.

no. 1. Chart one of this atlas includes the eastern Mediterranean coast region, the Ægean, the Black Sea, and the northern half of the Red Sea.
" 2. Chart two includes the central Mediterranean coast regions.
" 3. Chart three includes the west coast of Europe from Friesland to Gibralter with the east coast line of Spain, a section of the northwest coast of Africa, England, Scotland, Ireland, Iceland or "islanda," the debatable land of frixlanda, the ' yslad brasil" and "yslad de man."
" 4. Chart four represents a section of the Atlantic and Mediterranean coast of the Iberian peninsula, the northwest coast of Africa from a point somewhat to the east of "tanger" to the mouth of the Sénegal River, the Azores Islands, the Madeiras and the Canaries.
" 5. Chart five lays down the coast of Africa from "c. verde" to "Capo di bona Spirancza," with a number of islands in the Atlantic.

RAILROADS.

Cram, G. F.

Cram's standard american railway system atlas of the world. Accompanied with a complete and simple index of the United States, showing the true location of all railroads, towns, villages and post offices . . . Foreign maps are compiled largely from charts of the Royal geographical society, and are geographically correct. 2 p. l., 5–606 pp. incl. 178 col. maps. fol. Chicago, G. F. Cram, 1900. 4180

NOTE.—Contains plans of many prominent cities of the United States.

Cram's bankers, brokers and attorneys atlas. The United States and world. 13th federal census edition. A complete series of United States maps, showing both steam and electric railroads, maps of island possessions, foreign countries, world, polar regions, hemispheres, etc. A carefully prepared index of over 70,000 place names . . . 3 pl., 5–530 pp. incl. 144 col. maps, 1 diagr. illus. fol. Chicago, New York, G. F. Cram, 1913. 4181

NOTE.—Similar to *Cram's bankers, brokers and attorneys atlas . . . Chicago, New York, 1913* [*1912*] with the addition of "An encyclopedia of geography", pp. 531–638.

RELIEF.

Bacon, G. W., & co.

Bacon's excelsior contour-relief atlas. cover-title, 36 (*i. e.* 42) [7] pp. incl. 46 col. maps. 8°. London, G. W. Bacon & co., ltd. [1913?] 4182

Ravenstein, A.

Plastischer schul-atlas für die erste stufe des unterrichts in der erdkunde. Enthaltend die karten von Deutschland, Europa, Asien, Afrika, Nord- und Süd-Amerika und Australien, nebst einem ideal-bild physisch-geographischen verhältnisse. In relief geprägt und nach der physisch-geographischen beschaffenheit (in einer besonderen beigabe auch nach der politischen eintheilung) der länder in farben gedruckt. 3te ganz umgearbeitete aufl. . . . 1 p.l., 8 maps, 8 relief maps. 4°. Frankfurt am Main, B. Dondorf, 1854. 4183

NOTE.—Enclosed in pasteboard box.
Consult also titles under "Contour relief."

SCHOOL.

Agostini, G. de.

Atlante geografico ad uso delle scuole elementari del circondario de Genova. cover-title, 9 col. maps, col. illus. sm. fol. Novara, Istituto geografico de Agostini [1911?] 4184

Åkerman, A.

Atlas juvenilis, eller geographiska chartor till ungdomens tienst i methodisk ordning författade af And. Åkerman . . . andra uplagan . . . 1 p. l., 30 maps. obl. 16°. Upsala [1789?] 4185

NOTE.—The latest date found in the atlas, 1789, is found on map no. 3, Charta öfver Sverige copierad och utgifven af Fredr. Akrel . . . Stockholm, 1789.
Maps engraved by A. Söderberg, E. Osterberg and F. Akrel.
The following maps relate to America:
no. 1. Mappa universalis totius orbis terraquæi, eller, general charta öfver hela jordklotet. Utgifwen af And. Åkerman . . . 1768. E. Osterberg sculpsit.
" 28. Mappa generalis Americæ eller general charta öfwer America af. A. Åkerman. E. Osterberg sc.
" 29. Mappa geogr. Americæ Septent^s. eller geogr. Charta öfwer Norra America af A. Åkerman.
" 30. Mappa geogr. Americæ Merid^s. eller geogr. charta öfwer Södra America af A. Åkerman.

Bacon, G. W., & co.

School and college atlas, one hundred and three maps, physical, political and commercial, index. 104, [7] pp. incl. 103 col. maps. 4°. London, G. W. Bacon [1914] 4186

NOTE.—Title on reverse of front cover.

Bartholomew, J. G.

Atlas for Canadian schools; a new series of physical and political maps . . . 2 p. l., 48, 23 [1] pp. incl. 48 col. maps. 8°. London, New York [etc.] T. Nelson & sons [1912?] 4187

Bludau, A.

Schwann'scher schul-atlas. Ausgabe B. . . . Für den regierungsbezirk Düsseldorf bearbeitet unter mitwirkung praktischer schulmänner. 1 p. l., 20 pp. incl. 15 col. maps, 1 col. map. 4°. Düsseldorf, L. Schwann [1914?] 4188

NOTE.—One map on reverse of back cover.

Brunner, A., *and* **Voigt, L.**

Deutscher handelsschul-atlas . . . auf grund der neuesten auflage von Keil und Riecke: Deutscher schulatlas. 3. verb. aufl . . . 43 (*i. e.* 44) 8 pp. incl. 72 col. maps, diagrs. 4°. Leipzig & Berlin, B. G. Teubner [1913] 4189

Chisholm, G. G., *and* **Leete, C. H.**

Longmans' new school atlas. New ed. 1 l., iv, 32 pp., 40 col. maps. 4°. New York, Longmans, Green & co., 1912. 4190

Diercke, P.

Diercke schulatlas für höhere lehranstalten. Mittelausgabe. 1. aufl. 2 p. l., 4, 144 pp. incl. 86 col. maps. 4 pl. fol. Braunschweig, Berlin, Hamburg, G. Westerman, 1914. 4191

Franklin, T., *and* **Griffiths, E. D.**

The atlas geographies; a new visual atlas and geography combined . . . 2 v., v. 1, vi, [2] 88 pp. incl. 7 maps, 8 col. maps (incl. front.) on 5 pl., illus., diagrs.; v. 2, viii, 184 pp. incl. 84 maps, 23 col. maps, 7 maps in pocket. 8°. Edinburgh, W. & A. K. Johnston [1914] 4192

CONTENTS.

pt. 1. Physical geography . . . for secondary schools.
" 2. Junior geography . . . for secondary schools.

Frijlink, H.

Frijlink's kleine school-atlas. Tweede uitgave. cover-title, 1 p.l., 17 col. maps. 12°. Amsterdam, H. Frijlink, 1847. 4193

Gesellschaft der freunde des vaterländischen schul- und erziehungswesens. *Hamburg.*

Atlas für Hamburger schulen. Bearb. u. hrsg. unter benutzung von Diercke, Schulatlas, kleine ausgabe von der Gesellschaft der freunde des vaterländischen schul- und erziehungswesens in Hamburg . . . 1 p. l., 56, [2] 24 pp. incl. 47 col. maps, illus., diagrs. 4°. Braunschweig, G. Westermann, 1912. 4194

NOTE.—Maps on end-papers.

Homann heirs.

Maior atlas scholasticvs extriginta sex generalibvs et specialibvs mappis Homannianis quantum ad generalem orbis & inprimis [sic] Germaniæ notitiam sufficiunt in gratiam erudiendæ iuventutis compositvs in vulgarem usum scholarum et discentium a. 1752 exhibitus ab Homannianis heredibus. 1 pl., 36 col. maps, 1 col. pl. fol. [Norimbergae, cura Homann heredum, 1752-1773] 4195

NOTE.—Index in latin and german in title-page. Dates on maps vary from 1730 to 1773. Many of the maps have two titles, some in latin and french, some in latin and spanish, and some in latin and italian. Maps are by the following cartographers: Lowitz, Haas, Majer Schatz, Tannoni, Tollmann, Zürner, Hübner and Harenberg.

Many of these maps are also in *Atlas compendiarius, 1752-[1765]* by Homann heirs.

The following maps relate to America:

no. [1] Planiglobii terrestris mappa . . . designata a G. M. Lowizio . . . 1746.—Mappe-monde . . . dressée par m. G. M. Lowitz . . . 1746.

" [36] Americae mappa generalis . . . D. I. M. Hasii . . . delineata ab Aug. Gottl. Boehmio . . . 1746.

CONTENTS.

pl. b. Schematismvs geographiae mathematicae. 1753.

no. 1. Planiglobii terrestris mappa. Designata a G. M. Lowizio. 1746.—Mappe-monde dressée par m. G. M. Lowitz. 1746.

" 2. Europa. A Joh. Matth. Hasio. 1743.—L'Europe. Par Jean Matthias Has. 1743.

" 3. Imperii romano-germanici tabvla generalis. A Ioh. Bapt. Homanno.—L'Allemagne suivant les éléments de géographie de mr. Schatz, a. 1741.

" 4. Regni Bohemiae tabula designata a Tob. Majero. 1747.—Carte des états de Bohême. 1748.

" 5. Circvlvs Avstriacvs. A Tobia Majero. 1747.—Le Cercle d'Avtriche. Par Tobie Maier. 1747.

" 6. Circulus Rhenanus inferior. A Ioh. Baptista Homanno.

" 7. Circuli supe. Saxoniae pars meridionalis ex Zolmannianis et Zürnerianis subsidijs designata. 1757.

" 8. Tabvla marchionatvs Brandenbvrgici et dvcatvs Pomeraniæ, edita a Ioh. Baptista Homanno.

" 9. Circuli Franconiæ pars orientalis.—Erster und gröster theil des gantzen hochlöbl. Franckischen craisses.

" 10. Bavariæ circulus. Per Io. Baptistam Homannum.—La [!] cercle de Bavière.

" 11. Circvli Sveviæ mappa. A I. M. Hasio. 1743.

" 12. Circulus Rhenanus superior ex conatibus Ioh. Baptistæ Homanni.

" 13. Circuli Westphaliae tabula. 1761.

" 14. Circulus Saxoniæ Inferioris ex conatibus Io. Bapt. Homanni.

" 15. Belgii Universi nova tabula. A Tobia Majero. 1748.—Carte des XVII provinces ou de l'Allemagne inférieure. Par m^r. Tob. Majer. 1748.

" 16. Belgivm catholicvm. A Tob. Maiero. 1747.—Carte des Pais-Bas catholiqves ou des x provinces de l'Allemagne. Par S^r. Tobias Maier. 1747.

no. 17. Septem provinciae seu Belgivm foederatvm . . . Auctore Tobia Majero . . . 1748.
" 18. Helvetia . . . per Tobiam Mayervm . . . 1751.—La Svisse.
" 19. Regni Galliae . . . tabula . . . 1741.—Carte de France, dressée par Guillaume de L'Isle . . . 1741.
" 20. Italia . . . elementis insuper geographiæ Schazianis accomodata . . . —Gli stati d'Italia . . . del sgr. Schaz . . . 1742.
" 21. . . . Sicilia, Sardinia, Corsica, Malta . . . a Io. Ant. Rizzi Zannoni . . . 1762.—Li regni di Sicilia, e Sardegna colle adiacenti sole di Corsica, Elba, Malta . . . dal sigr. G. A. B. Rizzi Zannoni . . . 1762.
" 22. Magna Britannia.—A general map of Great Britain.
" 23. Regnorvm Hispaniæ . . . tabula . . . a Ioh. Bapt. Homanno.—El reyno de Espanna.
" 24. Mappa geographica regni Poloniae . . . à Tob. Mayero . . . 1773.—Carte des états de la covronne de Pologne . . . dessinée par mr. Tob. Mayer . . . 1773.
" 25. Regnum Borussiae . . . a Ioh. Baptista Homanno.
" 26. Hvngariae . . . tabvla . . . a I. M. Hasio . . . Carte d'Hongrie . . . par mons. I. M. Hasius.
" 27. Imperii Turcici Evropaei terra, in primis Graecia . . . adornavit Ioannes Christoph Harenberg . . . 1741.
" 28. Regni Daniae . . . tabula . . . a Io Baptista Homanno.
" 29. Scandinavia complectens Sueciæ, Daniæ & Norvegiæ regna ex tabulis Ioh. Bapt. Homanni.
" 30. Imperii Russici . . . tabula . . . opera Ioh. Mathiae Hasii.
" 31. Imperium Turcicum . . . sumtibus Io. Baptista Homanni . . . ad mentem de L'Islii . . . 1737.
" 32. Asia . . . designata a M. August Gottlob Boehmio . . . 1744.—Carte de l'Asie . . . dessinée par Aug. Gottl. Boehmius . . . 1744.
" 33. Tartariæ maioris . . . exacta opera Ioh. Matthiæ Hasii . . . 1730.
" 34. Palaestina . . . studio Iohannis Christoph Harenbergii . . . 1750.—Carte de la Terre Sainte . . . par Jean Christoph Harenberg . . . 1750.
" 35. Africa . . . a Ioh. Matthia Hasio.
" 36. Americae mappa generalis . . . delineata ab Aug. Gottl. Boehmio . . . 1746.

Johnston, W., & A. K.

W. & A. K. Johnston's new era school atlas. cover-title, 40, iii, [21] pp. incl. 40 col. maps, diagrs. 8°. Edinburgh, W. & A. K. Johnston, ltd. [1914] 4196

Lenglet Dufresnoy, N.

Kurzverfassete kinder geographie, in acht und vierzig lectionen eingetheilet, und mit benöthigten charten versehen. In französischer sprache ausgefertiget durch den herrn abt Lenglet du Fresnoy, and zum nutzen der jugend in die teutsche übersetzet, nunmehr aber von neuem übersehen, in vielen stücken deutlicher gemachet, mit nicht wenigen nützlichen zusätzen vermehret, und insonderheit zum gebrauch für teutsche eingerichtet. 5e. und vieles

Lenglet Dufresnoy, N.—Continued.

verbesserte, und vermehrte auflage. Mit allergnädigster freiheit. 2 p. l., 55 pp., 8 maps. 4°. Nürnberg, G. P. Monath, 1764. 4197

NOTE.—This is an abridgment of the *Méthode pour étudier la géographie*, published in 1719 in four parts. It has been slightly changed and augmented by the translator.

CONTENTS.

no. 1. Typus orbis terrarum.
" 2. Novæ Europæ
" 3. Germania.
" 4. Italiæ.
" 5. Novæ Asiæ.
" 6. Novæ Africæ.
" 7. Totius Americæ.
" 8. Palaestina sive Terra Sancta.

Liechtenstern, T. von, *and* **Lange, H.**

Th. von Liechtenstern und Henry Lange's Schul-atlas zum unterricht in der erdkunde. Für den gebrauch der oberen klassen der lehranstalten. In 45 karten. 50. aufl. neueste redaction. Neu bearb. von Henry Lange. 2 p. l., 44 (*i. e.* 45) maps. fol. Braunschweig, G. Westermann, 1880. 4198

Loreck, C., *and* **Winter, A.**

Schul-atlas für höhere lehranstalten . . . Ausgabe B. 2te. aufl. 4 p. l., 146 pp. incl. col. maps. sm. fol. München, Piloty & Loehle, 1913. 4199

NOTE.—Contains maps showing the topography, temperature, rainfall, industries, products, geology, religion, etc., of many countries. Also the environs of many cities.

Lüddecke, R., *and* **Haack, H.**

Deutscher schulatlas . . . 7 berichtige aufl. 1 p. l., 50 (i. e. 53) col. maps, 1 pl. 4°. Gotha, J. Perthes, 1914. 4200

NOTE.—3 smaller maps are inserted showing:
1. Boundaries in the Balkan peninsula.
2. & 3. Boundaries in Africa.

Marinelli, O.

Atlante scolastico di geografia moderna . . . 2 v. fol. Milano, Allbrighi, Segati & c. [etc., etc.] 1911–12. 4201

Meyer, J.

Neuester grosser schulatlas über alle theile der erde . . . 2 p. l., 35 l. incl. 33 maps. 2 pl. obl. 4°. Hildburghausen & New York, geographische anstalt des bibliographischen instituts., [1838?] 4202

NOTE.—Maps bear dates from 1830 to 1838. On 2d l. "Verzeichniss der fünf und dreissig karten." Plate 1. contains astronomical charts, plate 2. the comparative height of mountains.

The following maps relate to America:
no. 9. Welt-charte in Mercators projektion, 1830.
" 10. Die oestliche und westliche halbkugel der erde, 1831.
" 14. America, 1833.
" 32. West Indien und Mittel America, 1832.
" 33. Süd-America, 1830.
" 34. Vereinigte Staaten von Nord America und Mexico.

Mitchell, S. A.

Mitchell's new school atlas. Mitchell's modern atlas ... Compiled from the great atlases of Keith Johnston, Stieler and Andre; from the maps of the United States coast and geodetic surveys; of the General Land office, Hydrographic bureau, Post-office and War departments; official maps of the several states; and other reliable authorities. With important geographical tables, and an extensive pronouncing vocabulary of nearly ten thousand names. New and rev. ed. 1 p. l., 20 pp. 44 (*i. e.* 35) maps. 4°. Philadelphia, E. H. Butler & co., 1886. 4203

NOTE.—Book contains two title pages that are identical.

Philip, G.

Philips' elementary atlas of comparative geography, a series of 40 coloured plates, containing over 90 maps and plans, printed in colours; and 8 pages of introductory letterpress. 8, 40 pp. incl. 37 col. maps, plates, illus., diagrs. 4°. London, G. Philip & son, ltd., Liverpool, Philip, son & nephew, ltd. [1914] 4204

Philip, G. & son.

Philips' modern school atlas of comparative geography, a series of 80 coloured plates, containing 142 maps and diagrams, with introduction and complete index. New & enl. ed. xi, 80, 24 pp. incl. 63 col. maps, 1 pl. 4°. London, G. Philip & son, ltd., London geographical institute, 1913. 4205

Philips' new school atlas of comparative geography ... with a consulting index. 2 p. l., 72, 22 pp. incl. 72 col. maps, 1 pl. 4°. London, G. Philip & son, ltd.; Liverpool, Philip, son & nephew, ltd., 1913. 4206

Schrader, F., *and* **Gallouédec, L.**

Atlas clásico de geografía moderna trazado especialmente para los institutos y colegios de los estados de la América Latina ... 2 p. l., 52 pp. incl. 39 col. maps, 2 pl. sm. fol. Paris, Hachette & cia. 1908. 4207

Atlas classique de géographie ancienne et moderne dressé conformement aux programmes officiels à l'usage de l'enseignement secondaire. Ouvrage contenant 343 cartes et cartons en couleurs, avec 75 notices et 175 figures des statistiques graphiques en

Schrader, F., *and* **Gallouédec, L.**—Continued.
couleurs et un index alphabétique de tous les noms contenus dans l'Atlas. 4. éd. rev. et complétée . . . 96, viii, [14] pp. incl. 343 col. maps, 145 col. diagr. sm. fol. Paris, Hachette & cie. 1914. 4208

Switzerland. *Konferenz der kantonalen erziehungsdirektoren.*
Atlas für schweizerische mittelschulen. Mit bundesunterstützung herausgegeben von der Konferenz der kantonalen erziehungsdirektoren. 2. aufl. xii, 136 pp. incl. 105 col. maps. 4°. Winterthur, Kartographia Winterthur, 1911. 4209

Sydow, E. von.
Schul-atlas in zwei und vierzig karten. 29te aufl . . . 2 p. l., 15 pp., 6 pl., 35 maps. 8°. Gotha, J. Perthes, 1877. 4210

Zerolo, E.
Atlas de geografia elemental para los establecimientos de enseñanza secundaria . . . Compóese de 60 mapas y un indice alfabético de unos 5,000 nombres. 2. ed. 3 p. l., 64 pp. incl. 60 col. maps. 4°. Paris, Garnier hermanos, 1901. 4211

Note.—On cover, "Tercera edición."

SEAS.

Mediterranean Sea.

Hispanic society of America.
Facsimiles of portolan charts belonging to the Hispanic society of America, with an introduction by Edward Luther Stevenson. 2 p. l., 4 pp., 16 facs. fol. New York, 1916. 4212

Note.—Half-title: Publications of the Hispanic society of America. no. 104.
In portfolio.
A numbered edition of which this is no. 14.

CONTENTS.

no. 1. Giacomo Giroldi. Early fifteenth century.
" 2. Petrus Roselli. 1468.
" 3. Vesconte de Maiolo. 1512.
" 4. Conte Hoctomanno Freducci. 1524.
" 5. Anonymous. Early sixteenth century.
" 6. Anonymous. Early sixteenth century.
" 7. Bartolome Olivo. ca. 1550.
" 8. Hieronymo Giriva [?] After 1550.
" 9. Bartolome Olives. 1552.
" 10. Jaume Olives. 1566.
" 11. Anonymous. Late sixteenth century.
" 12. Anonymous. Late sixteenth century.
" 13. Vincentius Demetrei Volcius. 1600.
" 14. Maiolo e Visconte. 1605.
" 15. Placitus Caloiro et Olivo. Early seventeenth century.
" 16. Jouan Battista Cavallini. 1637.

STATISTICAL.

1909.

Hickmann, A. L.

Prof. A. L. Hickmann's geographical-statistic universal pocket atlas. 2. ed. 1909 . . . 79 pp., 26 col. maps, 9 pl., 26 tab. 16°. Vienna & Leipsic, G. Freytag & Berndt [1909] 4213

VOYAGES.

Freycinet, L. C. D. de.

Voyage autour du monde . . . Exécuté sur les corvettes de s. m. l'Uranie et la Physicienne, pendant les années 1817, 1818, 1819 et 1820, publié sous les auspices de son exc. m. le comte Corbière, secrétaire d'état de l'intérieur . . . et de s. exc. m. le comte Chabrol de Crouzol, secrétaire l'état de la marine et des colonies . . . Navigation et hydrographie. Atlas. 2 p. l., 22 maps. fol. Paris, Pillet ainé, 1826. 4214

Note.—To accompany author's text of same title.

CONTENTS.

no. 1. Carte de la baie des Chiens-Marins. 1803, 1818.
" 2. Carte d'une partie de l'île Timor et de quelques îles voisines, par mrs. Labiche et Bérard. 1818.—Esquisse de la ville de Coupang, par L. I. Duperrey. 1818.—Carte du détroit de Bouron, par L. I. Duperrey. 1818.
" 3. Carte d'une partie du grand archipel d'Asie, par L. I. Duperrey. 1818–1819.—Plan du port de l'île Guébé, 1772, par m. Mareau.—Plan du port de l'île Fohou, 1772, par m. Mareau.
" 4. Carte d'une partie des îles des Papous, par L. I. Duperrey. 1818.
" 5. Carte d'une partie de l'île Vaigiou, par L. I. Duperrey. 1818.
" 6. Plan de l'île et du mouillage de Rawak, par L. I. Duperrey. 1818.
" 7. Carte d'une partie des îles Carolines, par L. I. Duperrey 1819.—Plan des îles de la Passion, d'après D. F. Tompson.—Plan de Basse-Triste, d'après D. F. Tompson.—Plan des îles Guliay aux îles Carolines, d'après D. L. de Torres, en 1804.—Essai sur la géographie des îles Carolines, par. L. de F. 1824.
" 8. Carte générale de l'archipel des îles Mariannes, par L. I. Duperrey. 1819. (Partie méridionale. Partie septentrionale)
" 9. Carte générale de l'île Guam, par L. I. Duperrey. 1819.
" 10. Carte particulière de l'île Guam (1.ere feuille) par L. I. Duperrey. 1819.—Plan de îl'le Rota, par mrs. Duperrey & Bérard. 1819.
" 11. Carte particulière de l'île Guam (2e. feuille) Par L. I. Duperrey. 1819.
" 12. Plan de la baie d'Umata, par L. I. Duperrey. 1819.
" 13. Plan du port San-Luis d'Apra, par L. I. Duperrey. 1819.
" 14. Plan du havre de Tarofofo, par L. I. Duperrey. 1819.
" 15. Plan de la rade de Tinian.—Plan de l'île Guguan.—Plan du farallon de Médinilla.—Plan du farallon de Tores, par L. I. Duperrey. 1819.
" 16. Plan de la rade de Kayakakoua, par L. I. Duperrey. 1819.
" 17. Plan de la baie de Kohaï-Haï, par L. I. Duperrey. 1819.
" 18. Plan du port d'Onorourou, par L. I. Duperrey. 1819.

Freycinet, L. C. D. de—Continued.

no. 19. Plan de la rade de Raheina.—Plan de l'île Rose.—Plan de lîle Pylstaart, par L. I. Duperrey. 1819.

" 20. Carte de la partie de la Terre-de-Feu. 1820.—Plan du havre Christmas (à la Terre-de-Feu) d'après Cook en 1774.—Plan de la baie de Bon-Succès, d'après Cook, 1760.—Plan de la baie Saint-François, d'après le capne. d'Arquistade. 1717.

" 21. Plan de la baie Française (à la partie Orientale des îles Malouines) par L. I. Duperrey. 1820.—Plan de la baie Française, tiré du voyage de dom Pernetty. 1764.

" 22. Plan de l'anse Saint-Louis (baie Française; îles Malouines)—Plan du port Duperrey (baie Française; îles Malouines) par L. I. Duperrey. 1820.

WALL.

Vidal de La Blache, P.

Collection de cartes murales parlantes au recto, muettes au verso. 85 maps, 35¼ x 41 inches each with margin. Paris, A. Colin [1917] 4215

NOTE.—In portfolio.

Accompanied by his *Notices géographiques.*

At head of each map: *Atlas général Vidal-Lablache historique & géographique, 30 francs.—Atlas classique Vidal-Lablache historique & géographique, 15 francs.* Maps nos. 5 and 37 wanting.

CONTENTS.

no. 1– 1bis. Termes de géographie.
" 2– 2bis. France. Cours d'eau.
" 3– 3bis. " Relief du sol.
" 4– 4bis. " Départements.
" 5bis. " Villes.
" 6– 6bis. " Canaux.
" 7– 7bis. " Chemins de fer. Principales lignes de navigation.
" 8. " Agriculture.
" 8bis. " Industrie et commerce.
" 9– 9bis. " Provinces en 1789.
" 10. " Frontière Nord-Est et Alsace-Lorraine.
" 10bis. " Divisions militaires.
" 11. Algérie et Tunisie. Carte physique.
" 11bis. " Carte politique.
" 12–12bis. Europe. Relief du sol.
" 13–13bis. " Politique.
" 14–14bis. Asie. Physique.
" 15–15bis. " Politique.
" 16–16bis. Afrique. Physique.
" 17–17bis. " Politique.
" 18–18bis. Continent américain. Carte physique.
" 19–19bis. Amérique du Nord. Politique.
" 20–20bis. Amérique du Sud. folitique.
" 21–21bis. Océanie.
" 22–22bis. Planisphère colonies françaises.
" 23. Carte de l'Orient pour l'étude de l'histoire du peuple hébreu jusqu'aux premiers siècles de l'ère chrétienne.
" 23bis. Palestine divisée en 12 tribus.

no. 23ter. Palestine au temps de Jésus-Christ.

" 24. Paris. Capitale.

" 24bis. Paris et environs.

" 25. Belgique. Physique & agricole.

" 26. Suisse. Physique et agricole.

" 26bis. " Politique et industrielle.

" 27. Allemagne. Physique.

" 27bis. " Politique.

" 28. Iles Britanniques. Carte physique et agricole et lieux historiques.

" 28bis. " Carte politique et industrielle.

" 29. Pays-Bas. Carte physique et agricole.

" 29bis. " Carte politique et industrielle.

" 30. Italie. Carte physique et agricole et lieux historiques.

" 30bis. " Politique & industrielle.

" 31. Espagne et Portugal. Carte physique et agricole et lieux historiques.

" 31bis. Espagne et Portugal. Carte politique & industrielle.

" 32. Autriche-Hongrie. Carte physique et agricole.

" 32bis. " Carte politique et industrielle.

" 33. Péninsule des Balkans. Carte physique et agricole et lieux historiques.

" 33bis. Péninsule des Balkans. Carte politique.

" 34. Russie. Carte physique et agricole.—Lieux historiques.

" 35. Grèce et Archipel. Carte physique et agricoles et lieux historiques.

" 35bis. Grèce et Archipel. Carte politique et industrielle.

" 36. Madagascar.

" 36bis. Indo-Chine française.

" 37bis. Guyane française.

" 38. Tunisie. Carte physique. Par L. Machuel.

" 38bis. " Carte politique. Par L. Machuel.

" 39–39bis. France. Géologie. Par m. Welsch.

" 40. Cochinchine physique. Par m. Henri Russier.

" 40bis. " politique. Par m. Henri Russier.

" 41. Dép^{t}. d'Oran. Carte physique.

" 41bis. " Carte politique.

" 42. Dép^{t}. d'Alger. Carte physique.

" 42bis. " Carte politique.

" 43. Dép^{t}. de Constantine. Carte physique.

" 43bis. " Carte politique.

" 44. Maroc. Carte physique. Par mm. P. Vidal-Lablache & Gaston Loth.

" 44bis. Maroc. Carte politique. Par mm. P. Vidal de la Blache & Gaston Loth.

" 45. Delta du Tonkin. Par m. Henri Russier.

WAR.

Belgium. *Institut cartographique militaire.*

Atlas d'histoire militaire dressé par J. Cohy, A. de Callatay̆, E. Panhuys, capitaines commandants adjoints d'état-major, Ed. Martin et Ch. Marchand, capitaines en second adjoints d'état

Belgium. *Institut cartographique militaire*—Continued.

major . . . 2 p. l., 7 maps. fol. Bruxelles, Institut cartographique militaire, 1912. 4216

NOTE.—At head of title: École militaire.

Maps illustrating the following subjects:

1re serie. Batailles caractérisant les époques principales de l'histoire de la tactique.

2e " Campagnes de 1796–1797.

3e " Campagne de 1805, en Allemagne.

4e " Campagne de 1815, aux Pays-Bas.

5e " Guerre franco-allemande de 1870–1871.

6e " Guerre russo-japonaise de 1904–1905.

Also contains short bibliography on each subject.

Washington Post.

The Washington Post standard war atlas with marginal index. cover-title, 16 pp. incl. 13 col. maps. fol. [Washington, Washington Post, ©1898] 4217

NOTE.—The maps are copyrighted by Rand McNally & co.

Cram, G. F.

Atlas of the war in Europe containing large-scale maps of the battle-ground of the world's most gigantic conflict . . . cover-title, 16 col. maps. fol. New York, Chicago, G. F. Cram & co., 1914. 4218

Atlas of the war in Europe, containing large-scale maps of the battle-ground of the world's gigantic conflict: Europe, Austria, Servia, Germany, Britain, Belgium, France, Russia, Italy, Greece, the world, etc. Together with special data showing comparison of armies and navies involved. cover-title, 16 col. maps. sm. fol. New York, G. F. Cram, ©1915. 4219

NOTE.—Portraits of various rulers on outside cover.

Differs slightly from the edition of 1914.

Historical war atlas of Europe, past and present, for the library, the home and the school. Interesting, instructive, accurate . . . 18 [2] pp. incl. 10 col. maps. sm. fol. Chicago, G. F. Cram co. 1917. 4220

NOTE.—Maps ornamented with portraits of the rulers and the flags of the various nations.

The contents appear on the title-page, also a table of "Distances between important European cities."

History-atlas. "Story of the great war". European historical atlas . . . cover-title, 29 pp. incl. 8 col. maps, illus. sm. fol. Chicago, G. F. Cram co. 1919. 4220a

NOTE.—Text on reverse of front cover. Map on back cover.

Same atlas with different arrangement, omitting map entitled, "Probable divisions of the Austro-Hungarian monarchy and its protectorates Bosnia and Herzégovina," and including map entitled, "Bird's-eye view training camp map of the United States," was issued with title, "Story of the great war. European historical atlas," and marked, "Copyright 1918 by George F. Cram company, Chicago, Ill."

United States at war—American war atlas . . . cover-title, 8 col. maps. fol. New York, Chicago, G. F. Cram & co., 1917. 4221

United States at war. American war atlas, containing detailed maps and comprehensive pronouncing index of the fighting fronts, topographical United States map showing army, navy, marine, aviation training camps, etc. together with indexed maps and flags of nations involved. cover-title, [16] pp., incl. 10 col. maps. fol. Chicago, Ill., G. F. Cram co., °1918. 4222

Darbishire, B. V.

War atlas . . . cover-title, 16 pp. incl. 12 maps. sm. 4°. London, New York, etc., H. Milford (Oxford university press) 1915. 4223

Note.—At head of title: Oxford university press.
Text on reverse of covers.

Great Britain. *Ministry of information.*

Small atlas of the war (companion to the "Chronology of the war") issued under the auspices of the Ministry of information. 4 p. l., 31 pp. of maps. 8°. London, Constable & co. ltd. 1918. 4223a

Note.—"Chronology of the war . . . v. 1, 1918" and this atlas have been edited by major-general lord E. Gleichen. See Foot-note, p. [v]
Cover-title: Chronology of the war. Atlas.

Gross, A.

The daily telegraph pocket atlas of the war. With diary of the war. With comprehensive index. cover-title, 1 l., 56 pp., 39 maps. 12°. London, Geographia, ltd., [1917] 4224

Note.—Contents on inside of cover.

Hammond, C. S., & co.

Brentano's record atlas of the world war, with transparent interleaving for recording changes in battle-lines, dates, etc. cover-title, 12 col. maps. fol. New York, C. S. Hammond & co., 1918. 4225

Note.—Same as *Hammond's record atlas of the world war . . . 1918.* Map on cover-title shows army cantonments and training camps. Cover-title shows flags of various nations.

Hammond's record atlas of the world war, with transparent interleaving for recording changes in battle-lines, dates, etc. cover-title, 16 pp. incl. 11 col. maps. fol. New York, C. S. Hammond & co., °1918. 4226

Note.—"United States army map," and various flags on t.-p.

Hammond, C. S., & co.—Continued.

United States army and navy pictorial, with new war maps of the world. cover-title, 3 p. l., 16 pp., 4 l., incl. 14 col. maps. illus. fol. New York, C. S. Hammond & co., [1917] 4226a

NOTE.—Separate title-page for maps reads: New war maps of the world with large scale maps of the battle fronts . . . Portrait of president Wilson on cover. Contains also portraits of U. S. commanders of war, various guns in use, aeroplanes, battleships, &c.

War atlas. European situation at a glance; new maps of all countries involved in greatest conflict in modern history: Russia, Austria, Servia, Germany, England, France. cover-title, 8 pp., incl. 8 col. maps. fol. New York, C. S. Hammond & co., °1914. 4227

Istituto geografico de Agostini.

Atlante della nostra guerra. 16 tavole doppie a colori e numerose illustrazioni nel testo. Tavole redatte da Achille Dardano: Testo redatto da Luigi Filippo de Magistris. 2 p. l., [3]-64 pp. incl. illus., 16 col. maps. fol. Novara, Istituto geografica de Agostini, 1916. 4228

MAPS.

no. 1. Teatro della guerra europea.
" 2. Europa etnico-linguistica.
" 3. Scacchiere franco-belga-tedesco.
" 4. Scacchiere russo-austro-tedesco.
" 5. La guerra nei Balcani.
" 6. Regno d'Italia al 24 maggio 1915.
" 7. Venezia tridentina—Venezia giulia—Dalmazia.
" 8. Venezia tridentina: Trentino ed Alto Adige.
" 9. Venezia guilia: Friùli orientale ed Istria.
" 10. Toponomastica italiana delle Alpi trentine.
" 11. Trentino: Scacchiere occidentale.
" 12. Trentino: Scacchiere orientale.
" 13. Cadore e Càrnia.
" 14. Alto e Medio Isonzo.
" 15. Basso Isonzo—Carso—Trieste.
" 16. Istria e Fiume.

Istituto italo-britannico-milano.

Atlante della guerra mondiale. Pubblicato sotto gli auspici dell' Istituto italo-britannico-milano . . . 15 (*i. e.* 16) col. maps. sm. fol. Novarra, Istituto geografico de Agostini, 1918. 4229

CONTENTS.

no. 1–2. Il mondo in guerra secondo le alleanze.
" 3–4. L'Europa in guerra secondo le alleanze.
" 5. L'Italia e la terre irredente.
" 6. Gran Bretagna e Irlanda.
" 7. Scacchiere occidentale.
" 8. Scacchiere orientale.
" 9. Scacchiere italo-austriaco.
" 10. Scacchiere balcanico.

no. 11. Scacchiere mesopotamico.
" 12. Territori occupati dagli imperi centrali.—Superficie dei territori occupati dagli alleati ragguagliata all'Europa.
" 13. Processo formativo della Germania.—Aspirazioni della Germania verso le Indie . . .
" 14. Impero britannico.—La pressione degli alleati sugli imperi centrali.
" 15. Europa etnico-linguistica.

Kenyon co.

Atlas of the world war showing latest maps and pictures. [anon.] cover-title, [32] pp. incl. 10 col. maps, illus. fol. [Des Moines, Ia., Kenyon co., ©1918] 4230

Revised atlas of the world and history of the world war, showing latest maps and pictures. cover-title, 13 [3] pp., 13 col. maps, illus. fol. [Des Moines, the Kenyon co., 1919] 4230a

NOTE.—Text on inside of covers. Three maps on cover.

Larousse, Librairie.

Atlas de poche du théâtre de la guerre . . . [2. éd.] 2 p. l., 59 pp. incl. 56 maps. 12°. Paris, Larousse [1916] 4231

Literary (The) digest european war maps. 3 maps. sm. fol. New York, Literary digest [1914] 4232

CONTENTS.

no. [1] Western theatre of the war.
" [2] Eastern theatre of the war. Scale: 200 miles [to 2 inches] 10 x 15.
" [3] Scene of the western battles, detailed of the region of main military operations along the franco-belgian-german frontiers. Scale: 70 miles [to 2¾ inches] 10½ x 16½.

Third series. April 1, 1916. cover-title, 4 maps on 1 sheet. 4°. New York, the Literary digest, [1916] 4233

CONTENTS.

no. 1. Eastern campaign showing the present location of battle front and farthest advance of russians and teutons.
" 2. Western campaign showing present location of trenches and farthest advance of the french and germans.
" 3. Italian campaign showing lines of opposing armies.
" 4. Asiatic campaigns showing the field of british and russian operations against Turkey.

Matthews, J. N., co.

War atlas of Europe. cover-title, 13 pp. incl. 10 col. maps. 12°. [Buffalo, J. N. Matthews, 1914] 4234

Maurette, F.

Petit atlas de la guerre et de la paix; les pays où nous nous battons et pour lesquels nous nous battons. 19 [1] pp. incl. 9 col. maps. 8°. Paris, Hachette & c^ie^., 1918. 4235

NOTE.—Text and cover illustrated with small maps.

Nelson, T., & sons.

Map book of the world-wide war. Fifty-six maps and a diary of the war. 64 pp. incl. 56 maps. sm. 4°. London, New York, T. Nelson [1915?] 4236

Philip, G.

Philips' record atlas, a series of 128 pages of coloured political maps of the world, with complete index edited by George Philip . . . 2 p. l., 128, 127 [1] pp. incl. 68 col. maps. 4°. London, G. Philip & son, ltd.; Liverpool, Philip son & nephew, ltd., 1917. 4236a

Note.—Has colored half-title. Contains the following maps relating to the war:
no. 36–37. Belgium & eastern France showing the western theatre of the great war.
" 42–43. Poland and the eastern theatre of the great war.

Philip, G., & son, *ltd.*

The western front at a glance. A large-scale atlas of the allies' fighting line in the west. 1 l., 48, 24 pp., incl. 25 col. maps. 12°. London, G. Philip & son, ltd. [1917] 4237

Note.—Contents on title-page.

Rand, McNally & co.

Atlas of the European conflict containing detailed maps of the nations . . . 14, [3] pp., incl. 11 col. maps. fol. Chicago, Rand McNally & co. 1914. 4238

Atlas of the world war, showing detailed maps of all the nations engaged in the conflict; blockade conditions that arrayed the United States against Germany; continental and world maps, showing national interrelations, world commerce routes and colonial interests of warring nations, also, a chronological summary of the principal events of the great war from its inception to the present time; with general analysis of conditions and progress of the war. 16 pp. incl. 12 col. maps. sm. fol. Chicago, New York, Rand, McNally & co. 1917. 4239

Note.—Text on the inside of back cover.

Atlas of the world war; showing detailed maps of all the nations engaged in the conflict; blockade conditions that arrayed the United States against Germany; continental and world maps, showing national interrelations, world commerce routes and colonial interests of warring nations; also a chronological summary of the principal events of the great war from its inception to the present time; with a general analysis of conditions and progress of the war. 16, [4] p. front., illus. (maps) pl., fold. map. fol. Chicago, New York, Rand, McNally & co. °1918. 4240

Note.—Cover-title: Rand-McNally atlas of the world war.

Battle fields of today. cover-title, 10 maps. sm. fol. [Chicago, Rand, McNally & co. 1916] 4240a

NOTE.—Text on the reverse of covers.

On cover title: Compliments of Union trust co. . . . Rochester, N. Y.

Comprehensive atlas of the new Europe . . . cover-title, 32 pp. incl. 16 col. maps. sm. fol. [Chicago, Rand, McNally & co. 1919] 4240b

NOTE.—Text on reverse of covers.

Concise atlas of the world war with battleships. 1 p. l., 32 pp. incl. 18 col. maps, illus. sm. fol. Chicago and New York, Rand, McNally & co. 1917. 4241

Concise peace atlas, containing president Wilson's peace conditions, peace conference who's who, disposition of former german colonies, war cyclopedia, dates of notable battles, approximate value of foreign coins . . . cover-title, 16 pp. incl. 10 col. maps. 12°. Chicago, New York, Rand, McNally & co. 1919. 4242

NOTE.—Text on the reverse of covers.

Graphic representation of the battle fields of today. cover-title, 9 maps. fol. Chicago, New York, Rand McNally & co. [°1915] 4243

On the battle lines. cover-title, 9 maps. 12°. Chicago, New York, Rand, McNally & co. [1915] 4244

NOTE.—Text on reverse of covers.

War map of Europe.—The Rand-McNally new library atlas map of Europe. Scale of statute miles, 140 to 1 in. fol. [Chicago] Rand, McNally & co., 1914. 4245

NOTE.—Text on verso of map under the title of "The european conflict and conditions that brought it about."

Stanford, E., *ltd.*

The peace conference atlas, a series of maps to illustrate boundary & other questions under consideration at the peace conference, 1919. cover-title, 7 pp., 24 col. maps. text, 8°; maps, obl. 4°. London, E. Stanford, ltd. [1919] 4245a

CONTENTS.

no. 1. Europe, index-map.
" 2. Denmark and the duchies, Heligoland and the Kiel canal.
" 3. Alsace-Lorraine.
" 4. Antwerp and the Schelde.
" 5. Eastern Belgium and Luxembourg.
" 6. The Italian Trentino and Triest.
" 7. Poland.
" 8. Czecho-Slovakia.
" 9. Yugo-Slavia.
" 10. Rumania.
" 11. Sea of Marmara.—The Bosporus.—The Dardanelles.
" 12. Western Asia Minor.
" 13. Armenia.

Stanford, E., *ltd.*—Continued.

no. 14. Mesopotamia.
" 15. Syria and Palestine.
" 16. Siberia.
" 17. Finland, European Russia and the Caucasus.
" 18. Ukrainia.
" 19. Arabia.
" 20. Togoland and Cameroon.
" 21. East Africa.
" 22. South-west Africa.
" 23. New Guinea, commonwealth of Australia, and Kiaochow, China.
" 24. The Pacific islands (Solomon, Caroline, Pelew, Marshall and Marianne islands) and New Guinea.

Stanford's geographical establishment.

An atlas of the world war. cover-title, 14 col. maps. sm. fol. London, Stanford's geog[l]. estab[t]. [1917?] 4246

NOTE.—"Foreword" on the verso of the first map.
Printed by the Dangerfield printing co., ltd.

CONTENTS.

no. [1] The western theatre of war.
" [2] The eastern theatre of war.
" [3] The italian theatre of war.
" [4] The theatre of war in the Balkans.
" [5] The turkish theatre of war.
" [6] The british front in the west.
" [7] The men of the british empire; their homes and their battlefields.
" [8] The end of Germany's dream in the east.
" [9] The downfall of Germany's world-empire.
" [10] The isolation of Germany.
" [11] What Germany wants.
" [12] The growth of Prussia.
" [13] Subject nationalities of the german alliance.
" [14] The Allies' ring of steel: how Germany is hemmed in.

Times, The. *London.*

The Times war atlas. cover-title, 1 sheet, 24 maps on 10 sheets. fol. [London, the Times, 1914-1915] 4247

NOTE.—Text on 1 sheet entitled the Times war atlas gazetteer.

CONTENTS.

no. [1] Map of the area of the european war.
" [2] Map of the world.
" [3] The main fortresses of the western campaign.
" [4] The partition of Poland, 1772, 1793, 1795.—The partition of Poland, 1807, 1815, 1846.—The austro-montenegrin frontier with the fortress of Cattaro.—The austro-italian frontier.
" [5] Map of the Balkans. Showing recent territorial changes.
" [6] Map of the north-eastern theater of war.
" [7] Map of the frontiers of France.
" [8] Map of the North Sea.
" [9] Map of the western campaign.
" [10] Map of Paris & environs.

Supplement to the Times war atlas. 19 maps on 7 sheets. fol. London [the Times, 1915] 4248

CONTENTS.

no. [1] Posen and the silesian frontier.—East and west Prussia.—The area of fighting in Galicia.—Kamerun.—German Southwest Africa.—German East Africa.
" [2] The campaign in Lorraine.—Upper Alsace.—Heligoland.—Fortress of Posen.—Territory of Kiao-Chau.—Kiel and the Baltic entrance to the Kaiser Wilhelm canal.—Borkum and the mouth of the Ems.—Fortress of Tsingtau.
" [3] Map of Paris & environs.
" [4] Map of eastern Germany & Poland.
" [5] Map of western Germany.
" [6] Map of north-western France.
" [7] Map of north-eastern France.

Willsden, S. B. & co.

The world's greatest war. 1914. [24] pp. incl. 11 col. maps, illus. fol. [Chicago, S. B. Willsden & co., 1914] 4249

Willsden, S. B.

The world's greatest war . . . cover-title, 31 pp. incl. 13 col. maps, illus. sm. fol. Chicago, S. B. Willsden, 1917. 4250

GENERAL.

1375

[Atlas of the world. anon.] fasc. 2 pl., 3 maps. fol. [Paris, 1841] 4251

NOTE.—Known as "Atlas catalan." Maps similar to those published to accompany article by J. A. C. Buchon and J. Tastu, entitled: *Notice d' un atlas en langue catalane, manuscrit de l'an 1375 conservé parmi les manuscrits de la bibliothèque royale,* in *France. Académie des inscriptions et belles-lettres. Notices et extraits des manuscrits de la bibliothèque du roi. 4°. Paris, 1841. v. 14, pt. 2. pp. 1–152.*

Date 1375 found in pl. 2.

On the 1st pl. are four columns of text in gothic letters of the XIVth century. The first column contains an expose of the various influences of the moon during thirty days. In the 2nd column are two circular diagrams relating astronomy and geography. Below these is the drawing of a man with the names of the signs of the zodiac, and a table showing the corresponding months and days.—The third and fourth column contain text relating to geography and cosmography.—The second plate contains a large circular diagram formed of 37 circles. In the corners of the plate are four figures representing the four seasons. The first map contains the countries of western Europe and northwestern Africa. On the second map are eastern Europe as far as the eastern shore of the Black sea, and northeastern Africa and Palestine. The third map contains eastern Asia.

The maps to accompany the article above noted contain in the lower right corners their consecutive numbers and the reference to the pages where they should be inserted. These do not appear on the maps of this atlas.

1514

Ptolemaeus, C.

[Geographia] In hoc opere haec cōtinentur. | Noua translatio primi libri geographiæ Cl' Ptolemæi: quæ quidem translatio verbum: habet e | verbo fideliter expressum: Ioanne Vernero Nurenbergeñ interprete. | In eundem primum librum geographiæ Cl' Ptholomaei: argumēta, paraphrases quibus idem li | ber per sententias: ac summatim explicatur: & annotationes eiusdem Ioannis Veneri. | Libellus de quatuor terrarum orbis in plano figurationibus ab eodem Ioanne Vernero nouissi | me compertis & enarratis. | Ex fine septimi libri eiusdem geographiæ Cl' Ptolomæi super plana terrarum orbis descriptione | a priscis instituta geographis. Locus quidā, noua trāslatione, paraphrasi: & annotationibus expli | catus: quem recentium geographorum: vtipsorum id pace dicam. nemo hucusq sane ac medulli | tus intellexit. | De his quæ geographiæ debent adesse: Georgii Amirucii Constantinopolitani opusculum. | In idem Georgii Amirucii opusculum. Ioannis Verneri Appendices. | Ioannis de Regiomonte epistola. ad Reuerendissimū patrē & dominū Bessarionem Cardinalem | Nicenum. ac Constantinopolitanū patriarcham de compositione & vsu cuiusdā meteoroscopii. | Caesarea cautum est sanctione: ne quisquam hoc | opus infra sexaginta annos: praeter mani | festum opificis consensum imprimat | aut distrabat sub graui mulcta: | in Imperialibus his litte- | ris expressa. | [*Colophon:*] Explicit geographicus hic liber: per ipsius compositorem: atq̃ per Conradum Hein | fogel artium & philosophiæ magistrum: diuiq̃ Maximiliani Imperatoris Capel | lanum. Et haud mediocrem mathematicū fideliter emendatus recogni | tusq̃. Necnon a Ioanne Stuchs Nurenbergæ impressus. Anno | domini nostri Iesu christi. Millesimoquingentesimo | decimoquarto. [1514] pridie nonas Novembris | phebe ad Iouis contuber | nium defluente. | 4252

[68] l. comprising: 3 p. l. 129 pp. diagrs. in text. sm. fol. (sig. a–c in sixes; d in eights; e–h in sixes; i in eights; k in sixes; l in four.

sig. [a1] recto, title, verso [Imperial privilege]; recto a2–verso a3, Reuerendissimo & illustrissimo principi domino Matheo tituli sancti angeli, diacono Cardinali Gurceñ, Imperialis Maiestatis p Italiam locum tenenti generali Ioannes Verner Nurenbergeñ. perpetuam dicit fœlicitatem, dated Ex Nurenberga Anno domini Millesimoquingentesimodecimoquarto; verso a 3 Ioannis Verneri Nurenbergeñ. recens interpretamentum in primum librum Geographiæ Cl' Ptolomæi; a4–[b5] text of Ptolemaeus, book 1, incl. 4 diagrs.; [b6]–g4, Ioannis Verneri Norenbergen. in primi libri geographiae Cl. Ptolaemaei paraphrasim prooemivm, dated, Anno salutis humanæ, 1514, quarto Kl' Octobris, incl. 29 diagrs.; recto [g5] Ioannes Verner. Bilbaldo Percamero patricio Norenbergensi senatorii ordinis: sapientissimo philosopho: ac oratori facvndissimo: foelicitatem perpetvam; verso [g5]–h4, Libellus Ioannis Verneri Nurenbergeñ. de quatuor aliis planis terrarum orbis descriptionibus, incl. 8 diagr.; [h5]–i2, Sebaldo Schreyer Ciui Nurenbergeñ viro optimo Ioannes Verner Salutem perpetuam, incl. 4 diagr.; i2–[i7] De his quæ geographiæ adesse debent Georgii

Amirucii oposculum, incl. 9 diagr.; verso [i7]-l[1] Ioannis Verneri Nurenbergen. appendices, incl. 15 diagr.; li2-13, Ad Bessarionem Cardinalem Nicenumac patriarcham Costantinopolitanum: de compositione Metheoroscopii Ioannis de Regiomonte Epistola, incl. 1 diagr.; recto [14] Registrum huius libri; [Colophon]; verso [14] blank.

Nordenskiöld says that this incomplete edition, without maps, has been of no small importance to cartography on account of the treatise: *De quatuor terrarum orbis in plano figurationibus.*

1608

Mercator, G.

Atlas minor de Gverard Mercator traduict de latin en françois par [Lancelot Voisin] le sieur de la Popelinière gentilhomme françois anno 1608. 4 p. l., 655 (*i. e.* 653) [1] pp. incl. 146 maps, 1 pl. obl. 12°. Amsterodami excusum in ædibus Iudoci Hondij. veneunt etiam apud Corneliū Nicolai item apud Ioannem Ianssoniū Arnhemi [1608] 4253

NOTE.—Collation: engraved title-page, verso blank, p. l. [1].—Iodocus Hondius au lecteur salut, dated 1608, p. l. [2].—Pour l'vsage des tables, p. l. [3].—Indices des tables de c'est oeuvre ou de leurs descriptions, p. l. [4].—Pourtrait de la terre vnverselle, p. 1. Text and 146 maps, pp. 2–655.—Sonnet à monsievr Hondivs docte géographe de nostre aage, sur la traduction françoyse de son atlas, signed Iohannes Clusius Gallus, p. [656]

First french edition of the Mercator's *Atlas minor.*

The pagination is defective. There are no pages 145–146.

Jodocus Hondius reduced the large atlas of Mercator to a small quarto and first published it with latin text in 1607. The Library of Congress has many editions of the Atlas minor. See preceding volumes. The following maps relate to America:

p. 3. Typus orbis terrarum.
" 19. Americæ descrip.
" 23. Polus Arcticus cum vicinis regionibus.
" 623. Hispania Nova.
" 627. Virginia et Florida.
" 631. Cuba insul.—Hispaniola.—Havana portvs.—I. Iamaica.—I. S. Joannis.—I. Margareta.
" 635. America Meridionalis.
" 639. Fretum Magellani.
" 647. Designatio orbis Christiani.

1608

Quad, M.

Fascicvlvs geographicvs complectens totivs orbis regionum tabulas circiter centum. vnà cum earundem Enarrationibus. Ex quibus totivs mvndi sitvs vniuersaliter ac particulariter çognosci potest. fluuiorum scilicet, montium, syluarum, solitudinumq; qualitates: vrbium & origenes: populorum denig, diuersissimorum naturæ ac mores. In ordinem hunc compendiosum redactus per Matthiam Quadum sculptorem. 9 p. l. [352] pp. incl. 86 maps. 4°. Coln am Rein, bey Iohan Buxemacher kunstdrucker vffs Maximini strass daselbst, 1608. 4253a

NOTE.—The same maps as in Quad's *Geographisch handtbuch, 1600,* except

Quad, M.—Continued.

no. 36. Comitatvs Waldeck, which is a different map from the one in the earlier publication, and six additional maps as follows:
" 4. Barbaria Africana, et Biledvlgerid. 1603.
" 25. Salsburgensis jurisdictionis locorumque vicinorum vera descriptio. Auctore Marco Secznagel Salisburgense. Henricus Nagel fecit. 1590.
" 32. Thuringia comitatuum. 1603.
" 34. Lvnaebvrgensis dvcatvs . . . delineat$_g$ à Ioanne Mellingero Hallensi. 1593.
" 64b. Regni Neapolitani . . . Pyrrho Ligorio auctore.
" 65. Mediolanvm Lombardiae ducatus. 1604.

For note on this publication see v. 1, title 411.

Some of the maps are ornamented with portraits, many of them of the rulers and high church dignitaries of the countries represented, as William, duke of Bavaria, 1596, Frederick, duke of Würtemberg, Ernestus, archbishop of Cologne, John William, duke of Cleves, queen Elizabeth of England, sultan Mahumet II, 1595, Christian IV, king of Denmark, and others.

1634–1708

Wit, F. de.

Atlas minor. 2 v., 1 pl., 127 col. maps, 2 pl.; 1 pl., 124 col. maps. fol. Amstelodami, F. de Wit, [1634–1708] 4254

NOTE.—Each volume has an elaborate engraved, colored title-page, the first signed "G. Laeiresse invent. A. Blooteling sculp" and the second, "Laüwerens Scherm. delin. & sculp."

In v. 2, at head of title, "Londini apud Christophorum Browne."

Title-page to v. 1, gives no place, publisher or date; the place and publisher in v. 2, being repeated in dutch and between the two imprints a small circle contains the words, "Sold by Christopher Browne at y globe at the west end of Saint Paull's church".

Both volumes have manuscript lists of the maps.

Beside those by de Wit the maps are by various cartographers. Only a few of them are dated, the earliest being 1634 and the latest 1708.

CONTENTS

v. 1, no. [1] Novus planiglobii terrestris per utrumque polum conspectus.
" " [2] Planisphærium terrestre sive terrarum orbis. Auctore Carolo Allard.—Vlakke aardkloot gemeenlyk genaamd de geheele waereld. Door Carel Allard.
" " [3] Boussole des vents.
" " [4] Planisphærium cœleste. ex formis Petri Schenk.
" " [5] Accuratissima Europæ tabula. Authore Carolo Allard.
" " [6] Nouvelle carte géographique du grand royaume de Moscovie représentant la partie septentrionale &c. par Nicolas Wisscher.
" " [7] Nouvelle carte géographique du grand royaume de Moscovie représentant la partie meridionale &c. par Nicolas Visscher.
" " [8] Turcicum imperium. Inset: Occidentalior pars maris Mediterranei.
" " [9] Regni Poloniæ magni ducatus Lithuaniæ . . . tabula. Edita a Carolo Allard, Ph. Tideman del. G. v. Gouwen fecit.
" " [10] Ducatuum Livoniæ, et Curlandiæ, nova tabula.
" " [11] Magni ducatus Lithuaniæ.

v. 1, no. [12] Ukrainæ pars, quæ Podolia palatinatus vulgo dicitur. Per Guil. le Vasseur de Beauplan.
" " [13] Ukrainæ pars qvæ Pokutia vulgo dicitur. Per Guil. le Vasseur de Beauplan.
" " [14] Ukrainæ pars qvæ Barclavia palatinatus vulgo dicitur. Per Guilhelmum la Vasseur de Beauplan.
" " [15] Ukrainæ pars qvæ Kiovia palatinatus vulgo dicitur. Per Guilhelmum le Vasseur de Beauplan. Joh. Blaeu exc.
" " [16] Nova et accurata Wolgæ fluminis. Auctore Adamo Oleario. Amstelodami prostant apud Petrum Schenk et Gerardum Valk.
" " [17] Dwinæ fluvii Amstelodami vendibiles apud P. Schenk et G. Valk.
" " [18] Le royaume de Hongrie. Par Guillaume De l'Isle.
" " [19] Walachia, Servia, Bvlgaria, Romania. Typis Gerardi Valk et Petri Schenk.
" " [20] Principauté de Transilvania. H. Iaillot.
" " [21] Sclavonia, Croatia, Bosnia cum Dalmatiæ parte. Per Gerardum Mercatorem.
" " [22] Carta noua accurata del passagio et strada dalli Paesi Bassi par via de Allemagna per Italia. 1671.
" " [23] Per accurata S. Romani Imperii tabula. Per Nicolaum Visscher. G. v. Gouwen sc.
" " [24] Totius Danubii nova & accuratiss tabula. Auctore Jacobo de la Feuille.
" " [25] Exactissima tabula, qua tam Danubii fluvii pars inferior. Per Nicolaum Visscher.
" " [26] Exactissima tabula, qua tam Danubii fluvii pars media. Per Nicolaum Visscher.
" " [27] Exactissima tabula, qua tam Danubii fluvii pars superior. Per Nicolaum Visscher.
" " [28] Circuli Austriaci pars septentrionalis.
" " [29] Austriæ archiducatus pars inferior. Delineata per Nicol^{m}. Visscher.
" " [30] Moraviæ nova et post omnes priores accuratissima delineatio. Auctore I. A. Comenio. Inset views: Polna.—Olumts.—Brin.—Znaim.
" " [31] Ducatus Carintiæ et Carniolæ.
" " [32] Regnum Bohemiæ. Auctore Nicolao Visscher.
" " [33] Mappa geographica exactissma continens imperatoris hæreditarium dominum Silesiam. Edente Petro Schenck.
" " [34] Palatinatvs Posnaniensis. Per G. F. M. Joannes Blaeu. Gerard Coeck sculpsit.
" " [35] Territoire de Trente Pierre Mortier. Excudebat Guiljelmus Blaeu.
" " [36] Circuli austriaci pars occidentalior.
" " [37] R. I. Bavariæ circulus atque electoratus. Per Nicolaum Visscher.
" " [38] Bavariæ pars superior. Per Nicolaum Visscher.
" " [39] Bavariæ pars inferior. Per Nicolaum Visscher.
" " [40] Bavariæ palatinatus. Per Nicolaum Visscher.
" " [41] Saltzbvrg archiepiscopatvs et Carinthia dvcatvs. Auctore Ger. Mercatore. Amstelaedami apud G. Valk et P. Schenk.
" " [42] Le cercle de Souabe. Par H. Jaillot.

Wit, F. de—Continued.

v. 1, no. [43] Nouvelle carte du pais de Donawert et Hochstett. Insets: Donawert.—Hochstett.—Augsburg.

" " [44] Chorographia ducatus Wurtenburgici. Opere sumptuario Gerardi Valk.

" " [45] Vera totius marchionatus Badensis et Hochbergensis. Excudebant Janssonio-Waesbergii Moses Pitt et Stephanus Swart. Inset: Exemplum seu tabula geometriciæ arithmeticae et mechanicæ operationis.

" " [46] Circuli Franconiæ pars orientalis.

" " [47] La Suisse. H. Iaillot.

" " [48] Tabula geographica qua pars septentrionalis sive inferior Rheni, Mosæ, et Mosellæ. Per Nicolaum Visscher.

" " [49] Tabula geographica qua pars meridionalis sive superior Rheni, Mosæ, et Mosellæ. Per Nicolaum Visscher.

" " [50] Superioris atque inferioris Alsatiæ. Ex conatibus P. Schenk.

" " [51] Landgraviatus Alsatiæ inferioris novissima tabula. Per Nicolaum Visscher.

" " [52] Superioris Alsatiæ nec non Brisigaviæ et Suntgaviæ geographica tabula. Ex conatibus Nicolai Visscher.

" " [53] Hassia Lantgraviatus. Opera Gerardi Valk.

" " [54] Nassovia principatus. Delineatus â Joh. Jac. Stetter. Excudit Nic. Visscheri.

" " [55] Electoratus et palatinatus Rheni.

" " [56] Circulus Electorum Rheni.

" " [57] Moguntini archiepiscopat' et electoratus. Per Nic. Visscher. G. v. Gouwen. sc.

" " [58] Treverensis regio archiepiscopatus electoratusque titulô insignus. Pro ut edidit Gerardus Valk.

" " [59] Archiepiscopatus Coliensis; ducatibus Iuliacensi et Montensi. Prostant penes Gerardum Valk.

" " [60] Le cercle de Westphalie. Par H. Jaillot.

" " [61] Le duché de Westphalie. Par le s. Sanson. Amsterdam chez Pierre Mortier.

" " [62] Basse partie de l' évesché de Munster, et le comté de Benthem. Par le s^r. Sanson. Amsterdam chez Pierre Mortier.

" " [63] Oost-Frise, ou le comté d' Embden. Par le s^r. Sanson. Paris chez H. Iaillot.

" " [64] Haute partie de l'évesché de Munster. Par le s^r Sanson. Paris chez H. Iaillot.

" " [65] Episcopatvs Paderbornensis descriptio nova Ioanne Gigante Ludense. Auctore. Prostant Amstelaedami apud Petrum Schenk, et Gerardum Valk.

" " [66] Cliviæ ducatus et Marchiæ comitatus tabulam.

" " [67] Le duché de Berg.

" " [68] Le duché de Iuliers.

" " [69] Le comté de la Marck.

" " [70] Comitatus Meursensis et annexarum dinastiarum accuratam tabulam humillime offert A. von Heurdt.

" " [71] Saxoniæ electoralis. Sculpta â Petro Schenckio Amstelodamensi.

" " [72] Circuli Saxoniæ superioris pars meridionalis.

" " [73] Circulus Saxoniæ inferioris.

" " [74] Marchionatus Misniæ.

v. 1, no. [75] Marchionatus Brandenburgi et ducatus Pomeraniæ tabula.
" " [76] Ducatus Pomeraniæ.
" " [77] Rvgia insvla ac dvcatvs accuratissimè descripta ab E. Lubino.
" " [78] Ducatus Brunsuicensis.
" " [79] Ducatus Luneburgici et comitatus Dannebergensis per Nicolaum Visser.
" " [80] Ducatus Bremæ & Ferdæ.
" " [81] Ducatus Meklenburgicus.
" " [82] Holsatiæ tabula generalis.
" " [83] Regni Prussiæ et Prussiæ Polonicæ.
" " [84] Leodiensis episcopatus. Per Nicolaum Visscher.
" " [85] Leodiensis episcopatus pars septentrionalis. Per Nicolaum Visscher.
" " [86] Leodiensis episcopatus pars media. Per Nicolaum Visscher.
" " [87] Tractus inter Sabim et Mosam. Per Nicolaum Visscher.
" " [88] Les dix-sept provinces des Pays-Bas. Par G. Valk.
" " [89] Les provinces des Pays-Bas catholiques. Par le s^r^. Sanson.
" " [90] Ducatus Lurzenburgici tabula.
" " [91] Tabula ducatus Limburch. et comitatus Valckenburch.
" " [92] Nieuwe kaart van 't graafschap namen, met een groot gedeelte van 't hertogdom Brabant. By Nicolaus Visscher. Inset: Vervat van de maasstroom van Dinant tot omtrent Charlemont en Givet.
" " [93] Correctissima descriptio Hannoniæ comitatus.
" " [94] Le comté d'Artois . . . Amsteldam chez Nicolaum Visscher.
" " [95] Novissima et accuratissima comitatus Flandriæ.
" " [96] Flandriæ comitatus pars australis. Per Nicolaum Visscher.
" " [97] Flandriæ comitatus pars media. Per Nicol. Visscher.
" " [98] Flandriæ comitatus pars occidentalis.
" " [99] Flandriæ comitatus pars septentrionalis. per Nicol. Visscher.
" " [100] Nieuwe kaerte van t landt van Waes ende Hulster ambracht. Per Nicolaum Visscher.
" " [101] Flandriæ comitatus pars orientalis. Per Nicolaum Visscher.
" " [102] Flandriæ comitatus pars Batava. Per Nicolaum Visscher.
" " [103] Perfecte kaerte, van t' Berger en Broucborger ambracht. Per Nicolaus Visscher. Inset: Platte grond vande stad, kastel en haven van Duynkercke.
" " [104] Brabantiæ ducatus S. I. imperii marchionatus Mechliniæ dominii nova tabula.
" " [105] Brabantiæ Batavæ pars orientalis. Per Nicolaum Visscher.
" " [106] Brabantiæ Batavæ pars occidentalis. Per Nicolaum Visscher.
" " [107] Bruxellensis tetrarchia. Per Nicolaum Visscher.
" " [108] Lovaniensis tetrarchia. Per Nic. Visscher.
" " [109] Mechlinia dominium et Aerschot ducatus. Auctore Nicolao Visscher.
" " [110] Marchionatus Sacri Romani imperii. C. J. Visscher excudebat. Inset views: Antwerpen.—Templi d. virginis Mariæ vera delineatio.—S[t]. Michiels kercke.—Mariæ poort.—Kerck der Augustinẽ.—Bursa.—Domus senatoria Antwerpiensis.—Kercke der Iesuiten.—S. Ioris poort.—Kerck der Carmeliten.—Domus Hansæ Teutonicæ.

Wit, F. de—Continued.

v. 1, no. [111] Exactissima Belgii Foederati tabula cum annexis divisa in provincias. Per Casparum Specht. Inset: Land caerte van't verenigde Nederland met 'tgene daer onderhoort verdeelt in syn provincien. 1702.

" " [112] Ducatus Geldriæ et comitatus Zutphaniæ, tabula. Gesneden bÿ Abram Deur.

" " [113] Comitatus Zutphaniæ.

" " [114] Ducatus Geldriæ tetrachia Arnhemiensis sive Velavia.

" " [115] Tetrachia ducatus Geldriæ Neomagensis.

" " [116] Tetrachia ducatus Geldriæ Ruremondana sive Hispanica.

" " [117] 't Graavschap Holland en sticht van Utrecht nevens de voornaamste delen van Gelderland in haar minder verdeling op niews verbetert door Caspar Specht t Utrecht 1704. Inset: Trexel.—Vlieland.

" " [118] Hollandiæ pars meridionalior vulgo Zuyd-Holland. Auctore Nic. Visscher.

" " [119] Delflandia, Schielandia et circumjacentes insulæ ut Voorna, Overflackea, Goerea, Yselmonda et aliæ, ex conatibus geographicis Nicolai Visscher.

" " [120] Rhenolandia, Amstelandia. Per Nicolaum Visscher.

" " [121] Kennemaria et Westfrisia vulgo et vernaculé Noord-Holland. Per Nicolaum Visscher.

" " [122] Tabula nova provinciæ Ultrajectiniæ, quam jussu nob. hujus dominij ordinum emensus est Bernardus du Roy geometra et in lucem edidit Nicol. Visscher. L. von Anse sculp.

" " [123] Comitatvs Zelandiæ. Per Nicolaum Visscher.

" " [124] Frisiæ dominum vernacule Friesland. Door. Abraham Allard. Inset: Kaart van de Friesse eilanden.

" " [125] Transisalania provincia vulgo Over-Yssel. Auctore N. Ten Have emendata a F. de Wit.

" " [126] Groningæ et Omlandiæ dominium vulgo de provincie van Stadt en Land. Tabulam redactum per Lud. Tjardæ â Starckenburg et Nicol. Visscher.

" " [127] Illustribus ac potentibus comitatus Drentiæ d. d. statoribus eorumque deputatis viris nobilissimis eminemtissimis prudentissimisque reflorescentis provinciæ et Westerwoldiæ dominii typvm emendatum lmque dedicat Corneli Pynacker, 1634. Amstelodami apud Ioannem Ianssonium.

v. 2, no. [1] Accuratissima Galliæ tabula.

" " [2] Carte particulière du terroir et des environs des Paris. Dessinée par F. Viuier. Amsteldam par N. Visser.

" " [3] Gouvernement general de l'Isle de Franc.

" " [4] Comté et gouvernement général de Champagne.

" " [5] Arcihiepiscopatvs Cameracensis. Prostant Amstelaedami apud Petrum Schenk et Gerardum Valk.

" " [6] Nova Picardiæ tabula.

" " [7] Duché et gouvernement général de Normandie. Inset: Les isles de Garnezy Ierżay et Aurigny.

" " [8] Duché et gouvernement général de Bretagne.

" " [9] Gouvernement général dv pays Orleanois.

" " [10] L'Isle de Ré. Par Charles Allard. Inset view: Le bombardement d'Olone.

v. 2, no.[11] Tabula nova partis septentrionalis episcopatus Carnutensis ad usum serenissimi Burgundiæ ducis. Parisiis H. Iaillot.—Partie septentrionale de l'évesché de Chartres. Amsterdam chez Pierre Mortier.

" " [12] Partie méridionale de l'évesché de Chartres. Par N. Sanson.

" " [13] Nouvelle carte géographique de la partie méridionale de France. Par Nicolas Visscher.

" " [14] Govverement de la Gvienne & Gascogne.

" " [15] Carte de l'évesché de Nantes. Par H. Iaillot.

" " [16] Le diocèse de l'évechè de Nismes, dressé nouvellement sur lieux par le s^{r}. Gautier. Amsterdam chez Pierre Mortier. Insets: Plan de la ville Nismes.—Elévation perspective de l'amphithéâtre de Nismes.—Façade de pont du gard.—Façade de l'amphithéâtre.—Façade de la maison Quarrée de Nismes.—Plan de la maison Quarrée.—Plan du temple de Diane.—Profils du temple de Diane.

" " [17] Gouvernement général de Langvedoc.

" " [18] Le théâtre de la guerre dans les Sévennes, le Languedoc, et le pays aux environs. Amsterdam par Pierre Mortier.

" " [19] Comté et gouvernement général de Provence.

" " [20] Generalis Lotharingiæ.

" " [21] Comitatus sive liberæ Burgundiæ.

" " [22] Ducatus Bvrgvndiæ.

" " [23] Le gouvernement général du Dauphiné.

" " [24] Le gouvernement général du Lyonnois. Par le s^{r}. Sanson reveu et corrigé par P. Mortier.

" " [25] L'Italie. Par H. Iaillot.

" " [26] Status belli Italiam inter Galliam.

" " [27] Dvcatvs Chablasivs et Lacvs Lemanvs.

" " [28] Tabvla generalis Sabavdiæ. Ioannes Blaeu excudit. Thomas Borgonius invent. Ioannes de Broen sculp.

" " [29] Pedemontivm et reliquæ ditiones Italiæ regiæ celsitvdini Sabavdicæ subditæ, cum regionibus adjacentibus. Joannes Blaeu excudit. Thomas Borgonius invent. Joannes de Broen sculp.

" " [30] De stoel des oorlogs in Italien. Door Nicolaus Visser.

" " [31] Status et ducatus Mediolanensis et Parmensis. Per Carolum Allard.

" " [32] Territorio di Cremona. Ex typographia Amstelodami penes Petri Schenk et Gerardi Valk.

" " [33] Dominii Veneti. Auct. Carolo Allard. Inset: Istriam.

" " [34] Carte nouvelle du Cremasco à la république de Venise. Par le s^{r}. Sanson. Amsterdam chez Pierre Mortier.

" " [35] Carte nouvelle du Bergamasco faisant partie des états de la république de Venise. Par le s^{r}. Sanson. Amsterdam chez P. Mortier.

" " [36] Carte particulière du Bressan faisant partie des états de la république de Venise. Par le s^{r}. Sanson. Amsterdam chez Pierre Mortier.

" " [37] Territorio di Verona. Typis Amstelodami apud Pet. Schenk et G. Valk.

" " [38] Carte nouvelle du territoire de Vicenza. Par le s^{r}. Sanson. Amsterdam chez P. Mortier.

Wit, F. de—Continued.

v. 2, no. [39] Carte nouvelle du Padouan et le Polesin de Rovigo de la république de Venise. Par le s^{r}. Sanson. Amsterdam chez Pierre Mortier.

" " [40] Carte nouvelle du duché de Mantoue. Par le s^{r}. Sanson. Amsterdam chez P. Mortier.

" " [41] Dvché de Parma et de Piacenza. A Amsterdam chez Pierre Mortier.

" " [42] Carte nouvelle du duché de Moderne, de Regio et de Carpi. Par le s^{r}. Sanson. Amsterdam chez Pierre Mortier.

" " [43] Carte nouvelle du duché et légation de Ferrare. Par le s. Sanson. Amsterdam chez Pierre Mortier.

" " [44] Dominio Fiorentino. Amstelodam excudebat G. Valk et P. Schenk.

" " [45] Status ecclesiasticus et magnus ducatus Thoscanæ.

" " [46] Tabula nova geographica Natoliæ et Asiæ Minoris. Accuratissimè composita per Jacobum Cantelii et edita per Nicolaum Visscher.

" " [47] [Grand Tartarie] Inset: Carte des pays situés au Nord nord est de la Chine. Levée en voyage par le P. Verbiest.

" " [48] Imperii Persici delineatio ex scriptis potissimum geographicis Arabum et Persarum tentata ab Adriano Relando.

" " [49] Magni Mogolis imperivm.

" " [50] Carte particulière d'une partie d' Asie où sont d' Andemaon Ceylon, les Maldives. Amsterdam, chez Pierre Mortier.

" " [51] Partie occidentale d'une partie d' Asie où sont les isles de Zocotora, de l'Amirante. Amsterdam, chez Pierre Mortier.

" " [52] Insula Ceilon. Per Nicolaum Visscher.

" " [53] Sinus Gangeticus vulgo golfo de Bengala.

" " [54] Le royaume de Siam. Amsterdam chez Pierre Mortier.

" " [55] Svmatræ.

" " [56] Insulæ Iavæ cum parte insularum Borneo, Svmatræ.

" " [57] Molvccæ insvlæ celeberrimæ. Amstelodami Guiljelmus Blaeuw excudit. Inset: Bachian I.

" " [58] Iaponia regnvm.

" " [59] Indiæ orientalis.

" " [60] Novissima et perfectissima Africæ descriptio ex formis Caroli Allard.

" " [61] Fezzæ et Marocchi regna Africæ celeberrima describebat Abrah. Ortelius. Prostant Amstelaedami apud Petrum Schenk et Gerardum Valk.

" " [62] Sitvs terræ Canaan. Emendavit N. Sanson.

" " [63] Nova Ægypti tabula.

" " [64] Barbaria. Sold by Christopher Browne.

" " [65] Insulæ promontorii Viridis Hispanis islas de Cabo Verde, Belgis de Sonte eylanden.

" " [66] Insulæ Canariæ alias Fortunatæ dictæ.

" " [67] Regna Congo et Angola.

" " [68] Gvinea.

" " [69] Insvla S. Lavrentii vulgo Madagascar.

" " [70] Recentissima Novi Orbis sive Americæ Septentrion alis et Meridionalis tabula ex officina Caroli Allard.

" " [71] Le Canada ou partie de la Nouvelle France. Par H. Iaillot. Paris, 1696.

v. 2, no. [72] Extrema Americæ versus boream ubi Terra Nova, Nova Francia, adjacentiaque. Amsteledami Io. Blaeu exc.
" " [73] Virginiæ partis australis, et Floridæ partis orientalis.
" " [74] Carte particulière de la Caroline. Par le sieur S[anson] à Amsterdam chez Pierre Mortier.
" " [75] Carte générale de la Caroline. Par sieur S[anson] à Amsterdam chez Pierre Mortier. Inset: [Ashley river, Cooper river]
" " [76] Carte nouvelle contenant la partie d' Amérique la plus septentrionale. Par Nicolas Visscher.
" " [77] Nova tabula geographica complectens borealiorem Americæ partem. Amstlodami Nicolao Visscher.
" " [78] Jamaica Americæ Septentrionalis ampla insula. Per Nicolaum Visscher.
" " [79] Insula Matanino vulgo Martanico in lucem edita per Nicolaum Visscher.
" " [80] Téâtre de la guerre en Amérique telle qu'elle est à présent possédée par les Espagnols.
" " [81] Archipelague du Mexique où sont les isles de Cuba, Espagnole, Iamaïque &c. par Pierre Mortier. Inset: Isle de St. Jean Delua.
" " [82] Insvlarvm Hispaniolæ et Cvbæ.
" " [83] Insulæ Americanæ in Oceano Septentrionali ac regiones adaicentes. Per Nicolaum Visscher.
" " [84] Perv. Amstelodami, Guiljelmus Blaeuw excudit.
" " [85] Chili. Amstelodami Guiljelmus Blaeuw excudit.
" " [86] Nove et accurata Brasiliæ totius tabula auctore Ioanne Blaev i. f.
" " [87] L' état de la république de Venise par sr. Sanson à Amsterdam, chez Pierre Mortier.
" " [88] Regnum Neapolis.
" " [89] Regni et insulæ Siciliæ. Insets: Messina.—Milazzo.—Palermo.—Catania.—Trapano.
" " [90] Insularum Melitæ vulgo Maltæ Gozæ et Comini. 1707. Insets: Tabula hæc addita est ita ut insulæ regiones et Terræ Melitæ circumjacentes clarius ostendentur.—[La Valetta]
" " [91] Insularum Sardiniæ et Corsicæ.
" " [92] Archipelagus unà cum Græciâ antiquo-hodiernâ de edita a Carolo Allard.
" " [93] Macedonia Alexandri magna patria. Amstelodami P. Mortier.
" " [94] Peloponnesus hodie Morea. Per Nicolaum Visscher.
" " [95] Cyprvs insvla.
" " [96] Cretæ seu Candiæ. Per Nicolaum Visscher.
" " [97] Carte nouvelle de la mer Mediterranée divisée en mer de Levant et de Ponant. Dressée par le sr. Sanson. Amsterdam chez Pierre Mortier.
" " [98] Regnorum Portugalliæ et Algarbiæ. Auctor Carolus Allard.
" " [99] Novissima et accuratissima regnorum Hispaniæ et Portugalliæ. 1705.
" " [100] Andalvzia continens Sevillam et Corsvbam.
" " [101] Granata et Mvrcia regna.
" " [102] Valentia regnvm. Amsterdami apud Guiljelmum Blaeuw.

Wit, F. de—Continued.

v. 2, no. [103] Insvlæ Balearides et Pytivsæ. E. Symons Hamersveldt sculpsit. Ex typographia Amstelodami apud Petri Schenk et Gerardi Valk.

" " [104] Accuratissima principatus Cataloniæ et comitatuum Ruscinonis et Cerretaniæ.

" " [105] Regni Navarræ accurata tabula.

" " [106] Regni Arragoniæ. 1707.

" " [107] La Castille. Par Nicolas Visscher.

" " [108] Regnorum Castellæ veteris, Legionis, et Gallæciæ principatuum que Biscaiæ, et Asturiarum.

" " [109] Biscaia et Gvipvscoa Cantabriæ veteris pars. Typus Amstelodami apud P. Schenk et G. Valk.

" " [110] Regnorum Castellæ Novæ, Andalusiæ, Granadæ Valentiæ, et Murciæ accurata tabula.

" " [111] Tabula nova complectens præfecturas Normanniæ et Britanniæ una cum Angliæ, parte et Manica. Per Nicolaum Visscher.

" " [112] Regnorum Magnæ Britanniæ sive Angliæ Scotiæque nec non Hiberniæ. Edita a Carolo Allard. Inset: Deucaledonius oceanus.

" " [113] Regni Angliæ et Walliæ principatus tabula. Per Carolum Allard.

" " [114] Novissima regni Scotiæ septentrionalis et meridionalis tabula. Auctore Carolo Allard. Inset: Deucaledonius oceanus.

" " [115] Novissima et accuratissima regni et insulæ Hiberniæ. Per Petrus Schenk.

" " [116] Dania regnum.

" " [117] Carte des courones du Nord. Par Guillaume Del' Isle. A Amsterdam chez Pierre Schenk. 1708.

" " [118] Accurata Scaniæ Blekingiæ et Hallandiæ descriptio. Inset: Gothiæ pars, Hallandia septentrionalis.

" " [119] Ducatus Slesvicensis.

" " [120] Regni Sueciæ.

" " [121] Regni Gothiæ, tabula generalis.

" " [122] Suecicæ Lapponiæ et Norvegicæ nova tabula.

" " [123] Regni Norvegia nova tabula. Inset: Norvegiæ pars septentrionalis.

" " [124] Nova tabula magni ducatus Finlandiæ.

1637

Mercator, G.

Historia mvndi: or Mercator's atlas. Containing his cosmographicall description of the fabricke and figure of the world. Lately rectified in divers places, as also beautified and enlarged with new mâppes and tables; By the studious industry of Ivdocvs Hondy. Englished by W[ye] S[altonstall] generosus, & coll. regin. Oxoniæ. eng. title, 12 p. l., 930 [32] pp. incl. 183 maps (2 fold.) 4°. London, Printed by T. Cootes for Michaell Sparke, and Samuel Cartwright. 1635. 4255

NOTE.—Eng. title has imprint "London, printed for Michaell Sparke, and are to be sowld in Greene Arboure, 1637. Second edition." This copy has a map of Ægyptus folded and inserted between pages 818 and 819.

It contains the duplicate map of New Spain on page 907 but also includes the fold. map of Virginia, Ralph Hall sculpsit, 1636 inserted between pages 904 and 905.
The paging is regular except for several misprints, pages being misnumbered.
Title page illuminated.
The maps relating to America are the same as those of title 451 in v. I.

1641

Cluver, P.

Philippi Clvveri Introdvctionis in vniversam geographiam, tam veterem qvam novam, libri VI. Tabulis æneis illustrati, & gemino indice aucti, cui adjuncta est Danielis Heinsii Oratio in obitum ejusdem Philippi Clvveri . . . 10 p. l., 214, [76] pp. 33 fold. maps, fold. pl. 12°. Brvnsvigæ, typis B. Gruberi, sumptibus G. Mulleri, 1641. 4256

NOTE.—Added title-page, engraved.
First edition 1624.
Woltersdorf gives 33 editions and Tiele gives an edition of 1627 not given by Woltersdorf.
The following map relates to America:
no. 1. Typus orbis terrarum.

1641–1729

Ottens, R.

Atlas maior cvm generales omnivm totius orbis regnorvm rervmpvbl. atqve insularvm tvm particvlares praecipvarvm in iis provinciarvm dvcatvvm comitatvvm ceterarvm qve minorvm regionvm ac divisionvm tabvlas geographicas continens ex optimis ac novissimis qvibvsqve variorvm avtorvm tabvlis collectvs et eleganti ordine dispositvs ab Reinero Ottens. 7 v. fol. Amstelædami apud viduam ac filios Ioachimi Ottens [1641–1729] 4257

NOTE.—The atlas contains 835 miscellaneous maps by various cartographers and many plates, with a general title-page in each volume.
From the nature of the contents it is probable that few copies were placed on the market.
In all volumes except the first the imprint reads: "Amstelædami apud Reinervm et Iosvam Ottens," and the words, "In [blank] tomos divisvs," follow the title.
The cartouche on the title-page of each volume is signed, "F. Ottens inv. et fecit 1724," and is elaborately colored in v. 1. Tiele gives examples of this atlas from Bodel Nijenhuis in 3 v. and as quoted from Muller's *Cat. Amer. Pars. III*, in 4 v. which contain the map "Berbice, 1740," also an example in the University at Amsterdam in 7 v.
Maps in the present copy are dated from 1641–1729. The maps are engraved and handcolored and are richly ornamented with fruits, flowers, cupids, shields figures in the costumes of the time and country, small portraits, and views showing customs and historical events.
Many maps have short lists of explanations. The long lists are mentioned in the note to the map.
The maps of cities are very elaborate.
In v. 1, there is an elaborately engraved, colored secondary title-page with the word "Atlas" in a scroll at the top and the imprint, Amstelædami apud viduam

Ottens, R.—Continued.

ac folios Joachim Ottens, signed I. van Munnickhausen sculp., L. Webbers pinxit.

The first volume has several maps of the world in hemispheres, including Homann's map which appears also in v. 2 and v. 3. Maps of the world in hemispheres appear in the other four volumes, that in v. 7, being the same as the one in v. 4.

Volume 4 contains the whole of Schotanus à Sterringa's *Uitbeeldinge der heirliykheit Friesland,* published by F. Halma, 1718, including the elaborate title-page and large plates of coats of arms and the maps augmented by those of Alting. A series of maps by Fricx also appear in this volume. The atlas is an unusually fine one and contains many rare maps, the maps of America in v. 7 being of great interest and include Ottens' Totius Neobelgii, with the "Restitutio" view of New York.

The contents of the maps which follows has been carefully annotated.

CONTENTS

v. 1, no. 1. System solare et planetarium ex hypothesi Copernicana. Novissime collectum & exhibitum à Iohanne Bapt. Homanno Norigergæ.

" " 1a. Systema mundi Tychonicum secundum celeberrimorum astronomorum Tychonis de Brahe et Io. Baptistæ Riccioli. Hyptheses concinnatum à Ioh. Gabr. Doppelmajero. Operâ Ioh. Bapt. Homanni Norimbergæ.

" " 2. Nouvelle carte pour conduire, à l'astronomie et à la géographie et pour faire conoitre les différens sistemès du monde.

" " 3. Sphæra automatica auspiciis amp. Adriani Vroesii, calculus Nicolai Stampioen, per Trasium adornata. Quam d. Sebastiani Schepers. Vidua & heredes dispersam & collapsam publico usui destinarunt et ab artifice Bernardo Cloesio. Lugd. Batav. 1711. Spæræ Armillaris Copernicanæ brevis descriptio.

" " 4. La spere artificielle ou armilaire oblique. P. Stark-man sculpsit. A Paris chez le s^r. de Fer. 1716.

" " . Sphærarum artificialium typica repræsentatio.

" " 5. Sphæra mundi. Exhibita à Ioh. Gabr. Doppelmaiero. Opera Ioh. Bapt. Homanni. Noribergæ.

" " 6a. Hemisphærium coeli boreale in quo fixarum loca secundum eclipticæ ductum ad añum 1730 completum exhibenter à Ioh. Gabriele Doppelmaiero. Opera Ioh. Baptistæ Homanni Norimbergæ.

" " 6b. Hemisphærium coeli australe exhibentur à Ioh. Gabriele Doppelmaiero. Opera Ioh. Baptistæ Homanni. Norimbergæ.

" " 6c. Hemisphærivm coeli boreale. Sistuntur â Ioh. Gabriele Doppelmaiero. Operâ Ioh. Bapt. Homanni. Norimbergæ.

" " 6d. Hemisphærivm coeli avstrale.

" " 7-7e. Globi coelestis in tabulas planas redacti pars I-VI. Exhibentur â Ioh. Gabr. Doppelmayr. Operâ Ioh. Bapt. Homanni. Norimbergæ.

" " 8. Sterre kaert of hemels pleyn. Door dit hemels pleyn. Gemaeckt door Remmet Teunisse Backer tot Enckhuysen. I. de Broen sculp. tot Amsterdam vytgegeven door Reinier & Josua Ottens.

v. 1, no. 9. Motvs planetarvm svperiorvm. Exhibiti â Ioh. Gabr. Doppelmajero. Ioh. Bapt. Homanni Noribergæ.

" " 9a. Motus in coelo spirales. Pro exemplo ad annum. 1712 et 1713 geometricède scripti a Ioh. Gabriele Doppelmajero. Operâ Ioh. Baptistæ Homanni Noribergæ.

" " 9b. Theoria planetarum primariorum. Exhibente Ioh. Gabr. Doppelmayero. Sumptibus Ioh. Baptistæ Homanni. Noribergæ.

" " 9c. Ephemerides motuum coelestium geometricæ. Ad an̄. Chr. 1708 et 1709. Demonstrãtur à Ioh. Gabr. Doppelmajero. Operâ Ioh. Bapt. Homanni Norimbergæ.

" " 9d. Phænomena motvvm irregvlarivm quos planetæ inferiores Venvs et Mercvrivs ad annum salutis 1710. Demonstrata à Ioh. Gabrielle Doppelmajero. Operâ Ioh. Baptista Homanni Norimbergæ.

" " 10. Tabula selenographica. Exhibetur à Ioh. Gabr. Doppelmajero. Operâ Ioh. Baptistæ Homanni Norinbergæ.

" " 11. Introduction à la géographie de la corespondance du globe terrestre ou mappe-monde avec la sphère céleste par les cercles, les lignes et les points, qui sont imaginés dans celle-cy et ceux qui se décrivent sur l'autre. Dressée par N. de Fer. 1722.

" " 12. Basis geographæ recentioris astronomica designantur a Iohanne Gabriele Doppelmajero. Operâ Ioh. Bapt. Homanni. Norimbergæ.

" " 13. Plan de l'histoire universelle.

" " 14. Tabvla anemographica seu pyxis navtica ventorum nomina sex linguis repræsentans. Amstelodami apud Ioan Ianssonium.

" " 15. Nouvelle carte pour conduire à la connoissance de la marine et à demonstrer la plus part des instrumens qui servent à cet art et à connoitre la construction des vaisseaux et les agrets pour servir à aquérir cette connoissance avec des remarques.
Plate marked "Tom. 7, no. 42."

" " 16. Carte des pavillons.
Plate marked "Tom. 7, no. 43."

" " 17. Tafel in welke vertoont werden alle werk-tuygen behorende tot de krygs-kunde vestingbouw en artillerye als mede tot de belegeringe van steden velt-slagen, legertochtenen legerplaatzen alle de gedeeltens van de zee en't land, en eyndelyk allerley slag van schepen in't licht gebracht door Casper Specht 't Utrecht gedrukt tot Amsterdam by I. Ottens.
Title also in french at top of map.

" " 18. Carte pour contribuer à indiquer la connoissance des premiers principes des fortifications.
Plate marked "Tom. 7, no. 41."

" " 19. Carte du blazons ou la science de la noblesse avec des instructions pour conduire à cette connoissance.
Plate marked "Tom. 7, no. 39."

" " 20. Nouvelle carte des ordres militaires.
Plate marked "Tom. 7, no. 40."

" " 21. Carte pour servir à l'intelligence de l'histoire, de la cronologie, et de la géographie des empires, des Assiriens, des Perses, des Egiptiens, et des Chinois.
Has extensive border text.

Ottens, R.—Continued.

v. 1, no. 22. Orbis veteribus noti tabula nova. Auctore Guillelmo Del' Isle. Paris. 1714.

" " 23. De oude wereldt. Door Isaak Verburg. t Amsterdam by R. en G. Wetstein. Door J. Keiser getekent en gesneden. Insets: Peloponnesus.—[Part of Italy]

" " 24 Imperivm Romanum. Auth. Phil. Briet. Inset: [Part of Italy]

" " 25. Theatrum historicum ad annum Christi quadringentesimū in quo tum imperii Romani tu Barbarorum. Pars occidentalis. Auctore Guillelmo Del' Isle. Amstelodami apud I. Cóvens & C. Mortier. Inset: Supplementum theatro historico.

Map has explanatory notes.

Appears also in Delisle's *Atlas nouveau, 1733.*

" " 26. Theatrum historicum ad annum Christi quadringentesimū in quo tu imperii Romani tu Barbarorum. Pars orientalis. Autore Guillelmo Delisle. Amstelodami apud I. Cóvens & C. Mortier. Inset: Supplementum theatro historico.

Appears also in Delisle's *Atlas nouveau, 1733.*

" " 27. Planisphere terrestre. Par m^{r}. Cassini le fils. Leide chez Pierre vander Aa. J. Goeree del. G. v. Gouwen fecit.

Appears also in Guedeville's *Le nouveau théâtre du monde, 1713.*

" " 28. Nouveaux mappemonde ou globe terrestre avec des tables et des remarques pour conduire ă la connoissance de la géographie et histoire.

" " 29. Planiglobii terrestris cum utroq hemisphærio generalis exhibitio. Publice proponit Io. Bapt. Homann. Norimbergæ.

For description of this map see v. 2, no. 1, which is the same.

" " 30. Hémisphere Septentrional pour voir plus distinctement les terres Arctiques. Par Guillaume Delisle. Paris. 1714.

This map and the one following are found in Delisle's [*Collection of maps of the world, 1763*] and Homann heirs, *Atlas compendiarivs, 1752–[1755]*

" " 31. Hémisphere méridional pour voir plus distinctement les terres australes. Par Guillaume Del Isle. Paris. 1714.

" " 32. Nova & accuratissima totius terrarum orbis tabula nautica variationum magneticarum index juxta observationes anno 1700 habitas constructa per Edm. Halley. H. Halma excudit.

Large map on two sheets joined and folded. Has explanatory annotations.

Appears also in Ottens' *Atlas minor,* [*1695–1756?*] and [*1745?*]

" " 32a. La description & les usages d'une carte marine du monde entier, nouvelle & corrigée monstrant variation de la boussole.

This description given in french and dutch and signed E. Halley.

" " 32b. Tables géographiques des divisions du globe terrestre. Par le s^{r}. Sanson. Paris chez Hubert Iaillot.

" " 33. Europa antiqua cum finitimis Africæ & vtriusque Asiæ regionibus. Nicolavs Blancardvs. delineabat.

" " 34. L'Europe. Leide chez Pierre vander Aa. —Europe inpraecipuas ipsius partes distributa. a Petro vander Aa.

v. 1, no. 34a. Historishe en geographische tafel. gestelt door C. Specht t' Utrecht.

" " 34b. Le noble jeu des armories de l'Europe enrichy de cartes géographiques. Gravé par P. Stark-man. à la Haye chez Iacob de Iongh.

A description of the game is given in french and english. The dedication to "His most sacred majesty George king of Great Britain, France and Ireland, elector of Brunswick-Lunenburg." signed by I. I. Cheneviere.

" " 34c. Tables géographiques des divisions de l'Europe. Par le s^r. Sanson. Paris chez H. Iaillot.

" " 35. Nouvelle carte marine de tous les ports de l'Europe sur l'océan et sur la Méditerranée. Gravé. Par. Berey. Se vend à Paris chez Iaillot le fils.

" " 36. Magnæ Britanniæ tabula; comprehendens Angliæ, Scotiæ, ac Hiberniæ regna. per Nicol. Visscher. Amst. Bat. Nunc apud P. Schenk iun.

Cartouche elaborately illustrated and surmounted by a portrait of William III.

Appears also in Visscher's *Variae tabulae geographicae*, [*1700?* and *Atlas minor* [1710?]

" " 37. Carte des royaumes d'Angleterre d'Ecosse et d'Irland. Par C. Inselin. Paris chez le s^r. Jaillot. 1715.

large maps on two sheets joined and folded.

" " 37a. Tables des divisions de toutes les parties et isles comprises sous le nom des Isles britanniques. Par le s^r. Sanson. Paris chez H. Iaillot. 1696.

" " 38. Angliæ regnum. per Nicol^m. Visscher. Amst. Bat. Nunc apud P. Schenk iun.

Appears also in Ottens heirs, *Atlas*, [*1740?*]

" " 39. Orientalior districtus regni, Angliæ. Per F. de Wit.

" " 40. Occidentalior regni Angliæ districtus. Per F. de Wit Amstelodami. Ex officina P. Mortier.

" " 41. Tractus regni Angliæ septentrion. Per F. de Wit Amstel-[dam] Ex officina P. Mortier.

" " 42. Les environs de Londres. Amsterdam chez I. Cóvens et C. Mortier.

" " 43. Accurater grundriss u. gegend der koenigl. Gross-Brittannischen haupt und residentz-stadt London wie auch prospecte einiger kœnigl. pallæste u. lust-schlösser derselbē edirt von Ioh. Baptist Homanns. erben in Nürnberg. Inset views: Prospect des königl. hospitals zu Chelsey.—Der königliche palast zu Windsor.—Prospect königl. lust-schlosses Hampton-court.—Der königl. palast zu Kensington.

" " 44. La plus grande partie de la Manche, qui contient les côtes de Angleterre et celles de France. Amsterdam chez Ioachim Ottens.

" " 45. Exactissima regni Scotiæ tabula tam in septentrionalem et meridionalem. Per Nicolaum Visscher Amst. Bat.

An alphabetical list of place names on the reverse of map.

Appears also in Visscher's *Variæ tabulæ geographicæ*, [*1700?*] *Atlas minor*, [*1710?*] and [*1712?*] and Ottens heirs, *Atlas*, [*1740?*]

Ottens, R.—Continued.

v. 1, no. 46. Scotiæ prouintiæ inter Taum fluvium, et septentrionales oras Angliæ. Veneunt Amstelodami apud Petrum Schenk et Gerardum.Valk.

" " 47. Scotiæ provinciæ intra flumen Taum, et Murra fyth sitæ. Apud G. Valk et P. Schenk.

" " 48. Extrimæ Scotiæ pars septentrionalis. Veneunt Amstelodami penes Petrum Schenk et Gerardum Valk.

" " 49. Hiberniæ regnum tam in præcipuas Ultoniæ, Connaciæ, Lafeniæ, et Momoniæ. Per Guillelmum Petty et in lucem editum per Nicolaum Visscher Amst. Bat. Nunc apud Pet. Schenk iunior.

" " 50. Provincia Vltoniæ.—The provincie of Vlster. Prostant in officina Amstelodami apud P. Schenk et G. Valk.

" " 51. Provincia Connachtiæ.—The province of Connavgt. Prodeunt ex officina Amstelodami apud Petri Schenk et Gerardi Valk.

" " 52. Comitatvs Lageniæ.—The covntie of Leinster. Prostant in officina Amstelodami penes Petri Schenk et Gerardi Valk.

" " 53. Provincia Momoniæ.—The province of Movnster. Prodeunt ex officina Amstelodami apud Petri Schenk et Gerardi Valk.

" " 54. Exactissima totius Scandinaviæ tabula, qua tam Sueciæ, Daniæ, et Norvegiæ regna. Per Nicolaum Visscher Amst. Bat. Nunc ap[ud] P. Schenk iu.

An issue of this map without Schenk's name appears in Visscher's *Variæ tabulæ geographicæ*, [*1700?*] and [*1704?*] and in his *Atlas minor*, [*1710?*]

" " 54a. Tables des divisions de la Scandinavie. Par le s^r. Sanson. Paris chez H. Iaillot. 1696.

" " 55–56. Carte des couronnes du Nord. Par. Guilllaum De l'Isle. 1706. A Paris chez l'auteur et se trouve à Amsterdam chez Louis Renard. Gravé par Liebaux fils. A similar map brought out by Schenk in 1708, appears in Ottens heirs, *Atlas*, [*1740?*]

" " 57. Dania regnum. Per F. de Wit Amstelodami ex officina I. Cóvens et C. Mortier.

" " 58. Carte du royaume de Danemarc. Par Guill. Del 'Isle. 1710.

" " 58a. Tables des divisions du royaume de Dannemarck. Par le s^r. Sanson. Paris chez H. Iaillot, 1696.

" " 59. Insularum Danicarum. Per F. de Wit. Amstelodami ex officina I. Cóvens et C. Mortier.

Appears also in Cóvens and Mortier's *Atlas nouveau, 1683–1761* and without Cóvens & Mortier's name in Braakman's *Atlas minor, 1706*.

" " 60. Saltholm und Drako mit den zeichen aus der see.—Helsingburg.—Kopenhagen.—Lands-cron.—Die insul Ween.—Malmoo, Malmuyen oder Ellebogen. In Amsterdam bei Joachim Ottens.

" " 61. Accurate vorstellung der berühmten Meer-Enge, zwischen der Nord und Ost see der Svnd genant mit der herümligenden gegend von Seeland und Schonen, nebst der königlich-dähnischen haupt und residentz Copenhagen. Edirt von Ioh. Babtist Homann. In Nürnberg. Inset views: Helsingbvrg.—Landscron.—Malmoe.—Cronenbvrg.—Prospect der königl. danischen haupt u. residenz stadt Copenhagen.

Appears also in Homann heirs, *Stadt atlas, 1762*.

v. 1, no. 62. Iutiæ tabula. Per F. de Wit Amstelodami ex officina P. Mortier.

Appears also in Cóvens & Mortier's, *Atlas nouveau, 1683–1761*, and without Mortier's name, in Braakman's *Atlas minor, 1706*.

" " 63. Slesvicensis ducatis. Per Nicolaum Visser Amst. Bat. Nunc apud Petrum Schenk iunior.

" " 64. Holsatiæ ducatus. Per Nicolaum Visser Amst. Bat. Nunc apud Petrum Schenk iunior.

" " 65. Regni Norvegia. Per F. de Witt Amstelodami. Ex officina I. Cóvens et C. Mortier. Inset: Norvegiæ pars septentrionalis.

Appears also in Cóvens & Mortier, *Atlas nouveau, 1683–1761*, and in Ottens heirs, *Atlas [1740?]*

" " 66. Tractus Norwegiæ Danicus magnam dioeceos Aggerhusiensis partem sistens editus a Iohannis Baptistæ Homanni. Noribergæ anno 1729.

One-third of the plate covered by an illustration of mining operations.

" " 67. Plan der belagerung von Fridrichshall. Edirt von Iohann Baptist Homann. Nürnberg.

" " 68. Tractus Norvegiæ Suecicus præfecturam Bahusiæ finitimæqve Daliæ provinciæ partem sistens pvlico exhibitvs a Ioh. Bap. Homanno. Noribergæ ·anno· 1729. Insets: Die königl. schwedischestadt und vestung Marstrandt.—Die stadt Wennersburg.—Prospect der vestung Bahvs.—Die koenigl. schwedis vestung Gothenburg.

" " 69. Nieuwe afteekening van het eyland Spits-Bergen. Uytgegeven door Gerard van Keulen.

Appears also in Cóvens & Mortier, *Atlas nouveau, 1683–1761*, as does the map which follows.

" " 70. Het eyland Ysland. te Amsterdam by Gerard van Keulen.

" " 71. Regni Sueciæ tabula generalis. Per F. de Wit Amstelodami. Ex officina I. Cóvens et C. Mortier.

Appears also in Cóvens & Mortier, *Atlas nouveau, 1683–1761*, and without Cóvens & Mortier's name in Visscher's *Atlas minor, [1710?]*

" " 72. Regni Gothiæ tabula generalis. Correctore et editore F. de Witt, Amstelodami. Ex officina I. Cóvens et C. Mortier.

" " 73. Nova Gothiæ australis. Aúctore F. de Witt Amstelodami. Inset: Vestro-Gothiæ pars.

" " 74. Nova et accurata Scaniæ et maximæ partis Zeelandæ tabula. à Amsterdam chez la veuve de Pierre Mortier.

" " 75. Sueonia sive regni Sueciæ propriæ. Emendata. per F. de Witt Amstelodami. Ex officina I. Cóvens et C. Mortier.

Appears also in Cóvens & Mortier, *Atlas nouveau, 1683–1761*.

" " 76. Ducatus Uplandiæ. Per F. de Witt Amstelodami. Ex officina P. Mortier.

" " 77. Accurate carte der Upländischen Scheren mit der situation und gegend umb die königl. swedische haupt und residentz stadt Stockholm edirt von Ioh. Bapt. Homann. Nürnberg. Inset views: Prospect des königl. schwedischen residenzschloss in Stockholm mit dem Norder Malm.—Prospect der königlichen strasse in Stockholm mit Syder Malm.

Ottens, R.—Continued.

v. 1, no. 78. Accurater grundriss und prospect der kön. Schwed. reichs. u. haupt stadt Stockholm. edirt von Ioh. Baptist. Homann in Nür[nbe]rg.
Has explanatory list.
Appears also in Homann heirs, *Stadt atlas, 1762.*

" " 79. Dalecarliæ et Westmanniæ, nova et accurata descriptio. Amstelodami sumptibus apud P. Schenk et G. Valk.

" " 80. Nordlandia sive regni Sueciæ propriæ pars septentrionalis. Auctore F. de Witt Amstelodami ex officina P. Mortier.
Appears also in Cóvens & Mortier, *Atlas nouveau, 1683–1761.*

" " 81. Suecicæ Lapponiæ et Norvegicæ nova tabula. Per F. de Witt Amstelodami. Ex officina P. Mortier.
Appears also in Cóvens & Mortier, *Atlas nouveau, 1683–1761,* without P. Mortier's name.

" " 82. Nova tabula magni ducatus Finlandiæ. Aucta et correcta per F. de Witt. Amstelodami ex officina I. Cóvens et C. Mortier.
Appears also in Cóvens & Mortier, *Atlas nouveau, 1683–1761*.

" " 83. [De Oost Finsche golf]

" " 84. Nieuwe afteekening van de Finlandse golf of Bodem opgestelt en afgeteekent door Abraham Maas tot S[t]. Petersburg. nieuwlyks in't ligt gebragt door Joannes van Keulen.

" " 85. Carte nouvelle de tout l'empire de la Grande Russie dans l' estat ou il s'est trouvé à la mort de Pierre le Grand.

" " 86. Generalis totius imperii Russorum novissima tabula. Ex conatibus Iohannis Baptistæ Homanni Norimbergæ.

" " 87. Imperii Russici sive Moscoviæ. Ex tabula N. Witsen. Pro maiori parte exceptus per F. de Witt Amst. Ex officina I. Cóvens et C. Mortier,[a] at London by Christopher Browne.
Appears also in Braakman's *Atlas minor, 1706,* and Visscher's *Atlas minor, [1712?]* and in Visscher's *Atlas minor [1710?]* without either Cóvens & Mortier or Browne's name.

" " 88-89. Carte de Moscovie dressée par Guillaume De l'Isle. Amsterdam chez Iean Cóvens et Corneille Mortier.
Both sheets have additional titles at the top of the sheet, that on the first sheet being the same as the title given above, and on the second sheet reading: Partie méridionale de Moscovie, dressée par G. de l'Isle, à Amsterdam chez I. Cóvens et C. Mortier.
Appears also in Cóvens & Mortier, *Atlas nouveau, 1683–1761.*

" " 89a. Tables ou divisions de la Moscovie ou Russie Blanche, par le s[r]. Sanson. Paris chez H. Jaillot. 1692.

" " 90. Nieuwe afbeelding van de gelegentheid der stat S[t]. Petersburg.—Afbeelding van de nieuwe russische hooft-residentie en zee stadt S[t]. Petersburg benevens haare nieuwe vesting door zyne russisch-keizerlyke majesteit a[o]. 1703.
J. Kaiser sculp. Gedrukt t Amsterdam by de wed. I. Ottens.
Latin title at top of map: Nova ac verissima vrbis S[t]. Petersburg. A Reinero Ottens Amstelaedamensi. In lvcem edita.
An explanatory list on the map contains the date 1716.

v. 1, no. 91. Sedes belli in Polonia et in Moscoviæ, Turciæ terminis per Abrahamum Allard Amstelod. Inset: Wolgæ ostia.
Map on two sheets joined and folded.
Appears also in Cóvens & Mortier, *Atlas nouveau, 1683–1761.*

" " 92. Tabula geographica qua pars Russiæ Magnæ pontus Euxinus. A Ioh. Baptista Homanno. Noribergiæ.

" " 93. Tavrica Chersonesvs hodie Przecopsca et Gazara dicitur. Amstelædami impensis G. Valk et P. Schenk.

" " 94. Nouvelle carte géographique de la mer d' Asof ou de Zabache & des Palus Meotides exactement dessignée & mise en lumiére par Nicolas Visscher.
Appears also in Visscher's, *Atlas minor*, [*1717?*]

" " 95–96. Nieuwe zeer accurate, en naauwkeurige caart vande rivier den Don of Tanais, met aanwyzinge van alle des selfs dieptens, droogtens etc. afgemeeten in't iaar 1699, in tegenwoordigheÿd vander grooten heer, czaar, en grootvorst, Peter Alexiowits door. Cornelis Cruÿs. Te Amsterdam by Ioachim Ottens. Insets: Nieuwe kaart van den oorspronk en loop van den Don tot Woronitz, nevens de gebaande weg van Moscwa.—[View] De verlaringe van de grondt en voor gevel van zyn groot czaarse majestyten magazyn op Taganrock aen de zee zyde.—Aftekening van zyn czaerze mayesteyts haven by Tagenrock.—Nieuwe kaart verbeeldende de Doorgraving mit de riv. Ilafla tot in de Kamisinka. The last two insets appear on the second sheet.

" " 97. Dvcatvvm Livoniæ et Cvrlandiæ cum vincinis insulis. Editore Ioh. Baptista Homanno Norimbergæ.

v. 2, no. 1. Planiglobii terrestris cum utroq hemisphærio cælesti generalis exhibitio. Publice proponit Io. Bapt. Homann. Norimbergæ. View in one corner shows Mt. Etna in irruption, and "Norwegiian vorticis" in the opposite corner. The celestial hemispheres are entitled, "Hemisphærium boreale," and "Hemisphærium australe." Notes at the foot of the map. Ornamented with cupids and small heads.

" " 2. Europa christiani orbis domina in sua imperia regna et status exacte divisa per Iohan. Bapt. Homann. Norimbergæ.

" " 3. Tabula nova totius regni Poloniæ, in quo sunt ducatus et provinciæ Prussia, Cujavia, Mazovia, Russia Nigra, &c. Ducatus Lithuania, Ukrania, &c. in qua Volhynia, et Podolia cum suis Palatina ibus ac confinys. Authore N. Sansonio Abbevillensi. Amstelodami apud Nicolaum Visscher, nunc apud Petrum Schenk iun.

" " 4. Reipublicæ et status generalis Poloniæ nova tabula, comprehendens maioris et minoris Poloniæregni magni ducatus Lithuaniæ, ducatus Prussiæ, Curlandiæ, samogitiæ, Massoviæ, Volhyniæ, Podoliæ, Russiæ, Ucraniæ et de Moscoviæ pars. Amstelodami apud Joachimum Ottens. Jacob Keyser sculptor. The Sanson table following is of interest in connection with this map and the one preceding it.

" " 4a. Tables ou divisions de Pologne. Par le s[r] Sanson.

" " 5. Ducatuum Livoniæ, et Curlandiæ. Per F. de Witt Amstelodami.

Ottens, R.—Continued.

v. 2, no. 6. Magni ducatus Lithuaniæ. Per F. de Witt Amstelodami. Ex officina P. Mortier. The various cities are marked by a descriptive device and a list called "Signorum declaratio," gives explanation of these devices. Note to the reader in a cartouche.

" " 7. Palatinatvs Posnaniensis. Per G. F. M. Gerard Coeck sculpsit. Amsterdami exc. J. Cóvens et C. Mortier. [Dedication signed] G. Freudenhamerus Medicus. Note to the reader on a panel at the right side of maps.

" " 8. Typus generalis Ukrainæ. Penes Gerardum Valk et Petrum Schenk. Explanation of descriptive devices in cartouche.

" " 9. Vkrania quæ et terra Cosaccorvm cum vicinis Walachiæ, Moldaviæ, Minorisq, Tartariæ provinciis exhibita à Ioh. Baptista Homanno Noribergæ.

" " 10. Ukrainæ pars qvæ Pokutia vulgo dicitur. Per Guil. le Vasseur de Beauplan. Amstelodami exc. P. Mortier. Sieur de Beauplan, author of this and the three following maps of Ukraine is said to have served seventeen years in Ukraine as engineer to the king of Poland. He wrote a description of Ukraine in french which was translated into english and included in Churchill's Collection of voyages and travels, published in 1732. In a note preceeding the work the following statement is made, "Nothing is wanting, but the map which in some places he refers to; but in a short advertisement he informs the reader that all his papers and draughts, which it seems he had left to be engraved in Poland, had been there seized by the king, which has deprived us of the satisfaction of so exact a map as we might reasonably expect from him." These maps of Ukraine however were all published in Amsterdam by P. Cóvens, and Cóvens & Mortier.

" " 11. Ukrainæ pars, quæ Podolia palatinatus vulgo dicitur. Per Guil. le Vasseur de Beauplan. Amstelodami exc. P. Mortier.

" " 12. Ukrainæ pars qvæ Barclavia palatinatus vulgo dicitur. Per Guilhelmum le Vasseur de Beauplan. Amstelodami ex officina I. Cóvens & C. Mortier.

" " 13. Ukrainæ pars, qvæ Kiovia palatinatus vulgo dicitur. Per Guilhelmum le Vasseur de Beauplan. Amstelodami ex officina P. Mortier.

" " 14. Regni Prussiæ et Prussiæ Polonicæ. Auctore F. de Witt Amstelodami. Ex officina P. Mortier.

Contains list explaining the devices used to indicate cities, towns, parishes, churches, lakes, rivers, etc.

" " 15. Regnum Borussiæ gloriosis auspicÿs serenissimi e potentissimi princ Friderici III primi Borussiæ regis, march. et elect. Brand. A Ioh. Baptista Homanno Norimbergæ.

Ornamented with portrait of Frederick III, elector of Brandenburg, who was Frederick I, of Prussia, which is surrounded with symbolical figures bearing his coat of arms and the various insignia of his state.

v. 2, no. 16. Borussiæ regnum sub fortissimo Tutamine et justissimo regimine serenissimi ac potentissimi principis Friderici Wilhelmi. Mappa geographica delineatum cura et sumptibus Matth. Seuteri. Augustani. Inset: Princpatus Neocomensis seui Neufchatel ad Borussiæ regem.

Ornamented with portrait of Frederick William I, of Prussia, with figures, etc., following the idea carried out on the forgoing map.

" " 17. Prospect, grundris und gegend der Polnischen vesten reichs und handels-stadt Dantzig und ihrem Werder edirt von Io. Bapts Homann in Nürnberg. Inset: Prospect der stadt Danzig.

" " 18. Imperium Romano-Germanicum. A Ioh. Baptista Homanno. Norimbergæ.

Explanatory list in lower left hand corner of map.

" " 19. Tabula geographica totius Germaniæ qua differentium imperii trium religionum status et dominia diversis coloribus distincta exhibentur à Ioh. Bapt. Homanno.

Explanatory list in lower left hand corner of map.

" " 20. Hydrographia Germaniæ. Opera Ioh. Baptistæ Homani Noribergæ. [Dedication signed] Phil. Henr. Zollmanus. The Specht plate and the Sanson table which follow are of interest in connection with this and the preceeding map.

" " 20a. Kort begryp van Duytsland, de drie Ryx collegien in hunne wapens en zittingen kreits verdelingen en aantekeningen door C. Specht 't Utrecht. 1706. Inset: Duytsland in 9 kraitzen of circels nevens de keyserlyke erflanden verdeelt.

" " 20b. Tables des divisions de l' Allemagne. Par le S. Sanson.

" " 21. Circulus Saxoniæ Inferioris, divisa in ducatus Brunsuici, Zellæ, Holsatiæ, Meklenbergi et Bremæ, archiepiscopatum Magdeburgi et episcopatus Hildesii et Halberstadii, per Gerardi et Leonardi Valk.

" " 22. Slesvicensis ducatus incolis das hertzogtum Schleswieg. Per Nicolaum Visser Amst. Bat. Nunc apud Petrum Schenk iunior.

" " 23. Holsatiæ ducatus, vernaculé das hertzogtum Holstein. Per Nicolaum Visser Amst. Bat. Nunc apud Petrum Schenk iunior.

" " 24. Wagria quæ est pars orientalis Holsatiæ. Amstelodami veneunt apud P. Schenk et G. Valk.

" " 25. Dithmarsia, Rendesburgum, Kiel et Bordesholm, in occidentali parte Holsatiæ.

" " 26. Tabula geographica novissima ducatus Stormariæ, in meridionali parte Holsatiæ. Amstelodami prostant apud P. Schenk et G. Valk.

" " 27. Prospect und grundris der keiserl. freyen reichs und ansee stadt Hamburg samt ihrer gegend edirt durch Ioh. Bapt. Homann in Nürnberg. Inset: Prospect der stadt Hamburg gegen mittag anzusehen. Gives list of references to numbers and letters on the map. All prominent buildings showing in the inset are designated by name. Ornamented with groups of symbolical figures illustrating the prosperity and progress of the city.

Ottens, R.—Continued.

v. 2, no. 28. Ducatus Meklénburgicus in quo sunt ducatus Vandaliæ et Meklenburgi ducatus et comitatus Swerinensis Rostochiense et Stargardiense domin. Auctore F. de Witt.

" " 29. Ducatus Meklenburgici tabula generalis continens duc. Vandaliæ et Meklenburg comitatum et episcopatum Swerinensem Rostochiense et Stargardiense dominium excudente Io. Baptista Homanno Noribergæ.

" " 30. Particulier carte der gegend von Wismar nebst der insul Pöel und angedeuteter Bloquade zu wasser und lande 1715. duch herrn. Heinr. Varenium und edirt von Ioh. Bap. Homann. In Nürnberg. Inset: Stadt Wismar.

All prominent buildings showing in inset are designated by name. Illustrated with symbolical figures.

" " 31. Ducatus Bremæ & Ferdæ maximæque partis fluminis Visurgis descriptio per Fredericum de Wit. Amstelodami ex officina P. Mortier.

" " 32. Prospect und grundris der keiserl. freyen reich und ansee stadt Bremen samt ihrer gegend edirt durch Ioh. Bapt. Homann in Nürnberg. Inset: Die stadt Bremen.

Gives list of references to numbers and letters on the map. All prominent buildings showing in the inset are designated by name. Ornamented with groups of symbolical figures illustrating the prosperity and progress of the city.

" " 33. Typus geographicus ducat. Lauenburgici. A Ioh. Bapt. Homannis. Noribergæ. 1729. Rup. Al. Schneider sculp. Furth. Inset: Hadulorum regio.

" " 34. Ducatus Luneburgici et comitatus Dannebergensis per Nicolaum Visser Amst. Bat. Nunc apud Pet. Schenk iun.

" " 35. Saxoniæ tractus ducatum Magdeburgensem. Editus à Ioh Baptist. Homañi. Noribergæ. Inset view: Magdeburg.

" " 36. Geographische charte des hertzogthums Magdeburg und Halle ... Gestochen von P. Schenk iun. in Amsterdam.

On either side of the map a register of places appears.

" " 37. Ducatus Brunsuicensis in eiusdem tres principatus Calenbergicum scilicet et Grubenhagensem et in Guelpherbitanum Edita per F. de Wit. Amstelodami. Ex officina I. Cóvens et C. Mortier.

" " 38. Ducatus Brunsuicensis in ejusdem tres principatus Calenburgicũ scilicet & Grubenhagensē et in Geulpherbitanum Edita Ioh. Bapt. Homanni Norimbergæ.

" " 39. A general prospect of the royall house and garding at Hernhausen. I. von Sassa fecit. Amsterdam at Peter Schenk. At the sign of N. Visschers Athlas.

List of explanations at foot of map. Title and list also in french.

" " 40. Marchionatus Brandenburgicus et ducatus Pomeraniæ. Venundantur per Gerard^m. et Leonard^m. Valk.

" " 41. Ducatus Pomeraniæ. Per Fredericum de Wit. Amstelodami ex officina Petri Mortier.

" " 42. Eine accurate karte von Pomeran, wie auch dem landt Rügen neben Strahlsundt invent: Ioh. Himmerich gestochen von P. Schenk.

On a panel at foot of map, a list of explanatory references is given.

v, 2, no, 43. Insulæ et principatus Rugiæ cum vicinia Pomeraniæ littoribus. Edita â Ioh. Baptista Homanno. Noribergiæ.

" " 44. Land-charte des chur-fürstenthums Brandenburg. Amsterdam bey Johannes Cóvens und Cornelius Mortier.
Latin title at top of map. The various cities are marked by a descriptive device and a list entitled "Erklährung derer zeichen" gives explanation of these devices.

" " 45. Marchionatvs Brandenburgici partes duæ Ruppin comitatus & Prignits regiuncula. Auth. Olao Iohannis Gotho. Amstelodã ex officina Petri Mortier.

" " 46. Marchia Vetus vulgo Alte-Marck in March: Brandenburgico. Prostant Amstelaedami apud Petrum Schenk et Gerardum Valk.

" " 47. Marchia Media vulgo Mittel Marck in March: Brandenb. Prostant Amstelaedami apud Petrum Schenk et Gerardum Valk.

" " 48. Marchia Nova; vulgo New Marck in March: Brandenburg. Prostant Amstelaedami apud Petrum Schenk et Gerardum Valk.

" " 49. Circulus Saxoniæ Superioris. Per Gerard et Leonard Valk.

" " 50. Circulus Saxoniæ Superioris. A Iohanne Baptista Homanno Norimbergæ. Inset view: Leypzig.

" " 51. Neue Sächsischen post-charte. Gestochen von P. Schenk iun. in Amsterdam

" " 52. Nova Anhaltini principatus tabula autore Ioh. Tobia Schuchart architect. Anhalt. Pet. Schenck sculp. 1710.
Table of distances given in lower left hand corner of map.

" " 53. Darstellung des grundrisses und prospectus der. Haupt stadt Halle, welcher daselbst und verlag Iohann Baptistæ Homanns ist ausgemessen und geometrice verzeichnet warden von I. C. Homann. Zufinden in Nürnberg. Inset views: Prospect der stadt Halle.—Durchschnitt einer salz kothen wie solche von innen on zusehen.—Abbildung des saltzbrunnens teutsch genannt.—Das grosse auditorium.
Contains "Erklärung der zeichen."

" " 54. Geometrischer general ris des stiffts Merseburg, gestochen von P. Schenk in Amsterdam. Inset view: Merseburg.

" " 55. Geographischer entwurff des amtes Leipzig. Gestochen von P. Schenk iun. in Amsterdam.
A register of places appears on both margins of the map.

" " 56. Plan oder grundriss der chur Sæchsischen handels stadt Leipzig. Schenk exc Amst.
A list of references at foot of the map.

" " 57. Accurate geographische delineation der in dem Meisnischen creisse des churfürstenthums Sachsen liegenden dioeces oder superintendtur Grossen Hayn, 1711, von m. Adam Friedrich Zürner. Gestochen von Peter Schencken iun.
A register of places appears on both margins of map. Dedication at top of map. Contains "Erklaerung der zeichen," and explanatory note.

" " 58. Accurate geographische delineation der dioeces und ammtes Dresden. Edirt von m. Adam Friederich Zürner. Gestochen von Peter Schencken jun. Inset views: Alt-Dresden.—Neu-Dresde.

Ottens, R.—Continued.

A very extensive register of places and the coats of arms of the principal divisions appear on both margins. Dedication at top of map. Contains "Erklaerung derer zeichen."

v. 2, no. 59. Illustrissimo principi Ioanni Georgio duci Saxoniæ hanc Thuringiae lantgraviatus tabulam omni animi devotione offert et inscribit Petrus Schenk. Amst.

" " 60. Comitativs Mansfeldiæ descriptio. Auctore Tilemanno Stellg. sig. Prostant Amstelaeaimpudda Pet. Schenk et Ger. Valk.

" " 61. Nova territorii Erfordien. Auctore Ioh. Bapt. Homanno Norbergæ. Inset view: Die stadt Erfurt. Revidit Fridericus Zollmannus a 1717.

Map contains short explanatory note.

" " 62. Principatus Isenacensis. A Iohanne Bapt. Homanno Norimbergæ.

" " 63. Tabula geographica in qua serenissimi principis Friderici. Principatvs Gotha, Cobvrg et Altenburg. Ostenduntur à Ioh. Baptista Homanno, Norimbergae. Inset view: Die hoch fürstl. residenz stadt Gotha.

" " 64. Land-chart von fürstenthum Altenburg. Gestochen von P. Schenk in Amsterdam.

" " 65. Circulus Franconius. Per Ger. et Leon. Valk.

" " 66. Circuli Franconiæ pars occidentalis exhibens simul entegrum ferè electoratum Moguntinum. Author Io. Bapt. Homann Norimbergæ. Title also in german at top of map. Title ornamented with two portraits with the following inscription "Gens Schonborna duos tibi dat Germania, natos majores meritis non habitura patres."

" " 67. Circuli Franconiæ pars orientalis. Io. Bapt. Homann Norimbergæ.

Title also in german at top of map.

" " 68. Principatus Hennenbergensis. Amstelodami apud G. Valk et P. Schenk. [Dedication signed] Henricus Hondius.

" " 69. Sac. Rom. imperii principatus & episcopatus Bambergensis. A Io. Bapt. Homanno, Norimbergæ. Inset: Carinthiæ Bambergensis.—View: Bamberg.

" " 70. Serenissimo principi ac domino, domino Ernesto Friderico. Hanc ejusdem principatus Saxo-Hildburghusian novam et exactam tabulam submississime d. d. d. Ioannes Bapt. Homann, Norimbergæ. Inset view: Plan der hochfürstlichen residenz-stadt Hildburghausen.

Contains "Erklärung der zeichen," in an elaborate cartouche.

" " 71. Geographica descriptio montani cujusdam districtus in Franconia. A Ioh. Baptista Homann. Inset view: Thurnau.

Contains "Erklärung der zeichen."

" " 72. Ducatus Franciæ orientalis seu sac. rom. impreij principatus et episcopatus Herbipolensis vulgo Würtzburgensis. A Ioh. Bapt. Homann, Norimbergæ. Inset view: Grundriss der Würtzbur. stadt und vestung königshofen.—Prospect des neuen hoch fürstlichen palatÿ in der stadt von der Abentseiten anzusehen.

v. 2, no. 73. Accurate vorstellung der hoch fürstl. bischöffl. residenz und haupt-stadt Würtzburg des herzogthums Francken. Von I. B. Homann. A. 1723 in Nurnberg. List of explanations at foot of map.

" " 74. Comitatvs Wertheimici finitimarvmqve regionvm nova et exacta descriptio. Apud Gerardum Valk et Petrum Schenk Amstelædami.

" " 75. Erpach comitatus. Petrus Kærius cælavit Amstelædami typis Gerardi Valk et Petri Schenk.

" " 76. Territorivm Norimbergense. Prostant Amstelædami apud P. Schenk, G. Valk. Inset view: Nvrnberg.

" " 77. Prospect und grundris der des heil. rom. reichsstadt Nürnberg samt ihrem linien und gegend auf eine meil-wegs herumb. edirt von Ioh. Bap. Homann daselbst. Inset view: [Nürnberg] Map contains "Erklærung der ziffern," and view also has list of explanations.

" " 78. S. r. i. principatus et episcopatus Eistettensis. A Iohanne Baptista Homanno. Norimbergæ. Inset view: Prospect der hoch fürstl. bischöfflichen haupt und residenz-stadt Eichstett samt de schloss S[t]. Wilibaldsburg.

" " 79. Regni Bohemiæ. Sumptibus Ioh. B. Homanni Norib.

" " 80. Regnum Bohemiæ eique annexæ provinciæ ut ducatus Silesiæ marchionatus Moraviæ et Lusatiæ vulgo die Erb-landeren. Auctore Nicolao Visscher Amstelædami.

" " 81. Die herschaft Toeplitz im leutmeritzer creisse des königreichs Boehmen entworffen von M. A. F. Zurner, gestochen in Amsteldam von P. Schenk. Inset views: Der atle schloss berg.—Hoch graff liches schloss in Töplitz.—Südlicher prospect.—Nordlicher prospect.—Grundriss der warme haupt bades, wie auch derer übrigen neben bader in Töplitz.

A register of places appears on both margins and on the map. Contains "Erklærung der zeichen."

" " 82. Geographischer entwurff der stadt und gegend des welt berühmten kæyser Carlsbades in königreich Böhmen. Von M. A. F. Zurner gestochen von Peter Schencken jun. 1715. Inset views: Ellenbogen.—Kæyser Carlsbad.—Schlackenwerda.—Lusthäuser der herrn burger meister an der grossen wiese.—Ietziger prospect von der stadt Carlsbad.—Sciagraphia der Carlsbader. This last view has a long list of references to places which are indicated by numbers and letters. Register of places appears on both margins of the maps.

" " 83. Totius marchionatus Lusatiae. Revisa et aucta, â. Ioh, Hübnero et in lucem edita â Ioh. Baptista Homanno. Norimbergæ.

" " 84. Nova et accurata descriptio marchionatus Lusatiæ inferioris oder neue und accurate beschreibung der margrafthums Nieder Lausitz gestochen von Peter Schencken jun. in Amsterdam. The following note is attached to the cartouche containing the title, "Weil von diesen lande noch nicht sonderlich gestochen und dies der erste versuch hie bey so wird ein jeder der etwas mit grunde und raison daran zu verbessern weiss, solches zu communiciren gebethen."

" " 85. Lusatia superior. Auth. Bartholomaeo Sculteto Gorlitio. Prostant Amstlaedami apud Petrum Schenk, et Gerardum Valk.

114882°—19——6

Ottens, R.—Continued.

v. 2, no. 86. Mappa geographica exactissima continens imperatoris hæreditarium dominum Silesiam. Edente Petro Schenck.

" " 87. Superioris et inferioris ducatus Silesiæ. Edita à Ioh. Baptista Homaño Norimbergæ. Inset: Breslaw.

" " 88. Dvcatvs Silesiæ Glogani vera delineatio secundá curá as labore confecta a Iona Sculteta Sprotta Silesio. Prostant Amstelaedami apud Petrum Schenk et Gerardum Valk.

" " 89. Ducatus Silesiæ Wolanus. Authore Iona Sculteto Sprotta Silesio. Prostant Amstel. apud Petrum. Schenk et Gerard. Valk.]Dedication signed] Ionas Scultetus.

" " 90. Ducatus Breslanus sive Wratislaviensis. Joh. van den Aueele inv. et fecit. Prostant Amstelaedami apud Petrum Schenk et Gerardum Valk. Inset: Breslaw totius Silesiæ metropolis. The dedication is in english and is not signed. It reads, "To the right honourable s^r; George Cartwright bar. vice chamberline of the kings household.

" " 91. Ducatus Silesiæ Ligniciensis. Prostant Amstelaedami apud Pet. Schenk et Ger. Valk. Inset view: FVrstliche stadt Lignitz.

" " 92. Dvcatvs Silesiæ Schwidnicensis, authore Friduico Kuhnovio. Amstelo: apud P. Schenk et G. Valk.]Dedication signed] Petrum Schenk.

" " 93. Dvcatvs Silesiæ Grotganvs cum districtu episcopali Nissensi delineatore Iona Scvlteto, Silesio. Prostant Amstelaedami apud Petrum Schenk et Gerardum Valk. [Dedication signed] Iona Scvlteto.

" " 94. Comitatus Glatz. Authore Iona Sculteto. Prostant ap[ud] Petrum Schenk et Gerardum Valk.

" " 95. Tabula generalis marchionatus Moraviæ. Accuratè emensus hac mappa delineatos exhibet Ioh. Christoph. Müller. Editore Ioh. Bapt. Homanno Norimbergæ.

" " 96–97. Marchionatûs Moraviae circulus Olomucensis. Accuratè emensus hac mappa delineatum exhibet Io. Chr. Müller. Editore Ioh. Baptista Homann Norimbergæ.

At the foot of map no. 96, the following additional title appears, Circuli Olomucensis pars borealis. The main title is on map no. 97, with the following at top of map, Circuli Olomucensis pars australis.

" " 98–99. Marchionatus Moraviæ circulus Preroviensis. Hac mappa delineatum publicè exhibet Io. Chr. Müller. Editore Io. Baptista Homanno Norbergæ.

At the foot of map no. 98, the following additional appears, Circuli Preroviensis pars borealis. The following title appears at top of map no. 99, Circuli Preroviensis pars australis.

" " 100. Marchionatûs Moraviæ circulus Hradistiensis. Accurate emensus hac mappa delineatum exhibet Ioh. Christ. Müller. Editore Ioh. Baptista Homanno Noribergæ.

" " 101–102. Marchionatus Moraviæ circulus Brunnensis. Accuratè emensus hac mappa delineatum exhibet I. C. Müller. Editore Ioh. Baptista Homanno Noribergæ.

At foot of map no. 101, the following title appears: Circuli Brunnensis pars septentrionalis. The following title appears at top of map no. 102, Circuli Brunnensis pars meridionalis.

v. 2, no. 103. Marchionatus Moraviæ circuli Znoymensis et Iglaviensis. Accuratè emensus hâc mappâ delineatos exhibet Io. Chr. Müller. Editore Io. Baptista Homanno Noribergae.

" " 104. Moraviæ nova et post omnes priores accuratissima delineatio, auctore I. A. Comenio. per Nicolaum Visscher edita. Inset views: Polna.—Olmuts.—Brin.—Znaim. [Dedication signed] I. A. Comenius.

" " 105. Imperii circulus Bavaria. Denuò nunc exhibetur â Petro Schenk.

" " 106. Circulus Bavariæ. A Mathæo Seutter Augustiæ Vindelic.

" " 107. Bavariæ palatinatus vulgo die Ober-Pfaltz. Per Nicolaum Visscher Amst. Bat. Nunc apud Pet. Schenk iunior.

" " 108. Bavariæ pars superior. Per Nicolaum Visscher. Nunc apud Pet. Schenk iunior. Inset: Ut Superiorem Bavariae partem.

" " 109. Bavariæ pars inferior. Per Nicolaum Visscher Amst. Bat. Nunc apud Petrum Schenk.

" " 110–113. Sacri imperii romani circuli et electoratus Bavariæ.

Very finely engraved map on four sheets without author, but very similar to the maps of Nicolas Visscher. The various smaller divisions of Bavaria are ornamented through the map with small coats of arms. Map no. 111 contains the table of distances, and no. 113 contains a list of the number of cities, towns, monasteries, rivers, mountains, etc., which are shown.

" " 114. S. r. i. principtvs et archiepiscopatus Salisburgensis. Operâ Ioh. Bapt. Homann. Norimbergæ. Inset: Austria Salisburgensis.

Ornamented with portrait of "Franciscus Antonius archi- ep. Salisb.," to whom the map is dedicated, which surmounts a globe marked "Hierarchia Salisburgensi," surrounded by symbolical figures and coats of arms.

Contains "Erklärung der zeichen."

" " 115. Prospectus illustriores celeberrimæ archiepiscopalis urbis Salisburgensis præcipuorumque in ea magnificorum ac admirabilium tam sacrorum quam profanorum ædificiorum in ornamentum tabulæ geographicæ aeri incisi ac venum expositi a Matthæo Seuttero. Augusta Vind.

The plan of the city has extra title, "Die hoch fürstliche haupt und residentz stadt Saltzburg." There are ten views of buildings, each with separate title, several of which have explanatory lists.

v. 3, no. 1. Planiglobii terrestris cum utroq hemisphærio cælesti generalis exhibitio. Publice proponit Io. Bapt. Homann. Norimbergæ.

For description or this map see v. 2, no. 1, which is the same.

" " 2. Europa christiani orbis domina in sua imperia regna et status exacte divisa per Iohan Bapt. Homann Norimbergæ.

Same as v. 2, no. 2.

" " 3. S. imperium Romano-Germanicum oder Teutschland. Neulich entworffen und theils gezeichnet durch Iulium Reichelt . . . aber aussgeführt und aussgegeben durch Nicolaum Visscher zu Amsteldam. A. Hogeboom sculp. Nunc apud Petrum Schenk iunior.

Ottens, R.—Continued.

v. 3, no. 4. Imperium Romano- Germanicum. Ioh. Baptista Homanno Norimbergæ.
Same as v. 2, no. 18.

" " 5. Tabula geographica Europæ Austriacæ generalis. Edita à Ioh. Christophoro Homanno Noribergæ.
Dedicated to Charles VI, of Germany.
Map is ornamented elaborately with figures and shields. In the lower left hand corner a shaft is shown surmounted by a bust and entwined with a vine from which hang fifteen medalion portraits.

" " 6. Germania Austriaca. Auctore Io. Bapt. Homann Noribergæ.

" " 7. Maiestas Austriaca. Per Matthaeum Seutterum.

" " 8. Circuli Austriaci pars septentrionalis in qua archiducatu. Austriæ et ducatus Stiriæ. Per F. de Wit Amstelodami. Ex officina I. Córens et C. Mortier.

" " 9. Austriæ archiducatus pars inferior. Delineata per Nicol^m^ Visscher Amst. Bat. Nunc apud Petrum Schenk iunior.

" " 10. Viennense territorium ob res bellicas inter christianos et turos nuperrime editum per Nicolaum Visscher. Nunc apud Petrum Schenk junior.

" " 11. Prospect und grund-riss der kayserl. residenz stadt Wien. Ioh. Bapt. Homann in Nür[nberg] Inset view: Prospect der kayserl. residenz stadt Wien.
Map contains "Erklärung der zeichen."

" " 12. Ducatus Stiriæ novissima tabula. A Ioh. Bapti. Homanno Noribergæ. Inset view: Grätz.

" " 13. Circuli Austriaci pars occientalior. Per F. de Witt Amstelodami. Ex officina P. Mortier.

" " 14. Ducatus Carintiæ et Cariolæ. Per F. de Witt Amstelodami. Ex officina I. Córens et C. Mortier.

" " 15. Nova et accurata Carinthiæ ducatus.. Edita à Io. Bapt. Homanno. Norimbergæ. Inset views: Die stadt Clagenfurt.—Artige weis ehmaliger gewohnheit, einen ertz hertzog in Cärnthen einzusetzen.—Die strassen aus Cärnthen in Crain über und durch den berg Loibl.

" " 16. Carinthia ducatus. Per Matth. Seutter. Inset view: Clagenfurt.

" " 17. Tabula ducatus Carnioliæ. A Io. Bapt. Homanno. Noribergæs Inset: Der Czirknizer see.
View: Prospect der St. Laybach.

" " 18. Imp. Caes. Carolo VI. Avgvsto pio victori gentis svae sideri felicissimo chorographiam hanc exhibentem primar. regionvm Habspvrgicar sitvm positvmq. brevibvs exterarvm ditionvm intervallis vt permistvm et implicatvm ita variis tvrbis expositvm nec non vltvvm Imperii Germ. terminos perpetva transitvvm, obsidionvm hibernorvm coactionvm vexatione agitatos antiqvae fidei et invictae testes pietatis supplex dicat provincia Brisgoia. Avst. Ant. 1718. Ioh. Bapt. Homann edidit Noribergæ.
The following note at foot of map: "Alle stätt und dorffschafften, welche in dem rothen grund ligen, oder mit solcher farb umbfangen, seind Oesterreichisch.

v. 3, no. 19. Potentissimæ Helvetiorum reipublicæ. A Ioh. Baptista Ho manno Noribergæ.
Mountain view and interior showing cheese making in lower left hand corner.

" " 20. Same as map no. 19 with different coloring.

" " 21. La Suisse divisée en ses treze cantons, ses alliez & ses sujets- Par. H. Iaillot. Amsterdam, Pierre Mortier.
Latin title at top of map. Explanatory notes headed "Divi. sions géogaphiques de a Suisse." The coats of arms of the thirteen cantons and of eleven cities, also of nine divisions subject to the Swiss, are given on the margins.

" " 22. Carte de Suisse. Par Guillaume del Isle. Paris chez l'auteur, 1715.
The secondary title gives the thirteen cantons and allied divisions by name, with a small coat of arms of each appearing against the name in the title.
Explanatory notes headed "Advertissement".

" " 23–26. Nova Helvetiae tabula geographica illustrissimis et potentissimis cantonibus et rebuspublicis reformatæ religionis Tugurinae, Bernensi, Glaronensi, Basiliensi, Scaphusianae, Abbatis Cellamae. Dominis suis clementissimis humillime dictata a Ioh. Iacobo Scheuchzero Tigurino. Amstelædami ex officina Petri Schenkii.
An additional latin title appears at the top of the map on sheets nos. 23–24 giving the thirteen colonies by name and many lesser subdivisions. The whole map is elaborately ornamented with views of swiss scenery and legends, and illustrations of Swiss products. A descriptive list of these views appears on sheet no. 25. On sheet no. 24, a scroll upheld by a representation of "Father Time" is shown containing a list headed "Helvetiæ antiquæ geographicus index". The body of the map is further ornamented with small coats of arms of the various divisions. Sheet no. 26, has descriptive text. Listed in Hübner's Museum geographicum as published in 1712.

" " 27. Territory Basiliensis nova descriptio. Petrus Kærius cælavit. Amstelædami penes Gerardum Valk et Petrum Schenk.

" " 28. Zvrichgow et Basiliensis provincia. A vanden Broeck fecit. Amstelodami apud G. Valk et P. Schenk.

" " 29. Argow cum parte merid. Zvrichgow. Auctore Ger. Mercatore. Apud G. Valk et P. Schenk.

" " 30. Das Wiflispvrgergow. Gerardo Mercatore auctore. Apud G. Valk et P. Schenk.

" " 31. Carte de la souveraineté de Neuchatel et Vallangin dressée sur les mémoires du s^r. D. F. de Merveilleux . . . Rectifiéz par les observations de l'Académie royale des sciences. Dediée à messieur de la Vénérable classe et compagnie des pasteura du comté de Neuchâtel. Par leur très humble et très obéiss. serviteur De Merveilleux. Gravé par Liebaux le fils.
Explanatory text at the top and in the body of the map. List of devices in lower left hand corner of map.

Ottens, R.—Continued.

v. 3, no. 32. Lacvs Lemanni locorvmqve circvmiacentivm accvratissima descriptio. Auctore Iacobo Govlartio Genevensi. Amsterdam Pet. Schenk et Ger. Valk.
The following in small cartouche: "Benevole lectore, F. Franciam G. Genevam denotat.

" " 33. Alpinæ seu fœderatæ Rhætiæ subditarumque ei terrarum nova descriptio. Auctoribus Fortunato Sprechero à Berneck. Ac Phil Cluverio. Everardus Simonis Hamersveldt sculpsit. Amstelodami penes Gerardum Valk et Petrum Schenk.

" " 34. Nouvelle carte du pays de Grisons. Dressée sur les observations du Ph. Cluvere et du collonel Schmid de Gruenek. Johannes van Lugtenburg gesneden en door Jacob Keyzer gecorrigeert.
At head of map latin title reads: Rhæthia foederata cum subditis ei terris. Prostant Amstelædami apud R. Ottens, a°. 1724.

" " 35. Comitatus Burgundiæ. Per Nicol^m. Visscher. Amst. Bat. Nunc apud Petrum Schenk iunior.

" " 36. Circulus Suevicus. Edente Gerardô Valck.

" " 37. Partie septentrionale de la Souabe. Par G. De l'Isle. Paris chez l'auteur, 1704.

" " 38. Partie meridionale de la Souabe. Par Guillaume Del' Isle. Paris chez l'auteur, 1704.

" " 39–42. Totius S. R. I. circuli Suevici tabula chorographica T. Lamsvelt del. fc.

" " 43–51. Suevia universa IX. tabulis delineata, in quibus omnium, non solum ad circulum pertinentium episcopatuum, ducatuum, marchionatuum, principatuum, abbatiarum, comitatuum, dynastiarum, civitatum imperialium, ut et ordinis equestris, sed etiam omnium eidem inter: et adjacentium statuum territoria, urbes, oppida, monasteria, &. distincte et accuratessime reperiuntur; juxta recentissimam observationem exhibita â Iaques Michal. Sculpta à Matthæo Seuttero. August. Hubner's *Museum geographicum*, the preface of which is dated 1746, lists this map and notes it as an unusually fine one.

" " 52–53. Ducatus Würtenbergici. Per M. Iohannem Majer. Operâ Ioh. Baptistæ Homanni Noribergæ. Insets: Sylvæ Herciniæ pars superior, olim dicta Eremus Helvetiorum.—Views: Stuttgart.—Tübingen.
On the right and left margins of the map a series of 76 small coats of arms appear.

" " 54. Ducatus Wurtenbergensis. Per Nicolaum Visscher Amst. Bat. Nunc apud Pet. Schenk iun. G. v. Gouwen schulp.

" " 55. Nova et accurata territorii Vlmensis cum dominio Wainensi descriptio quam revidente e curante Iohanne Christophoro Lauterbach. In lucem edidit Ioh. Baptista Homann, Noribergæ. Inset: Grund und abriss der Ulmischen herrschafft zu Wain.

" " 56. Protoparchiæ Mindelhemensis. Io. Baptista Homann, Norimbergæ. Inset view: Die stadt Mindelheim.

v. 3, no. 57. Augspurg die haupt-stadt und zierde des Schwæbischen craisis verfertig't und verleg't von Matthæo Seutter daselbst. Gottfried Rogg del. Melchoir Rhein fecit. Inset view: Prospect dess hei röm. reich freÿen stadt Augspurg. Contains "Erklærung derer buchstaben u. ziffern."

" " 58. Accurata recens delineata ichnographia celeberrimæ liberæ imperii civitatis ac Sveviæ metropolis Augustæ Vindelicorum, cura et sumtibus Matth. Seutteri. Augustani. Ioh. Thomas Krauss architectus et perspectivicus.
Title also in german. At foot of map, explanatory list in latin and german.

" " 59. Vera totius marchionatus Badensis et Hochbergensis. Amstelædami apud Gerardum Valk et Petrum Schenk.
Contains a diagram and table headed, "Exemplum seu tabula geomrtricæ, arithmeticæ et mechanicæ operationis. Joan Morell et Daniel Beüch Ravenspurgani fecerunt."

" " 60. Duplicate of no. 18.

" " 61. Superioris et inferioris Rheni Mosæ & Mosellæ. Per Abrahamum Allard Amstelo-Batavum. Insets: Naarden.—Koblens.—Namur.—Trarbach.—Saar-Louis.—Fort Louis.—Bonn.—Maintz.—Frankfort.—Philipsburg.—Landaw.—Strasburg.
Title in dutch: Tooneel des oorlogs aan de Rhyn Moesel Maas Saar &c. uitgegeven door Abr. Allard. This title also in french.

" " 62. Pars summa. seu australis Superioris Rheni circuli. Per Gerardum Valk Amstel.

" " 63. Generalis Lotharingiæ. Auctore F. de Witt Amstelodami. Se vend à Amsterdam chez Pierre Mortier.

" " 64–69. Les estats du duc de Lorraine où sont les duchez de Lorraine et de Bar. Le temporel des eveschez de Metz, Toul et Verdun. Hubert Jaillot. 1705.
General title on second sheet,—in this atlas, no. 65. Each sheet has separate title as follows: 1. Le Verdunois. 1704.—2. Le pays Messin.—3. Le Toulois, 1704.—4. Partie meridionale du temporel de l'evesché de Metz, 1704.—5. Partie du balliage de Vosge, 1704.—6. Les prevotez, offices, senéchaussée et comté, qui font partie des balliages de Vosge, 1704.

" " 70. Totius Alsatiæ. Per Nicolaum Visscher Amst. Bat. P. Tideman del. G. v. Gouwen sculp.

" " 71. Landgraviatus Alsatiae tam superioris quam inferi[-] Editore Ioh. Baptista Homanno Noribergæ.

" " 72. Superioris Alsatiæ nec non Brisigaviæ et Suntgaviæ geographica tabula. Ex conatibus Nicolai Visscher. Nunc apud Petrum Schenk iun.

" " 73. Landgraviatus Alsatiæ inferioris novissima tabula. Per Nicoluam Visscher. Nunc apud Petrum Schenk iunior.

" " 74. Argentorati territorium, vulgo Strasburger gebiet. Auctore Carolo Allard. Amstelo Batavo.

" " 75. S. r. i. pars septentrionalior superioris circuli Rhenani. Auctore F. de Witt Amstelodami ex officina I. Cóvens & C. Mortier.

" " 76. Pars altera seu borealis circuli Rhenani vulgo qui superior. Per Gerardum Valk.

Ottens, R.—Continued.

v. 3, no. 77. Hassia lantgraviatus. Opera Gerardi Valk. Insets: Land gr. Hessen Rheinfeltz.—Land grafs Hessen Darmstat.

" " 78. Waldeck comitatvs. Prostant Amstelaedami apud Petrum Schenk et Gerardum Valk.

" " 79. Territorivm abbatiæ Heresfeldensis. Prostant Amstel. apud Pet. Schenk et G. Valk.

" " 80. S. r. i. principatus Fuldensis in Buchonia. A Ioh. Baptista Homanno Noribergæ.

" " 81. S. r. imp. comitatus Hanau. Per Fr. Zollmannum. Curante Ioh. Chr. Homanno Noribergæ, 1728. R. A. Schneider sculps. Fürth. Inset: Prospect der stadt Hanau.
Explanatory text in upper right hand corner.

" " 82. Nassovia principatus. Delineatus à Joh. Jac. Stetter. Excudit Nic. Visscheri vidua Amstelodami.

" " 83. Abbildung der weit- berümten keyserlichen -frey-reychs-wahl- und handel-stat Franckfurt am Mayn mit ihrem gebiet. Durch Nicolaus Visscher in Amsterdam. Nunc apud Petrum Schenk iunior.

" " 84. Circulus electorum Rheni sive Rhenanus inferior. Per F. de Wit. Amstelodami ex officina I. Cóvens et Mortier.

" " 85. Exactissima tabula sedis balli Palatinatus ad Rhenum. Per Nic. Visscher Am[!] nc [!] apud P. Schenk iunior.

" " 86. Electoratus et Palatinatus Rheni. Per F. de Wit. Amstelodami ex officina P. Mortier.

" " 87. Moguntini archiepiscopat' et electoratus. Per Nic. Visscher Amst. Bat. Nunc apud Petr. Schenk iunior.

" " 88. Archiepiscopatus ac electoratus Trevirensis ditio. Per Nicolaum Visscher Amst. Bat. Nunc apud Petr. Schenk iunior. G. v. Gouwen schulp.

" " 89. Novissima et accuratissima archiepiscopatus et electoratus Coloniensis ducatuum Iuliacensis et Montensis et Meursuæ comitatus. Per F. de Witt Amstelodami.

" " 90. Regionum Coloniense electoratu. Nunc apud Petr. Schenk iunior. Amstelaedami. Per Nicolaum Visscher.

" " 91. Descriptio agri civitatis Coloniensis.

" " 92. Circulus Westphalicus. Per Ger. et Leon. Valk.

" " 93. S. r. i. circulus Westphalicus. Editore et correctore F. de Witt Amstelodami. Ex officina P. Mortier.

" " 94. Frisia orientalis. Amstelodami Carolus Allard excudit.
Additional title at top of map: Nova tabula totius Frisiæ orientalis emendata auct. C. Allard.

" " 95. Oost-Frise, ou le comté d' Embden. Par le s^r^. Sanson, 1696.

" " 96. Oldenbvrg comitatvs. Prostant Amstelaedami apud Petrum Schenk et Gerardum Valk. Auctore Joanne vanden Avele.

" " 97. Monasteriensis episcopatvs. Sumptibus Gerardi Valk et Pertus Schenk.

" " 98. Basse partie de l'évesché de Munster, et le comté de Benthem. Par le s^r^. Sanson. Amsterdam chez Pierre Mortier.

" " 99. Haute partie de l'évesché de Munster. Dressé. par le s. Sanson. Paris chez H. Jaillot.

" " 100. Comitatvs Bentheim et Steinfvrt. Auctore Ioanne Westenberg. Prostant Amstelaedami apud Petrum Schenk et Gerardum Valk.

v. 3, no. 101. Osnabrvgensis episcopatvs. Auctore Ioanne Gigante Prostant Amstelaedami apud Petrum Schenk et Gerardum Valk. Inset view: Osenbrugge.—Map: Districtvs Reckengergensis. [Dedication signed] Ioannes Gigas.

" " 102. Episcopatvs Paderbornensis descriptio nova Ioanne Gigante, auctore. Prostant Amstelaedami apud Petrum Schenk et Gerardum Valk.

" " 103. Nova ducatus Westphaliæ. 1706.
Explanatory text in upper right hand corner of map.

" " 104. Celssissimo potentissimo invictissimoq, principi Frederico Guiljelmo II. Hanc exactissimam Cliviæ ducatus et Marchiæ comitatus tabulam humillime offert auctor Fredericus de Wit Amstelodami ex officina I. Cóvens & C. Mortier.

" " 105. Le duché de Cleves, la seigneurie de Ravenstein, et le comté de Meurs. Par le s^r^. Sanson. A Paris, chez H. Jaillot. Se vend à Amsterdam chez Iean Cóvens et Corneille Mortier.

" " 106. Illustrissimo cellissimoq, principi Guiljemo Henrico. Hanc comitatus Meursensis. Accuratam tabulam humillime offert A. von Heurdt.

" " 107. Le comté de la Marck. Par le s^r^. Sanson. Paris chez Hubert Iaillot, 1692.

" " 108. Novissima et accuratissima archiepiscopatus et electoratis Coloniensis ducatuum Iuliacensis et Montensis et Meursiae comitatus. Per F. de Witt Amstelodami. Ex officina P. Mortier.

" " 109. Le duché de Berg, le comté de Homberg, les seigneuries de Hardenberg et de Wildenborg. Par le s^r^. Sanson. Paris ches H. Jaillot, 1692.

" " 110. Le duché de Iuliers. l' abbaye de S^t^. Cornelis Munster, la baronie de Wickrad, et la ville impériale d'Aix la Chapelle. Par le s^r^. Sanson. Paris chez H. Jaillot, 1696.

" " 111. Episcopatus et principatus Leodiensis et Namurcensis comitatus. Auctore F. de Witt. Amstelodami.

" " 112. Leodiensis episcopatus pars septentrionalis. Per Nicolaum Visscher Amst. Bat.

" " 113. Leodiensis episcopatus pars media. Per Nicolaum Visscher Amst. Bat. Nunc apud Petrum Schenk iunior.

" " 114. Tractus inter Sabim et Mosam. Per Nicolaum Visscher Amst. Bat. Nunc apud Petrum Schenk iunior.

v. 4, no. 1. Nova orbis terraquei tabula accuratissime delineata. Leide chez Pierre vander Aa.
French title, Mappe-monde ou description générale du globe terrestre et aquatique.

" " 2. L'Europe selon les nouvelles observations de mess^r^. de l' Academie des sciences, etc. Leide chez vander Aa.
An additional title at the top of map.

" " 3. Neu-vermehte post-charte durch gantz Teutschland. Von herrn Ioh. Peter Nell. In kupfer gebracht und verlegt Iohann Baptist Homann in Nürnberg [Dedication signed] Ioannes Pet. Nell.
Latin title at top of map.

Ottens, R.—Continued.

v. 4, no. 4. Carta noua accurata del passagio et strada dalli Paesi Bassi per via de Allemagna per Italia et per via di Paesi suizeri à Geneua, Lione et Roma per seruizio delli Marchanti et viagianti in Geñale ad instanza delli S̃scherer et di Momforti speditori delli Marchantie in Bregens, dato in luce da Frederico de Wit di Amsterdam l'anno 1671.
Explanatory text at top of map.

" " 5. L'empire d'Allemagne. H. Jaillot.
Latin title at top of map.

" " 6. Germaniæ inferioris XVII provinciarum accuratissima tabula. Nuperrime edita per Nicolaum Visscher. [Dedicatiòn signed] Nicolaus Visscher.

" " 7. Belgium. Venundantur â Gerardo et Leonardo Valk.

" " 7a. Tafel vande XVII Nederlandze provincien. Door C. Specht. te Amsterdam by R. & J. Ottens.
Inset map: De XVII provincien.
This table and the Sanson table following are of interest in connection with the various maps of the Netherlands shown in this volume.

" " 7b. Tables des divisions des dix-sept provinces des Pays-Bas. Par le s^r. Sanson.

" " 8. Belgium foederatum. Per Nicolaum Visscher. Nunc apud P. Schenk iunior.

" " 9. Belgica foederata. Venalis habent Gerardus et Leonardus Valk.

" " 10. Exactissima Belgii fœderatii tabula cum annexis divisa in provincias. Per Casparum Specht Amsterdam by R. & I. Ottens.
Contains coats of arms and an explanatory table on a large scroll. Table headed: Land caerte van't Verenigde Nederland met'tgene daer onderhoort verdeelt in syn provincien.

" " 11. Dominii Groningæ nec non maximæ partis Drentiæ. Per Nicolaum Visscher. Nunc apud Pet. Schenk iun. Inset: Caerte vande Groeninger eylanden ende Watte.

" " 12. Corectissima nec non novissima dominii et provinciæ Groningæ et Omlandiæ. Per Fredericum de Witt Amstelodami. Ex officina I. Cóvens et C. Mortier.

" " 13. Transisalania provincia; vulgo Over-yssel. Auctor. N. ten-Have. Edita vero per Nicolaum Visscher. Nunc apud Pet: Schenk iunior.

" " 14. Drentia comitatvs. Transisulaniæ tabula II. Auctore Cornelio Pynacker. A. van den Broeck fecit. Prostant Amstelodami apud Pet. Schenk et Ger. Valk.

" " 15. Frisiæ dominium vernacule Friesland, verdeeld in de hoofddeelen van Oostergoo, Westergoo en Sevenwolde als ook der XI steden zynde noch onderscheiden in XXX grietenijen. Naar de niewst afineetingen getekend en uitgegeven door Francois Halma. Te Leeuwarden, 1718. Inset: Friesse eilanden met de omleggende zee plaaten enz.
A curious column, surmounted by the two heads of Janus in the lower left hand corner is marked, "Steenen man, bÿ Harlingen, op de zeedÿk." This is the first map of the Schotanus à Sterringa and Alting, *Uitbeelding der heerlijkheit*

Friesland. It is preceded by the title, a large engraved title signed "Joh. Hilarides invenieb. T. Folkema sculp. 1717," the three plates showing the coats of arms, and the preliminary leaves, and is followed by the other 38 maps which compose this atlas. A copy of the separate atlas with uncolored maps is in the Library of Congress. See. v. 1, title. 3088.

v. 4, no. 16. [Duplicate of no. 15]

" " 17. Leeuwerders deel de erste grietenije van Ooster goo. Door B. Schotanus a Sterringa. 1695. Vermeerdert uitgegeeven door François Halma, 1718.

" " 18. Ferwerda deel de tweede grietenije van Ooster goo. Weesentlyk vertoont door B. Schotanus à Sterringa. Vermeerdert uitgegeeven door François Halma, 1718.

" " 19. Donger deel west zyde der Pasens. De derde grietenije van Ooster goo. Afgemeeten en uytgegeven door B. Schotanus a Sterringa. Vermeerdert uitgegeeven door François Halma, 1718.

" " 20. Donger deel oost zyde der Pasens. De vierde grietenije van Ooster goo. Afgemeeten en op't papier gebracht door B. Schotanus à Sterringa 1690 en 1691. Vermeerdert uitgegeeven door François Halma, 1718.

" " 21. Kollumer land en het Nieuw Kruys land de vÿfde gritenije van Ooster goo. Vermeerdert uitgegeeven door François Halma, 1718.

" " 22. Achtker spelen de sefde grietenije van Ooster-goo. Afgemeeten en op't papier gebracht door B. Schotanus à Sterringa. Vermeerdert uitgegeeven door François Halma, 1718.

" " 23. Dantuma- deel de zevende grietenije van Ooster-goo. Weesentlyk vertoont door B. Schotanus à Sterringa. Vermeeder uitgegeeven door F. Halma, 1718.

" " 24. Tjietjerkstera deel de achtste grietenije van Ooster-goo. Afgemeeten door B. Schotanus à Sterringa. Vermeerdert uitgegeeven door François Halma, 1718.

" " 25. Smallingerland de negende grietenije van Oostergo. Wesentlyk afgebeeldt door B. Schotanus à Sterringa. Vermeerdert uitgegeeven door François Halma, 1718.

" " 26. Idaardera deel de tiende grietenije van Ooster goo. Door B. Schotanus à Sterringa aº 1694. Vermeerdert uitgegeeven door François Halma, 1718.

" " 27. Rauwerderhem de elfde grietenije van Ooster goo. Weesentlyk vertoont en afgemeeten door Bernardus à Schotanus à Sterringa. Vermeerdert uitgegeeven door François Halma, 1718.

" " 28. Menalduma deel. Wesentlyk vertoont door B. Schotanus à Sterringa. Vermeerdert uitgegeeven door F. Halma, 1718.

" " 29. De grietenije van Franeker deel de tweede van Wester goo. Weesentlyk vertoont door B. Schotanus à Sterringa 1693. Vermeerdert uitgegeeven door F. Halma, 1718.

" " 30. De. grietenije van Barra deel. Wesentlyk vertoont door B. Schotanus à Sterringa. Vermeerdert uitgegeeven door F. Halma, 1718.

Ottens, R.—Continued.

v. 4, no. 31. Baardera deel de vierde grietenije van Wester goo. Afgemeeten en wesentlyk vertoont door Bernhardus Schotanus à Sterringa. Vermeerdert uitgegeeven door F. Halma, 1718.

" " 32. Hennaardera deel de vyfde grietenije van Wester goo. Naukeurig afgemeeten en uytgebeelt door Bernhardus Schotanus à Sterringa. Vermeerdert uitgegeeven door François Halma, 1718.

" " 33. Wonzera deel de seste grietenije van Wester goo. Vermeerdert uitgegeeven door F. Halma, 1718.

" " 34. Wijmbritsera deel de zevende grietenije van Wester goo. Afgemeeten door B. Schotanus à Sterringa 1687 en 9. Vermeerdert uitgegeeven door François Halma, 1718.

" " 35. Hemelumer oude vaart en de Noort Woude, de achtste grietenije van Wester goo. Wesentlÿk vertoont door B. Schotanus à Sterringa. Nu vermeerdert uitgegeeven. Door François Halma, 1718.

" " 36. Hetbild de negende en laatste grietenije van Wester goo. Vermeerdert uitgegeeven door François Halma, 1718.

" " 37. Utingera deel d' eerste grietenije van de Zevenwolden. Door B. Schotanus à Sterringa 1693. Vermeerdert uitgegeeven door François Halma, 1718.

" " 38. De grietenije van Aengwerden de tweede van de Zevenwolden. Weesentlyk vertoont door B. Schotanus à Sterringa. Vermeerderd uitgegeeven François Halma, 1718.

" " 39. Donia Werstal de derde grietenije van de Zevenwolden. Weesentlyk afgebeelt door B. S. à Sterringa. Vermeedert uitgegeeven door François Halma, 1718.

" " 40. Haskerland de vierde grietenije van de Zevenwolden. Afgemeeten en weesentlyk afgebeelt door B. Schotanus à Sterringa 1685 . . . Vermeerderd uitgegeeven door Franç. Halma, 1718.

" " 41. Schooterlandt de vÿfde grietenije van de Sevenwolden. Door B. Schotanus à Sterringa. Vermeerdert uitgegeeven door François Halma, 1718.

" " 42. Lemsterland de sefte grietenije der Zevenwolden. Door B. Schotanus à Sterringa. Vermeerdert uitgegeeven door. François Halma, 1718.

" " 43. Gaasterland de zevende grietenije van de Zevenwolden. Afgemeten en vertoont door B. Schotanus à Sterringa, 1690 en 91. Vermeerdert uitgegeeven door François Halma, 1718.

" " 44. Opsterlandt de achtste grietenije van de Zevenwolden. Weesentlyk vertoont . . . 1693. Vermeerdert uitgegeeven door F. Halma, 1718. [Dedication signed by] B. Schotanus à Sterringa.

" " 45. Stellingwerf Oost- eynde de negende grietenije van de Sevenwolden. Weesentlyk afgebeelt. A. Ch. 1685 door Bernhardus Schotanus à Sterringa. Vermeerd uitgegeeven François Halma 1718.

" " 46. Stellingwerf west einde, de tiende en laaste grietenije van de Zevenwold. Weesentlyk vertoont. Door B. Schotanus à Sterringa. Vermeerderd uitgegeeven door François Halma, 1718.

v. 4, no. 47. Typus Frisiæ veteris. Disponente Bernhardo Schotano à Sterringa. Franciscus Halma excudebat. 1718. Inset [Sketch of plant]: Hodiè Belgicè sive botanicis water patich Hydrolapathum.
This with the set of 7 maps by Alting which follow belonging to the Schotanus à Sterringa and Alting atlas, have border text. The number of the map appears on the 7 maps at the head of the text.

" " 48. i. Descriptio veteris Agri Batavi et Frisii, omnisque regionis quæ hodie est in dicione vii Foederatorvm cis et ultra Rhenvm. Auctore Mensone Alting.

" " 49. ii. Descriptio Agri Frisii antiqvi. Auctore Mensone Alting.

" " 50. iii. Summaria descriptio Fresiae vniversae. Auctore Mensone Alting. Gerard. de Broen fecit Amstelodami.

" " 51. iiii. Descriptio Frisiae sub Francorum reditum. Auctore Mensone Alting. Ger. de Broen fec. Amstel.

" " 52. v. Descriptio Frisiae Liberae inter Kennemum et Amisiam. Auctore Mensone Alting. Ger. de Broen fecit Amstelodami.

" " 53. vi. Pars i. Frisiae Liberae quae Westfresia. Auctore Mensone Alting. J. Mulder in. et fc. Ger. de Broen fecit Amstelodami.

" " 54. vii. Pars ii. et iii. Frisiae Libera. Auctore Mensone Alting. Ger. de Broen fecit Amstelodami.

" " 55. Ducatus Geldriæ. Auctore Joachimo Ottens. Amstelodamensi.

" " 56. Ducatus Geldriæ tetrachia Arnhemiensis sive Velavia. Amstelodami ex officina P. Mortier. Gedruckt. By F. de Wit.

" " 57. Comitatus Zutphaniæ. Per F. de Witt. Amstelodami apud I. Cóvens et C. Mortier.

" " 58. Tetrachia ducatus Geldriæ Neomagensis. Per F. de Wit. Amstelodami apud I. Cóvens et C. Mortier.

" " 59. Tetrachia ducatus Geldriæ Ruremondana sive Hispanica. Per F. de Wit. Amstelodami apud P. Mortier.

" " 60. Fossa Eugeniana quæ a Rheno ad Mosam duci cœpta est, anno 1627 ductu comitis Henrici vanden Berge. Apud Janssonio-Waesbergios, Mosem Pitt et Stephanum Swart.

" " 61. Tabula nova provinciæ Ultrajectinæ. Edidit Nicol. Visscher. Nunc apud Petrum Schenk junior. L. van Anse schulp.

" " 62. Ultrajecti ejusdemque territorii, delineatio geometrica ex officina C. Specht nunc apud Ioac. Ottens. [Additional title], Caerte vande vryheyd der stadt Utrecht. Volgens decisie van den iare 1539.

" ' 63. Nieuwe kaart van Mynden en de 2 Loosdrechten. Door Nicolaas Visscher. Nunc apud P. Schenk iun. [Dedication signed] de weduwe van Nicolaus Visscher.

" " 64. Kaart van't graafschap Holland. te Amsterdam by de wed. I. Ottens en zoone. Inset: Kaart van Texel, Vlieland, de zanden en dieptens der Zuiderzee. [Additional title at top of map]: Hollandiæ comitatus una cum Ultrajectino dominio nec non maximis partibus Geldriae ducatus, per C. Specht.

" " 65. Kennemaria et Westfrisia vulgo et vernaculé Noord-Holland per Nicolaum Visscher Amst. Bat. Nunc apud Petrum Schenk iunior. [Dedication signed] Nicolaus Visscher.

Ottens, R.—Continued.

v. 4, no. 66. Hollandiæ septentrionalis & Frisiæ occidentalis accuratissima delineatio autore Amstelodami Ioachim Ottens. Inset: Insulæ adjacentes Texel, Vlieland, & Schelling.

" " 67. Rhenolandia, Amstelandia et circumjacentia aliquot territoria. Per Nicolaum Visscher. Nunc apud Petrum Schenk iunior. [Dedication signed by] Nicolaus Visscher.

" " 68–69. Afbeeldinge van de wydvermaarde en beroemde koopstad Amsteldam met d' omleggende landen gemeten en getekent door Gerrit Drogenham, landmeter, in t koper gebragt door Daniel Stopendaal en uitgegeven door Nicolaus Visser. Amsterdam by I. Ottens.

" " 70. Amsteldam. Inset view: [Amsterdam and water front]. [Dedication signed] J. de Ram.
Explanatory lists in both upper corners of the map.

" " 71. Accuratergrundis und prospect der weltberuhmter Hollandischen haupt und handels-stadt Amsterdam edirt von Iohann Baptist Homanns. In Nurnberg 1727. Inset view: Prospect der vortrefflichen kauff und handels stadt Amsterdam.
Explanatory lists in both upper corners of map.

" " 72. Deze nieuwe kaart van Gooilandt word met schuldige eerbiedigheidt aan den wel ed. gestr. heere den heere en m^r^. Henrick Bicker schepen der stadt Amsterdam. Opgedragen door. Reinier & Iosua Ottens. H. Post fecit.
Explanatory list headed: "Groote der landen Rynlandische maat."
Very curious map with a section showing the estates of m^r^. Henrick Bicker and his neighbors with their names attached, the whole called s'Gravenland.

" " 73. Nieuwe kaart van Myden, en de 2 Loosdrechten midtsgaders van s'Gravenland, nevens het gerecht van Breukelen, en Loendersloot. Uytgegeven door Nicolaas Visscher. Nunc apud P. Schenk iun. [Dedication signed] de weduwe van Nicolaus Visscher.
Neither this map nor the preceding Ottens map are dated but they are of about the same date as the names on the estates in the section called s'Gravenland are practically the same. On this map the estates along the Vechte and other streams are indicated by name also.

" " 74. Delflandia, Schielandia et circumjacentes insulæ ut Voorna, Overflackea, Goerea, Yselmonda et aliæ ex conatibus geographicis Nicolai Visscher Amst. Bat. Nunc apud Petrum Schenk iunior.

" " 75. Nieuwe platte grond van s'Gravenhage met de publicque gebouwen opgedraagen aan de edele achtbare heere burgemeesters en regeerds der selve stede. Door haar edelheÿts onderdanigste en gehoorsaamste dienaresse Anna Beek. J. Rouset delin.
A very elaborate cartouche contains a list headed: Namen der edele heeren van de magistraat. This cartouche and the one containing the title are ornamented with the coats of arms of the men mentioned in the list.
Contains explanatory list headed: Aan der cyffer letters.

v. 4, no. 76. Hollandiæ pars meridionalior, vulgo Zuyd-Holland. Auctore Nic. Visscher. Nunc apud P. Schenk jun.

" " 77. Comitatvs Zelandiæ. Per Nicolaum Visscher. Nunc apud Pet. Schenk. [Dedication signed] N. Visscher.

" " 78. Zelandiæ comitatus novissima tabvla, delineata per Nicolaum I. Visscherum nunc autem emendata et aucta per R. Ottens. [In a small cartouche an additional title appears,] Nieuwe kaart van't eiland Schouwen en Duiveland. te Amsterdam by de wed. Ottens en zoone.

" " 79. Nieuwe kaart van het eiland Overflakke. te Amsterdam by wed. Ottens en zoone.

" " 80. Nieuwe kaart van het eiland Walcheren. te Amsterdam by wed. Ottens en zoone.

" " 81. Nieuwe kaart van de eilanden Zuid en Noord Beveland Wolfersdyk en de heerlykheden van Vosmaar, Tolen Poortvliet-Martensdyk. te Amsterdam by de wed. Ottens en zoone.

" " 82. t'Meerderdeel van t'Oost-Vrye in Vlaenderen. t'Amsterdam gedruckt by de wed. Ottens en zoone. [Dedication signed] Jac. Mogge.

" " 83. t Meerder deel van staat Vlaenderen. te Amst. by d'wed. Ottens en zoone.

" " 84. Belgii pars meridionalis cum occidentalibus Germaniæ et septentrionalibus Franciæ confiniis. Per Nicolaum Visscher Amst. Bat. Nunc apud P. Schenk.

" " 85. Novissima et accuratissima decem austriacarum in Belgio provinciarum tabula. Auctore Joachimo Ottens, Amstelodami. [Dedication to Charles VI, signed] Joachim Ottens.

" " 86. Belgii regii accuratissima tabula auctore Fredricum de Witt. Ex officina R. & J. Ottens.

" " 87. La partie méridionale des Pays Bays, connuë sous le nom de Flandre diuisée en plusieurs prouinces qui sont possédées par les roys de France et d'Espagne et par les Estats Généraux des Provinces Vnies ou Hollandois par le P. Coronelli. Corigée et augmentée par le s. de Tillemont. Dédiée à son altesse royale monseigneur le duc d'Orléans. Par. I. B. Nolin. A Paris chez I. B. Nolin, 1701.

This map has been cut to the margin and mounted on an extra sheet of paper. Many of the more important places on the map have not only the french form of the name but the latin and in some cases have the old latin form in addition.

" " 88. Carte du comté Flandre. Par Guillaume de l'Isle. Paris chez l'auteur, 1704. Gravé par Lièbaus, le fils. Se trouve à Amsterdam chez L. Renard.

This map has also been cut to the margin and mounted on an extra sheet of paper.

" " 89. Novissima et accuratissima comitatus Flandriæ. F. de Witt. Ex officina I. Cóvens & Mortier.

" " 90. Flandriæ comitatus. Per Nicol^{m}. Visscher Amst. Bat. Nunc apud Petrum Schenk iunior. G. v. Gouwen schulp.

" " 91. Flandriæ comitatus pars Batava. Per Nicolaum Visscher. Nunc apud Petrum Schenk iunior.

" " 92. Niewe kaerte van t landt van Waes ende Hulster ambacht. Per Nicolaum Visscher. Nunc apud Pet. Schenk iunior. C. J. Visscher excudebat.

Ottens, R.—Continued.

v. 4, no. 93. Flandriæ comitatus pars septentrionalis. Per Nicol. Visscher Amst. Bat. Nunc apud Petrum Schenk iunior.

" " 94. Nouveau plan de la ville d'Ostende ville forte du comté de Flandre célèbre par l'octroy de l'empereur pour la navigation aux Indes Orientales. A Amsterdam chez R. & J. Ottens.

An uncolored map. Places indicated by numbers and an explanatory list appears on the map.

" " 95. Flandriæ comitatus pars orientalis. Per Nicolaum Visscher Amst. Bat. Nunc apud Petrum Schenk iunior.

" " 96. Flandriæ comitatus pars media. Per Nicol. Visscher Amst. Bat. Nunc apud Petrum Schenk iunior.

" " 97. Flandriæ comitatus pars australis. Per Nicolaum Visscher. Amst. Bat.

" " 98. Flandriæ comitatus pars occidentalis. Per Nicolaum Visscher Amst. Bat. Nunc apud Petrum Schenk iunior.

" " 99. Brabantiæ ducatus cum adjacentibus provinciis per Nicolaum Visscher Amst. Bat. Nunc apud P. Schenk jun.

" " 100. Brabantiæ Batavæ pars orientalis. Per Nicolaum Visscher Amst. Bat. Nunc apud Petrum Schenk iunior.

" " 101. Brabantiæ Bataviæ pars occidentalis. Per Nicolaum Visscher Amst. Bat. Nunc apud Petrum Schenk iunior.

" " 102. Tetrarchiæ Antverpiensis pars meridionalis. Per Nicolaum Visscher Amst. Bat. Nunc apud Petr. Schenk iunior.

" " 103. Marchionatus Sacri Romani Imperii. Inset map: Tabella hæc in gratiam spectatorum addita ut Ostium Scaldis videant simul etiam propugnacula, aggeres, terras que à mare absorptas.—[Three views]: Antwerpen. [Dedication signed] Nicolaus Jansenius Piscator.

Beside the views of Antwerp a number of views of buildings border the map. These include: Templi d. Virginis Maryæ vers delineatio.—De Burse gesticht anno 1531.—Domus senatoria Antwerpiensis.—Domus Hansæ Teutonicæ.

Contains explanatory text.

" " 104. Mechlinia dominium et Aerschot ducatus. Auctore Nicolao Visscher.

" " 105. Bruxellensis tetrarchia. Per Nicolaum Visscher Amst. Bat. Nunc apud Petr. Schenk iun.

" " 106. Lovaniensis tetrarchia una cum Arscotano ducatu. Per Nic. Visscher Amst. Bat. Nunc apud Petrum Schenk iunior.

" " 107. Le Limbourg. Par le s[r]. Sanson. Paris chez H. Jaillot.

" " 108. Ducatus Lutzenburgi. Per Nic. Visscher. Nunc apud Petr. Schenk iun.

" " 109. Les courans des rivières de Meuse de Mozel et de la Sar où se trouvent le Luxembourg et l'archevêché de Treves. Dressé par I. B. Nolin.

Map has been cut to the border and mounted on an extra sheet of paper.

" " 110. Le comté de Namur. Par F. de Witt.—Comitatus Namurcensis. Per F. de Witt nunc apud I. Ottens.

v. 4, no. 111. Le comté de Haynaut, à l'usage de monseigneur le duc de Bourgogne. A Paris chez H. Jaillot. Se vend à Amsterdam chez Pierre Mortier. [Latin title at top of page.]
Comitatus Hannoniæ et archiepiscopatus Cameracensis ad usum serenissimi Burgundiæ ducis.

" " 112. Correctissima descriptio Hannoniæ comitatus. Per F. de Witt. Amstelodami ex officina P. Mortier.

" " 113. Carte d'Artois et des environs. Par G. de l'Isle. Amsterdam chez Pierre Mortier.
Additional french title on upper margin of map.

" " 114. Comitatus Artesiæ et Flandriæ meridionalis et regionum circumjacentium nova descriptio ex tabulis G. de l'Isle, E. H. Fricx etc. excerpta per F. de Witt Amstelodami.—Nouvelle description du comté d'Artois de Flandre méridionale et des environs. Tirée des cartes de G. de l'Isle, E. H. Fricx, et des autres per F. de Witt à Amsterdam.

" " 115. Carte particulière d'une partie d'Angleterre, se vend à Amsterdam. Corrigée d'un grande nombre des fautes, sur la copie de Bruxelles chez Eugene Henry Fricx, cette carte contient 24 feuilles et se trouvent chez I. Cóvens et C. Mortier. Deur fecit.
The original maps by Fricx, from which this and the following twenty three maps were taken, were published from 1706 to 1712, except the one showing the environs of Luxembourg which was not engraved until 1727. With the exception of this one, the original engravings of the rest appeared in Fricx's *Tables des cartes des Pays-Bas et des frontières de France. 1712.* See v. 3, no. 4049. The editions of the maps numbered from 1 to 24, which appear in this Ottens atlas, were reissued by Cóvens and Mortier, and many of them appear also in the fourth volume of their *Atlas nouveau.* [*1683–1761*]
The maps which show the coast are profusely illustrated with shipping.

" " 116. 2. Carte particulière d'une partie d'Angleterre. Amsterdam chez I. Cóvens et Mortier. Sur la copie de Bruxelles par E. H. Fricx. Deur fecit.

" " 117. Le Canal et partie de la France. Amsterdam chez I. Cóvens et C. Mortier. Sur la copie de Bruxelles par E. H. Fricx.

" " 118. La mer du Nord. Amsterdam chez I. Cóvens et C. Mortier sur la copie de Bruxelles par E. H. Fricx.

" " 119. Carte particulière des environs de Dunkerque, Bergues, Furnes, Gravelines, Calais, et autres. Se vend chez I. Cóvens et C. Mortier, à Amsterdam sur la copie de Bruxelles chez E. H. Fricx.

" " 120. Carte particulière des environs d'Arthois du Boulenois. Se vend à Amsterdam chez I. Cóvens et C. Mortier, sur la copie de Bruxelles par E. H. Fricx.

" " 121. Carte particulière des environs de Bruges, Ostende, Damme, l'Ecluse et autres. Se vend chez Cóvens et Mortier, à Amsterdam sur la copie de Bruxelles chez Eugene Henry Fricx nouvellement corrigée.

114882°—19——7

Ottens, R.—Continued.

v. 4, no. 122. Carte particulière des environs de Menin, Courtray, Ypre, Dixmude, et Deynse. Se vend chez I. Cóvens et C. Mortier. Amsterdam, sur la copie de Bruxelles chez E. H. Fricx.

" " 123. Carte particulière des environs de Lille, Tournay, Valenciennes, Bouchain, Douay, Arras, Bethune. Se vend à Amsterdam chez Cóvens et Mortier, sur la copie de Bruxelles par E. H. Fricx.

" " 124. Carte particulière des environs d'Anvers, Gand, Hulst, et de tout le Pays de Waes, et la marquisat du S^t. Empire. Se vend à Amsterdam chez Cóvens et Mortier.

" " 125. Carte particulière des environs de Bruxelles, avec le Bois de Soigne, et d'une partie de la Flandre jusques à Gand. Se vend à Amsterdam chez Cóvens et Mortier sur la copie de Bruxelles par E. H. Fricx.

" " 126. Carte particulière des environs de Mons, d'Ath, de Charleroy, de Maubeuge, du Quesnoy, de Condé, &c. Se vend a Amsterdam chez Cóvens et Mortier, sur la copie de Bruxelles chez Eugene Henry Fricx. Nouvellement corregée.

" " 127. Carte particulière des environs de Lier et d'une partie de la Campine. Se vend à Amsterdam chez Cóvens et Mortier sur la copie de Bruxelles par E. H. Fricx.

" " 128. Carte particulière des environs de Louvain, Aerschot, Diest, Tirlemont, Leau, Iudogne, Malines, et de partie du pays de Liege. Se vend a Amsterdam. Corrigée d'un nombre des fautes sur la copie de Bruxelles chez E. H. Fricx. Chez Cóvens et Mortier.

" " 129. Comté de Namur. Amsterdam chez Cóvens et Mortier. Sur la copie de Bruxelles par E. H. Fricx.

" " 130. Carte particulière des environs de Roermonde, Venlo, la marais de Peel se vend à Amsterdam chez Cóvens et Mortier sur la copie de Bruxelles par E. H. Fricx.

" " 131. Carte particulière des environs de Maestricht, partie de Liège Faucquemont, et pays d'Outre-Meuse. Se vend à Amsterdam chez Cóvens et Mortier, sur la copie de Brussel par E. H. Fricx.

" " 132. Carte particulière des environs de Liege, Limbourg, et partie de Luxembourg. Se vend à Amsterdam chez Cóvens et Mortier sur la copie de Bruxelles par E. H. Fricx.

" " 133. Les embouchures de la Somme et de Bresle riv. ou est S^t. Valeri, Eu et Dieppe. Amsterdam chez I. Cóvens et C. Mortier. Sur la copie de E. H. Fricx. Corrigée et augmentée.

" " 134. Les environs d'Abbeville, Dourlens, Amiens, Corbie, et du cours de la Somme. Amsterdam chez I. Cóvens et C. Mortier sur la copie de E. H. Fricx.

" " 135. Carte particulière des environs de Cambray, Bappaumes, S^t. Quentin, Perone. Amsterdam chez Cóvens et Mortier sur la copie de Brussel par E. H. Fricx.

" " 136. Carte particulière des environs d'Avesnes Landrecy, La Capelle, Guise, à Amsterdam chez Cóvens et Mortier sur la copie de Brussel par E. H. Fricx.

v. 5, no. 137. Carte particulière des environs de Philippeville, Charlemont, Marienbourg, Rocroy, Charleville, Mezieres, Sedan. Sur la copie de Brussel par E. H. Fricx. Amsterdam chez I. Cóvens et C. Mortier.

" " 138. Cartes des environs de Luxembourg. Amsterdam chez Cóvens et Mortier sur la copie de Bruxelles par E. H. Fricx.

" " 1. Mappemonde à l'usage du roy. Par Guillaume Delisle. Paris chez G. Delisle, 1720.

" " 2. Carte d'Europe. Par G. Delisle. Paris, 1724.

" " 3. Carte de France. Par Guillaume Delisle. Paris, 1721.

" " 4. Carte nouvelle du royaume de France divisé en toutes ses provinces et ses acquisitions. La Haye chez Pierre Husson. Nouvellemet gravé par Luggerd van Anse. [Latin title at top of map] Galliæ regnvm in omnes suas procincias accurate divisum. Per Petrum Husson 1708.

Explanatory list at the right of the map entitled: La France divisée en ses douze anciens gouvernemens et en ses vingt-quatre nouveaux et l'on le remarque en cet ordre.

" " 5. La France. Par Charles Inselin. Paris chez B. Jaillot, 1713.

Large folded map with explanatory text. Maps by Charles Inselin appear in Placide de Sainte Hélène, *Cartes de géographie, [1714?]* and in Delisle and Buache, *Atlas géographique et universel. 1700–62.*

" " 5a. Tables des divisions des gouvernements du royaume de France. Par le s^r. Sanson. Paris chez H Iaillot, 1696.

" " 6. Nova Picardiæ tabula. Amsterdam chez P. Mortier.

" " 7. Praefectura Piccardiæ. Ex revisione Gerardi et Leonardi Valk.

" " 8. Carte d'Artois et des environs. Par Guillaume Del'Isle. Paris, 1711. Dersoier sculp.

" " 9. Partie méridionale de Picardie dressée sur les opérations. géometriques de m. Lesperon, et sur plusieurs autres mémoires. Par Guillaume Delisle. des Rosiers fec. Paris, 1712.

" " 10. Gouvernement général de Picardie qui comprend la généralité d'Amiens divisée en ses huit élections avec l'Artois, et les frontières des Pays Bas. Par le s^r. Jaillot.

The main title of this map is the general title to the four maps by Jaillot, each of the maps which follow having a separate title of its own.

Additional title at the foot of first map reads: Partie de la Flandre, et du Hayaut, ou sont les villes de Dixmude, Ipres, Lille, Douay, Courtray, Tournay, Oudenarde, Gand, Dendermonde, Mons, Valenciennes, Condé, S^t. Guislain, Ath, le Quesnoy, et Maubeuge. Par le s^r. Jaillot.

" " 11. Partie de la Picardie, de l'Artois et de la Flandres, où sont les villes de Calais, Ardres, Boulougne, Monstreuil, Rhue, Hesdin, Arras, Lens, Bethune, Aire, S^t. Omer, Graveline, Bourbourg, Donkerke, Bergue, Furnes, Nieuport, Ipres, Cassel et la Bassée. Par le s^r. Jaillot. [Dedication signed] B. Jaillot.

" " 12. Les élections d'Amiens, d'Abbeville, de Dourlens de Montdidier et partie de celle de Perone dans généralité d'Amiens par le s^r. Jaillot.

Ottens, R.—Continued.

v. 5, no. 13. L'élection de S. Quentin partie de celle de Pérone dans la généralité d'Amiens avec les élections de Guise, de Laon, et de Noyon dans la généralité de Soissons, par le s[r]. Jaillot. 1717.

" " 14. Description du gouvernement de la Cappelle, par P. Petit Bourbon. Amstelodami apud Petrum Schenk et Gerardum Valk.

" " 15. Gouvernement général de l'Isle de France. Amsterdam chez F. de Witt. Se vend chez P. Mortier.

" " 16. La généralité de Soissons divisée en sept élections scavoir Soissons, Laon, Noyon, Crespy, Clermont, Guise, Chateau-Thiery en Brie, en Picardie. Par le s[r]. Jaillot. Privilège du roy 1723.

" " 17–18. La généralité de Paris divisée en ses vingt-deux elections. Par. Bernard Jaillot. Gravé par Delahaye 1725.

" " 19. Carte du diocèse de Beauvais, dressée sur les mémoires de m. le Scellier. Par Guillaume Del Isle. Se trouve Beauvais chez Etienne Aleau. Inset: Plan de la ville de Beauvais. Inset has list of references to places indicated by letters and numbers.

" " 20. Carte topographique du diocèse de Senlis. Levée sur les lieux m[r]. Parent curé d'Aumont. Par Guillaume Del'Isle. Avec privilège du 28 aout 1709. Insets: Plan de Crespy.—Plan de la ville de Senlis.
Has table showing position of places and border text.

" " 21. Les environs de Paris à l'usage de monseigeur le duc de Bourgogne. Par G. de L'isle, à Amsterdam chez I. Cóvens & C. Mortier.
Latin title at top of map reads: Nova territorii Parisiensis tabula.

" " 22. Carte particulière du terroir et des environs des Paris qui est la plus grande partie de l'Isle de France parfaitement bien dessinée par F. Viuer donneè au public à Amsterdam par N. Visser.

" " 23. Carte de la prévosté et vicomté de Paris. Par G. Delisle. Paris. 1711. Des Rosiers fecit.

" " 24. La banlieüe de Paris. Par N. de Fer. Paris. 1717. P. Starck-man sculpsit.

" " 25. Le plan de Paris, ses faubourgs et ses environs, divisé suivant ses méridiens et parallèles par minutes et secondes. Gravé par Matthieu Seutter à Augsbourg.—Grund-riss des stadt Paris, welcher dieselbe nach ihren mittags-und parallel-linien in minuten und secunden abtheilet. Herausgegeben und verlegt von Matthæus Seutter.
Has explanatory text in both french and german.

" " 26. Nouveau plan de la ville et faubourgs de Paris. Comme il est à présent. Mis au jour par B. Jaillot. Très exactement levé et mesuré sur lieux, augmenté de tous les nouvelles ruës qui y ont été faites jus-qu'en 1717. J. B. Scotin le jeu. fec. Putbaux sculpsit. [Dedication signed] Bernard Jaillot 1723.
A map on four sheets mounted in one and folded. Each sheet has a list of explanatory references to the points on the map which are numbered.

v. 5, no. 27. Comté et gouvernement général de Champagne. Amsterdam chez F. de Witt. Se vend chez P. Mortier.

" " 28. Carte de la Champagne et des pays voisins où l'on voit la généralité de Chalons, partie de celle de Soissons, &c. Par Guillaume Del Isle. Paris. 1713.

" " 29. Partie méridionale de Champagne. Par Guillaume Del'Isle. Paris, 1713.

" " 30. Les sovverainetez de Sedan et de Ravcovrt et la prévosté de Doncheri. Amsterdami apud Guiljelium Blaeuw.

" " 31. Carte du pais de Retelois. Faicte par Iehan Iubrien Chalonnois. 1641. Amstelodami apud G. Valk et P. Schenk.

" " 32–33. Evesché de Meaux. Par. Hubert Jaillot. Levé par l'ordre de monseigneur l'évesque de Meaux. Par M. Chevallier. Cordier sculp. Paris chez le s^r. Iallot. 1717. Insets: Plan de la ville de Meaux.—Plan du palais épiscopal de Germigny l'évêque.

First sheet has title at foot of the map, Partie septentrionale de l'évesché de Meaux. Second sheet has title at top, Partie méridionale de l'évesché de Meaux.

" " 34. Generalis Lotharingiæ ducatus tabula. Per Nicolaum Visscher Amst. Bat.

" " 35. Duché et governement général de Normandie. Par F. de Witt. Se vend chez P. Mortier. Inset: Les isles de Garnezy Ierzay et Aurigny pont partie de la Normandie mais elles sont sous le domaine des Anglois.

" " 36. Le gouvernement général de Normandie en ses trois généralitez, sçavoir Roüen, Caen et Alencon. Par B. Jaillot. P. Starckman sculpsit. Paris, 1719. Inset: Les isles angloises.

A large map on 2 sheets which are mounted together, and folded. Hübner lists a map on 2 sheets and one on four sheets, by Jaillot.

" " 37. Carte de Normandie. Par Guillaume Del Isle. 1716.

" " 38. Tabula nova complectens praefecturas Normanniæ et Britanniæ, una cum Angliæ, parte et Manica. Per Nicolaum Visscher Amst. Bat. Nunc apud Petrum Schenk junior.

" " 39. Roüen. Ville capitale de Normandie, port de mer sur la rivière de Seine. Par N. de Fer. Paris chez le s^r. Danet. 1724.

" " 40. Le diocèse de Sees ses cinq archidiaconez dont trois sont situez en Normandie. Levé exactement sur les lieux par Fr. L. de la Salle. Dédié à monseigneur Dominique Barnabé Turgot. Par. B. Jaillot. Paris, chez le s^r. Iaillot, 1718. Jenvelliers sculp.

" " 41. Duché et gouvernement général de Bretagne. Par F. de Witt à Amsterdam. Ex officina Petri Mortier.

" " 42. Carte de l'évesché de Nantes. Par H. Iaillot. Paris chez le s^r. Iaillot.

Contains explanatory text.

" " 43. Gouvernement général dv pays Orléanois. Amstelodami ex officina P. Mortier.

" " 44. Le gouvernement général d'Orléans. Par B. Jaillot, 1721. Gravé par Delahaye.

" " 45. Carte de la Beauce du Gatinois de la Sologne et pays voisins. Par Guillaume Delisle. Paris chez le s^r. Del'Isle, 1718.

Ottens, R.—Continued.

v. 5, no. 46–47. L'évesché de Chartes divisé en archidiaconéz et doyennéz. Par Hubert Iaillot. Paris, 1695.

The first sheet has additional title at the foot of the map: Partie septentrionale de l'évesché de Chartes, par le s^r. Iaillot. Paris, 169–. Second sheet on which main title shows has additional title at top of map: Partie méridionale de l'évesché de Chartes, par le sieur Iaillot.

" " 48. Le Maine, l'Anjou et la Touraine, la Beauce et la Sologne, le Perche Goüet, le Vendomois, le Dunois, le Blaisois, l'Orleanois et le païs Chartrain. Par N. de Fer. Paris, 1713. P. Stark- man sculpsit.

" " 49. Carte des provinces du Maine et du Perche dans laquelle se trouve comprise la partie septentrionale de la généralité de Tours. Par Guillaume Del'Isle. Paris, 1719.

" " 50. Carte particulière d'Anjou et de Touraine ou de la partie méridionale de la généralité de Tour par Guillaume Delisle.

" " 51. La province de Poitou et le pays d'Aunis.—La généralité de Poitiers. Par A. H. Jaillot, 1707.

" " 52. Le Berri et le Nivernois, la Beauce et la Sologne. Par N. Fer. Paris chez Benard, 1713. P. Stark-man sculp.

" " 53. Généralité de la Rochelle. Par le s^r. Jaillot, 1722. Delahaye sculpsit.

" " 54. La généralité de la Rochelle comprenant le pays d'Aunis, la Saintonge. Par I. B. Nolin. Insets: Veüe de la Rochelle.—Veüe de Rochefort.—Plan de la tour de Cordoüan.—Coupe de la tour de Cordoüan.

Map on 2 sheets joined together and folded.

" " 55. L'Isle de Ré avec ses environs; où est représenté le bombardement de S^t. Martin, et d'Olone, par l'armée navalle de sa maiesté Britannique, le 15 & 16 juillet 1696. Par Charles Allard. Inset view: Le bombardement d' Olone.

" " 56. Vtrivsqve Bvrgvndiae, tum ducatus tum comitatus, descriptio. Amsterdami apud G. Valk et P. Schenk.

" " 57. Ducatus Bvrgvndiæ nova descriptio divisa, correcta et edita per F. de Witt. Ex officina I. Covens et C. Mortier.

" " 58–59. Carte du duché de Bourgogne et des comtez en dépend ans Par Guillaume del 'Isle. 1709. Desrosiers sc.

Map in two parts,—the first part has additional title at foot of map: Partie septentrionale du duché de Bourgogne. The second part has additional title at top of map: Partie meridionale du duché de Bourgogne.

Has explanatory text in cartouche on second sheet.

" " 60. La Bresse Chalonnoise.

" " 61. Bressia vulgo Bresse. Amsterdami Guiljelmus Blauw excudit.

" " 62. La sovverainete de Dombes. Apud Guiljelmum et Ioannem Blaeu.

" " 63. Superior Burgundiæ comitatus; vulgo la Franche comté. Per Gerard Valk.

" " 64. Gouvernement général du Lyonnois. Par F. de Witt. a Amsterdam. Apud I. Cóvens et C. Mortier.

v. 5, no. 65. Le governement général et militaire du Lyonnois. Par I. B. Nolin. Inset: Gouvernement général du Lyonnois suivant les estats généraux tenu à Paris en anne 1614.
Map on two sheets joined together and folded.
Title in very elaborate cartouche.

" " 66. Gouvernement général du Lyonnois. Par le s^r^. Jaillot. Paris, 1721. Jenvilliers sculpsit.
Large folded map.

" " 67. La généralité de Moulins. Par H. Jaillot.

" " 68. Borbonivm dvcatvs.—Bovrbonnois. Amstelodami prostant in officina apud Petrum Schenk et Gerardum Valk . . .

" " 69. La province d'Auvergne divisée en haute et basse. La généralité de Riom. Par B. Jaillot, 1715.

" " 70. Le governement général du Dauphiné divisé en haut en bas. Par F. de Witt. Ex officina Cóvens et Mortier.

" " 71. Le Dauphiné divisé en ses principales parties. Par H. Jaillot. Paris chez le s[r]. Jaillot, 1713.

" " 72. Comté et gouvernement général de Provence. Amsterdam par F. de Witt, se vend Pierre Mortier.

" " 73. Carte de Provence et des terres adjacentes. Par Guillau[me]. Del Isle. Paris, 1715. Derozier sc.

" " 74. La principavté d'Orange et comtat de Venaissin. Amstelodam apud Petrum Schenk et G. Valk. Evert Sÿmons z. Hamersveldt sculp.
Dedication signed Iudocus et Henricus Hondij.

" " 75. Gouvernement général de Langvedoc. Par F. de Witt.

" " 76. Le gouvernement général de Languedoc. Par N. de Fer. Paris chez Benard, 1712. P. Stark-man sculp. Inset: Le canal royal de Languedoc. Par N. de Fer. 1712. Inset has explanatory text.

" " 77. Gouvernement général de Languedoc. Paris chez le s[r]. Jaillot, 1721.
Large map in two parts jointed and folded.

" " 78. Les montagnes des Sévennes où se retirent les fanatiques de Languedoc et les plaines des environs où ils font leurs courses avec les grands chemins royaux faicts par l'ordre du roy pour rendre ces montagnes practicables sous les soins de m. de Basville. Paris I. B. Nolin, 1703.

" " 79. Carte du diocèse d'Uzès dressée sur les lieux par le s[r]. Gautier. Dédiée à monseigneur Michel Poncet. Par. J. B. Nolin fils du s[r]. Nolin. Paris chez la veuve du s[r]. Nolin. Inset: Uzès.—Plan de la ville, citadelle et pont S[t]. Esprit.—Plan du passage du Rhône, Fort S[t]. Andre pont, et enceinte de la ville d'Avignon.—Pont du S[t]. Esprit.—Façade du pont du Gard.

" " 79a. Table alphabétique des noms des villes, bourgs, paroisses, hameaux, châteaux ec. qui se trouvent dans cette carte du diocèse d'Usez.

" " 80. Diocèse de Nismes dressé nouvellement sur les lieux par le s[r]. Gautier. Dédié à monseigneur Esprit Flechier. Par I. B. Nolin 1698. Insets: Plan de la ville Nismes.—Elévation perspective de l'amphitéatre de Nismes.—Façade du pont du Gard.—Profils du temple de Diane.—Façade de la maison Quarrée de Nismes.—Façade de l'amphitéatre.—Plan de la maison Quarrée.—Plan du temple de Diane.

Ottens, R.—Continued.

v. 5, no. 81. Le diocèse de Montpellier. Par A. H. Jaillot. Paris, 1706.

" " 82. Carte du diocèse de Beziers dressée sur les lieux par le s. Gautier. Par G. Del 'Isle. Inset: Plan de Beziers.
Map has border text.

" " 83. Le Roussillon. Mis au jour par N. de Fer. Paris, 1706. H. van Loon sculp. Insets: Ville-Franche.—Bellegarde.—Perpignan.—Collioure.—Puicerda.—Mont-Louis.—Roses.

" " 84. Episcopatvs Albiensis.—Evesche d'Alby. Amstelaedami exc. Joannes Blaeu.

" " 85. Plan de Tolose divisé en hvit capitolae. Paris chez de Fer. [Dedication signed] m^{r}. Gouuin de Rochefort.

" " 86. Le gouvernement général de Guinne et Gascogne. Par m. G. de L'isle. Amsterdam chez Iean Cóvens et C. Mortier.
Same title repeated at top of map.

" " 87. Carte du Bourdelois du Perigord. Par G. del' Isle. Paris, 1714.
The northern part of the map which follows, though issued at an earlier date and with no general title.

" " 88. Carte du Bearn de la Bigorre de l'Armagnac. Par Guillaume Delisle, 1712.

" " 89. La généralité de Limoges. Par le sieur B. Iaillot. 1719. Desbruslins sc.
Has explanatory text.

" " 90. Dioecesis Sarlatensis vernacule le diocese de Sarlat. Ioannes Tardo delineabat. Amsterdami apud Guiljelmum Blaeu.

" " 91. Le dvché d'Aigvillon. Par le s^{r}. Pierre du Val.

" " 92. L'évesché d'Aire, tracé par le s^{r}. Pierre de Val.
Map cut to the margin and pasted on another sheet.

" " 93. Le pais de Bèarn. Evert Sÿmons z. Hamersveldt sculp. Amstelodami apud G. Valk et P. Schenk.

" " 94. Le diocèse de Comminge. Cordier sculpsit. Paris chez le s. Iaillot, 1700.

" " 95. Hispaniæ et Portugalliæ regna. Per Nicolaum. Nunc apud Petrum Schenk iunior.

" " 95a. Tables des toutes les parties de l'Espagne. Par le s^{r}. Sanson. Paris chez H. Iaillot, 1696.

" " 96. Carte nouvelle et curieuse du royaume d'Espagne dédiée et présentée au roy par. C. Inselin. F. Roettiers inv. et fecit. Paris chez B. Jaillot. 1713.
Has explanatory text.
Map on 2 sheets joined together and folded.

" " 97. Accuratissima et nunc novissimè revisa correctaque tabula regnorum Valentiæ et Murciæ, insularum Majorcæ, Minorcæ et Juicæ. Auctore Joachimo Ottens Amst Batavo.
Explanatory text in french and dutch, in large cartouche.

" " 98. Perfectissima geographica delineatio regnorum Vandalitiæ, Granatæ, et Algarbiæ; tractuum correcta et edita a Joachimo Ottens Amst. Batavo.

" " 99. Novissima et accuratissima tabula, quâ Galliæciæ et Legionis regna, Asturiarum principatus Portugalliæ tractus septentrionalis, ut et utriusque Castellæ, Extremaduræ et Biscajæ partes confines exactissime ostenduntur, auctore Joachimo Ottens Amst. Batavo.

v. 5, no. 100. Exactissima et postomnes alias nunc demum edita tabula continens perfectam descriptionem regnorum Arragoniæ et Navarræ, principatûs Cataloniæ, nec non partium conterminarum, Biscajæ utriusque Castellæ, ac Valentiæ. Auctore Joachimo Ottens Amst. Batavo.

" " 101. Les frontières de France et d'Espagne tant deça que de là les monts Pirénées, par de Fer. H. van Loon sculps. Paris chez G. Danet.

" " 102. Cataloniæ principatus, nec non Ruscinonensis et Cerretaniæ comitatus, per Nicolaum Visser Amst. Bat. Nunc apud Petrum Schenk iunior.

" " 103. La Catalogne dédiée au roy par le p. Placide. Paris chez melle. Duval, 1707.
Map on 2 sheets joined together and folded.
From Placide's *Cartes de géographie*, published ca. 1714.

" " 104. Carte très juste des terres et environs de Balaguer et Lerida, où l'on peut distinctement voir où la bataille s'est donnée, entre l'armée du roy Charles, et celle de Philippe V, le 27 iuillet 1710, chez Nicolas Visser.

" " 105. Regni Arragoniæ typus novissimus in episcopatus divisus et editus per F. de Witt Amstelodami, ex officina P. Mortier.

" " 106. Carte du royaume d'Aragon. Dédiée à monseigneur le duc d'Orléans régent; par Bourguignon d'Anville. Gravé par P. Starck-man. 1719.
Title at head of map, "Théâtre de la guerre d'Espagne."
Map on two sheets jointed together and folded.

" " 107. Regni Navarræ accurata tabula nuper correcta et in lucem edita per Fredericum de Wit Amstelodami ex officina I. Cóvens & C. Mortier.

" " 108. La Biscaye et le royaume de Navarre. Par I. B. Nolin.
Map has explanatory text.
Cut to the margin and pasted on another sheet.

" " 109. La Castille propre ou vielle, et la nouvelle; avec l'Estremadure Castillane dressé sur les mémoires de Rodrigo Mendes Silva, et autres à Amsterdam, par Nicolas Visscher.

" " 110. Accurater grundris der königl. Spanischen haupt und residentz stadt Madrit mit denen prospecten des königl. schlosses und andern lust gebæuen edirt von Iohann Bapt. Homanns kaÿser lichen geographi seeligen erben in Nürnberg. Insets: Prospect des königl. schlosses zu Madrid.—Prospect des place major in Madrid, mit dem grossen stiergesecht.—Der königl. Spanische lust palast buen retiro beÿ Madrid.—Aranjuez meil von Madrid.—Heremitage St. Antonio.

" " 111. Madrid. Par N. de Fer. P. Starck-man scrip. A Paris chez J. F. Benard, 1706.
Large map on 2 sheets joined and folded.
Map has explanatory text in cartouche.

" " 112. Les royaumes de Grenade et d'Andalousie. Par N. de Fer, Paris, 1707.
Map cut to margin and pasted on another sheet.

" " 113. Nieuwe en nauwkeurige kaart van het zuidelykst gedeelte van Spanje genaamt Andalusie. Amsterdam door R. en I. Ottens.

Ottens, R.—Continued.

v. 5, no. 114. Plan de Cadix, de baye, du Puntal, de Port Marie, de Rotta, & de l'entrée de la rivière de Guadalete. Dressé sur les lieux par mr. D** ingénieur de S. M. C. à la Haye chez Alberts & van der Kloot. 1727.

" " 115. De haven en straat van Gibraltar. Door Carel Allard, to Amsterdam. Insets: Estrecho de Gibraltar.—[View] Gibraltar.
Published after 1704, which date appears on the map.

" " 116. Carte de la baye de Gibraltar. Où l'on voit cette place, avec ses fortifications, celle des Alguecires, ses ouvrages projettés, l'Isle qui couvre son port, & le fortin qui y est projetté, lesquels son excellence monsieur le marquis de Verboom ingénieur général traça sur les lieux, comme aussi le village de St. Roques, où est le camp des Espagnols aujourd'hui. Fait par J. D. Grodmetz, ingénieur qui a été employé, sous le dit marquis de Verboom, pour tracer les susdits ouvrages. Hagæ comit. in Hollandiæ apud Iacob de Iongh.

" " 117. Nouveau plan de Gibraltar, avec ces fortifications &c. à Amsterdam chez Jean Cóvens et Corneille Mortier. 1727.—Vüe de la ville de Gibraltar du côté du détroit . . . —Vüe de Gibraltar du coté Nord ouest . . . —Nouvelle carte d'une partie d' Espagne, de la mer Méditerranée, et d' Afrique, montrant l' advantageuse situation de Gibraltar et de Port Mahon. A Amsterdam chez J. Cóvens et C. Mortier.
The two views have title in french, dutch and english.

" " 118. Plan de la ville de Gibaltar située au detroit de ce nom en 1706, mis au jour par Nicolas Visscher. Nunc apud Petrum Schenk iunior.—Plan de la ville de Ceuta.—Veue de la ville de Gibaltar.

" " 119. Nieuwe paskaart vant naauw van de Straat. Door. Hendrik Lynslager, anno 1726. H. de Leth fecit 1727. Uytgegeven by And. en Hend. de Leth. tot Amsterdam.

" " 120. Aftekening van't naauw van de Straat, uyt de Middelandsche zee te sien.—Vüe du détroit, comme il se représente du côté de la mer Méditerranée.
Small uncolored view.

" " 121. Portugalliæ et Algarbiæ regna, per Nicolaum Visscher. Nunc apud Petr. Schenk iunior.

" " 122. Les frontières d' Espagne et de Portugal. Par N. de Fer. Gravée par P. Starckman. Paris, 1703.

" " 123. Portugalliæ meridionales placæ, geo-hydrographicè descriptæ, et in lucem edita ab auctore Carolo Allard; Amstelo-Batavo. A. Allard fecit acu.

" " 124. Baleares seu Gymnesiae et Pityvsae insulæ dictæ Maiorca, Minorca et Yvica a R. et I. Ottens.
Descriptive text in cartouche contains date 1708.

" " 125. Nieuwe afteekening van het eyland Minorca geleegen in de Middellandsche zee. Te Amsterdam by Gerard van Keulen.

" " 126. Nieuwe afteekening van de rivier of Porto Mahon aen de z. o. hoek van het eyland Minorca in de Middlelandsche zee. Inset: De stadt Maon of Mahon of Minorca.
Contains the date 1712 on the map.

v. 6, no. 1. Planisphærium terrestre, sive terrarum orbis, planisphæricè constructi quintuplex. Adjunctis aliquibus astronomicæ-geographiæ Tyrociniis auctore Carolo Allard. Amastelo-Batavo. Vlakke aard-kloot, gemeenlyk genaamd de geheele waereld. Door Carel Allard.

" " 2. Accuratissima Europæ tabula multis locis correcta et nuperrimè edita authore Carolo Allard Amstelo-Batavo.

" " 3. Les marches ou frontières d' Allemagne, et d' Italie avec les routes que l'on tient ordinairement par les Alpes, pour passer de l'un l'autre de ces états par N. de Fer. Gravé par H. van Loon. Paris, 1703.

" " 4. Italia cum stationibus suis et viis publicis delineata à Jacobo Cantrelli da Vignola. Lugduni Batavorum excudit Petrus vander Aa.—Nouvelle carte de l'Italie, où sont exactement marquez les postes et les chemins, par Jaques Cantrelli da Vignola. A Leide chez Pierre vander Aa.

" " 5. L' Italie divisée en ses principaux estats, royaumes, et republiques où sont exactement remarquées toutes les routes des postes suivant qu' elles sont présentement établies par le s^r. Iaillot, à Paris, 1718.

" " 6. Novissima et accuratissima totius Italiæ Corsicæ et Sardiniæ descriptio. Per F. de Witt, Amstelodami, ex officina R. & I. Ottens.
Appears also in Atlas published by Ottens heirs ca. 1740.

" " 7. Italia in suos quoscunq̃ status divisa, iiq̃ iterum particulares ditiones distributi huic accedunt insulæ Sicilia, Sardinia, Corsica &c. Auctore Carolo Allard Amstelod. J. Deur delin. et sculp. Inset: Siciliam.

" " 7a. Tables ou divisions des principaux estats qui composēt l' Italie par le s^r. Sanson. Paris chez H. Iaillot 1696.

" " 8. Regiæ celsitudinis Sabaudiæ status per Nicolaum Visscher Amst. Bat. Nunc apud Petr. Schenk iunior.

" " 9–14. Les estats de Savoye et de Piémont par Hubert Iaillot. Paris chez le s^r. Iaillot, 1707.
A large map on 6 sheets each having a special title in addition to the general title which appears on no. 11. They are not arranged in proper order in this list, but a brief special title is here given in the order in which they appear: no. 9, La Bresse, le Bugey, le Valromay, la principauté de Dombes et le Viennois.—no. 10, les duchés Savoye, de Genevois, de Chablais, les comtés de Morienne, de Tarentaise et la baronie de Faussigny.—no. 11, Le duché d' Avost, la seigneurie de Verceil, le marquisat d' Yvrée.—Le Valentinois le Diois et les baroñies, dans le Dauphiné; le comtat Venaiscin et la principauté de Orange.—no. 13, Partie du Briançonnois, du Graisvaudan, du Gapençois et l' Ambrunois dans le Daufiné. 1706.—no. 14, La principauté de Piémont, les marquisats de Saluce et de Suzes, les comités de Nice et d' Ast, Montferrat &c.

" " 15. Tabvla generalis Sabavdiæ. Joannes Blaeu excudit. Thomas Borgonius invent. Joannes de Broen sculp.

" " 16. Dvcatvs Chablasive et Lacvs Lemamvs. Joannes Blaeu ex cudit. Th. Borgonius inv. Joannes de Broen sculp.

Ottens, R.—Continued.

v. 6, no. 17. Pedemontivm et reliquæ ditiones Italiæ regiæ celsitvdini Sabavdiæ subditæ. Joannes Blaeu excudit. Thomas Borgonius invent. Joannes de Broen sculps.

" " 18. Carte du Piemont et du Monferrat. Par Guillaume Del' Isle. Paris, 1707. Gravé par Liebaux le fils, à Paris chez l'auteur, 1707. Se trouve à Amsterdam chez I. Renard.
Has explanatory text in cartouche.

" " 19. Partie méridionale du Piémont et du Monferrat par Guillaume Del' Isle Desrosiers sc. à Paris chez l'auteur 1707 et se trouve à Amsterdam chez Louis Renard. Inset: Environs de Nice et de Ville-franche.

" " 20. Les vallées du Piemont. Paris chez I. B. Nolin. Small map with extensive border text entitled: Description des vallées de Piémont. Paris, chez Jean-Baptiste Nolin, 1690.
Plate cut to the edge of the text and mounted on another sheet.

" " 21. Signoria di Vercelli. Amsterodami apud Ioannem Ianssonium.

" " 22. Montisferrati dvcatvs. Amstelodami G. Valk et P. Schenk excudit. [Dedication signed] Henricus Hondius.

" " 23. De stroel des oorlogs in Italien, waar in vertoont werden de staat van Milano, de republicen van Venetien en Genoua, de landen van Parma, Mantoua, Modena, Ferrara. tot Amsteldam door Nicolaus Visser. Nunc apud Petrum Schenk iunior. Luggert van Anze schulp.

" " 24. Status Mediolanensis. Gerh. et Leonh. Valk.

" " 25. Nova et præ cæteris aliis status et ducatus Mediolanensis Parmensis et Montis Ferrati. Per F. de Witt Amstellod. Ex officina I. Cóvens et C. Mortier.

" " 26. Status reipublicæ Genuensis status et ducatus Mediolanensis et Montisferrati. Per F. de Wit Amstelodami ex officina I. Cóvens et C. Mortier.

" " 27. Belli typvs in Italia victricis Aquilæ progressus in statv Mediolanensi et dvcatv Mantvae demonstrans tabula recens emendata et aucta per Io. Bapt. Homannvm anno 1702.
Cartouche containing title ornamented with scene before Cremona entitled, "A. 1702, die 1 febr. Cæsarei Cremonam strata gemate ingessi Gallorum 2000 mactant sed capto Duce de Villeroy cum militie pra' fectis reversi eammox deseruerũt." Above the cartouche are the words, "Tandem bona causa triumphat anno 1707."

" " 28. Parte Alpestre dello stato di Milano con il lago Maggiore di Lugano, e di Como. Amstelodami apud G. Valk et P. Schēk.

" " 29. Dvcato ouero territorio de Milano. Ex typographia Amstelodami apud P. Schenk et G. Valk.

" " 30. Territorio di Pavia, Lodi, Novarra, Tortona, Alessandria et altri vicini dello stato di Milano. Sumptibus Amstelodami apud Pet. Schenk et Ger. Valk.

" " 31. Territorio di Cremona. Ex typographia Amstelodami penes Petri Schenk, et Gerardi Valk.

" " 32. Dvcato de Parma et di Piacenza. Amstelodami penes P. Schenk et G. Valk.

" " 33. Ligvria ò stato della republica di Genova. Amstelædami prodeunt ex officina apud Gerardi Valk et Petri Schēk.

v. 6, no. 34. Republicæ Genuensis dominium. Per Matth. Seutter.
Inset view: Genua.
The inset view of the city has explanatory list giving names of places indicated by figures, and at one end is illustrated by a view showing the processes of silk production, and at the other end by a view of a building with a symbolical figure representing plenty. The cartouche of the main map is elaborately illustrated to show the progress of the country.
Contained in Seutter's *Grosser atlas, 1734?*

" " 35. Venetia potentissima e la più magnifica, fiorentissima e la più ricca citta capitale della serenissima republica edificata sopra 72 isole piciole nello mare Adriatico, tagliata in rame di Matt. Seüttero. Aug. Inset view: Altra parte della piazza di S. Marco in Venetia. Der andere theil dess S. Marx plaz in Venedig.—Piazza de S. Marco di Venetia. Der St. Marx plaz in Venedig.
Map has same title in german.

" " 36. Carte nouvelle du duché de Mantoue levée par ordre exprès. à l' usage des armées en Italie: où sont exactement marqués les grands chemins les routes des impériaux &c. Par le s^r. Sanson, à Amsterdam chez J. Cóvens et C. Mortier.

" " 37. Carte nouvelle du duché de Modène, de regio et de Capri; avec la seigneurie de la Cafargnana &c. levée par ordre exprès à l' usage des armées en Italie, où sont exactement marqués les grands chemins, les routes des impériaux &c. Par le s^r. Sanson. Amsterdam chez Pierre Mortier . . .

" " 38. Dvcato di Modena regio et Carpi col dominio della Carfagnana. Amstelodami apud P. Schenk et G. Valk.

" " 39. Dominii Veneti in Italia in partes accurate divisi ac statuum ducum Parmæ, Mutinæ, Mantuæ et Mirandolæ. Per Fredericum de Witt Amstelodami, ex officina I. Cóvens et C. Mortier.

" " 40. Estat de la seigneurie et république de Venise en Italie. Par A. H. Jaillot. Cordier sculpsit. À Paris chez l'auteur le s^r. Iaillot, 1706.

" " 41. Territorio di Bergamo. Amstelodami penés G. Valk et P. Schenk.

" " 42. Territorio di Brescia et di Crema. Amstelodami apud G. Valk et P. Schenk.

" " 43. Les provinces du Veronese, du Vicentin du Padouan, de Polesine de Rovigo et du Dogado ou duché à la république de Venise. Par A. H. Iaillot, à Paris chez le s^r. Iaillot, 1705.
This map appears in Delisle *& others, Atlas géographique et universel, 1789.*

" " 44. Carte nouvelle du territoire de Verone levée par ordre exprès. à l'usage des armées en Italie; où sont exactement marqués les grands chemins, les routes des impériaux &c. Par le s^r. Sanson, à Amsterdam chez Pierre Mortier.

" " 45. Territorio de Vicenza. Amstelaedami prodeunt ex officina apud Gerardi Valk et Petri Schenk.

" " 46. Territorio Padovano. Venditant Amstelodami, apud P. Schenk et G. Valk.

" " 47. Polesino di Rovigo. Amstelodami sumptibus G. Valk et P. Schēk.

Ottens, R.—Continued.

v. 6, no. 48. Il Bellvnese con il Feltrino. Inpensis Amstelodami penes Petri Schenk et Gerardi Valk.

" " 49. Territorio Cremasco.—Il Cadorino. Amstelodami, ex officina G. Valk et P. Schenk.

" " 50. Territorio Trevigiano. Amstelodami, sumptibus P. Schenk et G. Valk.

" " 51. Istria olim Lapidia.

" " 52. Le golfe de Venise. Par N. de Fer. P. Starcknam sculpsit. Paris, 1716.
Map cut to the margin and pasted on another sheet.

" " 53. Status ecclesiasticus et magnus ducatus Thoecanæ. Per Fredericum de Wit. Amstelodami ex officina Petri Mortier.
Contained in Visscher's Atlas minor, 1684?.

" " 54. Estats de l'eglise et de Toscane. Par le s^r. B. Jaillot. Paris, 1721.

" " 55. Estats de l'église et de Toscane. Dressé sur les lieux, et mis au jour. Amsterdam par Cóvens et Mortier.
Additional title at the top of the map, Estat du grand duc de Toscane, & estats de l'eglise. Dressé sur les lieux par N. Sanson.
Large map on 2 sheets joined and folded.

" " 56. Dominio Fiorentino. Amstelodami excudebat G. Valk et P. Schenk.

" " 57. Stato della repvlica di Lvcca. Apud G. Valk et P. Schenk. Evardus Simonis Hamersveldt sculpsit.

" " 58. Territorio di Siena con il ducato di Castro. Typis Amstelodami, penes P. Schenk et G. Valk.

" " 59. Le Isle d'Elbe. Amsterdam chez Pierre Mortier.
Small map on one leaf.

" " 60. Toscana inferiore detta anticamente Tvscia svbvrbicaria. Prostant in officina Amstelodami apud Petri Schenk et Gerardi Valk.

" " 61. Carte nouvelle du duché et légation de Ferrare à l'eglisé levée par ordre exprès à l'usage des armées en Italie, où sont exactement marqués les grands chemins, les routes de impériaux &c. Par le s^r. Sanson. Amsterdam chez Pierre Mortier.

" " 62. Le comté et légation de Boulogne. Dressée sur Magin et rectifiée sur les mémoires de Pompeio Vizani et autres nouveaux auteurs par I. B. Nolin.
Map on one leaf.
Has explanatory text in lower right hand corner.

" " 63. Romagna olim Flaminia. Amstelodami G. Valk et P. Schenk.

" " 64. Dvcato di Vrbino. Amstelodami venundantur a P. Schenk et G. Valk.

" " 65. Marca d' Ancona olim Picenvm. Amstelodami G. Valk et P. Schenk excudit.

" " 66. Territorio Pervgino. In typographia Amstelodami penes P. Schenk et G. Valk.

" " 67. Territorio di Orvieto. Prodeunt ex officina Amstelodami penes Petri Schenk et Ger. Valk.

" " 68. Vmbria overo dvcato di Spoleto. Amstelodami, venundantur apud per P. Schenk et G. Valk.

v. 6, no. 69. Campagna di Roma; olim Latium patrimonio de S. Pietro et Sabina. Amstelodami excudebat G. Valk et P. Schenk.

" " 70. Veteris et modernæ urbis Romæ ichnographia et accurata designatio, cura et sumtibus Matthæi Seuteri. Inset: Die 7 berge der alten statt Rom.
Has explanatory text in cartouche on right hand side of map and in long scroll on left hand side. Contained in Seutter's *Grosser atlas, 1734*?

" " 71. Le chiese di Roma con le loro principali reliquie stationi, et indulgenze data in luce da Matteo Seuterro. Augusta.
Same title in german.
Each building has explanatory text.
Contained in Seutter's *Grosser atlas, 1734*?

" " 72. Dvcatvs Bracciani et Angvillariæ comitatvs olim Sabatia. Amstelædami prostant in officina penes Gerardi Valk et Petri Schenk. [Dedication signed] Iohannes Ianssonius.

" " 73–74. Le royaume de Naples. Par. A. H. Jaillot. Paris chez l'auteur, 1703.
Each part has an additional title, no. 73, Partie septentrionale du royaume de Naples, no. 74, Partie meridionale du royaume de Naples 1706.

" " 75. Regnum Neapolis. Per Fredericum de Witt. Amstelodami, ex officina P. Mortier.
Contained in Braakman's *Atlas minor, 1706*.

" " 76. Abrvzzo citra et vltra. Amstelodami, apud G. Valk et P. Schenk.

" " 77. Terra di Lavoro, olim Campania Felix. Amstelodami, penes G. Valk et P. Schenk.

" " 78. Urbis Neapolis cum præcipuis eius ædificiis secundum planitiem exacta delineatio, edita a Ioh. Bapt. Homanni. herede Norimbergae 1727.
The map of the city has additional title, Ichnographia Neapolis, and has explanatory list. The engravings at the top and foot of the map are: Veduta del palazzo del vice re.—Veduta di Castel Nuovo.—Veduta del castel del Ovo.—Veduta del Molo.—Piazza del Mercato.—Veduta del l' castel S[t]. Elmo.—Tabella antiquitatis Romanæ.—Vesuvius mons.

" " 79. Ischia isola olim Ænaria. Amstelodami apud G. Valk et P. Schenk.

" " 80. Contado di Molise et principato vltra. Impensis Amstelodami apud P. Schenk et G. Valk.

" " 81. Principato Citra olim Picentia. Prodeunt ex officina Amstelodami apud Petri Schenk et Gerardi Valk.

" " 82. Capitanata, olim Mesapiæ et Iapygiæ pars. Amstelodami apud G. Valk et P. Schenk.

" " 83. Insvlæ Tremitanæ, olim Diomedeæ dictæ. Par m[r]. Blaeu. Amsterdam chez P. Mortier.
Contained in J. Blaeu's *Atlas minor, 1662–1665*.

" " 84. Terra di Bari et Basilicata. Amstelodami, apud G. Valk et P. Schenk.

" " 85. Terra di Otranto olim Salentina et Iapigia. Amstelodami, apud Gerardi et Petrum Schenk.

" " 86. Calabria citra olim Magna Græcia. Amstelodami, apud G. Valk et P. Schenk.

Ottens, R.—Continued.

v. 6, no. 87. Calabria vltra, olim altera Magnæ Græciæ pars. Amstelodami, apud G. Valk et P. Schenk.

" " 88. Insulæ et regni Siciliæ novissima tabula, inventa par G. de L'Isle, et edita par Joachim Ottens Amstelodami.—Carte de l'isle et royaume de Sicile per G. de l'Isle et imprimé à Amsterdam chez Ioachim Ottens. J. Keyser sculptor. Inset: Carte particulière de l'isle de Malte et des isles voisines. An edition of this map was published by J. Cóvens and C. Mortier in Delisle's *Atlas nouveau, 1733.* Another edition of the map was published by Dezauche in 1781 and one in 1789.

" " 89. Palerme. — Messine. — Urbs Melazzo. — Catania. — Trapani. — Fort de Faro.—La Scaletta.—Augusta. A Amsterdam chez Joachim Ottens.
Eight small engravings on one folded leaf.

" " 90. Insularum Sardiniæ et Corsicæ descriptio per Fredericum de Wit. Amstelodami ex officina P. Mortier.

" " 91. Nieuwe en nette afteekening van het eyland of koninkryk Sardinia. tot Amsterdam by Gerard van Keulen. J. Keyser sculp.

" " 92. Insulæ Corsicæ noua & accurata descriptio. Prostant Amstelodami apud Petrum Schenk et Gerardum Valk.

" " 93. Insularum Melitæ vulgo Maltæ Gozæ et comini correctissima descriptio auctore F. de Witt Amstelodami. 1707. Insets: Tabula hæc addita est ita ut insulæ regiones et terræ Melitæ circumjacentes clarius ostendentur.—Citta Valetta.

" " 94. Danubii fluvii sive Turcici imperii in Europa. Per F. de Witt. Amstelodami, ex officina P. Mortier.

" " 95. Fluviorum in Europe principis Danubii cum adiacentibus regnis nec non totius Græciæ et Archipelagi novissima tabula authore Ioh. Baptista Homanno Norimbergæ.

" " 96. Regnum Hungaria in omnes suos comitatus accuraté divisum et editum. Per F. de Wit. Amstelodami ex officina P. Mortier.

" " 96a. Tables, ou divisions du royaume et des estats de la couronne de Hongrie par le s[r]. Sanson. Paris chez Hubert Iaillot, 1696.

" " 97. Novissima tabula regni Hungariæ. Auctore Joachimo Ottens geographo Amstelodamensi. J. Keyser schulpcit.

" " 98. Hungaria generalis. Venundantur â Gerardo et Leonardo Valk.

" " 99–102. Le royaume de Hongrie diuisé en Haute, et Basse Hongrie auec l'Esclavonie subdiuisées en leurs comtez. Par le p. Coronelli. Corrigée et augmentée par le s[r]. Tillemon. Paris chez I. B. Nolin, 1688.
Title on map no. 102. Additional titles, no. 99, Partie du royaume de Hongrie vers le septentrion, et l'occident.—no. 100, Partie du royaume de Hongrie, vers le septentrion et l'orient. Inset: Ancien royaume de Hongrie.—no. 101, Partie du royaume de Hongrie, vers le midy et l'occident.—Partie du royaume de Hongrie, vers le midy et l'orient.
Maps cut to the margin and pasted on extra sheets.

" " 103. Accurate karte des landes Belgrado, Temeswar und Peterwardeinn da die batalie furgefallen, zwischen dem keyser und grossen turck, den 5 August 1716. Amstelodami apud I. Ottens exc.

Has explanatory list and three small engravings at the foot of the map, Peter Wardein, Belgrad and Temeswar.

v. 6, no. 104. Dalmatia, Sclavonia, Croatia, Bosnia, Servia et Istria, una cum republica Ragusana et circumjacentibus regionibus. Venundantur per Gerardum et Leonardum Valk.

" " 105. Le royaume de Dalmacie, divisé en ses comtez, territoires etc. la Morlaquie, la Bosnie. Par le père Coronelli. Dédié à monseigneur Jérome Venier par le r. p. Coronelli et I. B. Nolin. N. Guerard fecit. Inset: Partie occidentale de la Dalmacie &c.

The following "Avertissement" appears in a cartouche, "Le p. Coronelli, autheur de cette carte en a fait une autre du royaume de Hongrie qui se peut joindre avec celle-cy: on trouve l'une et l'autre à Paris chez J. B. Nolin."

" " 106. Le gouvernement de Raguse, estant une partie de Dalmatie avec quelques isles, très exactement mis en escrit par le père Coronelle.—Cherso, et Ossoro isole del Quarner.

Two small maps on 1 leaf.

" " 107. Principatus Valachiæ, Moldaviæ et Transylvaniæ. Per Gerardum et Leonardum Valk.

" " 108. Principatus Transilvaniæ. Ex conatibus Ioh. Baptistæ Homanni, Noribergæ.

" " 109. Bulgaria et Romania. Per Ger. et Leon. Valk.

" " 110. Exactissima tabula qua tam Danubii fluvii pars superior. Per Nicolaum Visscher Amst. Bat. Nunc apud Petrum Schenk iunior.

This map with the two following form one map.

They appear also in Visscher's *Atlas minor, 1710?*

" " 111. Exactissima tabula qua tam Danubii fluvii pars media. Per Nicolaum Visscher Amst. Bat. Nunc apud Pet. Schenk iunior.

" " 112. Exactissima tabula qua tam Danubii fluvii pars inferior. Per Nicolaum Visscher Amst. Bat. Nunc apud Pet. Schenk iunior.

" " 113. Turcicum imperium sive Magni Turcarum sultani status in Europa Asia et in Africa. per F. de Witt Amstelodami. Ex officina P. Mortier. Inset: Occidentalior pars maris Mediterranei in hoc angelo posita est ita ut Turcicum imperium unius folii in majori forma demonstretur.

" " 113a. Tables, ou divisions de la Turquie en Europe. Par le s^r. Sanson. Paris chez H. Jaillot, 1696.

" " 114. Nouvelle carte de la mer Noire et du canal de Constantinople très exacte, mis au jour par N. Visscher. Inset: Canal de Constantinople.

Inset has explanatory text in cartouche.

" " 115. Accurate vorstellung der orientalisch-kayserlichen haupt-und residenz-stadt Constantinopel. Herausgegeben von Iohann Baptist Homann in Nürnberg. Inset views: Prospectivische vorstellung der Dardanellen vor Constantinopel.—Prospect der Türckisch haupt und residentz- stadt Stambul oder Constantinopel.

The inset views are uncolored. View of Constantinopel has explanatory list.

Ottens, R.—Continued.

v. 6, no. 116–117. Græciæ antiquæ tabula nova. Autore Guillelmo Delisle Parisius, 1707.

Large map issued in 2 parts. General title on map no. 117, and additional titles on each sheet: no. 116, Græciæ pars septentrionalis. Parisius, 1708.—Græciæ pars meridionalis.

" " 118. Græciæ et Archipelago. Per Gerardum et Leonardum Valk.

" " 119. Exactissima totius Archipelagi nec non Græciæ tabula. Per Nicolaum Visscher Amstelo- Bat^m. Nunc apud P. Schenk iunior.

Appears also in Visscher's *Atlas minor, 1710?*, and 1712?

" " 120. Achaia vetvs et nova à Io. Bapt. Homanno. Norimbergae. Io. Christoph^s I. B. Homanni filius designavit.

" " 121. Mare Mediterraneum, exhibens oras Hispaniæ, Galliæ, Italiæ, mare Hadriaticum, Archipelagus, Natoliam, Ægyptum, Levantum, Barcam, Tripolin, Tunetanum, Algeriam, Fezzam, Maurocum, quibus accedunt insulæ Majorca, Minorca, Ebusa, Corsica, Sardinia, Sicilia, Candia, et Cyprus. Venundantur. per Gerardum et Leonardum Valk.

Large map on two sheets joined and folded.

" " 122. Nova et accurata geographica tabula insulæ Corfu seu Corcyræ cum confiniis suis ac portubus ex adverso in Græcia iacentibus. Autore Joachimo Ottens Amstelodami. Insets: Mare Adriaricum.—Urbs Corfu in plano exhibita.

Appears also in Visscher's *Atlas minor, 1717?*

" " 123. Peloponnesus hodiè Morea. Per Nicolaum Visscher Amst. Bat. Nunc apud Petrum Schenk iunior.

Appears also in Visscher's *Atlas minor, 1710?* and 1717?

" " 124. Peloponnesus hodie Moreæ regnum. Auctore F. de Wit. Amstelodami ex officina P. Mortier.

The margin of the map is made up of fourteen small engravings of places as follows: Navarino.—Zarnata.—Cas^l. Tornese.—Corinto.—Malvasia.—Patrasso.—Coron.—Napoli di Romania.—Modon.—Lepanto.—S. Maura.—Cerigo.—Atene.—Misitra olim Sparta.

" " 125. Cretæ seu Candiæ insula et regnum. Per Nicolaum Visscher Amst. Bat.

" " 126. Insula Samos Polycratis reg. et Pythagorae Phil. Ex descriptione potissimum Iosephi Georgirene ab eodem edita. Fec. et exc. Petr. Schenk. Amst. Insets: Ins. Nicaria, olim Icaria.—Ins. Pathmos, vulgó Patino et Palmosa.

Appears also in v. 8 of Cóvens & Mortier's *Atlas nouveau. [1683–1761]*

v. 7, no. 1. Nova orbis terraquei tabula accuratissime delineata.—Mappemonde ou descriptio générale du globe terrestre et aquatique. Leide chez Pierre vander Aa.

" " 2. Asia antiqua cum finitimis Africæ et Europæ regionibus. Nicolaus Blancardus Belga, Leidensis, ad lucem ævi veteris delineabat.

On the lower part of the map there is a series of engravings of coins of different reigns.

v. 7, no. 3. L'Asie. Leide Pierre vander Aa.—Asia in praecipuas ipsius partes distributa a Petro vander Aa. Insets: Hæc tab. regionum ad partem septentrio- orientalem Sinæ sit. edita á defer. juxta relationes r. p. Martini jesuitæ.—Hæc tab. regionum sitarum ad partem septentrionalem, ad septentrio- orientalem et ad orientalem Sinæ, edita fuit á defer juxta relationes r. p. verbiest jesuitæ.

" " 4. Exactissima Asiæ delineatio. Per Carolum Allard Amstelo-Batavum. Extracta ex authenticis tabulis d. Nicolai Witsen. Ph. Tiedeman delin. G. v. Gouwen sculp. Inset: Tartariæ pars.
Appears also in Visscher's *Atlas minor, 1710?*

" " 5. Carte d'Asie. Par Guillaume Delisle. Paris, 1723.

" " 6. Asiae recentissima delineatio. Authore Ioh. Bapt. Homanno. Noriberg.
Has explanatory text in cartouche.

" " 6a. Tables géographiques des divisions de l'Asie. Par le s^r^. Sanson. Paris chez H. Iaillot, 1696.

" " 7. Magni Turcarum domini imperium in Europa, Asia, et Africa. Per Nicolaum Visscher Amst. Bat. Nunc apud Petrum Schenk iunior. Tideman f. G. v. Gouwen sc.
Large map on two sheets joined and folded.

" " 7a. Divisions de toutes les provinces de l'empire des Turcs. Par le s^r^. Sanson. Paris chez H. Iaillot, 1696.

" " 8. La Perse, la Géorgie, la Natolie les Arabies, l'Egipte et le cours du Nile. Par N. de Fer. Paris, 1720.

" " 9. Nova Persiæ Armeniæ Natoliæ et Arabiæ. Per Fred. de Witt ex officina R. & I. Ottens Amst.
Appears also in Visscher's *Atlas contractus, 1666?*

" " 10. Natolia, quæ olim Asia Minor. Amstelodami sumptibus penes Petrum Schenk, et Gerardum Valk.

" " 11. Tabula nova geographica Natoliæ et Asiæ Minoris. Per Jacobum Cantellii, et edita per Nicolaum Visscher Amst. Bat. Nunc apud Petrum Schenk iunior.

" " 12. Carte particulière des païs où les apôtres ont prêché l'éuangile; des lieux les plus renommez de leurs voyages, et de la route de St Paul à Rome. Dressée pour bien entendre l'Histoire sainte. Amsterdam chez I. Cóvens & C. Mortier. I. van Luchtenburg delin. et sculpsit.

" " 13. Assyria vetvs divisa in Syriam, Mesopotamiam, Babyloniam, & Assyriam propriè dictam. Auctore Phil. de la Ruë. Amstelodami apud I. Cóvens & C. Mortier.
Appears also in Le Clerc's *Atlas Antiquus*, [*1705*]

" " 14. Terrá Sancta, sive Promissionis, olim Palestina. Per Fredericum de Wit. Gedruckt tot Amsterdam by Pieter Mortier. Inset: Castorum populi Israelitici.

" " 15. Iudæa seu Terra Sancta, quae Hebræorum sive Israelitarum in suas duodecim tribus divisa. Amstelodami apud Petrum Mortier.—Iudæa, sive Terra Sancta induodecim tribus divisa. Autore N. Sanson. Amstelodami apud Petrum Mortier.

" " 16. Regnvm Ivdæorvm. Auctore Ph. de la Ruë. Amstelodami apud I. Cóvens & C. Mortier.

Ottens, R.—Continued.

v. 7, no. 17. Imperii Persici delineatio ex scriptis potissimum geographicis Arabum et Persarum tentata ab Adriano Relando. Ex formis [Pet]tri [!] Schenk [Amst]eldæmi [!] 1705.
Dedication to Nicolaes Witsen and latin verse in cartouche.

" " 18. [Persia]
Without title, author or date. Cut to the margin and pasted on another sheet.

" " 19. Imperii Persici in omnes suas provincias, exacte divisi luci publicæ exponit Io. Baptista Homann. Norimbergæ.

" " 20. Verschiedene prospecte dervornemsten stadten in Persien: Herausgegeben von Iohann Baptist Homann. Nürnberg.—Astrachan.—Derbent.—Teflis Kars.—Erzerum.—Baccu.—Sultania.—Schamachia.—Erivan.—Schiras.—Candahar.—Die stadt Ardebil.—Die stadt Kachan.—Isphanan.—Gamrom oder Bender Abassi.
Appears also in Homann heirs, *Stadt-atlas, 1762.*

" " 21. Carte des pays voisins de la mer Caspiene. Par Guillaume Delisle. Paris, 1723. Marin sculpsit.
Appears also in Cóvens *and* Mortier's *Atlas nouveau, [1683-1761]*

" " 22. Provinciarum Persicarum Kilaniæ à Io. Bapt. Homanno. Noribergæ. R. A. S. 1728. Inset: Prospect der rusischen stadt und vestung Tercki.

" " 23. Nova ac verissima maris Caspii, in lucem edita per Reinerum Ottens. Iacob Keyser sculp. Gedrukt t' Amsterdam by de wed. I. Ottens.

" " 24. Geographica nova ex oriente gratiosissima duabus tabulis specialissimis contenta quarum una mare Caspivm altera Kamtzadaliam seu terram Jedso curiosé exhibet. Editore Io. Bapt. Homann. Norimbergæ.
Each section of the map has a separate title: Das Caspische meer.—Das land Kamtzadalie sonst Jedso.

" " 25. Generalis totius imperii Rossorum novissima tabula. Ex conatibus Iohannis Baptistæ Homanni Norimbergæ.

" " 26. Tartaria, sive Magni Chami imperium, in lucem editum a Carolo Allard, Amst. Bat.
Appears also in Braakman's *Atlas minor, 1706.*

" " 27. Carte de Tartarie. Par Guillaume Del'Isle. Amsterdam chez Pierre Mortier.
Additional title at top of map: Tartaria, sive Magni Chami imperium.

" " 28. Magnæ Tartariæ, Magni Mogolis imperii, Iaponiæ, et Chinæ. Per F. de Witt Amstelodami, ex officina I. Cóvens et C. Mortier.

" " 29. Magni Mogolis imperivm de novo correctum et divisum per F. de Witt, Amstelodami ex officina I. Cóvens & C. Mortier.

" " 30. Sinus Gangeticus, vulgo golfo de Bengala nova descriptio. Amstelædami typiis G. Valk et P. Schenk.

" " 31. Nieuwe kaarte van't koninkryk Bengale, Opgestelt door Joh. van Leenen, J. van Braam et G. onder de Linden.

v. 7, no. 32. Indiæ orientalis nec non insularum adiacentium nova descriptio, per Nicolaum Visscher. Nunc apud Petrum Schenk junior.
Reproduced in *Remarkable maps of the xvth, xvith & xviith centuries reproduced in their original size*, published at Amsterdam by F. Muller & co., 1894–1899.

" " 33. Tabula Indiæ orientalis et regnorum adjacentium. J. van Braam et G. onder de Linden.

" " 34. Les Indies orientalis. Par. N. de Fer, 1721. Paris chez Dauet.
In the cartouche containing the title the latitude and longitude of the principal cities of the East Indies are given.

" " 35. Carte des côtes de Malabar et de Coromandel. Par G. Delisle. Marin sculpsit. Paris, 1723.

" " 36. Nova tabula terrarum Cucan, Canara, Malabaria, Madura, & Coromandellia cum parte septentrionali insulae Ceylon. Edente Hadriano Relando. tot Amsterdam by Gerard van Keulen.

" " 37. Nieuwe kaart van Choromandel ende Malabar opgesteld door François Valentyn. J. van Braam en G. onder de Linden.

" " 38. Insula Ceilon et Madura per Joachim Ottens.
Appears also in Ottens heirs. *Atlas*, [*1740?*]

" " 39. Nieuwe kaart van het eyland Ceylon, opgestelt door Francois Valentyn. J. van Braam et G. onder de Linden.

" " 40. Imperii Sinarvm nova descriptio. Auctore Joh. van Loon. Amstelædami ex typographia apud Gerardi Valk et Petri Schenk.
Appears also in Visscher's *Atlas contractus*, [*1666?*]

" " 41. Carte exacte de toutes les provinces, villes, bourgs, villages et rivières du vaste et puissant empire de la Chine, dressée par Jean Nieuhof et présentement mise au jour par Pierre vander Aa, à Leide.

" " 42. Pecheli, Xansi, Xantung, Homan, Nanking, in plaga regni Sinensis inter septentrionem ac orientem cecian versus sitæ provinciæ. Amstelodami venales apud P. Schenk et G. Valk.

" " 43. Suchuen; et Xensi, provinciæs eu praefecturæ regni Sinensis. Amstelodami typis apud Petrum Schenk et Gerardum Valk.

" " 44. Iunnan, Queicheu, Quangsi, et Quantong provinciæ regni Sinensis. Amstelædami sumptibus G. Valk et P. Schenk.

" " 45. Huquang, Kiangsi, Chekiang ac Fokien, provin. sivæ præfecturæ regni Sinen^s^. Amstelædami impensis Gerardi Valk et Petri Schenk.
The four preceding maps of provinces of China appear also in Visscher's *Atlas minor*, [*1717?*]

" " 46. Le royaume de Siam auec les royaumes qui luy sont tributaires et les isles de Sumatra, Amdemaon, etc. et les isles voisines. Amsterdam chez Ioachim Ottens.
Map on two sheets joined and folded. Title at top of map, "Le royaume de Siam avec les royaumes qui luy sont tributaires.

" " 47. Svmatræ et insularum locorumque nonnullorum circumiacentium tabula noua. Amstelodami apud P. Schenk et G. Valk.

" " 48. Nieuwe kaart van het eyland Sumatra verbeterd door François Valentyn. J. van Braam et G. onder de Linden exc.

Ottens, R.—Continued.

v. 7, no. 49. Insulae Iavae pars occidentalis edente Hadriano Relando.—Insulae Iavae pars orientalis edente Hadriano Relando. t Amsterdam by Gerard van Keulen. J. Keyser fecit. Insets: de have of reede van Batavia.—Afteekening vande stad ent kasteel van Batavia.
Map on two sheets joined and folded.
Appears also in Cóvens and Mortier's *Atlas nouveau*, [*1683–1761*]
Ornamented with a scene of natives offering to the Belgian lion the products of the island.

" " 50. Nieuwe en zeer naaukeurige kaart van t eyland Java Major of Groot Java verdeeld in seven bysondere besttekken door Françios Valentyn. J. van Braam et G. onder de Linden excud[nt].
Map on 7 leaves joined and folded.

" " 51. Kaart van het eyland Bali. J. van Braam en G. onder de Linden exc.

" " 52. Insula Borneo et occidentalis pars celebis cum adjacentibus insulis. Amstelodami apud Pet. Schenk et Ger. Valk.
Appears also in Visscher's *Atlas minor*, [*1717?*]

" " 53. Kaart van het eyland Borneo. J. van Braam et G. onder de Linden exc.

" " 54. Insularum Moluccarum nova descriptio. Amstelodami apud P. Schenk et G. Valk.
Appears also in Visscher's *Atlas minor*, [*1717?*]

" " 55. De landvoogdy der Moluccos met de aangrenzende eylanden. Inset: [Celebes]

" " 56. De landvoogdy Amboina met de elf onderhoorige eylanden.
Map cut to the margin and pasted on another sheet.

" " 57. Caart van het eyland Amboina in't bijsonder. Inset: Het Casteel Victoria.
Map cut to the margin and pasted on another sheet.

" " 58. Insvlarvm Bandanensivm novissima delineatio. Amstelodami apud P. Schenk et G. Valk.

" " 59. Nieuwe caart der eylanden van Banda. Gemaakt door François Valentyn. J. van Braam en G. O. Linden excud[it].

" " 60. Kaart der zuyd-wester eylanden van Banda. J. van Braam et G. o. Linden excud.

" " 61. Kaart van de zud-ooster eylanden van Banda. J. van Braam en G. onder de Linden exc.

" " 62. [Philippine islands]
Small map without author, title or date. Cut to the margin and pasted on another sheet.

" " 63. Kaart van het eyland Formosa en de eylanden van Piscadores. J. van Braam & G. onder de Linden exc.
Cut to the margin and pasted on another sheet.

" " 64. Nova et accvrata Iaponiæ terræ Esonis ac insularum adjacentium. Amstelodami vendibilis apud P. Schenk et G. Valk.

" " 65. Imperivm Japonicvm per regiones digestvm sex et sexaginta atqve ex ipsorvm Japonensivm mappis descriptvm ab Hadriano Relando. Inset: Conspectvs vrbis Nangasacki. Amstelodami apud I. Ottens.
Has explanatory text at foot of map.

This map without Ottens' name and marked "I. Goeree in. B. Ruyter sculpr.," and with the inset marked, "Trajecti Batavorvm apud Gvilielvm Broedelet, 1715," appears in Visscher's *Atlas minor*, [*1717?*]

v. 7, no. 66. Nieuwe kaart van het eyland Japan verbeterd door François Valentyn. J. van Braam et G. onder de Linden exc.

" " 67. Description exacte et fidele des villes, bourgs et villages qui les ambassadeurs de Hollande ont rencontrez dans leur voyage par terre de la ville d Osacca jusqu'a Iedo capitale du Japon.—Voyage des ambassadeurs de Hollande, par mer de Nangasacqui à Osacca exactement decrit presentement publié par P. vander Aa, à Leide.

" " 68. Africæ antiquæ et quarundam Europæ, Asiæque adiacentium regionum. Edita a Nicolao Blancardo Batavo.

" " 69. L'Afrique. Leide chez Pierre vander Aa.
Additional title at top of map: Africa in praecipuas ipsius partes distributa, ad observationes academiae regiae scientiarum et exquisitissimas tabulas, quae nunquam antehac l'ucem viderunt excusa a Petro vander Aa.

" " 70. Novissima et perfectissima Africæ descriptio ex formis Caroli Allard. Amstelo-Batavii. Ph. Tideman del. G. v. Gouwen.
Appears in Braakman's *Atlas minor, 1706.*

" " 71. Carte d'Afrique. Par Guillaume Delisle. Paris, 1722.
The same map with Buache's name in the lower right hand corner appears in Delisle and Buache's *Atlas géographique et universel, 1700–1762.*

" " 72. Totius Africas nova repræsentatio, a Io. Baptista Homanno, Norimbergæ.

" " 72a. Tables géographiques des divisions de l'Afrique. Par le s[r]. Sanson. Paris chez H. Iaillot, 1696.

" " 73. Carte de la Barbarie de la Nigritie at de la Guinée. Par Guillaume Del'Isle. Paris, 1707. Inselin sculpsit.
Editions of this and the two following maps with an additional line giving Buache's name and the date 1745, appear in Delisle and Buache's [*Atlas géographique & universal, 1700–1762*]

" " 74. Carte de l Egypte de la Nubie l'Abissinie &c. Par Guillaume De lisle. Desrosiers sculp. à Paris, 1707.

" " 75. Carte du Congo et du pays des Cafres. Par G. De l'Isle, à Paris, 1708.

" " 76. Africæ magna pars ad illustrationem historiæ ecclesiasticæ. Matth Seuteri. Augustæ Vindelicorum.
Contains explanatory text in latin and german.

" " 77. Nova Barbariæ descriptio. Prostant Amstelaedami apud Petrum Schenk et Gerardum Valk.

" " 78. Fezzæ et Marocchi regni Africæ celeberrima, describebat Abrah: Ortolius. Prostant Amstelaedami apud Petrum Schenk et Gerardum Valk.
An edition of this map appears in Blaeu's *Le théâtre dv monde, 1638–1640.*

" " 79. Statum Marocca Norum a Io. Chris. Homanno m. d. Noribergæ anno 1728. Inset view: Der stadt Marocco.—Prospect der königlichen residenz stadt Mequinetz.

Ottens, R.—Continued.

Appears also in Homann heirs, *Homannischer atlas von hundert landkarten, 1747–[1757]*

v. 7, no. 80. Ægypti recentior descriptio. Prostant Amstelaedami apud Petrum Schenk et Gerardum Valk.

Appears also in Visscher's *Atlas minor, [1717?]*

" " 81. Das heutige Ægypten aus der reyssbeschreibung des berühmten h[n] Paul Lucas gezoge, und mit folgenden denckwürdigkeiten herausgegeben von Iohann Bapt. Homann. Nürnbg. Ioannis Christophorus I. B. Homanni filius delineavit.

Additional title at top of map, Ægyptus hodierna ex itinerario celeberrimi viri Pauli Lucæ Franci desumta ac repræsentata à Iohanne Baptista Homann. Norimbergæ.

Ornamented with views of the wonders of Egypt.

" " 82. Nieuwe platte paskaart van de Roode zee in Oost-indien. Amsterdam by Gerard van Keulen.—Carte particulière de la mer Rouge. Amsterdam auparavant chez Pierre Mortier. Inset: Fortification de Monbasa.—Het eyland Babel Mandel.—L'isle de Monbasa.

" " 83. Nigritarum regnum. Amstelodami apud Gerardum Valk et Petrum Schenk.

Dedication signed Joannis Jansonii.

" " 84. Gvinæ.

" " 85. Æthiopia svperior vel interior; vulgo Abissinorvm sive Presbiteri Ioannis imperivm. Amstelædami penes G. Valk et P. Schenk.

Appears also in Visscher's *Atlas minor, [1717?]*

" " 86. Jobi Ludolfi Habessinia seu Abassia Presbyteri Johannis regio. Anno Christi 1683. Christianus Ludolfus j. filius delineavit ex autographo parentis. Apud G. Valk et P. Schenk.

Appears also in Visscher's *Atlas minor, [1717?]*

" " 87. Nieuwe kaart van caap der Goede Hoop in hare rechte jegenwoordige staat vertoond door François Valentyn. J. van Braam et G. onder de Linden exc. Inset: Kaart van de caap der Goede Hoop.

" " 88. Nieuwe naauwkeurige land-en zee-kaart, van het voorna amste gedeelte der Kaffersche kust, begrypende de Sardanje-bay en de camp de Bonne Esperanca.

Additional title at top of map, Nova et accurata tabula Promontórii Bonae Spei, vulgo cabo de Bona Esperança.

" " 89. Insulæ Canariæ olim Fortvnatæ dictæ. Amstelodami apud G. Valk et P. Schenk.

" " 90. L'Amerique. Leide chez Pierre vander Aa. I. Goeree delin. I. Baptist sculp.

Additional title at top of map, America in præcipuas ipsius partes distributa, ad observationes Academiæ regiæ scientiarum et exquisitissimas tabulas quæ nunquam antehac lucem viderunt, excusa a Petro vander Aa.

Cartouche containing title ornamented with medallions of Columbus and Americus Vespucius, and with an indian scene.

" " 91. Recentissima novi orbis sive Americæ Septentrionalis et Meridionalis tabula ex officina Caroli Allard. Ph. Tideman del. G. v. Gouwen sculp. Inset: Zeelandia Nova.

Appears also in Allard's *Atlas minor*, [*1696?*]—Braakman's *Atlas minor*, *1706*.—Visscher's *Atlas minor*, [*1710?*]—Ottens heirs *Atlas*, [*1740?*]

v. 7, no. 92. Carte d'Amérique. Par Guillaume Delisle. Paris, 1722.
The Library of Congress has a copy of this map in separate form.

" " 93. Totius Americæ Septentrionalis et Meridionalis novissima repræsentatio quam ex singulis recentium geographorum tabulis collectā luci publicæ accommodavit Iohannes Baptista Homann. Norimbergæ.
Appears also in Homann's *Neuer atlas*, *1710*–[*1731*] and *Kleiner atlas* [*1732?*]

" " 94. Amérique Septentrionale divisée en ses principales parties. Par H. Iaillot.—America Septentrionalis in suas præcipuas partes divisa.
A copy of this map with slight differences appears in Jaillot's *Atlas françois*, *1695*.

" " 95. L'Amérique Septentrionale. Par G. de l'Isle. Amsterdam chez Pierre Schenk, 1708.
Appears also in Ottens' *Atlas minor*, [*1703–1756?*] and in Visscher's *Atlas minor*, [*1717?*]

" " 95a. Tables géographiques des divisions de l'Amérique Septentrionale. Par le s^r. Sanson. Paris chez H. Iaillot, 1692.

" " 96. Carte du Canada ou de la Nouvelle France. Par Guillaume De l'Isle. Amsterdam chez Iean Cóvens et Corneille Mortier.
Appears also in Delisle's *Atlas nouveau*, *1730*, and without Cóvens and Mortier's name, published at Paris, dated 1703, and extending to the 260th meridian, in Delisle's *Atlas de géographie*, [*1700–1712*] and in Delisle and Buache's [*Atlas géographique et universel*, *1700–1762*]

" " 97. Nova tabula geographica complectens Borealiorem Americæ partem; in qua exacte delineatæ sunt Canada sive Nova Francia, Nova Scotia, Nova Anglia, Novum Belgium, Pensylvania, Virginia, Carolina, et Terra Nova cum omnibus littorum pulvinorumque profunditatibus. Amstlodami â Nicolao Visscher. Nunc apud Petrum Schenk iunior.—Carte nouvelle contenant la partie d' Amérique la plus Septentrionale ou sont exactement dêcrites les provinces suivantes comme le Canada ou Nouvelle France, la Nouvelle Ecosse, la Nouvelle Angleterre, les Nouveaux Païs Bas, la Pensylvanie, la Virginie, la Caroline et l' Jle de Terre Neuve avec les profundeuis le long des côtes et sur les bancs. Par Nicolas Visscher. Nunc apud Petrum Schenk iunior.
Large map on two sheets joined and folded. Published ca. 1685. The Library of Congress has a separate copy of the western half of this map with a border all the way around it, marked Luggardus van Anse schulp. It shows that it has been taken from an atlas, and while corresponding in all particulars with the same part of this map, it is evidently from a different plate.

" " 98. Amplissimæ regione Mississipi. Nova tabula edita â Io. Bapt. Homanno. Norimbergæ. Inset view: Catarrhacta ad Niagaram.

Ottens, R.—Continued.

Appears also in Homann heirs' *Atlas geographicvs maior, 1759–[1781]* and of copy dated *1759–[1784]*

v. 7, no. 99. Tabula Mexicae et Floridae terrarum Anglicarum, et anteriorum Americae insularum; item cursuum et circuituum fluminis Mississipi dicti. Amstel. prostant apud Petrum Schenck.

Appears also in Ottens heirs *Atlas, [1740?]*

" " 100. Nova Hispania, et Nova Galicia. Guiljelmus Blaeuw excudit.

Appears also in Blaeu's *Le theatre dv monde, 1638–1640,* and edition of *1644;* and in Blaeu's *Atlas maior, 1662–1665.*

" " 101. Totius Neobelgii nova et accuratissima tabula. Typis Ioachim Ottens Amstelodami. Inset view: Nieuw-Amsterdam onlangs Nieuw jorck genaemt, ende hernomen bij de Nederlanders op den 24 Aug. 1673 eindelÿk aan de Engelse weder afgestaan.

This inset view, drawn about 1673, is the "Restitutio" view (the word appearing beneath the group of figures surmounting the view), by Hugo Allard, used by Allard, Ottens, Seutter and Seller. A copy of the Ottens issue of this map is very rare.

" " 102. Nova Anglia Septentrionali Americæ implantata Anglorumque coloniis florentissima geographice exhibita à Ioh. Baptista Homann. Norimbergæ.

Appears also in Homann heirs *Atlas geographicvs maior, 1759–1781]*

" " 103. Virginia Marylandia et Caroline in America Septentrionali Britannorum industria excultæ repræsentatæ à Ioh. Bapt. Homann. Norimbergæ.

Appears also in Homann heirs, *Atlas geographicvs maior, 1759–[1781]*

" " 104. Carte général de la Caroline. Par le sieur S * * * [Sanson] à Amsterdam chez Pierre Mortier. Inset: [Charleston harbor]

Appears also in *Le Neptune françois, De fransche neptune, 1693–1700.*

" " 105. Carte particulière de la Caroline. Par le sieur S * * * [Sanson] à Amsterdam chez Pierre Mortier.

Shows many names of early settlers particularly those located along the rivers.

Appears also in *Le Neptune françois, De fransche neptunus, 1693–1700,* and Cóvens & Mortier's *Atlas nouveau, [1683–1761]*

" " 106. Carte nouvelle de la mer du Sud. Donné au public par And. & Henry de Leth à Amsterdam.—Nova maris Pacifici tabula.—Nieuwe kaart van de Zuyd zee. Insets: Plan du port et Mont Table au cap de Bonne Esperance.—Carte particulière du detroit de Magellan.—*Views:* Chute fleuve de St. Laurent nommé Mississipi.—La ville de Mexico.—Fort au cap de Bonne Esperance.—Le cap de Bonne Esperance.

Large map on 2 sheets joined and folded. Map profusely annotated with historical facts.

Another issue of this map of apparently a later date and with the inset maps changed, also a cartouche containing views of Vera Cruz, the bay of Rio Janeiro and Havana substituted for the cartouche containing the view of the "Chute fleuve de St. Laurent " appears in Ottens' *Atlas, [1756?]*

v. 7, no. 107. Nova isthmi Americani, qui et Panamiensis item Dariensis tabvla in qua vrbes Porto Bello, Panama et Carthagena. Edita a Reinere et Josva Ottens Amstelodami.
Appears also in Ottens' *Atlas minor*, [*1695–1756?*]

" " 108. Insulæ Americanæ in oceano Septentrionali ac regiones adiacentes, a C. de May usque ad lineam æquinoctialem. Per Nicolaum Visscher. Nunc apud Petrum Schenk iunior.
Appears without Schenk's name in the three copies of Visscher's *Atlas minor*, [*1690?*] in the Library of Congress, the contents of which differ slightly, also appears without Schenk's name in Visscher's *Atlas minor*, [*1684?*], [*1700?*], [*1712?*], [*1717?*] and in Visscher's *Variæ tabula geographicæ*, [*1704?*]

" " 109. Jamaica, Americæ Septentrionalis ampla insula, a Christophoro Columbo detecta in suas gubernationes peraccuratè distincta. Per Nicolaum Visser Amst. Bat. Nunc apud Pet. Schenk jun. L. v. Anse schulp.
Appears without Schenk's name in Visscher's *Atlas minor*, [*1690?*] and in Schenk's *Atlas contractus*, [*1705?*]

" " 110. L'isle St. Domingue ou Espagnole découverte l'an 1492 par les espagnols et dressé par N. Fer. Paris chez Danet, 1723.

" " 111. Nieuwe en aldereerste afteekening van 't eyland S^t^. Thomas, 1719. tot Amsterdam by Gerard van Keulen. Inset: de haven van S^t^. Thomas.—De ooster haven van 't eyland S^t^. Ian.
Same map with a row of five small insets at the foot of the map, showing the elevation of various points on the island, appears in Voogt's *De nieuwe groote lichtende zee-fakkel. 1782.*

" " 112. Tabula novissima atque accuratissima Caraibicarvm insularum sive Canni balvm quæ etiam Antillæ Gallicæ dicuntur, a Reinero Ottens Amstelædamensi. Gedrukt 't Amsterdam by de wed. I. Ottens.
Appears also in Ottens heirs, *Atlas*, [*1740?*]

" " 113. Insula Matanino vulgo Martanico in lucem edita per Nicolaum Visscher. Nunc apud P. Schenk iun.
Appears without Schenk's name in Visscher's *Atlas minor*, [*1690?*], and [*1717?*]

" " 114. L'Amérique Meridionale. Par G. De l'Isle. Amsterdam chez I. Cóvens & C. Mortier.
Appears also in Delisle's *Atlas nouveau, 1733*, and [*1741?*], and in Valck's *Nova totius geographica telluris projectio*, [*1748?*]

" " 114a. Tables géographiques des divisions de l'Amérique Meridionale. Par le s^r^. Sanson, à Paris chez H. Iaillot, 1696.

" " 115. Carte de la Terre Ferme du Pérou du Brésil et du pays des Amazones. Par Guillaume Del'Isle, à Amsterdam chez Iean Cóvens et Corneille Mortier.
Additional title at head of map, Tabula géographica Peruæ, Brasiliæ & Amazonum regionis.
Appears also in Delisle's [*Collection of maps, 1722–74*], and Delisle's *Atlas nouveau, 1733*, and [*1741?*]

" " 116. Nieuwe afteekening van het eyland Curacao. Tot Amsterdam by Gerard van Keulen. Insets: t Fort Amsterdam on't in koomen van baya S^t^. Anna geleegen op't eyland Curacao.—[View]: 't Fort Amsterdam voor aan de bay S^t^. Anna.

Ottens, R.—Continued.

Is illustrated with narrow view showing the elevation of the mountains, and has explanatory text.

Appears also in Voogt's *De nieuwe groot lichtende zee-fakkel, 1782.*

v. 7, no. 117. Nieuwe kaart van Suriname vertonende de stromen en landstreken van Suriname, Comowini, Cottica, en Marawini. t Amsterdam by J. Ottens.

Appears in Ottens' *Atlas minor, [1695–1756?]*

" " 118. Nova et accurata Brasiliæ totius tabula, auctore Ioanne Blaev. Nunc apud Petrum Schenk iunior.

Appears without Schenk's name in Allard's *Atlas minor, 1696?*

" " 119. Carte du Paraguay, du Chili, du detriot de Magellan. Par Guillaume de l'Isle. Amsterdam chez Pierre Mortier.

Appears also in Delisle's [*Collection of maps, 1722–74*] and in his *Atlas nouveau, 1730, 1733,* and [*1741?*] and in Valk's *Nova totius geographica telluris projectio* [*1748?*]

1644

Jansson, J.

Des nieuwen atlantis aenhang ofte des nieuwen wereld-beschrijvinghe ende volkome vertoogs ende afbeeldinghe vande voornaemste koninckrijcken ende landen des gantschen werelts. Vereiert met veele schoone nieuwe land-caerten die ten deele noyt voor desen uytghegeven ende ten deele seer verbetert ende vermeerdert zijn. 2 p. l., [464] pp. incl. 105 maps. fol. Amstelodami, I. Ianssonium, 1644. 4258

Note.—Tiele gives three editions of Jansson's Atlas which are earlier than this one,—a dutch edition of 2 v., 1639, a french edition of 3 v., 1639, and a german edition of 3 v., 1640, with other later editions, but does not mention this edition of 1 v., 1644.

Many maps have the title in latin followed by the same title in the vernacular. For maps of America, see nos. 103–106 of contents.

CONTENTS.

no. [1] Comitatus Northvmbria.
" [2] Comitatvs Nottinghamiensis.
" [3] Provincia Oxoniensis.
" [4] Comitatus Cantabrigiensis.
" [5] Comitatus Penbrochiensis.
" [6] Ceretica sive Cardiganensis comitatvs.
" [7] Merivinia comitatus.
" [8] Comitatvs Darbiensis.
" [9] Devoniæ descriptio.
" [10] Svffolciæ nova et accurata delineatio.
" [11] Provinciæ Cantii.
" [12] Rvssiæ. Auctore Isaaco Massa.
" [13] Moscoviæ pars avstralis. Auctore Isaaco Massa.
" [14] Nova et accurata tabula episcopatvvm Stavangriensis Bergensis et Asloiensis.

no. [15] Gothia.
" [16] Vplandia.
" [17] Selandiæ in regno Daniæ insulæ chorographica descriptio.
" [18] Lalandiæ et Falstriæ accurata descriptio.
" [19] Tractuum Borussiæ. Authore Olao Ioannis Gotho.
" [20] Saxonia inferior.
" [21] Albis fluvius.
" [22] Marchionatus Brandenburgicus. Authore Olao Iohannis Gotho.
" [23] Saxonia superior.
" [24] Lusatia superior. Ath. Bartholomæo Sculteto Gorlitio.
" [25] Marchionatus Misniæ una cum Voitlandia. Authore Olao Ioannis Gotho.
" [26] Thuringia lantgraviatus. Henricus Hondius.
" [27] Serenissimo principi ac domino, D. Christiano duci Brunsvicensi et Luneburgensi hanc accuratissimam sui ducatus Brunsuicensis tabulam dedicat consecratq, Ioannes Ianssonius.
" [28] Principatus Amhaldinus et Magdeburgensis archiepiscopatus.
" [29] Circvlvs Westphalicvs.
" [30] Territorivm Francofvrtense.
" [31] Principatus Hennenbergensis. Henricus Hondius.
" [32] Comitatvs Wertheimici Finitimarvmqve regionvm nova et exacta descriptio.
" [33] Palatinatvs ad Rhenvm.
" [34] Vtriusquæ Alsatiæ superioris ac inferioris nova tabvla.
" [35] Territorium Argentoratense.
" [36] Helvetiæ Rhetiæ & Valesiæ cum omnibus finitimis tabula.
" [37] Territory Basiliensis nova descriptio.
" [38] Comitatus Tirolensis.
" [39] Comitatus Glatz. Authore Iona Sculteto.
" [40] Silesiæ dvcatvs. Ionas Scultetus Sprotta.
" [41] Dvcatvs Silesiæ Glogani vers delinaetio secunda cura ac labore confecta a Iona Sculteto Sprotta.
" [42] Ducatus Silesiæ Wolanus. Authore Iona Sculteto Sprotta.
" [43] Ducatus Breslanus. A Georgio Vechnero et Iona Sculteto Sprotta. Inset: Breslaw totius Silesiæ metropolis.
" [44] Ducatus Silesiæ Ligniciensis. Ionas Scultetus. Inset: Fv̈rstliche stadt Lignitz.
" [45] Silesia inferior. A Jona Sculteto Sprotta-Silesio.
" [46] Avstria archidvcatvs. Auctore Wolfgango Lazio.
" [47] Karstia, Carniola, Histria, et Windorvm Marchia. Ger. Mercatore auctore.
" [48] Dvcatvs Gelriae pars secunda.
" [49] Dvcatvs Gelriac pars prima.
" [50] Dvcatvs Gelriae pars quarta.
" [51] Imperium Caroli Magni.
" [52] Picardia vera et inferior. Henricus Hondius.
" [53] Lotharingia dvcatvs noua descriptio.
" [54] Territorivm Metense. Auctore Ab. Fabert.
" [55] Le pais de Brie.
" [56] Beauvaisis.
" [57] Valesivm ducatus.
" [58] Belsia.
" [59] Bitvricvm dvcatvs.

Jansson, J.—Continued.

no. [60] Comitatus Burgundiæ.
" [61] Les environs de l'Estang de Longpendv, comprenant vne grande partie du comte de Charolois. Par Iean van Damme.
" [62] Bressia.
" [63] La principavte de Dombes.
" [64] Quercy.
" [65] Langvedoc.
" [66] Sabavdia dvcatvs.
" [67] Legionis regvm et Astrvriarvm principatvs.
" [68] Territorio Trevigiano.
" [69] Territorio Cremasco.—Il Cadorino.
" [70] Polesino di Rovigo.
" [71] Territorio di Bergamo.
" [72] Stato di Milano.
" [73] Territorio di Cremona.
" [74] Dvcato ouero territorio de Milano.
" [75] Territorio di Pavia, Lodi, Novàrra, Tortona, Alessandria et altri vicini dello stato de Milano.
" [76] Parte Alpestre dello stato di Milano con il Lago Maggiore di Lucano, è di Como.
" [77] Principatus Pedemontii, ducatus Augustæ prætoriæ Salutii marchionatus, Astæ, Vercellarum et Nicæ comitatus nova tabula.
" [78] Piemonte et Monferrato.
" [79] Ligvria ò stato della republica di Genova.
" [80] Riviera di Genova di ponente.
" [81] Riviera de Genova di levante.
" [82] Dvcato di Modena regio et Caprif col dominio della Carfagnana.
" [83] Domino Fiorentino.
" [84] Territorio de Siena con il ducato di Castro.
" [85] Ischia isola olim Ænaria.
" [86] Elba isola.
" [87] Dvcato di Ferrara.
" [88] Territorio di Bologna.
" [89] Romagna olim Flaminia.
" [90] Territorio di Orvieto.
" [91] Territorio Pervgino.
" [92] Dvcato di Vrbino.
" [93] Marca d'Ancona olim Picenvm.
" [94] Vmbria overo dvcato di Spoleto.
" [95] Abrvzzo citra et vltra.
" [96] Terra di Lavoro, olim Campania Felix.
" [97] Principato Citra olim Picentia.
" [98] Capitanata olim Mesapiæ et Iapygiæ pars.
" [99] Terra di Otranto olim Salentina et Iapigia.
" [100] Calabria citra olim Magna Græcia.
" [101] Calabria vltra olim Altera Magnæ Græciæ pars.
" [102] Magni Mongolis imperium.
" [103] India quæ orientalis dicitur, et insvlæ adiacentes, Henricus Hondius.
" [104] America Septentrionalis.
" [105] Virginiæ partis australis, et Floridæ partis orientalis, interjacentiumq regionum nova descriptio.
" [106] America pars meridionalis.

1655

Ortelius, A.

Theatro del mondo . . . nel quale distintamente si dimostrano in tauole, tutte le prouincie, regni & paesi del mondo. Con la descrittione delle città, territorij, castelli, monti . . . ridotto à intieta perfettione, & in questa picciol forma, per maggior commodità de' viaggianti. 4 p. l., 231, [16] 12 pp., 109 maps. 24°. Venetia, [G. M.] Turrini, [1655] 4259

Note.—Collation: 4 l. unsigned.—Sig. A–I, K–P in eights.—Q in four.—R in six. Dedication dated 1655. This date was taken as the date of publication. l. [1] recto: half title, "Theatro del mondo"; verso: blank.—l. [2] recto: title, with vignette and dedication to "il sig. Abbate Hondedei"; verso: blank.—l. [3] recto-verso: "Illvstriss e reverendiss Signore"; dated: "Di Venetia. Dalle mie stampe li 20. settembre 1655," signed: "Gio: Maria Turrini." l. [4] recto: "Lettore"; verso: "Carta marina." sig. A recto—[P4] recto: Theatro del mondo et prima della descrittione del mare"; [P4] verso: blank. [P5] recto—[Q3] verso: "Tavola delli nomi, et particolarità contenute nella presente opera." [Q4] recto-verso: "Libri volgari istorici, romanzi, belle lettre . . . stampati dal Turrini & altri."—R recto—[R5 verso]: "Poste per il mondo."—[R6] recto: "Tavola de' viaggi."—[R6] verso: Dichiaratione, per sapere quanto siano lunghe le poste, la legà francese."

This edition is not mentioned in Hessels' *Epistulæ Ortelianæ*, 1887, but there is listed another edition dated july 15, 1655, a copy of which is said to be in the British Museum.

The following maps relate to America:

no. [1] Carta marina. [World]
" [2] Typvs orbis terrarvm.
" [3] Evropa. [Gronlandiae pars]
" [6] Americae sive novi orbis nova descriptio.
" [99] Tartariae sive magni chami regni tipvs. [Americaè vel nov: orbis pars]
" [101] Indiaé orientalis insvlarvmqve adiacientivm tiipvs. [Americae siue Indie]

1658

Sanson, N., *d'Abbeville.*

Cartes générales de tovtes les parties dv monde, ov les empires, monarchies, republiques, estats, peuples, &c. de l'Asie, de l'Africqve, de l'Evrope, & de l'Américqve, tant anciens que nouveaux, sont exactement remarqués, & distingués suivant leur estenduë . . . 2 p. l., 113 (*i. e.* 117) maps. fol. Paris, l'avthevr; P. Mariette, 1658. 4260

Note.—"Table des cartes générales de toutes les parties du monde," on the two pages following the title-page. The "Table" contains the names of 113 maps, of which one map is wanting in this copy. Four maps not called for by the "Table" are inserted. The inserted maps follow:

Sardones. Evesché de Elne ou Perpignan. L. Cordier sc. 1660.
La Prusse. Somer sculp. 1659.
La Curlande. Somer sc. 1659.
Principauté de Catalogne. L. Cordier Abb. sculp. 1660.
The maps are dated from 1632 to 1660.

Sanson, N., *d'Abbeville*—Continued.

Of the maps in this edition Pierre Mariette appears as the publisher of forty two; Melchor Tavernier's name and address as well as Pierre Mariette's appears on sixteen maps; M. Tavernier on one; the author as publisher on twenty-eight; the author and P. Mariette on two; and on twenty-seven maps no publisher is given.

As engraver, the name of J. Somers, sometimes given Sommers and sometimes J. Somers Pruthenus, appears on thirty-six; A. Peyrounin on eight; Riuière on one; R. Cordier on fourteen; L. Cordier on three; A. de la Plaes or Plaets on four; fifty maps are without engraver's name.

The earliest date of which a record has been found of the collection of Sanson's maps with this title is found in Woltersdorf. *Repertorium der land-und see-karten*, p. 103. It reads:

"1645. *Sanson.* Cartes générales de toutes les parties du monde etc. par Sanson d'Abbeville Paris chez l'auter et Mariette gr. Af. 98 karten. Andere zälen 104 Bl. Dabei ist gewöhnlich Sansonis d'Abb. Systema geogr. per tabulas repraesentatum Paris 1644. 100 geogr. Tabellen."

A map entitled, Sabaudia, ducatus la Savoie, similar to the Sanson maps, has been inserted in place of map no. 76, Etats de Savoye, which is wanting.

CONTENTS

no. 1. Mappe-monde. Riuiere sculp. 1651.

" 2. L'Hydrographie ou description de l'eau. 1652.

" 3. Harmonie ou correspondance du globe auecq la sphère. Jean Somer Pruthenus sculpsit. 1659.

" 4. Asie. A. Peyrounin sculp. 1650.

" 5. Les estats de l'empire des Turqs en Asie. I Somer sculp.

" 6. Carte des trois Arabies. J. Somer sculp. 1654.

" 7. Description de l'empire du Sophi des Perses. I. Somer sculp.

" 8. L'Indie deçà et delà le Gange, où est l'empire du Grand Mogol. Somer sculp. 1654.

" 9. Partie meridionale de l'Inde. I. Somer sculp. 1654.

" 10. La Chine royavme. Johannes Somer Pruthenus sculpsit. 1656.

" 11. Description de la Tartarie. Somer sculp. 1654.

" 12. Les isles Philippines, Molucques et de la Sonde. I. Somer sculp. 1850.

" 13. Afriqve. A. Peyrounin sculp. 1650.

" 14. Estats et royaumes de Fez et Maroc; Darha et Segelmesse; tirés de Sanuto de Marmol &c. J. S. sculp. 1655.

" 15. Partie de la Barbarie. Partie du Biledulgerid. Tirées de Sanuto et d'autres. I. S. sculp. 1655.

" 16. Partie de la coste de Barbarie. Tirés de Sanuto et d'autres. I. Somer P. sculp. 1655.

" 17. Roy^{me}, et désert de Barca et l'Egypte. I. S. P. sculp. 1655.

" 18. L'Afrique Tirée en partie de Sanut, et de l'Arabe de Nubie. I. Somer Pruthenus sculp. 1655.

" 19. Haute Ethiope. Tirés de Sanut de Mercator &c. 1655.

" 20. Basse Æthiope. La costa deça le cap Nègre est tirée en partie de Samuel Blommaert en delà avecq l'Isle de Madagascar, de Sanuto; le dedans du pays, d'autres. I. Somer Pruthenus sculp. 1655.

" 21. L'Evrope.

" 22. Carte générale des royavme d'Angleterre Escosse et Irelande. tirée de Campdenespede & autres. 1658.

no. 23. Ancien royau^{me} de Northumberland. 1658.
" 24. Ancien royaumes de Mercie, et East-Angles. 1654.
" 25. Anciens royaumes de Kent, d'Essex, et de Sussex. 1654.
" 26. Provinces d'West; autrefois royaume d'Westsex. 1654.
" 27. Principauté de Galles. 1658.
" 28. La Scandinavie. 1647.
" 29. Royaume de Danemarq. R. Cordier Ab. scul. 1658.
" 30. Nort-Iutlande. 1659.
" 31. Sud-Gotlande. 1659.
" 32. Estats du czar ou grand dvc de la Rvssie Blanche. A. Peyrounin sculp.
" 33. Carte générale du royaume de France. 1658.
" 34. Carte des rivieres de la France. 1641.
" 35. Carte géographicque des postes qui trauersent la France. 1632.
" 36. Gouvernement général de la Picardie, Artois, Boulenois, et pays reconquis. I. Sommer sculp. 1651.
" 37. Duché et gouvernement de Normandie. R. Cordier Abbauil. sculp. 1650.
" 38. Isle de France, Champagne, Lorraine. R. Cordier Abbauil. sculp. 1648.
" 39. Duché et gouvernement de Bretagne. R. Cordier Abbauil. sculpsit. 1650.
" 40. Gouvernement général d'Orléans. 1651.
" 41. Les deux Bourgognes. 1648.
" 42. Gouvernem. gén^{ral} du Lyonnois.
" 43. Gouvernement général de Guienne et Gascogne. R. Cordier Abbauil. sculp. 1651.
" 44. Gouvernem^{t}. géné^{ral} du Languedoc. R. Cordier Abbavil. sculps. 1651.
" 45. Le gouvernement général du Daufiné. 1652.
" 46. Comté, et gouvernement de Provence. R. Cordier Abbav. sculp. 1651.
" 47. Carte générale de l'empire d'Allemagne. 1658.
" 48. Palatinat du Rhein, Alsace. R. Cordier Abbauil sculp. 1648.
" 49. Estate de la sussession de Cleves, et Iuliers. R. Cordier Abbauil. sculp. 1648.
" 50. Picardie et les Pays Bas Catholiqves. R. Cordier Abbauil. sculp. 1684.
" 51. Provinces vnies des Pays Bas. R. Cordier Abbauil. sculp. 1648.
" 52. Cercle de Westphalie. 1650.
" 53. Les Suisses. R. Cordier Abbauil. sculp. 1648.
" 54. Le Tirol. 1654.
" 55. Bayeran. R. Cordier graveur Abbeuille. 1655.
" 56. Ertz-hertzogthumb Oesterreich.. 1659.
" 57. Hertzogthüber Steyer, Karnten, Krain. 1657.
" 58. Konigreich Boheim. 1654.
" 59. Provinces unies, et incorporées à la couronne de Boheme. 1654. Inset: Marquisat de Moravie.
" 60. Haute Saxe. R. Cordier, graveur, Abbeuil. 1655.
" 61. Churfurstenthum, und March Brandeburg. 1654.
" 62. Hertzog thumb Pommern. 1654.
" 63. Haute partie de la Basse Saxe. 1657.
" 64. Basse partie de la Basse Saxe. 1657.

Sanson, N., *d'Abbeville*—Continued.

no. 65. Estate de la couronne de Pologne. Iohannes Somer Pruthenus sculp. 1655.
" 66. Carte générale d'Espagne. 1658.
" 67. Les états de la couronne de Castille. Somer sculp. 1652.
" 68. Royavme de Navarre. J. Sommer sculp. 1652.
" 69. Les estats de la couronne de Castille. J. Sommer sculpsit. 1652.
" 70. Les états de la couronne d'Arragon. Somer sculp. 1653.
" 71. Les états de la couronne de Portugal en Espagne. Somer sculp. 1653.
" 72. Parte septentrional do reyno de Portugal. 1654.
" 73. Parte meridional do reyno de Portugal. 1654.
" 74. Carte générale de l'Italie. 1658.
" 75. Haute Lombardie. A. de la plaes sculcit. 1648.
" 76. Estats de la Savoye. [Wanting]
" 77. Basse Lombardie. 1648.
" 78 Estats de l'eglise et Toscane. 1648.
" 79. Royaume de Naples. AB. de la plaets sculpcit. 1648.
" 80. Calabre citérieure et vltérieure le Far de Messine. AB. de la plaets sculpsit. 1648.
" 81. Isle et royavme de Sicile. AB. de la Plaets sculpcit. 1647.
" 82. Isle de Corse.—Isle et roy^{me} de Sardaigne.
" 83. Estats de l'empire dv grand seignevr des Turqs. 1654.
" 84. Estats de l'empire des Tvrqs en Evrope. 1655.
" 85. Ameriqve Septentrionale. A. Peyrounin. sculp. 1650.
" 86. Le Canada. I. Somer sculpsit. 1656.
" 87. Le Nouveau Mexique et la Floride. Somer sculp. 1656.
" 88. Mexicque. Somer sculp. 1656.
" 89. Les Isles Antilles. I. Somer sculpsit. 1656.
" 90. Ameriqve Meridionale. A. Peyrounin sculp. 1650.
" 91. Terre Ferme. Somer sculp. 1656.
" 92. Partie de la Terre Ferme. 1656.
" 93. Le Perou. Iohannes Somer Pruthenus sculp. 1656.
" 94. Le Chili. I. Somer Pruthen sculp. 1656.
" 95. Le Bresil. J. Somer sculp. 1656.
" 96. Le Paragvayr, le Chili, la Terre, et les isles Magellanicques. Somer Pruth. sculp. 1656.
" 97. Les deux Poles. Jean Somer Pruthenus sculpebat. 1657.
" 98. Orbis vetus. Jean Somer Pruthenus sculpebat. 1657.
" 99. Asie vetvs. A. Peyrounin sculp. 1650.
" 100. Africa vetve. A. Peyrounin sculp. 1650.
" 101. Europa vetvs. A. Peyrounin sculp. 1650.
" 102. Romani Imperii qua occidens est. 1637.
" 103. Romani Imperii qua oriens est. 1637.
" 104. Britannicæ insulæ. 1641.
" 105. Baltia, quæ et Scandia, Finningia, Cimbrica Chersonesus. 1654.
" 106. Sarmatia utraque Europæa et Asiatica. 1654.
" 107. Gallia vetus. 1649.
" 108. Calliæ antiquæ. 1641.
" 109. Germania antiqua. 1641.
" 110. Germano-Sarmatia. I. Somer Pruthenus sculpsit. 1655.
" 111. Hispaniæ antiquæ tabulæ. 1641.
" 112. Italia antiqua cum insulis Sicilia Sardinia & Corsica. 1641.
" 113. Graeciæ antiquæ. 1636.

1659

Cluver, P.

Philippi Cluverii introdvctionis in vniversam geographiam tam veterem quam novam libri VI. Tabulis aeneis illustrari. Accessit P. Bertii breviarium orbis terrarum. 4 p. l., 394, [12] pp. 38 maps, 2 pl. 24°. Amstelodami, ex officina Elzeviviriana, 1659. 4261

NOTE.—Engraved title-page.

First edition, 1624. Many editions appeared in different languages. See v. 1, title 573, v. 3, titles 3432, 3439.

Woltersdorf gives this edition and mentions the maps by Buno.

CONTENTS

no. [1] Orbis terrarum typus.
" [2] Europa.
" [3] Typvs Hispaniae veteris.
" [4] Galliae veteris descriptio.
" [5] Germaniæ Cisrhenanæ.
" [6] Helvetiæ.
" [7] Inferioris Germaniæ descriptio.
" [8] Britannicarum insularum typus.
" [9] Populorum Germaniæ inter Rhenum et Albim descriptio.
" [10] Sueviæ quæ cis Codanum fuit sinum antiqua descriptio.
" [11] Vindeliciæ et Norici.
" [12] Nova totius Germaniæ descriptio.
" [13] Dania, Svecia et Norvegia.
" [14] Italia.
" [15] Ligures, Taurini etc. item Rhætiæ pars.
" [16] Histr Carni, Veneti item Rhætiæ pars.
" [17] Etruria, Latium, Umbria, etc.
" [18] Picentes, Vestini, etc. Campania, Apulia, Lucania, Bruth, etc.
" [19] Italiæ recentioris descriptio.
" [20] Siciliæ antiqua tabula.
" [21] Corsicæ antiquæ tabula.—Sardiniæ antiquæ tabula.
" [22] Pannonia et Illyricum.
" [23] Græciæ descriptio.
" [24] Creta, Cyprus et Rhodus.
" [25] Thraciæ descriptio.
" [26] Moesiæ et Daciæ.
" [27] Russia cum confinijs.
" [28] Asia.
" [29] Imperii Sinarum nova descriptio.
" [30] India vetus.
" [31] India orientalis nova.
" [32] Persia ex Adamo Oleario.
" [33] Armenia, Syria, Mesopotamia, etc.
" [34] Natolia, quæ olim Asia Minor.
" [35] Palaestina et Phoenice cum parte Cœle-Syria.
" [36] Africa.
" [37] Africa minor.—Mauritania.—Aegyptus.
" [38] Americæ sive Indiæ occidentalis.

1659–1672

Blaeu, J.

[Atlas mayor, sino Cosmographia Blaviana, en la qual exact. se descrive la tierre, el mar y el cielo] 10 v. fol. [Amsterdam, J. Blaeu, 1659–1672] 4262

NOTE.—The spanish edition of Blaeu was brought out in 1659–1672. The arrangement is that of the latin edition of 1662–1665, though the volumes have not been numbered as in the latin edition. The volume numbers of the corresponding volumes of the latin edition have been assigned in this case. The eleventh volume containing America was never published, and Africa was omitted from v. 9, which contains the Africa section in the latin edition. Also the section, Suecia, appears in v. 1, in the spanish instead of v. 2, as in the latin edition. The spanish edition is very rare, as almost the whole edition was destroyed by fire in 1672, when the publishing house of Blaeu was burned. This copy does not contain the general title-page for the work and many of the parts lack any title-page at all.

The volumes of this set are bound in green velvet.

A list of the maps contained is found at the end of each volume. These maps are the same as those in the latin edition [1662–1665] described in v. 3, title 3430. The beauty of the coloring is unusually well preserved.

The differences between this copy of the spanish edition and the Library of Congress copy of the latin edition with other descriptive matter are here noted.

v. 1. Does not contain general title-page, title-page to volume or half-titles to sections. The general title-page is not contained in any volume of this set.
Pages 81–82 with the map of Europe, wanting.
Map, reyno de Gocia, wanting. Text included.
Pintura de Steleburg . . . wanting.
Quadrante mural, o de Ticho, wanting.
Manillas del Equador, wanting.
On p. xvij, Capatania de Tonderen, shows some difference from same map in latin edition.

v. 2. No title-page to the volume, and no half titles to the sections.

" 3. Title-page to the volume is dated 1662.
Pages 51–52, Grotkaw, o Nissa duquado, wanting.
" 323, Territorio de Francfort sobre el Mein, wanting.
" 335, El Danubio, map wanting.
Opp. p. 366, Territorii Lindaviensis pars septentrionalis, inserted.

" 4. Title-page to volume dated 1663. Has title-page to second part.

" 5. No title-page.
Pages 65–66, La Bretaña en la forma que se divido en tiempo de los Anglo-Saxones . . . wanting.

" 6. No title-page. Privilege dated 1664.

" 7. Title-page to volume dated 1662. Contains all preliminary leaves.
Opp. p. 74, Dioecesis Ebroicensis vulgo l'Eveschè d' Evreux, inserted.
Opp. p. 204, Episcapatvs Albiensis, inserted.

" 8. Title-page to volume dated 1669. Contains all preliminary leaves.

" 9. Title-page to volume dated 1672. Contains illuminated half title-page, with all preliminary leaves. Africa section omitted.

" 10. Title-page to volume dated 1658. Contains illuminated title to Martini's Novvs atlas Sinensis, dedication and privilege.

For extensive note on the latin edition, and table of contents of each volume, see v. 3, title 3430.

CONTENTS

v. 1. Hyparctica.—Norvega.—Suecia.—Dinamarka.
" 2. Russia.—Polonia.—Partes orientales d' Europa.—Grecia.
" 3. Alemania.
" 4. Paises Baxos, o Belgia.
" 5. Inglaterra.
" 6. Escocia ẏ Hibernia.
" 7. Francia y Helvecia.
" 8. Italia.
" 9. España.
" 10. Asia.

1662–1672

Blaeu, J.

Atlas maior sive Cosmographia Blaviana, qva solvm, salvm, coelvm, accvratissime describvntvr. 11 v. fol. [Amstelaedami, I. Blaev, 1662–1672] 4263

NOTE.—The dates and voluming of this edition are the same as in another copy dated 1662–1665, which is in the Library of Congress, except that v. 9 is dated 1672. See v. 3, title 3480.

Vol. 5, "Anglia," and v. 6, "Scotia, Hibernia," have half titles dated 1646 and 1654 respectively.

Although most of the maps are the same as in the other Library of Congress copy, many have a different arrangement of the text on the reverse, with varying signatures, and some of the maps are different. The text of v. 6, "Scotia, Hibernia," is from entirely different plates though the maps are the same. It has "Privileges" in dutch and latin and one in english granted by Oliver Cromwell and dated 1654, which indicates that this issue of v. 6 may have been part of a set brought out for use in England.

The ninth volume "Hispania, Africa," dated 1672, is in spanish and belongs to the spanish edition, "Atlas mayor, sino Cosmographia Blaviana," issued 1659–1672. See Tiele, *Nederlandsche bibliographie van land- en volkenkunde.*

In v. 10, Martini's China has a two page index not in the other Library of Congress copy.

In v. 11, which is devoted to American maps, the text is the same but printed from different plates. All maps are those called for by the index except map on p. 1–2, "Novissima et accuratissima totius Americæ descriptio per N. Visscher," which is substituted for "Americæ nova tabula. Auct. Guiljelmo Blaeuw," in other copy, and map on p. 213–214, "Nova et accurata Brasiliæ totius tabula, auctore Ioanne Blaev," which is substituted for "Brasilia . . . excudebat Iohannes Blaeu."

For contents of maps see v. 3, title 3480.

CONTENTS

v. 1. Arctica.—Norvegia.—Dania. 1665.
" 2. Suecia.—Russia.—Polonia.—Regiones orientales circa Danubium, ultra Germaniam.—Græcia. 1662.
" 3. Germania. 1662.
" 4. Belgica Regia.—Belgica Fœderata. 1662.
" 5. Anglia. 1662.
" 6. Scotia.—Hibernia. 1662.
" 7. Gallia.—Helvetia. 1662.

Blaeu, J.—Continued.

v. 8. Italia. 1662.
" 9. Hispania.—Africa. 1672.
" 10. Asia. 1662.
" 11. America. 1662.

1675?

Sanson, N. *d'Abbeville*, **Sanson, G.,** *and* **Sanson, N.** *fils*.

[Géographie universelle] 2 p. l. (ms). 76 col. ms. l., 35 engr. l. 44 maps. fol. [Paris, 1675?] 4264

NOTE.—Title-page wanting. Corrected from v. 1, title 484.

Compiled from *Cartes générales de la géographie ancienne et nouvelle . . . par les s*r*. Sanson. Paris, 1675*, from which all the maps are taken, with the exception of: Mappe-monde.—Natvlia, quae olim Asia Minor.—Gouvernement général d'Orléans.

Maps dated 1647–1674 (Flanders, no. 37)

Ms. dedication to the dauphin, Louis of France, son of Louis xiv, by "le très humble très obéissant et très fidèle serviteur et sujet f. Athanaze de Sainct Charles, relig^r carme ref^e. de la province de Tourajnne et du conuent des Pillettes."

Original binding bearing the arms of the dauphin of France.

Between the maps are inserted Sanson's engraved geographical tables, and the manuscript indexes to the most important places, written in red, blue and black ink, and showing the "Climat—Longitudes—Latitudes—Solstice" of the places listed.

Maps engraved by the following engravers: Jean Somer, R. Cordier, A. de la Plaetz, A. Peyrounin, Lud. Cordier, and R. Michault.

The following maps relate to America:

no. [1] Mappe monde.
" [43] Amérique septentrionale.
" [44] Amérique méridionale.

1680

Morden, R.

Geography rectified: or, A description of the world, in all its kingdoms, provinces, countries, islands, cities, towns, seas, rivers, bayes, capes, ports; their antient and present names, inhabitants, situations, histories, customs, governments, &c. As also their commodities, coins, weights, and measures, compared with those at London. Illustrated with above sixty new maps. The whole work performed according to the more accurate discoveries of modern authors. 7 p. l., 418 pp. incl. 62 maps. sm. 4°. London, for R. Morden and T. Cockeril, 1680. 4265

NOTE.—The following maps relate to America:

p. 7. A new map of ye world.
" 361. America.
" 363. The northwest part of America.
" 369. A new map of Virginia and Maryland.
" 373. New England and New York.
" 379. Carolina, Virginia and Maryland.

p. 384. Mexico or New Spaine.
" 390. The western islands.
" 393. Insulae Jamaicae.
" 397. The island of Barbados.
" 401. Bermuda.
" 403. The country of ye Amasones.
" 410. Chili and Paragay.
" 413. Brazile.
" 416. Terra Magellanica.

1685

Du Val, P.

[Maps to accompany Du Val's Geographia universalis. 1685] 51 maps. 24°. [Nurnberg; 1685?] 4266

Note.—No title page or cover title.
A 2d ed. corrected and enlarged was issued at London, 1691. A german edition was issued at Nurnberg, 1694.
The following maps relate to America:
no. [1] Typus orbis terrarum.
" [2] Terra arctica.
" [4] Terra antarctica.
" [6] America.
" [7] Canada.
" [8] Virginia.
" [9] Florida.
" [10] Nova Mexico.
" [11] Mexico, sive N. Hispania.
" [12] Insulæ Antilles.
" [13] Castilla Doro.
" [14] Gvaiana.
" [15] Perv.
" [16] Chili.
" [17] Terra Magellanica.
" [18] La Plata.
" [19] Brasilia.
" [50] Insulæ Philippinæ alias Manilhæ dictæ.

1690

Seller, J.

A new systeme of geography, designed in a most plain and easie method, for the better understanding of that science. Accommodated with new mapps, of all the countries, regions, empires, monarchies, kingdoms, principalities, dukedoms, marquesates, dominions, estates, republiques, soveraignties, governments, seignories, provinces, and countries in the whole world. With geographical tables, explaining the divisions in each map . . . 1 p. l., 112 pp. [36] l., 58 maps. 16°. [London] J. Seller & J. Seller, jr., 1690. 4267

Note.—An earlier issue has the date 1685 supplied from the *Term catalogue, 1683–1696*. The 1690 issue differs somewhat from the earlier one. Most of the maps are preceeded by an index to the map.

Seller, J.—Continued.

Imperfect copy. Indexes to the maps of the world and to Paraguay appear without the maps.

Error in pagination, there being no pages 30–31.

Contains map of Hamburg entitled, "A map of the city of Hambvrgh & adjacent countrey."

CONTENTS.

nc. [1] Europe.
" [2] Scotland.
" [3] Ireland.
" [4] The XVII provinces.
" [5] The ten spanish provinces.
" [6] Comitatus Holandiæ.
" [7] France.
" [8] Portugal.
" [9] Italy.
" [10] Germany.
" [11] Denmark.
" [12] A map of the city of Hambvrgh & the adjacent countrey.
" [13] Swedeland and Norway.
" [14] Moscovia or Russia.
" [15] Lesser Tartaria.
" [16] Poland.
" [17] Lithuania.
" [18] Hungaria and Sclavonia.
" [19] Turky in Europe.
" [20] The north part of Turky in Europe Transilvania Moldavia, Walachia Bessarabie.
" [21] The south part of Turky in Europe.
" [22] Morea olim Peloponesus.
" [23] Asia.
" [24] Turky in Asia.
" [25] The land of Canaan divided into 12 tribes.
" [26] Georgia.
" [27] Arabia.
" [28] Persia.
" [29] Empire of Mogol.
" [30] India on this side Ganges.
" [31] India beyond Ganges.
" [32] China.
" [33] Tartaria.
" [34] Africa.
" [35] The kingdom of Moroco in Barbary.
" [36] The kingdom of Fez.
" [37] The kingdom of Alger.
" [38] The kingdomes of Tunis and Tripoli.
" [39] The kingdom and desart of Barca.
" [40] Ægypt.
" [41] The island of Saint Hellena.
" [42] Mexico and New Spaine.
" [43] Carolina newly discribed.
" [44] Pensilvania.
" [45] New Iarsey.

no. [46] Insulæ Iamaicæ.
" [47] The island of Barbados.
" [48] Bermudas.
" [49] The island of Tobago.
" [50] Insula Matanino vulgo Martanico.
" [51] South America.
" [52] The Magellenick land.
" [53] Chili.
" [54] Peru.
" [55] Brasil.
" [56] The Amazone country.
" [57] Terra Firma.
" [58] A mapp of the South Pole.

1693

Morden, R.

Geography rectified; or, A description of the world, in all its kingdoms, provinces, countries . . . As also their commodities, coins, weights, and measures, compared with those at London. Illustrated with seventy eight maps. The 3d ed., enl. To which is added a compleat geographical index to the whole, alphabetically digested. The whole work performed according to the more accurate observations and discoveries of modern authors. 5 p. l., 574, [2] 575–626, [72] pp. incl. 77 maps, illus. 8°. London, for R. Morden & T. Cockerill, 1693. 4268

NOTE.—For note and list of maps of America, see v. 1, title 498.

1695

Thesaurus geographicus; a new body of geography: or, A compleat description of the earth . . . Collected with great care from the most approv'd geographers and modern travellers and discoveries, by several hands. 4 p. l., 44 pp., 1 l., [2], 506, [13], pp. illus., maps, plan. sm. fol. London, printed for A. Sewall & T. Child, 1695. 4269

NOTE.—Preface states, "The maps are drawn according to those of Sanson, De Wit and Vischer; and tho' the size of them be small, they contain the names of all the most considerable places."

The following maps relate to America:
opp. p. 44. The world in planisphere.
p. 473. America.
p. 480. A map of the English plantations in America.

1697

Cluver, P.

Philippi Cluverii introductio in universam geographiam tam veterem quam novam tabulis XLVI. ac notis olim ornata à Johanne Bunone, jam verò locupletata additamentis & annota-

Cluver, P.—Continued.

tionibus Joh. Frid. Hekelii & Joh. Reiskii. Cum privilegio ordinum Holl. & Westfrisiae. 10 p. l., 565 (*i. e.* 567) 60 pp., front., 43 maps, 3 pl., 2 tab. 8°. Amstelædami, J. Wolters, 1697. 4270

NOTE.—First edition published in 1624, followed by many other editions.
Elaborately engraved half title reads: Philippi Cluverii introductionis in universam geographiam cum notis I. Bunonis Hekelii et Reiskii. Lib. VI. Amstelædami, J. Wolters, A°. 1697.
For notes on other editions, see v. 1, no. 573, v. 3, titles 3432 and 3439.
A list of the maps appears under the edition of 1667?, see v. 3, title 3432.
In addition to these maps, this edition contains the following:
no. 23. Siciliae antiquæ descriptio.
" 24. Corsicæ antiquæ descriptio.
The following maps relate to America:
no. 4. Typus orbis terrarvm.
" 46. America.

1699

Lea, P.

[Collection of maps] 7 pp., 28 maps. fol. London, P. Lea, [1699?] 4271

NOTE.—The date of issue of many of these maps is supplied from the Term catalogue, 1668–1709. Many of the maps were accompanied by index sheets or "Alphabets" as they are headed. The "Alphabets" for Europe, Asia, Africa and America are found in this collection.
Contains manuscript index calling for one map which is wanting. Map no. [11] Map of the Channel, is dated 1695. The date given to the *Collection* is 1699 which is the date of issue of map no. 6, A new map of England and Wales, as given in the Term catalogue.

CONTENTS.

no. [1] A new mapp of Europe. [1690]
" [2] A new mapp of Asia. [1690]
" [3] A new mapp of Africa. [1690]
" [4] Spain and Portugal.
" [5] A new mapp of England, Scotland and Ireland. [1685]
" [6] A new map of England and Wales. [1699]
" [7] An epitome of S^r. William Petty's large survey of Ireland. Sutton Nicholls sculp.
" [8] The new and accurate mapp of France. R. Palmer sculp.
" [9] A new map of the courses of the Rhine and the Rhone.
" [10] Mapp of the sea coast of Europe and ye straits by R. Morden & P. Lea.
" [11] Mapp of the Channel. 1695.—The harbour of S. Malo.—The river Seine, from Havre de Grace to Rouen-Nieuport, Furnes, Dvnkirk.
" [12] A plat of all the straits.
" [13] A new map of Scandinavia.
" [14] Regni Poloniæ et ducatus Lithvaniæ Voliniæ, Podoliæ, Vcraniæ, Prussiæ et Curlandiæ. Per F. De Witt.
" [15] Tablula Russia vulgo Moscovia. T. Lhuilier fecit.
" [16] A new mapp of the kingdom of Hungary and the states that have been subject to it which are at present the northern parts of Turkey in

Europe. Inset views: Buda.—Novigrad.—Temeswar.—Canysa.—Belgrad.—Zygreth.—Great Waradin.—Gyula.—Alba Regalis. R. Palmer sculp.

no. [17] A new generall map of the seat of war from vpper Hungary to the isle of Candia. Inset views: Napoli di Romania.—Modon.—Navarin.—Bridge of Essecke. I. Oliver sculp.

" [18] Turky in Europe and in the lesser Asia.

" [19] The Spanish Netherlands. Herman Moll fecit.

" [20] The seven United Provinces of Netherland. James Moxon sculp. [1686]

" [21] A new map of Savoy, Piemont, and Switserland, also part of France, Germany and Spain, by P. Lea & H. Moll.

" [22] Italy.

" [23] A map of Canaan.

" [24] A new map of Carolina, by Iohn Thornton. Robert Morden and by Philip Lea. Inset: A perticuler [!] map of the going into Ashley and Cooper rivers.

" [25] A new map of New England and New York, New Iarsey, Pensilvania, Maryland and Virginia.

" [26] The island of Barbadoes. [Wanting]

" [27] A generall mapp of the continent and islands which bee adjacent to Jamaica.—A new mapp of the island of Jamaica. [1685]

" [28] A map of the principall part of Europe.

" [29] a [!] new groundplot of the citty of Hamburg. [1686] Herman Moll, sculpsit. Insets: [Albis flu.]—Hamburg with four lands.

1699–1702

Loon, J. van, *and* **Voogt, C. J.**

De nieuwe groote lichtende zee-fackel, behelfende 't eerste, 't weede, 't darde, 't vierde, vijfde of 't laetste deel. Alwaer klaer en volkomen in vertoont wort, alle bekende zee-kusten van de geheele Noord Ocean, en deszelfs inboesemen, met een partenente beschryvinge, van alle bekende haavens, bayen, reden, drooghten, strekkingen van kourissen, en op-doeninge van landen alles op haare waare pools-hooghte geleyt, uyt ondervindinge van veele ervaaren stuurlieden, lootsen, en liefhebbers der zeevaert. Vergaedert met groote kosten, en op het Nieuw in beter order gestelt als voor dese, en verrijckt met het vijde, of laetste deel, dat noyt voor dese in 't licht is geweest . . . 5 v. in 1. fol. t'Amsterdam, J. van Keulen, 1699–1702. 4272

NOTE.—Tiele, in his *Nederlandsche bibliographie van land-en volkenkunde,* gives an earlier edition of this work in one volume with the same general title-page, dated 1689.

In the 1699 edition, the title-pages of volumes 2 and 4 are preceeded by elaborately engraved plates giving the "Privilegie" on the verso. The title-pages of volumes 3 and 5, with the "Privilegie" on the verso, are very elaborately engraved. Volume 1 is without separate title-page or date, v. 2, is dated 1702; v. 3, 169–; v. 4, 1701; v. 5, 1687.

Loon, J. van, *and* **Voogt, C. J.**—Continued.

The following maps relate to America:

v. 1, no. [1a] Wassende graade kaart van alle bekende zeekusten op den geheele aardbodem.

v. 4, no. [1a] Paskaert vertonende behalven Europaes zuydelyckste een gedeelte van de custen of Africa een America.

" " 1. Pas kaart van West Indien.

" " 2. Pas-kaart van de zee-kusten van Guiana. Inset: t Fort van Cajana by de inwoonders genaemt Sobarbiob.

" " 3. Pas-kaart vande rivieren Commewini Suriname Cupaname.

" " 4. Pas kaart van de kust van Guiana.

" " 5. Pas kaart van Rio Oronoque, golfo de Paria met d' eylanden Trinidad, Tabago, Granada, Granadillos en Bequia.

" " 6. Pas kaart van de Caribes Insets: De westkust van Guardalupa.—de Rondom bay van S. Luzia.—De Santos.

" " 7. Pas kaart van t eyland S Iuan de Porto Rico.

" " 8. Pas-kaart vande zee kusten van Veneçuela.

" " 9. Pas-kaart van de zuyd-kust van Espanjola met de zee kust van nuevo reyne de Granada. Inset: Baya de Tiburaon.

" " 10. Pas kaart van de noord kust van Espaniola. Insets: t Eyland Turtuga.—Porto de Guanives.

" " 11. Pas-kaart van de zee kusten van Carthagena, Tierra Firma, Costa Rica ende Honduras. Insets: de Haaven van Carthagena.—d Ilhas de S Barnardo.—de Haavenen van Nombre de Dios en Porta Bella.

" " [12] Pas kaart van de zuyd kust van Cuba en van geheel Yamaica. Insets: Baya Oristan in Yamaica.—Baya Yamaica.

" " 13. Pas-kaart van de golff de Guanaios.

" " 14. Pas kaart van de golff van Mexico. Inset: De haaven van Iuan d'Ulhua.

" " 15. Pas kaart van de boght van Florida. Insets: Bahia de Matanças.—Havana.—Baja Hondo.

" " 16. Pas kaart vande noord oost kust van Cuba en d'oost kust van Florida.

" " 17. Pas kaart van Ila Barmuda.

" " 18. Pas kaart van de kust van Carolina. Inset: De kust van Carolina.

" " 19. Pas kaart van de zee kusten van Virginia

" " 20. Pas-kaart vande zee kusten van Niew Nederland anders genaamt Niew York. Insets: De Noord rivier.—De Versche rivier.

" " 21. Pas-kaart vande zee kusten inde boght van Niew Engeland.

" " 22. Pas-kaart vande zee kusten van Terra Nova met de byleggende zee-kusten van Francia Nova, Canada en Accadie.

" " 22½. Pas-kaart van de Grand Banq by Terra Neuff.

" " [23] Pascaarte vande noorder zee custen van America.

v. 5. " [1] Pascaarte vande zee custen van Guinea en Brasilia.

" " 10–19. Pas-kaartvan de zee-kusten van Brazilia.

" " [20] Pascaert van de zuyd zee en een gedeelte van Brasil.

1703?

Cóvens, J., *and* **Mortier, C.**

[Mappe monde ou globe terrestre—Europe—Asie—Afrique—Amérique] 5 maps on 25 sheets. fol. [Amsterdam, J. Cóvens & C. Mortier, 1703?] 4273

NOTE.—No title page. Latest date, 1701, found on the map of America. The map of the world and that of Europe both show "S^{t}. Petersburg" which was founded in 1703.

All the maps bear the mention "Dressée sur les observations de mrs. de l'Académie royale des sciences et de Sanson, Nolin, de Fer, Delisle et . . . sur la carte que . . . Nicolas Witsen . . . a donnée au public . . . et mis au jour par Cóvens et Mortier . . . à Amsterdam."

In addition to the titles in the upper margins, the maps of Europe, Asia, Africa, and America have titles within elaborately decorated cartouches, representing mythological and other symbolical subjects.

CONTENTS.

no. [1] Mappe-monde ou globe terrestre en deux plans hémisphères, dressée sur les observations de m^{rs}. de l'Académie royale des sciences, Sanson, Nolin, du Fer et principale^{mt} sur la carte que monsieur Nicolas Witsen. a donnée au public. Insets: [Arctic regions] 4½ in. diam.—]Antarctic regions 4½ in. diam.—Two astronomical hemispheres, each 4½ in. diam. In 4 sheets; sheets 1 & 3: 20×27; sheets 2 & 4: 21¼×27.—In two hemispheres, each 27 in. diam.; ornamented in the upper and lower border with engraved illustrations of passages of the Genesis; six of which are in circular frames in the upper margin, the others in the right and left corners.

The latest date found in the map is 1699—near the mouth of the Mississippi river is the note: "Col. françoise en 1699," also on the western coast of Scotland: "I. nouvellement découv. en 1699."

On this map is shown S^{t}. Petersbourg, which was founded in 1703.

The Library of Congress has a similar map of the world by J. B. Nolin, dated 1708, in two hemispheres, with the same border illustrations, with slight variations.

On that map is the notice "Débouchement du détroit d'Anian *par où un vaisseau hollandais communiqua* de la mer du Nord à la mer du Sud . . ." It also shows the "Detroit connecting the two oceans."

On the 1703? map, however, is the notice: "*On croît sur de fortes conjectures* que par le Détroit d'Anian *on peut communiquer* de la mer du Sud à la mer du Nord, mais personne n'a encor hazardé la navigation de ce détroit, on en a seulement reconnu les entrées." Besides these statements the 1708 map contains much more geographical information than the other, especially in North America.

In the Pacific ocean, on the 1708 map, near the straits of Magellan is the notice: "J'ai posé le détroit de Magellan entre les 50.51$^{d.}$ de latitude, ce qui est different de ce que les autres géographes ont cy devant fait . . . je n'étais contenté dans ma première mappemonde de marquer l'endroit au Sud où il avoit été jetté sans m'expliquer". In the 1703? map, the straits are shown at the 52° lat. south.

On the 1708 map, the course and mouth of the Mississippi river are more accurately delineated than in the other.

Cóvens, J., *and* Mortier, C.—Continued.

From the above, it may be assumed that the map must have been issued after 1703 but before 1708.

The 1703? map has in the left lower margin: "se vendent . . . à Amsterdam chez Jean Cóvens et Corneille Mortier."

The Library of Congress has also a separate copy of this map.

no. [2] L'Europe, dressée sur les n: observations faites en toutes les parties de la terre, rectifiée par m[rs]. de l'Académie royale des sciences &c.

In 5 sheets; sheets 1–3: 23×20½; sheets 4, 5: 19½×20½.

In this map is shown S[t]. Petersburg, which was founded in 1703.

In the lower right corner is an engraving representing a group of mythological figures, the pope, the emperor and other dignitaries; in the center is an imperial double-headed eagle.

The fourth and fifth sheets have special titles: "Carte nouvelle de la mer Mediterranée divisée en mer de Levant et de Ponant . . . dressée par le s[r]. Sanson.—Partie orientale de la mer Méditerranée."

" [3] L'Asie, dressée sur les n: observ[ations] faites en toutes les parties de la terre, rectifiée par m[rs]. de l'Académie royale des sciences, &c. Insets: "Carte des pays situés au nord nordest de la Chine, levée en voyage par le p. Verbiest." 4½×9.—"Groenland." 3½×5½.

In 5 sheets; sheet 1: 21×25; sheets 2–5: 21×19½.

Sheet no. [3] has separate title: "Carte nouvelle de la Grande Tartarie par . . . N. Witsen . . . à Amsterdam, dressée sur les degréez [!] de s[r]. Sanson."—Sheet no. [4] is entitled: "Troisième partie de l'Asie ou partie de la chine, les isles de Bornéo et Philippines, &c."

Shows a small part of Alaska: "Terre de la compagnie."

" [4] L'Afrique, dressée sur les n: observations faites en toutes les parties de la terre, rectifiée par mrs. de l'Académie royale des sciences, &c."

In 6 sheets; sheets 1, 2, 4, 5: 21×19; sheets 3, 6: 21×13½.

" [5] L'Amérique, dressée sur les n. observations faites en toutes les parties de la terre, rectifiée par m[rs]. de l'Académie royale des sciences, &c."

In 5 sheets: 20½×21. Latest date found 1701: "Isle de Beauchesne découverte en 1701."

1708

Cellarius, A.

Harmonia macrocosmica sev atlas universalis et novus, totius universi, creati cosmographiam generalem, et novam exhibens. In quâ ominium totius mundi orbium harmonica constructio, secundum diversas diversorum authorum opiniones, ut et vranometria, seu totus orbis cœlestis, ac planetarum theoriæ, et terristris globus, tàm planis et scenographicis iconibus, quam descriptionibus novis ab oculos ponuntur. Opus novum, antehac nunquam visum, cujuscunque conditionis hominibus utilissimum, jucundissimum, maximè necessarium, & adornatum . . . 2 p. l., 32 (*i. e.* 34) col. pl., maps. fol. Amstelodami, G. Valk & P. Schenk, 1708. 4274

Note.—Plates of the 1708 edition with title-page and index, without text.

An edition was published in 1660 and one in 1661.

Plates elaborately illuminated.

Index calls for 29 plates.

1709

Afferden, F. de.

El atlas abreviado, ó compendiosa geographica del mundo antiguo, y nuevo, conforme à las ultimas pazes generales del Haya . . . 3. ed. 5 p. l.,.230 [2] pp. 42 maps, 1 pl. 12°. Amberes, H. & C. Verdussen, 1709. 4275

NOTE.—Engraved half title reads: Atlas a solis ortu vsque ad occasum laudabile nomen Caroli . . . Half title and several maps engraved by Harrewyn. Many of the maps are by I. Peeters; others executed by him.

The Library of Congress has a reprint of this atlas issued by the widow of H. Verdussen, 1725, called 3. ed. There are no changes in either text or maps.

The following maps relate to America:

no. [1] [World] P. I. Peeters.
" [43] Americæ. I. P. Harrewyn f.

1709

Valck, G., ***and*** **Schenk, P.**

Atlantis sylloge compendiosa . . . 3 p. l., 37 [2] pp., 100 col. maps. fol. Amstelodami, G. Valk & P. Schenk, 1709. 4276

NOTE.—Col. eng. half-title reads: Nova totius geographica telluris projectio. Amstelodami.

Inserted between eng. half title and title-page is the "Inleidings tot de geographie . . . Door den heer Sanson d'Abbeville." Table of contents is on title-page.

Maps made by G. and L. Valck, P. Schenk, A. F. Zürner, Sr. Sanson, and N. Visscher.

CONTENTS.

no. 2. Planisphaerium terrestre. A. F. Zurner.
" 3. Novus planiglobii terrestris per utrumque polum conspectus. G. Valck.
" 4. Europae in tabula geographica delineatio. A. F. Zurner.
" 5. Scandinavia, vel regna septentrionalia Suecia, Dania, et Norvegia. G. et L. Valck.
" 6. Regni Norvegiae. Nova et accurata descriptio. G. Valk et P. Schenk.
" 7. Sueciae magnae, totius orbis regni antiquissimi, Hodierna in sex principales suas partes, Gothiam Nempe, Sueciam propriam sive stricté Sumptam, Nordlandiam, Finniam, Ingriam, Livoniam. G. & L. Valck.
" 8. Tabula ducatum Livoniae et Curlandiae. G. Valck.
" 9. Regnum Daniae. G. & L. Valck.
" 10. Totius Ivtiae generalis accurata delincatio.
" 11. Holsatiae tabula generalis in qua sunt ducatus Holsatiae, Ditmarsiae, Stormariae et Wagriae. P. Schenk. 1707.
" 12. Russia Alba, sive Moscovia. G. & L. Valck.
" 13. Magna Britannia, aut Anglia, Scotia, et Hibernia. G. et L. Valck.
" 14. Regnum Scotiae. G. et L. Valck.
" 15. Regnum Angliae. G. et L. Valck.
" 16. Regnum Hibernae. G. et L. Valck.
" 17. Belgium distributum in septemdecem provinciae. G. et L. Valck.
" 18. Belgica Foederata. G. et L. Valck.
" 19. Hollandiae comitatus. N. Visscher.

Valck, G., *and* **Schenk, P.**—Continued.

" 20. Belgium regium divisum in decem provincias. G. & L. Valck.
" 21. Brabantiae ducatus. P. Schenk.
" 22. Flandrinae comitatus. P. Schenk.
" 23. Germania. G. et L. Valck.
" 24. Totius Rheni tractus. G. Valck.
" 25. Fluminum princeps Danubius. G.Valck.
" 26. Circulus Westphalicus. G. et L. Valck.
" 27. Circulus Saxoniae inferioris. G. et L. Valck.
" 28. Circulus Saxoniae superioris. G. et L. Valck.
" 29. Marchionatus Brandenburgicus, et ducatus Pomeraniae. G. et L. Valck.
" 30. Uterque Rheni circulus, superior et inferior electoralis, com Palatinatu.
" 31. Archiepiscopatus Coloniensis; ducatibus Iuliacensi et Montensi intermedius. G. Valck.
" 32. Treverensis regio. G. Valck.
" 33. Moguntinorum. G. Valck.
" 34. Pars altera seu borealis circuli Rhenani. G. Valck.
" 35. Hassia lantgraviatus. G. Valck.
" 36. Pars summa, seu Australis superioris Rheni circuli. G. Valck.
" 37. Generalis Lotharingia. G. Valck.
" 38. Superioris atque inferioris Alsatiae. P. Schenk.
" 39. Circulus Franconicus. G. et L. Valck.
" 40. Le royaume de Boheme, duché de Silesie, les marquisat de Moravie et de Lusace. s[r]. Sanson.
" 41. Circulus Suevicus. G. Valck.
" 42. Chorographia ducatus Wurtenburgici. G. Valck.
" 43. Circulus Bavaricus. G. et L. Valck.
" 44. Circuli Austriaci orientalior pars. G. Valck.
" 45. Superior Burgundiae. G. Valck.
" 46. Helvetia divisa in tredecim cantones. G. et L. Valck.
" 47. Regnum Poloniae. G. et L. Valck.
" 48. Regnum Galliae. G. et L. Valck.
" 49. Praefectura Piccardiae. G. et L. Valck.
" 50. Normannia ducatus. G. et L. Valck.
" 51. Gubernatio insulae Franciae. G. et L. Valck.
" 52. Praefectura ducatus Britanniae. G. et L. Valck.
" 53. Campaniae praefectura. G. et L. Valck.
" 54. Aurelianensis praefectura generalis. G. et L. Valck.
" 55. Vtrivsqve Bvrgvndiae.
" 56. Praefectura Lugdunensis generalis. G. et L. Valck.
" 57. Novissimam hanc tabulam Aquantaniae et Vasconiae, Guascogne et Guienne dictae. G. Valck.
" 58. Praefectura generalis Languedociae, olim Occitania. G. et L. Valck.
" 59. Delphinatus praefectura. G. Valck.
" 60. Provincia. G. Valck.
" 61. Hispaniarum Portugalliaeque. G. Valck.
" 62. Gallaecia regnum. F. Fer.
" 63. Legionis regnum et Astruarum principatus.
" 64. Navarra regnum.
" 65. Utriusque Castiliae.
" 66. Arragonia regnum. J. B. Labanna.
" 67. Principatus Cataloniae, comitatus Perpiniani et Cerdannae. G. et L. Valck.

no. 68. Valentia regnum.
" 69. Andaluzia continens Sevillam et Cordubam.
" 70. Granata, et Murcia regna.
" 71. Corona Portugalliae et Algarbia. P. Schenk. 1703.
" 72. Italia. G. et L. Valck.
" 73. Status Sabaûdiae. G. et L. Valck.
" 74. Status Mediolanensis. G. et L. Valck.
" 75. Respublica Veneta, ducatus Mutinae, Parmae et Mirandulae. G. et L. Valck.
" 76. Ligvria, ò stato della republica di Genova.
" 77. Stato della repvblica di Lucca.
" 78. Magni ducis Hetruriae status. G. Valck.
" 79. Status Ecclesiasticus, magnus ducatus Florentiae. G. et L. Valck.
" 80. Regnum Neapolis. G. et L. Valck.
" 81. Hungaria generalis. G. et L. Valck.
" 82. Imperium Turcicum in Europa, Asia et Africa. G. et L. Valck.
" 83. Regni Hungariae, Graeciae, Moreae, totius Danubii, adiacentiumque regnorum. P. Schenk.
" 84. Asiae. A. F. Zurner.
" 85. Tartaria sive magni Chami imperium.
" 86. Imperii Percici delineatio. P. Schenk.
" 87. Magni Mogolis imperium.
" 88. Imperii Sinarum nova descriptio. J. van Loon.
" 89. Indiae orientalis, nec non insularum adiacentium. N. Visscher.
" 90. Insularum Indiae orientalis.
" 91. Africae. A. F. Zurneri.
" 92. Nova Barbariae descriptio.
" 93. Aegypti recentior descriptio.
" 94. Aethiopia superior vel interior.
" 95. Habessinia seu Abassia. C. Ludolfus.
" 96. Aethiopia inferior, vel exterior.
" 97. Americae tam septentrionalis quam meridionales. A. F. Zurner.
" 98. America Septentrionalis.
" 99. Insulae Americanae.
"100. Americae pars meridionalis.

1714

Aa, P. van der.

Nouvel atlas, très-exact et fort commode pour toutes sortes de personnes, contenant les principales cartes géographiques. Dressé suivant les nouvelles observations de m[rs]. de l'Académie royal des sciences, & rectifié sur les relations les plus récentes des plus fidéles des voyageurs. 5 p. l., 4 pp., 98 maps, 1 pl. 4°. Leide, P. vander Aa [1714] 4277

NOTE.—The date is supplied from van der Aa, *Catalogue de livres de cartes géographiques des villes châteaux &c. de l'univers. Leide,* [*1715*]

Van der Aa's *Atlas nouveau et curieux des plus célèbres itinéraires*, contains a table of contents of this atlas in 2 v. giving 199 entries.

An edition of the atlas was brought out by Cóvens & Mortier about 1735, which corresponds with this atlas. The maps have had the name of van der Aa removed and that of Cóvens & Mortier substituted, and the name of map no.

Aa, P. van der—Continued.

96 changed from La Floride to La Louisiane. See v. 3, title 3488, also Lowery's *Descriptive list of spanish possessions . . . ed. by P. L. Phillips.*

The three additional maps not called for by the index are evidently part of the atlas as they occur also in an imperfect copy in the Library of Congress collection. This imperfect copy has several plates not called for by the index and which are called for by the index of the Cóvens and Mortier edition. Beside the illustrated engraved title-page on two leaves, the atlas contains an elaborately illustrated engraved dedication on two leaves, both hand colored.

The first five numbers in the table of contents call for the title, dedication, etc.

CONTENTS.

no. 6. Mappe-monde.
" 7. L'Europe.
" 8. Les Isles Britanniques.
" 9. L'Angleterre.
" 10. L'Ecosse.
" 11. L'Irlande.
" 12. Scandinavie septentrionale.
" 13. Scandinavie méridionale.
" 14. Le Danemarc.
" 15. La Norvèque.
" 16. La Suède.
" 17. La Moscovie septentrionale.
" 18. La Moscovie méridionale.
" 19. La Pologne.
" 20. La Prusse.
" 21. La Hongrie.
" 22. L'Allemagne.
" 23. La Bohême.
" 24. Cercle d' Autriche.
" 25. " de Bavière.
" 26. " " Franconie.
" 27. " " la Souabe septentrionale.
" 28. " " la Souabe méridionale.
" 29. La Suisse.
" 30. Cercle du Haut Rhin.
" 31. L' Alsace.
" 32. Landgraviat de Hesse.
" 33. Cercle électoral du Rhin.
" 34. L' archevêché de Mayence.
" 35. " " Treves.
" 36. " " Cologne.
" 37. Cercle de Westphalie.
" 38. L' évêche de Liège.
" 39. Cercle de la Basse Saxe.
" 40. Le duché de Lunebourge.
" 41. " " " Brunswick.
" 42. Cercle de la Haute Saxe.
" 43. Brandenbourg et Pomeranie.
" 44. Les XVII provinces des Pays-Bas.
" 45. Les provinces unies des Pays-Bas.
" 46. La Hollande.
" 46a. Partie septentrionale de la Nord-Hollande.
" 46b. Partie méridionale de la Nord-Hollande.

no. 46c. La Sud Hollande.
" 47. La Zélande.
" 48. L' Utrecht.
" 49. La Gueldre.
" 50. La Frise.
" 51. L' Over-Issel.
" 52. La Groningue.
" 53. Carte des Pays Bas Catholiques.
" 54. Carte du Brabant.
" 55. " " comte de Flandre.
" 56. Carte des comtez de Hainaut de Namur et de Cambresis.
" 57. La duché de Limbourg.
" 58. " " " Luxembourg.
" 59. Carte d' Artois.
" 60. La France.
" 61. Carte du gouvernement de Picardie.
" 62. " " " " Normandie.
" 63. " " " " Bretagne.
" 64. " " " d'Orléanois.
" 65. " " " de l'Isle de France.
" 66. " " " " Chamagne.
" 67. Carte de Lorraine.
" 68. Carte du gouvernement de Bourgogne.
" 69. " " " " Lyonnois.
" 70. " " " " Dauphiné.
" 71. " " " " Province.
" 72. " " " " Languedoc.
" 73. " " " " Guyenne et Gascogne.
" 74. L'Espagne.
" 75. Le Portugal.
" 76. L' Italie.
" 77. La Savoye.
" 78. Le Piémont.
" 79. Seigneurie de Venise.
" 80. L' État de l' Eglise.
" 81. Le grand duché de Toscane.
" 82. Le royaume de Naples.
" 83. L' Isle de Sicile.
" 84. Turquie en Europe.
" 85. La Grèce.
" 86. L'Asie.
" 87. Turquie en Asie.
" 88. La Grande Tartarie.
" 89. Terre Sainte.
" 90. La Chine.
" 91. L' Inde de-ça le Gange.
" 92. L' Inde de-là le Gange.
" 93. L' Afrique.
" 94. Le cap de Bonne Espérance.
" 95. L' Amérique septentrionale.
" 96. La Floride.
" 97. Canada.
" 98. Mexique.
" 99. L' Amérique méridionale.
" 100. Le Brésil.

1716

English, The, pilot. The third book. Describing the sea-coasts, capes, headlands, straits, soundings, sands, shoals, rocks, and dangers. The islands, bays, roads, harbours, and ports in the oriental navigation. Shewing the properties and nature of the winds and moussons in those seas; with the courses and distances from one place to another: the setting of the tides and currents; the ebbing and flowing of the sea. Also a new table of variations; and a correct table of longitudes and latitudes. With many other things necessary to be known. Being furnished with new and exact large draughts of ports, islands, and descriptions; gathered from the practice and experience of divers able and expert navigators of our english nation. Divided into three parts. The first part, shewing the nature and properties of the winds and moussons in the navigation from England to the East-Indies, and all over the Oriental ocean; and thereby how to shape a course from one port to another, according to the time of year in those seas. The second part, containing necessary instructions for sailing between England and the East-Indies, in the spring and fall. The third part, describing the sea-coasts, capes, headlands, straits, soundings, sands, shoals, rocks, and dangers. The islands, bays, roads, harbours, and ports, from Cape Bona Esperance, all over the Oriental ocean, being very much corrected and augmented with several additions: not heretofore publish'd. Collected for the general benefit of our countrymen, by John Thornton . . . 76 pp., 39 maps. fol. London, for R. & W. Mount & T. Page, 1716. 4278

NOTE.—The Library of Congress has a copy of the *English pilot. Third book*, dated 1748, without John Thornton's name on the title-page, and in which the maps are similar to those in this edition but many of them are re-engraved on new plates. In this 1716 edition many of the old Seller plates have evidently been used with Seller's name removed and that of Sam[l]. Thornton substituted. In the 1748 edition where these same plates have been used, Thornton's name has been eraced. Dalrymple accuses Thornton of copying Seller verbatim in a 1703 edition and giving him no credit. See v. 3, title 3455.

CONTENTS

no. [1] A new and correct mapp of the world, according to m[r]. Edward Wright commonly called Mercator's projection.

" [2] A new chart of England Scotland and Ireland.

" [3] A new and correct draugh[t] of the channell between England & France.

" [4] A large draught of the Isle of Wight and Owers. By Sam[l]. Thornton.

" [5] A new & correct large draught of Plymouth sound Cattwater and Hamowse. By Sam[l]. Thornton.

" [6] A new chart of the Irish sea. By Sam[l]. Thornton.

" [7] A chart of the sea coast from England to the streights. Sam[l]. Thornton. 1714.

no. [8] A generall chart from England to Cape Bona Esperanca with the coast of Brasile. By Sam[l]. Thornton.

" [9] A chart of the coast of Barbaria with the Western, Canaria, & Cape de Verd isles. By Sam[l]. Thornton. Insets: Madera island.—I. Tenerifa.

" [10] A new mapp of the coast of Guinea from Cape de Verd to Cape Bona-Esperanca. By Sam[l]. Thornton.

" [11] A new mapp of the island of Saint Hellena. By Sam[l]. Thornton. Inset: A draught of the island of Trinidada.

" [12] A draught of Cape Bona Esperanca. By Sam[l]. Thornton.

" [13] A draught of the south part of Africa from Cape Bona Esperanca to Delagoa. By Sam[l]. Thornton.

" [14] A chart of the western part of the East-Indies with all the adjacent islands from Cape Bona Esperanca to the island of Zelone. By Sam[l]. Thornton.

" [15] A new draught of the island of Madagascar ats [!] S[t]. Lorenzo with Augustin bay and the island of Monbass at large.

" [16] A chart of the island of Mauritius. By Sam[l]. Thornton. Inset: Dangerous shoals of S[t]. Brandon.

" [17] A chart of the straits of Babelmandell and Moha. By Sam[l]. Thornton.

" [18] A large draught of the coast of Arabia from Maculla to Dofar. By Sam[l]. Thornton. Sutton Nicholls sculp.

" [19] A large draught of the golf of Persia. By Sam[l]. Thornton.

" [20] A large chart of part of the coast of Guzaratt & India from Diu Head to Bombay. By Sam[l]. Thornton.

" [21] A new map of the island of Bombay and Sallset. By Sam[l]. Thornton.

" [22] A large draught of part of the coast of India from Bombay to Bassalore. By Sam[l]. Thornton.

" [23] A large draught of the Mallabar coast from Bassalore to Cape Comaroone. By Sam[l]. Thornton.

" [24] A new mapp of the island of Zeloan. By Sam[l]. Thornton.

" [25] A large chart of part of the coast of Coremandell from Point Pedro to Armegon. By Sam[l]. Thornton.

" [26] A new chart of part of the coast of Coremandell from Armegon to Bimlepatam. By Sam[l]. Thornton.

" [27] A new chart of the coast of Orixa and Galconda. By Sam[l]. Thornton.

" [28] A new and correct chart shewing the goeing over the Braces with the sands shoals depth of water and anchorage from Point Palmiras to Hughley in the bay of Bengall. By Sam[l]. Thornton.

" [29] A mapp of the greate river Ganges as it emptieth it selfe into the bay of Bengala. Taken from a draught made uppon the place, by the agents for the English East India company. By Sam[l]. Thornton.

" [30] A chart of the eastermost part of the East Indies and China, from Cape Comarine to Iapan . . . by Sam[l] Thornton.

" [31] A new and correct chart of part of the island of Java from the west end to Batavia with the streights of Sunda. By Sam[l]. Thornton.

" [32] A large draught of the coast of Iava from Bantam Point to Batavia. By Sam[l]. Thornton.

" [33] A large draught of the east end of Java and Madura shewing the streights of Bally. By Sam[l]. Thornton.

" [34] A large chart describeing y[e] streights of Malacca and Sincapore. By Sam[l] Thornton.

English, The, pilot—Continued.

no. [35] A large draught of the coast of China from Amoye to Chusan with y[e] harbour of Amoye at large. By Sam[l]. Thornton.

" [36] A large draught of the north part of China. Shewing all the passages and chanells into the harbour of Chusan. By Sam[l]. Thornton.

" [37] A large draught from Benjar on the island of Borneo to Macasser on the island of Celebres shewing the streights of Bally . . . By Saml. Thornton.

" [38] A large draught of the south part of Borneo. By Saml. Thornton.

" [39] A draught of the coast of New Holland. By Saml. Thornton. Inset: A draught of Sharks bay on the coast of New Holland by cap[t] Dampier anno 1701.

1719

Chiquet, J.

Le nouveau et curieux atlas géographique et historique, ou le divertissement des empereurs, roys, et princes. Tant dans la guerre que dans la paix. Dédié à son A. R. mgr. le duc d'Orléans . . . 1 p. l., 3–56, 4 l. incl. 24 maps, diagrs. obl. 8°. Paris, Cheveanau, [1719] 4279

NOTE.—Date, 1719, found on maps. Engraved title-page and maps.
Bound at end: *Les véritables portrais des roys de France tirés sur leurs monuments, tombeaux, sceaux et sur des tableaux originaux fait de leurs temps avec l'époque de leurs règnes, la durée de chaque lignée, le lieu de leurs sépultures et le nombre des roys. engr. title, 6 illus. l. incl. 54 ports. 8°. Paris, veuve Chiquet, 1724.*

MAPS.

no. 9. Le globe céleste.
" 11. Le globe terrestre.
" 13. L'Europe.
" 15. L'Asie.
" 17. L'Afrique.
" 19. L'Amérique Septentrionale.
" 21. L'Amérique Méridionale.
" 23. Les royaumes de Portugal et d'Algarve.
" 25. L'Espagne.
" 27. Le royaume de France.
" 29. Les XVII provinces des Pays-bas.
" 31. L'empire d'Allemagne.
" 33. Les estats de la couronne de Pologne.
" 35. Estats du grand duc de Moscovie.
" 37. Les royavmes d'Angleterre, d'Escosse et d'Irlande.
" 39. Le royaume de Danemark, avec les isles adjacentes le duché de Slewick &c.
" 41. Le royaume de Norwège.
" 43. Estats de la couronne de Suède.
" 45. Estats de l'empire du grand seigneur dit sultan.
" 47. Le royaume de Hongrie.
" 49. Carte générale d'Italie et des isles adjacentes.
" 51. Les isles et coste de la Dalmatie, la république de Raguse et partie de la Servie.
" 53. La Grèce.
" 55. Isle et royaume de Candie.

1719

Mallet, A. M.

Beschreibung des gantzen weltkreises, darinnen I. Eine deutliche vorstellung der künstlichen und natürlichen sphæræ, der himmels- und erd-kugel, gestirne, lufftzeichen und der nord-länder. II. Des alten und jetzigen Asiæ. III. Des alten und neuen Africæ. IV. Des alten und neuen Europæ. V. Die fortsetzung des alten und neuen Europæ, wie auch der australischen oder mittgälichen länder und Americæ; nebst allgemeinen und besondern land-charten von denen kayserthümern, königreichen, fürstenthümern . . . zufinden. Hiebevor von dem authore zu Paris in frantzösischer sprache geschrieben, anno 1684. in die hochteutsche sprache übersetzet; jetzo aber auff verlangen durch einen hochgelährten historio-graphum durchgehends wohl auf den jetzigen welstand eingerichtet, auch mit neuen anmerckungen vermehret, und mit 650. künstlichen kupfferstücken gezieret. 5 v. in 2. 4° Franckfurt am Mayn, J. A. Jung, 1719. 4280

NOTE.—Each vol. has special t.-p. and added t.-p., engr.; general t.-p. with v. 1 only.

Maps are similar to those of the french edition of 1683, described in title 3447, but are not from the same plates, although they are in french, with french titles. German titles are also given outside the border.

1727?

Moll, H.

A set of thirty-two new and correct maps of the principal parts of Europe, &c. with the great or post-roads, and principal cross-roads, done in the year 1725, 1726 and 1727. All, except four, viz. England, Scotland, Ireland, and a general map of Turky in Europe; which has been done and printed before . . . 2 p. l., 32 maps. 8°. [London, 1727?] 4281

NOTE.—Contents on title-page.

Map no. 8, A pocket companion of ye roads of ye south part of Great Britain, imperfect.

A number of Moll's atlases listed at the foot of the title-page.

The following maps relate to America:

no. 1. A new map of the whole world with the trade winds. 1727.
" 28. Asia 1727.
" 30. Africa 1727.
" 31. America 1726.
" 32. A map of the West-Indies 1727.

1730–1769

Tirion, I.

Nieuwe en beknopte hand-atlas. Bestaande in eene verzameling van eenige der algemeenste en nodigste landkaarten; alle in de Nederduitsche taal en na de alderlaatste ontdekking- en van de L'Isle en anderen opgesteld, en in een voegzaame grootte uitgegeven; om op eene gemaklyke wyze by het leezen der nieuwstydingen en historien te konnen worden gebruikt. 2 p. l., 112 maps. fol. Amsterdam, I. Tirion [1730–1769] 4282

NOTE.—Tiele mentions another edition of this atlas of 1744 containing 67 maps, and Woltersdorf gives one of that date containing 74 maps.

The Library of Congress has a copy of the edition in which the register calls for 114 maps, which is quoted by Tiele, also this edition of 112 maps without date. Tiele states that in both of these editions the maps are dated from 1753–1754, but a comparison of the Library of Congress copies show that the dates of the maps vary from 1730 to 1769, and that the maps are the same in both copies with the exception of two.

The two extra maps are in the edition calling for 114 maps, and are as follows:

no. 4. Nieuwe wereld kaart, waar in de reizen van den h^r. Anson rondsom de wereld . . .

" 93. Kaart van de Papoasche eilanden. 1753.

For list of maps of America see v. 1, title 600.

1738?

Kilian, G. C.

I. Supplement oder zusaz zu dem Atlas curieux, bestehend aus 25. special land charten, gegenden ū. inslen, und solle diser atlas alle jahr mit 25. stüken vermehret und continuirt werden, heraus gegeben und verlegt von Georg Christoph Kilian. 2 v. in 1. 3 p. l., 50 col. maps; 3 l., 48 col. maps, 2 pl. (text) 12° Augspurg. [1738?] 4283

NOTE.—*Atlas curieux* brought out by Gabriel Bodenehr at Augsburg ca. 1704. See v. 1, title 545.

Maps in Supplement engraved by Gabriel Bodenehr, G. F. Riecke and G. C. Kilian.

Title to pt. 2 differs slightly.

Latest date in the atlas found in pt. 2, map no. 17, Passirung der Donau von der kayserlichen armee. 1738.

A number of maps have border text. Pt. 2, contains 2 pl. of text, no. 21, Beschreibung von America, and no. 25, Beschreibung von Africa.

The following maps relate to America:

pt. 1, no. 25. General charte von dem mitternächt America.
" 2 " 20. Americæ Septentrionalis et Meridional.
" " " 22. Die insulen in West America.
" " " 23. Accurate charte von der insul Curacao.

1738?

Wells, E.

A new sett of maps both of antient and present geography, wherein not only the latitude and longitude of many places are corrected, according to the latest observations; but also the most remarkable differences of antient and present geography may be quickly discern'd by a bare inspection or comparing of correspondent maps; which seem to be the most natural and easy method to lead young students (for whose use the work is principally intended) unto a competent knowledge of the geographical science. Together with A geographical treatise particularly adapted to the use and design of these maps. By Edward Wells, d.d. some time student of Christchurch, Oxon, and late rector of Cotesbach in Leicestershire. Imprimature, Gu. Paynter . . . 2 p. l., 41 maps. fol. London, printed by T. W. for J. Walthoe, R. Wilkin [etc. 1738 ?] 4284

Note.—For extensive note on this edition, see v. 3, title 3489.

Contains the three maps which are wanting in the first copy as follows:

no. 33. Travels of the patriarchs and children of Israel, &c.
" 34. Land of Canaan, &c.
" 35. Places in the New Testament.

The following maps differ from the corresponding maps in the first copy:

no. 27. Ancient Asia.
" 28. Present Asia.
" 40. A new map of South America.

A geographical treatise, to accompany this atlas, mentioned in the title, is wanting.

1739

Giustiniani, F.

El atlas abreviado ò el nuevo compendio de la geografia universal, politica, historica, i curiosa, segun el estado presente del mundo, illustrado con quarenta i tres mapas, i enriquecido con un breve tratado de la geografia antiqua mui util para los curiosos de la historia antiqua . . . 3 v. 12°. Leon de Francia, J. Certa, 1739. 4285

Note.—The following maps relate to America:

v. 1, no. [1] [The world]
" 2, pt. 1, no. [10] America.

1740–1747

Le Rouge, G. L.

[Collection of maps of all parts of the world] 77 maps. fol. [Paris, Le Rouge, 1740–1747] 4286

Note.—Without title-page. Possibly separate maps never published as an atlas, as no atlas corresponding to this by Le Rouge with a regular title-page has been found.

Le Rouge, G. L.—Continued.

CONTENTS.

no. 1. Mappe monde nouvelle. 1744.
" 2. L'Europe. 1747.
" 3. L'Asie. 1747.
" 4. L'Afrique. 1747.
" . L'Amérique. 1746.
" 6. Amérique Septentrionale. Suivant la carte de [H.] Pople faite à Londres en 20 feuilles. 1742.
" 7. La France divisée par gouvernemente et par provinces. 1745.
" 8. La Provence. 1747.
" 9. Le gouvernt général du Dauphiné. 1745.
" 10. La Champagne. 1744.
" 11. Carte contenant le pais entre Boulogne, Aire, Amiens, et Dieppe.
" 12. La Flandre le Hainaut le Brabant l'Artois une partie de la Picardie, et du Luxembourg. 1745.
" 13. Carte du pais situé entre Péronne Guise Mons Lille et Béthune.
" 14. La châtellenie de Lille et le bailliage de Tournay. 1744.
" 15. Carte topographique des environs de Charleroy jusqu'à Philippeville. 1746.
" 16. Carte du pais situé entre Namur Liège Meziere et Arlon. 1742.
" 17. Carte chorographique, des environs de Namur.
" 18. Plan de la bataille de Fontenoy le 11 may 1745. Inset: Mont de la Trinité.
" 19. Carte des Pais-Bas. 1742.
" 20. Carte contenant le pais entre Nieuport l'Ecluse Anvers Ypres et Bruxelles.
" 21. Carte contenant le pais entre Venlo, Liège, Louvain, et Malines. 1742.
" 22. La Hollande. 1746. Inset: Commerce hollandois dans les Indes.—Limbourg.
" 23. Les XVII provinces dites les Pays Bas. 1742.
" 24. La Haute et la Basse Alsace. 1743.
" 25. Le Brabant.
" 26. Le duché de Luxembourg. 1743.
" 27. L'empire d'Allemagne. 1742.
" 28. L'Allemagne par religions.
" 29. L'Allemagne ecclesiastique.
" 30. La Westphalie. 1742.
" 31. L'Electorat de Hannover 1741. Insets: Luneburg.—Haarburg.—Ultzen.—Stade.—Bremen.
" 32. Same. Insets: Nyenburg.—Hanover.—Bremerfurde.—Hildesheim.
" 33. Le cours du Rhin. 1744.
" 34. Théâtre de la guerre en Silesie. 1741. Inset: Plan de Breslaw.
" 35. Partie orientale du cercle de Franconie. 1743.
" 36. L'électorat de Mayence. 1742.
" 37. Partie de l'électorat de Mayence et du landgraviat de Darmstadt. 1745.
" 38. La Vederavie. 1745.
" 39. Cours du Danube, feuille 1 contenant la Suabe. 1742.
" 40. Le royaume de Bohême. 1742.
" 41. Théâtre de la guerre en Bohême. 1741. Insets: Koniggratz.—Clumnitz château.—Einbogen.—Chateau de Brandeis.—Prag.—Budweiss.—Eger.—Kolin.—Leutmaritz.—Pilsen.—Thabor.

no. 42. Carte particulière de la Moravie. 1742. Insets: Brunn.—Olmutz.—Iglaw.—Neustatt.
" 43. Théâtre de la guerre en Autriche. 1742.
" 44. L'Archeveché de Saltzbourg. 1743. Inset: Partie la Basse Autriche.
" 45. Le duché de Stirie. 1742.
" 46. Le duché de Carinthie. 1742. Inset: Clagenfurt.
" 47. Cours du Danube feuille 11e. contenant la Bavière. 1742. Inset: Saltzburg.—Ratisbonne.—Munich.—Donawerth.—Rain.—Lauingen
" 48. Le comte du Tirol. 1742.
" 49. Partie de la Souabe. 1745.
" 50. [Map without title. Probably part of no. 33, Le cours du Rhin. 1744]
" 51–55. Le cours du Rhin de Bâle à Hert près Philisbourg. 1745.
" 56. Le cours du Rhin de Constance.
" 57. Carte topographique du cours du Rhin de Philisbourg. 1745.
" 58. Carte d'Allemagne et d'Italie. 1742.
" 59. L'Italie. 1743.
" 60. Le duché Savoye. 1744.
" 61. Le Piemont et la Monferrat. 1744.
" 62. Succession de Charles VI en Italie. Le duché de Milan, de Mantoue, de Parme et de Plaisance. 1742.
" 63. Milanois Mantouan, Parmesan, et Ferrarois. 1745.
" 64. L'Etat de l'église et le gr. duché de Toscane. 1744.
" 65. Le royaume de Naples et de Sicile. 1745.
" 66. Les Isles Britanniques. 1744. Inset: Les isles de Jersey et Grenesey.
" 67. Le royaume d'Angleterre. 1745.
" 68. Les environs de Londres. 1745.
" 69. L'Ecosse. 1746.
" 70. Le royaume d'Irlande. 1745.
" 71. Théâtre de la guerre en Finlande. 1742.
" 72. Etats de Moscovie. 1744.
" 73. Le royaume de Pologne le grand duché de Lithuanie. 1745.
" 74. Le royaume de Hongrie, la Transilvanie, l'Esclavonie, la Croatie, et la Bosnie. 1742.
" 75. Le duché de Carniole. 1742. Inset: Lac Circknitz.
" 76. Le royaume de Prusse. 1742.
" 77. La Saxe. 1743.

1747

Lat, J. de.

Atlas portatif très exact ou livre de cartes géographiques. Qui est une suite à celui qui a précédé le globe terrestre & les royaumes de l'Europe. Et celui-ci comprend les cartes général particulières des royaumes, païs, isles & les côtes de l'Asie. Toutes les cartes sont construites sur le même méridien, suivant le sistéme de monsr. G. de l'Isle, & sur les meilleures observations faites jusqu' au temps present. Te tout construit & dirigé en cette forme, pour la comodité des amateurs de la géographie, qui pouront porter ce livre fort commodement, en poche.—Weerelds hand-atlas, of naauwkeurig geographische kaart- boekje. Zynde een vervolg op het weerlds deel en koninkryken van Europa. Hier in worden begrepen de generale en particuliere kaarten van alle de koninkryken, land-

Lat, J. de—Continued.

schappen, eilanden en zeekusten van Asia . . . v. 2, 4 p. l., 35 col. maps. nar. 12°. Deventer, J. de Lat; Almelo, J. Keyser, 1747. 4287

NOTE.—Maps are based on those of G. Delisle, M. Hasius and P. Lucas, and engraved by J. Keyser and J. de Lat.

[1750–1784]

Bellin, J. N., *& others.*

Hydrographie françoise. Receuil des cartes marines générales et particulières dressées au dépôt des cartes, plans et journaux, par ordre des ministres de la marine, depuis 1737 jusques en 1772, par feu m. Bellin . . . et autres. v. 2, 1 p. l., 48 maps on 91 l. fol. [Paris, dépôt général de la marine, 1750–1784] 4288

NOTE.—Engraved title-page marked: Arrivet delineavit & sculpcit 1765.
Maps dated 1750–1784.
This copy is like the 1737–1807 ed., see title 590, with the following exceptions:
no. 57. Carte réduite du golfe de S[t]. Laurent. 1754.
" 58. Suite de la carte reduite du golfe de S[t]. Laurent. 1753.
" 59. Carte réduite de la partie septentrionale de l'isle de Terre Neuve. 1764, corr. en 1767.
" 60. Carte réduite du grand banc et d'une partie de l'isle de Terre Neuve. 1764.
" 61. Carte des isles de Saint Pierre et Miquelon. 1763.
" 62. Carte de l'isle Saint Pierre. 1763.
" 65. Carte réduite des costes orientales de l'Amérique Septentrionale. 1757.
" 67. Carte réduite du golfe du Mexique et des l'isles de l'Amérique. Seconde édition année 17[!].
" 69. Carte hydrographique de la baye de la Havane avec le plan de la ville et de ses forts. 1762.
" 71. Carté particulière de l'isle de la Jamaique. 1758.
" 72. Carte réduite de l'isle de Saint Domingue et de ses débouquements. 1750.
" 73. Carte de l'isle de Saint Domingue. 1764.
" 74. Carte réduite des débouquemens de S[t]. Domingue. 1768.
" 75. Carte réduite des isles Antilles. 1758. Inset: Carte particulière des isles des Vierges.
" 87. Mapa y planta del Rio de la Plata. 1770.
" 100. Carte réduite des mere comprises entre l'Asie et l'Amérique. 1742. corr. en 1756.
The following maps, published in title 590, are omitted from this copy: 56, [67a] [67b] [67c] [68a] 69, [69a] [70a] 71–74, [74a] 75, [84a] [84b] 87, [87a]

1754–[1790]

Homann heirs.

Beqvemer hand atlas avs sechs vnd zwanzig Homannischen landkarten nach der vorschrifft des Hübnerischen Musei geographic n. 2 zum gebrauch der Hübnerischen geographischen fragen also eingerichtet a. 1754 . . . 1 p. l., 25 col. maps, 1 col. pl. fol. [Nuremberg, Homann heirs] 1754–[1790] 4289

NOTE.—The Library of Congress has another copy of this atlas, see title 604, in which the maps differ from those in this copy.

Maps are dated from 1736 to 1790.

CONTENTS.

no. a. Schematismvs geographiae mathematicae. 1753.

" 1. Planiglobii terrestris designata a G. M. Lowitzio. 1746. Fig. 1, dicitur Hemisphærum polare arcticum. Fig. 2, Hemisphærium antarcticum. Fig. 3, Hemisphærium sphæræ obliquæ pro horizonte Norimb. Fig. 4, ejus oppositum inferius cum Antipodibus Norimbergensibus.

" 2. Europa, a Ioh. Matth. Hasio. 1789.

" 3. Asia, a I. Matt. Hasio. 1744.

" 4. Africa, a Ioh. Matthia Hasio.

" 5. Americae mappa generalis delineata ab Aug. Gottl. Boehmio.. 1746.

" 6. Regnorum Hispaniæ et Portvgalliæ tabula generalis ad statum hodiernum in suas provincias divisa per D. T. Lopez in nonnullis emendavit F. L. Güssefeld. 1782.

" 7. Regnum Portugalliæ. Per Ioh. Bapt. Homannum.

" 8. Très nouvelle carte du royaume de France. Par I. A. B. Rizzi Zannoni. 1764.

" 9. Regnorum Magnae Britanniæ et Hiberniæ mappa geographica, a Tobia Majero. 1749. Inset: Insulæ Schetlandicæ.

" 10. Magnæ Britanniæ pars meridionalis in qua regnum Angliæ exhibit Ioh. Bapt. Homan.

" 11. Magnæ Britanniæ pars septentrionalis qua regnum Scotiæ accurata tabula ex archetypo Vischeriano desumta exhibitur imitatore Iohan Bapt. Homanno.

" 12. Hiberniæ regnum a Ioh. Bapt. Homanno.

" 13. Belgii Universi a Tobi Majero. 1748.

" 14. Belgivm Catholicvm a Tob. Maiero. 1747.

" 15. Septem provinciae seu Belgivm foederatvm. Auctore Tobia Mayero. 1748.

" 16. Helvetia delineata per d^m^. Tobiam Mayervm, 1751.

" 17. Italia in suos status divisa ex d' Anvilliano Rizzi Zannonique prototypis desumta curantibus Homannianis haeredibus a°. 1790.

" 18. Charte welche des Deutsche reich. Entworfen von Ioh. Bapt. Homann.

" 19. General charte vom königreich Dænemark. Entworfen duch F. L. Güssefeld. 1789.

" 20. Regni Sueciae, edita a Ioh. Bapt. Homanno.

" 21. Charte vom kônigreich Norwegen, entworfen von F. L. Güssefeld 1789. Insets: Der nordiche theil des stifts Drontheim.—Charte über die zu Norwegen gehörigen inseln Fårôer nach C. G Mengel.

" 22. Mappa geographica regni Poloniae, a Tob. Mayero. 1773.

" 23. Tabula geographica totam Borvssiam ut et districtvm Notecensem exhibens. Inset: Charte welche den Netz district vorstellet.

" 24. Totius Danubii, ab Augusto Gottlob Boehmio. 1766.

" 25. Charte das Russische reich und die von den Tatarn. Entworfen von F. L. Güssefeld. 1786.

1755–1771

Palairet, J., *& others.*

[Collection of maps] 33 maps. fol. [London, C. Bowles, & J. Bowles, 1755–1771] 4290

NOTE.—A collection of maps without title-page, similar to Palairet's "Bowles's Universal atlas" [1794–1798] see title 681, but of earlier date. Binders title: Bowles, General atlas.

Except for slight changes in the title, imprint and order, the following maps are the same in both atlases:

no. [11] A draught of Falkland islands.
" [19–20] The Cormandel coast.
" [31] An accurate map of Portugal.

Maps no. 27, 2e Carte de la Turquie européenne, and no. 28, 2e Carte de Hongrie, 1755, are the same with an added line of imprint, as in Palairet's Atlas méthodique, 1755.

Maps are by Palairet, Delarochette, Bowen, Rocque and Bayly, many of them drawn according to Anville, Majer, Petty, Delisle, Hübner and Homann.

A number of maps engraved by Gibson, Reynolds and Kitchin.

The following maps relate to America:

no. [1] A new and accurate map of the world. 1770.
" [2] A map of the whole continent of America.
" [9] South America. By De Larochette.
" [10] A map of the inhabited part of New England.
" [25] A map of the discoveries made by the Russians on the north west coast of America.
" [32] A new chart of the vast Atlantic or Western ocean including the sea coast of Europe, Africa, America and the West India islands.

1756–1758

Gendron, P.

Atlas ô compendio geographico del globo terestre, dividido en imperios, reynos, republicas, estados, provincias, islas, capitales, arzobispados, obispados, religiones y rios obra nui util y aun necesaria para saber la geographia que servira de introduction ô de suplemento al methodo geographico impresso en dos tomos de ovtavo . . . 2 v. in 1. 2 p. l., 34 pp. 29 maps. 8°. Madrid, Barthelemi; Cadiz, Bonardel, 1756–1758. 4291

NOTE.—Double page engraved title to each part. Second part dated 1758.

Most of the maps in pt. 1 are by Robert de Vaugondy and dated from 1754 to 1756. Several maps in pt. 2 are by Brion de la Tour, and one by d'Anville.

Text engraved and on one side of leaf only.

The following maps relate to America:

no. 2. Carta general de el mundo. Por el sr. Robert, 1754. Desbruslins sculpsit.
" 6. La America Meridional. Por el sr. Roberto, 1754.
" 7. La America Septentrional. Por el sr. Roberto, 1754.
" 24. Mapa de las islas de la America y de otros paises de Tiera Firme. Situados antes de estas islas y al rededor del golfo Mexico. Por el sr. d'Anville.

no. 25. Mapa de la parte mas septentrional de la America. 1758. Laurent sculp.
" 26. Mapa de la principal parte de la America Septentrional.
" 27. Mapa de la parte mas, septentrional de la America espanola. Por el s. Brion.
" 28. Mapa de la parte principal de la America Espanola. Por el s[r].Brion.
" 29. Mapa de la parte mas meridional de la America. Por el s[r]. Brion.

1757–1786

Robert de Vaugondy, G., *and* **Robert de Vaugondy, D.**

Atlas universel, par m. Robert, géographe ordinaire du roy et par m. Robert de Vaugondy son fils, géographe ord. du roy et de s. m. polonoise duc de Lorraine et de Bar, et associé de l'académie royale des sciences et belles lettres de Nancy. Avec privilège du roy. 1757. 2 p. l., 34 pp., 111 (*i. e.* 107) maps. fol. Paris, les auteurs; Boudet, 1757–[1786] 4292

Note.—Engraved title-page.
Dates on maps vary from 1749 to 1786.
The first twelve maps are devoted to ancient geography.
Maps no. [10, 14, 24, 79] are wanting.
Contains a noted map, no. [111] "Etats-Unis de l'Amérique Septentrionale avec les isles Royale, de Terre Neuve, de S[t]. Jean, l'Acadie &c. 1785. Paris, Boudet," which gives a list of the thirteen original states, with Vermont and the proposed names of the ten new states provided for in the Jeffersonian ordinance of 1784, and entitled, Sylvania, Michigania, Chersonesus, Arsenistpia, Metropotamia, Illinoia, Saratoga, Washington, Polypotamia, Pelisipia.
Contains two plans of Jerusalem, entitled, "Plan de Jérusalem moderne, sous la domination des Turcs.—Plan de Jérusalem du tems de N. S. J. C." They are insets to map no. [109] "La Judée depuis le retour de la captivité et particulierement sous Herode le grand et ses enfans. Tems de N. S. Jesus-Christ."
The following maps relate to America:
no. [1] Orbis vetus. 1752.
" [13] Mappemonde. 1783.
" [102] Amérique Septentrionale. Publiée en 1750 et corrigée en 1783. Inset: Partie nord-ouest de l'Amérique.
" [103] Partie de l'Amérique Septent. qui comprend la Nouvelle France. 1755. Inset: Supplément pour les lacs du Canada.
" [104] Partie de l'Amérique Septentrionale, qui comprend le cours de l'Ohio, la N[lle]. Angleterre, la N[lle]. York, le New Jersey, la Pensylvanie, le Maryland, la Virginie, la Caroline. 1755. Inset: Supplement pour la Caroline.
" [105] Carte de la Virginie et du Maryland. Dressée sur la grande carte angloise de m[rs]. Josué Fry et Pierre Jefferson. 1755.
" [106] Amérique Méridionale. 1783.
" [107] Partie de la mer du Nord, où se trouvent les grandes et petites isles Antilles et les isles Lucayes. 1750.
" [108] Isles de Saint Domingue ou Hispaniola et de la Martinique. 1750. Inset: Isle de la Martinique.
" [111] Etats-Unis de l'Amérique Septentrionale, avec les isles Royale de Terre Neuve, de St. Jean, l'Acadie &c. 1785.

1757-1794

Sayer, R.

[General atlas containing 41 colored maps of all countries of the world] 41 maps on 84 l. fol. [London, 1757-1794] 4293

NOTE.—The printed index on the reverse of the front cover calls for 41 maps of which one, no. 23, Ottoman empire, is wanting, and one, no. 7a, France divided into metropolitan circles, has been inserted. Title-page also wanting. Maps dated from 1757-1794.

CONTENTS.

no. 1. A new map of the world. 1791.
" 2. Europe. By Thomas Kitchen. 1790.
" 3. A new and compendious map of England and Wales. By Samuel Dunn. 1788.
" 4. A new map of Scotland or North Britain. By lieutenant Campbell. 1790.
" 5. A new map of Ireland. By Thos. Kitchen. 1786.
" 6. A new map of the kingdoms of Spain and Portugal. 1790.
" 7. A new map of the kingdom of France divided into its governments with all the post roads. Published by order of the Post-master general. 1792.
" 7a. France divided into metropolitan circles departments & districts; as decreed by the National assembly, jany. 15th. 1790. London, published by W. Faden. [Inserted]
" 8. A chart of the island of Jersey from the survey made by capt. Clement Lempriere. 1786.
" 9. A correct map of the island of Minorca, by John Armstrong. 1781. Insets: Mediterranean sea.—Harbour of Mahan.—North prospect of Mahon.—North east prospect of St. Philips castle.
" 10. A new map of the island and kingdom of Corsica. By Thomas Jefferys. 1794.
" 11. The island and kingdom of Sicily. By Robert Mylne. 1757.
" 12. A new map of Switzerland. 1790.
" 13. A new map of Italy with the islands of Sicily, Sardinia & Corsica. 1790.
" 14. A new map of Germany. 1793.
" 15. The German dominions of the king of Great Britain. By Thomas Jefferys.
" 16. A new map of the emperor's dominions, exhibiting the post roads of Germany, Hungary and the Netherlands, with those of the adjacent parts of France, Switzerland, Italy and Poland, from the large map published at Vienna by the order of Joseph II, emperor of the romans. Wigzell sculp. 1793.
" 17. A map of the Seven United Provinces with the land of Drent, and the generality lands. By W. Faden. 1789.
" 18. A map of the Austrial possessions in the Netherlands.
" 19. A new map of the northern states containing the kingdoms of Sweden Denmark, and Norway.
" 20. Greece, archipelago and part of Anadoli. By L. S. de la Rochette. 1790. London, published for Willm. Faden. 1791. W. Palmer sculp.
" 21. A new map of Turkey in Europe. F. Vivares sculpt. 1789.

no. 22. A new map of Turkey in Asia. By mons^{r}. d'Anville. 1789.
" 23. Ottoman empire. [Wanting]
" 24. Kingdom of Hungary, principality of Transilvania, Sclavonia, Croatia, with part of Valakia, Bulgaria, Bosnia and Servia. 1788.
" 25. A map of the kingdom of Poland and the grand duchy of Lithuania with their dismembered provinces and the kingdom of Prussia. By Willm. Faden. 1792. Inset: Warszawa.
" 26. The kingdom of Prussia, with its newly incorporated province of Polish Prussia now named Western Prussia; with the territory of Dantzick; by John Roberts. 1789.
" 27. The European part of the Russian empire. 1790.
" 28. The Asiatic part of the Russian empire. 1788.
" 29. Asia. By Thomas Kitchen. 1789.
" 30. A new map of the empire of Persia. 1790.
" 31. The peninsular of India. By J. Rennell.
This map engraved by J. Phillips & W. Harrison. 1788.
" 32. A new general map of the East Indies. By Thomas Jefferys with additions and emendations from the actual surveys made by Maj^{r}. James Rennel.
" 33. The empire of China. M. Borven sculp^{t}. 1790.
" 34. The empire of Japan. 1790.
" 35. Africa. By Thomas Kitchen. 1789.
" 36. America divided into north and south. 1789.
" 37. An accurate map of the United States of America with part of the surrounding provinces agreeable to the treaty of peace of 1783. By In^{o}. Cary. 1783.
" 38. A new map of Nova Scotia, and Cape Breton island and the adjacent parts of New England and Canada. By Thomas Jefferys. 1786.
" 39. A map of the inhabited part of Canada. By Claude Joseph Sauthier. Engraved by W^{m}. Faden. 1777.
" 40. A new and correct map of the province of Quebec. 1788. Insets: A particular survey of the isles of Montreal.—Plan of Montreal.—The city of Quebec.—Course of the river St. Laurence from la Valterie to Quebec.
" 41. The West Indies, including part of Virginia, North Carolina, South Carolina, Georgia, East Florida, West Florida, Louisiana, and the Gulf of Mexico, with part of the coast of South America: from the bay of Honduras, to the mouth of the river Oronoko. London. publish'd 1783 by Jno. Cary.

1763?

Moll, H.

Atlas minor; or a new and curious set of sixty-two maps, in which are shewn all the empires, kingdoms, countries, states in all the known parts of the earth; with their bounds, divisions, chief cities & towns, the whole composed & laid down agreable to modern history . . . 2 p. l., 62 (*i. e.* 60) maps. obl. 8°. London, J. Bowles; C. Bowles [1763?] 4294

NOTE.—2nd copy.
For note on copy no. 1, see v. 1, title 635.
Shows the imprint which has been cut from the title-page of the first copy.

Moll, H.—Continued.

Has perfect copy of map no. 36, India proper, or the Empire of the Great Mogul, which is imperfect in copy no. 1.

Following maps wanting:

no. 10. A chart of part of ye sea coast of England & Flanders.
" 49. New England, New York, New Jersey and Pensilvania[!]

1768–1793

Kitchin, T., *& others.*

A general atlas, describing the whole universe: being a complete collection of the most improved maps extant; corrected with greatest care, and augmented from the latest discoveries. The whole being an improvement of the maps of d'Anville and Robert . . . 1 p. l., 23 maps on 35 sheets. fol. London, R. Sayer, [1768–1793] 4295

NOTE.—The Library of Congress has a number of other editions of this atlas of varying dates, which all differ somewhat. See Index.

CONTENTS.

no. 1– 2. A general map of the world. By Saml. Dunn. 1787.
" 3– 4. Europe from the latest surveys and observations. 1787.
" 5. A compleat map of the British Isles. 1788.
" 6– 7. England and Wales. By John Rocque.
" 8– 9. A new and correct map of Scotland. By lieutenant Campbell. 1790. Inset: The Islands of Shetland.
" 10–11. A map of the kingdom of Ireland. By J. Rocque.
" 12. The Catholic Netherlands. 1793.
" 13. The Seven United Provinces. 1793.
" 14. A new map of the kingdom of France divided into its governments. 1792.
" 15. A new map of the kingdoms of Spain and Portugal. 1790.
" 16. A new map of Italy with the islands of Sicily, Sardinia & Corsica. From mons^r. d'Anville. 1790.
" 17–18. Map of the empire of Germany. By L. Delarochette.
" 19. A new map of the northern states containing the kingdoms of Sweden, Denmark and Norway. 1790.
" 20. A new map of the kingdom of Poland. 1787.
" 21. The European part of the Russian empire. 1790.—The Asiatic part of the Russian empire. 1788.
" 22–23. Asia and its islands according to d'Anville. 1787.
" 24–25. The East Indies with the roads. By Thomas Jefferys. 2nd edition. 1768.
" 26–27. Africa with all its states, kingdoms, republics, regions, islands, &c^a improved and inlarged from d'Anville's map; to which has been added a particular chart of the Gold Coast. By S. Boulton. 1787.
" 28–29. A new map of the whole continent of America, divided into North and South and West Indies. Compiled from m^r d'Anville's Maps of that continent. & corrected in the several parts belonging to Great Britain from the original materials of governor Pownall. 1786. Inset: The supplement to North America containing the countries adjoining Baffins & Hudsons Bay.

no. 30–31. A new map of North America, with the West India Islands. corrected from the original materials of govern. Pownall. 1783. Inset: A particular map of Baffin and Hudson's bay.—Passage by land to California.
" 32. An exact chart of the St. Laurence, from Fort Frontenac to the Island of Anticosti. By Thos. Jefferys. 1775. Inset: The Seven islands.—A continuation of the river from Quebec to Lake Ontario.—The Traverse or passage from Cape Torment into the south channel of Orleans island.—The road of Tadousac.
" 33. Course of the river Mississippi. By lieut. Ross. 1775.
" 34–35. A map of South America. From mr d'Anville. 1787. Inset: A chart of the Falkland islands.

1777

Kitchin, T., *& others.*

A general atlas describing the whole universe. Being a compleat [!] and new collection of the most approved maps extant; corrected with the utmost care, and augmented from the latest discoveries: the whole being an improvement of the maps of d'Anville and Robert [de Vaugondy] . . . 24 maps on 35 sheets. fol. London, R. Sayer & J. Bennett, 1777. 4296

NOTE.—Maps the same as in 1780 edition except map no. 1–2, Scentia terrarum et coelorum . . . by S. Dunn, which is dated 1772 in this edition and 1780 in the 1780 edition.

For contents of this atlas, see entry for 1780 edition in v. 1, title 653. For nótes see 1790 edition, v. 4, no. 4300 and the notes on the various other editions.

Parts of maps no. 3–4, Europe, and no. 17–18, Germany, by Delarochette, are wanting.

1783

Nolin, J. B.

Atlas général à l'usage des collèges et maisons d'éducation adapté aux différents ouvrages de géographie, pour l'intelligence de l'histoire ancienne et moderne, accordés aux observations de l'accadémie rle. des sciences. eng. title, 1 p., 48 sheets incl. 44 maps & 4 pl. 4°. Paris, Mondhare, 1783. 4297

NOTE.—The plates contain figures illustrating mathematical geography, the zones, climates, longitudes and latitudes, etc.

Table of contents at end.

Maps by De la Fosse, Buache and Nolin.

Maps are dated 1780 and 1781.

The following maps relate to America:

no. 7. Hémisphère occidental ou nouveau monde.
" 32. L'Amérique.
" 33. Amérique septentrionale avec les nouvelles découvertes fait au Nord, par les Russes, et les Anglois.
" 34. Partie septentrionale des possessions angloises en Amérique.
" 35. La Virginie, Pennsilvanie, Nouvelle Angleterre. 1781.
" 36. Partie méridionale des possessions angloises en Amérique.

Nolin, J. B.—Continued.

no. 37. Golfe du Mexique.
" 38. Carte du Brésil, le Pérou, Terre Ferme, et le pays des Amazones.
" 39. Terre Magellanique, le Chili et le Paraguay.
" 40. Carte phisique de la mer.

1784

Robert de Vaugondy, G.

Nouvel atlas portatif destiné principalement pour l'instruction de la jeunesse, d'après la Géographie moderne de feu l'abbé [Louis Antoine Nicolle] Delaroix . . . 9 pp. 52 (*i. e.* 53) maps. 4°. Paris, S. Delamarche, 1784. 4298

NOTE.—First published in 1762.

For note on other editions see v. 3, title 3528. Quérard gives an edition published by Delamarche in 1784, without date. The date in this copy appears on the title-page.

Maps dated from 1776 to 1780. Many maps engraved by E. Dussy.

The following maps relate to America:

no. 1. Mappe-monde. 1780.
" 2. " " 1778. [Division par religions]
" 3. " " 1778. [Division par. habitans]
" 4. " " 1778. [Division par la figure des hommes]
" 42. L'Amérique.
" 43. Canada, Louisane, possessions angl. 1778. Inset: Nouveau Méxique.
" 44. Nouvelle Espagne, Nouveau Méxique, Isles Antilles.
" 45. Terre-Ferme, Pérou, Brésil, Pays de l'Amazone.
" 46. Paraguay, Chili, Terre Magellan.

1787?

[Maps of the world] 20 col. maps. [n. p. 1787?] 4299

NOTE.—Title-page wanting.

Latest historical data in atlas, 1778.

Most of the maps contain chronological lists of the sovereigns, family trees of the reigning houses and coats of arms.

CONTENTS.

no. 1. Globus oder erd-kugel.
" 2. Europa.
" 3. Asia.
" 4. Africa.
" 5. America.
" 6. Teutschland.
" 7. Dænnemarck.
" 8. Norwegen und Schweden.
" 9. Rusland.
" 10. Preussen.
" 11. Pohlen.
" 12. Bohmen.
" 13. Ungarn.

no. 14. Türkische reich in Europa and Asia.
" 15. Portugall und Spanien.
" 16. Frankreich.
" 17. Gros-Brittannien.
" 18. Niederlande.
" 19. Republick Schweiz.
" 20. Italien.

1790

Kitchin, T., *& others.*

A general atlas describing the whole universe: being a complete collection of the most approved maps extant; corrected with the greatest care, and augmented from the latest discoveries. The whole being an improvement of the maps of d'Anville and Robert [de Vaugondy] 1 p. l., 23 maps on 35 sheets. fol. London [1790] 4300

NOTE.—The earliest issue of this atlas seems to be the one published in 1773. A number of editions followed. This edition is like the edition to which date 1768–1788 has been supplied from the maps, except for slight changes of date on several maps, five of them carrying the date 1790.

The issue of 1790 was also published by R. Sayer. The issue of 1795 being published by R. Laurie and J. Whittle successors to mr. Sayer.

An article in the Gentleman's magazine for may, 1858, states that this "publishing house dates from the commencement of english hydrography, (with perhaps the single exception of that excellent work, the '*English Coasting Pilot*' by Greenvile Collins, hydrographer to Charles II., published in 1693) . . . It is the oldest exhisting firm [1858] but one in Europe which has devoted itself to nautical works, the exception being the respectable and respected house of Gerard Hulst van Keulen and co., of Amsterdam."

CONTENTS.

no. 1–2. A general map of the world. By Samuel Dunn. 1787.
" 3–4. Europe. 1787.
" 5. A compleat map of the British Isles. 1788.
" 6–7. England and Wales. By John Rocque.
" 8–9. A new and correct map of Scotland. By lieutenant Campbell 1790. Inset: The islands of Shetland.
" 10–11. A map of the kingdom of Ireland. By J. Rocque.
" 12. The Catholique Netherlands. 1788.
" 13. The Seven United Provinces. 1788.
" 14. A new map of the kingdom of France divided into its government with all the post roads.
" 15. A new map of the kingdoms of Spain and Portugal. 1790.
" 16. A new map of Italy, with the islands of Sicily, Sardinia & Corsica. 1790.
" 17–18. Map of the empire of Germany, with the kingdom of Prussia, &c. By L. Delarochette.
" 19. A new map of the northern states containing the kingdoms of Sweden, Denmark, and Norway. 1790.
" 20. A new map of the kingdom of Poland. 1787.
" 21. The European part of the Russian empire. 1790.—The Asiatic part of the Russian empire. 1788.

Kitchin, T., *& others*—Continued.

no. 22–23. Asia and its islands. 1787.
" 24–25. The East Indies. By Thomas Jefferys. 2d ed. 1768.
" 26–27. Africa. By S. Boulton. 1787.
" 28–29. A new map of the whole continent of America. 1786. Inset: The supplement to North America.
" 30–31. A new map of North America, with the West India islands. 1786. Inset: A particular map of Baffin and Hudson's bay.—Passage by land to California.
" 32. An exact chart of the river St. Lawrence. 1775.
" 33. Course of the river Mississipi from the Balise to Fort Chartres; taken on an expedition to the Illinois in the latter end of the year 1765. By lieut. Ross. Improved from the surveys of that river made by the french.
" 34–35. A map of South America. From mr. d'Anville with several improvements and additions. 1787.

1794

Wilkinson, R.

A general atlas being a collection of maps of the world and quarters, the principal empires, kingdoms, e'c. with their several provvinces, & other subdivisions, correctly delineated. 2 p. l., 48 col. maps. sm. fol. London, R. Wilkinson, 1794. 4301

Note.—The engraved title-page is ornamented with a large cartouche commemorative of the achievements of Columbus, Drake, Raleigh and Cooke.
Map no. 2, Mercator's chart of the world, is mutilated.
The following maps relate to America:
no. 1. Map of the world from the latest discoveries.
" 45. A new map of North America agreeable to the latest discoveries. T. Conder sculp.
" 46. A map of the United States of America, with part of the adjoining provinces. T. Conder sculpt.
" 47. An accurate map of the West Indies from the latest improvements. W. Harrison sculp.
" 48. A new map of South America from the latest discoveries. I. Puke sc.

1798

Laurie, R., & Whittle, J.

A new and elegant imperial sheet atlas, comprehending general and particular maps of every part of the world. Principally compiled from the great french atlas, and others of the most distinguished geographers in Europe, forming the completest collection of single sheet maps hitherto published . . . engraved on fifty-one plates beautifully colored. 2 p. l., 51 (*i. e.* 52) col. maps (part fold). fol. London, R. Laurie & J. Whittle, 1798. 4302

Note.—Same maps in the editions described in titles 716 and 720. Map of the United States, 1794, has american flag in color over the title.

1798–1800

Payne, J.

A new and complete system of universal geography. [Atlas] 43 maps (part. fold.) 8°. [New York, Low & Willis, 1798–1800] 4303

Note.—Accompanies his *A new and complete system of universal geography.* Maps engraved by Rollinson, Tanner, Anderson, Barker, Tiebout and Scoles. The following maps relate to America:

no. [1] The world.
" [2] General chart on Mercator's projection.
" [23] A map of North America. 1799.
" [24] The United States of America.
" [25] Vermont. 1799.
" [26] The state of New Hampshire. 1799.
" [27] The state of Massachusetts. 1799.
" [28] The province of Maine. 1799.
" [29] Rhode Island.
" [30] A new map of Connecticut. 1799.
" [31] The state of New York. 1800.
" [32] State of New Jersey.
" [33] The state of Pennsylvania. 1800.
" [34] The states of Maryland and Delaware. 1799.
" [35] The state of Virginia. 1799.
" [36] The state of Kentucky with the adjoining territories. 1800.
" [37] North Carolina. 1800.
" [38] A map of the Tennessee government. 1799.
" [39] The state of South Carolina. 1799.
" [40] Georgia. 1799.
" [41] South America. 1799.
" [42] West Indies.
" [43] A chart shewing the tract of capt. Cook's last voyage. 1799.

1800?

Sharman, J.

[Collection of maps] 29 maps. obl. 12°. [1800?] 4304

Note.—Title-page wanting.
Date supplied from C. F. Carter's List no. 50.

CONTENTS.

no. [1] The world according to the latest discoveries.
" [2] Europe.
" [3] England and Wales. [Imperfect]
" [4] Scotland. Inset: Shetland isles.
" [5] Russia in Europe.
" [6] Sweden, Denmark & Norway.
" [7] Denmark k^{m}. A. Keith sc.
" [8] France divided into provinces.
" [9] France divided into departments, including the Netherlands, Savoy, Nice & Corsica.
" [10] The United Provinces and Netherlands.
" [11] Germany.
" [12] Poland and Prussia.

Sharman, J.—Continued.

no. [13] Spain and Portugal.
" [14] Italy.
" [15] Hungary and Turkey in Europe. Inset: Morea.
" [16] Switzerland. A. Keith sc.
" [17] Asia.
" [18] Turky in Asia.
" [19] A map of the Holy Land.
" [20] East Indies and China.
" [21] Persian empire.
" [22] Egypt.
" [23] Africa.
" [24] North America.
" [25] South America.
" [26] United States of America.
" [27] West Indies. A. Keith sculpt.
" [28] The Roman empire at its greatest extent.
" [29] Ancient Greece.

1804

Antillón y Marzo, I. de.

[Atlas of the world] 16, 32, 30, 52, [1], 31 pp., 5 fold. maps. 8°. [Madrid, real seminario de nobles, 1804] 4305

NOTE.—Maps dated 1801 & 1802. Engraved and drawn by J. Morata, Cardono, F. Selma, P. Gangoiti.

"On February 1, 1804, the 'Ephemerides de la ilustración de Espana' announced to its readers that Isidoro Antillon not only explained his plan [for the teaching of geography] based on sound geographical principles in relation with history, commerce, military, etc., but that he presented a map of the Pacific ocean, with an explanatory text, which gave him the idea of compiling an atlas to accompany his geographical works."

"He began by collecting and drawing maps with great accuracy, and this work may be called the first spanish atlas. To the Seminario de nobles belongs the honor of offering to the nation the realization of this useful and high project."

"Each map is accompanied by an analysis or memoire containing the extensive knowledge of the author." See Beltram y Rozpida, Ricardo. *Isidoro de Antillon. Madrid, 1903. p. 29.*

With reference to this atlas Navarette in his *Biblioteca maritima española. 1851. p. 668*, says:

"El atlas debia constar de treinta cartas, qui si se hubierdo concluido se tendria el primer atlas que podria llamarse español del cual estaban ya publicados y venales en la imprenta real cinco cuadernos."

CONTENTS.

Maps.

no. [1] El Grande oceano desde el paralelo 64. de latit. septentrional, hasta el 57 de latit. austral . . . 1801.
" [2] El oceano Atlantico . . . 1802.
" [3] El oceano reunido 7 el gran golfo de la India . . . 1802.
" [4] La America septentrional desde su extremo norte hasta 10° de latitud segun has ultimas observaciones 7 descubrimientos . . . 1802.
" [5] La Escandinavia ó Mar Caltico, Suecia, Noruega y Dinamarca . . . 1802.

1804

Kitchin T., *& others.*

Kitchin's general atlas, describing the whole universe: being a complete collection of the most approved maps extant: corrected with great care, and augmented from the last edition of d'Anville and Robert [de Vaugondy] . . . 1 p. l., 27 maps on 40 sheets. fol. London, R. Laurie & J. Whittle, 1804. 4305a

Note.—Maps same as in edition of 1801, except no. 34, "Europe . . . from the latest surveys and observations of mr. d'Anville," dated 1805 instead of 1794, and no. 18, "A new map of Germany," dated 1803 instead of 1794.

For contents see v. 3, title 3533.

1812

Malte-Brun, C., *originally* M. C. B.

Atlas complet du précis de la géographie universelle dressé conformément au texte de cet ouvrage et sous les yeux de l'auteur, par m. Lapie. 2 p. l., 11 [1] 80 maps. sm. fol. Paris, F. Buisson, 1812. 4306

Note.—Five maps have been inserted at the beginning of the atlas, as follows: Europe en 1829.—Royaume de France en 1829.—Confédération germanique en 1829.—Royaume de Pologne en 1829 depuis 1815.—Royaume des Pays-Bas en 1829.

The following maps relate to America:

no. 23. Mappe-monde sur la projection réduit de Mercator.
" 24. Mappe-monde en deux hemisphères.
" 25. Mappe-mondes sur diverses projections.
" 69. Amérique Septentrionale.
" 70. Amérique Méridionale.
" 71. États Unis et Grandes Antilles.
" 72. Mexique.
" 73. N^lle^. Grenade, Caracas et Guyanes.
" 74. Pérou et Brésil.
" 75. Buenos-Ayres, Chili et Patagonie.

1814

Laurie, R., *and* **Whittle, J.**

A new juvenile atlas, and familiar introduction to the use of maps: with a comprehensive view of the present state of the earth, and of the relative importance of its different nations: including a series of statistical tables, exhibiting at a general view, the extent, population, nature of government, principal towns, revenue, religion, chief products, articles of export, &c., of all the republics, empires, kingdoms, and states in the world, according to the most recent and accurate authorities . . . First american from the latest London edition, corrected and improved by John Melish. 38 pp., 10 col. maps. fol. Philadelphia, for J. Melish, J. Vallance, & H. S. Tanner by G. Palmer, 1814. 4307

Note.—"This work was originally published in London, by Laurie and Whittle, celebrated map publishers. The leading object in the compilation

Laurie, R., *and* Whittle, J.—Continued.

of it was to communicate, in the clearest manner, a general idea of the use of maps, and of the relative situation, with the comparative importance, of all the different states and nations of the earth.

In the present edition, the maps and geography of the latest London edition have been carefully revised and improved; and the American part has been much altered, in consequence of the revolutions that have taken place in that quarter. A new map and description of the United States, including part of Canada and Florida, is added."

On title-page: "The maps, which include the latest discoveries, consist of:

no. 1. Elementary map.
" 2. The world in general.
" 3. General map of America.
" 4. " " " Europe.
" 5. " " " Asia.
" 6. " " " Africa.
" 7. Map of the United States, with the roads.
" 8. " " England, with the same.
" 9. " " Scotland, " " "
" 10. " " Ireland, " " "

1814?

Playfair, J.

Atlas to Playfair's geography . . . cover-title, 7 maps. obl. fol. London, 1814. 4308

NOTE.—Six of the maps marked, "Drawn and engraved for dr. Playfair's Geography." Same maps found in Playfair's. *A new general atlas, ancient and modern. 1814.*

CONTENTS

no. [1] Italy. Drawn by W. W. Macpherson. Cooper sculpt 1809.
" [2] Eastern hemisphere. Engraved by B. Smith.—Roman wall in Britain. 1809.—Britannia antiquæ. Cooper sculpt. 1809.
" [4] Ancient and modern Ireland. Engraved by B. Smith.
" [5] Italia antiquæ. Cooper sculp. 1809.
" [6] Sweden, Denmark & Norway.
" [7] Poland. Engraved by B. Smith.

A new general atlas, ancient and modern . . . elegantly engraved by the most eminent artists in London. 2 p. l., 46 maps. fol. London, for the author, 1814. 4309

NOTE.—Most of the maps are marked, "Drawn and engraved for dr. Playfair's Geography."

Corrected title from v. 1, titles 137, 723.

CONTENTS

no. [1] The world as known to the ancients. B. Smith sculpt. 1808.
" [2] Map of the world according to Strabo. J. Bye sc.
" [3] Map of the world, constructed towards the conclusion of the xth century.
" [4–5] Map of the world, constructed in the xivth century.
" [6] Hispania. B. Smith sculpt. 1808.

no. [7] Gallia B. Smith sculpt. 1808.
" [8] Roman wall in Britain. 1809.—Britannia antiquæ. Cooper sculpt. 1809.
" [9] Germania antiqua. Neele sc.
" [10] Italia antiquæ. Cooper sculp. 1809.
" [11] Græcia antiqua. Neele sculpt. 1812.
" [12] Asia Minor. Neels sc.
" [13] Libyæ vel Africæ. Neele sc. 1814.
" [14] Western hemisphere. Drawn by N. Coltman. Eng. by E. Jones.
" [15] Eastern hemisphere. Engraved by B. Smith.
" [16] Europe. Drawn by N. Coltman. Engraved by J. Bye.
" [17] Asia. Neel sc. 1814.
" [18] Africa. Engraved by H. Cooper.
" [19] North America. Neele sculp.
" [20] South America. Neele sc. 1814.
" [21] Spain and Portugal. N. Coltman delt. B. Smith sculpt.
" [22] France in provinces. Drawn by N. Coltman. E. Jones sculpt. Inset: Corsica.
" [23] France in departments. E. Jones sculpt. Inset: Corsica.
" [24] England. Drawn by W. W. Macpherson. Cooper sculp. 1809.
" [25] Scotland. Cooper delt. et sculpt. 1809. Inset: The Shetland islands.
" [26] Ancient and modern Ireland. Engraved by B. Smith.
" [27] Sweden, Denmark & Norway.
" [28] The seven United Provinces. B. Smith sculpt. 1808.
" [29] The Netherlands.
" [30] Germany. Engraved by H. Cooper.
" [31] Switzerland. Engraved by H. Cooper.
" [32] Italy. Drawn by W. W. Macpherson. Cooper sculp. 1809.
" [33] Hungary, and Turkey in Europe. Neele sculpt. 1812.
" [34] Poland. Engraved by B. Smith.
" [35] Russia in Europe. S. I. Neele sculpt. 1812.
" [36] Map of Russian Asia with the adjacent countries. Neele sc. [Shows Bering strait]
" [37] Modern Asia Minor. Neele sc.
" [38] Palestine and Syria—Syria antiqua et Palæstina. Neele sc.
" [39] Ægyptus antiqua.—Egypt. Neele sc.
" [40] Arabia. Engraved by H. Cooper.
" [41] Persia. S. I. Neele.
" [42] Hindostan. S. I. Neele sculpt. 1814.
" [43] China and Japan Engraved by H. Cooper.
" [44] The Asiatic islands. Neele sc. 1814
" [45] West Indies. Engraved by H. Cooper.
" [46] Islands in the Pacific ocean. Neele sc. 1814.

1815

Bazeley, C. W.

The new juvenile atlas, illustrative of the various divisions which comprise the surface of the globe; intended also as an interesting companion to a view of the world or ancient and modern geographical delineations . . 1 p. l., 28 maps. 8°. Philadelphia, for the author, 1815. 4310

NOTE.—"Sold by B. B. Hopkins."

Index on title-page calls for 26 maps of which no. [19] Asiatic Turkey, is wanting. Three maps nos. [27–29] in atlas are not called for by the index.

The Library of Congress has a second very imperfect copy which has an additional title-page reading: *The academy of science and art, or ladies new preceptor: containing a complete system of useful and polite education, as well as general knowledge. Intended for use of schools and private students. By C. W. Bazeley . . , In six volumes.* Imprint same as above.

CONTENTS

no. [1] Chart of the world on Mercators projection.
" [2] The Roman empire at its greatest extent.
" [3] Ancient Greece.
" [4] Europe.
" [5] Sweden, Norway, &c.
" [6] Russia in Europe.
" [7] England & Wales.
" [8] Scotland.
" [9] Ireland.
" [10] France.
" [11] Holland.
" [12] Germany.
" [13] Poland.
" [14] Spain & Portugal.
" [15] Italy.
" [16] Turkey.
" [17] Asia.
" [18] China.
" [19] Asiatic Turkey. [Wanting]
" [20] Persia.
" [21] Hindoostan.
" [22] Africa.
" [23] North America.
" [24] United States.
" [25] West Indies.
" [26] South America.
" [27] A general map of the world from the most modern authorities.
" [28] Palestine.
" [29] Places mentioned in the Old and New Testament with those remote from the Holy Land.

1817

Carey, M.

Carey's general atlas, improved and enlarged: being a collection of maps of the world and quarters, their principal empires, kingdoms, &c. . . . 3 p. l., 58 maps. fol. Philadelphia, M. Carey & son, 1817. 4311

NOTE.—List of maps on title-page.

Library of Congress has editions of 1796, 1802, [1814?] 1814 and 1818. See v. 1 & 3.

CONTENTS

no. 1. A map of the world from the best authorities.
" 2. A chart of the world according to Mercators projection, showing the latest discoveries of capt. Cook.
" 3. A new and accurate map of North America. Bower sc.
" 4. The British possessions in North America. W. Robinson, sc. 1814.
" 5. A map of the United States of America. Gridley sc.
" 6. Vermont. Delineated & engraved by Amos Doolittle.
" 7. The state of New Hampshire. By Samuel Lewis, 1813.
" 8. The district of Maine. Engd. by John G. Warnicke.
" 9. The state of Massachusetts.
" 10. The state of Rhode Island; compiled from the surveys and observations of Caleb Harris, by Harding Harris.
" 11. Connecticut. Delineated & engraved by A. Doolittle.
" 12. The state of New York. S. Lewis del. J. G. Warnicke sc.
" 13. The state of New Jersey. Compiled by Samuel Lewis.
" 14. Pennsylvania.
" 15. Delaware.
" 16. Maryland.
" 17. A correct map of Virginia.
" 18. North Carolina. By Samuel Lewis.
" 19. The state of South Carolina. By Samuel Lewis. W. Barker, sculp.
" 20. The state of Georgia. Gridley sc.
" 21. Kentucky. Gridley sc.
" 22. The state of Tennesee.
" 23. The state of Mississippi and Alabama territory. Shallus sc.
" 24. The state of Ohio with part of upper Canada, &c.
" 25. The upper territories of the United States. Kneass & Delleker sc.
" 26. Louisiana.
" 27. Missouri territory formerly Louisiana. Bower sc.
" 28. Plat of the Seven Ranges of townships.
" 29. Mexico.
" 30. West Indies.
" 31. Carte de la partie françoise de St. Dominque. Faite par Bellin et depuis augmentée par P. C. Varlé.
" 32. A new map of South America.
" 33. A map of the Caracas. Warnicke sc.
" 34. Peru.
" 35. Chili and part of the viceroyalty of La Plata. W. Robinson sc.
" 36. A map of Brazil.
" 37. Europe. Bower.
" 38. Sweden, Denmark, Norway, and Finland. Engraved by S. Hill.
" 39. Russian empire.

Carey, M.—Continued.

no. 40. Scotland. Inset: Shetland islands.
" 41. An accurate map of England and Wales.
" 42. A map of Ireland.
" 43. Holland. S. Lewis delin.
" 44. Germany.
" 45. France.
" 46. Turkey in Europe and Hungary.
" 47. Spain and Portugal. S. Lewis del. J. G. Warnicke sculp.
" 48. Italy and Sardinia. Bower.
" 49. Switzerland.
" 50. Poland.
" 51. Asia.
" 52. China. B. Tanner.
" 53. An accurate map of Hindostan or India.
" 54. The islands of the East Indies with the channels between India, China & Holland.
" 55. A new and accurate map of New South Wales with Norfolk and Lord Howe's islands, Port Jackson.
" 56. Africa.
" 57. A map of the countries situate about the North Pole.
" 58. A map of the discoveries made by capts. Cook & Clerk in the years 1778 & 1779 between the eastern coast of Asia and the western coast of North America. Also mr. Hearn's discoveries to the North westward of Hudson's bay, in 1772.

1817

Steel & Horsburgh.

Steel & Horsburgh's new and complete East-India pilot, being a collection of charts, general and particular, from England to the cape of Good Hope, Bombay, Madras, Bengal and China . . . 1 p.l., 30 maps. fol. London, Steel & Goddard, 1817. 4312

NOTE.—14 maps wanting.

CONTENTS.

no. 2. The entrances of the river Thames. 1312. Inset: The river Thames from London to Leigh road.
" 3. Harbours and islands in the British Channel. 1813.
" 4. Principal harbours in the British Channel.
" 6. A new chart of the Açores or Western islands. 1813.
" 7. A chart of the Canary Islands. 1815.
" 8. Steel's new and improved chart of Cape Verd islands. 1809.
" 9. Steel's chart of the Southern Atlantic ocean. 1814.
" 14. Chart of Mauritius, or the isle of France, and of the isle of Bourbon. 1811.
" 15. Chart of the Persian Gulph. 1813.
" 21. Steel's new chart of the bay of Bengal. 1810.
" 22. [Indian Sea from Bengal to the China Seas]
" 23. Steel's new chart of the straits of Malacca and Singapore. 1809.
" 25. A new chart through the straits of Sunda to Batavia. 1815.
" 26. Steel's new chart of the straits of Macassar. 1812.
" 29. Chart of the islands and passages to the eastward of New Guinea. 1808.
" 30. Chart of Goa and Murmagoa roads. 1812, by David Inverarity.

1820

Cyclopaedia, The; or, universal dictionary of arts, sciences and literature. By Abraham Rees . . . with the assistance of eminent professional men . . . vol. 6. Ancient and modern atlas. 1 p. l. 61 maps. 4°. London, for Longman, Hurst, Rees, Orme & Brown; F. C. & J. Rivington, etc., 1820. 4312a

NOTE.—Maps engraved by Lowry, Alex[r]. Findlay, J. Russell, Cooper, J. Lodge, B. Smith, Hewitt, J. Bye, Sid. Hall, John Cooke, J. Pickett, E. Jones. The maps in the american edition, though apparently the same, are by different engravers.

The following maps relate to America:
no. [23] The world. 1806.
" [24] The world on Mercators projection. J. Lodge sculp. 1807.
" [53] Chart of the Pacific ocean. Cooper sculp. 1808.
" [57] North America. Engraved by J. Russell. 1809.
" [58] South America. Drawn and engraved by J. Russell. 1809.
" [59] British possessions in North America. Drawn and engraved by J. Russell. 1809.
" [60] United States. Engraved by E. Jones. 1805.
" [61] West Indies. B. Smith sculpsit. 1805.

1820

Potter, P.

[Atlas of the world] 7 maps. 8°. [Poughkeepsie, P. Potter, 1820] 4313

NOTE.—Title-page wanting.

The following maps relate to America:
no. [1] The world.
" [2] North America.
" [3] United States of America.
" [4] South America.

1824

Finley, A.

A new general atlas, comprising a complete set of maps, representing the grand divisions of the globe, together with the several empires, kingdoms and states in the world; compiled from the best authorities, and corrected by the most recent discoveries. 2 p. l., 58 col. maps, 2 tab. fol. Philadelphia, A. Finley, 1824. 4314

NOTE.—For other editions see v. 1, titles 752, 755, 760.

The following maps relate to America:
no. 1. Western hemisphere.
" 3. World.
" 4. North America.
" 5. Canada.
" 6. United States.
" 7. Maine.
" 8. New Hampshire.
" 9. Vermont.
" 10. Massachusetts.

Finley, A.—Continued.

no. 11. Rhode Island.
" 12. Connecticut.
" 13. New York.
" 14. New Jersey.
" 15. Pennsylvania.
" 16. Delaware.
" 17. Maryland.
" 18. Virginia.
" 19. North Carolina.
" 20. South Carolina.
" 21. Georgia.
" 22. Alabama.
" 23. Ohio.
" 24. Kentucky.
" 25. Tennessee.
" 26. Indiana.
" 27. Illinois.
" 28. Mississippi.
" 29. Louisiana.
" 30. Missouri.
" 31. Mexico.
" 32. West Indies.
" 33. South America.

1827

Vivien de Saint-Martin, L.

Atlas universel, pour servir à l'étude de la géographie et de l'histoire anciennes et modernes. 1 p. l., 1 l., 48 maps (12 fold.) fol. Paris, Ménard & Desenne, 1827. 4315

NOTE.—First published in 1825.

CONTENTS.

no. [1] Mappe-monde en deux hémisphéres. 1825.
" [2] Carte générale de l'Europe. 1824.
" [3] Carte de royaume de Suède, comprenant la Suède propre et la Norwège et du royaume de Danemarck. 1824.
" [4] Carte de la Russie d'Europe. 1824.
" [5] Carte des Isles Britanniques, formées de trois grandes parties: l'Irlande, l'Ecosse et l'Angleterre. 1824.
" [6] Carte du royaume des Pays-Bas, divisé en deux grandes parties, la Hollande et la Belgique. 1824.
" [7] Carte comparative de la France. 1824.
" [8] Carte du royaume de France. 1824.
" [9] Carte générale d'Allemagne, comprenant l'empire d'Autriche, la confédération germanique, le royaume de Prusse, la Pologne et la Suisse. 1824.
" [10] Carte générale du royaume de Prusse. 1824.
" [11] Carte générale du royaume de Pologne, avant son démembrement par la Prusse, l'Autriche et la Russie. 1825.
" [12] Carte du nouveau royaume de Pologne. 1824.
" [13] Carte générale des états composant la confédération germanique. 1824.
" [14] Carte générale de l'empire d'Autriche. 1824.

no. [15] Carte de la Suisse. 1824.
" [16] Carte générale de l'Italie. 1824.
" [17] Carte de la péninsule hispanique où sont compris les royaumes d'Espagne et de Portugal. 1824.
" [18] Carte de la Turquie d'Europe et de la Grèce. 1826.
" [19] Carte générale de l'Asie. 1825.
" [20] Carte générale de la Russie d'Asie ou Sibérie. 1825.
" [21] Carte générale de l'empire chinois. 1826.
" [22] Carte particulière de la Chine. 1825.
" [23] Carte générale de la Turquie d'Asie. 1824.
" [24] Carte générale du royaume de Perse, et du royaume de Caboul ou Afghanistan. 1825.
" [25] Carte générale des Indes. 1825.
" [26] Carte générale de l'Afrique. 1826.
" [27] Carte générale de la partie nord-ouest de l'Afrique où sont les états de Maroc, d'Alger, de Tunis et de Tripoli, le fezzan et le grand désert de Sahara. 1826.
" [28] Carte particulière de l'Egypte. 1825.
" [29] Carte d'une partie de l'Afrique septentrionale où se trouvent la Sénégambie, la Nigritie ou Soudan, la Nubie et l'Abyssinie. 1826.
" [30] Carte générale de l'Afrique méridionale. 1826.
" [31] Carte de l'Amérique septentrionale avec les régions polaires. 1825.
" [32] Carte de la partie septentrionale du nouveau monde, où sont comprises les possessions anglaises de l'Amérique du Nord, l'Amérique russe et les régions polaires arctiques. 1825.
" [33] Carte générale des Etats-Unis de l'Amérique septentrionale. 1825.
" [34] Carte générale du Mexique et des provinces-unies de l'Amérique centrale ou Guatemala. 1826.
" [35] Carte particulière des Antilles et du golfe du Mexique avec l'isthme de Panama. 1825.
" [36] Carte de l'Amérique méridionale. 1825.
" [37] Carte de la république de Colombia. 1826.
" [38] Carte générale d'une partie de l'Amérique du Sud où sont comprises les nouvelles républiques du Pérou, du Haut Pérou, et de Buenos-Ayres ou La Plata. 1826.
" [39] Carte générale de l'empire du Brésil. 1826.
" [40] Carte de l'Océanie. 1824.
" [40] Partis orbis veteribus Grœcis Romanisque notæ mappa generalis. 1826.
" [42] Imperii Romani, tam in occidente quam in oriental, mappa generalis pro Cæsarum tempore. 1826.
" [43] Italia vetus ad Augusti tempus. 1825.
" [44] Gallia vetus in regiones IV, in provincia XVII. 1824.
" [45] Græciæ antiquæ nec non et Macedoniæ. 1826.
" [46] Asiæ Minoris: mappa generalis ad Cæsarum tempus. 1826.
" [47] Syriæ: mappa generalis ubi Syria propria. 1826.
" [48] Ægyptus antiqua ad tempora Romana. 1825.

1827-1828

Brigham, J. C., *and* **Morse, S. E.**
Nuevo sistema de geografía, antigua y moderna, con diez y ocho laminas y cuatro mapas. 320 pp. illus. 12°. & atlas of 5 maps. 4°. Nueva York, White, Gallaher & White, 1827-28. 4316

NOTE.—Atlas dated 1828.
Title of atlas: *Atlas adaptado al systema nuevo de geografia*

1829?

Delamarche, F.
Atlas de la géographie ancienne et moderne, à l'usage de l'école royale de Saint-Cyr, des collèges et des maisons d'éducation, pour suivre les cours de géographie et d'histoire . . . 33 (*i. e.* 32) maps, 1 pl. sm. fol. Paris, F. Delamarche & C. Diem, [1829?] 4317

NOTE.—Maps have various dates from 1811-1820.
The following maps relate to America:
no. 2. Mappe-monde. 1820.
" 19. Amérique septentrionale. 1811.
" 20. Amérique méridionale. 1811.

1830-1834

Diccionario geográfico universal . . . Atlas. 42 maps. obl. fol. [Barcelona, J. Torner, 1830-1834] 4318

NOTE.—Atlas to accompany, *Diccionario geográfico universal . . . 10 v. 8°. Barcelona, J. Torner, 1830-1834.*
Maps are dated from 1830-1834.
Maps engraved by Domingo Estruc, Pablo Alabern, Ramon Alabern.

CONTENTS.

no. [1] Mapa-mundi en dos hemisferios. Domingo Estruc lo grabó. 1831.
" [2] Mundo conocido de los antiguos. Pablo Alabern lo grabó. 1830.
" [3] Imperia antiqua ad expeditiones Cyri et Alexandri precipuè relata, quorum itineraria sunt depicta. Ramon Alabern lo g°.
" [4] Planisferio que comprende los tres viages de Cook y tierras ultim.te descubiertas. Pablo Alabern lo grabó.
" [5] Europa. Pablo Alabern lo grabó. 1831.
" [6] España y Portugal. Inset: Islas Canarias.
" [7] Reino de Francia. Pablo Alabern lo grabó.
" [8] Las Galias. Ramon Alabern lo g°.
" [9] Islas Britanicas. Domingo Estruc lo grabó. 1830.
" [10] Italia é Iliria. Domingo Estruc lo grabó. 1831.
" [11] Italia antigua. Pablo Alabern lo grabó. 1832.
" [12] Suiza.
" [13] Paises-Bajos. Pablo Alabern lo grabó. 1831.
" [14] Alemania. Ramon Alabern lo g°.
" [15] Germania, Pannonia, Dacia, et Sarmatia. Domingo Estruc lo gravó, 1832.

no. [16] Prusia con sus adquisiciones sobre el Rin. Tallér de Estruc g°.
" [17] Reino de Polonia ò sea la parte unida ala Rusia por el repartimiento de 1795 que conserva el nombre de aquel antiguo reino. R. Alabern lo g°.
" [18] Mapa general de Polonia antes de su desmembramiento Tallér de Estruc g°.
" [19] Rusia Europea. Pablo Alabern lo grabó. 1833.
" [20] Suecia y Dinamarca. Domingo Estruc lo grabó. 1830.
" [21] Turquia Europea y Grecia. Pablo Alabern lo grabó.
" [22] Grecia antigua. Pablo Alabern lo g°. 1831.
" [23] Planos para la historia de la Grecia antigua: Campo de batalla de Marathon.—Cercanias de Athenas.—Las Thermopylas.—Campo de batalla de Platea.—Ruinas de Athenas.—Combate naval de Salamina. Domingo Estruc lo grabó. 1830.
" [24] Africa. Pablo Alabern lo grabó.
" [25] Nordest de África . . . Ramon Alabern lo grabó.
" [26] Egipto. Domingo Estruc lo grabó. 1831.
" [27] Syria. Ramon Arabern lo g°.
" [28] Asia. Domingo Estruc lo gravó. 1832.
" [29] Asiae Minoris mappa generalis ad Cæsarum tempus. Ramon Alabern lo g°.
" [30] Turquia Asiatica. Ramon Alabern lo grabó.
" [31] Persia, Afganistan y Beluchistan. Ramon Alabern lo g°.
" [32] Oceania ó Australasia y Polynesia. Pablo Alabern lo grabó. 1831.
" [33] Imperio Chino y Japon. Pablo Alabern lo grabó.
" [34] India á una y otra parte del Ganges. Ramon Alabern lo g°.
" [35] America del Sur. Ramon Alabern lo grabó.
" [36] Mapa de la Nueva Granada y Caracas. Ramon Alabern lo g°.
" [37] América Meridional. Domingo Estruc lo grabó. 1831.
" [38] Estados Unidos de la América Septentrioal. Pablo Alabern lo grabó. 1834.
" [39] Imperio del Brasil. En el tallér de P. Alabern.
" [40] América Septentrional. Pablo Alabern lo grabó.
" [41] Islas Antillas y golfo de Méjico.
" [42] Méjico. En el tallér de Pablo Alabern.

1833

Starling, T.

Geographical annual or family cabinet atlas designed and engraved by Thomas Starling. Specially patronized by their most gracious majesties William IV and Adelaide. 1 p. l., 96 l. incl. 45 col. maps, 2 col. pl. 16°. London, for the proprietors for Bull, 1833. 4319

NOTE.—Printed by Perkins & Bacon.
Title, text and maps engraved.
First published in parts as the *Family cabinet atlas* in 1830.
Leaves 1–4 wanting.
The following maps relate to America:
pl. 8. The world on Mercator's projection.
" 10–11. The world.
" 78. North America.

Starling, T.—Continued.

pl. 80. British possessions in North America.
" 82. Canada, with New Brunswick, Nova Scotia & Newfoundland.
" 84. United States.
" 86. Mexico and Guatimala.
" 88. West Indies.
" 90. South America.
" 92. Colombia.
" 94. La Plata, Chile and the Banda Orientalc.
" 96. Brazil with Guiana & Paraguay.

1833–1834

Tanner, H. S.

[A new universal atlas containing maps of the various empires, kingdoms, states and republics of the world] . . . 63 col. maps. fol. [Philadelphia, published by the author, 1833–1834] 4320

NOTE.—Issued in parts of not less than four maps each.
Title-page and the following maps wanted:
no. 2. North America.
" 3. Lower Canada.
" 4. United States.
" 31. South America.
" 32. Venezuela, New Grenada & Equador.
" 33. Brazil.
" 34. Peru and Bolivia.
" 35. Chile, La Plata and Montevideo.
" 47. Kingdom of Sardinia.
" 56. Russia in Asia and Tartary.
" 58. Persia, Arabia &c.
" 59. India.
" 63. Oceana or Pacific ocean.

1838–1839

Brué, A. H.

Atlas universel de geographie physique, politique, ancienne & moderne, contenant les cartes générales et particulières de toutes les parties du monde; rédigé conformément aux progrès de la science pour servir à l'intelligence de l'histoire, de la géograhpie et des voyages . . . 2. éd. 3 p. l., 64 maps. fol. Paris, C. Picquet, 1838–[1839] 4321

NOTE.—Maps bear dates from 1821 to 1839. The following maps relate to America:
no. 15. Mappemonde sur la projection de Mercator. 1838.
" 16. Mappemonde en deux hémisphères. 1839.
" 17. Mappemonde. 1838.
" 57. Carte générale de l'Amérique septentrionale et des îles qui en dépendent. 1838.
" 58. Carte générale des États-Unis, du haut et bas-Canada, de la Nouv[le]. Ecosse, du Nouv[au]. Brunswick, de Terre-Neuve, &c[a]. 1838.
" 59. Carte générale des etats-unis mexicains et des provinces-unies de l'Amérique centrale. 1825

no. 60. Carte des Îsles Antilles, des états-unis de l'Amérique centrale et de la mer du Mexique. 1837.
" 61. Carte particulière des Îles Antilles. 1828.
" 62. Carte générale de l'Amérique méridionale et des îles qui en dépendent. 1839.
" 63. Carte des républiques de la N[le]. Grenade, de Vénézuéla et de l'Équatuér formées de l'ancien état de Colombie, et des Guyanes française, hollandaise et anglaise. 1836.
" 64. Carte générale du Pérou, du haut-Pérou, du Chili et de La Plata. 1836.
" 65. Carte du Brésil et d'une partie des pays adjacents. 1836.

1840

Arrowsmith, J.

The London atlas of universel geography, exhibiting the physical & political divisions of the various countries of the world, constructed from original materials . . . 1 p. l. 50 (*i. e.* 62) col. maps. fol. London, J. Arrowsmith, 1840. 4322

CONTENTS.

no. 1. Orbis veteribus notus. 1832.
" 2. The world, on Mercator's projection. 1840.
" 3. Europe. 1840.
" 4. England. 1832.
" 5. Inland navigation, railroads, geology and minerals of England & Wales. 1840.
" 6. Scotland. 1834.
" 7. Ireland. 1832.
" 8. Sweden & Norway. 1832. Inset: Tornea to the North Cape.
" 9. Denmark. 1840. Inset: Iceland.
" 10. Holland & Belgium. 1840.
" 11. France. 1840. Insets: France divided into provinces. Corsica.
" 12. Western Germany. 1832.
" 13. Prussia & Poland. 1834.
" 14. Russia & Poland. 1832.
" 15. Austrian empire. 1832.
" 16. Switzerland &c. 1832.
" 17. North Italy &c. 1834.
" 18. South Italy. 1832.
" 19. Turkey in Europe. 1832.
" 20. Greece and the Ionian islands. 1832.
" 21. Spain & Portugal. 1832. Inset: Minorca.
" 22. Africa. 1840.
" 23. Northwestern Africa. 1834.
" 24. Cape of Good Hope. 1840.
" 25. Nubia and Abyssinia. 1832.
" 26. Egypt. 1832.
" 27. Asia. 1832.
" 28. Turkey in Asia. 1832.
" 29. Central Asia, comprising Bokhara, Cabool, Persia, the river Indus & countries eastward of it. 1840.
" 30. India. 1840.

Arrowsmith, J.—Continued.

no. 31. Burmah, Siam, and Cochin China. 1832.
" 32. China. 1840.
" 33. Northern Asia. 1834.
" 34. Asiatic Archipelago. 1840.—Inset: I. of Singapore.
" 35. Southeastern Australia. 1838.
"35a. Cockburn Sound, by J. S. Roe. 1840. Inset: Kingstown. King Georges Sound.—Inset: Peel harbour.
" 36. Western Australia. 1839.—Insets: Guildford, Freemantle, Perth, Augusta, Kelmscott, Cockburn Sound.
" 37. Van Diemens Land. 1834.
" 38. Pacific ocean. 1832.
" 39. America. 1840.
" 40. British North America. 1840.
" 41. Upper Canada &c. 1838.
" 42. Lower Canada. 1838.—Inset: Newfoundland.
" 43. United States. 1834.
" 44. Mexico. 1832.—Inset: Mexico, showing its connection with ports [etc.]
" 45. West Indies. 1832. Inset: Shows western boundary between Guatemala and Yucatan.
" 46. South America. 1839.—Insets: Galapagos islands, Port San Carlos, Falkland islands, Patagonia.
" 47. Colombia. 1834.
" 48. Peru & Bolivia. 1834.
" 49. Brazil. 1840.
" 50. La Plata, the banda oriental del Uruguay and Chile. 1839.—Inset: Patagonia.
" [51] Sketch of acqusitions of Russia since Peter 1st. 1838.
" [52] Australia. 1840.
" [53] Eastern Australia. 1838.—Insets: Torres Strait, Van Diemens land.
" [54] Maritime portion of South Australia. 1840.—Insets: Encounter Bay, Nepean Bay, City of Adelaide, and east shore of Gulf of St. Vincent.
" [55] District of Adelaide, South Australia. 1840.
" [56] Eastern townships of Lower Canada. 1839.
" [57] [Western townships of Lower Canada]—Inset: Plan of Quebec.
" [58] Jamaica. 1839.
" [59] Leeward islands (West Indies) 1839.
" [60] Windward islands (West Indies) 1839.
" [61] British Guiana. 1839.

1844

Johnston, A. K.

The national atlas of historical, commercial, and political geography, constructed from the most recent and authentic sources . . . accompanied by maps and illustrations of the physical geography of the globe by dr. Heinrich Berghaus . . . and an ethnographic map of Europe by dr. Gustaf Kombst . . . 4 p. l., [10] pp., 46 maps. fol. Edinburgh, J. Johnstone [!] & W. & A. K. Johnston, 1844. 4323

NOTE.—See title 4325 for complete contents.
The following maps relate to America:
no. 1. World in hemispheres.
" 2. World on Mercator's projection.

no. 29. Islands in the Pacific ocean.
" 37. North America.
" 38. Canada.
" 39. United States and Texas.
" 40. West India islands.
" 41. South America.
" 42. Humboldt's system of isotherm curves.
" 43. Geographical distribution of the currents of air.
" 44. Survey of the culture of plants.

1844

Tanner, H. S.

A new universal atlas containing maps of the various empires, kingdoms, states and republics of the world, with a special map of each of the United States, plans of cities . . . 3 p. l., 72 col. maps (incl. front.) fol. Philadelphia, Carey & Hart, 1844. 4324

NOTE.—For editions of 1836, 1842-[43] and 1846 see titles 774, 788, 3553.
Maps engraved by E. B. Dawson, J. Knight, J. & W. W. Warr, W. Brose, E. Gillingham, G. W. Boynton, F. Dankworth, W. Haviland.
Engraved title-page contains view of "First landing of Columbus in the new world."

CONTENTS.

no. 1. A new map of the world on the globular projection. 1843.
" 2. North America. 1836.
" 3. Canada East. Inset: Nova Scotia, New Brunswick &c.
" 4. Canada West. Inset: Lake Superior.
" 5. United States. 1839.
" 6. A new map of Maine. 1840.
" 7. New Hampshire & Vermont. 1840.
" 8. Massachusetts and Rhode Island. 1841. Inset: Boston.
" 9. Connecticut. 1839. Insets: Hartford &c.—New Haven &c.
" 10. New York. 1840.
" 11. City of New York. 1835.
" 12. New Jersey reduced from T. Gordons map. 1834.
" 13. A new map of Pennsylvania. 1840.
" 14. Philadelphia. 1836.
" 15. A new map of Maryland and Delaware. Inset: Baltimore.
" 16. City of Washington. 1836.
" 17. A new map of Virginia. 1836.
" 18. A new map of Nth. Carolina. 1841. Inset: Gold region.
" 19. A new map of South Carolina. 1841. Inset: Charleston.
" 20. A new map of Georgia. 1839.
" 21. Florida. 1839. Insets: Pensacola. — Tallahassee. — Harbour of St. Augustine.
" 22. A new map of Alabama. 1841.
" 23. A new map of Mississippi. 1836.
" 24. A new map of Louisiana. 1839. Inset: New Orleans.
" 25. A new map of Arkansas. 1841.
" 26. A new map of Tennessee. 1841. Insets: Environs of Nashville.—Environs of Knoxville.

Tanner, H. S.—Continued.

no. 27. A new map of Kentucky. 1839. Insets: [Environs of Lexington]—Falls of Ohio.—[Ohio river from Maysville to Clarksburg]
" 28. A new map of Ohio. 1841. Inset: Cincinnati.
" 29. A new map of Michigan. 1841. Inset: Western part of Michigan.
" 30. A new map of Indiana. 1841.
" 31. A new map of Illinois. 1841. Inset: Lead region.
" 32. A new map of Missouri. 1841.
" 33. Wisconsin.
" 34. Iowa.
" [35] Texas. 1838.
" 36. Mexico & Guatemala. 1834. Insets: Guatemala.—Valley of Mexico.
" 37. West Indies. 1834.
" 38. South America. 1836.
" 39. Venezuela, New Grenada & Equador. Inset: Plan of a proposed communication between the Atlantic & Pacific oceans.
" 40. Brazil. Insets: Paraguay.—Environs of Rio Janeiro.
" 41. Peru and Bolivia.
" 42. Chili, La Plata and Uruguay. Inset: South part of Patagonia.
" 43. Europe.
" 44. England. Insets: Environs of Liverpool.—Environs of London.
" 45. Scotland. Inset: The Shetland isles.
" 46. Ireland.
" 47. France. Insets: Environs of Paris.—Corsica.
" 48. Spain and Portugal.
" 49. Holland and Belgium.
" 50. Germany.
" 51. Sweden & Norway.
" 52. Denmark.
" 53. Prussia. Inset: Environs of Berlin.
" 54. Kingdom of Sardinia. Inset: Island of Sardinia.
" 55. Switzerland.
" 56. Austrian empire. Inset: Environs of Vienna.
" 57. Italy. North part.
" 58. Kingdom of Naples. Inset: Environs of Naples.
" 59. Turkey in Europe.
" 60. Russia in Europe.
" 61. Greece. 1834. Inset: Candia.
" 62. Asia. Inset: New Holland or Australia.
" 63. Russia in Asia and Tartary. Inset: Western part of Russia.
" 64. Turkey in Asia. Inset: Environs of Constantinople.
" 65. Persia, Arabia &c.
" 66. Hindoostan. Inset: Delta of the Ganges.
" 67. China.
" 68. Africa. 1834. Insets: Liberia.—Monrovia.
" 69. Egypt &c.
" 70. Oceana.
" 71. Palestine & adjacent countries. 1836. Inset: Environs of Jerusalem.
" 72. Lengths of the principal rivers in the world.—Heights of the principal mountains in the world. [Frontispiece]

1846

Johnston, A. K.

The national atlas of historical, commercial and political geography, constructed from the most recent and authentic sources. . . . Accompanied by maps and illustrations of the physical geography of the globe, by dr. Heinrich Berghaus . . . and an ethnographic map of Europe by dr. Gustaf Kombst . . . 4 p. l., [47]–56 pp. 46 maps. fol. Edinburgh, J. Johnstone, & W. & A. K. Johnston, 1846. 4325

NOTE.—Same maps found in title 4323.

CONTENTS.

no. 1. The world in hemispheres.
" 2. The world on Mercator's projection.
" 3. Europe. (Wanting)
" 4. England and Wales.
" 5. Scotland.
" 6. Ireland.
" 7. France.
" 8. Spain and Portugal.
" 9. Switzerland.
" 10. Italy: north part.
" 11. Italy: south part, and island of Sardinia.
" 12. Greece or Hellas, Ionian islands and Crete.
" 13. Turkey in Europe.
" 14. Austria.
" 15. Germany: western states.
" 16. Prussia.
" 17. Belgium.
" 18. Holland.
" 19. Denmark, Iceland and the Faröer.
" 20. Sweden & Norway.
" 21. Russia in Europe.
" 22. Asia.
" 23. Turkey in Asia.
" 24. Palestine.
" 25. Persia and Cabool.
" 26. India.
" 27. S. E. peninsula and Malaysia.
" 28. China.
" 29. Islands in the Pacific ocean.
" 30. Australia.
" 31. New South Wales and Australia Felix.
" 32. Van Diemen's land, or, Tasmania.
" 33. New Zealand.
" 34. Africa.
" 35. Egypt and Arabia Petræa.
" 36. Nubia and Abyssinia.
" 37. North America.
" 38. Canada.
" 39. United States and Texas.
" 40. West India islands.

Johnston, A. K.—Continued.

no. 41. South America.
" 42. Humboldt's system of the isothermal lines of the globe.
" 43. Geographical distribution of the currents of air.
" 44. Survey of the geographical distribution and cultivation of the most important plants.
" 45. Mountain chains in Asia and Europe.
" 46. Ethnographic map of Europe.

1846–1851

Society, The, for the diffusion of useful knowledge.

Maps of the Society for the diffusion of useful knowledge. A new edition, corrected to the present time. 3 v. 3 p. l., 72 maps; 2 p. l., 86 maps; 2 p. l., 2 l., 39 pp., 50 maps, 6 pl. fol. London, C. Knight, 1846–51. 4326

NOTE.—Appended to vol. 3 is *The stars in 6 maps on the gnomonic projection. Rev. by the rev. W. R. Dawes. Under superintendence of the society for the diffusion of useful knowledge. London, 1851.* Also *Index to the principal places in the world . . . by the rev. J. Mickleburgh. London, C. Knight, 1850.* vol. 1 and 2 dated 1846; vol. 3 dated 1847.

CONTENTS.

v. 1, no. 1. Western hemisphere. 1844.
" " 2. Eastern hemisphere. 1844.
" " 3–4. The world on Mercator's projection.
" " 5–6. The world as known to the ancients.
" " 7. World on gnomonic projection. I. Africa and south Europe.
" " 8. World on gnomonic projection, II. America.
" " 9. World on gnomonic projection, III. Polynesia.
" " 10. World on gnomonic projection, IV. Asia.
" " 11. World on gnomonic projection, V. From north pole to 45° N. Lat.
" " 12. World on gnomonic projection, VI. From south pole to 45° S. Lat.
" " 13. Europe.
" " 14. The British Isles. 1844.
" " 15. Geological map of England and Wales. 1843.
" " 16. England with its canals and railways. 1844.
" " 17–21. England and Wales. 5 sheets. 1848.
" " 22. Scotland.
" " 23–25. Scotland. 3 sheets.
" " 26–27. Ancient Britain. 2 sheets.
" " 28. Ireland. 1844.
" " 29–30. Ireland. 1844.
" " 31. The Netherlands and Belgium. 1844
" " 32. Ancient France, or Gallia transalpina
" " 33. France in provinces.
" " 34–36. France. 3 sheets.
" " 37. Switzerland. 1844.
" " 38. Italy. General map including Sicily, Malta, Sardinia, Corsica, &c.
" " 39. Ancient Italy. I. 1845.

v. 1, no 40. Italy. I. 1845.
" " 41. Ancient Italy. II. 1845.
" " 42. Italy. II.
" " 43. Ancient Italy part III and Sicily. 1845.
" " 44. Italy. III. 1845.
" " 45. Corsica, and Sardinia. Balearic islands. Valetta, the capital of the island of Malta.
" " 46. Ancient Spain & Portugal. 1845.
" " 47. Spain and Portugal. 1845.
" " 48–50. Spain. 3 sheets. 1845.
" " 51. Portugal. 1845.
" " 52. Germany. General map. 1845.
" " 53–56. Germany. 4 sheets. 1845.
" " 56–58. Austrian dominions. 1845.
" " 59. Poland. 1845.
" " 60. Sweden, Norway and Denmark. 1841.
" " 61. The southern provinces of Sweden.
" " 62. Denmark and part of Norway. 1845.
" " 63. The northern provinces of Sweden and Norway with part I, of Russia.
" " 64. Russia in Europe. General map.
" " 64–72. Russia in Europe. 9 sheets.
" " 73. Grecian archipelago (ancient) 1845.
" " 74. Ancient Macedonia, Thracia, Illyria, Mœsia, and Dacia. [1845]
" " 75. Turkey. I.
" " 76. The Turkish empire in Europe and Asia. 1845.
" " 77. Ancient Greece. Northern part. 1845.
" " 78. Greece.
" " 79. Turkey. II.
" " 80. Ancient Greece. Southern part.
v. 2, no. 81. Asia.
" " 82. Asia Minor Antiqua.
" " 83. Asia Minor.
" " 84. Ancient Syria.
" " 85. Syria.
" " 86. Palestine in the time of our Saviour.
" " 87. Palestine with the Hauran and the adjacent districts.
" " 88. Arabia with Egypt, Nubia and Abyssinia.
" " 89. The eastern part of the ancient Persian empire.
" " 90. Persia with part of the Ottoman empire.
" " 91. Western Siberia, Independent Tartary, Khiva, Bokhara, &c.
" " 92. Eastern Siberia.
" " 93. Siberia and Chinese Tartary. 1846.
" " 94. Bokhara, Kabool, Beloochistan &c.
" " 95. The Panjab with part of Afghanistan, Kashmeer, Sinde &c.
" " 96. India. 1846.
" " 97–107. India. 11 sheets.
" " 108. China. The interior.
" " 109. China and the Birman empire.
" " 110. Eastern islands, or Malay Archipelago.
" " 111. Islands in the Indian ocean.
" " 112. Empire of Japan.

Society, The, for the diffusion of useful knowledge—Continued.

v. 2, no. 113. Africa.
" " 114. North Africa or Barbary. I. Marocco.
" " 115. North Africa or Barbary. II. Algier.
" " 116. North Africa or Barbary. III. Tunis and part of Tripoli.
" " 117. North Africa or Barbary. IV. Tripoli.
" " 118. North Africa or Barbary. V. Parts of Tripoli and Egypt.
" " 119. Ancient Africa or Libya. 2 sheets.
" " 120. Ancient Africa or Libya.
" " 121. Ancient Egypt.
" " 122. Egypt.
" " 123–4. West Africa. 2 sheets.
" " 125. South Africa.
" " 126. Islands in the Atlantic.
" " 127. North America.
" " 128. British North America.
" " 129. North America. Canada and the United States.
" " 130. North America. I. Nova Scotia with part of New Brunswick and lower Canada.
" " 131. North America. II. Lower Canada and New Brunswick.
" " 132. North America. III. Upper Canada.
" " 133. North America. IV. Lake Superior.
" " 134. North America. V. Parts of Wisconsin and Michigan.
" " 135. North America. VI. New York, Vermont, Maine, New Hampshire, Massachusetts, Connecticut, Rhode Island, and New Jersey.
" " 136. North America. VII. Pennsylvania, New Jersey, Maryland, Delaware, Columbia and part of Virginia.
" " 137. North America. VIII. Ohio, with parts of Kentucky and Virginia.
" " 138. North America. IX. Parts of Missouri, Illinois and Indiana.
" " 139. North America. X. Parts of Missouri, Illinois, Kentucky, Tennessee, Alabama, Mississippi and Arkansas.
" " 140. North America. XI. Parts of North and South Carolina.
" " 141. North America. XII. Georgia with parts of North & South Carolina, Tennessee, Alabama & Florida.
" " 142. North America. XIII. Parts of Louisiana, Arkansas, Mississippi, Alabama & Florida.
" " 143. North America. XIV. Florida.
" " 144. The Antilles or West India Islands.
" " 145. The British Islands in the West Indies.
" " 146. Central America. I.
" " 147. Central America. II.
" " 148. South America.
" " 149–54. South America. 6 sheets.
" " 155. The Pacific Ocean.
" " 156. Polynesia or islands in the Pacific Ocean.
" " 157. Australia in 1846.
" " 158. New South Wales.
" " 159. Van-Diemen Island. Western Australia.
" " 160. The islands of New Zealand.
v. 3, no. 161. A map of the principal rivers.
" " 162. Amsterdam.
" " 163. Antwerp.

v. 3, no. 164. Athens. Inset.—Acropolis of Athens.
" " 165. Berlin.
" " 166. Birmingham. Inset.—Birmingham and its environs.
" " 167. Bordeaux.
" " 168. Boston, with Charleston and Roxbury.
" " 169. Brussels.
" " 170. Calcutta.
" " 171. Constantinople.
" " 172. Copenhagen.
" " 173. Dresden.
" " 174. Dublin.
" " 175. The environs of Dublin.
" " 176. Edinburgh.
" " 177. The environs of Edinburgh.
" " 178. Florence.
" " 179. Frankfort.
" " 180. Geneva.
" " 181. Genoa.
" " 182. Hamburg.
" " 183. Lisbon.
" " 184. Liverpool.
" " 185–6. London, 1848.
" " 187. The environs of London.
" " 188. Madrid.
" " 189. Marseille.
" " 190. Milan.
" " 191. Moscow.
" " 192. Munich.
" " 193. Naples.
" " 194. New York.
" " 195. Oporto.
" " 196–7. Paris.
" " 198. The environs of Paris.
" " 199. Parma.
" " 200. St. Petersburg.
" " 201. Philadelphia.
" " 202. Pompeii.
" " 203. Plan of ancient Rome.
" " 204. Plan of modern Rome.
" " 205. Stockholm, 1838.
" " 206. Syracuse, with the remaining vestiges of its five cities.
" " 207. Toulon.
" " 208. Turin.
" " 209–210. Venice.
" " 211. Vienna.
" " 212. Warsaw.
" " 213. Stars. I. Vernal eqinox.
" " 214. Stars. II. Simmer solstice.
" " 215. Stars. III. Autumnal equinox.
" " 216. Stars. IV. Winter Solstice.
" " 217. Stars. V. North pole.
" " 219. Stars. VI. South pole.

1849

Sharpe, J.

Sharpe's corresponding atlas, comprising fifty-four maps, constructed upon a system of scale and proportion, from the most recent authorities. Engraved on steel by Joseph Wilson Lowry. With a copious consulting index. 3 p. l., 22 pp., 54 (*i. e.* 52) maps. fol. London, Chapman & Hall, 1849. 4327

NOTE.—In 1850 a selection from the maps in this atlas were published under the title, *Sharpe's students atlas.* See v. 1, title 803.
Maps nos. 6 and 7 have joined in one, also nos. 19 and 20 making 52 maps in place of the 54 called for by the index.

CONTENTS

no. 1–2. The world in equal quarters—Sharpe's projection. 1847.
" 3. The world on Mercators projection. 1847.
" 4. Europe. 1847.
" 5. Great Britain and Ireland.
" 6–7. England and Wales. Railway map. 1847.
" 8. Scotland. 1847.
" 9. Ireland. 1847.
" 10. France–Belgium and Switzerland. 1847.
" 11. Holland and Belgium.
" 12. Prussia–Holland and the German states. 1847.
" 13. Switzerland. 1847.
" 14. Austrian empire. 1847.
" 15. Turkey and Greece.
" 16. Greece and the Ionian islands. 1847. Inset: Corfu.
" 17. Italy. 1847.
" 18. Spain and Portugal. 1847.
" 19–20. Northern Sweden and frontier of Russia.—Denmark, Sweden and Russia on the Baltic. 1847.
" 21. Western Russia from the Baltic to the Euxine. 1847.
" 22. Russia on the Euxine. 1847.
" 23. Russia at the Caucasus. 1847.
" 24. Russia in Europe. 1847.
" 25–27. Asia. 1848.
" 28. Australia and New Zealand. 1848.
" 29. Egypt and Arabia Petræa. 1848.
" 30. Nubia and Abyssinia to Bab el Mandeb. 1848.
" 31. Asia Minor. 1848.
" 32. Syria and provinces to the Persian gulf. 1848.
" 33–34. Persia. 1848.
" 35. Afghanistan and the Punjab. 1848.
" 36. Beloochistan and Sinde. 1848.
" 37. Central India. 1848.
" 38. The Carnatic, etc. 1848.
" 39. Bengal, etc. 1848.
" 40. India. 1848.
" 41–42. Africa. 1848. Inset: St. Helena.
" 43–44. North America. 1848.
" 45–46. United States. 1848.
" 49. Jamaica—Leeward and Windward islands. 1848.

no. 50. Mexico and Guatemala. 1848.
" 51. South America. 1848.
" 52. Columbian and Peruvian republics, etc. 1848.
" 53. La Plata-Chile and southern Brazil. 1848.
" 54. Eastern Brazil. 1848.

1851

Black, A., *and* **Black, C.**

Black's general atlas: comprehending sixty-one maps from the latest and most authentic sources. Engraved . . . by Sidney Hall, Hughes, &c. . . . With geographical descriptions, and an index of 59,280 names. 2 p. l., 12, 60 pp., 61 col. maps on 67 l. fol. Edinburgh, A. & C. Black, 1851. 4328

NOTE.—See also title 4330, which contains, with very few exceptions, the same maps.
For earlier and later editions see v. 1 & 3.

1851.

Ziegler, J.

Geographischer atlas über alle theile der erde; bearb. nach der ritterschen lehre und dem herrn dr. Carl Ritter . . . aus verehrung und dankbarkeit zugeeignet von J. M. Ziegler. 2 p. l. 24, [2] maps. fol. Berlin, D. Reimer, 1851. 4329

NOTE.—Accompanied by: Erläuterungen zum geographischen atlas. (Inserted before title-page.)

1852

Black, A., *and* **Black, C.**

Black's general atlas: comprehending seventy maps. Engraved . . . by Sidney Hall, William Hughes . . . New edition. Embracing all the latest discoveries . . . with introductory chapters on the geography and statistics of the various countries of the world, and a complete index of 65,000 names. 3 p. l., 12, 60 pp., 59 maps, illus. fol. Edinburgh, A. & C. Black, 1852. 4330

NOTE.—See also title 4328.
For earlier and later editions see v. 1-3.

1852

Dufour, A. H., *and* **Duvotenay, T.**

El globo. Atlas historico universal de geografia antiqua, de la edad media y moderna. Grabado en acero por don Ramon Alabern, acompañado de noticias geográficas é históricas. 292 pp. 45 maps, pl. 4°. Madrid, Gaspar & Roig, 1852. 4331

NOTE.—Many maps dated 1853.
At head of title: Biblioteca ilustrada de Gaspar y Roig.
The following maps relate to America:
no. [19] Mapa-mundi en dos hemisferios.

Dufour, A. H., *and* **Duvotenay, T.**—Continued.

no. [39] America Meridional.
" [40] Mejico. 1853. Inset: Guatemala.
" [41] Republica Argentina. 1853.
" [42] America Septentrional.
" [43] Estados-Unidos. 1853.
" [44] Antillas ó Indias Occidentales.

1853

Black, A., *and* **Black, C.**

Black's general atlas comprehending seventy maps. Engraved on steel, in the first style of art, by Sidney Hall, William Hughes . . . Embracing all the latest discoveries obtained from government surveys and expeditions, books of recent travel, and other sources. With introductory chapters on the geography and statistics of the various countries of the world, and a complete index of 65,000 names. New ed. 3 p. l., 12, 63 pp., 59 col. maps, 4 pl. fol. Edinburgh, A. & C. Black, 1853. 4332

Note.—For other editions see Author list.

Contents same as in 1854 edition except nos. 26^1, 48^1–48^3, 56^1–56^2, which do not appear here, and no. 41, Australasia, for which a new map entitled, Australia, has been substituted in the later edition. See title 4334.

1853.

Stieler, A.

Hand-atlas über alle theile der erde nach dem neuesten zustande, und über das weltgebäude. Bearbeitet von demselben so wie von F. v. Stülpnagel, H. Berghaus u. J. C. Bär. 4 p. l., iv, 48 [2] pp., 83 maps. sm. fol. Gotha, J. Perthes [1853] 4333

Note.—Contains plans of the following cities: Gotha.—Madrid.—Stockholm.—Berlin.—Wien.—Athen.—Athen und dem Piraeus.—Jerusalem.—Rio de Janeiro.

Plan of Gotha und umbegung, on title page.

Maps dated 1850–1853.

Inserted between maps nos. 39–40 is the map entitled, "Bergketten und flusssysteme in Afrika, 1850."

Below the map is the following note: "Interessante erläuterungen zu dieser dem Stieler'schen Hand-atlas als supplement beigegebenen neuesten darstellung von Afrika findet man in dem 11ten hefte des Berghaus'schen geographischen jahrbuchs."

1854

Black, A., *and* **Black, C.**

General atlas of the world, containing upwards of seventy maps. Engraved on steel, in the first style of art, by Sidney Hall, William Hughes . . . Embracing all the latest discoveries obtained from government surveys and expeditions, books of travel, and other sources, including the north-west passage discovered by h. m. ship Investigator. With introductory chapters on the geography and statistics of the various countries of the world, and a complete index of 65,000 names. New ed. 3 p. l., 12, 63 pp. 67 col. maps, 4 pl. fol. Edinburgh, A. & C. Black, 1854. 4334

NOTE.—For earlier and later editions see Author list. Contains map no. [28a] "Chart of the Baltic from admiralty & russian surveys," which is not called for by the index.

CONTENTS.

no. 1. The world.
" 2. The world on Mercator's projection. Eng^d. by G. Aikman.
" 2[1]. Chart of the world exhibiting its chief physical features. Inset: Chart shewing the distribution of rain & snow.—Chart shewing the distribution of the winds.—Ethnographical chart of the world shewing the distribution and varieties of the human race. Insets: Principal varieties of mankind.—Prevailing religions. Constructed & engraved by J. Bartholomew.
" 2[2]. Zoological chart of the world. Insets: Distributions of animals in a vertical direction.—Chart shewing the distribution of the principal birds. Chart of the world shewing the distribution of the principal plants. Insets: Distribution of plants in a vertical direction.—Chart shewing the region of the cultivation of the tea, sugar, coffee & cotton plants. Constructed and engraved by J. Bartholomew.
" 3[1]. A chart of magnetic curves of equal variation. By Peter Barlow. Eng^d. by G. Aikman.
" 3[2]. Chart of isothermal lines. Eng^d. by Geo. Aikman.
" 4. Physical geography. Geo. Aikman sculp^t.
" 5. Humboldt's distribution of plants in equinoctial America. Geo. Aikman sculp^t.
" 5[1]. Northern celestial hemisphere.—Southern celestial hemisphere. Constructed and engraved by J. Bartholomew.
" 5[2]. The solar system.—Theory of the seasons. Engraved by J. Bartholomew.
" 6. Europe.
" 7–8. England and Wales. Inset: Scilly isles.
" 8[1]. North & South Wales. Drawn & engraved by J. Bartholomew.
" 9–10. Scotland. Insets: Orkney isles.—Shetland isles.
" 11. Ireland.
" 12–13. Ireland.
" 14. France in provinces. Engraved by J. Bartholomew. Inset: Corsica.
" 15–16. France in departments. Inset: Corsica.
" 17. Switzerland.
" 18. Holland.
" 19. Netherlands now divided into Holland and Belgium.
" 20. Map of Central Europe, embracing Germany, Holland, Belgium, with parts of France and Switzerland; showing the roads, canals and railways . . .
" 21–22 Germany.
" 23. Austrian dominions.
" 24. Prussia
" 25. Denmark.

Black, A., *and* **Black, C.**—Continued.

no. 26. Sweden & Norway.
" 26[1]. Norway. Engraved by J. Bartholomew. Inset: Sketch map, shewing the relative position & climate of Norway.
" 27-28. Russia in Europe.
" 28a. Chart of the Baltic, from admiralty & russian surveys. Insets: Cronstadt and S[t]. Petersburg.—Sveaborg.—Port Baltic.—Chart of Reval.—Riga.
" 29-30. Spain & Portugal. Inset: Gibraltar.
" 31. Italy, north part. Inset: Environs of Rome.
" 32. Italy, south part. Inset: Malta and its dependencies.
" 33. Turkey in Europe. Insets: The Bosphorus.—Crete.
" 34. Hellas or Greece. Inset: Corfu.
" 35. Asia.
" 36. Turkey in Asia. Eng[d]. by Geo. Aikman. Inset: Ruins of Babylon.
" 37. Palestine according to its ancient divisions . . . Inset: The peninsula of Mount Sinai.
" 38. Persia and Afganistan.
" 39. India. Inset: Island of Singapore.
" 39[1]. Hindustan with parts of Caubul.
" 40. Eastern islands Birmah &c.
" 41. Australia. Constructed & engraved by J. Bartholomew. Inset: Van Dieman's land.
" 42. Africa. Insets: Madeira.—Port of Aden.
" 43. Egypt and Arabia Petraea. Insets: The ruins of Petra.—The Pyramids of Chizeh.—The ruins of Thebes.
" 44. Africa, north part.—Africa, south part.
" 44[1]. South Africa. Constructed & engraved by J. Bartolomew. Inset: Continuation of Africa south of the equator.
" 45. North America.
" 45[1]. Arctic regions and British America. Containing all the discoveries in the Arctic seas up to 1853. Constructed & engraved by J. Bartholomew. Insets: Chart of the territories discovered & examined by the searching expeditions under the command of cap. Austin & cap. Penny 1851.—Beechey island site of sir J. Franklin's winter quarters 1845-46.
" 46. Canada, New Brunswick &c. Inset: Continuation of Nova Scotia &c.
" 47-48. United States.
" 48[1]. New York, Vermont, New Hampshire, Rhode Island, Massachusetts & Connecticut. Drawn & engraved by J. Bartholomew.
" 48[2]. Kentucky and Tennessee. Drawn & engraved by J. Bartholomew.
" 48[3]. Maine. Drawn & engraved by J. Bartholomew.
" 49. Mexico, California & Texas. Inset: Guitimala.
" 50. West Indies. Insets: Panama railway.—Jamaica
" 51. South America.
" 52. Venezuela, New Granada, Equador, Peru, &c.
" 53. Chili, La Plata or the Argentine Republic & Bolivia.
" 54. Brazil, Uruguay, Paraguay & Guayana.
" 55. China.
" 56. Victoria, New South Wales and South Australia. Inset: Norfolk island.
" 56[1]. New South Wales. Drawn & eng[d] by J. Bartholomew. Inset: Plan of Sydney.

no. 56[2]. Victoria. Drawn & engd by J. Bartholomew. Inset: Mount Alexander gold region.
" 57. New Zealand. Insets: The settled portion of western Australia.—Van Diemens land.
" 58. The world as known to the ancients.
" 59. Map of the principal countries of the ancient world. Inset: The Roman empire.—The Persian empire.
" 60. The countries embraced within the travels of St Paul.—Lower Egypt.

1854

Johnston, A. K.

The national atlas of historical, commercial, and political geography, constructed from the most recent and authentic sources . . . With a copious index carefully compiled from the maps. 3 p. l., 11 pp. 42 maps. fol. Edinburgh, Cowan & co., [1854] 4335

NOTE.—Same maps as in the 1850 edition, title 799, with the exception of the "Chart of the North-west passage, 1850–1853," printed on the back of the map of North America.

1856

Mitchell, S. A.

A new universal atlas containing maps of the various empires, kingdoms, states and republics of the world. With a special map of each of the United States, plans of cities, &c. Comprehended in seventy-five sheets, and forming a series of one hundred and twenty-nine maps, plans, and sections. 2 p. l. 75 col. maps, front. fol. Philadelphia, C. Desilver, 1856. 4336

NOTE.—Colored picture of "First landing of Columbus in the new world," on title-page.

For the 1858 edition, see title 4340.

Dates of maps are copyright dates, 1850–1856.

The following maps relate to America:

no. 1. A new map of the world.
" 2. Map of North America.
" 3. Canada, east, formerly lower Canada. Inset: Nova Scotia, New Brunswick &c.
" 4. Canada, west, formerly upper Canada. Inset: Vicinity of the falls of Niagara.
" 5–6. A new map of the United States of America. Insets: Gold region of California.—District of Columbia.
" 7. A new map of Maine.
" 8. Map of New Hampshire & Vermont.
" 9. Map of Massachusetts and Rhode Island. Inset: Boston.
" 10. Map of Connecticut. Insets: Hartford &c.—New Haven &c.
" 11–12. Map of the state of New York. Insets: Vicinity of the falls of Niagara.—Vicinity of Rochester.—Vicinity of Albany.—Vicinity of New York.—Map of the Hudson river from New York to Albany.
" 13. Map of New Jersey.
" 14. New map of the state of Pennsylvania. Insets: Lehigh and Schuylkill coal regions.—Vicinity of Philadelphia.

Mitchell, S. A.—Continued.

no. 15. A new map of Maryland and Delaware.
" 16. City of Washington.
" 17. A new map of the state of Virginia. Inset: District of Columbia.
" 18. A new map of Nth. Carolina. Insets: [Vicinity of Trenton]—Gold region.
" 19. A new map of South Carolina. Inset: Charleston.
" 20. A new map of Georgia.
" 21. Map of Florida. Insets: Pensacola.—Tallahassee.—Harbour of St. Augustine.
" 22. A new map of Alabama.
" 23. A new map of Mississippi.
" 24. A new map of Louisiana. Inset: New Orleans.
" 25. Map of the state of Texas. Insets: Northern Texas.—Map of the vicinity of Galveston city.
" 26. A new map of Arkansas.
" 27. A new map of Tennessee. Insets: Environs of Nashville.—Environs of Knoxville.
" 28. A new map of Kentucky. Insets: Falls of Ohio.
" 29. A new map of the State of Ohio.
" 30. A new map of Michigan. Inset: Western part of Michigan.
" 31. A new map of Indiana.
" 32. A new map of the state of Illinois.
" 33. A new map of the state of Missouri.
" 34. A new map of the state of Wisconsin.
" 35. A new map of the state of Iowa.
" 36. Map of Minnesota territory.
" 37. A new map of the state of California, the territories of Oregon, Washington, Utah & New Mexico.
" [37a] A new map of Nebraska, Kansas, New Mexico, and Indian territories.
" 38. Mexico and Guatemala. Insets: The isthmus of Tehuantepec.—The isthmus of Nicaragua.—Guatemala or Central America.—Valley of Mexico.
" 39. West Indies.
" 40. South America.
" 41. Venezuela, New Grenada & Equador.
" 42. Brazil.
" 43. Peru and Bolivia.
" 44. Chili, La Plata and Uruguay.

1856

Stein, C. G. D.

Neuer atlas der ganzen erde für die gebildeten stände und für schulen. Vierundzwanzig karten, von welchen sechs doppelblätler, mit berücksichtigung der geographisch-statistischen werke von dr. C. G. D. Stein, entworfen und gezeichnet von G. Heck, A. H. Köhler, K. F. Muhlert, F. W. Streit u. a. gestochen von J. L. v. Baehr, H. Eberhard, H. Leutemann und R. Schmidt, nebst neun historischen und statistischen uebersichts-tabellen ausgearb. und neu verb. von prof. dr. K. Th. Wagner und dr.

T. E. Gumprecht . . . 28. aufl. 2 p. l., 24 maps (6 fold.) 9 fold. tabl fol. Leipzig, J. C. Hinrichs, 1856. 4337

NOTE.—The following maps relate to America:
no. 1. Die Hamisphären.
" 5. Nord-Amerika und West-Indien.
" 6. Süd-Amerika.
" 23–24. Die Vereinigten Staaten von Nord-Amerika nebst Mexico und Centralamerika.

1857

Colby, C. G.

The diamond atlas. With descriptions of all countries: exhibiting their actual and comparative extent, and their present political divisions, founded on the most recent discoveries and rectifications . . . The western hemisphere. 1 p. l., 239 pp., 54 col. maps, illus. sq. 12°. New York, Morse & Gaston, 1857. 4338

NOTE.—This atlas appeared in the same year, 1857, with the name of Samuel N. Gaston as publisher at the same address in New York. The only other differences in the atlas being that "Printed by C. A. Alvord" appears on the reverse of the title-page, instead of "Printed by E. O. Jenkins," and the issue of Samuel N. Gaston has an additional paragraph on p. iv, concerning the principal meridians in the western land surveys, and a page at the end on the Transatlantic telegraph. See v. 1, title 1180. For C. W. Morse. *The Diamond atlas . . . eastern hemisphere. New York, 1857*, see v. 1, title 824.

1858

Arrowsmith, J.

The London atlas of universal geography, exhibiting the physical & political divisions of the various countries of the world, constructed from original materials . . . 2 p. l., 68 maps (partly fold.) fol. London, J. Arrowsmith, 1858. 4339

1858

Mitchell, S. A.

A new universal atlas containing maps of the various empires, kingdoms, states and republics of the world. With a special map of each of the United States, plans, of cities, &c. Comprehended in eighty-one sheets, and forming a series of one hundred and forty-five maps, plans and sections. 2 p. l., 75 maps, front. fol. Philadelphia, C. Desilver, 1858. 4340

NOTE.—For the 1856 edition see title 4335, which contains same maps of America, with few minor changes. Map no. 40, "A new map of Central America, by J. L. Haggart, 1856," does not appear in the 1856 edition. Map no. 75 used as frontispiece.
Picture of the "First landing of Columbus in the new world," in title-page.

1859

Colton, G. W.

Colton's illustrated cabinet atlas and descriptive geography. Text—by Richard Swainson Fischer. 6 p. l., [9]-400 pp., 1 l. 52 col. maps. illus. fol. New York, J. H. Colton, 1859. 4341

1860

Colton, J. H.

Colton's general atlas, containing one hundred and eighty steel plate maps and plans, on one hundred and eight imperial folio sheets, accompanied by one hundred and sixty-eight pages letter. press descriptions, geographical, statistical, and historical, by Richard S. Fisher . . . [310] pp., incl. 103 maps. front. fol. New York, J. H. Colton, 1860. 4342

NOTE.—Dates in brackets are copyright dates. See also titles 4348, 4354, 4357, 4359, and entries in preceding volumes. Plans of principal cities of the world.

CONTENTS.

no. 1. Mountains & rivers.
" 2. Northern regions. [1855]
" 3. Southern regions. [1855]
" 4. Colton's map of the world on Mercator's projection. [1855]
" 5. Maps of the world illustrating co-tidal lines, ocean currents, meteorology, cultivation of the principal plants, animal kingdom, productive industry. [1855]
" 8. Comparative size of lakes and islands. [1855]
" 9. Western hemisphere. [1855]
" 10. Eastern hemisphere. [1855]
" 11. Colton's North America. [1859]
" 12. British, Russian & Danish possessions in North America. [1855]
" 13. Colton's New Brunswick, Nova Scotia, Newfoundland, and Prince Edward I[d]. [1855]
" 14. Colton's Canada, east or lower Canada, and New Brunswick. Inset: Vicinity of Montreal. [1855]
" 15. Colton's Canada, west or upper Canada. Insets: Wolf Island.—Vicinity of Welland canal & Niagara Falls. [1855]
" 16. Colton's United States of America. [1859]
" 17. Colton's Maine. [1859]
" 18. Colton's New Hampshire. [1855]
" 19. Colton's Vermont. [1859]
" 20. Colton's Massachusetts and Rhode Island. Inset: Vicinity of Boston. [1855]
" 21. Colton's map of Boston and adjacent cities. [1855]
" 22. Colton's Connecticut with portions of New York & Rhode Island. [1855]
" 23. Colton's New York. Insets: Oswego. — Buffalo. — Rochester. — Syracuse.—Albany.—Troy.—Vicinity of New York. [1858]
" 24. Colton's map of New York and the adjacent cities. [1855]
" 25. Colton's New Jersey. [1859]
" 26. Colton's Pennsylvania. [1859]
" 27. Philadelphia. [1855]

no. 28. Colton's Delaware and Maryland. Inset: District of Columbia. [1859]
" 29. Colton's city of Baltimore, Maryland. [1855]
" 30. Colton's Georgetown and the city of Washington. [1855]
" 31. Colton's Virginia. [1855]
" 32. Colton's North Carolina. [1855]
" 33. Colton's South Carolina. [1855]
" 34. Colton's the city of Charleston.—Colton's the city of Savannah. [1859]
" 35. Colton's Florida. [1855]
" 36. Colton's Alabama. [1859]
" 37. Colton's Mississippi. [1859]
" 38. Colton's Louisiana. [1855]
" 39. The city of Louisville, Kentucky.—The city of New Orleans, Louisiana. [1855]
" 40. Colton's new map of the state of Texas. [1855]
" 41. Colton's Arkansas. [1855]
" 42. Colton's Kentucky and Tennessee. [1855]
" 43. Colton's Ohio. [1855]
" 44. The cities of Pittsburgh and Allegheny.—The city of Cincinnati, Ohio. [1855]
" 45. Colton's Indiana. [1855]
" 46. Colton's Michigan. [1855]
" 47. Colton's Lake Superior and the northern part of Michigan. [1859]
" 48. Colton's Illinois. [1855]
" 49. The city of Chicago, Illinois.—The city of St. Louis, Missouri. [1855]
" 50. Colton's Missouri. [1855]
" 51. Iowa. [1855]
" 52. Colton's Wisconsin. [1859]
" 53. Colton's Minnesota and Dakota. [1855]
" 54. Colton's Kansas and Nebraska. [1859]
" 55. Colton's territories of New Mexico and Utah. [n. d.]
" 56. Colton's California. Inset: City of San Francisco. [1855]
" 57. Colton's Washington and Oregon. [1859]
" 58. Colton's Mexico. [1854]
" 59. Colton's Central America. [1855]
" 60. Colton's West Indies. [1855]
" 61. Colton's Cuba, Jamaica and Porto Rico. [1855]
" 62. Colton's South America. [1859]
" 63. Colton's Venezuela, New Granada, and Ecuador. [1855]
" 64. Colton's Peru and Bolivia. [1855]
" 65. Colton's Brazil and Guayana. [1855]
" 66. Colton's Argentine Republic, Chili, Uruguay & Paraguay. [1855]
" 67. Colton's Patagonia. Insets: South Orkney or Powell's group.—Falkland Islands.—South Georgia Island. [1855]
" 68. Colton's Europe. [1855]
" 69. Colton's England and Wales. [1855]
" 70. The environs of London. [1855]
" 71. Scotland. Insets: Shetland isles.—Orkney isles. [1855]
" 72. Colton's Ireland. [1855]
" 73. Colton's France. [1855]
" 74. The environs of Paris. [1855]
" 75. Colton's Spain and Portugal. [1855]
" 76. Colton's Holland and Belgium. [1855]
" 77. Colton's Denmark. [1855]
" 78. Colton's Germany. no. 1. [1855]

Colton, J. H.—Continued.

no. 79. Colton's Germany. no. 2. [1859]
" 80. Colton's Germany. no. 3. [1855]
" 81. Colton's Switzerland. [1855]
" 82. Colton's Prussia and Saxony. [1855]
" 83. Colton's Austria. Inset: Vicinity of Vienna. [1855]
" 84. Colton's northern Italy. [1859]
" 85. Colton's southern Italy, Kingdom of Naples, island Sardinia & Malta. [1855]
" 86. Colton's Sweden and Norway. [1855]
" 87. Russia. [1855]
" 88. Colton's Turkey in Europe. [1855]
" 89. Colton's Greece and the Ionian republic. [1854]
" 90. Colton's Asia. [1856]
" 91. Colton's Turkey in Asia. [1855]
" 92. Colton's Palestine. Inset: Arabia Petraea. [1855]
" 93. Colton's Persia, Arabia, &c. [1855]
" 94. Colton's China. [1859]
" 95. Colton's Japan, Nippon, Kiusiu, Sikok, Yesso and the Japanese kuriles. [1855]
" 96. Colton's Hindostan or British India. [1859]
" 97. Colton's East Indies. [1855]
" 98. Colton's Australia. [1855]
" 99. Colton's Hawaiian group or Sandwich islands. [1855]
" 100. Africa. North eastern sheet. [1855]
" 101. Africa. North western sheet. [1855]
" 102. Colton's Africa. Southern sheet. [1855]

1862

Johnson, A. J.

Johnson's new illustrated (steel plate) family atlas, with descriptions, geographical, statistical, and historical. Compiled, drawn, and engraved under the supervision of J. H. Colton and A. J. Johnson. 3 p. l. [5]-99 p front., 69 col. maps, illus., diagrs. fol. New York, Johnson & Browning, 1862. 4343

NOTE.—Same maps of America found in the other 1862 edition, title 837. See also titles 840, 843, 858, 913, 4345, 4346, 4349.

1862.

Petermann, A.

Ergänzungen zu Stieler's hand-atlas. Vier special-karten . . . cover-title, 4 pp., 4 maps. ob. fol. Gotha, J. Perthes, 1862. 4344

CONTENTS.

no. 1. Das festungs-viereck Verona, Peschiera, Mantua, Lecnaco, im maasstabe von 1:150.000.
" 2. Die meerenge von Gibraltar im maassstabe von 1:200.000. Insets: Das spanishe gebiet von Ceuta im maassstabe 1:40.000.—Gibraltar in maassstabe von 1:25.000.
" 3. Der Isthmus von Panama im maassstabe von 1:200.000.
" 4. Die Viti-oder Fiji-inseln im maassstabe von 1:500.000. Inset: Übersicht der politischen eintheilung & bevölkerung der Fiji-gruppe. Nach Williams & Wilks.

1865

Johnson, A. J.

Johnson's new illustrated . . . family atlas, with physical geography, and with descriptions geographical, statistical, and historical, including the latest federal census, a geographical index, and a chronological history of the civil war in America. By Richard Swainson Fisher . . . Maps compiled, drawn, and engraved under the supervision of J. H. Colton and A. J. Johnson . . . 3 p. l. [5] 123 [1] pp. 62 col. maps, 5 col. pl. fol. New York, Johnson & Ward, 1865. 4345

NOTE.—"Entered, according to the Act of Congress, in the year 1864, by A. J. Johnson, in the clerk's office of the district court of the United States for the southern district of New York."

See also titles 837, 840, 843, 858, 913, 4343, 4346.

Engraved half title.

On title-page, "The new plates, copyrighted by A. J. Johnson, are made exclusively for Johnson's New illustrated family atlas. Others are the same as used in 'Colton's General atlas' " "Johnson & Ward, successors to Johnson & Browning, successors to J. H. Colton & co."

Contains maps of the cities of New York and Washington; also insets of Oswego, Buffalo, Rochester, Syracuse, Albany and Troy.

The following maps relate to America:

no. 8. Map showing the geographical distribution of the animal kingdom.—Bird map.—Map illustrating productive industry.—Map showing the principal ocean currents. 1864.

" 9. Map illustrating the principal features of meteorology.—Rain map.—Map illustrating the principal features of the land and the co-tidal lines.—Map showing the distribution and limits of cultivation of the principal plants

" 11. Western hemisphere.

" 12. Eastern hemisphere.

" 13-14. Map of the world on Mercator's projection.

" 15-16. North America.

" 17. Lower Canada and New Brunswick.

" 18. Upper Canada. Insets: Vicinity of the Welland canal.—Wolf island.

" 19. New Brunswick, Nova Scotia, Newfoundland and Prince Edward I^d.

" 20-21. United States. 1864.

" 22. Maine.

" 23-24. Vermont, New Hampshire, Massachusetts, Rhode Island and Connecticut. 1864.

" 25-26. Massachusetts, Connecticut and Rhode Island. 1864.

" 27-28. New York. Insets: Oswego.—Buffalo.—Rochester.—Syracuse.—Albany.—Troy.—Vicinity of New York.

" 29-30. Map of New York and the adjacent cities. Inset: Continuation of the city & county of New York on a reduced scale.

" 31-32. Pennsylvania and New Jersey. 1864.

" 33-34. Virginia, Delaware, Maryland & West Virginia. 1864. Inset views: Fortress Monroe.—University of Virginia.—General Post Office.—Treasury buildings.—Patent office.

" 35-36. Map of the vicinity of Richmond, and peninsular campaign in Virginia. 1862.

Johnson, A. J.—Continued.

no. 37. Georgetown and the city of Washington. Inset: Smithsonian institution.—The capitol.—Washington monument.
" 38. Delaware and Maryland. Inset: District of Columbia.
" [39–40] North and South Carolina. Insets: Plan of Charleston vicinity and harbor.—Views, Chimney Rocks and French Broad river.—Table mountain.
" 41–42. Georgia and Alabama. 1863.
" 43. Florida. 1863. Inset: Florida Keys.
" 44. West Indies. 1864. Inset: The Bermuda islands.
" 45–46. Arkansas, Mississippi and Louisiana.
" 47–48. New map of the state of Texas. Insets: Plan of the northern part of Texas.—Plan of Galveston bay.—Plan of Sabine lake.
" 49–50. Kentucky and Tennessee.
" 51–52. Ohio. 1864. Inset: State capitol at Columbus.
" 53–54. Indiana. 1864.
" 55–56. Illinois. 1864.
" 57–58. Wisconsin and Michigan. 1864.
" 59–60. Missouri and Kansas. Inset views: Santa Fe from the great Missouri trail.—Fire on the prairie.—Spearing fish.
" 61–62. Iowa and Nebraska. 1864.
" 63. Nebraska, Dakota, Montana and Kansas.
" 64. Minnesota. 1865. Inset: N^th eastern part cf Minnesota.
" 65. Washington, Oregon and Idaho.
" 66–67. California, with Utah, Nevada, Colorado, New Mexico and Arizona. 1864.
" 68. Mexico. Inset: Territory and isthmus of Tehuantepec.
" 69. Central America. Insets: Isthmus of Panama.—Harbor of San Juan de Nicaragua.—The "Nicaragua route."
" 70–71. South America. 1863.

1866

Johnson, A. J.

Johnson's new illustrated family atlas of the world, with physical geography, and with descriptions geographical, statistical, and historical, including the latest federal census, and the existing religious denominations in the world. Text by Richard Swainson Fisher . . . 3 p. l., [5]–134 [3] pp. 61 maps, 5 pl. fol. New York, A. J. Johnson, 1866. 4346

NOTE.—"Entered, according to Act of Congress, in the year 1865, by A. J. Johnson, in the clerk's office in the district court of the United States of the southern district of New York."

See also titles 837, 840, 843, 858, 913, 4343, 4345, 4349.

Engraved half title.

On title-page, "The new plates, copyrighted and owned by A. J. Johnson, are made for 'Johnson's New illustrated family atlas.' Others are the same as used in 'Colton's General atlas,' now published by him."

Maps of the cities of New York and Washington.

The following maps relate to America:

no. 8. Map showing the geographical distribution of the animal kingdom.—Bird map.—Maps illustrating productive industry.—Map showing the principal ocean currents. 1864.

no. 9. Map illustrating the principal features of meteorology.—Rain map.—Map illustrating the principal features of the land and the co-tidal lines.—Map showing the distribution and limits of cultivation of the principal plants

" 11. Western hemisphere.

" 12. Eastern hemisphere.

" 13–14. Map of the world on Mercator's projection.

" 15–16. North America.

" 17. Lower Canada and New Brunswick.

" 18. Upper Canada. Insets: Vicinity of the Welland canal.—Wolf island.

" 19. New Brunswick, Nova Scotia, Newfoundland and Prince Edward I[d].

" 20–21. United States. 1864.

" 22–23. Maine. 1866.

" 24–25. Vermont, New Hampshire, Massachusetts, Rhode Island and Connecticut. 1864.

" 26–27. Massachusetts, Connecticut and Rhode Island. 1864.

" 28–29. New York. 1866. Inset: Long Island.

" 30–31. New York and Brooklyn. 1866. Inset: New York north of Central park.

" 32–33. Pennsylvania and New Jersey. 1864.

" [33a] New Jersey.

" 34–35. Virginia, Delaware, Maryland & West Virginia. 1864. Inset views: Fortress Monroe.—University of Virginia.—General Post Office.—Treasury buildings.—Patent office.

" 36–37. Map of the vicinity of Richmond, and peninsular campaign in Virginia. 1862.

" [37a] Delaware and Maryland. Inset: District of Columbia.

" 38. Georgetown and the city of Washington. Inset views: Smithsonian institution.—The capitol.—Washington monument.

" 39–40. North Carolina and South Carolina. 1865. Insets: Map of Charleston harbor.—Views, Table mountain.—Chimney Rocks and French Broad river.

" 41–42. Georgia and Alabama. 1863.

" 43. Florida. 1863. Inset: Florida Keys.

" 44–45. Arkansas, Mississippi and Louisiana. 1866.

" 46–47. Texas. 1866. Insets: Plan of Galveston bay and vicinity.—Northern part of Texas.

" 48–49. Kentucky and Tennessee. 1865.

" 50–51. Ohio. 1864. Inset view: State capitol at Columbus.

" 52–53. Indiana. 1864.

" 54–55. Illinois. 1864.

" 56–57. Wisconsin and Michigan. 1864.

" 58–59. Missouri and Kansas. 1865.

" 60–61. Iowa and Nebraska. 1864.

" 62–63. Nebraska, Dakota, Idaho and Montana. 1865.

" 64. Oregon and Washington. 1865.

" 65. Minnesota. 1865. N[th]. eastern part of Minnesota.

" 66–67. California, also Utah, Nevada, Colorado, New Mexico, and Arizona. 1864.

" 68. Mexico. Inset: Territory and isthmus of Tehuantepec.

" 69. Central America. Insets: Isthmus of Panama.—Harbor of San Juan de Nicaragua.—The "Nicaragua route."

" 70–71. West Indies. 1864.

" 72–73. South America. 1863.

1866

Smith, R. C.

Smith's atlas of modern and ancient geography, corrected and enlarged, to accompany Smith's Geography for schools, academies, and families. 8 [6] pp., 24 col. maps. 4°. Philadelphia, J. B. Lippincott & co., 1866. 4347

NOTE.—Maps irregularly numbered.
The following maps relating to America are dated 1853 except the map of South America:
no. 10. Map of the world.
" 16. Map of North America.
" 20. Map of the United States and Canada.
" 24. Map no. 1. United States.
" 26. Map no. 2. United States.
" 28. Map no. 3. United States.
" 30. Map no. 4. United States.
" 34. Map no. 5. United States.
" 35. Texas.
" 38. Map no. 6. United States.
" 40. Map no. 7. United States.
" 42. Map no. 8. United States.
" 44. Map no. 9. United States.
" 49. Map no. 10. United States.
" 51. Map of Mexico.—Map of Central America.
" 53. Map of the West Indies.
" 55. Map of South America. 1847.

1868

Colton, G. W.

Colton's general atlas, containing one hundred and eighty steel plate maps and plans, and one hundred and nineteen imperial folio sheets . . . 2 p. l., front. [313] pp. incl. 101 col. maps, 3 pl. fol. New York, G. W. & C. B. Colton & co. 1868. 4348

NOTE.—"Entered, according to Act of Congress, in the year 1863, by J. H. Colton, in the Clerks office of the District Court of the United States for the Southern District of the State of New York.
See also titles 4342, 4354, 4357, 4359, and entries in preceding volumes.
Maps of the following cities: Washington.—Boston.—New York.—Philadelphia. — Baltimore. — Savannah. — Charleston. — Louisville. — New Orleans.—Pittsburgh.—Cincinnati.—St. Louis.—Chicago.—London.—Paris.

1868

Johnson, A. J.

Johnson's new illustrated family atlas of the world . . . with physical geography, and with descriptions, geographical, statistical, and historical, including the latest federal census, and the existing religious denominations in the world . . . 1 p. l., [6] 6–134 [3] pp., front., 63 col. maps, 2 pl., 1 diagr. fol. New York, A. J. Johnson, 1868. 4349

NOTE.—For note describing early changes in this work see entry for editions of 1865 and 1866, titles 4345, 4346.

See also titles 837, 840, 843, 858, 913, 4343, 4346.

Maps of New York and Washington.

Frontispiece: United States Capitol. Executed under the supervision of Geo. E. Perine. 1866.

Contains, Chart of comparative height of mountains and length of rivers.—New chart of national emblems.—A diagram exhibiting the difference of time between the places shown & Washington.

The following maps relate to America:

no. [1] Map showing the geographical distribution & range of the principal members of the animal kingdom.—Bird map.—Map illustrating productive industry.—Map showing the principal ocean currents.

" [2] Map illustrating the principal features of meteorology.—Rain map.—Map illustrating the principal features of the land and the co-tidal lines.—Map showing the distribution and limits of cultivation of the principal plants.

" [3] Globular world. 1867.

" [4] World on Mercators projection. 1865.

" [5] North America. 1867. Inset: Hawaiian group.

" [6] Ontario. 1867. Inset: Niagara river and vicinity.

" [7] Quebec. 1867.

" [8] Quebec . . . Newfoundland, Prince Edward and Cape Breton Is. 1867.

" [9] United States. 1864.

" [10] Maine. 1866.

" [11] Vermont and New Hampshire. 1867.

" [12] Massachusetts, Connecticut and Rhode Island. 1864.

" [13] New York. 1866. Inset: Long Island.

" [14] New York and Brooklyn. 1866.

" [15] Pennsylvania and New Jersey. 1864.

" [16] New Jersey.

" [17] Virginia, Delaware, Maryland and West Virginia. 1864.

" [18] Map of the vicinity of Richmond, and peninsular campaign in Virginia. 1862.

" [18a] Georgetown and the city of Washington.

" [19] Delaware and Maryland. 1855. Inset: District of Columbia.

" [20] North Carolina and South Carolina. 1865. Inset: Map of Charleston harbor.

" [21] Georgia and Alabama. 1863.

" [22] Florida. 1863. Inset: Florida Keys.

" [23] Arkansas, Mississippi and Louisiana. 1866.

" [24] Texas. 1866. Insets: Plan of Galveston bay and vicinity.—Northern part of Texas.

" [25] Kentucky and Tennessee. 1865.

" [26] Ohio. 1864.

" [27] Indiana. 1864.

" [28] Illinois. 1864.

" [29] Wisconsin and Michigan. 1864.

" [30] Missouri and Kansas. 1865.

" [31] Iowa and Nebraska. 1864.

" [32] Nebraska, Dakota, Idaho and Montana. 1865.

" [33] Oregon and Washington. 1865.

" [34] Minnesota. 1865.

" [35] California, and Utah, Nevada, Colorado, New Mexico, and Arizona. 1864.

Johnson, A. J.—Continued.

no. [36] Mexico. 1867. Inset: Isthmus of Tehuantepec.
" [37] Central America. 1867. Inset: Isthmus of Panama.
" [38] West Indies. 1864. Inset: The Bermuda islands.
" [39] South America. 1863.

1868

Stieler, A.

Hand-atlas über alle theile der erde und über das weltgebäude . . . [10te aufl.] 3 p. l., 10 pp., 84 maps. obl. fol. Gotha, J. Perthes [1868] 4350

NOTE.—Date and edition taken from text.
Contains small inset maps of various cities throughout the world.
This copy differs slightly from another of the same date in that it contains a text of 10 pages, and the dates on some of the maps are later.

1868

Hand-atlas über alle theile der erde und über das weltgebäude. Erste ausg. 1817. Jubel ausg. 1867 . . . 2 p. l., 79 col. maps, 4 col. pl. obl. fol. Gotha, J. Perthes [1868] 4351

NOTE.—Maps are by A. Petermann, F. v. Stülpnagel, H. Berghaus, C. Vogel.
Contains small inset maps of various cities throughout the world.

1869

Chambers, W., & R.

Atlas to accompany Chambers's encyclopaedia: a series of thirty-nine colored maps and a map of the annual revolution of the earth round the sun. 3 p. l., 40 (*i. e.* 39) col. maps, 1 pl. 4°. Philadelphia, J. B. Lippincott & co. 1869. 4351a

NOTE.—The following maps relate to America:
no. 1. The world. Engraved by W. H. Holmes.
" 5. North America.
" 6–7. United States.
" 8. Canada. Illman bros. engravers.
" 9. Central America.
" 10. South America.
" 11. West India Islands. Engraved by W. H. Holmes.

1871–1875

Stieler, A.

Handatlas über alle theile der erde und über das weltgebäude . . . 4 p. l., 11 pp., 90 (i. e. 89) maps. fol. Gotha, J. Perthes [1871–75] 4352

NOTE.—Maps dated 1871 to 1875. Atlas issued in parts. Accompanied by a text of 8 pp. entitled: Vorbericht zu Stieler's handatlas.

1873?

Cortambert, E., *i. e.,* **P. F. E.**

Nouvel atlas géographie moderne . . . 2 p. l., 66 (*i. e.* 64) col. maps, 2 pl. obl. fol. Paris, Hatchette & c[ie] [1873?] 4353

NOTE.—Date found on map no. 66.

1874

Colton, G. W.

Colton's general atlas, containing one hundred and eighty steel plate maps and plans, on one hundred and nineteen imperial folio sheets . . . Letterpress descriptions, geographical, statistical, and historical, by Richard Swainson Fisher. 1 p. l., front., [25] pp. incl. 100 col. maps, 3 col. pl. fol. New York, G. W. & C. B. Colton & co., 1874. 4354

NOTE.—See also titles 4342, 4348, 4357, 4359 and entries in preceding volumes.

Maps of the following cities: Georgetown and the city of Washington.—Boston.—New York.—Philadelphia.—Baltimore.—Savannah.—Charleston.—Louisville.—New Orleans.—Pittsburgh and Allegheny.—Cincinnati.—St. Louis.—Chicago.

Corrected title. See v. 3, title 3564.

1877

Lippincott, J. B., & co.

Handy atlas. A series of forty maps for the use of the general reader. (Being the maps that accompany the subscription edition of Chambers's Encyclopaedia) 3 p. l., 39 col. maps, 1. pl. 4°. Philadelphia, J. B. Lippincott & co., 1877. 4355

NOTE.—Half title reads, Atlas to accompany Chambers's Encyclopaedia.

1879–1882

Stieler, A.

Adolf Stieler's hand-atlas über alle theile der erde und über das weltbebäude . . . [7th ed.] 2 p. l., 8 pp., 95 (*i. e.* 94) maps. obl. fol. Gotha, J. Perthes, [1879–82] 4356

NOTE.—Atlas was first issued in parts. Maps dated 1879 to 1881.

The dates 1879–82 are noted on outside cover.

Accompanied by 8 pp. of text entitled, "Vorbemerkungen zu Stieler's hand-atlas."

1880

Colton, G. W.

Colton's general atlas of the world . . . drawn by G. Woolworth Colton. Accompanied by geographical, statistical and historical letter-press descriptions. 2 p. l., front. [276] pp. incl. [104 maps, 2 pl. fol. New York, G. W. & C. B. Colton & co., 1880. 4357

NOTE.—See also titles 4348, 4354, 4359 and entries in preceding volumes.

Maps no. 9–10, "World, on Mercator's projection," and no. 44, "City of Baltimore," wanting.

Colton, G. W.—Continued.

Frontispiece by "F. A. Chapman del.," and "C. Wise, sc."

Plates showing "National & commercial flags of all nations," and the "Comparative size of lakes and islands."

Plans of the following cities:

no. 27. Georgetown and the city of Washington.
" 32. Map of Boston and adjacent cities.
" 35. Albany.—Troy.—Vicinity of New York.—Oswego.—Buffalo.—Rochester.—Syracuse.
" 37. . . . New York city.
" 42. Philadelphia.
" 43. District of Columbia [Washington]
" 45. Richmond. Norfolk, Portsmouth.
" 47. . . . Plan of Charleston, vicinity & harbor.
" 48. The city of Savannah, Georgia.—The city of Charleston, South Carolina.
" 54. Vicinity of New Orleans.
" 55. The city of Louisville, Kentucky.—The city of New Orleans, Louisiana.
" 61. Vicinity of Cleveland.
" 62. The cities of Pittsburgh and Allegheny. The city of Cincinnati, Ohio.
" 71. The city of St. Louis, Missouri.—The city of Chicago, Illinois.
" 96. Manzanilla I.—Aspinwall city, Panama.—City of Panama.
" 97. City & harbor of Havana.
" 101. Pernambuco.—Rio de Janeiro.
" 102. City of Lima.
" 108. The environs of London.
" 112. The environs of Paris.
" 114. Amsterdam.—Brussels.
" 119. Bremen.—Hamburg.
" 122. Vicinity of Vienna.

Map no. 26 shows the gradual development of the United States to 1865.

The plan of Baltimore wanting in this copy may be consulted in the 1881 edition of the same work, title 4359.

1880

Johnston, A. K.

The royal atlas of modern geography; exhibiting, in a series of entirely original and authentic maps, the present condition of geographical discovery and research in the several countries, empires, and states of the world . . . With a special index to each map. A new edition. 6 p. l., [152] pp. front., 50 maps. fol. Edinburgh and London, W. & A. K. Johnston, 1880. 4358

Note.—See also titles 835, 868, 905, 1103.

1881

Colton, G. W.

Colton's general atlas of the world . . . accompanied by geographical, statistical, and historical letter-press descriptions. 1 p. l., front. [286] pp. incl. 106 col. maps, 2 pl. fol. New York, G. W. & C. B. Colton & co. 1881. 4359

Note.—See also titles 4347, 4353, 4357 and entries in preceding volumes.

Maps of the following cities: Washington and Georgetown, Boston, New York, Brooklyn, Philadelphia, Baltimore, Charleston, Savannah, Louisville, New Orleans, Pittsburgh, Cincinnati, Chicago, St. Louis, London and Paris.

1883

Ivison, Blakeman, Taylor & co.

Handy atlas of the world. 33 pp., incl. 34 maps. 4°. New York and Chicago, Ivison, Blakeman, Taylor, & co. [c1883] 4360

Note.—Copyrighted in 1883.

1884

Rand, McNally & co.

Rand, McNally & co.'s indexed atlas of the world. Containing large scale maps of every country and civil division upon the face of the globe, together with historical, statistical and descriptive matter relative to each. Accompanied by a new and original compilation forming a ready reference index . . . 3 p. l., 918 pp., incl. 109 col. maps, illus. fol. Chicago, Rand, McNally & co., 1884. 4361

1885

Baldwin, M. C.

The popular atlas, being a series of maps delineating the whole surface of the globe, with many special and original features; and a copious index of 23000 names . . . 2 p. l., 74 pp., 55 col. maps. sm. fol. New York, M. C. Baldwin, 1885. 4362

Note.—Many maps are the same as in Letts's *Popular atlas being a complete series of maps delineating the whole surface of the globe, with special and original features, and a copious index of 23,000 names. 4 v. in 2. 1881–1883.*

See v. 1, no. 900.

All maps and the outside of the cover are marked Letts's Popular atlas.

The following maps relate to America:

no. 1–2. The world on Mercator's projection.
" 3. Statistical map of North America.
" 4–7. Statistical & general map of Canada.
" 8–9. United States of North America and part of Canada.
" 10–19. Eastern United States.
" 20. United States, west, & Mexico, north.
" 21. Mexico, south: and Central America.
" 22. The Antilles, or West Indies.
" 23. Statistical map of South America.
" 24–29. South America.

1885

Grant, A. A.

Grant's standard indexed atlas. Carefully prepared to fill the wants of business men. Containing the fullest, largest scale and clearest engraved maps of the United States and Canada ever published. Accompanied by a complete and simple index, showing the true location of all railroads, towns and villages, with their population, number of banks, designating all telegraph, post and money order offices and locals, the railroads on which the different

Grant, A. A.—Continued.

stations are located, and the express companies doing business over each road. 237 [21] pp. incl. 48 maps. 1 map. fol. New York, A. A. Brant [1885] 4363

NOTE.—Pages 47–50 wanting.

Large folded map at end of atlas entitled: Cram's new pictorial and railroad map of the United States and territories.

1887

Johnston, W., & A. K.

The cosmographic atlas of political, historical, classical, physical and scriptural geography and astronomy; with indices and descriptive letterpress. 3d ed. 3 p. l., [44] pp. 60 maps, 6 pl. fol. Edinburgh, London, W. & A. K. Johnston, 1887. 4364

NOTE.—Index follows each set of maps.

1887–1890

Niox, G. L.

Atlas de géographie générale avec notes statistiques, historiques et géographiques. 2 p. l., 38 col. maps (partly fold.). fol. Paris, C. Delagrave [1887–90] 4365

NOTE.—Accompanied by text with title: Atlas de géographie générale. Notices. Paris, C. Delagrave [1891?]

1889?

Bacon, G. W.

[Excelsior memory maps] 30 maps. 8°. [London, G. W. Bacon & co. 1889?] 4366

NOTE.—Title-page wanting.

The following maps relate to America:

no. [2] North America.
" [3] South America.
" [5] Atlantic ocean.
" [8] Dominion of Canada.
" [22] The world.
" [26] Pacific ocean.
" [28] Basin of the St. Lawrence.
" [29] United States.

1889

Conklin, G. W.

Conklin's handy manual of useful information and world's atlas . . . also a compilation of facts for ready reference on 2,000 subjects, being an epitome of matters historical, statistical, biographical, political, geographical, and of general interest. A universal hand-book for ready reference . . . Copyright, 1888, by Laird & Lee. Revised and corrected edition copyright, 1889, by Laird & Lee. 14,440 [1] pp. incl. 49 maps. 24°. Chicago, Laird & Lee, 1889. 4367

NOTE.—At head of title: Edition of 1889.

1890

Black, A., & Black, C.

Black's general atlas of the world; embracing the latest discoveries, new boundaries, and other changes accompanied by introductory letterpress and index. New and revised edition. 117 pp. 58 maps. front. fol. Edinburgh, A. & C. Black, 1890. 4368

NOTE.—Frontispiece, The flags of all nations.

1890

Johnston, A. K.

The royal atlas of modern geography exhibiting, in a series of entirely original and authentic maps the present condition of geographical discovery and research in the several countries, empires, and states of the world. By the late Alexander Keith Johnston . . . with additions and corrections to the present date by J. B. Johnston . . . With a special index to each map. New ed. VIII, [166] pp. front., 53 maps. fol. Edinburgh and London, W. & A. K. Johnston, 1890. 4369

NOTE.—Small insets of the following cities appear on various maps: Paris.—Marseille.—Genoa.—Valetta.—Alexandria.—Rome.—Naples.—Geneva.—Copenhaven.—Berlin.—Vienna.—Stockholm.—St. Petersburg.

The following maps relate to America:

no. 1. The world in hemispheres.
" 2. Chart of the world on Mercator's projection.
" 4. Basin of the North Atlantic ocean.
" 44. North America.
" 45–47. Dominion of Canada. Inset: Newfoundland.
" 48–49. United States of North America. Inset: The Atlantic states.
" 50. Mexico.
" 51. West India islands and Central America.
" 52–53. South America.

1891–1913

Année (L') cartographique, supplément annuel à toutes les publications de géographie et de la cartographie . . . 1891–1913. Pts. 1–23. 4°. Paris, Hachette & cie, 1891–1913. 4370

NOTE.—In progress.
Editor: 1891–1913, F. Schrader.

1892

Bartholomew, J. G.

The graphic atlas and gazetteer of the world. [8], 128 pp. 1 l., 268 pp. incl. 132 col. maps. 4°. New York, London, [etc] T. Nelson & sons, [1892] 4371

NOTE.—Plans of the following cities: District of Columbia.—Toronto.—Quebec.—Niagara.—Montreal.

1895

Debes, E.

Neuer handatlas über alle teille der erde in 59 haupt-und 120 nebenkarten mit alphabetischen namenverzeichnissen . . . Ausgeführt in der Geographischen anstalt der verlagshandlung. 2 p. l., [172] pp. 59 col. maps. fol. Leipzig, H. Wagner & E. Debes, 1895. 4372

NOTE.—Various pagings.
Contains ethnographical map of Europe.

1895

Times, The. *London.*

"The Times" atlas. Containing 117 pages of maps, and comprising 173 maps and an alphabetical index to 130,000 names. iv, 117, 118 pp., incl. 173 maps. fol. London, published at the office of "the Times," 1895. 4373

NOTE.—Inset maps of important cities.

1896?

Cram, G. F.

Cram's universal atlas, geographical, astronomical and historical, containing a complete series of maps of modern geography, exhibiting the world and its various political divisions as they are to-day. Also an elaborate series of authentic historical maps showing the world's progress and development from the earliest times to the present, to which is added a brief history of astronomy and a description of the geography of the heavens. Illustrated by numerous views and charts; the whole supplemented with valuable statistics, diagrams, and a complete gazetteer of the United States . . . 632 pp. incl. 273 maps, illus., ports., plans, tables, diagrs. fol. New York, G. F. Cram [1896?] 4374

NOTE.—Plans of the largest and most important cities of the world, and principal cities of the United States.

1897

Rand, McNally & co.

Rand, McNally & co.'s new standard atlas of the world, containing large scale maps of every country and civil division upon the face of the globe, together with historical, descriptive, and statistical matter relative to each . . . Accompanied by a new and original compilation forming a ready reference index . . . 460 pp. incl. 126 maps, diagrs. fol. Chicago, Rand, McNally & co., 1897. 4375

NOTE.—Plans of many of the important cities of the United States.

1899

Cram, G. F.

Cram's universal atlas, geographical, astronomical and historical, containing a complete series of maps of modern geography, exhibiting the world and its various political divisions as they are today. Also an elaborate series of authentic historical maps showing the world's progress and development from the earliest times to the present, to which is added a brief history of astronomy and a description of the geography of the heavens. Illustrated by numerous views and charts; the whole supplemented with valuable statistics, diagrams, and a complete gazetteer of the United States. 657 pp. incl. 272 col. maps, illus., tables, diagrs. fol. Chicago, New York, G. F. Cram, [1899] 4376

NOTE.—Plates showing the flags and arms of the various nations.

Maps of the following cities: Lowell, Lynn, Worcester and Springfield, Mass., Portland, Me., Boston, Greater New York, New York and vicinity, Brooklyn, Buffalo, Philadelphia, Baltimore, Washington, Pittsburgh, Richmond, Cincinnati, Columbus, Cleveland, Toledo, Grand Rapids, Detroit, Bay City, Mich., Saginaw, Mich., Indianapolis, Chicago, St. Louis, Kansas City, Sioux City, Omaha, Denver, Milwaukee, Superior, Wis., Duluth, Minneapolis, St. Paul, Fargo, Sioux Falls, S. Dak., Memphis, Nashville, Charleston, Atlanta, Birmingham, New Orleans, Dallas, San Francisco, Sacramento, Takoma, Halifax and Dartmouth, Quebec, Montreal, Toronto, Liverpool, Edinburgh, London, Dundee, Glasgow, Dublin, Marseilles, France, Nice, Paris, Madrid, Valletta, Valencia, Copenhagen, Rome, Naples, Athens, Genoa, Brussels, Berlin, Stockholm, St. Petersburg, Vienna, Constantinople, Alexandria, Calcutta, Jerusalem.

1899

Rand, McNally & co.

Expansion atlas; containing general maps covering every part of the world, and special maps and descriptive matter pertaining to the Philippines, Hawaii, Puerto Rico, Cuba, Manila and vicinity. Including a chronology of all important events of the Spanish-American war . . . cover-title, 16 pp. incl. 13 col. maps. fol. Chicago, Rand, McNally & co., [c]1899. 4377

1903

Rand, McNally & co.

Rand, McNally & co.'s indexed atlas of the world . . . Historical—descriptive—statistical. With a special index to each map. [Rev. ed.] 2 v. 300 pp. incl. 142 col. maps; 2 p. l., [4], 301–547 (*i. e.* 250) pp. incl. 129 col. maps fol. Chicago, London [etc.] Rand, McNally & co., 1903. 4378

NOTE.—Plans of the following cities: Boston—New York, showing portions of Brooklyn, Jersey city, Westchester co.—Philadelphia—Chicago—St. Louis—Havana harbor.

CONTENTS.

v. 1. United States.
" 2. Foreign countries.

1907

Johnston, W. & A. K.

The multum in parvo atlas of the world, with descriptive text and complete index. New and revised edition. vi, 106, 74 pp. 112 (*i. e.* 110) col. maps, 2 pl. 12°. Edinburgh and London, W. & A. K. Johnston, 1907. 4379

Note.—Maps of the following cities: London and environs.—Environs of Liverpool and Manchester.—Edinburgh and environs.—Glasgow and environs.—Paris.—Environs of Berlin & Potsdam.

1910

Bartholomew, J. G.

The graphic atlas of the world . . . iv, 128, 138 pp., 1 l. incl. 85 col. maps. 8°. London, J. Walker & co., ltd., 1910. 4380

1910?

Jeheber, J. H.

Atlas de poche universel. 20 cartes géographiques des principaux pays du monde . . . Tableaux statistiques mis à jour par W. H. J. cover-title, 20 col. maps. 48°. Genève, J. H. Jeheber, [1910?] 4381

1912

American exporter, *publishers.*

Concise atlas of the world . . . cover-title, 32 pp. incl. 30 col. maps. 8°. New York, American exporter [©1912] 4382

1912

Bacon, G. W.

New general atlas of the world, containing all the latest geographical discoveries with alphabetical gazetteer and index, edited by G. W. Bacon . . . 3 p. l., 16, 16 [14] pp. 34 (*i. e.* 35) col. maps, 2 pl. fol. London, G. W. Bacon & co., ltd. 1912. 4383

1912

Bartholomew, J. G.

The citizen's atlas of the world, containing 156 pages of maps and plans with an index, a gazetteer, and geographical statistics . . . xvi, 69, [3], 133, [1] pp. front., 97 col. maps on 156 l. fol. [Edinburgh] J. Bartholomew & co. 1912–[1914] 4384

Note.—Issued in 1914 with 1912 title-page. The same as 1912 edition with changes in the following maps: The Balkan states.—Greece and the archipelago.—India, section 2. Frontispiece shows principal national flags.

1912

Cram, G. F.

Cram's junior atlas of the world containing a complete series of newly engraved maps of each state, foreign countries and United States possessions with new census information. New census edition. 288 pp. incl. 116 maps. 16°. Chicago, G. F. Cram, ©1912. 4385

1912

Cram's modern new census atlas of the United States and world. 13th census edition. A complete series of maps, of United States and possessions, foreign countries, world, polar regions and hemispheres. A carefully prepared index of over 70,000 place names in the United States . . . 3 p. l., 5–638 pp. incl. 189 maps. fol. New York, Chicago, G. F. Cram, 1912. 4386

1912

Hammond, C. S., & co.

American exporter concise atlas of the world. Published for private distribution by the American exporter . . . cover-title, 32 pp. incl. 30 col. maps. 8°. [New York, C. S. Hammond & co., °1912] 4386a

NOTE.—"Copyright, 1912."

1912

The compact atlas of the world containing new maps of every country in the world . . . cover-title, 32 pp. incl. 29 maps. sm. 4°. New York, C. S. Hammond & co. °1912. 4387

1912

Hammond's illustrated atlas of the world . . . 1 p. l., 224, [8] 8 pp. incl. 107 col. maps, illus. diagr. fol. New York, C. S. Hammond & co. 1912. 4388

1912

Handy almanac encyclopedia and atlas, 1913. A book of knowledge for home and office containing a vast amount of information respecting government, population, commerce, industry, agriculture, etc., etc. xvi, 216 pp. incl. 42 maps. New York, C. S. Hammond & co. °1912. 4389

1912?

Schrader, F.

Atlas de poche; contenant 68 cartes en couleurs, un texte géographique et statistique, et un index alphabétique des noms contenus dans l'atlas avec renvoi aux cartes. Nouvelle éd., corr. et mise au courant des derniers changements géographiques. 131 [1] p. incl. 55 col. maps. fol. Paris, Hachette & c^ie. [1912?] 4390

1913

Cram, G. F.

Agricultural and industrial review of Minnesota with world atlas; containing newly engraved maps of every state in the United States, detailed maps of every country, state and kingdom, together with a complete and adequate locating index to all cities, towns, villages and post offices in the United States, giving populations to every incorporated city and village therein. Edited and compiled under the direction of Earl J. Robinson, assisted by J. S. and M. B. Beem . . . 4 p. l. [5]–276 (*i. e.* 282) pp. incl. 104 col. maps, illus. ports. fol. Chicago & New York, G. F. Cram [1913] 4391

1913

Cram's unrivaled atlas of the world. New census edition containing newly engraved maps and charts of each state in the United States, each grand division, and detailed maps of every country, state and kingdom in the world together with a carefully prepared description of every state and country, an interesting and scientific explanation of geography, and a wealth of special feature maps and latest statistical diagrams, charts, tables . . . 3 p. l., [9]–582 pp. incl. front. col. maps, illus. fol. New York, Chicago, G. F. Cram, 1913. 4392

Note.—Copyrighted 1912. Maps of the following cities: Washington, Philadelphia, New York, Chicago, Cincinnati, St. Louis, St. Paul, Minneapolis and Boston.

Also contains maps and tables giving much statistical information concerning the government of the United States, schools, religious denominations, transportation, manufactures, agricultural products, cost of living, temperature and rainfall, population, finance and other subjects.

Pages 304–306 contain portraits of the presidents of the United States.

1913

Ideal reference atlas of the world. New census edition containing newly engraved maps and charts of each state in the United States, each grand division, and detailed maps of every country, state and kingdom in the world, together with a complete index showing how to find every city, town, village and post office on all the state maps . . . and giving population of every incorporated city and village in the United States according to the new 1910 census . . . 276 pp. incl. front., 100 col. maps, illus., ports., diagrs. fol. Chicago & New York, G. F. Cram, 1913. 4393

1913

Debes, E.

Neuer handatlas über alle teile der erde in 65 haupt- und 131 nebenkarten mit alphabetischen namenverzeichnis . . . 4. verm. und verb. auf. fol. Leipzig, H. Wagner & E. Debes, 1913. 4394

NOTE.—Maps of the following cities: Berlin.—Budapest.—Lemberg.—Jerusalem.

Issued in 28 pts. from 1911–1913.

A second impression issued in 1914.

1913

Franklin, T., *and* Griffiths, E. D.

The atlas geographies, a new visual atlas and geography combined. pt. 2, viii. 184 pp., 88 maps, 7 maps in pocket. 4°. Edinburgh, W. & A. K. Johnston, ltd. [1913] 4394a

NOTE.—Many small maps in text.

CONTENTS.

pt. 2. Junior geography adapted to meet the requirements of the Board of education syllabus for secondary schools.

1913

González de la Rosa, M. T.

Nuevo atlas geográfico universal, dedicado á la juventud americana. Contiene 44 mapas grabados por E. Morieu y J. Besson. Va precedido de una nueva introducción, que contiene extensas nociones astronómicas, geográficas y estadisticas, con arreglo á los datos y noticias oficiales más recientes . . . 15th ed. enteramente reformada y revisada por el mismo autor á fines de 1909. 55 [4] pp., 43 (*i. e.*) l. incl. 39 col. maps 4 col. 1 fold. col. map at end. obl. 4°. Paris, Mexico, v[da] de C. Bouret, 1913. 4395

NOTE.—Special maps of Central and South American countries.

1913

Hammond, C. S., & co.

Hammond's comprehensive atlas of the world . . . 2 p. l., 256, 256 pp. incl. 135 col. maps, 1 diagr. 8°. New York, C. S. Hammond & co. 1913. 4396

NOTE.—Copyright dated on maps vary from 1902–1913.

1913

Telegram & times concise atlas of the world containing new maps of the countries of the world with latest sporting records, population and political statistics and other new features. 48 pp., incl. 33 maps. 12°. New York, C. S. Hammond & co. 1913. 4397

NOTE.—"Copyright, 1912."

1913

Rand, McNally & co.

Rand, McNally & company's atlas of foreign countries (a companion volume to the Commercial atlas of America) containing political maps of all the countries and principal divisions of the world outside of the United States of America; relief maps of all the continents . . . and inset detail maps of cities, ports, and important islands . . . an alphabetical index of more than 130,000 place names and names of physical features, with key to location on map; latest available population figures; altitudes of principal mountains and lengths of chief rivers . . . 1st ed. [228] 110–279 pp. incl. 77 col. maps. fol. Chicago, Rand, McNally & co. 1913. 4398

1913

Rand, McNally & company's new family atlas of Canada and the world containing maps of the continents, the provinces of Canada, the United States and its dependencies, and all other countries of the world. Also an alphabetical list . . . 2 p. l., 185 pp., incl. 63 maps. fol. Chicago, New York, 1913. 4399

1913

Schrader, J. D. F., Prudent, F. P. V., *and* **Anthoine, E.**

Atlas de géographie moderne . . . contenant 64 cartes doubles imprimées en couleurs, accompanpagnées au verso d'un texte géographique, statistique et éthnographique avec 600 cartes de détail et d'un index alphabétique d'environ 50,000 noms. Nouv. éd. corr. et mise à jour. 2 p. l., 43 pp., 1 l. 64 col. maps. fol. Paris, Hachette & cie. 1913. 4400

Note.—Each map has text on reverse including small maps.

1913

Walker, H. B.

Walker's new international atlas; from the latest surveys and strictly up to date . . . These maps drawn and compiled especially for this new atlas: the United States maps from the very latest railway and government surveys; the dominion of Canada from crown land, railway and government surveys; the european and foreign maps from the Royal geographical society, London . . . 3 p. l., 5–638 pp. incl. 154 maps, illus., ports., diagrs. fol. Chicago & New York, H. B. Walker, 1913. 4401

Note.—Maps of the following cities: Honolulu.—Washington, D. C.—Philadelphia.—New York.—Chicago.—Milwaukee.—Cincinnati.—St.Louis.—St. Paul.—Minneapolis.—Boston.

1914

Adams, J. Q., & co.

The new international atlas of the world. 6 p. l. [528] pp. incl. 109 col. maps, illus., ports., diagrs. fol. Boston, J. Q. Adams & co., 1914. 4402

NOTE.—Various paging.

1914

Bartholomew, J. G.

The comparative atlas, physical & political . . . 11th ed., rev. and improved. 3 p. l., 64, 26 [1] pp. incl. front., 65 col. maps, diagrs. 4°. London, Meiklejohn & son, ltd. [1914]
[Professor Meiklejohn's geographical series] 4403

NOTE.—Frontispiece shows flags of all nations.

1914

Cram, G. F.

The ideal reference atlas of the world . . . containing newly engraved maps and charts of each state in the United States, each grand division, and detailed maps of every country, state and kingdom in the world; together with a complete index showing how to find every city, town, village and post office on all the state maps . . . and giving population of every incorporated city and village in the United States according to the new 1910 census, All carefully edited and brought up to the latest date. 1 p. l.. 5–276 pp. incl. 101 col. maps, illus., ports., diagrs. fol. Chicago & New York, G. F. Cram, 1914. 4404

1914

Debes, E.

Neuer handatlas über alle teile der erde in 65 haupt- und 131 neben-karten mit alphabetischen namenverzeichnis . . . 4. verm. und verb. auf. 2. abdruck. 2 p. l., 134 pp., 59 (*i. e.* 57) col. maps. fol. Leipzig, H. Wagner & E. Debes, 1914. 4405

NOTE.—Maps of the following cities: Berlin.—Budapest.—Lemberg.—Jerusalem. Earlier impression issued in 28 pts. from 1911–1913.

1914

Hammond, C. S., & co.

Handy almanac, encyclopedia and atlas. 1914. A book of knowledge for home and office, containing a vast amount of information respecting government, political history, commerce, industry, customs, tariffs, income taxes, population, agriculture . . . xxxii, 192, 16 pp. incl. 21 col. maps, illus., diagrs. 8°. New York, C. S. Hammond & co. 1914. 4406

1914

Hammond, C. S., & co.—Continued.

Hammond's home and office atlas of the world. 1 p. l., 240 [8] 15 [1] p. incl. 108 col. maps, illus., diagrs. fol. New York, C. S. Hammond & co. [c1914] 4407

1914

Hammond's illustrated atlas of the world . . . 1 p. l., 240 [8] 15 [1] p. incl. 106 col. maps, illus., diagrs. fol. New York, C. S. Hammond & co. 1914. 4408

1914

Hammond's modern atlas of the world; a new series of physical, political and historical maps compiled from government surveys and exhibiting the latest results of geographical research, accompanied by a gazetteer of the principal towns of the world. 1 p. l., 176, 15 [1] pp. incl. 105 col. maps, illus., diagrs. fol. New York, C. S. Hammond & co. 1914. 4409

NOTE.—On page 42 is found map of the Balkan states and Greece, giving the new boundaries.

1914

Hammond's pictorial atlas of the world. A new series of over one hundred maps in colors, based upon the latest official surveys and accompanied by a gazetteer of cities and towns and a descriptive gazetteer of the states, countries and physical features of the globe . . . 1 p. l., 176 pp., 1 l., 106 [4] 15 [1] p. incl. 109 col. maps, illus., diagrs. fol. New York, C. S. Hammond & co. 1914. 4410

1914

The new reference atlas of the world. A new series of physical, political and historical maps compiled from government surveys and exhibiting the latest results of geographical research . . . 1 p. l., 176, 15 [1] p. incl. 106 col. maps, illus., diagrs. fol. New York, C. S. Hammond & co. [c1914] 4411

1914

Hammond's standard atlas of the world, containing a new series of large scale maps based upon official surveys including maps of each state of the United States, the territory of Alaska, each province of the dominion of Canada and of Mexico and Cuba, showing . . . each railroad and railroad system, all interurban electric lines and all inland and coastwise water routes, etc. Also new maps of all foreign countries, together with a new postal and shipping guide of the United States and Canada . . . Also a new descriptive gazetteer of the principal citties of the world . . . 1st ed. 212 pp. incl. 113 col. maps. fol. New York, C. S. Hammond & co. 1914. 4412

1914

Istituto geografico de Agostini.

Calendario-atlante de Agostini, 1914, con notiziario redatto da L. F. de Magistris. Edizione accresciuta d' un ritratto, di due nuove carte e notevolmente ampliata nel testo. VIII, 152 pp. 26 (*i. e.* 23) col. maps. 3 pl., port. 18°. Novara, Istituto geografico de Agostini, [1914] 4413

NOTE.—At head of title: Anno XI. Series II—vol. I.

1914

Perthes, J.

Atlas portátil. Arreglado y traducido de la 51ª edición alemana por H. Habenicht y Br. Domann . . . Con noticias geográfico-estadisticas por H. Wichmann. 8. ed. Edición sudamericana. 36 pp., 28, 4 vol. maps. 16°. Gotha, J. Perthes, 1914. 4414

NOTE.—"Suplemento" consisting of three maps of Argentina and one of Paraguay.

1914

Poates, L. L., & co.

L. L. Poates & co.'s handy atlas of the world, containing maps of the United States, its 48 states, territories and insular possessions, dominion of Canada, each of the provinces and foreign countries. 78, [19] pp. incl. 75 maps. 12°. New York, L. L. Poates pub. co. [c1914] 4415

1914

Collier, P. F., & son.

The new encyclopedic atlas and gazetteer of the world. Edited and revised by Francis J. Reynolds . . . The Panama-Pacific edition. World maps revised to 1914. Showing new boundaries of all foreign states and their dependencies. Newly organized counties and other state changes within the United States. New Canadian maps. Latest population statistics of all countries and cities of the world. The Panama canal and the Panama-Pacific exposition . . . 264 pp. incl. 145 maps, front., illus. fol. New York, P. F. Collier & son, [c1914] 4416

NOTE.—Maps of the following cities: Atlanta, Baltimore, Berlin, Boston, Buffalo, Chicago, Cincinnati, Cleveland, Denver, Detroit, Indianapolis, Kansas City, London, Los Angeles, Louisville, Memphis, Milwaukee, Minneapolis & St. Paul, Quebec, Newark, New Orleans, New York, Paris, Philadelphia, Pittsburgh, Portland, Providence, Rochester, St. Louis, San Francisco, Seattle, Toronto, Washington, D. C.

1915

Hammond, C. S., & co.

The compact atlas of the world containing new maps of every country in the world . . . cover-title, 32 pp. incl. 29 col. maps. sm. 8°. New York, C. S. Hammond & co. ©1915. 4417

1915

Hammond's modern atlas of the world. A new series of physical, political and historical maps compiled from government surveys and exhibiting the latest results of geographical research, accompanied by a gazetteer of the principal towns of the world. 1 p. l., 176, 16 pp. incl. 106 col. maps, illus. sm. fol. New York, C. S. Hammond & co. 1915. 4418

NOTE.—"Parcels post map of the United States."

1915

Hickmann, A. L.

Prof. A. L. Hickmanns geographisch-statistischer universal-taschen-atlas. 1 p. l., 63, [1] 16 pp., 25 col. maps, 38 col. pl. 16°. Wien und Leipzig, G. Freytag & Berndt [1915] 4419

NOTE.—Plates illustrate the size of the rivers, religion, coats of arms, flags, commerce and legal tender of the various nations.

1915

Istituto geografico de Agostini.

Calendario-atlante de Agostini, 1915, con notiziario redatto da L. F. de Magistris. XL, 132 pp., 26 (*i. e.* 25) col. maps, 2 pl. 18°. Novara, Istituto geografico de Agostini, [1915] 4420

NOTE.—At head of title: Anno XII. Serie II—vol. II.

1915

Polish american publishing co.

Atlas historyczny i geograficzny zawiera: dziewięć Poskich historysznych map i dziewięć Angielskich geograficznysh map. 1 p. l., 16 col. maps. 8°. Chicago, Polish american publishing co. ©1915. 4421

NOTE.—Map on the reverse of title.
Nine historical maps of Poland.

1915

Rand, McNally & co.

Rand McNally ideal atlas of the world, containing large scale colored maps of each state, territory, and outlying possession of the United States, the provinces of Canada, and the various countries in Europe and South America, continent maps of Asia,

Africa, and Oceania, each state map accompanied by a page of letter press, covering area, population, resources, industries, climate, etc., of the state, an alphabetical index, giving the name, location and population of every county, city and incorporated village in each state, also a ready reference index on the margin of each map. 2 p. l., 193 pp. incl. 96 col. maps, front. col. plates, tables. fol. Chicago, New York, Rand McNally & co. 1915. 4422

NOTE.—Front., The Capitol, Washington, D. C.
Illustrated by colored lithograph plates, showing scenes of the various states, remarkable for their history or natural beauty.

1915

Rand McNally international atlas of the world, containing large scale colored maps op[!] each state, territory, and outlying possession of the United States, the provinces of Canada, and every country in the world; each map accompanied by a page of letter press, covering area, population, resources, industries, climate, etc. of each state or country. An alphabetical index, giving the name, location and population of every county, city, and incorporated village in each state, as well as the principal cities and towns of foreign countries. Also a ready reference index on the margin of each map . . . 2 p. l., xx, 329 pp. incl. 105 col. maps, 25 col. pl., 4 diagr. fol. Chicago, New York, Rand McNally & co. 1915. 4423

NOTE.—The following notice on title-page: "The publishers of this atlas desire to call attention to the fact that this is not a revised, but an essentially new atlas, that is herewith presented to the attention of the public for their consideration."

1915

Rand-McNally pocket atlas of the world, historical, political, commercial . . . 5 p. l., 387 pp. incl. 93 col. maps. 16°. Chicago and New York, Rand, McNally & co. 1915. 4424

NOTE.—Appended: Population of the United States, Census of 1910, by states, counties, cities, towns, boroughs, and villages. 114 pp. 16°. Chicago, New York [etc.] Rand, McNally & co. °1915.

1916

Cram, G. F., co.

The ideal reference atlas of the world. Newly engraved maps and charts of each state in the United States, each grand division, and detailed maps of every country, state and kingdom in the world. Accompanied by a complete index showing every city, town, village and post office on all the maps at a moment's glance,

Cram, G. F., co.—Continued.

and giving population of every incorporated city and village in the United States according to the latest census. Population of foreign countries according to latest available figures. A history and descriptive gazetteer of every state, country and kingdom of the world. All carefully edited and brought up to the latest date . . . 278 pp. incl. 106 col. maps, illus. fol. New York, Chicago, G. F. Cram co. 1916. 4425

NOTE.—Portraits of the presidents of the United States, and a list of the presidents with their respective cabinets.

1916

Funk & Wagnalls co.

Funk & Wagnalls new comprehensive atlas of the world; containing colored maps of all the states and territories in the United States, the Canal Zone, showing the Panama canal and the provinces of the Dominion of Canada, also full page maps of every country and civil division upon the face of the globe. 96 pp. incl. maps. 12°. New York and London, Funk & Wagnalls co. 1916.
[*With* The comprehensive standard dictionary of the english language. 12°. [New York & London ©1915]] 4426

1916

Hammond, C. S., & co.

Hammond's popular atlas of the world. Containing maps of all states, territories and principal foreign countries, together with lists of principal cities and towns giving latest population figures and a new gazetteer of United States. [274] pp., incl. 144 maps. 8°. New York, C. S. Hammond & co., 1916. [©1915] 4427

NOTE.—Atlas copyrighted in 1915.

1916

Istituto geografico de Agostini.

Calendario-atlante de Agostini, 1916, con notiziario redatto da Luigi Filippo de Magistris. Edizione accresciuta di due nuove tavole e corredata d'un quadro geografico-statistico-politico-commerciale-militare degli stati indipendenti della terra. xxiv, 148 pp., 26 col. maps, 2 pl., 1 fold. tab. 16°. Novara, Istituto geografico de Agostini, [1916] 4428

NOTE.—At head of title: Anno XIII. Serie II—vol. III.

1916

Matthews-Northrup co.

Handy atlas of the world. 34 pp., 1 l., incl. 33 maps. 12°. Buffalo, N. Y., Matthews-Northrup works, ©1916. 4429

Note.—Contents list on title-page.

1916

National map co.

New standard atlas of the world. A new series of over 100 maps in colors, based upon the latest official surveys, with a complete index showing location and population of all cities and towns, including an encyclopedia of the states and foreign countries. The population figures are according to the latest official census. [3]–244 pp., incl. 102 col. maps, illus. fol. Indianapolis, New York, National map co. ©1916. 4430

1916

Rand, McNally & co.

Rand-McNally dollar atlas of the world, historical, political, commercial . . . 2 p. l., 192 pp. incl. 93 col. maps. 12°. Chicago and New York, Rand, McNally & co. 1916. 4431

Note.—Appended: Population of the United States, Census of 1910, by states, counties, cities, towns, boroughs, and villages . . . 61 pp. 12°. Chicago and New York, Rand, McNally & co. [1916].

1916

Rand McNally & co.'s new family atlas of the world, containing maps of the continents, the states and dependencies of the United States, the provinces of Canada, and all other countries of the world; the constitution of the United States, and a facsimile, with signatures, of the declaration of independence; and portraits of the presidents and portraits and sketches of eminent statesmen, patriots, army and naval commanders, writers, and inventors; also an index by states, giving the latest population figures for states, counties, incorporated cities, towns, boroughs, and villages, and an index of nearly 2000 foreign cities, with location on maps. 2 p. l., 156 pp. incl. 100 maps, ports. tables. fol. Chicago, New York, Rand McNally & co. 1916. 4432

1916

Rand McNally universal atlas of the world, containing large scale colored maps of each state, territory, and outlying possession of the United States, the provinces of Canada, and every country in the world; each map accompanied by a page of letter press, covering area, population, resources, industries, climate, etc., of

Rand, McNally & co.—Continued.

each state or country. An alphabetical index, giving the name, location, and population of every county, city, and incorporated village in each state, as well as the principal cities and towns of foreign countries. Also a ready reference index on the margin of each map . . . 2 p. l., xx, 329 pp. incl. 105 col. maps, 25 col. pl., 4 diagrs. fol. Chicago, New York, Rand, McNally & co. 1916. 4433

NOTE.—The following notice on title-page: "The publishers of this atlas desire to call attention to the fact that this is not a revised, but an essentially new atlas, that is herewith presented to the attention of the public for their consideration."

Published also in 1905 under title, *Rand McNally international atlas of the world.*

On verso of title-page, "Copyright, 1915, by Rand McNally & co., under Rand McNally international atlas of the world."

1917

Collier, P. F., & son.

The new encyclopedic atlas and gazetteer of the world, edited and revised by Francis J. Reynolds . . . World maps revised to 1917—showing new boundaries of all foreign states and their dependencies—newly organized counties and other state changes within the United States—up-to-date information on Alaska and America's insular possessions—new canadian maps—latest population and production statistics of all countries and cities of the world—latest maps of the war zones . . . 264 pp. incl. 145 maps, front., illus. fol. New York, P. F. Collier & son, 1917. 4434

NOTE.—Beside many small maps in the text, contains the following maps of cities: Atlanta.—Baltimore.—Part of the inner city of Berlin.—Boston.—Buffalo. — Chicago. — Cincinnati. — Cleveland. — Denver. — Detroit. — Indianapolis. — Kansas City. — London. — Los Angeles. — Louisville. —Memphis. — Milwaukee. — Minneapolis. — Montreal. — Newark. — New Orleans. — New York. — Brooklyn. — Paris. — Petrograd. — Philadelphia. — Pittsburgh. — Portland. — Providence. — Rochester. — St. Louis. — San Francisco.—Seattle.—Toronto.—Washington.

1917

Cram, G. F., co.

Cram's modern reference atlas. The United States and world. A complete series of maps of the United States and possessions, foreign countries, the world, polar regions and hemispheres. A carefully prepared index of over 150,000 place names in the United States, of counties, cities, towns, villages, post offices and railroad stations. A complete and comprehensive index of all foreign countries. A concise history and descriptive gazetteer of each state and foreign country, area, population, capital, physiography, drainage, products, climate, resources, etc., facts carefully compiled from latest reliable official information. 496 pp., incl. 137 col. maps. fol. New York, Chicago, G. F. Cram co. 1917. 4435

Note.—"An entirely new set of maps, many of them on a greatly increased scale, have been specially made for this edition . . ." See introduction.

Maps of the following cities: Boston.—New York city.—Philadelphia.—Washington, D. C.—St. Louis.—Chicago.—Milwaukee.—Cincinnati.—St. Paul.—San Francisco.—Minneapolis.

1917

Cram's unrivaled atlas of the world. New historical edition. Newly engraved maps and charts of each state in the United States, each grand division, and detailed maps of every country, state and kingdom in the world. Historical maps, graphically showing the rise and fall of the various kingdoms, states and empires, from the first great empires, B. C. 3000 to A. D. 500, Roman empire A. D. 200–300, and Europe A. D. 500 to Europe A. D. 1878, accompanied by historical description of every state and country, comprising a descriptive gazetteer of the world, and a wealth of special feature maps and latest statistical diagrams, tables, etc. All carefully edited and brought up to the latest date. Fully indexed. 478 pp. incl. 155 col. maps, front., illus. sm. fol. Chicago, New York, G. F. Cram co. 1917. 4436

Note.—Illustrations include flags and arms of various nations, and the flags of the United States.

Special feature maps show production, elevations, rainfall, geological formation, and government reclamation projects of the United States.

Maps of the following cities: Boston, New York, Philadelphia, Washington, St. Louis, Chicago, Milwaukee, Cincinnati, St. Paul, San Francisco, and Minneapolis.

1917

Hammond, C. S., & co.

Compact atlas of the world. Compliments of the Equitable trust company. cover-title, 31 pp. incl. 29 col. maps. 12°. [New York, C. S. Hammond & co. 1917] 4437

Note.—Map of Europe showing "German barred zones." pp. 16–17.

1917

Hammond's comprehensive atlas of the world . . . 2 p. l., 256, 256 (*i. e.* 258) pp. incl. 132 col. maps. 8°. New York, C. S. Hammond & co. 1917. 4438

Note.—Copyright dates on maps vary from 1904–1916, many being reprinted from the 1913 edition of the atlas.

1917

Hammond, C. S., & co.—Continued.

Hammond's standard atlas of the world, containing a new series of large scale maps based upon official surveys including individual maps of each state of the United States, the territory of Alaska, each province of the dominion of Canada and of Mexico and Cuba, showing in separate colors each railroad and railroad system, all interurban electric lines and all inland and coastwise water routes, etc. Also new maps of all foreign countries, together with a new postal and shipping guide of the United States and Canada . . . also a new descriptive gazetteer of the principal cities of the world . . . 231 (*i. e.* 329) pp. incl. 116 col. maps, front. fol. New York, C. S. Hammond & co. 1917. 4439

NOTE.—At head of title: Fourth export edition.

All maps except those of North America are by George Philip & son, ltd., London; and appear also in their Mercantile marine atlas of the world. 1916.

1917

Mawson, C. O. S.

Doubleday, Page & co.'s geographical manual and new atlas . . . Maps of to-day and to-morrow. New maps will replace old after the great war. xxxii, 380 pp. incl. 180 col. maps. sm. fol. Garden City, N. Y., Doubleday, Page & co. 1917. 4440

NOTE.—Maps are by C. S. Hammond & co., New York.

Contains a few special maps devoted to the war conditions in Europe, also physical maps, and maps of various parts of the world showing racial distribution, language, rainfall, vegetation, production, population and transportation.

"Authors and books quoted or referred to": pp. viii–ix.

1917

Rand, McNally & co.

Rand, McNally & co.'s complete atlas of the world, containing colored maps, with marginal indexes, of every country and civil division in the world; also portraits and sketches of leading statesmen, generals, writers, and inventors, together with a complete and up-to-date ready reference index, including the latest official population figures available, for the United states and all the principal cities, towns, and villages of foreign countries. 2 p. l., 258 pp. incl. 120 col. maps, ports. sm. fol. Chicago, New York, Rand, McNally & co. 1917. 4441

NOTE.—Contains the same maps as Rand, McNally & co.'s *Imperial atlas of the world*, and two other maps of Alberta and Saskatchewan, also additional text.

Contains maps of the following cities: Boston.—New York city.—Brooklyn.—Pittsburgh.—Philadelphia.—Baltimore.—Washington, D. C.—Cincinnati.—Cleveland.—Chicago.—Detroit.—Milwaukee.—St. Paul.—Minneapolis. — St. Louis.—Kansas City, Kan., and Kansas City, Mo.—New Orleans.—San Francisco.

1917

Rand, McNally & co.'s excelsior atlas of the world, containing colored maps, with marginal indexes, of every country and civil division in the world; also portraits and sketches of leading statesmen, generals, writers, and inventors, together with a complete and up-to-date ready reference index, including the latest official population figures available, for the United States and all the principal cities, towns, and villages of foreign countries. 2 p. l., 258 pp. incl. 120 col. maps, ports. sm. fol. Chicago, New York, Rand, McNally & co. 1917. 4442

NOTE.—Published also under title, Rand McNally & co.'s *Complete atlas of the world. 1917.*

The same maps and index as in Rand McNally & co.'s *New imperial atlas of the world. 1917.*

1917

Rand-McNally dollar atlas of the world, historical, political, commercial . . . 2 p. l., 192 pp. incl. 93 col. maps. 12°. Chicago and New York, Rand, McNally & co. 1917. 4443

NOTE.—Appended: Population of the United States, latest census, by states, counties, cities, towns, boroughs, and villages . . . 63 pp. 12°. Chicago and New York, Rand, McNally & co. [1917]

1917

Rand, McNally & co.'s new family atlas of the world, containing maps of the continents, the states and dependencies of the United States, the provinces of Canada, and all other countries of the world; the constitution of the United States, and a facsimile, with signatures, of the declaration of independence; and portraits of the presidents and portraits and sketches of eminent statesmen, patriots, army and naval commanders, writers, and inventors; also an index of states, giving the latest population figures for states, counties, incorporated cities, towns, boroughs, and villages, and an index of nearly 2000 foreign cities, with location on maps. 2 p. l., 159 pp. incl. 102 col. maps, diagrs. sm. fol. Chicago, New York, Rand, McNally & co. 1917. 4444

NOTE.—Maps are the same as the corresponding maps used in Rand, McNally & co.'s *Imperial atlas of the world,* and their *Complete atlas of the world,* excepting the map of the world and the map of the polar regions.

1917

Rand, McNally & co.'s new imperial atlas of the world, containing large scale colored maps of each state and territory in the United States, provinces of Canada, the continents and their subdivisions. A ready reference marginal index is shown upon the

Rand, McNally & co.—Continued.

maps of all the countries of the earth. 2 p. l., 191 pp. incl. 118 col. maps. sm. fol. Chicago, New York, Rand, McNally & co. 1917. 4445

NOTE.—Same maps and index used in Rand, McNally & co.'s *Complete atlas of the world.*

Contains a map showing acquisition of territory by the United States at various periods, and maps of the following cities: Boston.—New York city.—Brooklyn.—Pittsburgh.—Philadelphia.—Baltimore.—Washington, D. C.—Cincinnati.—Cleveland.—Chicago.—Detroit.—Milwaukee.—St. Paul. — Minneapolis.—St. Louis.—Kansas City, Kan., and Kansas City, Mo.—New Orleans.—San Francisco.

1917

Rand-McNally pocket atlas of the world, historical, political commercial . . . 5 p. l., 387 pp. incl. 94 col. maps. 16°. Chicago and New York, Rand, McNally & co. 1917. 4446

NOTE.—Appended: Population of the United States, latest census figures by states, counties, cities, towns, boroughs, and villages. 116 pp. 16°. Chicago, New York, Rand, McNally & co. 1917.

1918

Collier, P. F., & son.

The new encyclopedic atlas and gazetteer of the world, edited and revised by Francis J. Reynolds . . . World maps revised to 1918—showing new boundaries of all foreign states and their dependencies—Latest and revised maps of all war zones—New maps of each state of the United States, including all newly organized counties and other boundary changes to 1918—The very latest revised Canadian maps—Latest population and production statistics of all the countries and cities of the world—Up-to-date information on Alaska and America's insular possessions—Illustrated gazetteer of cities and towns of the world . . . 272 pp. incl. 153 maps, front., illus. fol. New York, P. F. Collier & son, 1918. 4447

NOTE.—Beside many small maps in the text, contains the following maps of cities: Atlanta.—Baltimore.—Part of the inner city of Berlin.—Boston.—Buffalo. — Chicago. — Cincinnati. — Cleveland. — Denver. — Detroit. — Indianapolis.—Kansas City.—London.—Los Angeles.—Louisville. — Memphis. — Milwaukee. — Minneapolis. — Montreal. — Newark. — New Orleans.—New York. — Brooklyn. — Paris. — Petrograd. — Philadelphia. — Pittsburgh. — Portland. — Providence. — Rochester. — St. Louis. — San Francisco.—Seattle.—Toronto.—Washington.

1918

Mawson, C. O. S.

Doubleday, Page & co.'s geographical manual and new atlas . . . Maps of to-day and to-morrow. New maps will replace old after the great war. xxxii, 392 pp, incl. 180 col. maps. sm. fol. Garden City, N. Y., Doubleday, Page & co. 1918. 4447a

NOTE.—Maps are by C. S. Hammond & co., New York.
Maps of the following cities: New York.—Washington.
Contains a few special maps devoted to the war conditions in Europe, physical maps, and maps of various parts of the world showing racial distribution, language, rainfall, vegetation, production, population and transportation; also a general index not found in the first edition, 1917.
"Authors and books quoted or referred to": pp. viii–ix.

1918

Perthes, J.

Justus Perthes' taschen-atlas . . . Vollständig neu bearbeitet von Hermann Habenicht . . . Mit geographisch-statistischen notizen von Hugo Wichmann. 55. aufl. 80 pp., 24 col. maps. 16°. Gotha, J. Perthes, 1918. 4448

1918

Rand, McNally & co.

Rand McNally new reference atlas of the world and the war. Containing detailed maps of european war areas, strategic maps in minute detail of the battle regions in Belgium, France, and Italy, and a large-scale map of every country in the world, with an introductory war summary and an enlightening talk on war maps and how to use them in studying the events of the war, by S. J. Duncan-Clark . . . Supplemented by gripping war facts and figures, reference diagrams, ready reference indexes with pronunciations and population figures, and many other features of value for a complete comprehension of the war situation. 148 pp. incl. 67 col. maps. sm. fol. Chicago, New York, Rand McNally & co. [1918] 4449

NOTE.—The eight strategic maps of european war areas are accompanied by a key map and a separate index to accompany each map.
Contains a military map of the United States, and an industrial map of the United States.

1919

Hammond, C. S., & co.

Hammond's commercial and library atlas of the world. 1 p. l., 296 pp. incl. illus., ports., maps. 4°. New York, C. S. Hammond & co. 1919. 4449a

NOTE.—"Principal cities of the world." pp. 129–180.
"Weather bureau and laws of weather forecasting." pp. 181–183.
"Descriptive gazetteer of the principal cities of the world." pp. 184–216.
"Presidents of the United States." pp. 217–223.
"Parcel post guide of the United States." pp. 225–284 with map.

1919

Hammond, C. S., & co.—Continued.

Hammond's historical and statistical atlas of the world war; maps of all the areas figuring in the conflict of 1914–1918; an historic record of life-long interest. [24] pp. incl. illus., ports., maps. fol. New York, C. S. Hammond & co., inc., 1919. 4450

Reynolds, F. J.

Reynolds' after-war atlas and gazetteer of the world . . . World maps remade by world's treaty of peace, Paris, 1919—Showing new boundaries of all foreign states and their dependencies—Revised maps of all war zones—New maps of each state of the United States, including all newly organized counties and other boundary changes to 1919—New Canadian maps—Latest population and production statistics of all the countries and cities of the world—Up-to-date information on Alaska and America's insular possessions—Illustrated gazetteer of the cities and towns of the world—40 pages tabulated events of the great war from 1914 to peace conclusion, with maps showing all military operations. 40 maps of automobile routes throughout the United states. 1 p. l., 364 (*i. e.* 370) pp. incl. 230 maps, front., illus. fol. New York, Reynolds publishing co. incorporated [1919] 4450a

Note.—Many small maps in text.

A republication with many additions and revised indexes of P. F. Collier & son's *The new encyclopedic atlas and gazetteer of the world*, which was edited by Francis J. Reynolds and issued in 1907–1909, 1911–1912, 1914, 1917–1918. For titles see v. 1–3.

For list of the maps of cities see title 4447.

1919

Wilner, M. M.

A new atlas of the world, corrected according to the peace terms, together with a graphic story of the great war, 1914–1919 [32] pp., maps. 12°. New York, F. F. Lovell, ©1919. 4450b

Note.—Text on pp. 2, 3 and 4 of cover.

AMERICA.

COMMERCIAL.

Rand, McNally & co.

Rand McNally & co.'s commercial atlas of America. Containing large scale maps of all states in the United States and of its outlying possessions, of the provinces of the dominion of Canada, of Newfoundland, the republic of Mexico, Central America, Panama, the West Indies, Cuba, Japan, China, and South Africa: large continental maps of North America, South America, Europe,

Africa, Asia and Australasia . . . 3d ed. LVII, 22, 13–449 pp. incl. 117 col. maps, diagr. fol. Chicago, Rand, McNally & co. 1913. 4451

NOTE.—Lists of all the railroads, electric lines, steamship and steamboat lines, also maps showing parcel post rates, inland waterways, lake traffic, time, acquisition of territory in the United States, recent discoveries in North Polar regions, United States forest reservations, industrial conditions, etc.

Maps of the following cities: Boston.—New York, Brooklyn, and Jersey City. — Brooklyn. — Buffalo. — Philadelphia. — Pittsburgh. — Baltimore. — Washington, D. C. — Cincinnati. — Cleveland. — Toledo. — Indianapolis. — Chicago. — Detroit. — Milwaukee. — Minneapolis. — St. Paul. — St. Louis.—Kansas City, Kan., and Kansas City, Mo.—New Orleans.—San Francisco.—Montreal.—Toronto.

1914

Rand, McNally & co.'s commercial atlas of America. Containing large-scale maps of all states in the United States and of its outlying possessions, of the provinces of the dominion of Canada, of Newfoundland, the republic of Mexico, Central America, Panama, Bermuda, the West Indies and Cuba; large continental maps of North America, South America, Europe, Africa, Asia, and Australia . . . 4th ed. 2 p. l., iii–xliv, 428 pp. incl. 113 col. maps, diagr. fol. Chicago, Rand, McNally & co. 1914. 4452

NOTE.—Lists of all the railroads, electric lines, steamship and steamboat lines; also maps showing lake traffic, time, industrial conditions, freight traffic and passenger association territories, etc.

Maps of the following cities: Boston.—New York.—Jersey city.—Brooklyn.—Buffalo.—Philadelphia.—Pittsburgh.—Washington, D. C.—Baltimore.—Cincinnati.—Cleveland.—Toledo.—Indianapolis.—Chicago.—Detroit.—Milwaukee.—St. Paul.—Minneapolis.—St. Louis.—Kansas city, Kans.—Kansas city, Mo.—New Orleans.—San Francisco.—Montreal.—Toronto.

1915

Rand, McNally & co.'s commercial atlas of America. Containing large-scale maps of all states in the United States and of its outlying possessions, of the provinces of the Dominion of Canada, of Newfoundland, the republic of Mexico, Central America, Panama, Bermuda, the West Indies and Cuba; large continental maps of North America, South America, Europe, Africa, Asia, and Australasia . . . 5th ed. 1 p. l., l, 442 pp. incl. 121 col. maps, diagr. fol. Chicago, Rand, McNally & co. 1915. 4453

NOTE.—Lists of all railroads, steamship and steamboat lines; postal information, irrigation projects, travel distance table, diagram showing American tariff from 1791 to 1914; also maps showing lake traffic, time, industrial conditions, freight traffic, passenger association territories; and North and South Polar regions.

Maps of the following cities: Baltimore.—Boston.—Brooklyn.—Buffalo.—Chicago.—Cincinnati.—Cleveland.—Detroit.—Indianapolis.—Kansas City, Kan.—

Rand, McNally & co.—Continued.

Kansas City, Mo.—Milwaukee.—Minneapolis.—Montreal.—New Orleans.—New York.—Philadelphia.—Pittsburgh.—San Francisco.—St. Louis.—St. Paul.—Toledo.—Toronto.—Washington.

1916

Rand, McNally & co.'s commercial atlas of America . . . 1 p. l., L, 446 pp., incl. 122 maps. 47th ed. fol. Chicago, Rand, McNally & co. 1916. 4454

NOTE.—Table of maps on cover.—Table of contents on inside of cover.

Lists of all the railroads, electric lines, steamship and steamboat lines, also maps showing inland waterways, lake traffic, time, acquisition of territory in the United States, recent discoveries in North Polar regions, United States forest reservations, industrial conditions, etc.

Maps of the following cities: Boston.—New York, Brooklyn and Jersey City.—Brooklyn.—Buffalo.—Philadelphia.—Pittsburgh.—Baltimore.—Washington, D. C.—Louisville.—Cincinnati.—Cleveland.—Toledo.—Indianapolis.—Chicago.—Detroit.—Milwaukee.—Minneapolis.—St. Paul.—St. Louis.—Kansas City, Mo., and Kansas City, Kan.—New Orleans.—San Francisco.—Montreal.—Toronto.

1917

Rand, McNally & co.'s commercial atlas of America. Containing large-scale maps of all the states in the United States and of its outlying possessions, of the provinces of the Dominion of Canada, of Newfoundland, the republic of Mexico, Central America, Panama, Bermuda, the West Indies, Cuba, Polar regions and various other useful maps; also large continental maps of North America, South America, Europe, Africa, Asia, and Oceania, and a new map of South America in four sections including complete and revised indices . . . 1 p. l., L, 448 pp. incl. 123 col. maps, diagr. fol. Chicago, Rand, McNally & co. 1917. 4455

NOTE.—At head of title 48th edition. 1st edition published 1911.

Lists of railroads, steamship lines, postal information, travel distance table, and diagram showing American tariff from 1791 to 1915.

Maps of the following cities: Boston.—New York, Brooklyn and Jersey City.—Buffalo.—Philadelphia.—Pittsburgh.—Baltimore.—Washington.—Louisville.—Cincinnati.—Cleveland.—Toledo.—Indianapolis.—Chicago.—Detroit.—Minneapolis.—St. Paul.—St. Louis.—Kansas City.—New Orleans.—San Francisco.—Montreal.—Toronto.

1918

Rand, McNally & co.'s commercial atlas of America. Containing large-scale maps of all the states in the United States and of its outlying possessions, of the provinces of the Dominion of Canada, of Newfoundland, the republic of Mexico, Central America, Panama, Bermuda, the West Indies, Cuba, Polar regions and various other useful maps; also large continental maps of North

America, South America, Europe, Africa, Asia, and Oceania, and a new map of South America in four sections including complete and revised indices . . . 1 p. l., LII, 448 pp. incl. 126 col. maps, diagr. fol. Chicago, Rand, McNally & co. 1918. 4456

NOTE.—At head of title, 49th edition. 1st edition published 1911.

List of railroads, steamship lines, postal information, travel distance tables, and diagram showing American tariff from 1791 to 1916.

Maps of the following cities: Boston.—New York, Brooklyn and Jersey City.—Buffalo.—Philadelphia.—Pittsburgh.—Baltimore.—Washington.—Louisville.—Cincinnati.—Cleveland.—Toledo.—Indianapolis.—Chicago.—Detroit.—Milwaukee.—Minneapolis.—St. Paul.—St. Louis.—Kansas City.—New Orleans.—San Francisco.—Montreal.—Toronto.

LITERARY AND HISTORICAL.

Bartholomew, J. G.

A literary & historical atlas of America . . . xiv, 231 pp. inc. 92 maps, 8 pl., 3 diagrs. 12°. London, J. M. Dent; New York, E. P. Dutton [1918]
[Everyman's library. Edited by Ernest Rhys. Reference]
4457

NOTE.—Contains a "Gazetteer of towns and places in America having a literary or historic interest."

SCHOOL.

Estévanez, N.

Atlas geográfico de América. Comprende los mapas de: la América del Sur, República Argentina, Uruguay, Paraguay, Chile, Bolivia, Brasil, Perú, Colombia y Ecuador, Venezuela, América Central (Guatemala, San Salvador, Honduras, Nicaragua y Costa Rica), Antillas, Isla de Cuba, Isla de Santo Domingo, América del Norte, Méjico y Estados Unidos. Trazados con el mayor esmero en vista de datos originales y recientes, y conteniendo en escala mayor las islas de Puerto Rico, Galápagos, etc., los istmos de Nicaragua y Panamá, tierras árticas, planos de ciudades y puertos, etc., etc. Con un resumen geográfico (dispueto con arreglo al plan de enseñanza de los colegios nacionales de la República Argentina) . . . 22 [2] pp., 17 col. maps. sm. fol. Paris, Garnier hermanos, [1896] 4458

NOTE.—On cover, "Tercera edición."

GENERAL.

1611

Wytfliet, C.

Histoire vniverselle des Indes Occidentales et Orientales, et de la conversion des Indiens. Diuisée en trois parties, par Cornille Wytfliet, & Anthoine Magin, & autres historiens . . . 3 pts. in 1 v. 8 p. l., 108 [12] 62 [2] 54 [4] pp. 19 maps. sm. fol. a Dovay, F. Fabri. 1611. 4459
[Thatcher collection]

NOTE.—Collation: title, l. 1; Sommaire des chapitres de l'histoire des Indes Occidentales, recto l. 2, to verso l. 3; Description des Indes Occidentales, verso l. 3; Av lectevr, recto l. 4; Approbatio, dated 12. Iunij. 1607, signed Bartholomæus Petrus, verso l. 4; Table tres-ample des-plvs notables choses contenves en la presente histoire des Indes Occidentales divisée en deux livres, recto l. 5—verso l. 7; In historiam Indiarvm, recto l. 8; printer's mark verso, l. 8; text, 108 pp. with 19 maps, 4 maps wanting; Table des chapitres de l'histoire des Indes Orientales, [9] pp.; Av lectevr, and Approbatio, dated 12. Iunij. 1607, signed Bartholomæus Petrus, [1] p.; engraved title-page to second part, 1 l., verso blank; text, 66 pp. with 4 small maps; engraved title-page to third part, 1 l., verso blank; text, 54 pp.; Table de l'histoire des Indes Orientales contenant la conversion des Indiens. [3] pp.; printer's mark, 1 p. First edition published in 1597 and according to Nordenskiöld an English edition also published in that year. Other editions in 1598, 1603, 1605 and 1607.

For note on first and other editions see v. 1–3.

Elaborately engraved title-pages to each part which are of same design as earlier editions but re-engraved.

Title-page of second part reads: *Histoire vniverselle des Indies Orientales. Diuisée en deux liures, faicte en latin par Antoine Magin. Nouuellement traduicte. Contenant la descouuerte, nauigation, situation & conqueste, faicte tant par les Portugais que par les Castillans. Ensemble leurs moeurs & religion. Seconde partie. à Dovay, F. Fabri, 1611.* Title page of third part reads: *La svite de l'histoire des Indes Orientales. De la conversion des Indiens. La troisieme partie. A Dovay, F. Fabry, 1611.*

Maps are the same as in earlier editions.

CONTENTS.

no. 1. Vtrivsqve hemispherii delinætio. [Wanting]
" 2. Chica sive Patagonica et Avstralis Terra. [Wanting]
" 3. Chili provincia amplissima.
" 4. Plata America provincia.
" 5. Brasilia.
" 6. Pervani regni descriptio.
" 7. Castilia avrifera cvm vicinis provinciis.
" 8. Residvvm continentis cvm adiocentibus insvlis.
" 9. Hispaniola insvla.
" 10. Cvba insvla et Iamaica.
" 11. Ivcatana regio et Fondvra.
" 12. Hispania Nova.
" 13. Granata Nova et California.
" 14. Limes occidentis Quiuira et Anian.

no. 15. Conibas regio cvm vicinis Gentibvs.
" 16. Florida et Apalche. [Wanting]
" 17. Norvmbega et Virginia. [Wanting]
" 18. Nova Francia et Canada.
" 19. Estotilandia et Laboratoris terra.
" [20] India Orientalis.—Iapaniæ regnvm.—Chinæ regnvm.—Insvlæ Philippinæ. [These four small maps usually appear on one double plate, but in this case they have been cut apart and are scattered through the text. "India Orientalis" has been misplaced and appears at the beginning of the first part.]

1789

English, The, pilot. Describing the West-India navigation, from Hudson's bay to the river Amazones. Particularly delineating the coasts, capes, headlands, rivers, bays, roads, havens, harbours, streights, rocks, sands, shoals, banks, depths of water, and anchorage, with all the islands therein; as Jamaica, Cuba, Hispaniola, Barbadoes, Antigua, Bermudas, Porto Rico, and the rest of the Caribbee and Bahama islands. Also a new description of Newfoundland, New England, New York, East and West New Jersey, Dellawar bay, Virginia, Maryland, Carolina, &c. Showing the courses and distances from one place to another; the ebbing and flowing of the sea, the setting of the tides and currents, &c. With many other things necessary to be known in navigation. The whole being much enlarged and corrected, with the additions of several new charts and descriptions. By the information of divers able navigators of our own and other nations. 66 (*i. e.* 68) pp., 20 maps, 6 maps in text. fol. London, for Mount & Davidson, 1789. 4460

NOTE.—Map no. 1, "A new and correct chart of the Western and Southern oceans," has border text pasted on both sides of the map.

CONTENTS.

no. [1] A new and correct chart of the Western and Southern oceans shewing the variations of the compass. According to the latest and best observations. [Without signature of Halley. See title 1157. Border text]
" [2] A new generall chart for the West Indies of E. Wright's projection vut. Mercators chart.
" [3] A new and accurate chart of the vast Atlantic or Western ocean, including the sea coast of Europe and Africa on the east, and the opposite coast of the continent of America, and the West India Islands on the west. By Eman: Bowen.
" [4] The harbour of Casco bay, and islands adjacent.
" [5] A new and correct chart of the coast of Newfoundland from Cape Raze to Cape Bonavista with Chebucto harbour in Nova Scotia. Insets: Chebucto harbour.—Trinity harbour.—St. John's harbour.
" [6] A chart of the south-east coast of Newfoundland.

English, The, pilot—Continued.

p. 18. Island of St. Peters.
no. [7] A map of the coast of New England from Staten island to the Island of Breton, as it was actualy [!] survey'd by capt. Cyprian Southack. Insets: The town of Boston in New England.—A chart of the Atlantic ocean shewing the situation of Nova Scotia with respect to the British Isles.
" [8] A chart of New York harbour with banks soundings and sailing marks from the most accurate surveys & observations.
" [9] Virginia, Maryland, Pennsilvania, East & West Jersey.
p. 25. Tobago Road.
" 26. Barbados.
no. [10] A draught of Virginia from the Capes to York in York river and to Kuiquotan or Hamton in James river by Mark Tiddeman.
p. 30. A large draft of the island Antegua.
no. [11] A new mapp of the island of St. Christophers being an actual survey taken by mr. Andrew Norwood, surveyr. genll. Insets: A new mapp of the island Martineca.—A new mapp of the island Guardalupa.
" [12] A draught of South Carolina and Georgia from Sewee to St. Estaca. By Andrew Hughes.
" [13] A correct chart of the Caribbee islands.
" [14] A correct chart of Hispaniola with the Windward Passage. By C. Price.
" [15] A draught of the west end of the island of Porto Rico and the island of Zachee.—A draught of Sam bay, on the south side of Hispaniola.—A draught of the island of Beata on the sough side of Hispaniola.—Platform bay on the south side of Cape Nicholas.—The west end of the island of Heneago.
" [16] A new & correct chart of Cuba, streights of Bahama, Windward Passage, the current through the gulf of Florida, with the soundings &c. By an officer in the navy. Inset: A plan of the harbour & town of Havana.
p. 44. A draught of the bay of Honda.
no. [17] A new and correct draught of the bay of Matanzas. By Robt. Pearson.
p. 50. Bermudas.
no. [18] A new and correct chart of the island of Jamaica.
" [19] A chart of the coast of Guayana, from the entrance of the river Orinoco to the entrance of the river Amazones. By R. Waddington. Insets: The river Orinoco, from the entrance thereof to St. Thomas's.—The river of Surinam and places adjacent.
" [20] A new and correct chart of the trading part of the West Indies.

1803

Luffman, J.

[Geographical principles. Maps] 9 col. maps. fol. [London, Booth, 1803] 4461

NOTE.—These maps are marked "Engrav'd for Luffman's Geographical principles," and "Publish'd may 1, 1803, by J. Luffman, no. 28, Little Bell alley, Coleman street, London."
The *London catalogue of books, 1800–1822*, published by William Brent, gives Luffman's *Geographical principles* issued by Booth.

1818-1823

Tanner, H. S.

A new american atlas containing maps of the several states of the North American union. eng. title, 2 p. l., [3], 18 pp., 18 col. maps on 22 l. fol. Philadelphia, H. S. Tanner, [1818]-1823. 4462

NOTE.—Copy 2. Issued in 5 pts. dated 1818-1823. Pts. I, II pub. by "Tanner, Vallance, Kearny & co., no. 10 Library street," 1818 and 1819 respectively; pt. III pub. by "Henry S. Tanner, no. 29 South Tenth street, 1821"; pt. IV by "H. S. Tanner, no. 8 Sansom street, 1822"; and pt. V by "Henry S. Tanner, no. 99 Walnut street, 1823."

Pt. I contains an announcement: "New and elegant American atlas now publishing by Tanner, Vallance, Kearny and co. engravers, Philadelphia," dated "July 10, 1818."

Pt. III has a notice "To the public" dated "January 1st. 1821." On the reverse of the back cover is a "List of maps and geographical works lately published and for sale by H. S. Tanner."

On the title-page below the date of imprint is the following: "Writing drawn and engraved by Joseph Perkins."

The maps of the world, South America, New York, America have the following imprint "Engraved & published by Tanner, Vallance, Kearny & co., Philadelphia"; in the other 1823 edition of this atlas in the Library of Congress, these maps have "Published by H. S. Tanner Philada."

Some of the maps differ from those in the other 1823 edition. On the map of South America, the title reads "South America and West Indies, 1818." The "Note" placed near the coast of French Guiana reads "The boundary line between the Spanish & Portuguese possessions is arranged agreably to the Treaties of St. Ildefonso in 1778 and that with France in 1815"—The lower right corner does not contain the inset diagram and table of "Comparative altitudes of the mountains, towns &c of South America" as shown in the other edition.

The map of New York contains in the lower left corner outside the border, "Constructed from materials furnished by J. H. Eddy esqr., of New York, and from the works of De Witt, Darby, Spafford, Lay, Smith, Bouchette & other authentic sources."—The "Boundary as fixed by the Commissioners under the 6th article of the Treaty of Ghent" shown in lake Ontario on the map of the 1823 ed., does not appear in this map.—The map also shows different county lines.

In the lower left corner of the map of Ohio & Indiana outside the border is the following: "Constructed from materials furnished by A. Bourne & S. Williams, esqrs. of Chillicothe; and from the works of De Ferrer, Ellicott, Volney, Darby, Brown, Drake, Cramer, Kilbourn &c. &c."—Shows also different land cession lines and boundaries; "Delaware's cession. 1818" and "Line of Pattawatima cession. 1818."

The map of Louisiana and Mississippi does not show the line of Chocktaw bounds as marked in the other edition.

Maps of pt. V. have in the lower right corner outside the border: "Engraved by H. S. Tanner & assistants."

CONTENTS.

Pt. I, no. [1] The world on Mercators projection.
" " [2] Europe.
" " [3] South America and West Indies. 1818.

Tanner, H. S.—Continued.

Pt. II. " [4] New York. 1819.
" " [5] Ohio and Indiana. 1819.
" " [6] America.
" " [7] Asia.
Pt. III. " [8] Map of the states of Maine, New Hampshire, Vermont, Massachusetts, Connecticut & Rhode Island. 1820.
" " [9] Virginia, Maryland and Delaware. 1820.
" " [10] Louisiana and Mississippi. 1820.
" " [11] Africa.
Pt. IV. " [12] A map of North America . . . 1822.
" V. " [13] Map of Pennsylvania and New Jersey. 1823.
" " [14] Kentucky, Tennessee and part of Illinois. 1823.
" " [15] Map of North & South Carolina. 1823.
" " [16] Georgia and Alabama. 1823.
" " [17] Illinois and Missouri. 1823.
" " [18] Map of Florida. 1823.—Inset: West part of Florida.

1819–1821

The new american atlas. pts. 1–3. fol. Philadelphia, Tanner. Vallance, Kearny & co. 1819–1821. 4463

NOTE.—Copy 3. Imperfect; pts. IV & V wanting. Cover-titles of the parts have same imprint as in copy 2.

The following maps differ from those in copies 1 & 2: "The world"—below the lower border are the following, in the center: "Published by H. S. Tanner, Philad[a]."; in the right corner: "Engraved by Tanner, Vallance, Kearny & co." South America has the title and imprint: "South America with improvements to 1821."—Below the lower border is the following: "Entered according to act of Congress, the 8th day of June 1818."—Engraved & published by H. S. Tanner, Philadelphia."

"New York" has the following imprint, below the lower border: "Constructed from materials furnished by J. H. Eddy of New York.—Engraved & published by H. S. Tanner, Philadelphia"—"Entered the 12th day of May, 1819."

Pt., I contains a circular-announcement entitled: *New and elegant american atlas* dated "July 10. 1818."

Pt., III has two pages of text entitled: "To the public."

CONTENTS.

Pt. 1, no. [1] The world on Mercators projection.
" " [2] Europe.
" " [3] South America with improvements to 1821.
Pt. 2, no. [4] New York. 1819.
" " [5] Ohio and Indiana. 1819.
" " [6] America.
" " [7] Asia.
" " [8] Map of the states of Maine, New Hampshire, Vermont, Massachusetts, Connecticut & Rhode Island. 1820.
" " [9] Virginia, Maryland, Delaware. 1820.
" " [10] Louisiana and Mississippi. 1820.
" " [11] Africa.

1823

Carey, H. C., & Lea, I.

A complete historical, chronological, and geographical american atlas, being a guide to the history of North and South America, and the West Indies: exhibiting an accurate account of the discovery, settlement, and progress of their various kingdoms, states, provinces, &c. Together with the wars, celebrated battles, and remarkable events, to the year 1822. According to the plan of Le Sage's [pseud. of M. J. A. E. D., comte de Las Cases] atlas, and intended as a companion to Lavoisne's improvement of that celebrated work. 3 p. l., [119] l. incl. 46 col. maps, 2 pl. fol. Philadelphia, H. C. Carey & I. Lea; London, J. Miller, 1823. 4464

NOTE.—The Library of Congress has another copy of this atlas without the "London, J. Miller" in the imprint. Both these copies contain the same maps. For contents see v. 3, title 3660a.

Maps have border text.

1907

Estrada, A., & cia.

Atlas general de las dos Américas publicado para el uso de los establecimientos de educacion de la república Argentina . . . Conteniendo 18 mapas y un indice de cada palabra contenida en el atlas. Construido y grabado por los s. s. W. & A. K. Johnston, ltd., de Edimburgo . . . 2 p. l., 9 [3] pp., 18 col. maps. sm. fol. Buenos Aires, A. Estrada & cia. 466 Bolivar, 1907. 4465

NORTH AMERICA.

HISTORICAL.

Hart, A. B.

Epoch maps illustrating American history . . . 3 p. l., 14 col. maps. obl. 16°. New York, Longmans, Green, & co. 1893. 4466

NOTE.—For contents see v. 1, title 1188.

HOTELS.

American hotel register co.

Leahy's hotel guide and railway distance maps of America . . . 126 [2] pp. incl. 63 maps. sm. fol. Chicago, American hotel register co. 1916. 4467

NOTE.—Maps on the reverse of covers.

The following notes on title-page: Established nearly half a century. Published semi-annually. Revised edition no. 27, august, 1916. Copyrighted august, 1916.

114882°—19——16

REPRODUCTIONS.

Hulbert, A. B.

The crown collection of photographs of american maps. From the colonial office library, London. Series III. fol. [1914–1916] 4468

NOTE.—The third series of the Crown collection consists of a set of maps on 250 sheets, with a table of contents on 10 pp., reproduced in London for Hulbert. The first 50 sheets were issued as v. 1, in 1914, the remainder at one time in 1916. There is no division into volumes. The numbering on the maps is continuous, and they are grouped according to locality.

Where size is given here, it is taken from Hulbert's table of contents.

CONTENTS.

no. 1. [Map of a portion of North America from the Great Lakes to the gulf of Mexico, and from the river Mississipi to the Atlantic ocean. About 75 miles to one inch. 1680] [The date signed to this map is incorrect. St. Denis' expedition in 1713 and his return route in 1716 are plainly given with the dates]

" 2–4. Same continued.

" 5. [A sketch of the confluance or streigts between Lakes Huron and Michigan, etc. 100 perches to 1 inch. [17–]]

" 6. Plan of the stockaid garrison of Michillimakinac, situate in latitude 45° 15′ northwest. Longitude from London, 84°. 80 feet to one inch.

" 7. A map describing the situation of the several nations of Indians between South Carolina and the Massisipi river; was copyed from a draught drawn and painted upon a deerskin by an Indian Cacique, and presented to Francis Nicholson, esq. governor. [1725]

" 8. Same continued.

" 9. [Map of a part of North America, showing proposed new western states. About 52 miles to 1 inch. [1790]]

" 10–12. Same continued.

" 13. [Map of North and South Carolina and Florida. 30 miles to 1 inch. 1715]

" 14–16. Same continued. Moll's map of New France evidently pasted on sheet no. 15.

" 17. [Map of Carolina. Showing the route of the forces sent in the years 1711, 1712, and 1713, from South Carolina to the relief of North Carolina, and in 1715 of the forces sent from North Carolina to the assistance of South Carolina, also showing the controverted bounds between Virginia and Carolina. About 15 miles to 1 inch. [1715]

" 18. Same continued.

" 19. Mapp of Beaufort in South Carolina. 1721. Five chain in an inch.

" 20. Same continued.

" 21. The ichonography or plann of the fortification of Charlestown and the streets, with the names of the bastions, quantity of acres of land, number of gunns and weight of their shott. By his excellency's faithful and obedient servant, John Herbert. October 27, 1721. A scale of ten chains 66 feet in a chain and two chains in an inch.

no. 22. This plan sheweth part of the southern boundary of the lands granted the 17th day of september anno dom̄ 1744 by his majesty King George the second to the right honourable John Lord Carteret now Earl Granville as the same was laid out and marked in the month of October anno dom̄ 1746 by Eleazer Allen, Matthew Rowan, William Forbes and George Gould esqrs. commissioners on the part of his majesty and Edward Moseley, James Hasell, George Moore and John Swann Esqrs commissioners on the part of the Earl Granville. Certified by us the tenth day of January anno dom̄ 1746. [Signed] J. Hawks. [North Carolina]

" 23-24. Same continued.

" 25. [Sketch map of the rivers Santee, Congaree, Wateree, Saludee, &c. with the road to the Cuttauboes. 1750]

" 26. Same continued.

" 27. [Map showing the indian country west of Carolina. By capt. George Haigh] 10 miles to 1 inch. 1751. [Certified as an exact copy by George Hunter, sur. genl.]

" 28-30. Same continued.

" 31. A map of the Catawba indian land surveyed agreeable to an agreement made with them by his majesty's governors of South Carolina, North Carolina, Georgia & Virginia and superintendent of indian affairs at a congress lately held at Augusta by his majesty's special command. Surveyed by order of his excellency Thomas Boone Esqr. Executed and certified by me this 22d day of February 1764. Saml. Wyly.

" 32-34. Same continued.

" 35. [A plan of the temporary boundary-line between the province of North and South Carolina, run agreeable to the instructions given us by his excellency Arthur Dobbs, esq. governor of North Carolina, and his honour William Bull, esq., lieut.-governor of South Carolina, and finished; as witness our hands this 24th september, 1764. Laid down by a scale one mile to an inch.— Ja. Moore, George Pawley, Saml. Wyly, Arthur Mackay, survrs.]

" 36-42. Same continued.

" 43. . . . Boundary line between the province of South Carolina, and the Cherokee indian country, [marked out] in presence of the headmen of the Upper Middle and Lower Cherokee Towns whose hands and seals are hereunder affixed which line is represented in the above deliniated plat. John Pickins, surveyor. Witness my hand at Fort Prince George this eighth day of may, 1766. Edward Wilkinson commiss.

" 44. Same continued.

" 45. Boundings of New Cambridge county in New England. Beginning at the middle part of the mouth or entrance of Connecticut in New England, and from thence to proceed along the coast of the sea to the Narragansets river, or harbour, there to be accounted sixty miles, and so up the western arme of the river to the head thereof, and unto the land north west ward till sixty miles be finished, and so to cross overland south west ward to meet with the end of sixty miles to be accounted from the mouth of Connecticutt up north west, and also all islands and isletts as well

Hulbert, A. B.—Continued.

in bayed as within five leagues distances from the premises and abutting upon the same or any part or parcel thereof. By M. C., 1697. [About 8 miles to 1 inch]

no. 46. Same continued.

" 47. [Sketch map (french) of the delta of the river Mississippi. About 18 miles to 1 inch. 1760?]

" 48–50. Same continued.

" 51. Plan and sections of the fort at Pensacola [!] 1763. Scale for the plan 230 feet [to 3 $\frac{3}{16}$ in.] [19 in. × 14 in.]

" 52. Same continued.

" 53. [Sketch of the castle of St. Augustin with ms. notes. 40 feet to 1 inch. 1763. 12½ in. × 8 in.]

" 54. [Map of part of East Florida from St. John's River to Bay of Mosquitos, showing names of proprietors of estates. Drawn from the originall plan of John Gordons, Esquire, given to Governor Grant. Jas. Moncrief, Engineer. 1 league to 1 inch. 1764. 40 in. × 15 in.]

" 55–57. Same continued.

" 58. Plan of Fort Picalata on St. John's River. Distance from St. Augustine seven leagues. [By James Moncrief. 20 feet to 1 inch. 1765. 11 in. × 9½ in.] Inset: Section.

" 59. A plan of the Fort and Harbour of Matanzas distant from St Augustine five leagues. Scale of 400 feet to an inch. [By James Moncrief. 400 feet to 1 inch. 1765. 19 in. × 12 in.] Inset: Sections.

" 60. Same continued.

" 61. Plan of the Harbour of Musquitos distant from St Augustine 72 miles. [By James Moncrief. 200 yards to 1 inch. 1765. 22 in. × 17 in.]

" 62. Same continued.

" 63. Plans Elevation and Section of one of the Blockhouses proposed for the Defence of the Town of Pensacola. Scale of 10 feet to an inch. [1765. 18 in. × 16 in.]

" 64. Same continued.

" 65. Estimate of one of the proposed Block Houses for defence of the Town of Panzacola.

" 66. Plan of the New Town of Panzacola. E. Durnford. Scale to the Plan 200 Feet to an Inch.

" 67–68. Same continued.

" 69. Sketch of part of the coast of East Florida from St Augustine to the Bay of Musquitos. [By James Moncrief. 3 miles to 1 inch. 1765. 28 in. × 8 in.]

" 70. Same continued.

" 71. [Sketch map of the river Iberville. 3 miles to 1 inch. 1765. 30 in. × 21 in.]

" 72. Same continued.

" 73. [Chart of Pensacola bay. 2 inches to 1 mile. 1765? 30 in. × 21 in.]

" 74–75. Same continued.

" 76. Scetch shewing the kings ground at St Augustine. [By W. Brasier. 1765? 36 in. × 14½ in.]

" 77–78. Same continued.

no. 79. A Plan of the City, Harbour, Fortifications and Environs of Saint Augustine. Scale one Mile to an Inch. [1765? 14 in. × 10 in.]

" 80. A Sketch of the Harbours near Cape Florida. Inset text: Some Account of the Harbours &c. [1765? 17 in. × 12 in.]

" 81. Scetch of the City and Environs of St Augustine. [1 mile to 1 inch. 1765? 16 in. × 9½ in.]

" 82. Plan of Fort Rosalia [or Natches, on the River Missisippi. 150 feet to 1 inch. 1765? 16 in. × 12 in.]

" 83. A Draught of the River Mobile. [From Mobile to Tombeché. 2 miles to 1 inch. 1765? 70 in. × 12 in.]

" 84–87. Same continued.

" 88. Scetch of the bay of Pensecola. [About 2½ miles to 1 inch. 1765? 17 in. × 9 in.]

" 89. [Plan of Fort Tombeckbee. 100 feet to 1 inch. 1765? 17 in. × 15 in.]

" 90. A Plan of the Bar and Entrance of the Harbour of Mobille. W. Brasier. [1 mile to 1 inch. 1766. 14 in. × 10 in.]

" 91. Field Survey of the River Mobile and part of the Rivers Alabama and Tensa, with the different Settlements . . . [Surveyed by Elias Durnford, engineer. 1 mile to 1 inch. 1770? 48 in. × 14 in.]

" 92–94. Same continued.

" 95. Reference to the Land surveyed on the Rivers Mobile and Alabama since the Establishment of the Civil Government in the Province of West Florida.

" 96. Plan of the Castle & Barr at Matansas. [400 feet to 1 inch. 1770? 17 in. × 11 in.] Inset: Plan Sections and Elevations of the Castle.

" 97. Plan of the River Mississippi from the River Yasons to the River Ibberville in West Florida . . . Scale 4 Miles to an Inch. [Showing lands granted and names of proprietors. By Elias Durnford. 1771. 48 in. × 14 in.]

" 98–100. Same continued.

" 101. [Sketch map of part of the Rivers Iberville, Amit, and Comit. By Elias Durnford, engineer] Scale 800 Feet to an Inch. [1771? 108 in. × 16 in.]

" 102–107. Same continued.

" 108. A Map of the road from Pensacola in Wt Florida to St Augustine in East Florida. From a Survey made by Order of the late Hon. Col. John Stuart, Esq. His Majesty's Superintendt of Indian Affairs Southern District in 1778. By Joseph Purcell.—General Remarks on the Roads or Paths.—Itinerary Along the Roads from Pensacola toward St. Augustine. [4 miles to 1 inch. 98 in. × 28 in.]

" 109–115. Same continued.

" 116. Chactaw Lands ceded to His Majesty by the Chactaws, [from the north boundary of West Florida on the Yazo river to the river Pasca Ocoola, in two sheets] Certified at Pensacola this 24th day of June 1779. By Joseph Purcell Surveyor. [1½ miles to 1 inch. 98 in. × 24 in.]

" 117–120. Same continued.

" 121. [Second sheet of same. 90 in. × 23 in.]

" 122–125. Same continued.

Hulbert, A. B.—Continued.

no. 126. [Spanish map of part of East Florida. 1 spanish league to 1 inch. 1785? 40 in. × 15 in.]

" 127–128. Same continued.

" 129. [Spanish map of a portion of the inland parts of East Florida. 1785? 24 in. × 18 in.]

" 130. Same continued.

" 131. [Spanish map of Bahia de Tampa. 3½ spanish leagues to 1 inch. 1785? 11 in. × 10 in.]

" 132. A Plan of King George's Fort at Allatamaha South Carolina. Latitude 31°, 12. North. [1722. 11 in. × 8 in.]

" 133. [Plan of Fort King George and part of the Alatamaha river. With] An Abstract of the Journall of the Voyage from Fort King George in South Carrolina to St. Simons Island & Barr in the Elizabeth Sloop Capt Sollard, Commander. [1722. 22 in. × 17 in.]

" 134. Same continued.

" 135. The Ishnography or Plan of Fort King George. By a scale of twenty feet in an Inch. [1722. 18 in. × 11 in.] Inset: The profil of the ffort King George by a scale of ten feet in an Inch.

" 136. Same continued.

" 137. [Sketch plan of Fort King George in Georgia] A Scale of Feet of 32 to an Inch. [1722? 22 in. × 18 in.]

" 138. A Plan of the Town of Charlottenbourg. [16½ perches to 1 inch. 1735? 17 in. × 12 in.]

" 139. [Projects and profiles for Savana, Ft. Hardwicke and Ft. Frederica, in Georgia. By William de Brahm. 300 feet to 1 inch. 1755. 19 in. × 11 in.]

" 140. Same continued.

" 141. A Map of Georgia and Florida. Taken from the latest & most Accurate Surveys Delineated & drawn by a Scale of 69 English Miles to a Degree of Latitude by Thomas Wright. 1763. [About 19 miles to 1 inch. 37 in. × 16 in.]

" 142–143. Same continued.

" 144. . . . Sketch of the Boundary Line as it is now mark'd, between the afforesaid province and the Creek Indian Nation Is most humbly Dedicated by his Excellencys Most obedient Serv't Saml Savery D. Surveyor. A Scale of Twenty one English Miles, Four in one inch. 1769. [55 in. × 14 in.]

" 145–147. Same continued.

" 148. Carte composée des differens ouvrages des Messieurs les Ingenieurs qui out été a la Louisiane, avec les renvois alphabetiques de chaque partie. [About 15 miles to 1 inch. 1750. 38 in. × 24 in.]

" 149–151. Same continued.

" 152. Partie de la Carte a grands points. [Sketch plan of part of the coast of Louisiana. About 9 miles to 1 inch. 1750? 38 in. × 24 in.]

" 153. Same continued.

" 154. Saco River and Winter Harbour. Anno 1699. [About 1⅓ miles to 1 inch. 17 in. × 11 in.]

" 155. Saco Fort. 1699. Inset: The Prospect of Saco Fort. 1699. [17 feet to 1 in. 22 in. × 16 in.]

" 156. Same continued.

no. 157. Casco-bay. Anno 1699. [1⅓ miles to 1 inch. 20 in. × 14 in.]
" 158. Same continued.
" 159. [Plan of the old fort of Pemaquid and the proposed new fort] 1699. [About 19 feet to 1 inch. 28 in. × 20 in.]
" 160. Same continued.
" 161. [A draught of the land about Pemaquid river. 17—. 22 in. × 14 in.]
" 162. Same continued.
" 163. [A part of the above map on a larger scale. 17—. 27 in. × 20 in.]
" 164. Falmouth old Fort. [1700? 20 feet to 1 in. 17 in. × 10 in.]
" 165. Pemaquid Fort in the Province of Main in America. Latitude 43° 55. J. Redknap, 1705. [20 feet to 1 inch. 22 in. × 17½ in.]
" 166. Profile of Pemaquid Fort. [8 feet to 1 inch. 20 in. × 14 in.]
" 167. Casco Bay Fort in the Province of Main in America. Latitude 44° 00. J. Redknap. 1705. [About 45 feet to 1 inch. 22 in. × 18 in.]
" 168. A Survey for six Townships on the east side of the River Penobscot in the territory of Sagadehock in New England. 1763. [1 mile to 1 in. 29 in. × 21 in.]
" 169. Same continued.
" 170. A Draught of a Rout from Fort Pownall on Penobscot River by way of Piscataquess River, Lake Sabin, Wolf River, and the River Chaudiere, to Quebec, and back again to Fort Pownall, by Penobscot River. Taken by order of His Excellency Francis Bernard, Esq. Governor &c. of His Majesty's Province of the Massachusetts Bay in New England, 1764. [4 miles to 1 inch. 46 in. × 30 in.]
" 171. Same continued.
" 172. A Plan of seven Townships laid out on the East Side of Mount Desert River in the Territory of Sagadehock. 1764. [1 mile to 1 inch. 43 in. x 18 in.]
" 173–174. Same continued.
" 175. A Plan of the Bay and River of Penobscot & the Islands lying therein commonly called the Fox Islands and the Sea Coast on the East side thereof so far as 13 Township have been lately laid out also of part of the Passage from Penobscot to Quebec by two different routs; also of the Bay of S^t^. Croix & a Passage from thence thro' the west branch of the River Passimaquoddy & by the River Passadamkee to Penobscot; also of a Passage from Penobscot thro' the River Sebesticoke to Fort Halifax on the River Kennebec; also of a Road cut from Fort Pownall to S^t^. George's Fort being the utmost extreamity of the Settlem̃ts in Sagadehock west-ward of Penobscot. All which were Surveyed by order of his Excellency Francis Bernard Esq. Governor and the General Court of the Province of the Massachusetts Bay, In the Year 1764 excepting the 13 Townships which were Surveyed by the same order in the Year 1762 & 1763. To which's added part of the passage of Lieutenant Montresor between Quebec and Fort Halifax by two different Routs made in the Year 1761 and the Sea Coast on the west side of Penobscot taken from an actual Survey. [1764. 4 miles to 1 inch. 42 in. x 25 in.]
" 176–178. Same continued.

Hulbert, A. B.—Continued.

no. 179. [Map of a portion of the Province of Maine showing Pine Forrests. Received from Mr. Scammell, October 2, 1772. 4 miles to 1 inch. 30 in. x 23 in.]

" 180–182. Same continued.

" 183. [Map of Maryland showing division of the Province into Counties. [10 miles to 1 inch. 1700? 21 in. x 20 in.]

" 184. Same continued.

" 185. The Draught of Castle Island in ye Bay of Boston in America. 1699. [100 feet to 1 inch. 22 in. x 17 in.]

" 186. [The Profiels belonging to Castle Island in the Massachusetts Bay in America. 1699. 10 feet to 1 inch. 22 in. x 16 in.]

" 187. Same continued.

" 188. Salem Fort in the province of the Massachusetts Bay in America. Latitude 42° 40′. Novr. 1705. J. Redknap. [125 feet to 1 inch. 18 in. x 11 in.]

" 189. The South Battery In the Town of Boston In the Province of the Massachusetts Bay in America. Latitude 42—25. [By J. Redknap, November, 1705. 10 feet to 1 inch. 22 in. x 17 in.]

" 190. Same continued.

" 191. The North Battery in the Town of Boston in ye province of the Massachusetts Bay in America. Latitude 42—25. J. Redknap, 1705. [About 40 feet to 1 inch. 22 in. x 17 in.]

" 192. Same continued.

" 193. Marblehead Fort in the province of the Massachsetts Bay in America. Latitude 42—34. [By J. Redknap, 1705. 11 feet to 1 inch. 22 in. x 17 in.]

" 194. Same continued.

" 195. This Plan describes the Northern Boundary Line of the Province of Massachusetts Bay in New England as it is called in his Majesties Royall Order for running the Same, extending from Three Miles due North of Pentucket Falls, in Merrimack River on a Course West allowing Ten degrees Variation till it comes to Hudson's River, with the Remarkable Mountains, Hills, Rivers, Streams, ponds etc. that fell in or near the course, taken by the Direction of his Excellency Jonathan Belcher Esqr. Governour of Said Province, to whom it is Humbly Dedicated by . . . Richard Hazzen. Haverhill, May ye 8th 1741. [3 miles to 1 inch. 53 in. x 10 in.]

" 196–198. Same continued.

" 199. A Plan of the Sea Coast from Little Rocks near Hampton to Normans Woe near Cape Anne including Cape Anne, Ipswich, Newbury and Hampton Harbors. Surveyed By Messrs. James Grant & Thos. Wheeler, Deputy Surveyors of Lands for the Northern District of North America. Under the Directions of Samuel Holland Esqr. . . . Drawn by Charles Blaskowitz. [1760. ¾ mile to 1 inch. 36 in. x 24 in.]

" 200–202. Same continued.

" 203. [Sketch map of New England. 14 miles to 1 inch. 17—. 19 in. x 14 in.]

" 204. Same continued [2nd Portion].

" 205. [Sketch map of New England and part of Nova Scotia. With] Explanation of the Letters, Marks, and Cyphers used in this Map. [17—. 18 in. x 14 in.]

no. 206. Same continued.

" 207. The Fort upon Great Island in Piscataqua River. 1699.—An explanation on the prospect draft of Fort William & Mary on Piscataqua River in the Province of Neu-Hampshir on the continent of Ameri. [1699. 22 in. x 8½ in.]

" 208. [Sketch map of Great Island or New Castle Island, showing plan of Town and Fort, etc.] 1699. [About 180 yards to 1 inch. 28 in. x 20 in.]

" 209. Same continued.

" 210. [Fort William and Mary upon Newcastle Island att the Entrance of Piscataqua River in the Province of Novo Hampshire. Latitude 43° 30′. By J. Dudley. 55 feet to 1 inch. 1699. 20 in. x 16 in.]

" 211. Same continued.

" 212. A Plan of Piscataqua Harbour. 2000 feet to 1 inch. [17—? 21 in. x 17 in.]

" 213. Same continued.

" 214. A Survey of Piscataqua Riv. by I. B. [About 1¼ inches to 1 mile. 1700? 28 in. x 26 in.]

" 215. Same continued.

" 216. The Profil upon the Pickt lyne G. H. belonging to the Fort Willm & Mary in Piscataqua River, America, 1705. [13 feet to 1 inch. 14 in. x 6½ in.]

" 217. [A map of Piscataqua River in New England, 1708. 1 mile to 1 inch. 25 in. x 17 in.]

" 218. Same continued.

" 219. A Draught of that part of the Province of New Hampshire Lying to the eastward of the River accatuckenuck that coms out of Winnipissiokee pond or Lake and the River Pimegawasset and Other Rivers that Empty themselves out att merrimack. Drawn by James Jeffry. May 2, 1720. [2 miles to 1 inch. 36 in. x 23 in.]

" 220–222. Same continued.

" 223. [Sketch Map of New Hampshire divided into Townships] June 5, 1730, Rec^d. from Col. Dunbar, with his Letter to the Secr^y. dated at Boston 2^d May, 1730. [3 miles to 1 inch. 23 in. x 18 in.]

" 224. Same continued.

" 225. A Map of the River Merrimack from the Atlantick Ocean to Pantuckett Falls describing Bounds between His Maj^ts. Province of New Hampshire & the Massachusetts Bay agreeable to His Maj^ts. Order in Council, 1741. To His Excellency Benning Wentworth Esqr. . . . inscribed By . . . Geo. Mitchell, Surv^t. [1 mile to 1 inch. 28 in. x 20 in.]

" 226. Same continued.

" 227. Province of New Hampshire, May 22, 1741. Mr. Walter Bryent personally appeared before me and made oath that this is a true and exact Plan of part of one of the divisional boundaries between His Majestys Provinces of New Hampshire & the Massachusets Bay, Made by him according to the best of his skil and remarks. Sworn Before Rich^d. Waldron, J^t. Peace.

" 228. Same continued.

Hulbert, A. B.—Continued.

no. 229. A Plan of His Maiestys Province of New Hampshire collected from Surveys made by Persons appointed to run Boundary Lines agreeable to His Majestys determination in Council Describing the principal Townships Granted by the Said Province and the Massachusetts Bay. By Order of His Excellency Benning Wentworth Esq[r]. . . . By Geo. Mitchell. This was Copy'd from a Plan sent over by Governor Wentworth to Capt[n]. Thomlinson, who communicated it to the Board, August . . . 1745. [4 miles to 1 inch. 30 in. x 21 in.]

" 230–232. Same continued.

" 233. [The first design of a stone Fort for the plan of Albany in America] Profiel upon the pickt Line i. k. of the old Fort called the Fort of Orange in the City of Albany. [20 feet to 1 inch. 1675? 22 in. x 17 in.]

" 234. Same continued.

" 235. [The second design of a stone Fort in the city of Albany in America. 20 feet to 1 inch. 1675. 28 in. x 20 in.]

" 236. Same continued.

" 237. [Plan de la Vile d'Albanie dans la Province de la Nouvelle Yorck en Amerique. 175 feet to 1 inch. 1677. 22 in. x 17 in.]

" 238. Same continued.

" 239. [Plan of parts of New York and New Hampshire, showing Land grants and the boundary between New Hampshire and Massachusets. 6 miles to 1 inch. 1680? 29 in. x 24 in.]

" 240–242. Same continued.

" 243. [Chart of the Port of New York and of the surrounding country. About 1½ miles to 1 inch. 1690? 27 in. x 19 in.]

" 244. Same continued.

" 245. [Plan of Schenectady Town in the Province of New York in America. About 180 feet to 1 inch. 1695? 22 in. x 17 in.]

" 246. Same continued.

" 247. [A Map of the Province of New Yorke in America and the Territorys Adjacent. By Augustin Graham, Survey. Generall. 10 miles to 1 inch. 1698? 38 in. x 28 in.]

" 248–250. Same continued.

VIEWS.

1829

Hall, B.

Forty etchings, from sketches made with the camera lucida, in North America, in 1827 and 1828 . . . 1 p. l., ii pp., 21 l. 20 pl., fold. map. 4°. Edinburgh [etc.] Cadell & co. [etc.] 1829. 4469

Note.—Two etchings to the page, with descriptive text opposite each.
All views marked, "Drawn with the camera lucida by capt[n]. B. Hall. Engraved by W. H. Lizars."

CONTENTS.

Map of the United States and Canada shewing capt[n]. Hall's route through those countries in 1827 & 1828. Engraved on steel by W. H. Lizars (frontispiece)

no. 1. Niagara from below.

" 2. Niagara from above.

no. 3. Niagara on the American side.
" 4. General view of Niagara Falls.
" 5. Bridge across the rapids at Niagara.
" 6. Bridge across Lake Cayuga.
" 7. Buffalo on Lake Erie.
" 8. The river Niagara flowing into Lake Ontario.
" 9. Newly cleared land in America.
" 10. The village of Rochester.
" 11. View from Mount Holyoke in Massachusetts.
" 12. Western end of the Great Erie canal.
" 13. Canadian voyageurs of captn Franklin's canoe.
" 14. Mississagua indians in Canada.
" 15. The river St. Lawrence below Quebec.
" 16. Village of Peterborough in upper Canada.
" 17. Bridge across the Congaree in South Carolina.
" 18. Frame work of the bridge across the Congaree.
" 19. Rice fields in South Carolina.
" 20. Two drivers and a backwoodsman with his rifle.
" 21. Village of Riceborough in the state of Georgia.
" 22. Log house in the forests of Georgia.
" 23. Pine barren of the southern states.
" 24. American forest on fire.
" 25. Swamp plantation on the banks of the Altamaha.
" 26. Embryo town of Columbus on the Chatahoochie.
" 27. A family group in the interior of the state of Georgia.
" 28. Chiefs of the nation, & a Georgian squatter.
" 29. The Balize at the mouth of the Mississippi.
" 30. The Mississippi at New Orleans.
" 31. The Mississippi overflowing its banks.
" 32. Wooding station on the Mississippi.
" 33. Steam boat on the Mississippi.
" 34. An Ohio steam boat on the Mississippi.
" 35. Shipping-port on the Ohio in Kentucky.
" 36. Backwoodsmen and steam boat pilot.
" 37. Island of logs on the Missouri.
" 38. Banks of the Missouri falling in.
" 39. Prairie at the confluence of the Missouri & Mississippi.
" 40. American stage coach.

1848

Warre, H. J.

Sketches in North America and the Oregon territory. 2 p. l., 5 pp., 1 map. 8 pl. fol. [London] Dickinson & co. [1848] 4470

NOTE.—In the text, 20 sketches are specified. 10 wanting in this copy; of these 6 are contained in another copy.

CONTENTS.

no. [1] Buffalo hunting on the W. prairies.
" [2] Forcing a passage through the burning prairie.
" [3] Distant view of the Rocky mountains.
" [4] Fort Garry.

Warre, H. J.—Continued.

no. [5] Falls of the Kamanis Taquoih river.
" [6] The Rocky mountains.
" [7] Source of the Columbia river.
" [8] Fort Vancouver.
" [9] Indian tomb.
" [10] Les Dalles Columbia river.
" [11] [Map showing the route traveled]

1848

Sketches in North America and the Oregon Territory. 2 p. l., 5 pp., 13 col. pl. on 11 l., 1 map. fol. [London] Dickinson & co. [1848] 4471

NOTE.—Dedication, second prelim. leaf, wanting.
20 "sketches" are specified in the text. 7 wanting in L. C. copy; of these, 3 are in another copy in L. C.: Buffalo hunting on the w. prairies—Forcing a passage through a burning prairie—The Rocky Mountains.

CONTENTS.

no. [1] Les Dalles Columbia river.
" [2] Fort Vancouver.
" [3] Indian Tomb.
" [4] Mount Hood from Les Dalles.
" [5] Fort Garry.
" [6] Valley of the Willamette river.
" [7] The american village.
" [8] Distant view of the Rocky mountains.
" [9] Source of the Columbia river.
" [10] Falls of the Kamanis Taquoih river.
" [11] Fall of the Peloos river.
" [12] Fort George formerly Astoria.
" [13] McGillivray or Kootoonai river.
" [14] [Map of the route traveled]

GENERAL

1761

Pownall, T.

Six remarkable views in the provinces of New-York, New-Jersey, and Pennsylvania, in North America. Sketched on the spot by his excellency governor Pownall; painted by mr. Paul Sandby; and engraved by mess. Sandby, Elliot, Benazech, &c. . . . 1 p. l., 6 pl. obl. fol. London, T. Jefferys [1761] 4472

NOTE.—Type-written title page of the original, which is wanting.

CONTENTS.

no. [1] A view in Hudson's river of the entrance of what is called the Topan Sea.—Vue sur la rivière d'Hudson, de l'entrée counue sous le nom de mer de Topan.
" [2] A view of the falls on the Passaick, or second river in the province of New Jersey.—Vue de l'cataracte du Passaick, ou seconde rivière, dans la province du Nouveau-Jersey.
" [3] A view in Hudson's river of Pakepsey & the Catts-Kill mountains, from Sopos island in Hudson's river.—Vuè sur la rivière d'Hudson dans Pakepsey et des montagnes de Catts-Kill, prise de l'isle de Sopos, située dans cette rivière.
" [4] A view of the great Cohoes falls, on the Mohawk river.—Vue de la grande cataracte de Cohoes, sur la rivière des Mohawks.
" [5] A view of Bethlem, [!] the great Moravian settlement in the province of Pennsylvania.—Vue de Bethlem, principal éstablissement des frères Moraves dans la province de Pennsylvania.
" [6] A design to represent the beginning and completion of an American settlement or farm.—Dessein qui représente la manière d'établir et de parachever une habitation ou ferme américaine.

1774–1781

The Atlantic Neptune, published for the use of the royal navy of Great Britain, by Joseph F. W. Des Barres . . . under the directions of the right hon'ble, the lords commissioners of the admiralty. 5 l., [68] maps, [8] pl. fol. [London, 1774–1781] 4473

NOTE.—Copy no. 15. Contains leaves giving general remarks and tables.

No. 37a, showing Cardigan bay and Bear harbour, not contained in any other edition of the Library of Congress.

No. 56 shows a colored view of the entrance to Boston harbour, without date.

No. 64 gives a colored view of New York, with the entrance of the North and East rivers, 1777.

CONTENTS.

no. [1] The coast of Nova Scotia, New England, New York, New Jersey, the gulph and river of St. Lawrence. The islands of Newfoundland, Cape Breton, St. John, Antecosty, Sable, &c. 1780.
" [2] A chart of Nova Scotia.
" [3] [Isle of Sable]
" [4] A view of the east end of the Isle Sable.—The eastern end of the Isle Sable [View]—A view taken from the south side of the n. e. barr.—A view taken from the ridge of the n. e. barr.—A view of the north shore of the Isle Sable. [Colored]
" [4a] Remarks on the Isle Sable.
" [5] The south west coast of the peninsula of Nova Scotia. 1776.
" [6] The south east coast of Nova Scotia. 1776.
" [7] Barrington bay.
" [8] Port Amherst. Port Haldimand. 1775.
" [9] Port Campbell. 1776.
" [10] Port Mills. Port Mansfield. Gambier harbour. 1776.
" [11] Liverpool bay. 1779.
" [12] Port Jackson. 1777.

The Atlantic Neptune—Continued.

no. [13] Kings bay. Lunenburg. 1776.
" [14] Cape Prospect.—The high lands of Haspotagoen.—The Ovens.—Cape Sable. Cape Sable. [Views]
" [15] Mecklenburgh bay. 1776.
" [16] Charlotte bay. 1776.
" [17] Leith harbour. Prospect harbour. Bristol bay. Sambro harbour. 1775. Inset view: Hopsons nose.
" [18] Halifax harbour.—Appearance of the shore at three miles off [Colored]—4 miles off shore.—Sambro light-house [Colored]—Sambro light-house.—Chebucto head [Colored] 1777. [Views]
" [19] Halifax harbour.—Catch harbour. Inset views: Light house.—Chebucto head.—Citadel hill.
" [20] Egmont harbour. [Two inset views]
" [21] Cape Egmont and Winter rock.—Entrance of Egmont harbor.—Entrance of Keppel harbor.—Falls of Hinchinbroke river.—Entrance into Chisetcooke inlet.—Dartmouth shore in the harbor of Halifax. [Views]
" [22] Knowles harbour. Tangier harbour. Keppell harbour. Saunder's harbour. Deane harbour. Inset views: Entrance of Keppel harbour.—Cape Southampton.
" [23] Spry harbour. Port Pallisser. Port North. Port Parker. Beaver harbour. Fleming river. 1776. Inset view: Cape Spry.—Beaver isles.—Pegasus Wing.
" [24] White islands harbour. Port Stephen's. Siscomb harbour. Houlton harbour River St. Mary. 1776.
" [25] Sandwich bay. 1776.
" [26] [Torbay] 1775. Inset view: Berry head & White head island.
" [27] [Canso harbor, Port George, Glasscow harbor, &c.] 1775. Inset: View of Port George.
" [28] White haven. Port Howe. 1774. [Inset view]
" [29] Crow harbor. Philip inlet. [Inset view]
" [30] Milford haven. [Inset view]
" [31] The Gut of Canso.
" [32] A chart of Cape Breton and St. John's islands, &c.
" [33] [St. Peters bay, Lenox passage, Bay of Rocks] Inset: View of Cape Round.
" [34] The south east coast of Cape Breton island surveyed. By Samuel Holland. 1779.
" [35] A chart of the n. e. coast of Cape Breton island, from Cape Ann bay to Cape Morien.
" [36] Port Hood. 1776.
" [37] The south east coast of the island of St John surveyed. By Saml. Holland. 1780.
" [37a] [Cardigan bay, Bear harbour, &c.]
" [38] Frederick bay. Ramsheg harbour. Pictou harbour. Port Luttrell.
" [39] Port Shediack. Cocagne.
" [40] The harbours of Rishibucto & Buctush. 1778.
" [41] [Miramichi bay] 1777.
" [42] [Bay of Chaleurs, Mall bay, Gaspey bay, &c.] 1777.
" [43] [Bay and harbour of the Seven islands] 1778.
" [44] [River St. Lawrence up to Quebec] 1781.
" [45] The Magdalen-isles in the gulph of St Lawrence. 1778.

no. [46] Annapolis Royal. St. Mary's bay. 1776. Inset: View of Guliver's hole.
" [47] The Isthmus of Nova Scotia. 1777.
" [48] River St. John. 1780. Inset view: The entrance of the river St. John.
" [49] The Wolves.—Grand-Manan island.—Shore westward of St. John's river. [Views]
" [50] [Grand bay of Passamaquody, St. Croix river, Copscook, Deer island, &c.]
" [50a] [Grand-Manan island]
" [51] The coast of New England. 1776.
" [52] [Moose harbour, Mechias bay, Chandler river, Gouldsborough bay, &c. 1776.
" [53] [Falmouth harbour, Portland sound, &c.]
" [54] [Wells bay, Piscataqua harbour, &c.] 1776.
" [55] [Boston harbour, Nachant bay, Nantasket road, Broad sound, &c.] 1775.
" [56] Boston, seen between Castle William and Governors island.—High lands of Agameticus.—Boston bay. [Views] The entrance of Boston harbor. [Colored view]
" [57] [Plymouth bay]
" [58] [Nantucket island, part of Martha's Vineyard, &c.] 1776.
" [59] [Buzzards bay, Elizabeth islands, Vineyard sound, &c.] 1776.
" [60] Cape Poge.—Sandy Point. [Views] Gay Head. [Colored view] Gay Head.—Sankoty Head. [Views] Sankoty Head. [Colored view]
" [61] A chart of the harbour of Rhode Island and Narraganset bay. 1776.
" [62] A chart of the coast of New York, New Jersey, Pensilvania, Maryland, Virginia, North Carolina, &c. 1780.
" [63] A chart of New York harbour, composed from surveys of lieutenants John Knight, John Hunter. Inset views: Bond Hollow.—Mount Pleasant.
" [64] Highland of Neversunk.—South shore of Long Island. [Views] New York and the entrance of the North and East rivers.—Light house on Sandy hook.—The Narrows. [Colored views] 1777.
" [65] Oyster bay and Huntington. Huntington bay. Inset: Hell Gate.
" [66] A chart of Delaware bay, with soundings. By Capt. sir Andrew Snape Hammond. 1779.
" [67] A chart of the Delaware river from Bombay hook to Ridley creek, with soundings . . . by Lt. Knight. 1779.—A plan of the Delaware river from Chester to Philadelphia. By Lieutenant John Hunter. 1777.
" [68] The harbour of Charles Town in South Carolina from the surveys of Sr. Jas. Wallace. 1777. [Inset view]
" [69] Port Royal in South Carolina. 1777.
" [70] The coasts, rivers and inlets of the province of Georgia, surveyed by Joseph Avery. 1780.
" [71] A plan of the harbour of St. Augustin in the province of Georgia [Florida]
" [72] [The north east shore of the gulph of Mexico]
" [73] A chart of the bay and harbour of Pensacola in the province of West Florida. 1780.
" [74] [Gulph of Mexico from Pensacola to Apelousa river]

1775-1780

The Atlantic Neptune, published for the use of the royal navy of Great Britain, by Joseph F. W. Des Barres, under the directions of the right hon'ble the lords commissioners of the admiralty. v. 3. fol. [London, 1775-1780] 4474

NOTE.—Copy no. 16. Volume 1 & 2 wanting.
Index sheet for pt. II. which belongs to v. 2, in v. 3. Table of contents for v. 3 is missing.

CONTENTS.

v. 3, no. 1. The coast of Nova Scotia, New England, New York, Jersey, the gulph and river of St. Lawrence. 1778. Publish'd . . . 1777.
" " 2. The coast of New England. 1776. [Inserted]
" " 3. [Coast from Moose harbr. to Gouldsborough] 1776.
" " 4. [Coast from Moose Point to Frenchmans bay] 1776. [Inserted]
" " 5. [Frenchmans bay.—Mount Desart island] 1776. [Inserted]
" " 6-7. [Belfast bay.—Penobscot bay.—Isle Haut bay.—Great Blue Hill bay] 1776. [Inserted]
" " 8. [Coast from Penmaquid point to Seal harbour] 1776. [Inserted]
" " 9. [Coast from Portland sound to Rogers bay] 1776. [Inserted]
" " 10. [Coast from Cape Elizabeth to Moose pt.] 1776. [Inserted]
" " 11. [Falmouth harbour]
" " 12. [Piscataqua harbour] 1779.
" " 13. [Coast from Newbury harbour to Cape Elizabeth] 1776. [Inserted]
" " 14. [Coast from Marblehead harb. to Hampton harbor] 1776.
" " 15. [Massachusetts bay] 1776. [Inserted]
" " 16. [Part of Martha's Vineyard.—Nantucket island] 1776. [Inserted]
" " 17. [Boston bay. Inserted]
" " 18. A chart of the harbour of Boston, composed from different surveys in 1769, by mr. George Callendar. 1775.
" " 19. [Plymouth bay]
" " 20. [Coast from Nantucket island to Rhode Island]
" " 21. [Coast of Long Island from Yellow hook to Cow harbour] [Inserted]
" " 22. [Buzzards bay.—The Elizabeth islands.—Vineyard sound] 1776.
" " 23. A chart of the harbour of Rhode Island & Narraganset bay. 1776.
" " 24. A chart of the coast of New York, New Jersey, Pensilvania, Maryland, Virginia, North Carolina, etc. with soundings & nautical remarks from lt. Jno. Knight. 1780.
" " 25. Hell gate.—Oyster bay and Huntington.—Huntington bay.
" " 26. [Coast of Connecticut.—Gardner's bay] 1779.
" " 27. A chart of Delawar bay, with soundings and nautical observations taken by capt. sir Andrew Snape Hammond. 1779.
" " 28. A chart of Delawar river from Bombay hook to Ridley creek, with soundings &c taken by lt. Knight. 1779.—A plan of Delawar river from Chester to Philadelphia. Shewing the situation of his majesty's ships &c. on the 15th. novr. 1777. By lieutenant John Hunter.
" " 29. A sketch of the operations before Charlestown the capital of South Carolina. Inset: [Charlestown harbour] [Inserted]
" " 30. The harbour of Charles Town in South Carolina from the surveys of sr. Jas. Wallace. 1777. Inset: Colored view.

v. 3, no. 31. [The north east shore of the gulph of Mexico] 1780.
" " 32. A chart of the bay and harbour of Pensacola. Surveyed by George Gould. 1780.
" " 33. A plan of the town of Newport. 1776. [Inserted]
" " 34. A chart of Port Royal and Kingston harbours, in the island of Jamaica.

1792

Norman, J.

The american pilot containing the navigation of the sea coast of North America, from the streights of Belle-Isle to Cayenne, including the island and banks of Newfoundland, the West-India islands, and all the islands on the coast. With particular directions for sailing to, and entering the principal harbours, rivers, etc. Describing also the capes, head lands, rivers, bays, roads, harbours, straits, rocks, sands, shoals, banks, depths of water, and anchorage. Shewing the courses and distances from one place to another, the ebbing of the sea, the setting of the tides and currents, with many other things necessary to be know [!] in navigation. Likewise, necessary directions for those who are not fully acquainted with the use of charts ... 2 p. l., 11 maps. fol. Boston, J. Norman, 1792. 4474a

CONTENTS.

no. [1] A chart of Nantucket shoals surveyed by capt. Paul Pinkham. 1791.
" [2] A new chart of the sea coast from the island of Cyenne [!] to the river Poumaron. By Osgood Carleton.
" [3] A new general chart of the West Indies . . . 1789.
" [4] A chart of South Carolina and Georgia. Inset: A chart of the bar and harbour of Charles Town.
" [5] Chart of the coast of America from Cape Hateras to Cape Roman, from the actual surveys of Dl. Dunbibine, esq.
" [6] A chart from New York to Whimble shoals.
" [7] Chart from New York to Timber island including Nantucket shoals.
" [8] [Coast of Maine]
" [9] [Bay of Fundy]
" [10] [Streights of Belle Isle]
" [11] A chart of the Banks of Newfoundland. 1785.

1794

Norman, J.

The american pilot containing the navigation of the sea coast of North America, from the streights of Belle-Isle to Cayenne, including the island and banks of Newfoundland, the West India islands, and all the islands on the coast, with particular directions for sailing to, and entering the principal harbours, rivers, &c. Describing also the capes, headlands, rivers, bays, roads, havens, harbours, straits, rocks, sand shoals, banks, depths of water, and anchorage. Shewing the courses and distances from one place to

Norman, J.—Continued.

another, the ebbing of the sea, the settling of the tides and currents, &c. With many other things necessary to be known in navigation. Likewise necessary directions for those who are not fully acquainted with the use of charts . . . 2 p. l., 11 maps. fol. Boston, J. Norman, 1794. 4475

NOTE.—A similar atlas with practically the same title-page was issued in 1798 and 1803 by William Norman. The title was changed to read, "from the streights of Belle Isle to Essequebo," and the date of the "Certificate" is 1794. See v. 1, title 1217.

Though usually spoken of as an american, John Norman, was an englishman who came to America some time previous to 1774. An advertisement of his business appeared in the Pennsylvania Journal, may 11, 1774. He first established himself in Philadelphia and then in Boston.

See also title 4477.

A "Certificate" on the title-page is signed by Osgood Carleton, and dated september 10th, 1791.

CONTENTS.

no. [1] A chart of Nantucket shoals surveyed by capt. Paul Pinkham. 1791.
" [2] A new chart of the sea coast from the island of Cyenne [!] to the river Poumaron. By Osgood Carleton.
" [3] A new general chart of the West Indies. 1789.
" [4] A chart of South Carolina and Georgia. Inset: A chart of the bar and harbour of Charles Town.
" [5] Chart of the coast of America from Cape Hateras to Cape Roman, from the actual surveys of Dl. Dunbibine, Esq.
" [6] A chart from New York to Whimble shoals.
" [7] Chart from New York to Timber island including Nantucket shoals.
" [8] [Coast of Maine]
" [9] [Bay of Fundy]
" [10] [Streights of Belle Isle]
" [11] A chart of the Banks of Newfoundland.

1799

North American, The, pilot. The first part of the North American pilot, for Newfoundland, Labradore, and the gulf and river St. Lawrence: being a collection of sixty-one accurate charts and plans, drawn from original surveys: taken by captain James Cook and Michael Lane, surveyor, Joseph Gilbert, and other experienced officers in the king's service . . . Chiefly engraved by the late Thomas Jefferys . . . New ed. 3 p. l., 23 maps on 25 sheets. fol. London, R. Laurie & J. Whittle, 1799. 4476

NOTE.—For other editions see v. 1, titles 1209, 1236.

CONTENTS.

no. 1. A general chart of the island of Newfoundland. By James Cook and Michael Lane and others. 1794.
" 2. A chart of the Banks of Newfoundland, drawn from a great number of hydrographical surveys, chiefly from those of Chabert, Cook and Fleurieu. 1794.

no. 3. A chart of the south-east part of Newfoundland, containing the bays of Placentia, St. Mary, Trepassey and Conception. 1794.

" 3a. A new survey of Trinity harbour in Newfoundland, communicated by our worthy friend Francis Owen. 1801.

" 4. Trinity harbour.—Carboniere and Grace harbours.—St. Johns harbour.—Cape Broyle harbour, Ferryland harbour, Aquafort harbour, Fermouse harbour. 1794.

" 4a. A chart of St. John's harbour in Newfoundland, surveyed in october 1798, by Francis Owen. 1799.

" 5. The harbour of Trepassey with Mutton and Biscay bays.—The road and harbour of Placentia. By James Cook.—St. Mary's harbour. T. Jefferys sculp. 1794.

" 5a. A chart of the road and harbour of Great Placentia, in Newfoundland. Surveyed in august 1800 by Francis Owen. 1801.

" 6. A chart of part of the south coast of Newfoundland. By James Cook. Insets: Port aux Basque.—St. Peters island. 1763.—Great Jervis harbour.—Harbour Briton.—Harbour of St. Lawrence.

" 7. A new chart of the coast of Nova Scotia with the south coast of New Brunswick. By capt. Holland. 1798.—Insets: Plan of river St. John.—Plan of Port Roseway harbour.—Plan of the entrance or harbour of river St. John.

" 8. The island of Sable. 1794.

" 9. The harbour of Halifax in Nova Scotia; by Thomas Backhouse. 1798.

" 10. A plan of Port Dauphin on the eastern side of Cape Breton Island. Surveyed in 1743.—A plan of Murgain or Cow Bay. Surveyed in august 1760.—A draught of the Gut of Canso. Surveyed by the king's ships in 1761.

" 11. A chart of the Gulf of St. Laurence. 1794.

" 12. A chart of the Magdalen islands in the Gulf of St. Lawrence surveyed in 1765. 1794.

" 13. A map of the island of St. John. Improved from the late survey of captain Holland. 1794. Inset: Gulf of St. Laurence.—A list of lots and proprietor names.

" 14. A plan of Chaleurs bay. Surveyed by his majesty's ship Norwich in 1760. 1794.

" 15. A plan of Ristigouche harbour in Chaleur bay. Surveyed in 1760, by the king's ship Norwich. 1794.

" 16. A chart of the west coast of Newfoundland, Labradore &c. &c. By James Cook. 1794. Insets: A plan of Hawkes harbour, Port Saunders and Keppel harbour.

" 17. A chart of the straights of Bellisle, taken in 1766, by James Cook and by Michael Lane in 1769. 1794. Insets: Bradore harbour.—Red bay.—York or Chateaux bay.—Quirpon harbour.—Croque harbour.

" 18. A chart of part of the coast of Labradore, from the straights of Bell Isle to Cape Bluff. Surveyed by Joseph Gilbert in 1767. And engraved by Thomas Jefferys. Insets: Petty harbour.—The three harbours of Sophia, Charlotte and Mecklenburg.

" 19. A chart of part of the coast of Labradore, from Grand Point to Shecatica. Surveyed by Michael Lane in 1768, and engraved by Thomas Jefferys. Insets: Plan of Mecatina harbour.—Plan of St. Augustine.—Plan of Cumberland harbour.

North American, The, pilot—Continued.

no. 20-22. A new chart of the river St. Laurence, from the island of Anticosti to the Falls of Richelieu. Taken by order of Charles Saunders, commander in chief of his majesty's ships in the expedition against Quebec in 1759. Engraved by Thomas Jefferys. 1794. Parokett island.—Mingan harbour.—Gaspee bay.—Harve S. Nicholas by Desjardins.—Bay of the Seven islands.—Pointe aux Allouettes or Larks Point.

1803

Norman, W.

The American pilot: containing the navigation of the seacoast of North-America, from the streights of Belle-Isle to Essequibo, including the island and banks of Newfoundland, the West-India islands, and all the islands on the coast. With particular directions for sailing to, and entering the principal harbours, rivers, &c. Describing also the capes, headlands, rivers, bays, roads, havens, harbours, straits, rocks, sands, shoals, banks, depths of water, and anchorage. Shewing the courses and distances from one place to another, the ebbing of the sea, the setting of the tides and currents, &c. With many other things necessary to be known in navigation. Likewise, necessary directions for those who are not fully acquainted with the use of charts . . . 4 p. l., 11 maps. fol. Boston, W. Norman, 1803. 4477

NOTE.—"Certificate," on title-page signed by Osgood Carleton, dated sept. 10th, 1794.

A list of publications issued by William Norman pasted on the reverse of the front cover.

See also title 4475.

CONTENTS.

no. [1] A chart of Nantucket Shoals surveyed by cap^t. Paul Pinkham. 1791.

" [2] A new general chart of the West Indies from the latest marine journals and surveys. 1789.

" [3] A chart of South Carolina and Georgia. Inset: A chart of the bar and harbour of Charlestown.

" [4] Chart of the coast of America from Cape Hateras to Cape Roman from the actual surveys of D^l. Dunbibin esq^r.

" [5] A new and accurate chart of the bay of Chesapeak including Delaware bay with all the shoals, channels, islands, entrances, soundings, & sailing marks as far as the navigable part of the rivers Patowmack Patapsco & N East. Drawn from several draughts made by the most experienced navigators chiefly from those of Anthony Smith.

" [6] Chart from New York to Timber Island including Nantucket shoals. From the latest surveys.

" [7] A chart of the coast of New England from the south shoal to Cape Sable including Georges Bank. From Holland's actual surveys. Inset: A plan of Boston harbour.

" [8] A chart of the coast of America from Wood Island to Good Harbour. From Hollands surveys.

no. [9] [A chart of the coast of Nova Scotia from Port Haldimand to Forked harbour]
" [10] A chart of the streights of Bell Isle.
" [11] A chart of the banks and part of the coast of Newfoundland including the islands of Sable and Cape Breton. From actual surveys of Jos: F. W. Des Barres esq[r].

1810

Randle, C.

83 drawings in manuscript. 37 maps, 46 col. pl. sm. fol. [1810]
4477a

Note.—A series of maps and water color views many of which are dated 1810 and are signed C. Randle.
The title as it appears above, is written on a slip and pasted on the outside cover. On the inside of the cover is written, "Drawings by cap[n]. Charles Randle. T. W. brother in law who died 1833, may 29—aged 84."

CONTENTS.

no. a. [Map of the coast of the United States from Virginia to Georgia]
" 1. View of Hamstead Heath.
" 2. Porchester castle.
" 3. Mamhead.
" 4. A scetch [!] of the New England armed vessels in Valcure bay on Lake Champlain . . . 11th october 1776.
" 5. A scetch [!] of his majestys armed vessels on Lake Champlain october 11th 1776.
" 6. Stamford bridge Yorkshire.
" 7. New Inn Undercliff Isle of Wight.
" 8. Carnarvon castle.
" 9. Newsteads Nottingham shire.
" 10. Pont Aberglass Llyn.
" 11. Crapstone near Reborough down Devonshire.
" 12. Wemburry Church near Yealm river Devon.
" 13–15. Views of the lands &c. in New England taken in the years 1772 a 1776.
" 16. SSE view of Boston lighthouse as in 1775.
" 17. View of Piscataque lighthouse from Kitterie point.
" 18. View of Kitterie point from Piscataque lighthouse . . . taken in 1775.
" 19. Nova Scotia &c.
" 20. Gulph of S[t]. Lawrence &c.
" 21. Charlotte Town. I. S[t]. Iohns as taken in 1773.
" 22–24. Gulph S[t]. Lawrence.
" 25. Gulph & river S[t]. Lawrence.
" 26–27. River S[t]. Lawrence.
" 28. Piscataqua river. Inset: Isle of Shoals.
" 29. Cape Ann.
" 30. Mount Desart island.
" 31. Roach rocks & chapel—Cornwall.
" 32. Isle of Sables.
" 33. Bay of Fundy.
" 34. Passamquiddi bay.

Randle, C.—Continued.

no. 35. Bay of Gaspee.
" 36. Cape Cod.
" 37. Rhode Island.
" 38. New England coast from Block Island to Passamaquiddi.
" 39. Gulf of Saint Lawrence.
" 40. View of Quebec.
" 41. River S^t. Lawrence. Inset: Seven Island bay.
" 42. Scetch [!] of the river Saint Lawrence from Quebec to Lake Ontario. Inset: [Ticonderago to Crownpoint].
" 43. Island of Saint Johns.
" 44. Tinmouth castle.
" 45. Lady Darce at Lee in Kent.
" 46. Island of Anticosti.
" 47. Cape Breton island. Inset: Bryon I. [and] Bird islands.
" 48. [Boston Harbor].
" 49. Magellan islands.
" 50. West Cowes—Isle of Wight.
" 51. Halifax harbor.
" 52. Penobscott river.
" 53. Scetch [!] of Falmouth harbor.—Isle Bic.
" 54. View of Snowden hill.
" 55. Port Royal Harbor in the island of Jaimaca.
" 56. Scetch [!] of Port l'Ioy or Hillsbrough harbor on the South side of the island of S^t. Johns.—1773.—Rough scetch [!] of Poictou harbor.—1774. Inset: Poictou island.
" 57. Port Royal harbor in South Carolina.
" 58. View at Taltrum—Devonshire.
" 59. Entrance to Cape Fear harbor.
" 60. View of Algers.
" 61. Island of Newfoundland.
" 62. Mitchel Grove park. Sussex.
" 63. Canterbury cathedral.
" 64. Mouths of the Mississippi. from a plan in the 1760.
" 65. View at Hoo near Cat Water Plymouth.
" 66. Scetch [!] of Florida from an old map of 1760.
" 67. View near Barnett.
" 68. Scetch [!] of the harbor of the Havanna.
" 69. Lake Superior, Lake Huron, Lake Michigan.
" 70. Isle of Montreal.
" 71. Tunbridge priory.
" 72. Quebec.
" 73. Goree.—[Map of] C. Verde.
" 74. Lake Ontario.
" 75. Fancy.
" 76. Jasmine from the cape of Good Hope.
" 77. Hatswell Sommersett.
" 78. Monte Video. 1811.
" 79. Rio de la Plata.
" 80. [Coast of Oaxaca state, Mexico] Inset: La Vera Cruz.—[Coast of Vera Cruz state, Mexico].
" 81. [Sketch] 1811.
" 82. [Sketch] 1811.
" 83. Island of Bourbon formerly Mascarenhas. From an old map of 1762.

1914

Philip, G., & son.

Philip's comparative wall atlas of North America. Edited by J. F. Umstead . . . & E. G. R. Taylor . . . 8 col. fold. maps, 41¼ x 33½ each. Scale 1:9,000,000. fol. London, G. Philip & son, 1914. 4478

NOTE.—Accompanied by *Explanatory handbook, North America. cover-title, 20 pp. 8° London, G. Philip & son, 1914.*

CONTENTS.

no. [1] Climate, summer conditions.
" [2] Climate, winter conditions.
" [3] Density of population.
" [4] Economic.
" [5] Natural vegetation.
" [6] Political divisions.
" [7] Relief of land & communications.
" [8] Temperature.

CANADA.

LAKES AND RIVERS.

Canada. *Geological survey.*

Plans of various lakes and rivers between Lake Huron & the river Ottawa, to accompany the geological reports of Canada, for 1853-54-55-56. 2 p. l. 22 maps. fol. Toronto, J. Lovell, 1857. 4479

GENERAL.

1760

Smyth, H.

[Views of the most remarkable places in the gulf and river of St. Lawrence. Drawn on the spot by captain Hervey Smyth, aid du camp to the late genl. Wolfe] 7 views, 12¼ x 19½ each. obl. fol. [London, T. Jeffreys, 1760] 4480

NOTE.—Five of the set of six views drawn by captain Smyth with english and french titles, also two other views by him.

The first view of the set of six entitled, "A view of the city of Quebec," carries the dedication: "To the right honourable William Pitt, one of his majesties most honourable privy council & principal Secretary of state. These six views of the most remarkable places in the gulf and river St. Laurence are most humbly inscribed by his most humble servant Hervey Smyth. Aid du camp to the late gen[l]. Wolfe."

The sixth view belonging to this series, which is wanting, is a view entitled, "A view of Pierced Island, a remarkable rock in the gulf of St. Lawrence."

Of the two additional views, the one entitled, "A view of the landing place," etc., is "Inscrib'd to the right hon[ble]. field marshal lord viscount Ligonier,"

Smyth, H.—Continued.

and the other, "A view of Quebec from the Bason," was published by T. Bowles.

Captain Hervey Smyth, afterwards Sir Hervey, entered the army in 1753, and retired in 1769. He made a number of sketches of Quebec in 1759. The sketches in this series were engraved by Paul Sandby, 1725–1809, Pierre Charles Canot, b. ca. 1710, William Elliot, 1727–1766, Peter Mazell and P. Benazech. For information concerning these men, see Bryan's *Dictionary of painters and engravers.*

"A view of the fall of Montmorenci," "A view of the landing place above Quebec," "A view of Cape Rouge," are all reproduced in Doughty's *The siege of Quebec and the battle of the plains of Abraham.*

CONTENTS.

no. 1. A view of the city ot Quebec, the capital of Canada, taken partly from Pointe des Peres, and partly on board the Vanguard man of war.
" 2. A view of the fall of Montmorenci and the attack made by general Wolfe. july 31, 1759.
" 3. A view of Cape Rouge or Carouge, nine miles above the city of Quebec.
" 4. A view of Gaspe bay, in the gulf of St. Laurence.
" 5. A view of Miramichi, a french settlement in the gulf of St. Laurence. (The above maps all marked, "Drawn on the spot")
" 6. A view of the landing place above the town of Quebec describing the assault of the enemys post, on the banks of the river St. Lawrence, with a distant view of the action between the british & french armys, on the Hauteurs d'Abraham, sep^{br}. 13th. 1759.
" 7. A view of Quebec from the Bason.

1876

Walling, H. F.

Tackabury's atlas of the dominion of Canada. With general descriptions by T. Sterry Hunt, Robert Bell, A. R. C. Selwyn, & others . . . Drawn, compiled and edited by H. F. Walling . . . 276 pp., incl. 52 maps. fol. Montreal, London, G. M. Tackabury, 1876. 4481

NOTE.—Plans of Hamilton, Kingston, London, Montreal, Ottawa, Quebec, Toronto.

Picture of Parliament buildings, Ottawa, on title-page.

1881

Macdonald, D.

Illustrated atlas of the dominion of Canada, containing maps of all the provinces, the north-west territories and the island of Newfoundland. From the latest official surveys and plans, by permission of the general and provincial government, together with a general descriptive history &c. Also maps of Europe, Asia, Africa, North and South America, United States, Oceanica, the world, &c., &c., and local maps prepared under the direction of D. Macdonald . . . 2 p. l., liii, viii, 107 (*i. e.* 136), [4] pp. incl. 30 col. maps, plates, ports. fol. Toronto, Ont., H. Parsell & co. 1881. 4482

1914

Canada. *Department of agriculture.*

Atlas of Canada, issued under the direction of hon. Martin Burrell, minister of agriculture. cover-title, 68 pp. incl. 12 maps, illus. 4°. Ottawa, Can. 1914. 4483

PROVINCES.

ONTARIO.

Postal.

Canada. *Post-office department.*

Postal map of the province of Ontario with adjacent counties of the province of Quebec. Published by authority of the honorable the post master general. Le f. Ans. Maingy, draughtsman. I. Dewe, chief post office inspector. Scale six miles to one inch. 1 p. l., 1 map on 6 sheets. fol. Ottawa, 1883. 4484

Note.—Photo lith. by the Burland lith. co., Montreal.
Title on sheet no. 1 of map.

Cities.

TORONTO.

1884

Goad, C. E.

Atlas of the city of Toronto and suburbs. From special survey and registered plans showing all buildings and lot numbers. 163 pp., 40 pl. fol. Montreal, Toronto, C. E. Goad, 1884. 4485

Note.—Blank verso of plates have been pasted together.

1890

Atlas of the city of Toronto and vicinity. From special survey founded on registered plans and showing all buildings and lot numbers. 2nd ed. . . . 3 p. l., 50 maps. fol. London, Montreal, [etc.] 1890. 4486

Miscellaneous.

Lake of the Woods.

International joint commission (U. S. and Canada) 1909.

Atlas to accompany Report to International joint commission relating to official reference re Lake of the Woods levels. By Adolph F. Meyer, Arthur V. White, consulting engineers. 2 p. l., 42 col. maps. obl. fol. Ottawa, Government printing department, 1915. 4487

Note.—At head of title: International joint commission.

QUEBEC.

Postal.

Canada. *Post-office department.*

Postal map of the province of Ontario with adjacent counties of the province of Quebec. Published by authority of the honorable the post master general Le F. Ans. Maingy, draughtsman. I. Dewe, chief post office inspector. Scale six miles to one inch. 1 p. l., 1 map on 6 sheets. fol. Ottawa, 1883. 4488

NOTE.—Photo lith. by the Burland ligh. co., Montreal.
Title on sheet no. 1 of map.

Postal map of the province of Quebec, shewing post offices, money order offices, p. o. savings banks, telegraph stations, and mail routes in operation on 1st january, 1880; also, railways, canals and principal rivers together with the intermediate distances between post offices. Published by order of the honorable the post master general. 3 p. l., 11 maps. fol. [Ottawa] 1880. 4489

NOTE.—Photo lith. by the Burland lith. co., Montreal.

NEWFOUNDLAND.

MARITIME.

Cook, J., Lane, M., *& others.*

Le pilote de Terre-neuve, ou, recueil de plans des côtes et des ports de cette île. Pour l'usage des vaisseaux du roi, et des navires de commerce destinés à la pêche. D'après les plans levés par mm. James Cook et Michael Lane . . . Précédé de deux cartes réduites, l'une de Terre-neuve avec les bancs et côtes voisines, l'autre de cette île en particulier; dressées sur les mêmes plans et assujetties aux observations astronomiques de mm. m^is^. de Chabert en 1750 et 1751, J. Cook et autres officiers anglois en 1766, le m^is^. de Verdun, le ch^er^. de Borda et Pingré en 1772. Publié par ordre du roi, au dépôt général des cartes, plans et journaux de la marine. Sous le ministère de m. le maréchal de Castries, comte d'Alais . . . 1784. 1 p. l., 12 (*i. e.* 14) maps. fol. [Paris] 1784. 4490

NOTE.—See also v. 1, title 1254.

CONTENTS.

no. 1. Carte réduite des bancs et de l'île de Terre-neuve, avec les côtes du golfe de S^t^. Laurent et de l'Acadie. 1784.
" 2. Carte réduite de l'île de Terre-neuve. 1784.
" 3. Plan des côtes de Terre-neuve: 1ère. feuille.—Contenant la partie méridionale depuis le cap de Raze jusqu'au cap du Chapeau-Rouge. 1784. Insets: Havre de Plaisance.—Havre de S^t^. Marie.—Havre des Trépassés.—Havres de S^t^. Laurent.—Havres de Burin.

no. 4. 2e. feuille.—Contenant la partie méridionale depuis le cap du Chapeau Rouge jusqu'aux îles de Burgeo, avec les îles de St. Pierre et Miquelon. 1784. Insets: Havre du Grand Jervis.—Havre Breton.

" 5. 3e. feuille.—Contenant la partie méridionale depuis les îles de Burgeo jusqu'au cap de Raye, avec l'entrée du golfe de St. Laurent comprise entre ce cap et le cap de Nord de l'île Royale. 1784. Inset: Port aux Basques.

" 6. 4e. feuille.—Contenant la partie occidentale depuis le cap de Raye jusqu'au cap de St. Grégoire. 1784. Inset: Plan des havres d'York et de Lark dans la baye des Iles.

" 7. 5e. feuille.—Contenant la partie occidentale depuis le cap de St. Grégoire jusqu'à la pointe de Ferolle. 1784. Inset: Plan du havre de Hawke, du port de Saunder et du havre de Keppel.

" 8. 6e. feuille.—Contenant la partie septentrionale, depuis la pointe de Ferolle jusqu'à l'île de Quirpon, avec le Détroit de Bell'-ile et les côtes de Labrador, situées sur ce détroit. 1784. Insets: Havre de Labrador.—Red bay ou baye Rouge.—Baye des Châteaux ou d'York.—Vieux Férolle.

" 9. 7e. feuille.—Contenant la partie orientale depuis l'île de Quirpon jusques au cap de St. Jean, vulgairement appellée le Petit Nord. 1784. Insets: Havre de Quirpon et baye de Griguet.—Havre de Croc.—Supplément ou fond de la baye Blanche.

" [10] Carte particulière des îles de St. Pierre et de Miquelon, levée par m. Fortin. 1782.

" 11. Plan de l'île de Saint Pierre au sud de Terre-neuve, levé par le sr. Fortin. 1763.

" 11 (*i. e.* 12) Plan des côtes de Terre-neuve: 9e. feuille.—Contenant la partie orientale. 1792. Insets: Plans particuliers des havres d'Aquafort et Fermouse.—Des havres du cap Broyle et Ferryland.—De Bulss-bay et Witless-bay.

" 12 (*i. e.* 13) Plan de la baye de St. Lunaire à la côte du nord-est de Terre-neuve, par m. de Granchain. 1785.

" 12 (*i. e.* 14) Carte de l'île de Fogo à la côte orientale de Terre-neuve. 1785. Insets: Plan du Port-Fogo.—Plan de Shoal-bay.

UNITED STATES.

AGRICULTURE.

United States. *Department of agriculture. Office of farm management.*

Atlas of american agriculture. Prepared under the supervision of O. E. Baker, agriculturist. pt. 5, The crops, section A, Cotton, by O. C. Stine . . . and O. E. Baker . . . 28 pp. incl. 74 maps, 24 diagrs. fol. Washington, Govt. print. office, 1918.

[Advance sheets 4. Issued december 15, 1918] 4491

NOTE.—At head of title: United States. Department of Agriculture. Office of farm management. W. J. Spillman, chief.

The title-page contains a list of the men engaged on the different subjects pertaining to this atlas as follows: Principal commercial types—O. F. Cook.—Geography of production—H. D. Smith, Hugh H. Bennett.—Economics and methods of production—A. G. Smith.—History of production—L. C. Gray.—Marketing and distribution—Fred Taylor.

BOUNDARY.

International boundary commission. *United States and Mexico,* 1893–

Proceedings of the International (water) boundary commission, United States and Mexico, treaties of 1884 and 1889. Equitable distribution of the waters of the Rio Grande. United States section. Anson Mills, brig. gen. U. S. A., retired, commissioner. W. W. Follett, consulting engineer. W. W. Keblinger, secretary. 2 v. plates, double maps. fol. Washington, govt. print. off. 1903. 4492

NOTE.—Paged continuously. English and spanish.

CONTENTS.

Extracts from treaties of 1848, 1854, 1884 and 1889.
Rules of the commission, etc.
The Brownsville and Matamoros jetties.
Defensive works on the Rio Grande at Brownsville, Texas, and Matamoros, Tamaulipas.
Eagle Pass bridges.
Bridges connecting Laredo, Texas, and Nuevo Laredo, Tamaulipas.
El Chamizal.
La isla de San Elizario.
Cattle seizure.
Obstructions opposite Columbia.
Construction of jetties and fences.
Obstructions under El Paso street-car bridge, etc.
Protest against jetties in violation of treaties, etc.
"El banco de Camargo," and others, on the lower Rio Grande.
Elimination of bancos on the Rio Grande.
Equitable distribution of the waters of the Rio Grande.
Construction of an international dam on the Rio Grande.
Protest of mexican citizens against the construction of dams by the Rio Grande dam and irrigation company.
Testimony submitted to the committee on foreign affairs on bill (H. R. 9710. 56th Cong., 1st sess.) to provide for the equitable distribution of the waters of the Rio Grande.
Measurement of flow of the Rio Grande and tributaries.
Report of the investigation of the diversion of water from the Colorado River in the State of California.
Index.
Index to names.

CLIMATIC.

United States. *Department of Agriculture. Weather bureau.*

Climatic charts of the United States . . . Prepared under the direction of Willis L. Moore . . . 1 p. l., 26 maps. fol. Washington, weather bureau, 1904.
[W. B. no. 301] 4493

CONTENTS.

pt. 1. Six Washington daily weather maps, for the dates february 1 to 6,
" 1903 inclusive showing the movement of a typical storm with full explanation of symbols, etc.
" 2. Five charts, normal precipitation.
" 3. Three charts, normal sunshine.
" 4. Three charts, normal barometric pressure.
" 5. Three charts, normal temperature of the air at the surface of the earth.
" 6. Six charts, temperature.

COAL DISTRIBUTION.

Rand, McNally & co.

Rand McNally atlas of the zonal system of bituminous coal distribution as ordered by the United States fuel administration and director general of railroads . . . 15 pp. incl. 14 col. maps. sm. fol. Chicago, New York, Rand, McNally & co. [1918] 4494

NOTE.—Letterpress on reverse of front cover.

COMMERCIAL.

Blum's commercial map publishing co., inc.

Blum's commercial atlas. 1918–1919 edition. 70 [1] l., incl. 34 maps. fol. New York, Blum's commercial map publishing co., inc. [1918] 4495

NOTE.—Index on title page.

Rand, McNally & co.

Rand, McNally & co.'s commercial atlas of America. Containing large-scale maps of all the states in the United States and of its outlying possessions, of the provinces of the Dominion of Canada, of Newfoundland, the republic of Mexico, Central America, Panama, Bermuda, the West Indies, Cuba, Polar regions, and various other useful maps; also large continental maps of North America, South America, Europe, Africa, Asia, and Oceana, and a new map of South America in four sections including complete and revised indices . . . 1 p. l., lii, 448 pp. incl. 126 col. maps, diagrs. fol. Chicago, Rand, McNally & co. 1918. 4496

NOTE.—At head of title, 49th edition. 1st edition published 1911.

Contains list of railroads, steamship lines, postal information, travel distance table, and diagram showing American tariff from 1791 to 1916.

Maps of the following cities: Boston.—New York, Brooklyn and Jersey City.—Buffalo.—Philadelphia.—Pittsburgh.—Baltimore.—Washington.—Louisville.—Cincinnati.—Cleveland.—Toledo.—Indianapolis.—Chicago.—Detroit.—Milwaukee.—Minneapolis.—St. Paul.—St. Louis.—Kansas City.—New Orleans.—San Francisco.—Montreal.—Toronto.

COTTON.

Price, T. H.

Atlas of the cotton-producing states, and production by counties; with history and statistics of the cotton trade . . . 1 p. l., 79 pp. 11 maps. fol. New York, T. H. Price, 1902. 4497

DIPLOMATIC.

Hawes, J. B.

[Maps showing the consular and diplomatic offices of the United States. Drawn by J. B. Hawes] 8 maps. fol. [Washington? dept. of state? 189-?] 4498

NOTE.—These maps have many places entered in manuscript.

EXPLORATIONS.

Lewis, M., *and* **Clark, W.**

Atlas accompanying the original journals of the Lewis and Clark expedition, 1804–1806, being facsimile reproductions of maps chiefly by William Clark, illustrating the route of the expedition, with sights of camping places and indian villages, besides much miscellaneous data. Now for the first time published, from the original manuscripts in the possession of mrs. Julia Clark Voorhis and miss Eleanor Glasgow Voorhis, together with a modern map of the route prepared especially for this volume. Edited, with introduction, by Reuben Gold Thwaites . . . v. 8, xvi, pp. 54 (*i. e.* 56) maps on 62 fold. sheets. 8°. New York, Dodd, Mead & co. 1905. 4499

CONTENTS.

no. 1. The upper Mississippi, lower Ohio, and lower Missouri rivers. Evidently copied from a contemporary french manuscript map.

" 2. "A topogr[aphical] sketch of the Missouri and upper Mississippi, exhibiting the various nations and tribes of indians who inhabit the country. Copied from the original spanish ms. map."

" 3. The upper Mississippi system, and the Missouri system as far as the Mandans.

" 4. The neighborhood of Camp River Dubois, 1803–04.

" 5. The Missouri, from St. Charles to Isle au Parish, showing route from may 21–about june 20, 1804.

" 6. The Missouri, in South Dakota, from Mud island (Isle au Vase) on the south, to Elk island (Isle au Biche) on the north, route from september 10–23, 1804.

" 7. The Missouri from just below Antelope creek to about the northern limit of Sully county, South Dakota. The route is shown from september 24–october 2, 1804.

" 8. The Missouri, about forty miles above the mouth of Cheyenne river. The route is shown for october 2–5, 1804.

" 9. The region of the Arikara villages, on the Missouri—the route for october 7–15, 1804.

" 10. The Missouri in North Dakota, from about the point where it enters that state from South Dakota to just below the site of Bismarck—the route for october 15–21, 1804.

No. 11. The Missouri, in the neighborhood of Fort Mandan.
" 12. Trail from the Mandans to the Yellowstone.
" 13. From the Mandans to the Rockies.
" 14, pts. 1-3. Sketch of the Missouri from Fort Mandan to the Rocky mountains—"from the 7th april to the 15th july, 1805."
" 15. The Missouri from Fort Mandan to above Goose Egg lake—the route of april 7-13, 1805.
" 16. The Missouri from Goose creek to White Earth river—the route of april 13-22, 1805.
" 17. The Missouri from White Earth river to twenty miles above Martha's river, showing the mouth of the Yellowstone—the route of april 21-30, 1805.
" 18. The Missouri from Martha's river to just below Milk river—the route of april 30-may 7, 1805.
" 19. The Missouri from below Milk river to Pine creek—the route from may 7-12, 1805.
" 20. The Missouri from Pine creek to just below Musselshell river—the route of may 12-19, 1805.
" 21. The Missouri from below Musselshell river to South Mountain creek—the route of may 19-24, 1805.
" 22a. Junction of the [Mussel] Shell and the Missouri, may 20, 1805.
" 23. The Missouri from South Mountain creek to Judith's river—the route of may 24-28.
" 24. The Missouri from Judith's river to Maria's river, may 29-june 11, 1805.
" 25. The Missouri from the entrance of Maria's river to the Great Falls, showing camping places for june 11-29, 1805.
" 26. Junction of Missouri and Medicine [Sun] rivers.
" 26a. Sketches of Great, Handsome, and Crooked Falls.
" 27. Gates of the Rocky mountains. july 16-20, 1805.
" 28. Missouri river from Pryor's [Mitchell's] creek [Montana] to the Three Forks of the Missouri—the route of july 21-24, 1805.
" 29. Missouri river from Gass's [Hot Springs] creek to Three Forks; and Jefferson river to Philanthrophy [Stinking Water] river—route of july 25-august 7, 1805.
" 29a. Jefferson river from Philanthropy to the Forks—the route of august 8-20, 1805.
" 30, pts. 1-3. "From Jeffersons river to the Forks of Kooskooske over the Rocky mountains from the 25th of august to the 9th of october, 1805."
" 31, " 1-2. "Sketch of Kooskooske & Lewis's river from the 7th to the 19th of Oc^{tr}. 1805.
" 32, " 1-2. "Sketch of the Columbia river from the forks, & the 19th of october 1805 to the 1st of jany on the Pacific ocean."
" 33. Rapids of the Columbia; with camps of october 26-28, 1805.
" 34. The Columbia river from the rapids to Wappato island, october 29-november 4, 1805.
" 35, pt. 1. Pacific coast, in neighborhood of Haley's bay, november 8-17, 1805.
" " " 2. Camp of november 7; detail.
" " " 3. Camp of november 8; detail.
" " " 4. Lower reaches of Columbia, november 4-6, 1805.
" 36. Sketch map of Haley's bay, november 18, 19, and 26, 1805.
" 37. Lewis's sketch-map of Vancouver's island, Nootka sound, etc.

Lewis, M., *and* **Clark, W.**—Continued.

no. 38. Sketch-map of the mouth of Columbia river and the route of Clark, january 6–10, 1806.
" 39. Sketch-map "given by a Clattsopp ind^{n}.," showing the mouth of the Columbia.
" 40. Sketch given by indians, april 18, 1806, at the Great Narrows of the Columbia, showing the basin of Lewis's river.
" 41. Sketch given by Cutnose, etc., may 3, 1806.
" 42. Sketch by Hohastillpilp, may 29, 1806.
" 43. Sketch obtained from indians at Flathead river camp, may 29–31, 1806.
" 44. Sketch map of the Lewis river system.
" 45. Crossing the mountains, showing the mountains, showing camps july 4–8, 1806.
" 46. "Sketch of cap^{t} Clarks rout from Clark river to the head of Jeffersons river"—july 5–9, 1806.
" 47. Sketch map of Gallatin and Madison rivers, with Clark's trail in the Yellowstone, july 13, 14, 1806.
" 48. Indian trails of a route from the Three Forks of the Missouri to the Yellowstone, july 13–15, 1806.
" 49. The Yellowstone, from the place where Clark reached it to Stillwater creek, july 15–7 [17], 1806.
" 50. The Yellowstone, from Rose [Stillwater] creek to Pryor's river, july 18–24, 1806.
" 51. The Yellowstone, from Pompey's Pillar to Little Wolf river, july 25–27, 1806.
" 52. The Yellowstone, from Little Wolf to Big Dry river, july 27, 1806.
" 53. The Yellowstone, near its junction with the Missouri, august 1, 1806.
" 54. Route of the Lewis and Clark expedition, showing its relation to modern geographical conditions.

FORESTRY.

United States. *Forest service.*

Forest atlas. Geographic distribution of North American trees . . . Pt. 1. Pines. By George B. Sudworth, dendrologist. 2 p. l., 36 col. maps. fol. [Washington] geological survey, 1913. 4500

NOTE.—At head of title: United States. Department of agriculture. Forest service. Henry S. Graves.

GEOLOGICAL.

United States. *Geological survey.*

Geologic atlas of the United States. Library ed. fol. Washington, engraved and printed by the survey, 1914. 4501

CONTENTS.

Reprint 3, 5 and 11. California.—Placerville, Sacramento, and Jackson. Scale $\frac{1}{125000}$.

Geologic atlas of the United States. Library ed. Folios 183–208. fol. Washington, engraved and printed by the survey, 1912–1919. 4502

NOTE.—Folios 1–159 catalogued in v. 1, title 1283. For folios 160–182, consult v. 3, title 3678.

CONTENTS.

(Subjects)

Arkansas.—Eureka Springs-Harrison. fol. 202.
California.—San Francisco. fol. 193.
Colorado.—Apishapa. fol. 186.
  Castle Rock. fol. 198.
  Colorado Springs. fol. 203.
Georgia.—Ellijay. fol. 187.
Illinois.—Colchester-Macomb. fol. 208.
  Belleville-Breese. fol. 195.
  Galena-Elizabeth. fol. 200.
  Murphry-Herrin. fol. 185.
  Tallula-Springfield. fol. 188.
Iowa.—Galena-Elizabeth. fol. 200.
Kansas.—Leavenworth-Smithfield. fol. 206.
Kentucky.—Kenova. fol. 184.
Maine.—Eastport. fol. 192.
Maryland.—Tolchester. fol. 204.
Michigan.—Detroit. fol. 205.
Minnesota.—Minneapolis-St. Paul.
Missouri.—Eureka Springs-Harrison. fol. 202.
  Leavenworth-Smithfield. fol. 206.
Montana.—Philipsburg. fol. 196.
New Jersey.—Raritan. fol. 191.
New Mexico.—Deming. fol. 207.
  Silver City. fol. 199.
New York.—Niagara. fol. 190.
North Carolina.—Ellijay. fol. 187.
Ohio.—Columbus. fol. 197.
  Kenova. fol. 184.
Pennsylvania.—Barnesboro-Patton. fol. 189.
Tennessee.—Ellijay. fol. 187.
Texas.—Llano-Burnet. fol. 183.
  Van Horn. fol. 194.
West Virginia.—Kenova. fol. 184.

(Numerical)

Folio 183. Texas.—Llano-Burnet. Scale $\frac{1}{125000}$.
" 184. Kentucky-West Virginia-Ohio.—Kenova. Scale $\frac{1}{125000}$.
" 185. Illinois.—Murphysboro-Herrin. Scale $\frac{1}{62500}$.
" 186. Colorado.—Apishapa. Scale $\frac{1}{125000}$.
" 187. Georgia-North Carolina-Tennessee.—Ellijay. Scale $\frac{1}{125000}$.
" 188. Illinois.—Tallula-Springfield. Scale $\frac{1}{62500}$.
" 189. Pennsylvania.—Barnesboro-Patton. Scale $\frac{1}{62500}$.
" 190. New York.—Niagara. Scale $\frac{1}{125000}$.

United States. *Geological survey*—Continued.

Folio 191. New Jersey.—Raritan. Scale $\frac{1}{625000}$.
" 192. Maine.—Eastport. Scale $\frac{1}{125000}$.
" 193. California.—San Francisco. Scale $\frac{1}{6250}$.
" 194. Texas.—Van Horn. Scale $\frac{1}{125000}$.
" 195. Illinois.—Belleville-Breese. Scale $\frac{1}{65000}$.
" 196. Montana.—Philipsburg. Scale $\frac{1}{125000}$.
" 197. Ohio.—Columbus. Scale $\frac{1}{125000}$.
" 198. Colorado.—Castle Rock. Scale $\frac{1}{125000}$.
" 199. New Mexico.—Silver City. Scale $\frac{1}{125000}$.
" 200. Illinois-Iowa.—Galena-Elizabeth. Scale $\frac{1}{62500}$.
" 201. Minnesota.—Minneapolis—St. Paul. Scale $\frac{1}{62500}$.
" 202. Arkansas-Missouri.—Eureka Springs-Harrison. Scale $\frac{1}{125000}$.
" 203. Colorado.—Colorado Springs. Scale $\frac{1}{125000}$.
" 204. Maryland.—Tolchester. Scale $\frac{1}{125000}$.
" 205. Michigan.—Detroit. Scale $\frac{1}{62500}$.
" 206. Missouri-Kansas.—Leavenworth-Smithfield. Scale $\frac{1}{62500}$.
" 207. New Mexico.—Deming. Scale $\frac{1}{125000}$.
" 208. Illinois.—Colchester-Macomb. Scale $\frac{1}{62500}$.

HARBORS.

Quinette de Rochemont, É. T., *and* **Vétillart, H.**

Les ports maritimes de l'Amérique du Nord sur l'Atlantique . . . III. Les ports des États Unis. 1 p. l., 24 col. maps, 22 pl. obl. fol. Paris, v^{ve} C. Dunod, 1904. 4503

NOTE.—To accompany their work entitled, *Les ports maritimes de l'Amérique du Nord sur l'Atlantique. 3 v. 1898–1904.*

HISTORICAL.

Baker, M. M.

Baker's historical geography maps of the United States. 1 p. l., 44 col. maps. fol. Philadelphia, McConnell school supply co. [1914] 4504

NOTE.—Title-page contains index. Large sheets on roller and printed on each side.

Croscup, G. E.

History made visible; a synchronic chart and statistical tables of United States history, by George E. Croscup, with a chronological text, by Ernest D. Lewis . . . 94 pp. front., illus. (maps, tables) 2 col. fold. charts. sm. fol. New York, Windsor publishing co. 1910. 4505

NOTE.—Bibliography: pp. [4]–5.

History made visible; United States history with synchronic charts, maps and statistical diagrams, by George E. Croscup. Chronological text, by Ernest D. Lewis . . . National ed. 127 pp. front., illus. (maps, tables) 2 col. fold. charts. sm. fol. New York, Windsor publishing co. 1911. 4506

NOTE.—Bibliography: pp. [4]–5.

Hodder, F. H.

Outline maps for a historical atlas of the United States, illustrating territorial growth and organization . . . Revised edition. 51 pp. incl. 24 maps. fol. Boston, Ginn & co. 1913. 4507

United States. *Treasury department. Bureau of statistics.*

Territorial development of the United States, compiled 1901. cover-title, 6 pp. 35 blue print maps. obl. fol. [Washington, 1901] 4508

NOTE.—The pages of text are typewritten and signed O. P. Austin.

RAILROADS.

Cram, G. F.

Cram's standard american railway system atlas of the world. Accompanied with a complete and simple index of the United States, showing the true location of all railroads, towns, villages and post offices . . . Foreign maps are compiled largely from charts of the Royal geographical society, and are geographically correct. 2 p. l., 5–606 pp. incl. 178 col. maps. fol. Chicago, G. F. Cram, 1900. 4509

NOTE.—Plans of many prominent cities of the United States.

Shelton, W. A.

Atlas of railway traffic maps. 1 p. l., 16 [4] maps (part fold.) 4°. Chicago, La Salle extension university, [©1913] 4510

Atlas of railway traffic maps . . . by William Arthur Shelton . . . 4 l., 16, [5] maps (part fold.) 4°. Chicago, La Salle extension university, [©1914] 4511

NOTE.—One of a series of texts on interstate commerce and railway traffic.
Lettered on cover: Railway traffic maps.
Text on verso of some of the maps.

United States express co.

Express and railway guide, february, 1895. 1 p. l., xxii, 86 pp. incl. 56 maps. sm. fol. Buffalo, N. Y., Matthews-Northrup co. [1895] 4512

RIVERS.

Mississippi and Ohio.

Cumings, S.

The western pilot; containing charts of the Ohio river and of the Mississippi, from the mouth of the Missouri to the Gulf of Mexico; accompanied with directions for navigating the same, and a gazetteer; or description of the towns on their banks, tributary streams, etc., also a variety of matter interesting to travelers, and all concerned in the navigation of those rivers; with a table of distances from town to town on all the above

Cumings, S.—Continued.

rivers. By Samuel Cummngs [!] Rev. and cor. by capt. Charles Ross & Geo. Conclin. 144 pp. illus. (maps) 8°. Cincinnati, G. Conclin, 1840. 4513

NOTE.—At head of title: New edition.

A revised and altered edition of the author's *Western navigator.* 1822. See v. 1, title 1318.

"Cumings' editions of the 'Navigator' and 'Pilot' . . . were amplifications of [The navigator of Zadok] Cramer . . . without acknowledgment of the main source of their material."—Sabin, *Bibl. amer., v. 5, p. 126.*

The western pilot; containing charts of the Ohio river and of the Mississippi, from the mouth of the Missouri to the Gulf of Mexico; accompanied with directions for navigating the same, and a gazetteer; or description of the towns on their banks, tributary streams, etc., also, a variety of matter interesting to travelers, and all concerned in the navigation of those rivers; with a table of distances from town to town on all the above rivers. By Samuel Cummings. Containing the population of the principal towns on the river in 1840. Rev. and cor. every year: by Capt. Charles Ross & George Conclin. 144 pp. incl. 44 maps. 8°. Cincinnati, G. Conclin, 1843. 4514

NOTE.—At head of title: New edition.

A revised and altered edition of the author's "Western navigator."

"Cumings editions of the 'Navigator' and 'Pilot' . . . were amplifications of [The navigator of Zadok] Cramer . . . without acknowledgment of the main source of the material."—Sabin, *Bibl. amer., v. 5, p. 126.*

The western pilot; containing charts of the Ohio River and of the Mississippi, from the mouth of the Missouri to the Gulf of Mexico; accompanied with directions for navigating the same, and a gazetteer; or description of the towns on their banks, tributary streams, etc., also a variety of matter interesting to travelers, and all concerned in the navigation of those rivers; with a table of distances from town to town on all the above rivers. By Samuel Cummings . . . Corrected by Capts. Charles Ross & John Klinefelter. 140, [2] pp. illus. (maps) 8°. Cincinnati, J. A. & U. P. James, 1854. 4515

NOTE.—At head of title: Latest revised edition.

A revised and altered edition of the author's "Western navigator."

"Cumings' editions of the 'Navigator' and 'Pilot' . . . were amplifications of [The navigator of Zadock] Cramer . . . without acknowledgment of the main source of their material."—Sabin, *Bibl. amer., v. 5, p. 126.*

ROADS.

Bullard co.

The red road book for all New England and eastern New York. Forty-four sectional plates, sixty-four city street maps. Detailed topographical road maps of the White Mountains. Detailed topographical maps showing camps, trails, lakes and ponds in the fishing and hunting sections of Maine. 112 pp. incl. 108 maps. 4°. Boston, Bullard co. ©1914. 4516

SEATS.

Birch, W.

The country seats of the United States of North America, with some scenes connected with them . . . [Part 1] [2] pp., 4 l., 19 pl. obl. 8°. Springland near Bristol, Penn., 1808. 4516a

NOTE.—Title-page and added t.-p., engr.

Title-page illustrated by a view: "The capitol at Washington," showing the wings without the central portion, surmounted by an eagle.

CONTENTS.

no. [1] The view from Springland.
" [2] Hoboken in New Jersey, the seat of m.r John Stevens.
" [3] Hampton the seat of gen.l Cha.s Ridgley, Maryland.
" [4] Landsdown the seat of the late W.m Bingham esq.r Pennsylvania.
" [5] The sun reflected on the dew, a garden scene. Echo, Pennsylv.a a place belonging to m.r D. Bavarage.
" [6] Mount Vernon, Virginia, the seat of the late gen.l G. Washington.
" [7] Fountain Green Pennsylv.a the seat of m.r S. Meeker.
" [8] Solitude in Pennsylv.a belonging to m.r Penn.
" [9] Devon in Pennsylv.a the seat of m.r Dallas.
" [10] Mount Sidney, the seat of gen.l John Barker, Pennsylv.a
" [11] The seat of m.r Duplantier near New Orleans & lately occupied as head quarters by gen.l J. Wilkinson.
" [12] Montibello the seat of gen.l S. Smith Maryland.
" [13] Woodlands the seat of m.r W.m Hamilton Pennsylvan.a
" [14] Sedgley the seat of m.r W.m Crammond Pennsylv.a
" [15] View from Belmont Pennsylv.a the seat of judge Peters.
" [16] York—Island, with a view of the seats of m.r A. Gracie, m.r Church &c.
" [17] Mendenhall ferry, Schuylkill, Pennsylvania.
" [18] China retreat Pennsyl.a the seat of m.r Manigault.
" [19] View from the Elysian bower, Springland Pennsylv.a the residence of m.r W. Birch.

STATISTICAL.

United States. *Census office, 13th census, 1910.*

Statistical atlas of the United States. Prepared under the supervision of Charles S. Sloane, geographer of the census. 99, [27] xi pp., 503 pl. 4°. Washington, govt. print. off., 1914. 4517

NOTE.—At head of title: Department of commerce. Bureau of the census. Wm. J. Harris, director.

United States. *Census office, 13th census, 1910*—Continued.

Plates give statistical maps and diagrams illustrating population, agriculture, manufactures, mines and quarries, cotton, financial statistics of cities, vital statistics, religious bodies, marriage and divorce, and insane in hospitals.

Contains map of the United States showing original area and acquisitions of territory from 1790 to 1910, and set of maps showing distribution of the rural population in 1790, 1800, 1810, 1820, 1840, 1850, 1860, 1870, 1880, 1890, 1900, 1910.

VIEWS.

Carey, M., & son.

Picturesque views of american scenery, 1820. [116] pp., 19 col. pl. fol. Philadelphia, published by M. Carey & son, printed by J. Shaw, 1820. 4518

NOTE.—Colored engraved title-page and plates.
Printed by J. Shaw and engraved by J. Hill.

CONTENTS.

no. 1. Washington's sepulchre, Mount Vernon.
" 2. View of the spot where gen. Ross fell near Baltimore.
" 3. View near the falls of Schuylkill.
" 4. Jones' falls near Baltimore.
" 5. View above the falls of Schuylkill.
" 6. Falls of St. Anthony on the Mississippi.
" 7. Lynnhaven bay.
" 8. Spirit creek; near Augusta, Georgia.
" 9. View by moonlight, near Fayetteville.
" 10. Burning of Savannah.
" 11. Norfolk; from Gosport, Virginia.
" 12. View on the Wisahiccon, Pennsylvania.
" 13. Bolling's dam, Petersburgh, Virginia.
" 14. View on the North river.
" 15. Passaic river, below the falls.
" 16. Passaic falls, New Jersey.
" 17. Hell gate.
" 18. Oyster cove.
" 19. Monument near North Point.

WARS.

Civil.

Van Horne, T. B.

History of the army of the Cumberland; its organization, campaigns, and battles, written at the request of major-general George H. Thomas chiefly from his private military journal and official and other documents furnished by him; by Thomas B. Van Horne . . . Illustrated with campaign and battle maps, compiled by Edward Ruger. [Atlas] 3 p. l., 22 maps. 8°. Cincinnati, R. Clarke & co. 1875. 4519

CONTENTS.

no. 1. Map exhibiting the operations of the armies of the Cumberland and Ohio while commanded respectively by brig. gen. Robert Anderson, brig. gen. (now gen.) Sherman, and maj. gen. G. H. Thomas.

no. 2. Map of the battlefield of Logan's Crossroads, or Mill Springs, january 19th, 1862.
" 3. Map of the field of Shiloh, near Pittsburgh Landing, Tenn. on the 6th and 7th of april, 1862.
" 4. Map of the country between Monterey, Tenn., and Corinth, Miss., showing the lines of entrenchments made & the routes followed in may 1862.
" 5. Map of the battlefield of Perryville, Ky.
" 6. Map exhibiting the campaigns of the army of the Cumberland while under the command of maj. gen. W. S. Rosecrans.
" 7. Map of the battlefield of Stone river, near Murfreesboro, Tenn., december 30th, 1862, to jan. 3rd, 1863.
" 8. Map of the battle of Chickamauga, september 19th and 20th, 1863.
" 9. Map exhibiting the Chattanooga & East Tennessee campaigns.
" 10. Battlefield of Chattanooga during the battles of nov. 23, 24 & 25, 1863.
" 11. Map illustrating the first epoch of the Atlanta campaign.
" 12. Map illustrating the second epoch of the Atlanta campaign.
" 13. Map illustrating the third epoch of the Atlanta campaign.
" 14. Map illustrating the fourth epoch of the Atlanta campaign.
" 15. Map illustrating the fifth epoch of the Atlanta campaign.
" 16. Map exhibiting the operations conducted pursuant to the orders of maj. general George H. Thomas.
" 17. Battlefield in front of Franklin, Tenn. november 30th, 1864.
" 18. Map of the battlefields in front of Nashville, dec. 15th & 16th, 1864.
" 19. Map of Selma, Ala., and its defences, captured by assault by the cav. corps m. d. m., april 2, 1865.
" 20. Map showing the marches of the U. S. forces under maj. gen. W. T. Sherman during the campaigns of Georgia and the Carolinas embracing the region from Atlanta to Savannah and thence to Durham Station, N. C.
" 21. Map of the battlefield of Bentonville, N. C., may 19th, 1865.
" 22. Map prepared to exhibit the campaigns in which the army of the Cumberland.

Revolutionary.

Marshall, J.

Atlas to Marshall's Life of Washington. Engraved by J. Yeager. 1 p. l., 10 maps. 8°. Philadelphia, J. Crissy [1850] [*With his* Life of George Washington . . . compiled under the direction of the hon. Bushrod Washington, from original papers. 8°. Philadelphia, Crissy & Markley, & Thomas, Cowperthwait & co. 1850. v. 2] 4520

NOTE:—Same maps as title 1341, but smaller scale.

Spanish American.

Rand, McNally & co.

War atlas with marginal index. cover-title, 16 pp. incl. 8 col. maps, illus. sm. fol. Chicago and New York, Rand, McNally & co. 1898. 4521

NOTE.—Reverse of the front cover shows map of Philippine Islands, and reverse of back cover shows "Strength of the navies of the United States and Spain." Contains map of the city and harbor of Havanna.
Page 1 gives flags of all nations.

GENERAL.

1796

Scott, J.

An atlas of the United States. cover title, [19] maps. 12°. Philadelphia, F. & R. Bailey, B. Davis, & H. & P. Rice, 1796. 4521a

NOTE.—Earliest atlas of the United States. Same maps, however, found in Scott's *The United States gazetteer. 16°. Philadelphia. F. R. Bailey, 1795.*

CONTENTS.

no. [1] A map of the United States.
" [2] Maine.
" [3] New Hampshire.
" [4] State of Vermont.
" [5] Massachusetts.
" [6] Rhode Island.
" [7] Connecticut.
" [8] New York.
" [9] New Jersey.
" [10] Pennsylvania.
" [11] Delaware.
" [12] Maryland.
" [13] Virginia.
" [14] North Carolina.
" [15] South Carolina.
" [16] Georgia.
" [17] S. W. Territory.
" [18] Kentucky.
" [19] N. W. Territory.

1809?

Spain. *Dirección de hidrografia.*

[Portulano de los Estados Unidos de America] 11 maps. sm. fol. [Madrid? 1809?] 4522

NOTE.—Probably from some part of the *Portulano de la America Settentrional*, published in Madrid and Mexico, though not in any part which is in the Library of Congress.

The signature T G, on Plano de la barra y puerto de Charleston, appears on two maps in the 1809 edition of the Portulano, and the maps are all of similar construction.

CONTENTS.

no. [1] Plano de Puerto Real en la Carolina del S.
" [2] Plano de la barra y puerto de Charleston.
" [3] Plano de la bahia y rio de Delaware.
" [4] Plano del puerto de Nueva York.
" [5] Plano de Newport en la Isla Rode.
" [6] Plano de la bahia y puerto de Boston.
" [7] Plano del puerto de Newburyport.
" [8] Plano del puerto de Portsmouth.
" [9] Plano de la entrada y puerto del rio de Sⁿ Juan en la bahia de Fundi.
" [10] Plano del puerto de Halifax.
" [11] Plano del puerto de Sⁿ Juan de Terranova.

1813

Carey, M.

Carey's american pocket atlas; containing twenty maps . . . With a brief description of each state and territory: also the census of the inhabitants of the United States, for 1810; the exports from the United States for twenty years. 4th ed., greatly improved and enlarged. iv, 168 pp., 23 maps, 2 tables. 12°. Philadelphia, M. Carey, 1813. 4523

NOTE.—Index on title-page.
Maps engraved by W. Barker, J. H. Seymour, and A. Doolittle. Map no. 3, New Hampshire, by Saml. Lewis.

CONTENTS.

no. 1. United States.
" 2. Vermont, from actual survey.
" 3. The state of New Hampshire.
" 4. Maine.
" 5. Massachusetts.
" 6. Rhode Island.
" 7. Connecticut.
" 8. New York.
" 9. New Jersey.
" 10. Pennsylvania.
" 11. Delaware.
" 12. Ohio.
" 12a. Upper territories of the United States.
" 13. Maryland.
" 14. Virginia.
" 15. Kentucky.
" 16. North Carolina.
" 17. Tennessee.
" 18. South Carolina.
" 19. Georgia.
" 19a. Mississippi territory.
" 20. Louisiana.
" 20a. Missouri territory.

1823

Tanner, H. S.

A new american atlas, containing maps of the several states of the North American union. Projected and drawn on a uniform scale from documents in the public offices of the United States and state governments, and other original and authentic information . . . 3 p. l., i i [2] 18 pp., 22 col. maps. fol. Philadelphia, H. S. Tanner, 1823. 4523a

NOTE.—Issued in three parts, pt. 1–2, 1819; pt. 3, 1822. Title-page dated 1823. The cover titles are bound in with the atlas. The Library of Congress has another copy of this atlas in which the date of pt. 1, is 1818 and of pt. 3, 1823, and which lacks an advertizing sheet dated Philadelphia, July 10, 1818, and an address "To the Public," both found in this copy.

The engraved title-page is ornamented with an engraving entitled "First landing of Columbus in the New World." At the foot of the title-page a line reads, "Writing drawn and engraved by Joseph Perkins."

For contents see v. 1, no. 1374.

1828

Tanner, H. S.

A new pocket atlas of the United States, with the roads and distances, designed for the use of travellers . . . 1 p. l., 12 maps. 24°. Philadelphia, published by the author, 1828. 4524

NOTE.—Appended: A list of maps, charts, and geographical works, recently published, and for sale by H. S. Tanner . . . Philadelphia.

CONTENTS.

no. 1. Part of Maine &c. with the boundary claimed by Gr[t]. Britain.
" 2. New England.
" 3. New York.
" 4. Falls of Niagara and adjacent country.
" 5. Pennsylvania and New Jersey.
" 6. Virginia, Maryland and Delaware. J. Knight sc.
" 7. Ohio and Indiana.
" 8. Kentucky and Tennessee. J. Knight sc.
" 9. North & South Carolina. J. Knight sc.
" 10. Georgia and Alabama. J. Knight sc.
" 11. Louisiana and Mississippi. J. Knight sc.
" 12. Illinois and Missouri. J. Knight sc.

1839

Burr, D. H.

The american atlas; exhibiting the post offices, post roads, railroads, canals, and the physical and political divisions of the United States of North America; constructed from the government surveys & other official materials. Under the direction of the post master general . . . 1 p. l., 13 col. maps (fold.) fol. [London, J. Arrowsmith, 1839] 4525

NOTE.—Maps bearing name of J. Arrowsmith in lower right-hand corner. Shows county lines. They are copyrighted july 10, 1839.

CONTENTS.

no. 1. The United States & part of the adjacent countries.
" 2. Maine, New Hampshire, Vermont, Massachusetts, Rhode I^d. & Connecticut.
" 3. New York.—Inset: New York City.
" 4. New Jersey & Pennsylvania.
" 5. Virginia, Maryland & Delaware.
" 6. North & South Carolina.
" 7. Georgia & Alabama.
" 8. Florida.
" 9. Mississippi, Louisiana & Arkansas.
" 10. Ohio & Indiana.
" 11. Kentucky & Tennessee.
" 12. Illinois & Missouri.
" 13. Michigan & part of Wisconsin territory.

1874

Gray, O. W.

Gray's atlas of the United States, with general maps of the world. Accompanied by descriptions geographical, historical, scientific, and statistical. 175 pp. incl. 72 maps. fol. Philadelphia, Stedman, Brown & Lyon, 1874. 4526

NOTE.—Contains plans of principal cities in the United States.

1895

Rand, McNally & co.

Rand, McNally & co.'s indexed atlas of the world (complete in two volumes) v. [2] fol. Chicago and New York, Rand, McNally & co. 1895. 4527

NOTE.—Paged continuously: v. 2, 2 p. l., 225–460 pp. incl. 69 col. maps, tab., diagrs.

CONTENTS.

v. 1. Foreign countries (wanting)
v. 2. United States.

1911

Geographical publishing co.

[Maps of the United States. Popular series.] 1 p. l., 59 pp. 48 col. maps. sm. fol. [Chicago, Geographical publishing co. 1911] 4528

NOTE.—Atlas consists of sheets bound in patent device marked "Educational device. Fanning & Frady, inventors. Dallas, Texas."

1912

Cram, G. F.

Cram's travelers' atlas of the United States containing specially engraved double-page maps of each state and the United States . . . 1 p. l., 208 (*i. e.* 254) pp., incl. 48 maps. 24°. Chicago, G. F. Cram [©1912] 4529

1913

Trolley press.

Traveler's atlas-guide to New England . . . New York city, eastern New York. 75 town and city plans; hotels, theatres, stores . . . automobile routes, railroads, steamboats, trolleys . . . cover-title, 96 pp. incl. 62 maps. fol. [Hartford] Trolley press, ©1913. 4530

1914

Denver weekly post.

Denver weekly post atlas containing colored sectional maps Colorado, Utah, Wyoming, Idaho, New Mexico and Montana. United States homestead laws, grazing laws; Carey act; desert land act; reclamation act; mining laws and other valuable information. [17] pp., incl. 7 col. maps. fol. [Denver] Denver weekly post, ©1914. 4531

1914

Murray-Aaron, E.

Home and library map-atlas of the United States. Indexed with locations and populations of the cities, towns and villages, 96 pp. incl. 50 col. maps. fol. Indianapolis, Ind., American geographic institute, ©1914. 4532

1916

National map co.

New standard atlas of the United States. A new series of over 50 maps in colors, based upon the latest official surveys, with a complete index showing location and population of all cities, towns and villages. The population figures are according to the latest official census. 1 p. l., 5–132 pp. incl. 50 col. maps. fol. Indianapolis, New York, National map co. ©1916. 4533

NOTE.—Contains 32 pp. of Statistics and information.

1916

New standard atlas of the United States. A new series of over 50 maps in colors, based upon the latest official surveys, with a complete index showing location and population of all cities, towns and villages. The population figures are according to the latest official census. 1 p. l., 5–100 pp. incl. 50 col. maps. fol. Indianapolis, New York, National map co. ©1916. 4533a

NOTE.—Without section of Statistics and information found in atlas of same title and date, published by National map co.

1917

New standard atlas of the United States. A new series of over 50 maps in colors, based upon the latest official surveys, with a complete index showing location and population of all cities, towns and villages. The population figures are according to the latest official census. 1 p. l., 5–100 pp. incl. 50 col. maps. fol. Indianapolis, New York, National map co. 1917. 4534

1918

Hammond, C. S., & co.

Hammond's pocket atlas of the United States with index of cities and towns giving population . . . 160 pp. incl. 71 maps. 16°. New York, C. S. Hammond & co. 1918. 4535

NOTE.—Cover-title: Hammond's indexed pocket atlas of the United States. Thin paper edition.

STATES.

ALABAMA.

Cities.

BIRMINGHAM.

Walter, T. U.

The quadrangle. Birmingham. Map book of business district showing ownership, etc., with complete index. 1 p. l., [93] l. 2 maps on 54 l. 4°. Birmingham, Ala., T. U. Walter, ©1914. 4536

ALASKA.

1869

United States. *Coast and geodetic survey.*

Harbors in Alaska. 1 p. l., 9 maps. sm. fol. [Washington] 1869. 4537

NOTE.—At head of title: U. S. Coast survey. Benjamin Peirce, superintendent.
Table of contents on title-page.

CALIFORNIA.

Petroleum.

California. *State mining bureau.*

Petroleum industry of California. Map folio accompanying Bulletin no. 69. cover-title, 13 maps, 4 pl. fol. San Francisco, Cal., State mining bureau, 1914. 4538

Counties.

YOLO.

Historical.

Gilbert, F. T.

The illustrated atlas and history of Yolo county, Cal., containing a history of California from 1513 to 1850, a history of Yolo county from 1825 to 1880, with statistics of agriculture, education, churches, elections, lithographic views of farms, residences, mills, &c. Portraits of well-known citizens, and the official county map. IV, 105 pp., 6 col. maps, 59 pl. fol. [San Francisco] De Pue & co. 1879. 4539

Cities.

LOS ANGELES.

Baist, G. W.

Baist's real estate atlas of surveys of Los Angeles, Cal. Complete in one volume. Compiled and published from official records, private plans and actual surveys . . . 1 p. l., index map, 44 col. maps. fol. Philadelphia, G. W. Baist, 1914. 4540

Miscellaneous.

San Francisco Bay.

Dumbarton land and improvement co.

Property on San Francisco bay. cover-title, 28 maps. fol. [San Francisco] Dumbarton land and improvement co. [c1914] 4541

Sunset-Midland oil field.

Kern trading & oil co.

Topographic atlas of the Sunset-Midland oil field, California. Scale 1 inch 1000 feet. cover-title, 1 p. l., 19 maps. obl. fol. [San Francisco] Kern trading & oil co. 1916. 4542

NOTE.—The preliminary leaf containing the "Legend" and the index map are marked "W. F. J. del." and the index map is dated, nov. 13, 1913.

COLORADO.

Lands.

Colorado. *State board of land commissioners.*

Atlas of the state lands of Colorado, issued under the authority of the state of Colorado . . . 1st ed. [12] pp. incl. 9 maps. illus. fol. Denver, Col., Clason map co. 1914. 4543

Counties.

LOGAN.

Ogle, G. A., & co.

Standard atlas of Logan county, Colorado, including a plat book of the villages, cities and townships of the county. Map of the state, United States and world. Patrons directory, reference business directory and departments devoted to general information. Analysis of the system of U. S. land surveys, digest of the system of civil government . . . 2 p. l., 7–81, viii, x–xxii pp. incl. 58 col. maps, illus. fol. Chicago, G. A. Ogle & co. 1917. 4544

MORGAN.

Ogle, G. A., & co.

Standard atlas of Morgan county, Colorado, including a plat book of the villages, cities and townships of the county. Map of the state, United States and world. Patrons directory, reference business directory and departments devoted to general information . . . 2 p. l., 7–69, viii, x-xxiii pp. incl. 46 col. maps, illus. fol. Chicago, G. A. Ogle & co. 1913. 4545

CONNECTICUT.

Counties.

TOLLAND.

Gray, O. W.

Atlas of Windham and Tolland counties, with a map of Connecticut. From actual surveys . . . 1 p. l., 37 col. maps on 45 l. fol. Hartford, C. G. Keeney, 1869. 4546

Note.—On title-page, "Engraved, printed and colored by Kellogg & Bulkely . . . Letter press and binding at Case, Lockwood & Brainard's."

WINDHAM.

Gray, O. W.

Atlas of Windham and Tolland counties, with a map of Connecticut. From actual surveys . . . 1 p. l., 37 col. maps on 45 l. fol. Hartford, C. G. Keeney, 1869. 4547

Note.—On title-page, "Engraved, printed and colored by Kellogg & Bulkely . . . Letter press and binding at Case, Lockwood & Brainard's."

DELAWARE.

Cities.

WILMINGTON.

Price, F. A.

Atlas of Wilmington, Delaware, showing former subdivisions of property. Compiled and prepared from city and county records and old plans . . . 1 p. l., 7 maps. fol. [Wilmington] F. A. Price, 1914. 4548

DISTRICT OF COLUMBIA.

Real estate.

Carpenter, B. D.

Map of the real estate in the county of Washington, D. C., outside of the cities of Washington and Georgetown from actual surveys. Authorized by acts of Congress approved June 4th 1880. 1 p. l., 30 maps. fol. [Washington] 1881. 4549

NOTE.—Printed pages entitled, "Alphabetical index for the county of Washington," have been pasted on the inside of the front cover.

WASHINGTON.

1913–1915.

Baist, G. W.

Baist's real estate atlas of surveys of Washington, District of Columbia. Complete in four volumes. Compiled and published from official records, private plans and actual surveys . . . 4 v. fol. Philadelphia, G. W: Baist, 1913–1915. 4550

CONTENTS.

v. 1. . W. section. 1913.
" 2. . E., S. E. and S. W. section. 1915.
" 3. . W. suburbs. 1915.
" 4. N. E. and S. E. suburbs. 1913.

1916

United States. *Engineer department.*

Map of the public lands under federal jurisdiction in the District of Columbia compiled under the direction of the secretary of war in the office of public buildings and grounds from information obtained by the Commission to investigate title of United States lands in the District of Columbia, 1915. 64th Congress. 1st sess. House of Representatives. Doc. no. 1055. 4 p. l., 41 (*i. e.* 42) col. maps. obl. fol. [Washington, government printing office, 1916] 4551

NOTE.—On cover: "Title of the United States to lands in the District of Columbia. Letter from the secretary of war transmitting final report of the com-

mission to investigate the title of the United States to lands in the District of Columbia, created by the act approved may 30, 1908 (35 Stat. L., 543) april 24, 1916—Referred to the committee on the District of Columbia and ordered to be printed, with illustrations."
Following this is the letter signed by Newton D. Baker, secretary of war, T. W. Gregory, attorney general, O. P. Newman, president of board of commissioners, District of Columbia, Claude A. Swanson, chairman of committee on public buildings and grounds, United States Senate, and Frank Clark, chairman of committee on public buildings and grounds, House of representatives.

1919

Baist, G. W.

Baist's real estate atlas of surveys of Washington, District of Columbia. Complete in four volumes. Compiled from official records, private plans, actual surveys. By G. Wm. Baist, Wm. E. & H. V. Baist, surveyors. 4 v., v. 1, 3. fol. Philadelphia [G. W. Baist] 1919. 4552

NOTE.—Title on reverse of front covers. The work to be complete in 4 volumes. At head of titles: Volume one; Volume three.

CONTENTS.

v. 1. N. W. section. 1919.
" 3. Suburbs, 1919.

IDAHO.

Counties.

CANYON.

Ogle, G. A., & co.

Standard atlas of Canyon county, Idaho, including a plat book of the villages, cities and townships of the county. Map of the state, United States and world. Patrons directory, reference business directory and departments devoted to general information. Analysis of the system of U. S. land surveys, digest of the system of civil government . . . 2 p. l., 8–79, viii, x–xxiii pp. incl. 31 col. maps, illus. fol. Chicago, G. A. Ogle & co. 1915. 4553

LATAH.

Ogle, G. A., & co.

Standard atlas of Latah county, Idaho, including a plat book of the villages, cities and townships of the county. Map of the state, United States and world. Patrons directory, reference business directory and departments devoted to general information. Analysis of the system of U. S. land surveys, digest of the system of civil government . . . 2 p. l., 7–71, viii, x–xxiii pp. incl. 41 col. maps, illus. fol. Chicago, G. A. Ogle & co. 1914. 4554

ILLINOIS.

State.

1879

Edwards, D. C.

Atlas of the state of Illinois to which are added various general maps, history, statistics, illustrations. 292 pp. incl. 118 maps, front., illus., ports. fol. Chicago, D. C. Edwards, 1879. 4555

NOTE.—Contains plans of cities; biographical sketches; patrons' directory; business directory of the patrons of the Illinois state atlas. Picture of "State House" as front.

1914

Rand, McNally & co.

Landowner's directory of northeast Illinois, comprising the counties of Boone, Cook, De Kalb, Dupage, Grundy, Kane, Kankakee, Kendall, Lake, part of Livingston, La Salle, McHenry and Will, as compiled from the county assessors' records exclusive of lands within the corporate limits of cities, towns and incorporated villages. 1 p. l., 228, [29] pp. incl. 13 maps. sm. fol. [Chicago, Rand, McNally & co. ©1914] 4556

NOTE.—No title-page. Caption title.

Counties.

BOND.

Ogle, G. A., & co.

Standard atlas of Bond county, Illinois, including a plat book of the villages, cities and townships of the county. Map of the state, United States and world. Patrons directory, reference business directory and departments devoted to general information . . . 2 p. l., 7–43, [15], viii, x–xxii pp. incl. 16 col. maps, illus., diagrs. fol. Chicago, G. A. Ogle & co. 1900. 4557

CARROLL.

Ogle, G. A., & co.

Standard atlas of Carroll county, Illinois, including a plat book of the villages, cities and townships of the county. Map of the state, United States and world. Patrons directory, reference business directory and departments devoted to general information . . . 2 p. l., 7–81, viii, x–xxii pp. incl. 24 col. maps, illus. fol. Chicago, G. A. Ogle & co. 1908. 4558

CHAMPAIGN.

Ogle, G. A., & co.

Standard atlas of Champaign county, Illinois, including a plat book of the villages, cities and townships of the county. Map of the state, United States and world. Patrons directory, reference business directory and departments devoted to general information. Analysis of the system of U. S. land surveys, digest of the system of civil government . . . compiled and published by G. A. Ogle & co. . . . assisted by Champaign county abstract co. . . . 2 p. l., 7–163, ii, vii–viii, x–xxiii pp. incl. 70 col. maps, illus., diagrs. fol. Chicago, G. A. Ogle & co. 1913. 4559

CLARK.

Ogle, G. A., & co.

Standard atlas of Clark county, Illinois, including a plat book of the villages, cities and townships of the county. Map of the state, United States and world. Patrons directory, reference business directory and departments devoted to general information. Analysis of the system of U. S. land surveys, digest of the system of civil government . . . 2 p. l., 7–83, viii, x–xxiii pp. incl. 24 col. maps, illus. fol. Chicago, G. A. Ogle & co. 1916. 4560

CLINTON.

Ogle, G. A., & co.

Standard atlas of Clinton county, Illinois, including a plat book of the villages, cities and townships of the county. Map of the state, United States and world. Patrons directory, reference business directory and departments devoted to general information . . . 2 p. l., 7–81, viii, x–xxiii pp. incl. 23 col. maps, illus. fol. Chicago, G. A. Ogle & co. 1913. 4561

COLES.

Ogle, G. A., & co.

Standard atlas of Coles county, Illinois, including a plat book of the villages, cities and townships of the county. Map of the state, United States and world. Patrons directory, reference business directory and departments devoted to general information. Analysis of the system of U. S. land surveys, digest of the system of civil government . . . 2 p. l., 7–95, viii, x–xxiii pp. incl. 38 col. maps, illus., diagrs. fol. Chicago, G. A. Ogle & co. 1913. 4562

DE KALB.

Ogle, G. A., & co.

Standard atlas of De Kalb county, Illinois, including a plat book of the villages, cities and townships of the county. Map of the state, United States and world. Patrons directory, reference business directory and departments devoted to general information. Analysis of the system of U. S. land surveys, digest of the system of civil government . . . 2 p. l., 7–69 [20] 89–95, viii, x–xxii pp. incl. 31 col. maps, illus. fol. Chicago, G. A. Ogle & co. 1905. 4563

DE WITT.

Ogle, G. A., & co.

Standard atlas of De Witt county, Illinois, including a plat book of the villages, cities and townships of the county. Map of the state, United States and world. Patrons directory, reference business directory and departments devoted to general information. Analysis of the system of U. S. land surveys, digest of the system of civil government . . . 2 p. l., 7–83, viii, x–xxiii pp. incl. 23 col. maps, illus. fol. Chicago, G. A. Ogle & co. 1915. 4564

DOUGLAS.

Ogle, G. A., & co.

Standard atlas of Douglas county, Illinois, including a plat book of the villages, cities and townships of the county. Map of the state, United States and world. Patrons directory, reference business directory and departments devoted to general information. Analysis of the system of U. S. land surveys, digest of the system of civil government . . . Compiled and published by Geo. A. Ogle & co. . . . assisted in record work and platting by the Douglas county abstract and loan company, Tuscola, Illinois . . . 2 p. l., 7–83, viii, x–xxiii pp. incl. 15 col. maps, illus. fol. Chicago, G. A. Ogle & co. 1914. 4565

FAYETTE.

Ogle, G. A., & co.

Standard atlas of Fayette county, Illinois, including a plat book of the villages, cities and townships of the county. Map of the state, United States and world. Patrons directory, reference business directory and departments devoted to general information. Analysis of the system of U. S. land surveys, digest of the system of civil government . . . 2 p. l., 7–107, viii, x–xxiii pp. incl. 27 col. maps, illus. fol. Chicago, G. A. Ogle & co. 1915. 4566

FORD.

Ogle, G. A., & co.

Standard atlas of Ford county, Illinois, including a plat book of the villages, cities and townships of the county. Map of the state, United States and world. Patrons directory, reference business directory and departments devoted to general information. Analysis of the system of U. S. land surveys, digest of the system of civil government . . . 2 p. l., 7-79, viii, x-xxiii pp. incl. 21 col. maps, illus. fol. Chicago, G. A. Ogle & co. 1916. 4567

FULTON.

Ogle, G. A., & co.

Standard atlas of Fulton county, Illinois, including a plat book of the villages, cities and townships of the county. Map of the state, United States and world. Patrons directory, reference business directory and departments devoted to general information. Analysis of the system of U. S. land surveys, digest of the system of civil government . . . 2 p. l., 7-133, viii, x-xxii pp. incl. 42 col. maps, illus. fol. Chicago, G. A. Ogle & co. 1912. 4568

GREENE.

Ogle, G. A., & co.

Standard atlas of Greene county, Illinois. Including a plat book of the villages, cities and townships of the county. Map of the state, United States and world. Patrons directory, reference business directory and departments devoted to general information. Analysis of the system of U. S. land surveys, digest of the system of civil government . . . 2 p. l., 7-85, viii, x-xxiii pp. incl. 22 col. maps, illus., ports., diagrs. fol. Chicago, G. A. Ogle & co. 1915. 4569

HENDERSON.

Standard map co.

Atlas and farm directory of Mercer & Henderson counties, Illinois, compiled from county records and actual surveys. 61 pp. incl. 19 col. maps. fol. [Chicago] Standard map co. 1914. 4570

IROQUOIS.

1884

Brink, W. R., & co.

Illustrated atlas map of Iroquois county, Illinois. Carefully compiled from official records and personal examinations. 103 [53] pp. incl. 37 maps, illus. fol. Edwardsville, Ill., W. R. Brink & co. 1884. 4571

NOTE.—Pagination irregular.

1904

Ogle, G. A., & co.

Standard atlas of Iroquois county, Illinois, including a plat book of the villages, cities and townships of the county. Map of the state, United States and world. Patrons directory, reference business directory and departments devoted to general information. Analysis of the system of U. S. land surveys, digest of the system of civil government . . . 2 p. l., 7–129, viii, x–xxii pp. incl. 36 col. maps, illus. fol. Chicago, G. A. Ogle & co. 1904. 4572

JERSEY.

Ogle, G. A., & co.

Standard atlas of Jersey county, Illinois, including a plat book of the villages, cities and townships of the county. Map of the state, United States and world. Patrons directory, reference business directory and departments devoted to general information. Analysis of the system of U. S. land surveys, digest of the system of civil government . . . 2 p. l., 7–71, viii, x–xxiii pp. incl. 21 maps, illus. fol. Chicago, G. A. Ogle & co. 1916. 4573

JO DAVIESS.

Ogle, G. A., & co.

Standard atlas of Jo Daviess county, Illinois, including a plat book of the villages, cities and townships of the county. Map of the state, United States and world. Patrons directory, reference business directory and departments devoted to general information. Analysis of the system of U. S. land surveys, digest of the system of civil government . . . 2 p. l., 8–117, viii, x–xxiii pp. incl. 48 col. maps, illus., diagrs. fol. Chicago, G. A. Ogle & co. 1913. 4574

LAKE.

Ogle, G. A., & co.

Standard atlas of Lake county, Illinois, including a plat book of the villages, cities and townships of the county. Map of the state, United States and world. Patrons directory, reference business directory and departments devoted to general information. Analysis of the system of U. S. land surveys, digest of the system of civil government . . . 2 p. l., 7–131, [11] pp. incl. 49 col. maps. fol. Chicago, G. A. Ogle & co. 1907. 4575

NOTE.—Does not contain the text called for on title-page.

McDONOUGH.

Ogle, G. A., & co.

Standard atlas of McDonough county, Illinois, including a plat book of the villages, cities and townships of the county. Map of the state, United States and world. Patrons directory, reference business directory and departments devoted to general information . . . 2 p. l., 7–99, viii, x–xxiii pp. incl. 27 col. maps, illus., diagrs. fol. Chicago, G. A. Ogle & co. 1913. 4576

McHENRY.

Everts, Baskin & Stewart.

Combination atlas map of McHenry county, Illinois. Compiled, drawn and published from personal examinations and surveys . . . Duval & Hunter, pr. Phila. 66 pp. incl. 24 col. maps, illus. fol. Chicago, Everts, Baskin & Stewart, 1872. 4577

McLEAN.

Ogle, G. A., & co.

Standard atlas of McLean county, Illinois, including a plat book of the villages, cities and townships of the county. Map of the state, United States and world. Patrons directory, reference business directory and departments devoted to general information. Analysis of the system of U. S. land surveys, digest of the system of civil government . . . Compiled and published by Geo. A. Ogle & co. . . . assisted in record work and platting by A. H. Bell . . . 2 p. l., 7–151, viii, x–xxiii pp. incl. 53 col. maps, illus. fol. Chicago, G. A. Ogle & co. 1914. 4578

MACOUPIN.

Morse-Warren engineering co.

Plat book of Macoupin county, Illinois, containing maps of villages and townships of the county and of the state, and United States . . . Engraved by W. W. Hixson & co., Rockford, Ill. 2 p. l., 7–142 pp. incl. 52 col. maps. fol. Carlinville, Ill., Morse-Warren engineering co. 1911. 4579

MARION.

Ogle, G. A., & co.

Standard atlas of Marion county, Illinois. Including a plat book of the villages, cities and townships of the county. Map of the state, United States and world. Patrons directory, reference business directory and departments devoted to general information. Analysis of the system of U. S. land surveys, digest of the system of civil government . . . 2 p. l., 7–101, viii, x–xxiii pp. incl. 31 col. maps, illus., ports., diagrs. fol. Chicago, G. A. Ogle & co. 1915. 4580

MERCER.

Standard map co.

Atlas and farm directory of Mercer & Henderson counties, Illinois, compiled from county records and actual surveys. 61 pp. incl. 19 col. maps. fol. [Chicago] Standard map co. °1914. 4581

MONROE.

Centennial atlas co.

Plat book of Monroe county, Illinois, compiled from county records and actual surveys. 1 p. l., 43 [25] pp. incl. 16 col. maps, illus. fol. Waterloo, Ill., Centennial atlas co. 1916. 4582

NOTE.—On title-page, "The Kenyon company, map makers, Des Moines, Iowa."

MONTGOMERY.

Ogle, G. A., & co.

Standard atlas of Montgomery county, Illinois, including a plat book of the villages, cities and townships of the county. Map of the state, United States, and world. Patrons directory, reference business directory and departments devoted to general information. Analysis of the system of U. S. land surveys, digest of the system of civil government . . . 2 p. l., 7–125, viii, x–xxiii pp. incl. 52 maps, illus. fol. Chicago, G. A. Ogle & co. 1912. 4583

MOULTRIE.

Ogle, G. A., & co.

Standard atlas of Moultrie county, Illinois, including a plat book of the villages, cities and townships of the county. Map of the state, United States and world. Patrons directory, reference business directory and departments devoted to general information . . . 2 p. l., 7–67, viii, x–xxiii pp. incl. 17 col. maps, illus. fol. Chicago, G. A. Ogle & co. 1913. 4584

OGLE.

Ogle, G. A., & co.

Standard atlas of Ogle county, Illinois, including a plat book of the villages, cities and townships of the county. Map of the state, United States and world. Patrons directory, reference business directory and departments devoted to general information. Analysis of the system of U. S. land surveys, digest of the system of civil government . . . 2 p. l., 8–129, viii, x–xxiii pp. incl. 63 maps, illus. fol. Chicago, G. A. Ogle & co. 1912. 4585

PIATT.

Warner & Beers.

Atlas of Piatt county and the state of Illinois, to which is added an atlas of the United States, maps of the hemispheres &c. 39, 2–93 pp. incl. 54 maps, 4 pl. fol. Chicago, Warner & Beers, 1875. 4586

NOTE.—Corrected from vol. 1, title 1560.

PIKE.

Ogle, G. A., & co.

Standard atlas of Pike county, Illinois, including a plat book of the villages, cities and townships of the county. Map of the state, United States and world. Patrons directory, reference business directory and departments devoted to general information. Analysis of the system of U. S. land surveys, digest of the system of civil government . . . 2 p. l., 7–105, [3] 111–121, viii, x–xxiii pp. incl. 39 maps, illus. fol. Chicago, G. A. Ogle & co. 1912. 4587

SANGAMON.

Sangamon county abstract co.

Plat book of Sangamon county, Illinois, showing all cities, villages and towns, acreage and ownership of all lands not platted, nature of soil as classified by U. S. Government survey. Compiled directly from the records . . . 3 p. l., 6–151 pp. incl. 77 col. maps. fol. Springfield, Ill., Sangamon county abstract co. 1914. 4588

NOTE.—Drawings by A. Russell Thayer, Frank L. Mellin and Alfred S. Harkness.

SCHUYLER.

Ogle, G. A., & co.

Standard atlas of Schuyler county, Illinois, including a plat book of the villages, cities and townships of the county. Map of the state, United States and world. Patrons directory, reference business directory and departments devoted to general information. Analysis of the system of U. S. land surveys, digest of the system of civil government . . . 2 p. l., 7–67, viii, x–xxiii pp. incl. 34 col. maps, illus., diagrs. fol. Chicago, G. A. Ogle & co. 1913. 4589

SHELBY.

Ogle, G. A., & co.

Standard atlas of Shelby county, Illinois, including a plat book of the villages, cities and townships of the county. Map of the state, United States and world. Patrons directory, reference business directory and departments devoted to general information . . . 2 p. l., 7–117, viii, x–xxiii pp. incl. 35 col. maps, illus., diagrs. fol. Chicago, G. A. Ogle & co. 1914. 4590

STEPHENSON.

Ogle, G. A., & co.

Standard atlas of Stephenson county, Illinois, including a plat book of the villages, cities and townships of the county. Map of the state, United States and world. Patrons directory, reference business directory and departments devoted to general information. Analysis of the system of U. S. land surveys, digest of the system of civil government . . . 2 p. l., 7–121, [1] viii, x–xxiii pp.

Ogle, G. A., & co.—Continued.

incl. 28 col. maps, illus. fol. Chicago, G. A. Ogle & co. 1913. 4591

UNION.

Ogle, G. A., & co.

Standard atlas of Union county, Illinois, including a plat book of the villages, cities and townships of the county. Map of the State, United States and world. Patrons directory, reference business directory and departments devoted to general information. Analysis of the system of U. S. land surveys, digest of the system of civil government . . . 2 p. l., 7–73, [1] viii, x–xxiii pp. incl. 22 col. maps, illus. fol. Chicago, G. A. Ogle & co. 1908. 4592

VERMILION.

Ogle, G. A., & co.

Standard atlas of Vermilion county, Illinois. Including a plat book of the villages, cities and townships of the county. Map of the state, United States and world. Patrons directory, reference business directory and departments devoted to general information. Analysis of the system of U. S. land surveys, digest of the system of civil government . . . 2 p. l., 8–189, viii, x–xxiii pp. incl. 48 col. maps, illus., ports., diagrs. fol. Chicago, G. A. Ogle & co. 1915. 4593

NOTE.—Contains also chronological arrangement of ancient, medieval and modern history. Supplement, p. x.

WILLIAMSON.

Ogle, G. A., & co.

Standard atlas of Williamson county, Illinois, including a plat book of the villages, cities and townships of the county. Map of the state, United States and world. Patrons directory, reference business directory and departments devoted to general information. Analysis of the system of U. S. land surveys, digest of the system of civil government . . . Historical sketch of Williamson county by judge Geo. W. Young of the Marion bar. Record work and platting by T. J. Youngblood . . . 2 p. l., 7–111, viii, x–xxii pp. incl. 30 col. maps, illus. fol. Chicago, G. A. Ogle & co. 1908. 4594

WINNEBAGO.

Ogle, G. A., & co.

Standard atlas of Winnebago county, Illinois, including a plat book of the villages, cities and townships of the county. Map of the state, United States and world. Patrons directory, reference business directory and departments devoted to general information. Analysis of the system of U. S. land surveys, digest of the system of civil government . . . Record work and platting by the Rockford abstract company . . . 2 p. l., 7–105, viii, x–xxii pp. incl. 40 col. maps, illus. fol. Chicago, G. A. Ogle & co. 1905. 4595

Cities.

CHICAGO.

1912–1913

Chicago real estate index co.

Atlas and ownership index . . . Chicago. Containing maps with full legal description showing the divisions of ownership with the owners name and address; also showing all house numbers with official allotted house numbers for all unimproved properties. Compiled from the records of the city of Chicago & of Cook county . . . v. 11–15. fol. [Chicago] Chicago real estate index co. 1912–1913. 4596

1913

Tillotson, M. D.

Tillotson's pocket map and street guide of Chicago and suburbs of Highland Park, Glencoe, Winnetka, Kenilworth, Wilmette, Evanston, Franklin Park, Maywood, River Forest, Oak Park, Riverside, La Grange, Morgan Park, Indiana Harbor and Gary, Indiana . . . 45, ii–xxxviii, 210 pp. incl. 172 maps. 12°. Chicago, M. D. Tillotson, c1913. 4597

1915

Chicago real estate index co.

Book of valuations of the central business district of Chicago. Covering property located within the following boundaries: Chicago river on the north, Twelfth street on the south, Chicago river (south branch) on the west, rail road property (Illinois central, etc.) on the east . . . 1 p. l., 55 maps. fol. [Chicago] Chicago real estate index co. 1915. 4598

1916

Kandul, S.

Kandul's atlas map guide of Chicago, a complete street, avenue, number and car-line guide to the city with sectional page maps showing ward, township, range and section lines, also blocks, streets, parks, boulevards, elevated, electric and steam railroads and their stations. Location of city, country, state and federal government offices and principal buildings, banks, cemeteries, clubs, express companies and foriegn consuls, golf club courses, hospitals, hotels, lake and ocean steamship offices and docks, restaurants, summer gardens, theatres and places of amusement . . . A correct list of re-named streets showing changes of august 15, 1913, up to and including april 1st, 1916. Compiled, published and revised april of each year . . . vi, 122 pp. incl. 69 maps. 8°. Chicago, S. Kandul, 1916. 4599

1916

Rand, McNally & co.

Atlas of the city of Chicago. cover-title, 1 p. l., 22 pp. incl. 20 maps. fol. Chicago, Rand, McNally & co. 1916. [1915] 4600

1917

Kirk, F. W.

Kirk's map of Chicago. Scale: 1 mile [to 2¾ inches]. Pages 12, 27, 44, 45, 47, 48 & 49. 1 mile [to 2½ inches]. 60 pp. incl. 1 map on 50 pp. and 1 index map. 8°. Chicago, F. W. Kirk [1917] 4601

CICERO.

Real estate map publishing co.

Real estate map publishing co.'s atlas of township of Cicero, Cook county, Ills., except that part lying east of 40th ave. Being the west two-thirds of township 39 north range 13 east of the 3rd principal meridian. Embracing the villages of Oak Park, Austin, Berwyn, Cicero, Morton Park, Hawthorne, Clyde and Ridgeland . . . Compiled and corrected to date from surveyors notes, official records... original plats and deeds or authentic copies thereof, and drawn to a scale of 200 ft. to an inch by Real estate map publishing co. A. C. Ebbesen, draughtsman. 1 p. l., iv, 48 l. fol. Chicago, Real estate map publishing co. 1913. 4602

NOTE.—Leaf no. 47 wanting.

PROVISO.

Real estate map publishing co.

Real estate map publishing co.'s atlas of township of Proviso, Cook county, Illinois . . . embracing the villages of Maywood, Melrose park, Forest Park, River Forest, Riverside, Brookfield, Bellwood, La Grange Park and Hillside . . . A. C. Ebbesen, draughtsman . . . v. 2. fol. Chicago, Real estate map publishing co. 1914. 4603

NOTE.—Collation: v. 2. 1 p. l., iv, 72 l., incl. 74 maps. Scale 200 feet to an inch. Index map follows title-page.

Miscellaneous.

Chicago river.

United States. *Engineer department.*

Atlas containing maps of Chicago river, Illinois, and its branches showing result of improvement by the U. S. government under direction of major W. L. Marshall . . . in 1896 to 1899. 1 p. l. 29 maps. fol. [Washington, D. C., A. B. Graham, photo. lith. 1899] 4604

[U. S. House of representatives. Document no. 95. 56th congress, 1st session]

NOTE.—Atlas to accompany report of W. L. Marshall, dated november 14, 1899.

INDIANA.

State.

Bowen, B. F., & co., *inc.*

Bowen's Indiana state altas containing a separate map of each county, showing section, township and range lines, railroad and interurban lines, churches and school houses and public highways, with a historical sketch of each county. Improved roads shown in colors. Also containing maps of Indiana, the United States and the world; population of counties, townships, incorporated cities and towns, with estimated population for 1920; geographical and other tables; a history of the growth of the state, and an explanation of the system of land surveys. 108, [2] 109–220 pp. incl. 96 col. maps, tab. fol. Indianapolis, B. F. Bowen & co. inc. 1917. 4605

Counties.

ALLEN.

Ogle, G. A., & co.

Standard atlas of Allen county, Indiana, including a plat book of the villages, cities and townships of the county. Map of the state, United States and world. Patrons directory, reference business directory and departments devoted to general information. Analysis of the system of U. S. land surveys, digest of the system of civil government . . . 2 p. l., 7–104, [1] viii, x–xxii pp. incl. 37 col. maps, illus. fol. Chicago, G. A. Ogle & co. 1898. 4606

BENTON.

Ogle, G. A., & co.

Standard atlas of Benton county, Indiana, including a plat book of the villages, cities and townships of the county. Map of the state, United States and world. Patrons directory, reference business directory and departments devoted to general information . . . Record work and platting by Robert A. Swan . . . 2 p.l, 7–65, viii, x–xxii pp. incl. 18 col. maps. fol. Chicago, G. A. Ogle & co. 1909. 4607

CASS.

Chadwick, C. W.

Chadwick farm atlas of Cass county, Indiana. 5 maps. fol. Ann Arbor, Mich., C. W. Chadwick, °1916. 4608

NOTE.—Caption title.

ELKHART.

Ogle, G. A., & co.

Standard atlas of Elkhart county, Indiana, including a plat book of the villages, cities and townships of the county. Map of the state, United States and world. Patrons directory, reference busi-

Ogle, G. A., & co.—Continued.

ness directory and departments devoted to general information. Analysis of the system of U. S. land surveys, digest of the system of civil government . . . 2 p. l., 7–109, viii, x–xxiii pp. incl. 31 col. maps, illus. fol. Chicago, G. A. Ogle & co. 1915. 4609

JASPER.

Ogle, G. A., & co.

Standard atlas of Jasper county, Indiana, including a plat book of the villages, cities and townships of the county. Map of the state, United States and world. Patrons directory, reference business directory and departments devoted to general information. Analysis of the system of civil government. Record work and platting by the Farmers' loan and abstract company . . . 2 p. l., 7–77, [1] viii, x–xxii pp. incl. 20 col. maps, illus. fol. Chicago, G. A. Ogle & co. 1909. 4610

KOSCIUSKO.

Ogle, G. A., & co.

Standard atlas of Kosciusko county, Indiana, including a plat book of the villages, cities and townships of the county. Map of the state, United States and world. Patrons directory, reference business directory and departments devoted to general information. Analysis of the system of U. S. land surveys, digest of the system of civil government . . . 2 p. l., 7–101, xxiii pp. incl. 64 col. maps, 6 pl., 1 map in text. fol. Chicago, G. A. Ogle & co. 1914. 4611

MONTGOMERY.

Ogle, G. A., & co.

Standard atlas of Montgomery county, Indiana, including a plat book of the villages, cities and townships of the county. Map of the state, United States and world. Patrons directory, reference business directory and departments devoted to general information. Analysis of the system of U. S. land surveys, digest of the system of civil government . . . Assisted in compiling and platting of the city of Crawfordsville by prof. J. A. Cragwall . . . and Otto F. Fitzpatrick . . . 2 p. l., 7–54, [4] 57–61, xxii pp. incl. 26 col. maps, illus. fol. Chicago, G. A. Ogle & co. 1917. 4612

NEWTON.

Ogle, G. A., & co.

Standard atlas of Newton county, Indiana, including a plat book of the villages, cities and townships of the county. Map of the state, United States and world. Patrons directory, reference business directory and departments devoted to general information. Analysis of the system of U. S. land surveys, digest of the system of civil government . . . 2 p. l., 7–71, viii, x–xxiii pp. incl. 19 maps, illus. fol. Chicago, G. A. Ogle & co. 1916. 4613

NOBLE.

Coil, R. C., *and* **Cleland, S.**

Complete survey and atlas of Noble county, Indiana, containing complete maps of all townships, cities and villages . . . 49 pp. incl. 20 col. maps. fol. Chicago, Standard map co. °1914. 4614

PULASKI.

Ogle, G. A., & co.

Standard atlas of Pulaski county, Indiana, including a plat book of the villages, cities and townships of the county. Map of the state, United States and world. Patrons directory, reference business directory and departments devoted to general information . . . 2 p. l., 7–53, viii, x–xxii pp. incl. 19 col. maps, illus. fol. Chicago, G. A. Ogle & co. 1906–1907. 4615

ST. JOSEPH.

Higgins, Belden & co.

An illustrated historical atlas of St. Joseph county, Indiana. Compiled, drawn and published from personal examinations & surveys . . . 2 p. l., [3]–4, 7–105 pp. incl. 21 col. maps (1 fold.) illus. fol. Chicago, Higgins, Belden & co. 1875. 4616

TIPPECANOE.

Parker, R. G.

Road and sectional map of Tippecanoe county, Indiana. 13 maps. fol. [La Fayette, Ind.?] °1913. 4617

WHITLEY.

Ogle, G. A., & co.

Standard atlas of Whitley county, Indiana, including a plat book of the villages, cities and townships of the county. Map of the state, United States and world. Patrons directory, reference business directory and departments devoted to general information. Analysis of the system of U. S. land surveys, digest of the system of civil government . . . 2 p. l., 7–50, 61–73, viii, x–xxiii pp. incl. 20 col. maps, illus. fol. Chicago, G. A. Ogle & co. 1916. 4618

Cities.

INDIANAPOLIS.

Baist, G. W.

Baist's real estate atlas of surveys of Indianapolis and vicinity, Indiana . . . Compiled and published from official records, private plans and actual surveys . . . 2 p. l., 35 (*i. e.* 36) col. maps. fol. Philadelphia, G. W. Baist, 1916. 4619

IOWA.

State.

Robinson, E. J., & co.

Illustrated review showing commercial, industrial, agricultural, historical development of the state of Iowa. Descriptive text covering counties, cities and villages based on the latest official sources, with special articles by well known state authorities . . . Newly engraved charts showing principal automobile roads, including the Lincoln highway and its feeders, detailed railroad maps of every state, with complete index; also maps of foreign countries. 192 pp. incl. 57 col. maps. 1 col. map at end. fol. Chicago, E. J. Robinson & co. [G. F. Cram, printer, 1915] 4620

NOTE.—Large map at end entitled, *Cram's superior map of Iowa. Corrected and revised edition. 1915. 34½ x 48.*

Also contains map entitled, *The Panama canal . . . Drawn from official data at Culebra, C. Z., by Wm. Dubois with sanction of the Isthmian canal commission.*

Counties.

ALLAMAKEE.

Anderson publishing co.

Atlas of Allamakee county, Iowa, containing maps of villages, cities and townships of the county. Maps of state, United States and world. Farmers directory, analysis of the system of U. S. land surveys . . . 47 [16] pp., incl. 27 col. maps. fol. Mason City, Iowa, Anderson publishing co. °1917. 4621

APPANOOSE.

Midland map co.

Atlas of Appanoose county, Iowa, 1915. Made from the county records and personal surveys . . . index-title, 3–73 pp. (*i. e.* 42 l.) incl. 38 maps. fol. Knoxville, Iowa, Midland map co. 1915. 4622

NOTE.—Pagination irregular.

BENTON.

Anderson publishing co.

Atlas of Benton county, Iowa, containing maps of townships of the county. Maps of state, United States and world. Farmers directory, analysis of the system of U. S. land surveys . . . 44 [16] pp., incl. 24 col. maps, illus. fol. Mason City, Iowa, Anderson publishing co. °1917. 4623

BOONE.

Anderson publishing co.

Atlas of Boone county, Iowa, containing maps of townships of the county. Maps of state, United States and world. Farmers directory, analysis of the system of U. S. land surveys . . . 53 pp.

incl. 22 col. maps. fol. Mason City, Iowa, Anderson publishing co. 1918. 4624

NOTE.—Copyrighted by G. W. Anderson.

BREMER.

Ogle, G. A., & co.

Standard atlas of Bremer county, Iowa, including a plat book of the villages, cities and townships of the county. Map of the state, United States and world. Patrons directory, reference business directory and departments devoted to general information. Analysis of the system of U. S. land surveys, digest of the system of civil government . . . 2 p. l., 7–57, viii, x–xxiii pp., incl. 25 col. maps, illus. fol. Chicago, G. A. Ogle & co. 1917. 4625

BUTLER.

Anderson publishing co.

Atlas of Butler county, Iowa, containing maps of townships of the county. Maps of state, United States and world. Farmers directory, analysis of the system of U. S. land surveys . . . 36 [16] pp. incl. 21 col. maps. fol. Mason City, Iowa, Anderson publishing co. 1917. 4626

NOTE.—Copyrighted by G. W. Anderson.

CASS.

Anderson publishing co.

Atlas of Cass county, Iowa, containing maps of townships of the county. Maps of state, United States and world. Farmers directory, analysis of the system of U. S. land surveys . . . 36, [16] pp. incl. 21 col. maps. fol. Mason City, Iowa, Anderson publishing co. 1917. 4627

NOTE.—Copyrighted by G. W. Anderson.

CEDAR.

Anderson publishing co.

Atlas of Cedar county, Iowa, containing maps of townships of the county. Maps of state, United States and world. Farmers directory, analysis of the system of U. S. land surveys . . . 37 [18] pp. incl. 22 col. maps. fol. Mason City, Iowa, Anderson publishing co. 1916. 4628

NOTE.—"Copyrighted by G. W. Anderson, 1916."

CHICKASAW.

Anderson publishing co.

Standard historical atlas of Chickasaw county, Iowa, containing maps of villages, cities and townships of the county. Maps of state, United States and world. Farmers directory, business directory and general information. 59 [16] 8 pp. incl. 26 col. maps. fol. Chicago, Anderson publishing co. 1915. 4629

CLARKE.

Osceola sentinel.

Complete atlas of Clarke county, Iowa . . . 28 pp. incl. 13 col. maps. sm. fol. [Osceola, Iowa] Osceola sentinel, 1909. 4630

CLAY.

Anderson publishing co.

Atlas of Clay county, Iowa, containing maps of townships of the county. Maps of state, United States and world. Farmers directory, analysis of the system of U. S. land surveys. 35 [16] pp. incl. 22 col. maps. fol. Mason City, Iowa, 1919. 4630a

NOTE.—"Copyrighted by G. W. Anderson, 1919."

CLAYTON.

Webb publishing co.

Atlas and farm directory with complete survey in township plats of Clayton county, Iowa, containing plats of all townships with owners' names; also maps of the state, United States and world; also an outline map of the county showing location of townships, villages, roads, schools, churches, railroads, streams . . . Published by the Farmer. 52, 12 pp. incl. 26 col. maps, illus. fol. St. Paul, Minn., Webb publishing co. ©1914. 4631

DALLAS.

Anderson publishing co.

Atlas of Dallas county, Iowa, containing maps of townships of the county, maps of state, United States and world. Farmers directory, analysis of the system of U. S. land surveys . . . 36 [17] pp. incl. 22 col. maps. fol. Mason City, Iowa, Anderson publishing co. 1916. 4632

NOTE.—"Copyrighted by G. W. Anderson, 1916."

DAVIS.

Ogle, G. A., & co.

Standard atlas of Davis county, Iowa, including a plat book of the villages, cities and townships of the county. Map of the state, United States and world. Patrons directory, reference business directory and departments devoted to general information. Analysis of the system of U. S. land surveys, digest of the system of civil government . . . 2 p. l., 7–67, [1], viii, x–xxiii pp. incl. 34 maps, illus. fol. Chicago, G. A. Ogle & co. 1912. 4633

DES MOINES.

Northwest publishing co.

Plat book of Des Moines county, Iowa . . . 2 p. l., 3–39 [13] pp. incl. 28 col. maps. fol. [Philadelphia] Northwest publishing co. 1897. 4634

Note.—Eng. by Balliet & Volk . . . Phila. Printed by F. Bourquin . . . Philad.

EMMET.

Ogle, G. A., & co.

Standard atlas of Emmet county, Iowa, including a plat book of the villages, cities and townships of the county. Map of the state, United States and world. Patrons directory, reference business directory and departments devoted to general information. Analysis of the system of U. S. land surveys, digest of the system of civil government . . . 2 p. l., 7–51, xxii pp. incl. 24 col. maps, illus. fol. Chicago, G. A. Ogle & co. 1918. 4635

FAYETTE.

Ogle, G. A., & co.

Standard atlas of Fayette county, Iowa, including a plat book of the villages, cities and townships of the county. Map of the state, United States and world. Patrons directory, reference business directory and departments devoted to general information. Analysis of the system of U. S. land surveys, digest of the system of civil government . . . 2 p. l., 7–129, viii, x–xxiii pp., incl. 35 maps, illus. fol. Chicago, G. A. Ogle & co. 1916. 4636

FLOYD.

Anderson publishing co.

Atlas of Floyd county, Iowa . . . Drawn from actual surveys and county records . . . 29 pp. incl. 14 col. maps. fol. Chicago, Anderson publishing co. 1913. 4637

GREENE.

1909

Midland map co.

Atlas of Greene county, Iowa. 35 [7] pp. incl. 17 col. maps. sm. fol. Knoxville, Iowa, Midland map co. 1909. 4638

Note.—Contains a "Digest of the system of United States land survey." 7 pp.

1917

Ogle, G. A., & co.

Standard atlas of Greene county, Iowa, including a plat book of the villages, cities and townships of the county. Map of the state, United States and world. Patrons directory, reference business directory and departments devoted to general information.

Ogle, G. A., & co.—Continued.

Analysis of the system of U. S. land surveys, digest of the system of civil government . . . 2 p. l., 7–61, xxii pp., incl. 26 col. maps, illus. fol. Chicago, G. A. Ogle & co. 1917. 4639

HAMILTON.

Ogle, G. A., & co.

Standard atlas of Hamilton county, Iowa, including a plat book of the villages, cities and townships of the county. Map of the state, United States and world. Patrons directory, reference business directory and departments devoted to general information. Analysis of the system of U. S. land surveys, digest of the system of civil government . . . 2 p. l., 7–59, xxii pp. incl. 30 col. maps, illus. fol. Chicago, G. A. Ogle & co. 1918. 4640

HANCOCK.

Anderson publishing co.

Atlas of Hancock county, Iowa, containing maps of villages, cities and townships of the county. 55 pp. incl. 26 col. maps. fol. Chicago, Anderson publishing co. °1914. 4641

Note.—Copyrighted by G. W. Anderson.

HENRY.

Ogle, G. A., & co.

Standard atlas of Henry county, Iowa, including a plat book of the villages, cities and townships of the county. Map of the state, United States and world. Patrons directory, reference business directory and departments devoted to general information. Analysis of the system of U. S. land surveys, digest of the system of civil government . . . 2 p. l., 7–57, xxii pp. incl. 26 col. maps, illus. fol. Chicago, G. A. Ogle & co. 1917. 4642

IOWA.

Anderson publishing co.

Atlas of Iowa county, Iowa, containing maps of townships of the county. Maps of state, United States and world. Farmers directory, analysis of the system of U. S. land surveys . . . 53 pp. incl. 21 col. maps. fol. Mason City, Iowa, Anderson publishing co. 1917. 4643

Note.—Copyrighted by G. W. Anderson, 1917.

JONES.

Ogle, G. A., & co.

Standard atlas of Jones county, Iowa, including a plat book of the villages, cities and townships of the county. Map of the state, United States and world. Patrons directory, reference business directory and departments devoted to general information.

Analysis of the system of U. S. land surveys, digest of the system of civil government . . . 2 p. l., 7–97, viii, x–xxiii pp. incl. 27 col. maps, illus. fol. Chicago, G. A. Ogle & co. 1915. 4644

KEOKUK.

Foote, C. M., *and* **Hood, E. C.**

Plat book of Keokuk county, Iowa . . . 46 pp. incl. 29 col. maps. fol. Minneapolis, Minn., C. M. Foote & co. 1887. 4645

Note.—Eng. by Wm. Bracher . . . Philad. Printed by Wm. Hart . . . Philad.

KOSSUTH.

Anderson publishing co.

Atlas of Kossuth county, Iowa, containing plats of all townships with owners names; also drainage districts, rural routes and outline map of the county showing location of townships, villages, roads, schools, churches, railroads, streams . . . 59 pp. incl. 29 col. maps. fol. Chicago, Anderson publishing co. 1913. 4646

LEE.

Ogle, G. A., & co.

Standard atlas of Lee county, Iowa, including a plat book of the villages, cities and townships of the county. Map of the state, United States and world. Patrons directory, reference business directory and departments devoted to general information. Analysis of the system of U. S. land surveys, digest of the system of civil government . . . 2 p. l., 7–79, viii, x–xxiii pp., incl. 33 maps, illus. fol. Chicago, G. A. Ogle & co. 1916. 4647

LOUISA.

Ogle, G. A., & co.

Standard atlas of Louisa county, Iowa. Including a plat book of the villages, cities and townships of the county. Map of the state, United States and world. Patrons directory, reference business directory and departments devoted to general information. Analysis of the system of U. S. land surveys, digest of the system of civil government . . . 2 p. l., 7–51, viii, x–xxiii pp., incl. 24 col. maps, illus. fol. Chicago, G. A. Ogle & co. 1917. 4648

MAHASKA.

Midland map co.

Atlas of Mahaska county, Iowa, 1913. Drawn from the county records and field surveys by the Midland map co. 61 (*i. e.* 67) pp. incl. 33 col. maps. fol. Knoxville, Iowa, Midland map co. ©1913. 4649

MILLS.

Bee publishing co.

Atlas of Douglas, Sarpy and Washington counties, Nebraska, and Mills and Pottawattamie counties, Iowa, containing maps of the townships of the counties, maps of Omaha and South Omaha, Nebraska and Council Bluffs, Iowa, drawn from actual surveys and county records. Comp. by the Anderson publishing company . . . for the Bee publishing company . . . 83, [4] pp. incl. 78 maps. fol. Omaha, Nebr., Bee publishing co. 1913 [1912] 4650

MONONA.

Anderson publishing co.

Atlas of Monona county, Iowa, containing maps of townships of the county. Maps of state, United States and world. Farmers directory, analysis of the system of U. S. land surveys. 41 [16] pp. incl. 25 col. maps. fol. Mason City, Iowa, 1919. 4651

NOTE.—"Copyrighted by G. W. Anderson."

MUSCATINE.

Anderson publishing co.

Atlas of Muscatine county, Iowa, containing maps of villages, cities, and townships of the county. Maps of state, United States and world . . . 49, [16] pp., incl. 21 maps, illus. fol. Mason City, Ia., Anderson publishing co. ©1916. 4652

NOTE.—Copyrighted 1916 by G. W. Anderson.

PLYMOUTH.

Le Mars sentinel.

Atlas and farm directory with complete survey in township plats of Plymouth county, Iowa, containing map of county and plats of all townships with owners name, showing townships, school districts, towns, county roads, township roads, rural routes, railroads, streams, schools, churches . . . Drawn and engraved by the Anderson publishing co., Chicago, Ill.. 67 pp. incl. 31 maps, illus. fol. Le Mars, Iowa, Le Mars sentinel, ©1914. 4653

POCAHONTAS.

Anderson publishing co.

Atlas of Pocahontas county, Iowa, containing maps of townships of the county. Maps of state, United States and world. Farmers directory, analysis of the system of U. S. land surveys . . . 35 [17] pp. incl. 22 col. maps. fol. Mason City, Iowa, Anderson publishing co. 1918. 4654

NOTE.—Copyrighted by G. W. Anderson.

POTTAWATTAMIE.

Bee publishing co.

Atlas of Douglas, Sarpy and Washington counties, Nebraska, and Mills and Pottawattamie counties, Iowa, containing maps of the townships of the counties, maps of Omaha and South Omaha, Nebraska, and Council Bluffs, Iowa, drawn from actual surveys and county records. Comp. by the Anderson publishing company . . . for the Bee publishing company . . . 83, [4] pp., incl. 78 maps. fol. Omaha, Nebr., Bee publishing co. 1913. [1912] 4655

RINGGOLD.

Ogle, G. A., & co.

Standard atlas of Ringgold county, Iowa, including a plat book of the villages, cities and townships of the county. Map of the state, United States and world. Patrons directory, reference business directory and departments devoted to general information. Analysis of the U. S. land surveys, digest of the system of civil government . . . 2 p. l., 7–81, viii, x–xxiii pp. incl. 24 col. maps, illus. fol. Chicago, G. A. Ogle & co. 1915. 4656

SAC.

Midland map co.

Atlas of Sac county, Iowa. 1912. 35 pp. incl. 17 col. maps. sm. fol. Knoxville, Iowa, Midland map co. 1912. 4657

SCOTT.

Huebinger, M.

Atlas of Scott county, Iowa, containing also maps of the three cities, Davenport, Rock Island, and Moline, Rock Island arsenal, Rock Island rapids and the Hennepin canal . . . 112 pp. incl. 42 col. maps. fol. Davenport, M. Huebinger & co. 1894. 4658

NOTE.—Contains, Directory of the leading [Davenport] business houses, and Directory of the leading farmers of Scott county. Also, Historischer ueberblick der stadt Davenport und umgegend.

SIOUX.

Anderson publishing co.

Atlas of Sioux county, Iowa. Containing plats of all townships with owners' names; also map of county . . . 53 pp. incl. 24 col. maps, illus. fol. Chicago, Anderson publishing co. 1913. 4659

NOTE.—Head of title: Alton Democrat, Jno. F. D. Aue, publisher. Copyright 1913, by the Alton Democrat, Alton, Iowa.

TAMA.

Anderson publishing co.

Atlas of Tama county, Iowa. Containing maps of villages, cities and townships of the county. Maps of state, United States and world . . . 43 pp., 6 l., incl. 25 col. maps, illus. fol. Chicago, Anderson publishing co. ©1916. 4660

NOTE.—Copyrighted 1916 by G. W. Anderson.

UNION.

Ogle, G. A., & co.

Standard atlas of Union county, Iowa, including a plat book of the villages, cities and townships of the county. Map of the state, United States and world. Patrons directory, reference business directory and departments devoted to general information. Analysis of the system of U. S. land surveys, digest of the system of civil government . . . 2 p. l., 7–73, viii, x–xxiii pp. incl. 24 col. maps, illus. fol. Chicago, G. A. Ogle & co. 1916. 4661

VAN BUREN.

Ogle, G. A., & co.

Standard atlas of Van Buren county, Iowa, including a plat book of the villages, cities and townships of the county. Map of the state, United States and world. Patrons directory, reference business directory and departments devoted to general information. Analysis of the system of U. S. land surveys, digest of the system of civil government . . . 2 p. l., 7–63, xxii pp. incl. 26 col. maps, illus. fol. Chicago, G. A. Ogle & co. 1918. 4662

WARREN.

Midland map co.

Atlas of Warren county, Iowa, 1915. Made from the county records and field surveys . . . 37 pp. incl. 18 col. maps. fol. Knoxville, Iowa, Midland map co. 1915. 4663

NOTE.—Pages 19–[20] misplaced.

WINNEBAGO.

Anderson publishing co.

Atlas of Winnebago county, Iowa, containing maps of villages, cities and townships of the county . . . 49, [16] pp. incl. 24 col. maps, illus. fol. Chicago, Anderson publishing co. 1913. 4664

WINNESHIEK.

Webb publishing co.

Atlas and farm directory with complete survey in township plats of Winneshiek county, Iowa. Containing plats of all townships with owners' names; also maps of the state, United States and world; also an outline map of the county showing location of townships, villages, roads, schools, churches, railroads, streams,

. . . published by the Farmer . . . Drawn and engraved by the Anderson publishing co., Chicago, Ill. 43, [12] pp. incl. 25 col. maps, illus., ports. fol. St. Paul, Minn., Webb publishing co. 1915. 4665

WOODBURY.

Anderson publishing co.

Atlas of Woodbury county, Iowa, containing maps of villages, cities and townships of the county. Maps of state, United States and world. Farmers directory . . . 99 [26] pp., incl. 46 col. maps. fol. Mason City, Iowa, Anderson publishing co. ©1917. 4666

WORTH.

Anderson publishing co.

Standard historical atlas of Worth county, Iowa, containing maps of villages, cities and townships of the county. Maps of state, United States and world. Farmers directory, business directory and general information. [118] pp. incl. 26 col. maps, illus. diagrs. fol. Chicago, Anderson publishing co. 1913. 4667

NOTE.—Various paging.

WRIGHT.

Ogle, G. A., & co.

Standard atlas of Wright county, Iowa, including a plat book of the villages, cities and townships of the county. Map of the state, United States and world. Patrons directory, reference business directory and departments devoted to general information. Analysis of the system of U. S. land surveys, digest of the system of civil government . . . 2 p. l., 7–87, viii, x–xxiii pp. incl. 27 maps, illus. fol. Chicago, G. A. Ogle & co. 1912. 4668

Cities.

DES MOINES.

Hartley, F. G.

Hartley's atlas of business district of Des Moines, Iowa. 3 p. l., 114 pp. incl. 115 maps. fol. [Des Moines ? F. G. Hartley] ©1913. 4669

KANSAS.

Counties.

BARTON.

Kenyon co.

Atlas and plat book of Barton county, Kansas. Containing outline map of the county; plats of all the townships with owners' names; Kansas state map showing automobile roads; and maps of the United States and world. 2 p. l., 4–55 pp., 9 l., incl. 26 col.

Kenyon co.—Continued.

maps, illus. fol. Great Bend, Kan., the Barton county daily democrat, ©1916. 4670

NOTE.—Map of Cheyenne township, pp. 26–27 appears twice, consecutively. Index on title-page.

BUTLER.

Ogle, G. A., & co.

Standard atlas of Butler county, Kansas, including a plat book of the villages, cities and townships of the county. Map of the state, United States and world. Patrons directory, reference business directory and departments devoted to general information . . . 2 p. l., 7–121, viii, x–xxiii pp. incl. 39 col. maps, illus. fol. Chicago, G. A. Ogle & co. 1905. 4671

CLAY.

Ogle, G. A., & co.

Standard atlas of Clay county, Kansas, including a plat book of the villages, cities and townships of the county. Map of the state, United States and world. Patrons directory, reference business directory and departments devoted to general information. Analysis of the system of U. S. land surveys, digest of the system of civil government, etc., etc. Assisted in record work and platting by Eric H. Swenson . . . 2 p. l., 7–57, xxii pp. incl. 31 col. maps, illus. fol. Chicago, G. A. Ogle & co. 1918. 4672

CLOUD.

Ogle, G. A., & co.

Standard atlas of Cloud county, Kansas, including a plat book of the villages, cities and townships of the county. Map of the state, United States and world. Patrons directory, reference business directory and departments devoted to general information. Analysis of the system of U. S. land surveys, digest of the system of civil government . . . 2 p. l., 7–93, xxii pp. incl. 29 col. maps, illus. fol. Chicago, G. A. Ogle & co. 1917. 4673

COFFEY.

Ogle, G. A., & co.

Standard atlas of Coffey county, Kansas, including a plat book of the villages, cities and townships of the county. Map of the state, United States and world. Patrons directory, reference business directory and departments devoted to general information. Analysis of the system of U. S. land surveys, digest of the system of civil government . . . 2 p. l., 7–57, xxii pp. incl. 29 col. maps, illus. fol. Chicago, G. A. Ogle & co. 1919. 4674

COWLEY.

Ogle, G. A., & co.

Standard atlas of Cowley county, Kansas, including a plat book of the villages, cities and townships of the county. Map of the state, United States and world. Patrons directory, reference business directory and departments devoted to general information. Analysis of the system of U. S. land surveys, digest of the system of civil government . . . 2 p. l., 7–129, [1] viii, x–xxiii pp. incl. 37 col. maps, illus. fol. Chicago, G. A. Ogle & co. 1905. 4675

ELLSWORTH.

Ogle, G. A., & co.

Standard atlas of Ellsworth county, Kansas, including a plat book of the villages, cities and townships of the county. Map of the state, United States and world. Patrons directory, reference business directory and departments devoted to general information. Analysis of the system of U. S. land surveys, digest of the system of civil government . . . 2 p. l., 7–59, xxii pp. incl. 29 col. maps, illus. fol. Chicago, G. A. Ogle & co. 1918. 4676

FORD.

1905-1906

Ogle, G. A., & co.

Standard atlas of Ford county, Kansas, including a plat book of the villages, cities and townships of the county. Map of the state, United States and world. Patrons directory, reference business directory and departments devoted to general information . . . 2 p. l., 7–93, viii, x–xxii. pp. incl. 37 col. maps, illus. fol. Chicago, Alden publishing co.; G. A. Ogle & co. 1905–1906. 4677

1916

Kenyon co.

Atlas and plat book of Ford county, Kansas. Containing outline map of the county; plats of all the townships with owners' names; Kansas state map showing automobile roads; parcel post map of the United States and map of the world. 82 pp., 2 l., incl. 37 col. maps. illus. fol. Dodge City, Kan., Dodge City journal, ©1916. 4678

Note.—Pages 68–74 found between pp. 6–7.
Index on title-page.

GRAHAM.

Ogle, G. A., & co.

Standard atlas of Graham county, Kansas, including a plat book of the villages, cities and townships of the county. Map of the state, United States, and world. Patrons directory, reference

Ogle, G. A., & co.—Continued.
business directory and departments devoted to general information . . . 2 p. l., 7–87, viii, x–xxii pp. incl. 31 col. maps, illus. fol. Chicago, G. A. Ogle & co. 1906. 4679

HARPER.

Ogle, G. A., & co.
Standard atlas of Harper county, Kansas, including a plat book of the villages, cities and townships of the county. Map of the state, United States and world. Patrons directory, reference business directory and departments devoted to general information. Analysis of the system of U. S. land surveys, digest of the system of civil government . . . 2 p. l., 65, xxii pp. incl. 29 col. maps, illus. fol. Chicago, G. A. Ogle & co. 1919. 4680

HARVEY.

Ogle, G. A., & co.
Standard atlas of Harvey county, Kansas, including a plat book of villages, cities and townships of the county. Map of the state, United States and world. Patrons directory, reference business directory and departments devoted to general information. Analysis of the system of U. S. land surveys, digest of the system of civil government . . . 2 p. l., 7–59, xxii pp. incl. 32 col. maps, illus. fol. Chicago, G. A. Ogle & co. 1918. 4681

JEFFERSON.

Ogle, G. A., & co.
Standard atlas of Jefferson county, Kansas, including a plat book of the villages, cities and townships of the county. Map of the state, United States and world. Patrons directory, reference business directory and departments devoted to general information. Analysis of the system of U. S. land surveys, digest of the system of civil government . . . 2 p. l., 7–83, viii, x–xxiii pp., incl. 21 maps, illus. fol. Chicago, G. A. Ogle & co. 1916. 4682

LABETTE.

1906

Ogle, G. A., & co.
Standard atlas of Labette county, Kansas, including a plat book of the villages, cities and townships of the county. Map of the state, United States, and world. Patrons directory, reference business directory and departments devoted to general information . . . 2 p. l., 7–87, viii, x–xxii pp. incl. 27 col. maps, illus. fol. Chicago, G. A. Ogle & co. 1906. 4683

1916

Kenyon co.

Atlas and plat book of Labette county, Kansas. Containing outline map of the county; plats of all the townships with owners' names, cities and towns, and Kansas state map showing automobile roads. 51 pp., 2 l., incl. 21 col. maps. fol. Parsons & Oswego, Kan., C. A. Wilkin & co. ©1916. 4684

NOTE.—Copyright 1916 by the Kenyon company, map makers, Des Moines, Iowa. Index on title-page.

LINCOLN.

Ogle, G. A., & co.

Standard atlas of Lincoln county, Kansas, including a plat book of the villages, cities and townships of the county. Map of the state, United States and world. Patrons directory, reference business directory and departments devoted to general information. Analysis of the system of U. S. land surveys, digest of the system of civil government . . . 2 p. l., 7–59, xxii pp. incl. 22 col. maps, illus. fol. Chicago, G. A. Ogle & co. 1918. 4685

LYON.

1878

Edwards bros.

An illustrated historical atlas of Lyon county, Kansas. Compiled, drawn and published from personal examination and surveys . . . 65 pp. incl. 36 col. maps, illus. 2 maps. fol. Philadelphia, Edwards brothers. 1878. 4686

1918

Ogle, G. A., & co.

Standard atlas of Lyon county, Kansas, including a plat book of the villages, cities and townships of the county. Map of the state, United States and world. Patrons directory, reference business directory and departments devoted to general information. Analysis of the system of U. S. land surveys, digest of the system of civil government . . . 2 p. l., 7–77, xxii pp. incl. 39 col. maps, illus. fol. Chicago, G. A. Ogle & co. 1918. 4687

MITCHELL.

Ogle, G. A., & co.

Standard atlas of Mitchell county, Kansas, including a plat book of the villages, cities and townships of the county. Map of the state, United States and world. Patrons directory, reference business directory and departments devoted to general information. Analysis of the system of U. S. land surveys, digest of the system of civil government . . . 2 p. l., 7–61, xxii pp., incl. 30 col. maps, illus. fol. Chicago, G. A. Ogle & co. 1917. 4688

NEOSHO.

Ogle, G. A., & co.

Standard atlas of Neosho county, Kansas, including a plat book of the villages, cities and townships of the county. Map of the state, United States and world. Patrons directory, reference business directory and departments devoted to general information . . . 2 p. l., 7–79, viii, x–xxii pp. incl. 23 col. maps, illus. fol. Chicago, G. A. Ogle & co. 1906. 4689

NORTON.

Ogle, G. A., & co.

Standard atlas of Norton county, Kansas, including a plat book of the villages, cities and townships of the county. Map of the state, United States and world. Patrons directory, reference business directory and departments devoted to general information. Analysis of the system of U. S. land surveys, digest of the system of civil government . . . 2 p. l., 59, viii, x–xxiii pp. incl. 35 col. maps, illus. fol. Chicago, G. A. Ogle & co. 1917. 4690

OSAGE.

Ogle, G. A., & co.

Standard atlas of Osage county, Kansas, including a plat book of the villages, cities and townships of the county. Map of the state, United States and world. Patrons directory, reference business directory and departments devoted to general information. Analysis of the system of U. S. land surveys, digest of the system of civil government . . . 2 p. l., 7–77, xxii pp. incl. 31 col. maps, illus. fol. Chicago, G. A. Ogle & co. 1918. 4691

OSBORNE.

Ogle, G. A., & co.,

Standard atlas of Osborne county, Kansas, including a plat book of the villages, cities and townships of the county. Map of the state, United States and world. Patrons directory, reference business directory and departments devoted to general information. Analysis of the system of U. S. land surveys, digest of the system of civil government . . . 2 p. l., 7–69, xxii pp., incl. 31 col. maps, illus. fol. Chicago, G. A. Ogle & co. 1917. 4692

OTTAWA.

Ogle, G. A., & co.

Standard atlas of Ottawa county, Kansas, including a plat book of the villages, cities and townships of the county. Map of the state, United States and world. Patrons directory, reference business directory and departments devoted to general information. Analysis of the system of U. S. land surveys, digest of the system of civil government . . . 2 p. l., 7–63, xxii pp., incl. 32 col. maps, illus. fol. Chicago, G. A. Ogle & co. 1918. 4693

PHILLIPS.

Ogle, G. A., & co.

Standard atlas of Phillips county, Kansas, including a plat book of the villages, cities and townships of the county. Map of the state, United States and world. Patrons directory, reference business directory and departments devoted to general information. Analysis of the system of U. S. land surveys, digest of the system of civil government . . . 2 p. l., 7–67 pp. viii, x–xxiii pp. incl. 38 col. maps, illus. fol. Chicago, G. A. Ogle & co. 1917. 4694

POTTAWATOMIE.

Ogle, G. A., & co.

Standard atlas of Pottawatomie county, Kansas, including a plat book of the villages, cities and townships of the county. Map of the state, United States and world. Patrons directory, reference business directory and departments devoted to general information . . . 2 p. l., 7–93, viii, x–xxii pp. incl. 31 col. maps, illus. fol. Chicago, G. A. Ogle & co. 1905. 4695

RENO.

Ogle, G. A., & co.

Standard atlas of Reno county, Kansas, including a plat book of the villages, cities and townships of the county. Map of the state, United States and world. Patrons directory, reference business directory and departments devoted to general information. Analysis of the system of U. S. land surveys, digest of the system of civil government . . . Compiled and published by Geo. A. Ogle & co., Chicago. Assisted in record work and platting by the Hall abstract co., Hutchinson, Kansas. 2 p. l., 7–101, xxii pp. incl. 55 col. maps, illus. fol. Chicago, G. A. Ogle & co. 1918. 4696

RICE.

Ogle, G. A., & co.

Standard atlas of Rice county, Kansas, including a plat book of the villages, cities and townships of the county. Map of the state, United States and world. Patrons directory, reference business directory and departments devoted to general information. Analysis of the system of U. S. land surveys, digest of the system of civil government . . . 2 p. l., 7–61, xxii pp. incl. 34 col. maps, illus. fol. Chicago, G. A. Ogle & co. 1919. 4697

SEDGWICK.

Edwards bros.

[Historical atlas of Sedgwick county, Kansas] 58 pp. incl. 31 col. maps. fol. [Philadelphia, Edwards brothers] 1882. 4698

Note.—t.-p., p. 23–24, 31–32, 43–44 wanting.
Binder's title.

SHAWNEE.

Kansas farmer co.

Plat book, directory and survey of Shawnee county, Kansas. 1913. Compiled from latest data on record . . . 44 pp. incl. 12 maps, illus. fol. Topeka, Kansas farmer co. 1913. 4699

SHERIDAN.

Ogle, G. A., & co.

Standard atlas of Sheridan county, Kansas, including a plat book of the villages, cities and townships of the county. Map of the state, United States and world. Patrons directory, reference business directory and departments devoted to general information . . . 2 p. l., 7–79, viii, x–xxii pp. incl. 32 col. maps, illus. fol. Chicago, G. A. Ogle & co. 1906–1907. 4700

SMITH.

Ogle, G. A., & co.

Standard atlas of Smith county, Kansas, including a plat book of the villages, cities and townships of the county. Map of the state, United States and world. Patrons directory, reference business directory and departments devoted to general information. Analysis of the system of U. S. land surveys, digest of the system of civil government . . . 2 p. l., 7–58 [4] 61–71 xxii pp. incl. 36 col. maps, illus. fol. Chicago, G. A. Ogle & co. 1917. 4701

STAFFORD.

Ogle, G. A., & co.

Standard atlas of Stafford county, Kansas, including a plat book of the villages, cities and townships of the county. Map of the state, United States and world. Patrons directory, reference business directory and departments devoted to general information . . . 2 p. l., 7–79, viii, x–xxii pp. incl. 26 col. maps, illus. fol. Chicago, G. A. Ogle & co. 1904. 4702

SUMNER.

Ogle, G. A., & co.

Standard atlas of Sumner county, Kansas, including a plat book of the villages, cities and townships of the county. Map of the state, United States and world. Patrons directory, reference business directory and departments devoted to general information. Analysis of the system of U. S. land surveys, digest of the system of civil government . . . 2 p. l., 7–97, xxii pp. incl. 37 col. maps, illus. fol. Chicago, G. A. Ogle & co. 1918. 4703

WABAUNSEE.

Ogle, G. A., & co.

Standard atlas of Wabaunsee county, Kansas, including a plat book of the villages, cities and townships of the county. Map of the state, United States and world. Patrons directory, reference business directory and departments devoted to general information. Analysis of the system of U. S. land surveys, digest of the system of civil government . . . 2 p. l., 7–81, xxii pp. incl. 24 col. maps, illus. fol. Chicago, G. A. Ogle & co. 1919. 4704

KENTUCKY.

Counties.

JEFFERSON.

Louisville title co.

Louisville title co.'s . . . new map of Louisville and Jefferson county, Kentucky. Compiled from actual surveys, and official records . . . Compiled and drawn by William B. Hunter. 1 p. l., 114 maps. obl. fol. Louisville, Ky., Louisville title co. ©1913. 4705

LOUISVILLE.

Louisville title co.

Louisville title co.'s . . . new map of Louisville and Jefferson county, Kentucky. Compiled from actual surveys, and official records . . . Compiled and drawn by William B. Hunter. 1 p. l., 114 maps. obl. fol. Louisville, Ky., Louisville title co. ©1913. 4706

LOUISIANA.

Louisiana. *Department of education.*

Thirty maps showing the public school situation in a few essential respects. Session of 1914–15. 36 pp. incl. 30 maps. sm. 16°. [Baton Rouge, 1915] 4707

MARYLAND.

Oysters.

Maryland. *Shell fish commission.*

Charts of Maryland oyster survey, 1906–1912. [Surveyed by Maryland shellfish commission in cooperation with United States bureau of fisheries and United States coast and geodetic survey: prepared under the direction of C. C. Yates] 1 p. l. 42 (*i. e.* 44) maps. fol. [Washington, government printing office, 1913] 4708

NOTE.—To accompany: *United States coast and geodetic survey. Summary of survey of oyster bars of Maryland, 1906–1912, by C. C. Yates. 1913.* (In pocket on inside of front cover)

Maryland. *Shell fish commission*—Continued.

CONTENTS.

Index chart of natural oyster bars etc. in 2 sheets.
no. 1. Fort Carroll to Magothy river.
" 2. Magothy river to Annapolis roads.
" 3. Annapolis roads to Horseshoe Point.
" 4. Horseshoe Point to Holland Point.
" 5–10. Somerset county and adjacent waters.
" 11–12. Wicomico county and adjacent waters.
" 13–15. Worcester county.
" 16–18. Calvert county.
" 19. Calvert, St. Marys and Charles counties.
" 20. Calvert and St. Marys counties.
" 21–25. St. Marys county.
" 26. Charles and St. Marys counties.
" 27. Baltimore county.
" 28. Kent county.
" 29–30. Kent and Queen Annes counties.
" 31–32. Queen Annes and Talbot counties.
" 33–34. Talbot county.
" 35–37. Talbot and Dorchester counties.
" 38–42. Dorchester county.

Counties.

BALTIMORE.

Bromley, G. W., & W. S.

Atlas of Baltimore county, Maryland. From actual surveys and official plans . . . 1 p. l., 44 maps (part. col.) fol. Philadelphia, G. W. Bromley & co. 1915. 4709

MONTGOMERY.

Deets, E. H., *and* **Maddox, C. J.**

A real estate atlas of the part of Montgomery county, Maryland, adjacent to the District of Columbia, comprising all of Rockville, Potomac, Bethesda and Wheaton election districts and parts of Colesville, Gaithersburg, and Olney election districts, showing property owners, with their outlines, acreage, and references to the land records, also, roads, streams, district lines, subdivisions and lots, as given by the Montgomery county assessment books for 1916. 1 p. l., 45 maps. fol. Rockville, Md., E. H. Deets & C. J. Maddox, 1917. 4710

Cities.

BALTIMORE.

Baltimore. *Topographical survey commission.*

Atlas of the city of Baltimore, Maryland, made from surveys and official plans. By the topographical survey commission. 2 p. l., index map, 34 col. maps. fol. [Baltimore, A. Hoen & co.] 1914. 4711

MASSACHUSETTS.

Cities.

1912

Massachusetts. *Harbor and land commission.*

Atlas of the boundaries of the towns of Amherst, Enfield, Greenwich, Hadley, Pelham, Prescott, Hampshire county; Leverett Shutesbury, Sunderland, New Salem, Franklin county; Barre, Dana, Hardwick, New Braintree, Petersham, Worcester county . . . 1 p. l., [30] 31 pp. incl. 10 maps. fol. [Boston] 1912. 4712

1913

Atlas of the boundaries of the cities of North Adams and Pittsfield; and towns of Adams, Cheshire, Clarksburg, Dalton, Florida, Hancock, Lanesborough, New Ashford, Savoy, Williamstown, Windsor, Berkshire county; Ashfield, Buckland, Charlemont, Colrain, Conway, Deerfield, Greenfield, Hawley, Heath, Leyden, Monroe, Rowe, Shelburne, Franklin county; Cummington, Plainfield, Hampshire county . . . 1 p. l., [79] pp. incl. 10 maps. fol. [Boston] 1913. 4713

1914

Atlas of the boundaries of the city of Holyoke and towns of Agawam, Blandford, Chester, Granville, Montgomery, Russell, Southwick, Tolland, Westfield, West Springfield, Hampden county; city of Northampton and towns of Chesterfield, Easthampton, Goshen, Hatfield, Huntington, Southampton, Westhampton, Williamsburg, Worthington, Hampshire county; Whatley, Franklin county . . . 21 p. l., 38 pp. incl. 12 maps. fol. [Boston] 1914. 4714

1915

Atlas of the boundaries of the towns of Alford, Becket, Egremont, Great Barrington, Hinsdale, Lee, Lenox, Monterey, Mount Washington, New Marlborough, Otis, Peru, Richmond, Sandisfield,

Massachusetts. *Harbor and land commission*—Continued.

Sheffield, Stockbridge, Tyringham, Washington, West Stockbridge, Berkshire county; and Middlefield, Hampshire county . . . 1 p.l., [36] 35 pp. incl. 11 maps. fol. [Boston] 1915. 4715

Note.—For other entries see v. 1, titles 1828–1846, and v. 3, titles 3770–3771a.

BOSTON.

1883-1885

Bromley, G. W., & co.

Atlas of the city of Boston . . . From actual surveys and official records . . . Engraved by A. H. Mueller . . . F. Bourquin, lith. v. 1, 3–6. fol. Philadelphia, G. W. & W. S. Bromley, 1883–1885. 4716

CONTENTS.

v. 1. City proper.
" 2. [Wanting]
" 3. Dorchester.
" 4. South & East Boston.
" 5. West Roxbury.
" 6. Charlestown and Brighton.

1890

Bromley, G. W., & W. S.

Atlas of the city of Boston, city proper and Roxbury. From actual surveys and official plans . . . Engraved by Rudolph Spiel. Printed by F. Bourquin. 2 p. l., 39 (*i. e.* 40) col. maps. fol. Philadelphia, G. W. Bromley & co. 1890. 4717

1894

Hales, J. G.

Plans and records of the streets, lanes, courts, places &c. in the town of Boston, taken from actual survey under the direction of the hon^ble^. board of selectmen in the year m.dccc.xix–m.dccc.xx. [Reprint] Maps of the street-lines of Boston, made for the selectmen in 1819 and 1820. Reproduced in fac-simile, and published by the city registrar. 2 v. in 1. 4 p. l., 285 pp. incl. 140 maps. 1 fold. map at end. fol. Boston, Rockwell & Churchill, 1894. 4718

Note.—Contains the following maps of Boston: *Map of Boston . . . surveyed by J. G. Hales, 1814;* in 16 plates.

The town of Boston in New England, a reprint of John Bonner's map of 1722.

A plan of Boston from actual survey, by Osgood Carleton. The contents of this atlas gives it under date of 1803. It is a reproduction of Carleton's map of 1796, and is contained also in a reprint of the Boston directory of that year.

A new and correct plan of the town of Boston, noted in contents of this atlas, to be Norman's map of 1789, whereas it is a reproduction of an anonymous map in *The gentleman's magazine, v. 45, 1775, p. 493.* This map is also reproduced in a reprint of the Boston directory, 1789.

A short sketch of the author of the atlas, is given in the preface.

1912

Bromley, G. W., & W. S.

Atlas of the city of Boston. Boston proper and Back Bay. From actual surveys and official plans . . . 2 p. l., 37 col. maps. fol. Philadelphia, G. W. Bromley & co. 1912. 4719

BROOKLINE.

French & Bryant.

Atlas of the town of Brookline, Mass. . . . 1 p. l., [2] pp. 27 (*i. e.* 28) col. maps. fol. Brookline, French & Bryant, 1897. 4720

NOTE.—Noted on title-page: Printed under the direction of Geo. W. Stadly & co., by Forbes lith. mfg. co., Boston.

CHELSEA.

Bromley, G. W., & W. S.

Atlas of the city of Chelsea and the towns of Revere and Winthrop. From actual surveys and official plans . . . Printed by F. Bourquin. 1 p. l., 18 col. maps. fol. Philadelphia, G. W. Bromley & co. 1886. 4721

LEE.

Beirne, J. P.

Atlas of the garden spots of Berkshire: Stockbridge, Lenox and Lee, Massachusetts. Made by Barnes and Jenks . . . and from plans loaned by W. H. Barnes . . . 1 p. l., 1 l., 9 maps. fol. Housatonic (?) J. P. Beirne [1894?] 4722

NOTE.—On title-page, Draughtsmen: J. P. Barnes, H. E. Jenks, T. W. Hill.

LENOX.

Beirne, J. P.

Atlas of the garden spots of Berkshire: Stockbridge, Lenox and Lee, Massachusetts. Made by Barnes and Jenks . . . and from plans loaned by W. H. Barnes . . . 1 p. l., 1 l., 9 maps. fol. Housatonic (?) J. P. Beirne [1894?] 4723

NOTE.—On title-page, Draughtsmen: J. P. Barnes, H. E. Jenks, T. W. Hill.

REVERE.

Bromley, G. W., & W. S.

Atlas of the city of Chelsea and the towns of Revere and Winthrop. From actual surveys and official plans . . . Printed by F. Bourquin. 1 p. l., 18 col. maps. fol. Philadelphia, G. W. Bromley & co. 1886. 4724

STOCKBRIDGE.

Beirne, J. P.

Atlas of the garden spots of Berkshire: Stockbridge, Lenox and Lee, Massachusetts. Made by Barnes and Jenks . . . and from plans loaned by W. H. Barnes . . . 1 p. l., 1 l., 9 maps. fol. Housatonic (?) J. P. Beirne [1894?] 4725

NOTE.—On title-page, Draughtsmen: J. P. Barnes, H. E. Jenks, T. W. Hill.

WINTHROP.

Bromley, G. W., & W. S.

Atlas of the city of Chelsea and the towns of Revere and Winthrop. From actual surveys and official plans . . . Printed by F. Bourquin. 1 p. l., 18 col. maps. fol. Philadelphia, G. W. Bromley & co. 1886. 4726

WORCESTER.

Richards, L. J., & co.

Atlas of the city of Worcester, Massachusetts. Based upon, and carefully compiled from, the official plans, surveys and records of the city engineer's and other municipal departments, together with numerous private plans and actual surveys and investigations by the publishers' special corps of engineers. 1 p. l., [6] pp., 33 (*i. e.* 34) col. maps. fol. Springfield, Mass., L. J. Richards & co. 1896. 4727

NOTE.—Street index on reverse of index map.

A list of the names of consulting local civil engineers, the publishers' corps of civil engineers, assistants and business representatives appears on the title-page.

MICHIGAN.

Railroads.

Farmer, A. J.

[Farmer's twenty-one plate series railroad and political atlas of Michigan. 1911 ed.] 21 pl. 4°. [Detroit, A. J Farmer, 1911] 4728

NOTE.—Title wanting.

Contains maps showing railroads, congressional districts, senatorial districts, representative districts, judicial circuits.

Farmer's twenty-one plate series railroad and political atlas of Michigan. 1915 ed. cover-title, 21 plates. obl. 4°. Detroit, A. J. Farmer, 1915. 4729

NOTE.—Maps show railroads, congressional districts, senatorial districts, representative districts, judicial circuits.

Farmer, S., & co.

Farmer's twenty-one plate series railroad and political atlas of Michigan. cover-title, 21 maps. 8°. Detroit, S. Farmer & co. [©1913] 4730

State.

1916

Bowen, B. F., & co.

Bowen's Michigan state atlas containing a separate map of each county, showing section, township and range lines, railroad and interurban lines, churches and school houses and public highways, with a historical sketch of each county. Improved roads shown in colors. Also containing maps of Michigan, the United States and the world, and the official soil map of Michigan; population of townships, cities and villages and geographical and other tables of value. 196 pp. (*i. e.* 200) incl. 88 maps. fol. Indianapolis, B. F. Bowen & co. 1916. 4731

Counties.

ALLEGAN.

Ogle, G. A., & co.

Standard atlas of Allegan county, Michigan, including a plat book of the villages, cities and townships of the county. Map of the state, United States and world. Patrons directory, reference business directory and departments devoted to general information. Analysis of the system of U. S. land surveys, digest of the system of civil government . . . 2 p. l., 7–127, viii, x–xxiii pp. incl. 73 col. maps, illus., diagrs. fol. Chicago, G. A. Ogle & co. 1913. 4732

ARENAC.

Ogle, G. A., & co.

Standard atlas of Arenac county, Michigan, including a plat book of the villages, cities and townships of the county. Map of the state, United States, and world. Patrons directory, reference business directory and departments devoted to general information . . . 2 p. l., 7–57, viii, x–xxii pp. incl. 18 col. maps, illus. fol. Chicago, G. A. Ogle & co. 1906. 4733

BARRY.

Ogle, G. A., & co.

Standard atlas of Barry county, Michigan, including a plat book of the villages, cities and townships of the county. Map of the state, United States and world. Patrons directory, reference business directory and departments devoted to general information. Analysis of the system of U. S. land surveys, digest of the system of civil government . . . 2 p. l., 7–105, viii, x–xxiii pp. incl. 56 col. maps, illus., diagrs. fol. Chicago, G. A. Ogle & co. 1913. 4734

BENZIE.

Ogle, G. A., & co.

Standard atlas of Benzie county, Michigan, including a plat book of the villages, cities and t wnships of the county. Map of the state, United States and world. Patrons directory, reference business directory and departments devoted to general information. Analysis of the system of U. S. land surveys, digest of the system of civil government . . . 2 p. l., 7–87, viii, x–xxiii pp. incl. 24 col. maps, illus. fol. Chicago, G. A. Ogle & co. 1915. 4735

BRANCH.

Ogle, G. A., & co.

Standard atlas of Branch county, Michigan, including a plat book of the villages, cities and townships of the county. Map of the state, United States and world. Patrons directory, reference business directory and departments devoted to general information. Analysis of the system of U. S. land surveys, digest of the system of civil government . . . 2 p. l., 7–123, viii, x–xxiii pp. incl. 27 col. maps, illus. fol. Chicago, G. A. Ogle & co. 1915. 4736

CALHOUN.

Ogle, G. A., & co.

Standard atlas of Calhoun county, Michigan, including a plat book of the villages, cities and townships of the county. Map of the state, United States and world. Patrons directory, reference business directory and departments devoted to general information. Analysis of the system of U. S. land surveys, digest of the system of civil government . . . Record work and platting of Battle Creek City by Harlan K. Whitney . . . 2 p. l., 7–155, viii, x–xxiii pp. incl. 48 col. maps, illus. fol. Chicago, G. A. Ogle & co. 1916. 4737

CASS.

Ogle, G. A., & co.

Standard atlas of Cass county, Michigan, including a plat book of the villages, cities and townships of the county. Map of the state, United States and world. Patrons directory, reference business directory and departments devoted to general information . . . 2 p. l., 7–71, viii, x–xxiii pp. incl. 41 col. maps, illus., diagrs. fol. Chicago, G. A. Ogle & co. 1914. 4738

CHEBOYGAN.

Consolidated publishing co.

Plat book of Cheboygan county, Michigan. Drawn from actual surveys and the county records by P. A. & J. W. Myers, surveyors and draughtsmen. 52 pp. incl. 36 col. maps. fol. Minneapolis, Consolidated publishing co. 1902. 4739

CLINTON.

Ogle, G. A., & co.

Standard atlas of Clinton county, Michigan, including a plat book of the villages, cities and townships of the county. Map of the state, United States and world. Patrons directory, reference business directory and departments devoted to general information. Analysis of the system of U. S. land surveys, digest of the system of civil government . . . 2 p. l., viii, x–xxiii pp. incl. 30 maps, illus. fol. Chicago, G. A. Ogle & co. 1915. 4740

DELTA.

Ogle, G. A., & co.

Standard atlas of Delta county, Michigan, including a plat book of the villages, cities and townships of the county. Map of the state, United States and world. Patrons directory, reference business directory and departments devoted to general information. Analysis of the system of U. S. land surveys, digest of the system of civil government . . . 2 p. l., 7–93, viii, x–xxiii pp. incl. 57 col. maps, illus., diagrs. fol. Chicago, G. A. Ogle & co. 1913. 4741

EATON.

Ogle, G. A., & co.

Standard atlas of Eaton county, Michigan, including a plat book of the villages, cities and townships of the county. Map of the state, United States and world. Patrons directory, reference business directory and departments devoted to general information . . . Record work and platting by M. E. Newcomb . . . 2 p. l., 7–105, viii, x–xxiii pp. incl. 30 col. maps. fol. Chicago, G. A. Ogle & co. 1913. 4742

GRATIOT.

Chadwick, C. W.

Chadwick farm atlas of Gratiot county, Michigan. 2 maps on 5 sheets. fol. Ann Arbor, Mich., C. W. Chadwick, °1914. 4743

Note.—Caption title.
J. H. Stevens, draughtsman.

HILLSDALE.

Ogle, G. A., & co.

Standard atlas of Hillsdale county, Michigan, including a plat book of the villages, cities and townships of the county. Map of the state, United States and world. Patrons directory, reference business directory and departments devoted to general information. Analysis of the system of U. S. land surveys, digest of the system of civil government . . . 2 p. l., 7–79, viii, x–xxiii pp. incl. 32 col. maps, illus. fol. Chicago, G. A. Ogle & co. 1916. 4744

HURON.

Chadwick, C. W.

Chadwick farm atlas of Huron county, Michigan. 3 maps on 7 sheets. fol. Ann Arbor, Mich., C. W. Chadwick [1913] 4745

INGHAM.

Chadwick, C. W.

Chadwick farm atlas of Ingham county, Michigan . . . 2 maps on 5 sheets. fol. Ann Arbor, Mich., C. W. Chadwich ©1914. 4746

NOTE.—Caption title.
J. H. Stevens, draftsman.

IONIA.

Ogle, G. A., & co.

Standard atlas of Ionia county, Michigan, including a plat book of the villages, cities and townships of the county. Map of the state, United States and world. Patrons directory, reference business directory and departments of general information . . . 2 p. l., 7–93, viii, x–xxii pp. incl. 29 col. maps, illus. fol. Chicago, G. A. Ogle & co. 1906. 4747

ISABELLA.

1899

Foote, C. M., *and* **Hood, E. C.**

Plat book of Isabella county, Michigan, drawn from actual surveys and the county records. 1 p. l., 42 pp. incl. 28 col. maps. fol. Minneapolis, C. M. Foote co. 1899. 4748

1915

Standard map co.

Atlas and farm directory of Isabella county, Michigan, compiled from county records and actual surveys. Published by Standard map co. . . . map publishers for the Prairie farmer . . . 38 pp. incl. 18 col. maps. fol. Chicago, Standard map co. 1915. 4749

NOTE.—Cover-title: Plat book of Isabella county, Michigan.

LAPEER.

Chadwick, C. W.

Chadwick farm atlas of Lapeer county, Michigan. 6 maps. fol. Ann Arbor, Mich., C. W. Chadwick, ©1915. [1916] 4750

NOTE.—Caption title.

LENAWEE.

Ogle, G. A., & co.

Standard atlas of Lenawee county, Michigan, including a plat book of the villages, cities and townships of the county. Map of the state, United States and world. Patrons directory, reference business directory and departments devoted to general information. Analysis of the system of U. S. land surveys, digest of the system of civil government . . . 2 p. l., 7–143, viii, x–xxiii pp. incl. 39 col. maps, illus. fol. Chicago, G. A. Ogle & co. 1916. 4751

LIVINGSTON.

Ogle, G. A., & co.

Standard atlas of Livingston county, Michigan, including a plat book of the villages, cities and townships of the county. Map of the state, United States and world. Patrons directory, reference business directory and departments devoted to general information. Analysis of the system of U. S. land surveys, digest of the system of civil government . . . 2 p. l., 7–85, viii, x–xxiii pp. incl. 25 col. maps, illus. fol. Chicago, G. A. Ogle & co. 1915. 4752

MACOMB.

Ogle, G. A., & co.

Standard atlas of Macomb county, Michigan, including a plat book of the villages, cities and townships of the county. Map of the state, United States and world. Patrons directory, reference business directory and departments devoted to general information. Analysis of the system of U. S. land surveys, digest of the system of civil government . . . 2 p. l., 7–127, viii, x–xxiii pp. incl. 35 maps, illus. fol. Chicago, G. A. Ogle & co. 1916. 4753

MASON.

1904

Ogle, G. A., & co.

Standard atlas of Mason county, Michigan, including a plat book of the villages, cities and townships of the county. Map of the state, United States and world. Patrons directory, reference business directory and departments devoted to general information. Analysis of the system of U. S. land surveys, digest of the system of civil government . . . 2 p. l., 7–81, viii, x–xxii pp. incl. 32 col. maps, illus., diagrs. fol. Chicago, G. A. Ogle & co. 1904. 4754

1915

Standard map co.

Atlas and farm directory of Mason county, Michigan. Compiled from county records and actual surveys . . . Map published for The prairie farmer. 36 pp., incl. 17 col. maps. fol. Chicago, Standard map co. °1915. 4755

NOTE.—Cover-title, Plat book of Mason county, Michigan.

MECOSTA.

Willits, W. W.

Willits farm atlas of Mecosta county, Michigan. 4 sheets. fol. Ann Arbor, Mich., C. W. Chadwick, 1915. 4756

MIDLAND.

Ogle, G. A., & co.

Standard atlas of Midland county, Michigan, including a plat book of the villages, cities and townships of the county. Map of the state, United States and world. Patrons directory, reference business directory and departments devoted to general information. Analysis of the system of U. S. land surveys, digest of the system of civil government . . . 2 p. l., 7–69, viii, x–xxiii pp. incl. 26 col. maps, illus. fol. Chicago, G. A. Ogle & co. 1914. 4757

MISSAUKEE.

Ogle, G. A., & co.

Standard atlas of Missaukee county, Michigan, including a plat book of the villages, cities and townships of the county. Map of the state, United States and world. Patrons directory, reference business directory and departments devoted to general information. Analysis of the system of U. S. land surveys, digest of the system of civil government . . . 2 p. l., 7–67, [1] viii, x–xxii pp. incl. 21 col. maps, illus. fol. Chicago, G. A. Ogle & co. 1906. 4758

MONTCALM.

Chadwick, C. W.

Chadwick's farm atlas of Montcalm county, Michigan. Compiled and sold under supervision of E. N. Billings . . . 5 sheets. fol. Ann Arbor, C. W. Chadwick, ©1913. 4759

NOTE.—Caption title.

OCEANA.

Ogle, G. A., & co.

Standard atlas of Oceana county, Michigan, including a plat book of the villages, cities and townships of the county. Map of the state, United States and world. Patrons directory, reference business directory and departments devoted to general information . . . 2 p. l., 7–83, viii, x–xxiii pp. incl. 26 col. maps, illus. fol. Chicago, G. A. Ogle & co. 1913. 4760

OSCEOLA.

Chadwick, C. W.

Chadwick farm atlas of Osceola county, Michigan . . . 2 maps on 5 sheets. fol. Ann Arbor, Mich., C. W. Chadwick, 1916. 4761

NOTE.—Caption title.

Indexes on reverse of maps.

SAGINAW.

Ogle, G. A., & co.

Standard atlas of Saginaw county, Michigan, including a plat book of the villages, cities and townships of the county. Map of the state, United States and world. Patrons directory, reference business directory and departments devoted to general information. Analysis of the system of U. S. land surveys, digest of the system of civil government . . . 2 p. l., 7–117, viii, x–xxiii pp. incl. 57 col. maps, illus. fol. Chicago, G. A. Ogle & co. 1916. 4762

ST. CLAIR.

Ogle, G. A., & co.

Standard atlas of St. Clair county, Michigan, including a plat book of the villages, cities and townships of the county. Map of the state, United States and world. Patrons directory, reference business directory and departments devoted to general information. Analysis of the system of U. S. land surveys, digest of the system of civil government . . . 2 p. l., 7–107, viii, x–xxiii pp. incl. 48 col. maps, illus. fol. Chicago, G. A. Ogle & co. 1916. 4763

SANILAC.

Ogle, G. A., & co.

Standard atlas of Sanilac county, Michigan, including a plat book of the villages, cities and townships of the county. Map of the state, United States, and world. Patrons directory, reference business directory and departments devoted to general information . . . 2 p. l., 7–125, viii, x–xxii pp. incl. 36 col. maps, illus. fol. Chicago, G. A. Ogle & co. 1906. 4764

Chadwick, C. W.

Chadwick farm atlas of Sanilac county, Michigan . . . 2 maps on 8 sheets. fol. Ann Arbor, Mich., C. W. Chadwick, 1916. 4765

NOTE.—Caption title.
Indexes on reverse of maps.

SHIAWASSEE.

Ogle, G. A., & co.

Standard atlas of Shiawassee county, Michigan, including a plat book of the villages, cities and townships of the county. Map of the state, United States and world. Patrons directory, reference business directory and departments devoted to general information. Analysis of the system of U. S. land surveys, digest of the system of civil government . . . 2 p. l., 7–107, viii, x–xxiii pp. incl. 32 col. maps. fol. Chicago, G. A. Ogle & co. 1915. 4766

WASHTENAW.

Ogle, G. A., & co.

Standard atlas of Washtenaw county, Michigan, including a plat book of the villages, cities and townships of the county. Map of the state, United States and world. Patrons directory, reference business directory and departments devoted to general information. Analysis of the system of U. S. land surveys, digest of the system of civil government . . . 2 p. l., 7–119, viii, x–xxiii pp. incl. 33 col. maps, illus. fol. Chicago, G. A. Ogle & co. 1915. 4767

WAYNE.

Sauer bros.

Detailed official atlas of Wayne county, Michigan. Containing general maps of Wayne county and city of Detroit, general township maps, showing areas of land and owners' names, railroads, wagon roads, streams, location of school houses, churches, cemeteries, etc., and detail plats of interior villages; also detail plats of all recorded subdivisions and additions in the county outside the city limits of 1914. Compiled and drawn from authentic records and private surveys . . . 1 p. l., 54 plates. fol. [Detroit] Wolverine news co. ©1915. 4768

NOTE.—Copyright by Wm. Sauer.
Table of contents on inside of cover.
Plates numbered 47B, 48B, 49B, not counted as separate maps.

WEXFORD.

Cadillac evening news.

Atlas of Wexford county, Michigan, containing complete maps of all townships, names of property owners, maps of the county, city of Cadillac, United States and state of Michigan. 1 p. l., 43 pp. incl. 19 col. maps. fol. [Cadillac, Mich., Cadillac evening news, 1914] 4769

NOTE.—Copyrighted 1914 by Standard map co., Chicago.

Cities.

DETROIT.

1915

Baist, G. W.

Baist's real estate atlas of surveys of Detroit and suburbs, Mich. . . . Compiled and published from official records, private plans and actual surveys . . . 2 v. 1 p. l., 30 (*i. e.* 31) col. maps; 1 p. l., 30 (*i. e.* 31) col. maps. fol. Philadelphia, G. W. Baist, 1915. 4770

NOTE.—Maps in both volumes numbered continuously.

1916

Baist's plat book of the city of Detroit and suburbs, Mich. . . . Index, 60 maps. sm. fol. Philadelphia, G. W. Baist, °1916. 4771

NOTE.—Title-page on inside of cover.

1918

Baist's real estate atlas of surveys of Detroit and suburbs, Michigan . . . Compiled from official records, private plans and actual surveys. 2 v., 30 (*i. e.* 31) col. maps; 31 col. maps. fol. Philadelphia, G. W. Baist, 1918. 4772

NOTE.—Titles on reverse of front cover. Index maps contain indexes to streets.
Maps continuously numbered.

MINNESOTA.

Agricultural—Industrial.

Cram, G. F.

Agricultural and industrial review of Minnesota with world atlas; containing newly engraved maps of every state in the United States, detailed maps of every country, state and kingdom, together with a complete and adequate locating index to all cities, towns, villages and post offices in the United States, giving populations to every incorporated city and village therein. Edited and compiled under the direction of Earl J. Robinson, assisted by J. S. and M. B. Beem . . . 4 p. l., [5]–276 [*i. e.* 282] pp. incl. 104 col. maps, illus., ports. fol. Chicago & New York, G. F. Cram [1913] 4773

Counties.

ANOKA.

Webb publishing co.

Atlas and farmers' directory of Anoka county and the eleven northern townships of Hennepin county, Minnesota. Containing plats of townships with owners' names; also maps of the state and United States, with an outline map of the county showing location of townships, villages, roads, schools, churches, railroads, streams . . . Published by the Farmer . . . [3]–52 (*i. e.* 56) [8] pp. incl. 27 col. maps. St. Paul, Minn., Webb publishing co. °1914. 4774

BENTON.

Webb publishing co.

Atlas and farm directory with complete survey in township plats, Benton county, Minnesota, containing plats of all townships with owners' names; also maps of the state, United States and world; also an outline map of the county . . . Compiled from latest

Webb publishing co.—Continued.

data on record. Published by the Farmer . . . Drawn and engraved by the Kenyon company, Des Moines, Ia. 29, [12] pp. incl. 18 col. maps, illus. fol. St. Paul, Minn., Webb publishing co. [1914] 4775

BLUE EARTH.

Ogle, G. A., & co.

Standard atlas of Blue Earth county, Minnesota, including a plat book of the villages, cities and townships of the county. Map of the state, United States and world. Patrons directory, reference business directory and departments devoted to general information. Analysis of the system of U. S. land surveys, digest of the system of civil government . . . 2 p. l., 7–131, viii, x–xxiii, pp. incl. 59 col. maps, illus., diagrs. fol. Chicago, G. A. Ogle & co. 1914. 4776

BROWN.

Webb publishing co.

Atlas and farmers' directory of Brown county, Minnesota. Containing plats of all townships with owners' names; also maps of the state and United States, with an outline map of the county showing location of townships, villages, roads, schools, churches, railroads, streams . . . Published by the Farmer . . . 37, [8] pp. incl. 19 col. maps. fol. St. Paul, Minn., Webb publishing co. °1914. 4777

CHIPPEWA.

Webb publishing co.

Atlas and farm directory with complete survey in township plats, Chippewa county, Minnesota, containing plats of all townships with owners' names; also maps of the state, United States and world; also an outline map of the county showing location of townships, villages, roads, schools, churches, railroads, streams . . . Published by the Farmer . . . Drawn and engraved by the Kenyon co., Des Moines, Iowa. 43, [12] pp. incl. 24 col. maps, illus. fol. St. Paul, Minn., Webb publishing co. °1914. 4778

CROW WING.

Ogle, G. A., & co.

Standard atlas of Crow Wing county, Minnesota, including a plat book of the villages, cities and townships of the county. Map of the state, United States and world. Patrons directory, reference business directory and departments devoted to general information. Analysis of the system of U. S. land surveys, digest of the system of civil government . . . 2 p. l., 8–91, viii, x–xxiii pp. incl. 72 col. maps, illus., diagrs. fol. Chicago, G. A. Ogle & co. 1913. 4779

DAKOTA.

Webb publishing co.

Atlas and farm directory with complete survey in township plats, Dakota county, Minnesota, containing plats of all townships with owners' names; Minnesota state map showing automobile roads; also maps of the United States and world; also an outline map of the county showing townships, villages, roads, schools, churches, railroads, streams . . . Compiled from latest data on record. Published by the Farmer . . . Engraved by the Kenyon company, Des Moines, Iowa . . . 38 [12] pp. incl. 29 col. maps. fol. St. Paul, Minn., Webb publishing co. ©1916. 4780

DODGE.

Webb publishing co.

Atlas and farm directory with complete survey in township plats, Dodge county, Minnesota, containing plats of all townships with owners' names; also maps of the state, United States and world; also an outline map of the county showing location of townships, villages, roads, schools, churches, railroads, streams . . . Published by the Farmer. 28, [12] pp. incl. 16 col. maps, illus. fol. St. Paul, Minn., Webb publishing co. ©1914. 4781

FARIBAULT.

Webb publishing co.

Atlas and farmers' directory of Faribault county, Minnesota. Containing plats of all townships with owners' names; also maps of the state and United States, with an outline map of the county showing location of townships, villages, roads, schools, churches, railroads, streams . . . Published by the Farmer . . . 43 [8] pp. incl. 23 col. maps. fol. St. Paul, Minn., Webb publishing co. ©1913. 4782

FILLMORE.

Webb publishing co.

Atlas and farm directory with complete survey in township plats of Fillmore county, Minnesota, containing plats of all townships with owners' names; also maps of the state, United States and world; also an outline map of the county showing location of townships, villages, roads, schools, churches, railroads, streams . . . Published by the Farmer . . . Drawn and engraved by the Anderson publishing co. Chicago, Ill. 53, 13 pp. incl. 30 col. maps, illus. fol. St. Paul, Minn., Webb publishing co. ©1915. 4783

FREEBORN.

Webb publishing co.

The farmers' atlas and directory with complete survey in township plats, Freeborn county, Minnesota. Containing plats of all townships with owners' names; also maps of the state and United States, with an outline map of the county showing location of townships, villages, roads, schools, churches, railroads, streams . . . Published by the Farmer . . . 44 (*i. e.* 54) [8] pp. incl. 23 col. maps. fol. St. Paul, Minn., Webb publishing co. ©1913. 4784

GOODHUE.

Webb publishing co.

Atlas and farmers' directory of Goodhue county, Minnesota. Containing plats of all townships with owners' names: also maps of the state and United States, with an outline map of the county showing location of townships, villages, roads, schools, churches, railroads, streams . . . Published by the Farmer . . . [3]–51 (*i. e.* 55) [8] pp. incl. 23 col. maps. fol. St. Paul, Minn., Webb publishing co. ©1914. 4785

GRANT.

Webb publishing co.

Atlas and farm directory with complete survey in township plats, Grant county, Minnesota, containing plats of all the townships with owners' names; also maps of the state, United States and world; also an outline map of the county showing location of townships, villages, roads, schools, churches, railroads, streams . . . Published by the Farmer . . . Drawn and engraved by the Kenyon co., Des Moines, Iowa. 35, [12] pp. incl. 21 col. maps, illus. fol. St. Paul, Minn., Webb publishing co. 1914. 4786

HENNEPIN.

Webb publishing co.

Atlas and farmers' directory of Anoka county and the eleven northern townships of Hennepin county, Minnesota. Containing plats of townships with owners' names: also maps of the state and United States, with an outline map of the county showing location of townships, villages, roads, schools, churches, railroads, streams . . . Published by the Farmer . . . [3]–52 (*i. e.* 56) [8] pp. incl. 27 col. maps. St. Paul, Minn., Webb publishing co. ©1914. 4787

ISANTI.

Webb publishing co.

Atlas and farmers' directory of Isanti county, Minnesota. Containing plats of all townships with owners' names; also maps of the state and United States, with an outline map of the county showing location of townships, villages, roads, schools, churches, railroads, streams . . . Published by the Farmer . . . 31 (*i. e.* 39) [8] pp. incl. 16 col. maps. fol. St. Paul, Minn., Webb publishing co. ©1914. 4788

JACKSON.

Ogle, G. A., & co.

Standard atlas of Jackson county, Minnesota, including a plat book of the villages, cities and townships of the county. Map of the state, United States and world. Patrons directory, reference business directory and departments devoted to general information. Analysis of the system of U. S. land surveys, digest of the system of civil government . . . Record work and platting by P. D. McKellar . . . and I. W. Mahoney . . . 2 p. l., 7–85, viii, x–xxiii pp. incl. 42 col. maps, illus., diagrs. fol. Chicago, G. A. Ogle & co. 1914. 4789

KANABEC.

Webb publishing co.

Atlas and farmers' directory with complete survey in township plats of Kanabec county, Minnesota. Containing plats of all townships with owners' names; also maps of the state, United States and world; also an outline map of the county showing location of townships, villages, roads, schools, churches, railroads, streams. Compiled from latest data on record. Published by the Farmer . . . 33 [12] pp., incl. 20 maps, illus. fol. St. Paul, Minn., Webb publishing co. ©1915. 4790

KANDIYOHI.

Webb publishing co.

Atlas and farm directory with complete survey in township plats, Kandiyohi county, Minnesota. Containing plats of all townships with owners' names; Minnesota state map showing automobile roads; also maps of the United States and world; also an outline map of the county showing location of townships, villages, roads, schools, churches, railroads, streams. Compiled from latest data on record. Published by the Farmer. 51 pp., 6 l., incl. 29 maps, illus. fol. St. Paul, Minn., Webb publishing co. 1915. 4791

KITTSON.

Ogle, G. A., & co.

Standard atlas of Kittson county, Minnesota, including a plat book of the villages, cities and townships of the county. Map of the state, United States and world. Patrons directory, reference business directory and departments devoted to general information. Analysis of the system of U. S. land surveys, digest of the system of civil government . . . 2 p. l., 7–71, [1], viii, x–xxiii pp. incl. 47 maps, illus. fol. Chicago, G. A. Ogle & co. 1912. 4792

LAC QUI PARLE.

Webb publishing co.

Atlas and farmers' directory of Lac Qui Parle county, Minnesota. Containing plats of all townships with owners' names: also maps of the state and United States with an outline map of the county showing location of townships, villages, roads, schools, churches, railroads, streams . . . Published by the Farmer . . . 49 [8] pp. incl. 25 col. maps. fol. St. Paul, Minn., Webb publishing co. °1913. 4793

LE SUEUR.

Webb publishing co.

The farmers' atlas and directory with complete survey in township plats. Le Sueur county, Minnesota. Containing plats of all townships with owners names; also maps of the state and United States, with an outline map of the county showing location of townships, villages, roads, schools, churches, railroads, streams . . . Published by the Farmer . . . 33 (*i. e.* 39) [8] pp. incl. 18 col. maps, illus. fol. St. Paul, Minn., Webb publishing co. °1912. 4794

LINCOLN.

Webb publishing co.

Atlas and farm directory with complete survey in township plats, Lincoln county, Minnesota. Containing plats of all townships with owners' names; Minnesota state map showing automobile roads; also maps of the United States and world; also an outline map of the county showing location of townships, villages, roads, schools, churches, railroads, streams, etc., etc. Compiled from latest data on record. Published by the Farmer. 23 pp., 6 l., incl. 20 maps, illus. fol. St. Paul, Minn., Webb publishing co. 1915. 4795

LYON.

Webb publishing co.

Atlas and farm directory with complete survey in township plats of Lyon county, Minnesota, containing plats of all townships with owners' names; also maps of the state, United States and world; also an outline map of the country showing location of townships, villages, roads, schools, churches, railroads, streams . . . Published by the Farmer . . . Drawn and engraved by the Anderson publishing co. Chicago, Ill. 43, [12] pp. incl. 25 col. maps, illus. fol. St. Paul, Minn., Webb publishing co. °1914. 4796

McLEOD.

Webb publishing co.

Atlas and farmers' directory of McLeod county, Minnesota. Containing plats of all townships with owners names; also maps of the state and United States, with an outline map of the county showing location of townships, villages, roads, schools, churches, railroads, streams . . . Published by the Farmer . . . 31 (*i. e.* 41) [8] pp. incl. 17 col. maps. fol. St. Paul, Minn., Webb publishing co. ©1914. 4797

MEEKER.

Webb publishing co.

Atlas and farmers' directory of Meeker county, Minnesota. Containing plats of all townships with owners names; also maps of the state and United States, with an outline map of the county showing location of townships, villages, roads, schools, churches, railroads, streams . . . Published by the Farmer . . . 37 (*i. e.* 41) [8] pp. incl. 20 col. maps. fol. St. Paul, Minn., Webb publishing co. ©1913. 4798

MILLE LACS.

Webb publishing co.

Atlas and farm directory with complete survey in township plats, Mille Lacs county, Minnesota, containing plats of all townships with owners' names; also maps of the state, United States and world; also an outline map of the county . . . Compiled from latest data on record. Published by the Farmer . . . Drawn and engraved by the Kenyon company, Des Moines, Ia. 42, [12] pp. incl. 24 col. maps, illus. fol. St. Paul, Minn., Webb publishing co. [1914] 4799

MOWER.

Webb publishing co.

Atlas and farmers' directory with complete survey in township plats of Mower county, Minnesota, containing plats of all townships with owners' names; also maps of the state, United States and world; also an outline map of the county showing location of townships, villages, roads, schools, churches, railroads, streams . . . Published by the Farmer . . . Drawn and engraved by Webb company . . . 43, [12] pp. incl. 25 col. maps, illus. fol. St. Paul, Minn., Webb publishing co. ©1915. 4800

NICOLLET.

Webb publishing co.

Atlas and farm directory of Nicollet county, Minnesota. Containing plats of townships with owners names; also maps of the state and United States, with an outline map of county showing location of townships, villages, roads, schools, churches, railroads, streams . . . Published by the Farmer . . . Compiled by the Anderson publishing co. . . . 29 (*i. e.* 31) [9] pp. incl. 16 col. maps. fol. St. Paul, Minn., Webb publishing co. ©1913. 4801

NOBLES.

Ogle, G. A., & co.

Standard atlas of Nobles county, Minnesota, including a plat book of the villages, cities and townships of the county. Map of the state, United States and world. Patrons directory, reference business directory and departments devoted to general information . . . 2 p. l., 7–95, viii, x–xxiii pp. incl. 29 col. maps, illus., diagrs. fol. Chicago, G. A. Ogle & co. 1914. 4802

OLMSTEAD.

Webb publishing co.

Atlas and farmers' directory of Olmstead county, Minnesota. Containing plats of all townships with owners' names; also maps of the state and United States, with an outline map of the county showing location of townships, villages, roads, schools, churches, railroads, streams . . . Published by the Farmer . . . 39 (*i. e.* 41) [8] pp. incl. 21 col. maps. fol. St. Paul, Minn., Webb publishing co. ©1914. 4803

PIPESTONE.

Webb publishing co.

Atlas and farm directory with complete survey in township plats, Pipestone county, Minnesota, containing plats of all townships with owners' names; also maps of the state, United States and world; also an outline map of the county . . . Compiled from latest data on record. Published by the Farmer . . . Drawn and engraved by the Kenyon company, Des Moines, Ia. 27, [12] pp. incl. 17 col. maps, illus. fol. St. Paul Minn., Webb publishing co. [1914] 4804

POLK.

Webb publishing co.

Atlas and farmers' directory with complete survey in township plats of Polk county, Minnesota, containing plats of all townships with owners' names; also maps of the state, United States and world; also an outline map of the county showing location of townships, villiages[!] roads, schools, churches, railroads, streams . . . Published by the Farmer . . . 121 [12] pp. incl. 63 col. maps. fol. St. Paul, Minn., Webb publishing co. 1915. 4805

REDWOOD.

Webb publishing co.

Atlas and farm directory with complete survey in township plats of Redwood county, Minnesota, containing plats of all townships with owners' names; also maps of the state, United States and world; also an outline map of the county showing location of townships, villages, roads, schools, churches, railroads, streams . . . Published by the Farmer . . . Drawn and engraved by the

Anderson publishing co. Chicago. 57, [12] pp. incl. 31 col. maps, illus. fol. St. Paul, Minn., Webb publishing co. °1914. 4806

RENVILLE.

Webb publishing co.

Atlas and farm directory with complete survey in township plats, Renville county, Minnesota. Containing plats of all townships with owners' names: also maps of the state and United States with an outline map of the county showing location of townships, villages, roads, schools, churches, railroads, streams . . . Published by the Farmer . . . [3]–59, [8] pp. incl. 30 col. maps. fol. St. Paul, Minn., Webb publishing co. °1913. 4807

RICE.

Webb publishing co.

Atlas and farm directory with complete survey in township plats, Rice county, Minnesota, containing plats of all townships with owners' names; Minnesota state map showing automobile roads; also maps of the United States and world; also an outline map of the county showing location of townships, villages, roads, schools, churches, railroads, streams . . . Published by the Farmer . . . Drawn and engraved by the Kenyon company, Des Moines, Iowa . . . 32 (*i. e.* 36) [12] pp. incl. 19 col. maps. fol. St. Paul, Minn., Webb publishing co. 1915. 4808

ROCK.

Ogle, G. A., & co.

Standard atlas of Rock county, Minnesota, including a plat book of the villages, cities and townships of the county. Map of the state, United States and world. Patrons directory, reference business directory and departments devoted to general information . . . 2 p. l., 7–75, viii, x–xxiii pp. incl. 21 col. maps, illus., diagrs. fol. Chicago, G. A. Ogle & co. 1914. 4809

ROSEAU.

Ogle, G. A., & co.

Standard atlas of Roseau county, Minnesota, including a plat book of the villages, cities and townships of the county. Map of the state, United States and world. Patrons directory, reference business directory and departments devoted to general information. Analysis of the system of U. S. land surveys, digest of the system of civil government . . . 2 p. l., 7–87, viii, x–xxiii pp. incl. 60 col. maps, illus., diagrs. fol. Chicago, G. A. Ogle & co. 1913. 4810

SCOTT.

Webb publishing co.

Atlas and farmers' directory of Scott county, Minnesota. Containing plats of all townships with owners' names; also maps of the state and United States, with an outline map of the county showing location of townships, villages, roads, schools, churches, railroads, streams . . . Published by the Farmer . . . 27 [8] pp. incl. 15 col. maps. fol. St. Paul, Minn., Webb publishing co. ©1913. 4811

SHERBURNE.

Webb publishing co.

Atlas and farm directory with complete survey in township plats, Sherburne county, Minnesota. Containing plats of all townships with owners' names; also maps of the state, United States and world; also an outline map of the county showing location of townships, villages, roads, schools, churches, railroads, streams. Compiled from latest data on record. Published by the Farmer. Drawn and engraved by the Kenyon company, Des Moines, Ia. 29 [12] pp. incl. 16 col. maps, illus. fol. St. Paul, Minn., Webb publishing co. ©1914. 4812

SIBLEY.

Webb publishing co.

Atlas and farmers' directory of Sibley county, Minnesota. Containing plats of all townships with owners' names; also maps of the state and United States, with an outline map of the county showing location of townships, villages, roads, schools, churches, railroads, streams . . . Published by the Farmer . . . 37 [8] pp. incl. 20 col. maps. fol. St. Paul, Minn., Webb publishing co. ©1914. 4813

STEELE.

Webb publishing co.

Atlas and farm directory with complete survey in township plats, Steele county, Minnesota, containing plats of all townships with owners' names; also maps of the state, United States and world; also an outline map of the county showing location of townships, villages, roads, schools, churches, railroads, streams . . . Published by the Farmer. 28, [12] pp. incl. 17 col. maps, illus. fol. St. Paul, Minn., Webb publishing co. ©1914. 4814

TODD.

Webb publishing co.

Atlas and farm directory of Todd county, Minnesota. Containing a double page map of the world, the United States and the state of Minnesota. This atlas also contains an outline map of the county . . . Also a full page plat of each and every township in the county . . . Compiled from latest data on record. Published by the Farmer . . . 61, [12] pp. incl. 33 col. maps, illus, fol. St. Paul, Minn., Webb publishing co. [1914] 4815

TRAVERSE.

Webb publishing co.

Atlas and farm directory with complete survey in township plats, Traverse county, Minnesota; containing plats of all townships with owners' names; Minnesota state map showing automobile roads; also maps of the United States and world; also an outline map of the county . . . Compiled from latest data on record. Published by the Farmer. 35 [12] pp. incl. 21 col. maps, illus. fol. St. Paul, Minn., Webb publishing co. [1915] 4816

WABASHA.

Webb publishing co.

Atlas and farm directory with complete survey in township plats, Wabasha county, Minnesota, containing plats of all townships with owners' names; also maps of the state, United States and world; also an outline map of the county . . . Compiled from latest data on record. Published by the Farmer . . . Drawn and engraved by the Kenyon company, Des Moines, Ia. 41 [12] pp. incl. 22 col. maps, illus. fol. St. Paul, Minn., Webb publishing co. [1915] 4817

WASECA.

Webb publishing co.

Atlas and farm directory with complete survey in township plats, Waseca county, Minnesota, containing plats of all townships with owners' names; also maps of the state, United States and world; also an outline map of the county showing location of townships, villages, roads, schools, churches, railroads, streams . . . Published by the Farmer. 27, [12] pp. incl. 16 col. maps, illus. fol. St. Paul, Minn., Webb publishing co. °1914. 4818

WASHINGTON.

Webb publishing co.

The farmers' atlas and directory with complete survey in township plats, Washington county, Minnesota. Containing plats of all townships with owners' names; also maps of the state and United States, with an outline map of the county showing location of townships, villages, roads, schools, churches, railroads, streams . . . Published by the Farmer . . . 30 (*i. e.* 34) [8] pp. incl. 16 col. maps, illus. fol. St. Paul, Minn., Webb publishing co. °1912. 4819

WATONWAN.

Webb publishing co.

Atlas and farm directory with complete survey in township plats, Watonwan county, Minnesota. Containing plats of all townships with owners' names; Minnesota state map showing automobile roads; also maps of the United States and world; also an

Webb publishing co.—Continued.

outline map of the county showing location of townships, villages, roads, schools, churches, railroads, streams, etc., etc. Compiled from latest data on record. Published by the Farmer . . . 27, [12] pp., 17 maps, illus. fol. St. Paul, Minn., Webb publishing co. °1915. 4820

WILKIN.

Webb publishing co.

Atlas and farmers' directory with complete survey in township plats of Wilkin county, Minnesota, containing plats of all townships with owners' names; also maps of the state, United States and world; an outline map of the county showing location of townships, villages, roads, schools, churches, railroads, streams . . . Published by the Farmer . . . 47 [12] pp. incl. 26 col. maps. fol. St. Paul, Minn., Webb publishing co. 1915. 4821

WINONA.

Webb publishing co.

Atlas and farmers' directory of Winona county, Minnesota, containing plats of all townships with owners' names; also maps of the state and United States, with an outline map of the county showing location of townships, villages, roads, schools, churches, railroads, streams . . . Published by the Farmer . . . 43 [8] pp. incl. 23 col. maps. fol. St. Paul, Minn., Webb publishing co. °1914. 4822

WRIGHT.

Webb publishing co.

Atlas and farm directory with complete survey in township plats, Wright county, Minnesota, containing plats of all townships with owners' names; Minnesota state map showing automobile roads; also maps of the United States and world; also an outline map of the county showing location of townships, villages, roads, schools, churches, railroads, streams . . . Published by the Farmer . . . Drawn and engraved by the Kenyon company, Des Moines, Iowa . . . 50 (*i. e.* 53) 12 pp. incl. 25 col. maps. fol. St. Paul, Minn., Webb publishing co. 1915. 4823

YELLOW MEDICINE.

Webb publishing co.

The farmers' atlas and directory with complete survey in township plats, Yellow Medicine co., Minnesota. Containing plats of all townships with owners' names; also maps of the state and United States, with an outline map of the county showing location of townships, villages, roads, schools, churches, railroads streams . . . Published by the Farmer . . . 49 [8] pp. incl. 24 col. maps. fol. St. Paul, Minn., Webb publishing co. °1913. 4824

Cities.

MINNEAPOLIS.

1892

Foote, C. M., & co.

Atlas of the city of Minneapolis, Minnesota. Compiled and drawn from actual surveys and official records. 2 p. l., 53 col. maps. fol. Minneapolis, C. M. Foote & co. 1892. 4825

NOTE.—Incomplete: map no. 5 wanting.

1913–1916

Real estate index co.

Atlas and ownership index. . . . Minneapolis . . . compiled from the records of the city of Minneapolis & of Hennepin county . . . v. 1–3. fol. Minneapolis, Real estate index co. [c]1913–1916. 4826

NOTE.—Vol. 1, copyrighted by Real estate index co., 1913; v. 2–3 copyrighted by Minneapolis real estate index co. 1914.

ST. PAUL.

Hopkins, G. M., co.

Plat book of the city of Saint Paul, Minn., and suburbs from official records, private plans and actual surveys . . . 1 p. l., 62 maps, 3 l. fol. Philadelphia, G. M. Hopkins co. 1916. 4827

MISSOURI.

Counties.

ANDREW.

Edwards bros.

An illustrated historical atlas of Andrew county, Missouri. Compiled, drawn and published from personal examinations and surveys. 52 pp. [4] l., incl. 20 col. maps. 9 pl. fol. Philadelphia, Edwards bros. 1877. 4828

AUDRAIN.

Ogle, G. A., & co.

Standard atlas of Audrain county, Missouri, including a plat book of the villages, cities and townships of the county. Map of the state, United States and world. Patrons directory, reference business directory and departments devoted to general information. Analysis of the system of U. S. land surveys, digest of the system of civil government . . . 2 p. l., 7–63, xxii pp. incl. 29 col. maps, illus. fol. Chicago, G. A. Ogle & co. 1918. 4829

BARRY.

Ogle, G. A., & co.

Standard atlas of Barry county, Missouri, including a plat book of the villages, cities and townships of the county. Map of the state, United States, and world. Patrons directory, reference business directory and departments devoted to general information. Analysis of the system of U. S. land surveys, digest of the system of civil government . . . 2 p. l., 7–93, [1] viii, x–xxii, pp. incl. 32 col. maps, illus. fol. Chicago, G. A. Ogle & co. 1909. 4830

BOONE.

Ogle, G. A., & co.

Standard atlas of Boone county, Missouri, including a plat book of the villages, cities and townships of the county. Map of the state, United States and world. Patrons directory, reference business directory and departments devoted to general information. Analysis of the system of U. S. land surveys, digest of the system of civil government . . . 2 p. l., 7–79, viii, x–xxiii, pp. incl. 32 col. maps, illus. fol. Chicago, G. A. Ogle & co. 1917. 4831

CALDWELL.

1876

Edwards bros.

An illustrated historical atlas of Caldwell county, Missouri. Compiled, drawn and surveyed from personal examinations and surveys . . . 52 (*i. e.* 54) pp. incl. 18 col. maps, illus. 2 maps (1 fold.) at end. fol. Philadelphia, Edwards bros. 1876. 4832

1917

Ogle, G. A., & co.

Standard atlas of Caldwell county, Missouri. Including a plat book of the villages, cities and townships of the county. Map of the state, United States and world. Patrons directory, reference business directory and departments devoted to general information. Analysis of the system of U. S. land surveys, digest of the system of civil government . . . 2 p. l., 7–51, viii, x–xxiii pp. incl. 24 col. maps, illus. fol. Chicago, G. A. Ogle & co. 1917. 4833

CALLAWAY.

1876

Edwards bros.

An illustrated historical atlas of Callaway county, Mo. Compiled, drawn and published from personal examinations and surveys. 58 pp. [4] l., incl. 29 col. maps. 7 pl. fol. Philadelphia, Edwards bros. 1876. 4834

1919

Ogle, G. A., & co.

Standard atlas of Callaway county, Missouri, including a plat book of the villages, cities and townships of the county. Map of the state, United States and world. Patrons directory, reference business directory and departments devoted to general information. Compiled by Geo. A. Ogle & co. . . . Assisted in record work and platting by W. P. Divers . . . and Sam K. Black . . . 2 p. l., 7–71, xxii pp. incl. 24 col. maps, illus. fol. Chicago, G. A. Ogle & co. 1919. 4835

CARROLL.

Ogle, G. A., & co.

Standard atlas of Carroll county, Missouri, including a plat book of the villages, cities and townships of the county. Map of the state, United States and world. Patrons directory, reference business directory and departments devoted to general information. Analysis of the system of U. S. land surveys, digest of the system of civil government . . . 2 p. l., 7–125, viii, x–xxiii pp. incl. 31 col. maps, illus. fol. Chicago, G. A. Ogle & co. 1914. 4836

CHARITON.

1876

Edwards bros.

An illustrated historical atlas of Chariton county, Mo. Compiled, drawn and published from personal examinations and surveys. 61 (*i. e.* 62) pp. [4] l., incl. 27 col. maps. 9 pl. fol. Philadelphia, Edwards bros. 1876. 4837

NOTE.—Page no. 18½ inserted.

1915

Tuttle & Pike.

Atlas of Chariton county, Missouri. 1915 . . . 61 pp. incl. 28 maps, 3 diagrs. fol. Higginsville, Mo., G. Scott, 1915. 4838

NOTE.—Contains the *System of United States land surveys.*

CLARK.

Ogle, G. A., & co.

Standard atlas of Clark county, Missouri, including a plat book of the villages, cities and townships of the county. Map of the state. United States and world. Patrons directory, reference business directory and departments devoted to general information. Analysis of the system of U. S. land surveys, digest of the system of civil government . . . 2 p. l., 7–79, viii, x–xxiii pp. incl. 20 col. maps, illus., ports., diagrs. fol. Chicago, G. A. Ogle & co. 1915. 4839

CLAY.

1877

Edwards bros.

An illustrated historical atlas of Clay county, Missouri. Compiled, drawn and published from personal examinations and surveys . . . 50 pp. incl. 19 col. maps, 10 pl., illus. 2 fold. maps at end. fol. Philadelphia, Edwards bros. 1877. 4840

1914

Ogle, G. A., & co.

Standard atlas of Clay county, Missouri, including a plat book of the villages, cities and townships of the county. Map of the state, United States and world. Patrons directory, reference business directory and departments devoted to general information. Analysis of the system of U. S. land surveys, digest of the system of civil government . . . 2 p. l., 7–79, xxiii pp. incl. 47 col. maps, 3 pl., 1 map in text. fol. Chicago, G. A. Ogle & co. 1914. 4841

COLE.

Ogle, G. A., & co.

Standard atlas of Cole county, Missouri, including a plat book of the villages, cities and townships of the county. Map of the state, United States and world. Patrons directory, reference business directory and departments devoted to general information . . . 2 p. l., 7–83, viii, x–xxiii pp. incl. 23 col. maps, illus., diagrs. fol. Chicago, G. A. Ogle & co. 1914. 4842

COOPER.

Ogle, G. A., & co.

Standard atlas of Cooper county, Missouri, including a plat book of the villages, cities and townships of the county. Map of the state, United States and world. Patrons directory, reference business directory and departments devoted to general information. Analysis of the system of U. S. land surveys, digest of the system of civil government . . . 2 p. l., 7–87, viii, x–xxiii pp. incl. 27 col. maps, illus., ports., diagrs. fol. Chicago, G. A. Ogle & co. 1915. 4843

DAVIESS.

Ogle, G. A., & co.

Standard atlas of Daviess county, Missouri, including a plat book of the villages, cities and townships of the county. Map of the state, United States and world. Patrons directory, reference business directory and departments devoted to general information. Analysis of the system of U. S. land surveys, digest of the system of civil government . . . 2 p. l., 7–85, viii, x–xxiii pp., incl. 25 maps, illus. Chicago, G. A. Ogle & co. 1916. 4844

DE KALB.

Ogle, G. A., & co.

Standard atlas of De Kalb county, Missouri, including a plat book of the villages, cities and townships of the county. Map of the state, United States and world. Patrons directory, reference business directory and departments devoted to general information. Analysis of the system of U. S. land surveys, digest of the system of civil government . . . 2 p. l., 7–47, viii, x–xxiii pp. incl. 24 col. maps, illus. fol. Chicago, G. A. Ogle & co. 1917. 4845

FRANKLIN.

Ogle, G. A., & co.

Standard atlas of Franklin county, Missouri, including a plat book of the villages, cities and townships of the county. Map of the state, United States and world. Patrons directory, reference business directory and departments devoted to general information. Analysis of the system of U. S. land surveys, digest of the system of civil government . . . 2 p. l., 7–111, xxii pp. incl. 39 col. maps, illus. fol. Chicago, G. A. Ogle & co. 1919. 4846

GASCONADE.

Ogle, G. A., & co.

Standard atlas of Gasconade county, Missouri, including a plat book of the villages, cities and townships of the county. Map of the state, United States and world. Patrons directory, reference business directory and departments devoted to general information. Analysis of the system of U. S. land surveys, digest of the system of civil government . . . . 2 p. l., 7–95, viii x–xxiii pp. incl. 40 col. maps, illus., diagrs. fol. Chicago, G. A. Ogle & co. 1913. 4847

GENTRY.

Ogle, G. A., & co.

Standard atlas of Gentry county, Missouri, including a plat book of the villages, cities and townships of the county. Map of the state, United States and world. Patrons directory, reference business directory and departments devoted to general information . . . Compiled and published by Geo. A. Ogle & co. . . . assisted in record work and platting by the Holden abstract & investment company . . . 2 p. l., 7–85, viii, x–xxiii pp. incl. 23 col. maps, illus., diagrs. fol. Chicago, G. A. Ogle & co. 1914. 4848

GRUNDY.

Ogle, G. A., & co.

Standard atlas of Grundy county, Missouri, including a plat book of the villages, cities and townships of the county. Map of the state, United States and world. Patrons directory, reference

Ogle, G. A., & co.—Continued.

business directory and departments devoted to general information. Analysis of the system of U. S. land surveys, digest of the system of civil government . . . 2 p. l., 7–69, viii, x–xxiii pp. incl. 23 maps, 3 pl., 1 map in text. fol. Chicago, G. A. Ogle & co. 1915. 4849

HARRISON.

1876

Edwards bros.

An illustrated historical atlas of Harrison county, Missouri. Compiled, drawn and published from personal examinations and surveys . . . 54 pp. incl. 29 col. maps, illus. 2 fold. maps at end. fol. Philadelphia, Edwards bros. 1876. 4850

1917

Ogle, G. A., & co.

Standard atlas of Harrison county, Missouri, including a plat book of the villages, cities and townships of the county. Map of the state, United States and world. Patrons directory, reference business directory and departments devoted to general information. Analysis of the system of U. S. land surveys, digest of the system of civil government . . . 2 p. l., 7–85, viii, x–xxiii pp., incl. 34 col. maps, illus. fol. Chicago, G. A. Ogle & co. 1917. 4851

HOLT.

Ogle, G. A., & co.

Standard atlas of Holt county, Missouri, including a plat book of the villages, cities and townships of the county. Map of the state, United States and world. Patrons directory and departments devoted to general information. Analysis of the system of U. S. land surveys, digest of the system of civil government . . . 2 p. l., 7–73, xxii pp. incl. 21 col. maps, illus. fol. Chicago, G. A. Ogle & co. 1918. 4852

JOHNSON.

Stinson, A. R.

Plat book of Johnson county, Missouri. Compiled and published by A. R. Stinson. Engraved by Albert Volk. 2 p. l., 40 pp. incl. 21 col. maps, 5 fold. maps. fol. Philadelphia, A. R. Stinson, 1914. 4853

Note.—Fold. maps of the state, United States and world. Also business directory of the county.

KNOX.

Ogle, G. A., & co.

Standard atlas of Knox county, Missouri, including a plat book of the villages, cities and townships of the county. Map of the state, United States and world. Patrons directory, reference business directory and departments devoted to general information. Analysis of the system of U. S. land surveys, digest of the system of civil government . . . 2 p. l., 7–65, viii, x–xxiii pp. incl. 20 col. maps, illus. fol. Chicago, G. A. Ogle & co. 1916. 4854

LAFAYETTE.

Tuttle & Pike.

Atlas of Lafayette county, Missouri, 1914 . . . 61 pp. incl. 26 maps. fol. Higginsville, Mo., G. Scott, [c1914] 4855

NOTE.—Contains the *System of United States land surveys.*

LEWIS.

Ogle, G. A., & co.

Standard atlas of Lewis county, Missouri, including a plat book of the villages, cities and townships of the county. Map of the state, United States and world. Patrons directory, reference business directory and departments devoted to general information. Analysis of the system of U. S. land surveys, digest of the system of civil government . . . 2 p. l., 7–81, viii, x–xxiii pp., incl. 23 maps, illus. fol. Chicago, G. A. Ogle & co. 1916. 4856

LINN.

Tuttle & Pike.

Atlas of Linn county, Missouri, 1915 . . . 51 pp. incl. 23 maps, 3 diagrs. fol. Higginsville, Mo., G. Scott, 1915. 4857

NOTE.—Contains the *System of United States land surveys.*

LIVINGSTON.

1878

Edwards bros.

An illustrated historical atlas of Livingston county, Missouri. Compiled, drawn and published from personal examinations and surveys . . . 54 pp. incl. 25 col. maps, illus. 2 fold. maps at end. fol. Philadelphia, Edwards bros. 1878. 4858

1917

Ogle, G. A., & co.

Standard atlas of Livingston county, Missouri, including a plat book of the villages, cities and townships of the county. Map of the state, United States and world. Patrons directory, reference business directory and departments devoted to general information. Analysis of the system of U. S. land surveys, digest of the system of civil government . . . 2 p. l., 7–61, viii, x–xxiii pp., incl. 27 col. maps, illus. fol. Chicago, G. A. Ogle & co. 1917. 4859

MCDONALD.

Ogle, G. A., & co.

Standard atlas of McDonald county, Missouri, including a plat book of the villages, cities and townships of the county. Map of the state, United States and world. Patrons directory, reference business directory and departments devoted to general information. Analysis of the system of U. S. land surveys, digest of the system of civil government . . . 2 p. l., 7–73, [1] viii, x–xxii pp., incl. 24 col. maps, illus. fol. Chicago, G. A. Ogle & co. 1909. 4860

MACON.

Ogle, G. A., & co.

Standard atlas of Macon county, Missouri, including a plat book of the villages, cities and townships of the county. Map of the state, United States and world. Patrons directory, reference business directory and departments devoted to general information. Analysis of the system of U. S. land surveys, digest of the system of civil government . . . 2 p. l., 7–69, xxii pp. incl. 36 col. maps, illus. fol. Chicago, G. A. Ogle & co. 1918. 4861

MARION.

Ogle, G. A., & co.

Standard atlas of Marion county, Missouri, including a plat book of the villages, cities and townships of the county. Map of the state, United States and world. Patrons directory, reference business directory and departments devoted to general information. Analysis of the system of U. S. land surveys, digest of the system of civil government . . . 2 p. l., 7–97, viii, x–xxiii pp. incl. 36 maps, illus., diagrs. fol. Chicago, G. A. Ogle & co. 1913. 4862

MONROE.

1876

Edwards bros.

An illustrated historical atlas of Monroe county, Missouri. Compiled, drawn and published from personal examinations and surveys. 60 pp. [3] l., incl. 24 col. maps, 8 pl. fol. Philadelphia, Edwards bros. 1876 4863

1917

Ogle, G. A., & co.

Standard atlas of Monroe county, Missouri, including a plat book of the villages, cities and townships of the county. Map of the state, United States and world. Patrons directory, reference business directory and departments devoted to general information. Analysis of the system of U. S. land surveys, digest of the system of civil government . . . 2 p. l., 7–61, viii, x–xxiii pp., incl. 29 col. maps, illus. fol. Chicago, G. A. Ogle & co. 1917. 4864

MONTGOMERY.

Ogle, G. A., & co.

Standard atlas of Montgomery county, Missouri, including a plat book of the villages, cities and townships of the county. Map of the state, United States and world. Patrons directory, reference business directory and departments devoted to general information. Analysis of the system of U. S. land surveys, digest of the system of civil government . . . 2 p. l., 7–63, xxii pp. incl. 25 col. maps, illus. fol. Chicago, G. A. Ogle & co. 1918. 4865

OSAGE.

Ogle, G. A., & co.

Standard atlas of Osage county, Missouri, including a plat book of the villages, cities and townships of the county. Map of the state, United States and world. Patrons directory, reference business directory and departments devoted to general information. Analysis of the system of U. S. land surveys, digest of the system of civil government . . . 2 p. l., 7–81, viii, x–xxiii pp. incl. 42 col. maps, illus., diagrs. fol. Chicago, G. A. Ogle & co. 1913. 4866

PERRY.

Ogle, G. A., & co.

Standard atlas of Perry county, Missouri, including a plat book of the villages, cities and townships of the county. Map of the state, United States and world. Patrons directory, reference business directory and departments devoted to general information. Analysis of the system of U. S. land surveys, digest of the system of civil government . . . 2 p. l., 7–75, viii, x–xxiii pp. incl. 17 col. maps, illus., ports., diagrs. fol. Chicago, G. A. Ogle & co. 1915. 4867

PUTNAM.

Edwards bros.

An illustrated historical atlas of Putnam county, Missouri. Compiled, drawn and published from personal examinations and surveys. 50 pp. [4] l., incl. 19 col. maps, 5 pl. fol. Philadelphia, Edwards bros. 1877. 4868

RAY.

1877

Edwards bros.

An illustrated historical atlas of Ray county, Missouri. Compiled, drawn and published from personal examinations and surveys . . . 52 (*i. e.* 56) pp. incl. 21 col. maps, 8 pl. 2 fold. maps at end. fol. Philadelphia, Edwards bros. 1877. 4869

1914

Ogle, G. A., & co.

Standard atlas of Ray county, Missouri, including a plat book of the villages, cities and townships of the county. Map of the state, United States and world. Patrons directory, reference business directory and departments devoted to general information. Analysis of the system of U. S. land surveys, digest of the system of civil government . . . 2 p. l., 7-85, xxiii pp. incl. 45 col. maps, 3 pl., 1 map in text. fol. Chicago, G. A. Ogle & co. 1914. 4870

SALINE.

Ogle, G. A., & co.

Standard atlas of Saline county, Missouri, including a plat book of the villages, cities and townships of the county. Map of the state, United States and world. Patrons directory, reference business directory and departments devoted to general information. Analysis of the system of U. S. land surveys, digest of the system of civil government . . . 2 p. l., 7-75, viii, x-xxiii pp., incl. 35 maps, illus. fol. Chicago, G. A. Ogle & co. 1916. 4871

SCHUYLER.

Ogle, G. A., & co.

Standard atlas of Schuyler county, Missouri, including a plat book of the villages, cities and townships of the county. Map of the state, United States and world. Patrons directory, reference business directory and departments devoted to general information. Analysis of the system of U. S. land surveys, digest of the system of civil government . . . 2 p. l., 8-65, viii, x-xxiii pp., incl. 15 maps, illus. Chicago, G. A. Ogle & co. 1916. 4872

SCOTLAND.

Harrison, R. H.

Illustrated historical atlas of Scotland county, Missouri, in connection with a general atlas of the United States and the state of Missouri. 2 p. l., 3-6, [9]-35 [17] 55-83 pp. incl. 32 col. maps, illus., diagrs. fol. Philadelphia, R. H. Harrison, 1876. 4873

SULLIVAN.

Edwards bros.

An illustrated historical atlas of Sullivan county, Missouri. Compiled, drawn and published from personal examinations and surveys . . . 52 pp. incl. 22 col. maps, 5 pl., 2 fold. maps at end. fol. Philadelphia, Edwards bros. 1877. 4874

Cities.

KANSAS CITY.

Spencer, H. A.

H. A. Spencer ownership service . . . Book of plats containing 946 maps of the most valuable property in Kansas City, Missouri, drawn to an exact scale from surveys and plats, of record, in the city engineers office. cover-title, 2 v., 1 p. l., 1082 maps; 1 p. l., [150] l. obl. 8°. Kansas City, Mo., H. A. Spencer, 1915. 4875

NOTE.—Volume 2, contains key to owners' names and addresses.

MONTANA.

Counties.

RICHLAND.

Janson, W.

Atlas of Richland county, Montana. cover-title, 92 maps. sq. fol. [Watford City, W. Janson] ©1917. 4876

NOTE.—Maps blue print.

NEBRASKA.

Counties.

BOX BUTTE.

Ogle, G. A., & co.

Standard atlas of Box Butte county, Nebraska, including a plat book of the villages, cities and precincts of the county. Map of the state, United States and world. Patrons directory, reference business directory and departments devoted to general information. Analysis of the system of U. S. land surveys, digest of the system of civil government . . . 2 p. l., 7–57, viii, x–xxiii pp. incl. 17 col. maps, illus., diagrs. fol. Chicago, G. A. Ogle & co. 1913. 4877

BUTLER.

Anderson publishing co.

Atlas of Butler and Polk counties, Nebraska, containing maps of townships of the county. Maps of state, United States and world. Farmers directory, analysis of U. S. land surveys . . . 58 [16] 59–61 pp. incl. 31 col. maps. fol. Mason City, Anderson publishing co. 1918. 4878

NOTE.—"Copyrighted by G. W. Anderson, 1918."

CASS.

Anderson publishing co.

Atlas of Cass county, Nebraska, containing maps of townships of the county. Maps of state, United States and world. Farmers directory, analysis of the system of U. S. land surveys . . . 34, 16

Anderson publishing co.—Continued.

pp. incl. 21 col. maps. fol. Mason City, Anderson publishing co. 1918. 4879

NOTE.—"Copyrighted by G. W. Anderson, 1918."

CEDAR.

Ogle, G. A., & co.

Standard atlas of Cedar county, Nebraska, including a plat book of the villages, cities and townships of the county. Map of the state, United States and world. Patrons directory, reference business directory and departments devoted to general information. Analysis of the system of U. S. land surveys, digest of the system of civil government . . . 2 p. l., 7–65, viii, x–xxiii pp. incl. 31 col. maps, illus. fol. Chicago, G. A. Ogle & co. 1917. 4880

CHEYENNE.

Ogle, G. A., & co.

Standard atlas of Cheyenne county, Nebraska, including a plat book of the villages, cities and townships of the county. Map of the state, United States and world. Patrons directory, reference business directory and departments devoted to general information. Analysis of the system of U. S. land surveys, digest of the system of civil government . . . 2 p. l., 7–83, viii, x–xxiii pp. incl. 35 col. maps, illus., diagrs. fol. Chicago, G. A. Ogle & co. 1913. 4881

COLFAX.

Ogle, G. A., & co.

Standard atlas of Colfax county, Nebraska, including a plat book of the villages, cities and precincts of the county. Map of the state, United States and world. Patrons directory, reference business directory and departments devoted to general information. Analysis of the system of U. S. land surveys, digest of the system of civil government . . . 2 p. l., 7–53, viii, x–xxiii pp. incl. 21 col. maps, illus. fol. Chicago, G. A. Ogle & co. 1917. 4882

CUMING.

Anderson publishing co.

Atlas of Cuming county, Nebraska, containing maps of townships of the county. Maps of state, United States and world. Farmers directory, analysis of the system of U. S. land surveys . . . 35 [14] pp. incl. 21 col. maps. fol. Mason City, Iowa, Anderson publishing co. 1918. 4883

NOTE.—"Copyrighted by G. W. Anderson, 1918."

DAWES.

Ogle, G. A., & co.

Standard atlas of Dawes county, Nebraska, including a plat book of the villages, cities and townships of the county. Map of the state, United States and world. Patrons directory, reference business directory and departments devoted to general information. Analysis of the system of U. S. land surveys, digest of the system of civil government . . . 2 p. l., 7–73, viii, x–xxiii pp. incl. 47 col. maps, illus., diagrs. fol. Chicago, G. A. Ogle & co. 1913. 4884

DODGE.

Anderson publishing co.

Atlas of Dodge county, Nebraska, containing maps of townships of the county. Maps of state, United States and world. Farmers directory, analysis of the system of U. S. land surveys . . . 31, 16 pp. incl. 19 col. maps. fol. Mason City, Iowa, Anderson publishing co. 1918. 4885

NOTE.—Copyrighted by G. W. Anderson.
Contains table entitled, "Distances saved by Panama Canal."

DOUGLAS.

Bee publishing co.

Atlas of Douglas, Sarpy and Washington counties, Nebraska, and Mills and Pattawattamie counties, Iowa, containing maps of the townships of the counties, maps of Omaha and South Omaha, Nebraska, and Council Bluffs, Iowa, drawn from actual surveys and county records. Comp. by the Anderson publishing company. 83, [4] pp., incl. 78 maps. fol. Omaha, Nebr., Bee publishing co. 1913. [1912] 4886

FILLMORE.

Anderson publishing co.

Atlas of Fillmore county, Nebraska, containing maps of townships of the county. Maps of state, United States and world. Farmers directory, analysis of the system of U. S. land surveys . . . 35, 16 pp. incl. 21 col. maps. fol. Mason City, Iowa, Anderson publishing co. 1918. 4887

NOTE.—"Copyrighted by G. W. Anderson."

GARFIELD.

Ogle, G. A., & co.

Standard atlas of Garfield county, Nebraska, including a plat book of the villages, cities and townships of the county. Map of the state, United States and world. Patrons directory, reference business directory and departments devoted to general information. Analysis of the system of U. S. land surveys, digest of the system of civil government . . . 2 p. l., 7–45, viii, x–xxiii pp. incl. 21 col. maps, illus. fol. Chicago, G. A. Ogle & co. 1916. 4888

HOWARD.

Ogle, G. A., & co.

Standard atlas of Howard county, Nebraska, including a plat book of the villages, cities and townships of the county. Map of the state, United States and world. Patrons directory, reference business directory and departments devoted to general information. Analysis of the system of U. S. land surveys, digest of the system of civil government . . . 2 p. l., 7–53, viii, x–xxiii pp., incl. 26 col. maps, illus. fol. Chicago, G. A. Ogle & co. 1917. 4889

JEFFERSON.

Ogle, G. A., & co.

Standard atlas of Jefferson county, Nebraska, including a plat book of the villages, cities and precincts of the county. Map of the state, United States and world. Patrons directory, reference business directory and departments devoted to general information. Analysis of the system of U. S. land surveys, digest of the system of civil government . . . 2 p. l., 7–63, viii, x–xxiii pp. incl. 29 col. maps, illus. fol. Chicago, G. A. Ogle & co. 1917. 4890

JOHNSON.

Ogle, G. A., & co.

Standard atlas of Johnson county, Nebraska, including a plat book of the villages, cities and precincts of the county. Map of the state, United States and world. Patrons directory, reference business directory and departments devoted to general information. Analysis of the system of U. S. land surveys, digest of the system of civil government . . . 2 p. l., 7–53, xxii pp. incl. 19 col. maps, illus. fol. Chicago, G. A. Ogle & co. 1918. 4891

KEITH.

Ogle, G. A., & co.

Standard atlas of Keith county, Nebraska, including a plat book of the villages, cities and townships of the county. Map of the state, United States and world. Patrons directory, reference business directory and departments devoted to general information. Analysis of the system of U. S. land surveys, digest of the system of civil government . . . 2 p. l., 7–71, viii, x–xxiii pp. incl. 44 col. maps, illus., diagrs. fol. Chicago, G. A. Ogle & co. 1913. 4892

MADISON.

Ogle, G. A., & co.

Standard atlas of Madison county, Nebraska, including a plat book of the villages, cities and precincts of the county. Map of the state, United States and world. Patrons directory, reference business directory and departments devoted to general information. Analysis of the system of U. S. land surveys, digest of the system of civil government . . . 2 p. l., 7–73, xxii pp., incl. 29 col. maps, illus. fol. Chicago, G. A. Ogle & co. 1918. 4893

MERRICK.

Ogle, G. A., & co.

Standard atlas of Merrick county, Nebraska, including a plat book of the villages, cities and townships of the county. Map of the state, United States and world. Patrons directory, reference business directory and departments devoted to general information. Analysis of the system of U. S. land surveys, digest of the system of civil government . . . 2 p. l., 7–65, viii, x–xxiii pp., incl. 24 col. maps, illus. fol. Chicago, G. A. Ogle & co. 1917. 4894

MORRILL.

Ogle, G. A., & co.

Standard atlas of Morrill county, Nebraska, including a plat book of the villages, cities and townships of the county. Map of the state, United States and world. Patrons directory, reference business directory and departments devoted to general information. Analysis of the system of U. S. land surveys, digest of the system of civil government . . . 2 p. l., 7–71, [1] viii, x–xxiii pp. incl. 42 col. maps, illus. fol. Chicago, G. A. Ogle & co. 1913. 4895

NEMAHA.

Ogle, G. A., & co.

Standard atlas of Nemaha county, Nebraska, including a plat book of the villages, cities and precincts of the county. Map of the state, United States and world. Patrons directory, reference business directory and departments devoted to general information . . . 2 p. l., 7–75, viii, x–xxiii pp. incl. 23 col. maps, illus., diagrs. fol. Chicago, G. A. Ogle & co. 1913. 4896

NUCKOLLS

Ogle, G. A., & co.

Standard atlas of Nuckolls county, Nebraska, including a plat book of the villages, cities and precincts of the county. Map of the state, United States and world. Patrons directory, reference business directory and departments devoted to general information. Analysis of the system of U. S. land surveys, digest of the system of civil government . . . 2 p. l., 7–65, viii, x–xxiii pp. incl. 27 col. maps, illus. fol. Chicago, G. A. Ogle & co. 1917. 4897

PAWNEE.

Ogle, G. A., & co.

Standard atlas of Pawnee county, Nebraska, including a plat book of the villages, cities and precincts of the county. Map of the state, United States and world. Patrons directory, reference

Ogle, G. A., & co.—Continued.

business directory and departments devoted to general information. Analysis of the system of U. S. land surveys, digest of the system of civil government . . . 2 p. l., 7–43, viii, x–xxiii pp. incl. 20 col. maps. illus. fol. Chicago, G. A. Ogle & co. 1917. 4898

PERKINS.

Ogle, G. A., & co.

Standard atlas of Perkins county, Nebraska, including a plat book of the villages, cities and townships of the county. Map of the state, United States and world. Patrons directory, reference business directory and departments devoted to general information. Analysis of the system of U. S. land surveys, digest of the system of civil government . . . 2 p. l., 7–45, viii, x–xxii pp. incl. 28 col. maps, illus. fol. Chicago, G. A. Ogle & co. 1917. 4899

PLATTE.

Goodwin, I. B.

Plat book of Platte county, Nebraska. Compiled from county records and actual surveys . . . 5, [1] 9–50 pp. incl. 21 col. maps. fol. Chicago, I. B. Goodwin, ©1914. 4900

POLK.

Anderson publishing co.

Atlas of Butler and Polk counties, Nebraska, containing maps of townships of the county. Maps of state, United States and world. Farmers directory, analysis of U. S. land surveys . . . 58 [16] 59–61 pp. incl. 31 col. maps. fol. Mason City, Iowa, Anderson publishing co. 1918. 4901

NOTE.—"Copyrighted by G. W. Anderson, 1918."

RICHARDSON.

Ogle, G. A., & co.

Standard atlas of Richardson county, Nebraska, including a plat book of the villages, cities and precincts of the county. Map of the state, United States and world. Patrons directory, reference business directory and departments devoted to general information. Analysis of the system of U. S. land surveys, digest of the system of civil government . . . 2 p. l., 7–87, viii, x–xxiii pp. incl. 30 col. maps, illus., diagrs. fol. Chicago, G. A. Ogle & co. 1913. 4902

SALINE.

Anderson publishing co.

Atlas of Saline county, Nebraska, containing maps of townships of the county. Maps of the state, United States and world. Farmers directory, analysis of the system of U. S. land surveys . . . 35, 16 pp. incl. 22 col. maps. fol. Mason City, Iowa, Anderson publishing co. 1918. 4903

NOTE.—"Copyrighted by G. W. Anderson, 1918."

SARPY.

Bee publishing co.

Atlas of Douglas, Sarpy and Washington counties, Nebraska, and Mills and Pottawattamie counties, Iowa, containing maps of the townships of the counties, maps of Omaha and South Omaha, Nebraska, and Council Bluffs, Iowa, drawn from actual surveys and county records. Comp. by the Anderson publishing company . . . for the Bee publishing company . . . 83, [4] pp. incl. 78 maps. fol. Omaha, Nebr., Bee publishing co. 1913 [1912] 4904

SAUNDERS.

Anderson publishing co.

Atlas of Saunders county, Nebraska, containing maps of townships of the county. Maps of state, United States and world. Farmers directory, analysis of the system of U. S. land surveys . . . 47 [16] pp. incl. 28 col. maps, 1 tab. fol. Mason City, Iowa, Anderson publishing co. 1916. 4905

NOTE.—"Copyrighted by G. W. Anderson, 1916."
Contains table of "Distances saved by Panama canal."

SHERIDAN.

Ogle, G. A., & co.

Standard atlas of Sheridan county, Nebraska, including a plat book of the villages, cities and townships of the county. Map of the state, United States and world. Patrons directory, reference business directory and departments devoted to general information. Analysis of the system of U. S. land surveys, digest of the system of civil government . . . 2 p. l., 8–101, xxiii pp. incl. 75 col. maps, 3 pl., 1 map in text. fol. Chicago, G. A. Ogle & co. 1914. 4906

SIOUX.

Ogle, G. A., & co.

Standard atlas of Sioux county, Nebraska, including a plat book of the villages, cities and townships of the county. Map of the state, United States and world. Patrons directory, reference business directory and departments devoted to general information. Analysis of the system of U. S. land surveys, digest of the system of civil government . . . 2 p. l., 7–85, viii, x–xxiii pp. incl. 60 col. maps, illus. Chicago, G. A. Ogle & co. 1916. 4907

STANTON.

Ogle, G. A., & co.

Standard atlas of Stanton county, Nebraska, including a plat book of the villages, cities and precincts of the county. Map of the state, United States and world. Patrons directory, reference business directory and departments devoted to general information. Analysis of the system of U. S. land surveys, digest of the

Ogle, G. A., & co.—Continued.
system of civil government . . . 2 p. l., 7–45, xxii pp. incl. 19 col. maps, illus. fol. Chicago, G. A. Ogle & co. 1919. 4908

THAYER.

Ogle, G. A., & co.
Standard atlas of Thayer county, Nebraska, including a plat book of the villages, cities and townships of the county. Map of the state, United States and world. Patrons directory, reference business directory and departments devoted to general information. Analysis of the system of U. S. land surveys, digest of the system of civil government . . . 2 p. l., 7–81, viii, x–xxiii pp. incl. 31 col. maps, illus. fol. Chicago, G. A. Ogle & co. 1916. 4909

WASHINGTON.

Bee publishing co.
Atlas of Douglas, Sarpy and Washington counties, Nebraska, and Mills and Pottawattamie counties, Iowa, containing maps of the townships of the counties, maps of Omaha and South Omaha, Nebraska, and Council Bluffs, Iowa, drawn from actual surveys and county records. Comp. by the Anderson publishing company . . . for the Bee publishing company . . . 83 [4] pp. incl. 78 maps. fol. Omaha, Nebr., Bee publishing co. 1913. [1912] 4910

WAYNE.

Ogle, G. A., & co.
Standard atlas of Wayne county, Nebraska, including a plat book of the villages, cities and precincts of the county. Map of the state, United States and world. Patrons directory, reference business directory and departments devoted to general information. Analysis of the system of U. S. land surveys, digest of the system of civil government . . . 2 p. l., 7–55, xxii pp. incl. 23 col. maps, illus. fol. Chicago, G. A. Ogle & co. 1918. 4911

WHEELER.

Ogle, G. A., & co.
Standard atlas of Wheeler county, Nebraska, including a plat book of the villages, cities and townships of the county. Map of the state, United States and world. Patrons directory, reference business directory and departments devoted to general information. Analysis of the system of civil government . . . 2 p. l., 7–41, xxii pp. incl. 23 col. maps, illus. fol. Chicago, G. A. Ogle & co. 1917. 4912

Cities.

OMAHA.

Baist, G. W.

Baist's real estate atlas of surveys of Omaha, Neb. Complete in one volume. Compiled from official records, private plans and actual surveys. 2 p. l., 30 (*i. e.* 31) col. maps. fol. Philadelphia, G. W. Baist, 1918. 4913

NOTE.—Copyrighted, 1918, by G. Wm. Baist.

NEW JERSEY.

Counties.

MONMOUTH.

Wolverton, C., *and* **Breou, F.**

Wolverton's atlas of Monmouth county, New Jersey. Compiled from actual surveys, state and county official records and private plans . . . 2 p. l., 55 col. maps on 43 pl. fol. New York, C. Wolverton, 1889. 4914

Cities.

ATLANTIC CITY.

Mueller, A. H.

Atlas of Absecon island, N. J. . . . Compiled from actual surveys, official records and private plans . . . 2 v., 2 p. l., 23 col. maps; 2 p. l., 19 col. maps. fol. Philadelphia, A. H. Mueller, 1914. 4915

NOTE.—Maps continuously numbered.

CONTENTS.

v. 1. Atlantic City.
" 2. Ventnor City, Margate City and Longport borough including Atlantic county map.

LANDIS.

Seward, W. H.

Tax map of Landis township, Cumberland county, New Jersey. title, 163 (i. e. 172) maps. obl. fol. [Vineland, N. J.] 1919. 4915a

NOTE.—Blueprint. "Copyright . . . by Walter H. Seward."

Titles of maps read: "Landis township tax map . . . surveyed map completed by West Jersey engineering co. for the estate of Augustus Clark Seward."

LONGPORT BOROUGH.

Mueller, A. H.

Atlas of Absecon island, N. J. . . . Compiled from actual surveys, official records and private plans . . . 2 v., 2 p. l., 23 col. maps; 2 p. l., 19 col. maps. fol. Philadelphia, A. H. Mueller, 1914. 4916

NOTE.—Maps continuously numbered.

CONTENTS.

v. 1. Atlantic City.
" 2. Ventnor City, Margate City and Longport borough including Atlantic county map.

MARGATE CITY.

Mueller, A. H.

Atlas of Absecon island, N. J. . . . Compiled from actual surveys, official records and private plans . . . 2 v., 2 p. l., 23 col. maps; 2 p. l., 19 col. maps. fol. Philadelphia, A. H. Mueller, 1914. 4917

NOTE.—Maps continuously numbered.

CONTENTS.

v. 1. Atlantic City.
" 2. Ventnor City, Margate City and Longport borough including Atlantic county map.

PATERSON.

Mueller, A. H.

Atlas of the city of Paterson, New Jersey. Compiled from actual surveys, official records and private plans, by J. M. Lathrop, civil engineer, assisted by E. Robinson. Under the direct management and supervision of . . . 2 p. l., 26 (*i. e.* 27) col. maps. fol. Philadelphia, A. H. Mueller, 1915. 4918

VENTNOR CITY.

Mueller, A. H.

Atlas of Absecon island, N. J. . . . Compiled from actual surveys, official records and private plans . . . 2 v., 2 p. l., 23 col. maps; 2 p. l., 19 col. maps. fol. Philadelphia, A. H. Mueller, 1914. 4919

NOTE.—Maps continuously numbered.

CONTENTS.

v. 1. Atlantic City.
" 2. Ventnor City, Margate City and Longport borough including Atlantic county map.

Miscellaneous.

Absecon Island.

Mueller, A. H.

Atlas of Absecon island, N. J. . . . Compiled from actual surveys, official records and private plans . . . . 2 v., 2 p. l., 23 col. maps; 2 p. l., 19 col. maps. fol. Philadelphia, A. H. Mueller, 1914. 4920

Note.—Maps continuously numbered.

CONTENTS.

v. 1. Atlantic City.
" 2. Ventnor City, Margate City and Longport borough including Atlantic county map.

NEW YORK.

State.

1836

Gordon, T. F.

Gazetteer of the state of New York: comprehending its colonial history; general geography, geology, and internal improvements; its political state; a minute description of its several counties, towns, and villages; statistical tables, exhibiting the area, improved lands, population, stock, taxes, manufactures, schools, and cost of public instruction, in each town. With a map of the state, and a map of each county, and plans of the cities and principal villages. xii, [1] 801 pp., incl. 68 maps. 12°. Philadelphia, for the author, 1836. 4921

1914

Cram, G. F.

A descriptive review of the commercial, industrial, agricultural, historical development of the state of New York, with special charts, detail maps and profuse half-tone illustrations from all parts of the Empire state; containing in addition, statistical charts pertaining to the increased cost of living, newly engraved maps of every state in the United States, detailed maps of every country, state and kingdom. Together with a complete and adequate locating index to all cities, towns, villages and post offices in the United States, giving populations to every incorporated city and village therein. 300 pp. incl. illus., maps, plans. fol. Chicago, New York, G. F. Cram [©1914] 4922

Counties.

CHEMUNG.

Miller, D. L.

Atlas of Chemung county, New York, embracing detailed plans of the city of Elmira. From official records, private plans and surveys under the direction and personal supervision of D. L. Miller . . . assisted by E. B. Foote, T. Flynn and A. R. Whipple. 1 p. l., 1 l., 25 col. maps. fol. Philadelphia, D. L. Miller, 1904. 4923

ERIE.

Century map co.

New century atlas Erie county, New York. From government surveys, official records, and general compilations and notations, by the company's corps of expert engineers and draughtsmen, Lew. J. G. Ogden . . . E. E. Whittemore . . . William Westgard . . . 1 p. l., 2 [2] 4–153 pp. incl. 83 col. maps, 1 pl. fol. Philadelphia, Buffalo, Century map co. 1909. 4924

NOTE.—Index on reverse of front cover.

NASSAU.

Hyde, E. B.

Atlas of Nassau county, Long Island, N. Y. . . . Historical, statistical. Based upon maps on file at the county seat in Mineola and upon private plans and surveys furnished by surveyors and individual owners . . . [173] pp. incl. 118 col. maps. fol. New York, E. B. Hyde, 1914. 4925

NOTE.—Various paging.

NEW YORK.

New York City. *Department of taxes and assessments.*

The land map of the county of New York prepared by the board of taxes and assessments under authority of the greater New York charter, chapter xxiv, amended by chapter 514 of the laws of 1916. January 1, 1917. 1 p. l., 24 (*i. e.* 25) maps. obl. fol. [New York, 1917] 4926

NOTE.—"Certified november 29, 1916." Signed, "Lawson Purdy, president. Charles T. White, A. L. Kline, F. B. Shipley, J. J. Halleran, John T. Knewitz, Collin H. Woodward, commissioners. Henry W. Vogel, surveyor."

NIAGARA.

Beers, Upton & co.

Atlas of Niagara and Orleans counties, New York. From actual surveys and official records. Engd. by Worley & Bracher. Printed by J. H. Toudy & co. 113 pp. incl. 77 col. maps. fol. Philadelphia, Beers, Upton & co. 1875. 4927

NOTE.—At foot of title-page the following names appear: D. G. Beers, W. Upton, J. H. Doty, J. Lanagan.

ONTARIO.

Nichols, B.

Atlas of Ontario county, New York, from actual surveys by and under the direction of Beach Nichols. Eng[d]. by Worley & Bracher. Printed by F. Bourquin. 83 pp. incl. 28 col. maps. fol. Philadelphia, Pomeroy, Whitman & co. 1874. 4928

ORLEANS.

Beers, Upton & co.

Atlas of Niagara and Orleans counties, New York. From actual surveys and official records. Engd. by Worley & Bracher. Printed by J. H. Toudy & co. 113 pp. incl. 77 col. maps. fol. Philadelphia, Beers, Upton & co. 1875. 4929

Note.—At foot of title-page the following names appear: D. G. Beers, W. Upton, J. H. Doty, J. Lanagan.

QUEENS.

New York State.

Land map of the county of Queens, city and state of New-York, as per chapter 434, Laws of 1914. Jamaica, July, 1915. 1 p. l., 8, 65 (*i. e.* 70) maps. fol. [New York, R. A. Welcke, 1915] 4930

Note.—Scale: 1″=600′.

Copyrighted, 1915, by Leonard Ruoff, county clerk of Queens county, N. Y.

SUFFOLK.

1915–1916

Hyde, M. B.

Atlas of a part of Suffolk county, Long Island, New York. South side, ocean shore . . . Based upon actual measurements by our own corps of engineers, maps on file at county offices, also maps from actual surveys furnished by surveyors and individual owners. 2 v. 2 p. l., 40 (*i. e.* 41) col. maps; 2 p. l., 29 (*i. e.* 31) col. maps. fol. Brooklyn, Manhattan, E. B. Hyde, 1915–1916. 4931

CONTENTS.

v. 1. Including townships of Babylon, Islip and lower portion of Brookhaven.
" 2. Including townships of Southampton and Easthampton, Shelter island.

1917

Atlas of a part of Suffolk county, Lond Island, New York. North side, Sound shore . . . Complete in two volumes. Based upon actual measurements by our own corps of engineers, maps on file at county offices, also maps from actual surveys furnished by surveyors and individual owners. v. 1, 2 p. l., 36 (*i. e.* 38) maps., fol. Brooklyn, Manhattan, E. B. Hyde, 1917. 4932

CONTENTS.

v. 1. Including townships of Huntington, Smithtown and part of Brookhaven.
" 2. Wanting.

WAYNE.

Beers, D. G., & co.

Atlas of Wayne co., New York. From actual surveys and official records. Engd. by Worley & Bracher . . . Printed by J. H. Toudy & co. . . . 87 pp. incl. 31 col. maps. fol. Philadelphia, D. G. Beers, 1874. 4933

NOTE.—Title-page contains the names, D. G. Beers, W. Upton, J. H. Doty, J. Lanagan.

WESTCHESTER.

Bromley, G. W., & co.

Atlas of Westchester county, N. Y. Pocket, desk and automobile edition . . . 2 v., 10 p. l., 9 col. maps on 268 pp. 1 col. map; 8 p. l., 13 col. maps on 293 pp. 1 col. map. 8°. New York, G. W. Bromley & co. 1914. 4934

NOTE.—Colored maps of the county pasted to back of front covers.

CONTENTS.

v. 1. Mt. Vernon, Pelham, New Rochelle, Mamaroneck, Rye, Harrison, White Plains, Scarsdale and Eastchester.

" 2. Yonkers, Greenburg, Mt. Pleasant, Ossining, Cortlandt, New Castle, North Castle, Yorktown, Somers, Bedford, Poundridge, Lewisboro, and North Salem.

YATES.

Everts, Ensign & Everts.

Combination atlas map of Yates county, New York. Compiled, drawn and published from personal examinations and surveys. 111 pp. incl. 20 col. maps, illus. fol. Philadelphia, Everts, Ensign & Everts, 1876. 4935

Cities.

ALBANY.

Lodge, B., & co.

Ward maps of Albany, N. Y., showing block numbers as designated in the assessors' books . . . Maps drawn by Arthur B. Murphy. cover-title, 19 maps. obl. 4°. [Albany, N. Y.] B. Lodge & co. c1916. 4936

NOTE.—The following noted on title-page: "The maps in this book can be revised periodically at a nominal cost."

BROOKLYN.

Hyde, E. B.

Miniature atlas of the borough of Brooklyn . . . 2 v., 4 p. l., 36, 675 (*i. e.* 677) pp.; 4 p. l., 34, 713 pp. 8°. Brooklyn, Manhattan, E. B. Hyde, 1912. 4937

CONTENTS.

v. 1. Brooklyn proper.

" 2. Outlying wards (29th, 30th, 31st and 32nd)

ELMIRA.

Miller, D. L.

Atlas of Chemung county, New York, embracing detailed plans of the city of Elmira. From official records, private plans and surveys under the direction and personal supervision of D. L. Miller . . . assisted by E. B. Foote, T. Flynn and A. R. Whipple. 1 p. l., 1 l., 25 col. maps. fol. Philadelphia, D. L. Miller, 1904. 4938

FAR ROCKAWAY.

Hyde, E. B.

Miniature atlas of Far Rockaway and Rockaway Beach, Queens (5th ward) 8 p. l., 6, 1–120 pp. incl. 123 col. maps. 8°. New York, Brooklyn, E. B. Hyde, 1912. 4939

NEW UTRECHT.

Dripps, M.

Atlas of New Utrecht, Kings county, N. Y. 1 p. l., 7 maps. fol. New York, M. Dripps, [1887] 4940

NOTE.—Index map on reverse of title-page.

NEW YORK.

Views.

Fay, T. S.

Views in New-York and its environs, from accurate, characteristic & picturesque drawings, taken on the spot, expressly for this work, by Dakin, architect; with historical, topographical & critical illustrations . . . 3 p. l., [62] pp., 1 map, 15 pl. 4°. New York, Peabody & co. London, O. Rich, 1831. 4941

NOTE.—Engraved title page and plates.

CONTENTS.

no. 1. New York.—Broadway from the Park.
" 2. Bowling Green.—Residence of Philip Hone, esq.
" 3. City Hall.—Navy yard, Brooklyn.
" 4. Leroy Place.—Shot tower.
" 5. Elysian fields, Hoboken.—City hotel, Trinity and Grace churches.
" 6. Lunatic asylum.—Merchants room, Exchange.
" 7. Washington institute and city reservoir.—Hudson river from Hoboken.
" 8. Coffee-house slip.—Park theatre.—Park Row.
" 9. Broad Street.—Holt's new hotel.
" 10. Map of the city of New-York, compiled and surveyed by William Hooker.
" 11. Webb's Congress hall.—Merchants exchange, Wall Street.—Masonic hall, Broadway.
" 12. Pearl street house & Ohio hotel.—Deaf and dumb asylum.
" 13. Rotunda, Chambers street.—Grace church, Broadway.—U. S. Branch bank, Wall street.—St. George's church, Beekman st.—St. Patricks cathedral, Mott st.

Fay, T. S.—Continued.

no. 14. Presbyterian church, Carmine street.—St. Thomas' church, Broadway.—2nd Unitarian church, Mercer cor. Prince st.—Washington hotel, Broadway.—Bowery theatre.
" 15. Episcopal seminary.—Oil cloth manufactory.—Fulton market.—Penitentiary, Blackwell's Island.
" 16. La Grange terrace—Lafayette place.—City of New York.

General.

1879

Bromley, G. W., & co.

Atlas of the city of New York . . . From actual surveys and official records. 1 p. l., 41 (*i. e.* 42) maps. fol. New York, G. W. Bromley & E. Robinson, 1879. 4942

NOTE.—Printed by F. Bourquin . . . Philadelphia.

1882

Bromley, G. W., & co.

Atlas of the 23rd. ward, city of New York. From actual surveys and official records. Engraved by A. H. Mueller . . . 1 p. l., 21 maps. fol. Philadelphia, G. W. & W. S. Bromley, 1882. 4943

1892

Colton, G. W., & C. B., & co.

Complete ward atlas of New York city, with key locating wards. cover-title, 13 maps. 4°. New York, New York record publishing co. ©1892. 4944

NOTE.—" Copyright 1892 by G. W. & C. B. Colton & co. N. Y.".

1912

Hyde, E. B.

Miniature atlas of the borough of the Bronx complete in two volumes . . . 2 v., v. 1. 8°. New York, Brooklyn, E. B. Hyde, 1912. 4945

CONTENTS.

v. 1. 23rd and 24th wards.
" 2. Wanting.

1912

Hyde, E. B.

Miniature atlas of the borough of Manhattan in one volume. 24 pp., 2 l., 472 pp. 8°. Brooklyn, Manhattan, E. B. Hyde, 1912. 4946

1913–1915

Bromley, G. W., & W. S.

Atlas of the city of New York, borough of Manhattan . . . From actual surveys and official plans . . . 5 v. fol. Philadelphia, G. W. Bromley & co. 1913–1915. 4947

NOTE.—Outline maps on verso of front covers.

CONTENTS.

v. 1. Battery to 14th street.
" 2. 14th street to 59th street.
" 3. 59th street to 110th street.
" 4. 110th street to 145th street.
" 5. 145th street to Spuyten Duyvil.

1915

Hammond, C. S., & co.

Hammond's atlas of New York city and the metropolitan district, containing new maps of each borough on large scale, showing streets, avenues, tunnels, all transportation routes, etc., including the subways now under construction and proposed; also detailed highway and township maps of the country adjacent to New York city, showing quality of roads, interurban electric lines, railroads, etc. cover-title, 16 pp. incl. 11 col. maps. 4°. New York, C. S. Hammond & co. [1915] 4948

NOTE.—Col. map on inside of each cover.

1915

Hammond, C. S., & co.

Hammond's atlas of the metropolitan district, a new collection of detailed maps of all boroughs of New York city, together with road maps of the Hudson valley, Long Island, northern New Jersey, central New Jersey. Showing in the borough maps all streets, avenues and transportation lines. And showing in the road maps all interurban electric lines, ferries, steam railroads, and stations, good roads, fair roads, etc. 2 p. l., 32 pp. incl. 22 col. maps. sm. fol. New York, C. S. Hammond & co. 1915. 4949

1916

Bromley, G. W., & co.

Atlas of the borough of Manhattan, city of New York. Desk and library edition. 3 p. l., 191 (*i. e.* 196) col. maps. obl. 4°. New York, G. W. Bromley & co. ©1916. 4950

NOTE.—Copyrighted, 1916, by G. W. Bromley & co.
Block index on reverse of front cover.

1916

Unz & co.

Atlas of New York city and the metropolitan district. cover-title, 10 pp. incl. 10 col maps. sm. fol. New York, Unz & co. 1916. 4951

1916–1917

New York City. *Department of taxes and assessments.*

Tentative land value maps of the city of New York prepared by the Department of taxes and assessments . . . 2 v. sm. fol. New York, 1916–1917. 4952

NOTE.—Lawson Purdy, president of the dept.

"Published under arrangement with the Department . . . [by] the Record and guide"

Volume for 1913 issued as section 3 of the *Real estate record and builders guide, v. 90, no. 2324.*

1917

Bromley, G. W., & W. S.

Atlas of the city of New York, borough of Richmond, Staten Island . . . From actual surveys and official plans . . . 2 p. l., 43 (*i. e.* 44) col. maps. fol. Philadelphia, G. W. Bromley & co. 1917. 4953

CONTENTS.

v. 1. Wanting.
" 2. Wards 4 & 5.

1918

New York City. *Department of taxes and assessments.*

The land map of the county of Bronx prepared by the board of taxes and assessments under authority of the greater New York charter, chapter xxiv, amended by chapter 514 of the laws of 1916. January 1, 1918 . . . 2 v., 1 p. l., 20 maps; 1 p. l., 26 maps. obl. fol. [New York, 1918] 4954

NOTE.—Maps numbered consecutively.

Copyrighted, 1918, by Lawson Purdy, John J. Halleran, Charles T. White, Collin H. Woodward, Ardolph L. Kline, Frederic B. Shipley, John J. Knewitz, commissioners of taxes and assessments of the city of New York.

Title-pages signed, Henry W. Vogel, surveyor, and certified dec. 5th 1917, Lawson Purdy, Joh Halleran, Chas. T. White, John J. Knewitz, commissioners.

ROCHESTER.

Hopkins, G. M., co.

Plat book of the city of Rochester, N. Y., and vicinity, from official records, private plans and actual surveys . . . 1 p. l., 4 pp., 52 (*i. e.* 54) col. maps. fol. Philadelphia, G. M. Hopkins co. 1918. 4955

ROCKAWAY BEACH.

Hyde, E. B.

Miniature atlas of Far Rockaway and Rockaway Beach, Queens (5th ward). 8 p. l., 6, 1–120 pp. incl. 123 col. maps. 8°. New York, Brooklyn, E. B. Hyde, 1912. 4956

Miscellaneous.

Hudson River.

Views.

Milbert, J. G.

Itinéraire pittoresque du fleuve Hudson et des parties laterales. L'Amérique du Nord d'après les dessins originaux pris sur les lieux . . . 1 p. l., 1 map, 53 pl. fol. Paris, H. Gaugain & cie. [1828–1829] 4957

Note.—Engraved title-page and plates.
To accompany text of the same title.
Dates taken from text.
Explanations of the plates given in french, latin, english, and german.

CONTENTS.

no. 1. Carte pour servir à l'Itinéraire pittoresque du fleuve Hudson et des parties latérales de L'Amérique du Nord.
" 2. Vue de New York prise de Weahawk.
" 3. Distillerie de mr. Pierpont sur l'isle Longue.
" 4. Intérieur de New York, rue de Provost et Chapel.
" 5. Bourg de Tarry-Town ou le major André fut pris.
" 6. Bourg de Sing-sing ou Mont Plaisant.
" 7. Port d'Haverstraw ou de Warren.
" 8. Plaine de West Point au moment de l'exercice.
" 9. Vue générale de l'école militaire de West Point.
" 10. Indian Brook dans la campagne du cpte. Phillips.
" 11. Chûte inférieure près l'habitation de me. Montgomery.
" 12. Ville d'Hudson.
" 13. Vue du port de la ville d'Hudson et des montagnes Catskill.
" 14. Ville d'Albany. Capitale de l'état de New York.
" 15. Intérieur de la ville d'Albany, maison de l'ancien gouverneur hollandais.
" 16. Chûte dans le Mont Ida, audessus de la ville de Troye.
" 17. Chûte de Cohoes, de la rivière Mohawk.
" 18. Place où le gal. anglais Burgoyne se rendit au génal. américain Gates.
" 19. Bains de Saratoga.
" 20. Chûtes générales de l'Hudson à Sandy Hill.
" 21. Cours de l'Hudson et moulins, près Sandy Hill.
" 22. Port du Lac Champlain à White Hall.
" 23. Chûtes de l'Hudson au village de Gleens.
" 24. Moulins à scies au village de Glenns.
" 25. Lac George et village de Caldwell.
" 26. Pont sur l'Hudson, près Luzerne.
" 27. Débarcadaire de Jessups.
" 28. Extrêmité de la chûte d'Adley's.
" 29. Rapides de l'Hudson à Adley's.

Milbert, J. G.—Continued.

no. 30. Vue générale des chûtes de l'Hudson à Adley's.
" 31. Pont et route près la rivière Mohawk.
" 32. Entrée des chûtes de l'ouest Canada Creek.
" 33. Grande chûte du Canada Creek.
" 34. Chûte de la rivière des Pierres àchaux.
" 35. Fer à cheval de la chûte du Niagara côté du Canada.
" 36. Chûte générale du Niagara, côté du Canada.
" 37. Chûte du Niagara prise du côté américain.
" 38. Chûte de la rivière Genésée.
" 39. Chûte du Deer Creek ou rivière des Daims.
" 40. Port militaire à Sacketts Harbourg.
" 41. Manufacture de coton sur la rivière Noire.
" 42. Chûte de Thérèze sur la rivière Indienne.
" 43. Moulins près de Luzerne, vers les sources de l'Hudson.
" 44. Vue de Boston prise du pont du Sud.
" 45. Chûte du Pawtucket.
" 46. Vue du côté du nord de la ville de Providence.
" 47. Chûte de la Passaic.
" 48. Vue de la rivière Passaic.
" 49. Entrée des chûtes de la Passaic.
" 50. Chûte près des bains de Schooley's.
" 51. Vallée de Schooley.
" 52. Machine à vapeur sur la rivière Schuylkill.
" 53. Machine pour élever les fardeaux sur les rapides de la Susquehanna.
" 54. Fonderié sur la rivière Jone's près Baltimore.
" 55. Pont naturel en Virginie.

Wall, W. G.

[The Hudson river portfolio from drawings made by W. G. Wall] 20 pl. ca. 14⅝ x 21½ each. [New York, H. I. Megarey, 1828] 4958

NOTE.—An uncolored set of these plates without title, or the descriptions which come with the earlier edition.

First published in parts of four prints each from about 1821 to 1825.

The first issue of the views was in aquatint. They were advertised to be engraved by I. R. Smith, most of them are, however, engraved by I. Hill.

An edition issued in 1828 has the words "and transferred to G. & C. & H. Carvill, New York," added to the imprint.

In the present edition the name, G. & C. & H. Carvill, New York, has been erased from all the plates except no. 15, "View from Fishkill looking to West Point," and no. 16, "West Point," leaving the phrase, "and transferred to," on all the other plates.

On views nos. 2, 3, 5, 11, the imprint reads, "Published by H. I. Megarey & W. B. Gilley, New York, and John Mill, Charleston, S. C. All views are painted by W. G. Wall. Engraved by I. Hill," except nos. 2, 3, 5 and 11. See contents for titles.

Views nos. 2, 3, were "Painted by W. G. Wall. Finished by J. Hill." Nos. 5, 11, "Painted by W. G. Wall. Eng. by I. R. Smith. Finished by J. Hill."

Pl. no. 20, "New York, from Governors Island," is reproduced in Stokes, *The iconography of Manhattan Island*, v. 3, pl. 89, with a bibliographical note on pp. 571–575.

CONTENTS.

no. 1. Little Falls at Luzerne.
" 2. The junction of the Sacandaga and Hudson Rivers.
" 3. View near Jessups Landing.
" 4. Rapids above Hadleys Falls.
" 5. Hadley's Falls.
" 6. Glenns Falls.
" 7. View near Sandy Hill.
" 8. Baker's Falls.
" 9. View near Fort Miller.
" 10. Fort Edward.
" 11. Troy from Mount Ida.
" 12. View near Hudson.
" 13. Hudson.
" 14. Newburg.
" 15. View from Fishkill looking to West Point.
" 16. West Point.
" 17. View near Fishkill.
" 18. View near Fort Montgomery.
" 19. Palisades.
" 20. New York, from Governors Island.

NORTH DAKOTA.

State.

House, W. M.

North Dakota and Richland county chart, compiled and published from official records and personal examination. To which is added a map of the world, a map of the United States, a map of Alaska, historical features, etc. 53 [4] pp. incl. 17 maps (5 col.), illus., front. fol. Chicago, Rand McNally & co. 1897. 4959

Counties.

ADAMS.

Ogle, G. A., & co.

Standard atlas of Adams county, North Dakota, including a plat book of the villages, cities and townships of the county. Map of the state, United States and world. Patrons directory, reference business directory and departments devoted to general information. Analysis of the system of U. S. land surveys, digest of the system of civil government . . . 2 p. l., 7–59, viii, x–xxiii pp. incl. 36 col. maps, illus. fol. Chicago, G. A. Ogle & co. 1917. 4960

BOWMAN.

Ogle, G. A., & co.

Standard atlas of Bowman county, North Dakota, including a plat book of the villages, cities and townships of the county.

Ogle, G. A., & co.—Continued.

Map of the state, United States and world. Patrons directory and departments devoted to general information. Analysis of the system of U. S. land surveys, digest of the system of civil government . . . 2 p. l., 7–69, xxii pp. incl. 42 col. maps, illus. fol. Chicago, G. A. Ogle & co. 1917. 4961

BURKE.

Ogle, G. A., & co.

Standard atlas of Burke county, North Dakota, including a plat book of the villages, cities and townships of the county. Map of the state, United States and world. Patrons directory, reference business directory and departments devoted to general information. Analysis of the system of U. S. land surveys, digest of the system of civil government . . . 2 p. l., 7–65, xxiii pp. incl. 48 col. maps, 4 pl., 1 map in text. fol. Chicago, G. A. Ogle & co. 1914. 4962

DIVIDE.

Ogle, G. A., & co.

Standard atlas of Divide county, North Dakota, including a plat book of the villages, cities and townships of the county. Map of the state, United States and world. Patrons directory, reference business directory and departments devoted to general information. Analysis of the system of U. S. land surveys, digest of the system of civil government . . . 2 p. l., 8–87, viii, x–xxiii pp. incl. 40 col. maps, illus. fol. Chicago, G. A. Ogle & co. 1915. 4963

EMMONS.

Ogle, G. A., & co.

Standard atlas of Emmons county, North Dakota, including a plat book of the villages, cities and townships of the county. Map of the state, United States and world. Patrons directory, reference business directory and departments devoted to general information. Analysis of the system of U. S. land surveys, digest of the system of civil government . . . 2 p. l., 7–79, viii, x–xxiii pp. incl. 53 col. maps, illus. fol. Chicago, G. A. Ogle & co. 1916. 4964

GRANT.

Ogle, G. A., & co.

Standard atlas of Grant county, North Dakota, including a plat book of the villages, cities and townships of the county. Map of the state, United States and world. Patrons directory, reference business directory and departments devoted to general information. Analysis of the system of U. S. land surveys, digest of the system of civil government . . . 2 p. l., 7–93, xxii pp. incl. 56 col. maps, illus. fol. Chicago, G. A. Ogle & co. 1918. 4965

HETTINGER

Ogle, G. A., & co.

Standard atlas of Hettinger county, North Dakota, including a plat book of the villages, cities and townships of the county. Map of the state, United States and world. Patrons directory, reference business directory and departments devoted to general information. Analysis of the system of U. S. land surveys, digest of the system of civil government . . . 2 p. l., 7–71, viii, x–xxiii pp. incl. 40 col. maps, illus. fol. Chicago, G. A. Ogle & co. 1917. 4966

LAMOURE

Ogle, G. A., & co.

Standard atlas of Lamoure county, North Dakota, including a plat book of the villages, cities, and townships of the county. Map of the state, United States, and world. Patrons directory, reference business directory and departments devoted to general information . . . Compiled and published by G. A. Ogle & co. . . . Assisted in record work and platting by Elliott-Holbert co. . . . 2 p. l., 7–85, viii, x–xxiii pp. incl. 41 col. maps, illus. fol. Chicago, G. A. Ogle & co. 1913. 4967

LOGAN.

Ogle, G. A., & co.

Standard atlas of Logan county, North Dakota, including a plat book of the villages, cities and townships of the county. Map of the state, United States and world. Patrons directory, reference business directory and departments devoted to general information. Analysis of the system of U. S. land surveys, digests of the system of civil government . . . 2 p. l., 8–93, viii, x–xxiii pp. incl. 37 maps, 3 pl., 1 map in text. fol. Chicago, G. A. Ogle & co. 1916. 4968

McKENZIE.

Janson, W.

[McKenzie county, North Dakota. In township form] 87 maps. fol. [Watford, N. Dak. 1916] 4969

NOTE.—Blue print.
In portfolio.

McLEAN.

Ogle, G. A., & co.

Standard atlas of McLean county, North Dakota, including a plat book of the villages, cities and townships of the county. Map of the state, United States and world. Patrons directory, reference business directory and departments devoted to general information. Analysis of the system of U. S. land surveys, digest of the system of civil government . . . 2 p. l., 8–111, xxiii pp.

Ogle, G. A., & co.—Continued.
incl. 77 col. maps, 4 pl., 1 map in text. fol. Chicago, G. A. Ogle, 1914. 4970

MERCER.

Ogle, G. A., & co.
Standard atlas of Mercer county, North Dakota, including a plat book of the villages, cities and townships of the county. Map of the state, United States and world. Patrons directory, reference business directory and departments devoted to general information. Analysis of the system of U. S. land surveys, digest of the system of civil government . . . 2 p. l., 7–69, xxii pp. incl. 42 col. maps, illus. fol. Chicago, G. A. Ogle & co. 1918. 4971

MORTON.

Ogle, G. A., & co.
Standard atlas of Morton county, North Dakota, including a plat book of the villages, cities and townships of the county. Map of the state, United States and world. Patrons directory, reference business directory and departments devoted to general information. Analysis of the system of U. S. land surveys, digest of the system of civil government . . . 2 p. l., 7–103, xxii pp. incl. 66 col. maps, illus. fol. Chicago, G. A. Ogle & co. 1917. 4972

MOUNTRAIL.

Ogle, G. A., & co.
Standard atlas of Mountrail county, North Dakota, including a plat book of the villages, cities and townships of the county. Map of the state, United States and world. Patrons directory, reference business directory and departments devoted to general information. Analysis of the system of U. S. land surveys, digest of the system of civil government . . . 2 p. l., 7–103, viii, x–xxiii pp., incl. 64 col. maps, illus. fol. Chicago, G. A. Ogle & co. 1917. 4973

OLIVER.

Ogle, G. A., & co.
Standard atlas of Oliver county, North Dakota, including a plat book of the villages, cities and townships of the county. Map of the state, United States and world. Patrons directory, reference business directory and departments devoted to general information. Analysis of the system of U. S. land surveys, digest of the system of civil government . . . 2 p. l., 7–51, viii, x–xxiii pp., incl. 28 col. maps, illus. fol. Chicago, G. A. Ogle & co. 1917. 4974

RENVILLE.

Ogle, G. A., & co.

Standard atlas of Renville county, North Dakota, including a plat book of the villages, cities and townships of the county. Map of the state, United States and world. Patrons directory, reference business directory and departments devoted to general information . . . 2 p. l., 7–57, viii, x–xxiii pp. incl. 32 col. maps, illus., diagrs. fol. Chicago, G. A. Ogle & co. 1914. 4975

SHERIDAN.

Ogle, G. A., & co.

Standard atlas of Sheridan county, North Dakota, including a plat book of the villages, cities and townships of the county. Map of the state, United States and world. Patrons directory, reference business directory and departments devoted to general information. Assisted in record work and platting by the Sheridan county abstract co. . . . 2 p. l., 7–63, viii, x–xxiii pp. incl. 37 col. maps, illus., diagrs. fol. Chicago, G. A. Ogle & co. 1914. 4976

STARK.

Ogle, G. A., & co.

Standard atlas of Stark county, North Dakota, including a plat book of the villages, cities and townships of the county. Map of the state, United States and world. Patrons directory, reference business directory and departments devoted to general information. Assisted in record work and platting by Current-Heffron abstract company . . . 2 p. l., 8–89, viii, x–xxiii pp. incl. 51 col. maps, illus., diagrs. fol. Chicago, G. A. Ogle & co. 1914. 4977

WARD.

1913

Frahm, H. C.

Pocket plat-book of Ward county, North Dakota. 1 p. l., 118 pp., incl. 58 maps. 12°. Minot, N. Dak., H. C. Frahm, 1913. 4978

1914

Pocket plat-book of Ward county, North Dakota. 1 p. l., 118 pp. incl. 58 maps. 12°. Minot, N. Dak., H. C. Frahm, 1914. 4979

1915

Ogle, G. A., & co.

Standard atlas of Ward county, North Dakota, including a plat book of the villages, cities and townships of the county. Map of the state, United States and world. Patrons directory, reference business directory and departments devoted to general informa-

Ogle, G. A., & co.—Continued.
tion. Analysis of the system of U. S. land surveys, digest of the system of civil government . . . 2 p. l., 8–121, viii, x–xxiii pp. incl. 70 col. maps, illus. fol. Chicago, G. A. Ogle & co. 1915. 4980

WILLIAMS.

Ogle, G. A., & co.
Standard atlas of Williams county, North Dakota, including a plat book of the villages, cities and townships of the county. Map of the state, United States and world. Patrons directory, reference business directory and departments devoted to general information. Analysis of the system of U. S. land surveys, digest of the system of civil government . . . 2 p. l., 7–103, viii, x–xxiii pp. incl. 65 col. maps, illus. fol. Chicago, G. A. Ogle & co. 1914. 4981

OHIO.

Roads.

Ohio. *Highway department.*
Highway maps of Ohio. vi pp., 88 maps. obl. fol. [Columbus, Ohio] state highway department, 1919. 4981a

NOTE.—Copyright 1919 by Clinton Cowen, state highway commissioner.

Counties.

BUTLER.

Republican publishing co.
Butler county atlas and pictorial review, including soil surveys, geological reports, township, village and city maps. 112 pp. incl. 52 col. maps, illus., ports. fol. Hamilton, O., Republican publishing co. 1914. 4982

NOTE.—At end is also map of the state, United States and world. By the Rand-McNally co.

CARROLL.

Lee, R. H.
Lee's farm atlas of Carroll county, Ohio. 5 maps. fol. Ann Arbor, Mich., C. W. Chadwick, ©1915. [1916] 4983

NOTE.—Caption title.

CUYAHOGA.

Hopkins, G. M., co.
Plat book of Cuyahoga county, Ohio, complete in one volume . . . From official records, private plans and actual surveys . . . 1 p. l., 3 l., 46 col. maps. fol. Philadelphia, G. M. Hopkins co. 1914. 4984

NOTE.—First three maps are indexes.
Volume three, on cover and at head of title-page. Volumes one and two are, *Plat-book of Cleveland, Ohio. 1912.* See title 4994.

FAIRFIELD.

Hannum, E. S.

Hannum's atlas of Fairfield county, Ohio. Engraved & printed at P. McGuigan's establishment, Philadelphia. 2 p. l., 26 maps. 4°. Lancaster, Ohio, E. S. Hannum. 1866. 4985

NOTE.—Contains "Outline map of Fairfield co., Ohio. From official surveys by E. S. Hannum." 26 x 24.

MIAMI.

Everts, L. H., & co.

Illustrated historical atlas of Miami county, Ohio, with an atlas of Ohio, and general maps of the United States and grand divisions . . . 64 (*i. e.* 66) [85] pp. incl. 19 col. maps, illus., 3 col. maps. fol. Philadelphia, L. H. Everts & co. 1875. 4986

NOTE.—Contains the title-page and contents of the Atlas of Ohio but the atlas is wanting, and a number of miscellaneous maps and views have been inserted instead, many of them of Orange co., N. Y. General maps of the world, United States and New York state appear.

MUSKINGUM.

Geographic institute.

Atlas of Muskingum county, Ohio . . . 64 pp., incl. 26 maps. 4°. Indianapolis, Ind., Geographic institute, 1916. 4987

PAULDING.

Ogle, G. A., & co.

Standard atlas of Paulding county, Ohio, including a plat book of the villages, cities and townships of the county. Map of the state, United States and world. Patrons directory, reference business directory and departments devoted to general information. Analysis of the system of U. S. land surveys, digest of the system of civil government . . . 2 p. l., 7–55, viii, x–xxiii pp., incl. 25 col. maps, illus. fol. Chicago, G. A. Ogle & co. 1917. 4988

SUMMIT.

Tackabury, Mead & Moffett.

Combination atlas map of Summit county, Ohio, compiled, drawn and published from personal examinations and surveys, by Tackabury, Mead & Moffett. 139 pp. incl. 32 col. maps, illus., plates, ports. fol. Philadelphia, Tackabury, Mead & Moffett, 1874. 4989

UNION.

Harrison, Sutton & Hare.

Atlas of Union county, Ohio, from records and original surveys, revised and corrected by A. S. Mowry . . . Illustrated by H. G. Howland . . . [1]–108 pp. incl. 24 col. maps, illus. fol. Philadelphia, Harrison, Sutton & Hare, 1877. 4990

WILLIAMS.

Ogle, G. A., & co.

Standard atlas of Williams county, Ohio, including a plat book of the villages, cities, and townships of the county. Map of the state, United States and world. Patrons directory, reference business directory and departments devoted to general information. Analysis of the system of U. S. land surveys, digest of the system of civil government . . . 2 p. l., 7–61, xxii pp., incl. 25 maps, illus. fol. Chicago, G. A. Ogle & co. 1918. 4991

Cities.

AKRON.

Hopkins, G. M., co.

Plat book of the city of Akron, Ohio, and vicinity, including Barberton, Cuyahoga Falls and Kenmore, from official records, private plans and actual surveys . . . 1 p. l., [2] pp., 35 (*i. e.* 36) col. maps. fol. Philadelphia, G. M. Hopkins co. 1915. 4992

CLEVELAND.

Mohr, J.

Atlas of Cleveland, O., showing wards and precincts. 1 p. l., 31 maps. obl. 8°. Cleveland, Mohr & co. [1906] 4993

Hopkins, G. M., co.

Plat-book of the city of Cleveland, Ohio, and suburbs, complete in two volumes . . . From official records, private plans and actual surveys. 2 v. 1 p. l., [4] l., 50 (*i. e.* 51) col. maps; 1 p. l., [4] l. 46 (*i. e.* 47) col. maps. fol. Philadelphia, G. M. Hopkins co. 1912. 4994

CONTENTS.

v. 1. North-east and south-east divisions of the city and eastern suburbs.
" 2. North-west and south-west divisions of the city and western suburbs.

DAYTON.

1908

Cellarius, F. J.

Map of Dayton, Ohio, showing wards and precincts, also street directory by precincts . . . 1 p. l. [8] l., 12 maps. obl. 8°. [Dayton] F. J. Cellarius, ©1908. 4995

1918

Atlas of the city of Dayton, Ohio, and adjoining territory. Compiled from original surveys and official records . . . 4 p. l., 30 (*i. e.* 31) maps. fol. [Dayton, F. J. Cellarius] 1918. 4996

NOTE.—For edition of 1907, see v. 1, title 2432.

TOLEDO.

Hopkins, G. M., co.

Plat-book of the city of Toledo, Ohio, and suburbs. Complete in one volume. From official records, private plans and actual surveys . . . 1 p. l., 3 l., 39 col. maps. fol. Philadelphia, G. M. Hopkins co. 1913. 4997

OKLAHOMA.

State.

1913

Adams engineering & blue printing co.

Atlas of Oklahoma. cover-title, 62 maps. obl. fol. Oklahoma City, Okla., Adams engineering & blue printing co. 1913. 4998

NOTE.—Blue print.

1916

Logan, L., *jr.*

Logan's Oklahoma history map book . . . 1 p. l., 42 pp. incl. 20 maps. obl. 8°. Oklahoma City, Oklahoma journal of education [©1916] 4999

1917

Burke, M. P.

Burke's township plats of the oil fields in north central Oklahoma. 395 pp. of plans. fold. map. 8°. [Tulsa, Okla., Tulsa Indian trading co. ©1917] 5000

NOTE.—Title taken from cover.

Counties.

GARFIELD.

Ogle, G. A., & co.

Standard atlas of Garfield county, Oklahoma, including a plat book of the villages, cities and townships of the county. Map of the state, United States and world. Patrons directory, reference business directory and departments devoted to general information . . . 2 p. l., 7–105, viii, x–xxii pp. incl. 41 col. maps, illus. fol. Chicago, G. A. Ogle & co. 1906. 5001

GRANT.

Ogle, G. A., & co.

Standard atlas of Grant county, Oklahoma, including a plat book of the villages, cities and townships of the county. Map of the state, United States and world. Patrons directory, reference business directory and departments devoted to general information . . . 2 p. l., 7–90, viii, x–xxii pp. incl. 25 col. maps, illus. fol. Chicago, G. A. Ogle & co. 1907. 5002

KINGFISHER.

Ogle, G. A., & co.

Standard atlas of Kingfisher county, Oklahoma, including a plat book of the villages, cities and townships of the county. Map of the state, United States and world. Patrons directory, reference business directory and departments devoted to general information. Analysis of the system of U. S. land surveys, digest of the system of civil government . . . 2 p. l., 7–85, [1] viii, x–xxii pp. incl. 33 col. maps, illus. fol. Chicago, G. A. Ogle & co. 1906. 5003

NOBLE.

Ogle, G. A., & co.

Standard atlas of Noble county, Oklahoma, including a plat book of the villages, cities and townships of the county. Map of the state, United States and world. Patrons directory, reference business directory and departments devoted to general information. Analysis of the system of U. S. land surveys, digest of the system of civil government . . . 2 p. l., 7–75, viii, x–xxiii pp. incl. 27 maps, illus. fol. Chicago, G. A. Ogle & co. 1912. 5004

OKLAHOMA.

Ogle, G. A., & co.

Standard atlas of Oklahoma county, Oklahoma, including a plat book of the villages, cities and townships of the county. Map of the state, United States and world. Patrons directory, reference business directory and departments devoted to general information. Analysis of the system of U. S. land surveys, digest of the system of civil government . . . 2 p. l., 7–119, [1] viii, x–xxii pp. incl. 54 col. maps, illus. fol. Chicago, G. A. Ogle & co. 1907. 5005

SEMINOLE.

Hastain, E.

Hastain's township plats of the Seminole nation. 60 pp. incl. 28 maps. 16°. Muskogee, Okla., Model printing co. ©1913. 5006

WOODS.

Ogle, G. A.; & co.

Standard atlas of Woods county, Oklahoma, including a plat book of the villages, cities, and townships of the county. Map of the state, United States and world. Patrons directory, reference business directory and departments devoted to general information . . . 2 p. l., 7–135, viii, x–xxii pp. incl. 87 col. maps, illus. fol. Chicago, G. A. Ogle & co. 1906. 5007

OREGON.

Counties.

SHERMAN.

Ogle, G. A., & co.

Standard atlas of Sherman county, Oregon, including a plat book of the villages, cities and townships of the county. Map of the state, United States and world. Patrons directory, reference business directory and departments devoted to general information. Analysis of the system of U. S. land surveys, digest of the system of civil government . . . 2 p. l., 7–87, viii, x–xxiii pp. incl. 38 col. maps, illus., diagrs. fol. Chicago, G. A. Ogle & co. 1913. 5008

UMATILLA.

Ogle, G. A., & co.

Standard atlas of Umatilla county, Oregon, including a plat book of the villages, cities and townships of the county. Map of the state, United States and world. Patrons directory, reference business directory and departments devoted to general information . . . 2 p. l., [7]–119, viii, x–xxiii pp. incl. 85 col. maps, illus., diagrs. fol. Chicago, G. A. Ogle & co. 1914. 5009

PENNSYLVANIA.

Railroads.

Hopkins, G. M.

Atlas of properties near the Philadelphia and Trenton railroad. Frankford to Trenton. (New York div. Penna. R. R.) 1 p. l., 21 (*i. e.* 22) col. maps. fol. Philadelphia, G. M. Hopkins, 1885. 5010

NOTE.—Corrected from title 2148.

Mueller, A. H.

Atlas of properties on main line Pennsylvania railroad from Overbrook to Paoli, embracing Lower Merion, Haverford and Radnor townships and parts of Upper Merion, Easttown and Tredyffrin townships. Compiled from actual surveys, official records and private plans by Ellis Kiser and J. M. Lathrop . . . 1 p. l., 33 col. maps. fol. Philadelphia, A. H. Mueller, c1913. 5011

State.

1916

Cram, G. F., co.

Descriptive review showing historical, agricultural, commercial, industrial development of the state of Pennsylvania with detail maps and profuse half-tone illustrations from all parts of the

Cram, G. F., co.—Continued.

keystone state. Containing in addition newly engraved maps of every state in the United States, and detail maps of every country, state and kingdom. Together with a complete locating index to all cities, towns, villages and post offices in the United States, giving populations to every incorporated city and village therein. 1 p. l., [5]-338 pp., incl. 100 maps, illus. fol. Chicago, New York, G. F. Cram co. °1916. 5012

NOTE.—Title-page contains view of Pennsylvania state capitol, Harrisburg.

1917

Descriptive review showing historical, agricultural, commercial, industrial development of the state of Pennsylvania, with detail maps and profuse half-tone illustrations from all parts of the Keystone state, containing in addition newly engraved maps of every state in the United States, and detail maps of every country, state and kingdom. Together with a complete locating index to all cities, towns, villages and post offices in the United States, giving populations to every incorporated city and village therein. 1 p. l., [1] 6-374 pp. incl. 100 col. maps, illus., diagr. fol. Chicago, New York, G. F. Cram co. 1917. **5013**

NOTE.—Pages 367-374 are duplicated.

Counties.

ALLEGHENY.

Pennsylvania. *Department of internal affairs.*

Warrantee atlas of Allegheny county, Pennsylvania, constructed from the records on file in the Department of internal affairs, and surveys made on the grounds during 1909, 1910, 1912, under the direction of honorable Henry Houck, secretary of internal affairs, in pursuance of an act of the general assembly of Pennsylvania. 3 p. l., 51 l. incl. 72 col. maps. fol. [Harrisburg, 1914] 5014

NOTE.—"The commonwealth of Pennsylvania, department of internal affairs. In testimony, that the several maps contained in this atlas were constructed from and compared with the original drafts and other official data on file in the department of internal affairs of Pennsylvania, and surveys made on the ground during 1909, 1910, 1912, by my direction, under authority of an act of assembly approved the 13th., day of june, 1907:—(Pamphlet laws for 1907, page 621) I have hereunto set my hand and caused the seal of said department to be affixed at Harrisburg, the ninth day of april, anno Domini, one thousand nine hundred and fourteen." [Signed] Henry Houck, secretary of internal affairs.

DELAWARE.

1880

Smith, B. H.

Atlas of Delaware county, Pennsylvania, containing nineteen maps exhibiting the early grants and patents, compiled from official records; together with a history of the land titles in the county. 3 p. l., xxiii [2] 8–10 pp., 19 col. maps. fol. Philadelphia, H. B. Ashmead, 1880. 5015

NOTE.—A letter from the author, dated march 25, 1880, presenting this copy of his *Atlas of Delaware county* to Prof. G. B. Keen, is pasted in the front of the atlas.

1909–1913

Mueller, A. H.

Atlas of Delaware county . . . Compiled from actual surveys, official records and private plans by Ellis Kiser and J. M. Lathrop . . . 2 v. 1 p. l., 32 (*i. e.* 33) col. maps; 1 p. l., 25 col. maps. fol. Philadelphia, A. H. Mueller, 1909–1913. 5016

NOTE.—Vol. 2. Compiled by J. M. Lathrop and St. Julian Ogier.
Contains maps of the following cities: Chester, Upland and Marcus Hook, and Aston, Bethel, Birmingham, Chester, Concord, Edgmont, Middletown, Thornbury, Upper and Lower Chichester townships.

CONTENTS.

v. 1, East of Ridley creek, embracing Darby, Upper Darby, Ridley, Springfield, Marple, Newtown, Upper and Nether Providence, Tinicum, and part of Haverford townships.
v. 2, West of Ridley creek embracing city of Chester, Upland and Marcus Hook, and Aston, Bethel, Birmingham, Chester, Concord, Edgmont, Middletown, Thornbury, Upper and Lower Chichester townships.

LANCASTER.

Bridgens, H. F.

Bridgens' atlas of Lancaster co., Penna. 1 p. l. [2]–3 pp., 40 col. maps. fol. Lancaster, D. S. Bare, ©1864. 5017

NOTE.—Map of Pennsylvania, with table of distances from Lancaster, and population of Pennsylvania, on inside of front cover.

MONTGOMERY.

Mueller, A. H.

Atlas of the North Penn section of Montgomery county, Pa. Embracing Cheltenham, Abington, Springfield, Upper Dublin and parts of Moreland, Whitemarsh, Whitpain, Lower & Upper Gwynedd townships. Compiled from actual surveys, official records and private plans . . . 1 p. l., 29 (*i. e.* 30) col. maps. fol. Philadelphia, A. H. Mueller, 1916. 5018

SNYDER.

Beers, D. G.

Atlas of Union & Snyder counties, Pennsylvania, from actual surveys. 1 p. l., 67 pp. incl. 29 col. maps, table. fol. Philadelphia, Pomeroy & Beers, 1868. 5019

NOTE.—Statistics, p. 67.

UNION.

Beers, D. G.

Atlas of Union & Snyder counties, Pennsylvania, from actual surveys. 1 p. l., 67 pp. incl. 29 col. maps, table. fol. Philadelphia, Pomeroy & Beers, 1868. 5020

NOTE.—Statistics, p. 67.

Cities.

ERIE.

Mueller, A. H.

Atlas of the city of Erie, Pa., and all adjoining sub-divisions. Compiled from actual surveys, official records and private plans . . . 2 p. l., 25 (*i. e.* 26) col. maps. fol. Philadelphia, A. H. Mueller, 1917. 5021

LANCASTER.

Baist, G. W.

Atlas of the city of Lancaster, Pennsylvania, compiled from official records, actual surveys & private plans . . . 1 p. l., 17 (*i. e.* 18) col. maps. fol. Philadelphia, J. L. Smith, 1886. 5022

NOTE.—"Copyright, 1886, by J. L. Smith, Philadelphia, Pa."

PHILADELPHIA.

Views.

Childs, C. G.

Views in Philadelphia and its environs, from original drawings taken in 1827–30. 4 p. l., 65 pp., 24 pl., 1 plan. 8°. Philadelphia, C. G. Childs [1830] 5023

CONTENTS.

no. 1. Philadelphia from Kensington. Drawn by T. Birch. Engraved by J. Cone. 1828.

" 2. Swedish lutheran church. Drawn by Thos. Sully. Engraved by C. G. Childs. 1828.

" 3. Christ church. Drawn by Geo. Strickland. Engraved by C. G. Childs. 1829.

" 4. Friends meeting house at Merion. Hugh Reinagle pinx^t^. Engraved by J. W. Steel., 1830.

" 5. Saint Stephen's church. Drawn by Geo. Strickland. Engraved by C. G. Childs. 1829.

" 6. First congregational unitarian church. Drawn by H. Reinagle. Engraved by C. G. Childs. 1829.

" 7. State house. Drawn by Geo. Strickland. Engraved by C. G. Childs. 1828.

" 8. Fairmount water works. From the west bank of the Schuylkill. Drawn by T. Doughty. Engraved by J. Cone. 1828.

" 9. Fairmount water works. From the reservoir. Painted by T. Doughty. Engraved by W. E. Tucker. 1829.

" 10. View of the Schuylkill. From the old water works. Drawn by cap^t^. R. J. Watson. Engraved by C. G. Childs. 1827.

no. 11. Bank of the United States. Drawn by Geo. Strickland. Engraved by C. G. Childs. 1828.
" 12. Bank of Pennsylvania. Drawn by Geo. Strickland. Engraved by Wm. E. Tucker. 1827.
" 13. Girard's bank. Late United States bank. Drawn by Geo. Strickland. Engraved by C. G. Childs. 1829.
" 14. Pennsylvania hospital. Drawn by Geo. Strickland. Engraved by C. G. Childs. 1828.
" 15. Pennsylvania institution for the deaf and dumb. Drawn by Geo. Strickland. Engraved by C. G. Childs. 1827.
" 16. University. Drawn by Geo. Strickland. Engraved by J. W. Steel. 1828.
" 17. Pennsylvania academy of the fine arts. Drawn by Geo. Strickland. Engraved by C. G. Childs. 1828.
" 18. Eastern penitentiary of Pennsylvania. Drawn by W^{m}. Mason. Engraved by C. G. Childs. 1829.
" 19. Plan of the eastern penitentiary. J. Haviland arch^{t}. del. C. G. Childs sc.
" 20. United States mint. Designed & drawn by W^{m}. Strickland. Engraved by W^{m}. H. Hay. 1830.
" 21. Widows' and orphans' asylum. Drawn by Geo. Strickland. Engraved by J. W. Steel. 1827.
" 22. Schuylkill canal at Manayunk. Drawn by Geo. Lehman. Engraved by C. G. Childs. 1829.
" 23. Eaglesfield. Drawn by W^{m}. Mason. Engraved by C. G. Childs. 1830.
" 24. Sedgeley Park. Drawn by E. W. Clay. Etched by J. W. Steel & W. H. Hay. Engraved by C. G. Childs. 1828.
" 25. Academy of natural sciences. Drawn by Geo. Strickland. Engraved by C. G. Childs. 1830.

Wild, J. C.

Panorama and views of Philadelphia, and its vicinity. Embracing a collection of twenty views, from paintings by J. C. Wild. With poetical illustrations of each subject, by Andrew M'Makin . . . 1 p. l., [22] pp., 24 pl. sm. fol. Philadelphia, J. T. Bowen, 1838. 5024

NOTE.—Descriptive text signed E. H. Copyrighted by J. T. Bowen.

Another edition, lithographed and copyrighted by Wild and Chevalier, was also published in 1838, the Library of Congress copy of which lacks title-page and has binder's title: *Views in Philadelphia.*

Sabin gives another edition of this publication issued in 1838 with title, *Views in Philadelphia, consisting of 20 small and 4 large plates on India paper, engraven on stone by J. C. Wild, with descriptions.*

CONTENTS.

no. [a–d] Panorama of Philadelphia from the state house steeple.
" 1. Fairmount.
" 2. U. S. bank.
" 3. Merchant's exchange.
" 4. View from the inclined plane near Philadelphia.
" 5. The Girard college.

Wild, J. C.—Continued.

no. 6. The Eastern penitentiary.
" 7. U. S. Naval asylum.
" 8. Alms house.
" 9. Moyamensing prison.
" 10. Philadelphia from the Navy yard.
" 11. State house.
" 12. Pennsylvania institution for the instruction of the blind.
" 13. Pennsylvania hospital.
" 14. Market street, from Front st.
" 15. University of Pennsylvania.
" 16. U. S. mint.
" 17. Christ church.
" 18. Manayunk near Philadelphia.
" 19. St. John's church.
" 20. Laurel hill cemetery.

General.

1859

Hexamer, E., & son.

Maps of the city of Philadelphia surveyed by Ernest Hexamer & William Locher . . . 1859. v. 5. fol. [Philadelphia] E. Hexamer & W. Locher, 1859. 5025

NOTE.—Firm name Ernest Hexamer in 1872 and Ernest Hexamer & son in 1887.

1872–1911

Insurance maps of the city of Philadelphia . . v. 1–37. fol. Philadelphia, E. Hexamer & son, 1872–1911. 5026

NOTE.—Vols. 1–5, revised edition.
Two issues of v. 6, 1876, and of v. 8, 1879.
Firm name Ernest Hexamer & William Locher in 1859, Ernest Hexamer in 1872, and Ernest Hexamer & son in 1887.
Changes and additions to these volumes when not sufficient to justify a re-issue, are issued from time to time on sheets.

1885–1888

Bromley, G. W., & W. S.

Atlas of the city of Philadelphia . . . From actual surveys and official plans of the survey department . . . v. 1, 6. fol. Philadelphia, G. W. Bromley & co. 1885–1888. 5027

CONTENTS.

v. 1. 5th, 6th, 7th, 8th, 9th & 10th wards.
" 6. 28th & 32nd wards.

1887–1891

Hexamer, E., & son.

Insurance maps of the city of Philadelphia . . . v. 2–3. fol. Philadelphia, E. Hexamer & son, 1887. 5028

Insurance maps of the city of Philadelphia . . . v. 4–5. fol. Philadelphia, E. Hexamer, 1889. 5029

Insurance maps of the city of Philadelphia . . . v. 1. fol. Philadelphia, E. Hexamer & son, 1890. 5030

Insurance maps of the city of Philadelphia . . . v. 8. fol. Philadelphia, E. Hexamer & son, 1891. 5031

1894

Bromley, G. W., & W. S.

Atlas of the city of Philadelphia, 23rd. & 35th. wards. From actual surveys and official plans . . . 2 p. l., 29 (*i. e.* 30) col. maps. fol. Philadelphia, G. W. Bromley & co. 1894. 5032

1894–1914

Hexamer, E., & son.

Insurance maps of the city of Philadelphia . . . v. 2. fol. Philadelphia, E. Hexamer & son, 1894. 5033

Insurance maps of the city of Philadelphia . . . v. 1. fol. Philadelphia, E. Hexamer & son, 1895. 5034

Insurance maps of the city of Philadelphia . . . v. 2–4. fol. Philadelphia, E. Hexamer & son, 1896. 5035

Insurance maps of the city of Philadelphia . . . v. 1, 5, 9. fol. Philadelphia, E. Hexamer & son, 1897. 5036

Insurance maps of the city of Philadelphia . . . v. 1, 8. fol. Philadelphia, E. Hexamer & son, 1898. 5037

Insurance maps of the city of Philadelphia . . . v. 6. fol. Philadelphia, E. Hexamer & son, 1899. 5038

Insurance maps of the city of Philadelphia . . . v. 2. fol. Philadelphia, E. Hexamer & son, 1900. 5039

Insurance maps of the city of Philadelphia . . . v. 1, 3–4. fol. Philadelphia, E. Hexamer & son, 1901. 5040

Insurance maps of the city of Philadelphia . . . v. 10. fol. Philadelphia, E. Hexamer & son, 1902. 5041

Insurance maps of the city of Philadelphia . . . v. 7, 11. fol. Philadelphia, E. Hexamer & son, 1904. 5042

Insurance maps of the city of Philadelphia . . . v. 2, 12. fol. Philadelphia, E. Hexamer & son, 1905. 5043

Insurance maps of the city of Philadelphia . . . v. 1–2, 8–9. fol. Philadelphia, E. Hexamer & son, 1906. 5044

Hexamer, E., & son.—Continued.

Insurance maps of the city of Philadelphia . . . v. 4–5. fol. Philadelphia, E. Hexamer & son, 1907. 5045

Insurance maps of the city of Philadelphia . . . v. 3, 16. fol. Philadelphia, E. Hexamer & son, 1908. 5046

Insurance maps of the city of Philadelphia . . . v. 6, 8, 13, 15. fol. Philadelphia, E. Hexamer & son, 1909. 5047

Insurance maps of the city of Philadelphia . . . v. 17, 25. fol. Philadelphia, E. Hexamer & son, 1910. 5048

Insurance maps of the city of Philadelphia . . . v. 22, 33. fol. Philadelphia, E. Hexamer & son, 1912. 5049

Insurance maps of the city of Philadelphia . . . v. 19. fol. Philadelphia, E. Hexamer & son, 1913. 5050

Insurance maps of the city of Philadelphia . . . v. 10, 28. fol. Philadelphia, E. Hexamer & son, 1914. 5051

PITTSBURGH.

Hopkins, G. M., co.

Real estate plat-book of the city of Pittsburgh . . . From official records, private plans and actual surveys . . . v. 2, 6, 7, 8. fol. Philadelphia, G. M. Hopkins co. 1914–1917. 5052

NOTE.—Titles vary, v. 8, *Plat book of the eastern vicinity of Pittsburgh.*

CONTENTS.

v. 2. Comprising the wards 1–6 & 9. 1914.
" 6. Comprising south side and southern vicinity, east half. 1916.
" 7. Comprising south side and southern vicinity, west half. 1917.
" 8. Plat book of the eastern vicinity of Pittsburgh. 1915.

RHODE ISLAND.

State.

1891

United States. *Geological survey.*

Topographical atlas of the state of Rhode Island and Providence plantations . . . in cooperation with the state. Triangulation and topography by the U. S. geological and the U. S. coast & geodetic surveys surveyed 1885–1888 . . . 22 numb. l., incl. 12 col. maps. fol. Boston, New York, G. H. Walker & co. 1891. 5053

NOTE.—For sale by J. C. Thompson, 269 Westminster St., Providence, R. I. Under the direction of the commission.

Cities.

PROVIDENCE.

1914

Chace, H. R.

Maps of Providence, R. I., 1650–1765–1770. 3 p. l., 18 l. incl. 6 maps. obl. 8°. [Providence, R. I.] H. R. Chace, 1914. 5054

CONTENTS.

Owners of home lots in the Providence plantations, 1650.
no. [1] Tax list 1650. Town papers 039. Providence, R. I.
Highways in the town of Providence, 1765.
no. [2] Highways in the town of Providence showing proposed division of 1765.
Owners of houses in the compact part of Providence, 1770.
no. [3–6] Owners or occupants of buildings in the central part of . . . Providence, R. I., 1770.

1914

Owners and occupants of the lots, houses and shops in the town of Providence, Rhode Island, in 1798, located on maps of the highways of that date. Also owners or occupants of houses in the compact part of Providence in 1759, showing the location and in whose names they are to be found on the map of 1798. 28 pp., 19 maps (1 index map). 4°. Providence, H. R. Chace [c1914] 5055

CONTENTS.

no. 1. Index map and highways and lanes in the town of Providence, R. I. 1798.
" 2. Owners of lots in Providence, R. I. Power st. to Fox Point. 1798.
" 3. Owners of lots in Providence, R. I. From India bridge to George st. 1798.
" 4. Owners of lots in Providence, R. I. Power st. to Smith st. 1798.
" 5. Owners of lots in Providence, R. I. George st. to Olney st. 1798.
" 6–19. Owners of lots in Providence, R. I. 1798.

1918

Hopkins, G. M., co.

Plat book of the city of Providence, Rhode Island. From official records, private plans and actual surveys . . . 1 p. l., [2] pp., 43 (*i. e.* 44) col. maps. fol. Philadelphia, G. M. Hopkins & co. 1918. 5056

SOUTH DAKOTA.

Counties.

BEADLE.

Ogle, G. A., & co.

Standard atlas of Beadle county, South Dakota, including a plat book of the villages, cities and townships of the county. Map of the state, United States and world. Patrons directory,

Ogle, G. A., & co.—Continued.

reference business directory and departments devoted to general information. Analysis of the system of U. S. land surveys, digest of the system of civil government . . . 2 p. l., 7–77, [1] viii, x–xxiii pp. incl. 44 col. maps, illus. fol. Chicago, G. A. Ogle & co. 1913. 5057

BON HOMME.

Ogle, G. A., & co.

Standard atlas of Bon Homme county, South Dakota, including a plat book of the villages, cities and precincts of the county. Map of the state, United States and world. Patrons directory, reference business directory and departments devoted to general information. Analysis of the system of U. S. land surveys, digest of the system of civil government . . . 2 p. l., 7–85, viii, x–xxiii pp. incl. 25 maps, illus. fol. Chicago, G. A. Ogle & co. 1912. 5058

CHARLES MIX.

Ogle, G. A., & co.

Standard atlas of Charles Mix county, South Dakota, including a plat book of the villages, cities and townships of the county. Map of the state, United States and world. Patrons directory, reference business directory and departments devoted to general information. Analysis of the system of U. S. land surveys, digest of the system of civil government . . . 2 p. l., 7–113, viii, x–xxiii pp. incl. 32 maps, illus. fol. Chicago, G. A. Ogle & co. 1912. 5059

DAVISON.

Nelson, J. L.

Nelson's township map and manual of Davison county, South Dakota. Together with general information relating to useful rules and tables; the altitude of various places . . . 1 p. l., 3 pp., 13 maps. 8°. [Mitchell, S. Dak., J. L. Nelson, 1915] 5060

EDMUNDS.

Ogle, G. A., & co.

Standard atlas of Edmunds county, South Dakota, including a plat book of the villages, cities and townships of the county. Map of the state, United States and world. Patrons directory, reference business directory and departments devoted to general information. Analysis of the system of U. S. land surveys, digest of the system of civil government . . . 2 p. l., [7]–73, viii, x–xxiii pp. incl. 39 col. maps, illus. fol. Chicago, G. A. Ogle & co. 1916. 5061

HUGHES.

Ogle, G. A., & co.

Standard atlas of Hughes county, South Dakota. Including a plat book of the villages, cities, and townships of the county. Map of the state, United States and world. Patrons directory, reference business directory and departments devoted to general information. Analysis of the system of U. S. land surveys, digest of the system of civil government . . . 2 p. l., 7–97, viii, x–xxiii pp., incl. 33 maps, illus. fol. Chicago, G. A. Ogle & co. 1916. 5062

SULLY.

Ogle, G. A., & co.

Standard atlas of Sully county, South Dakota, including a plat book of the villages, cities and townships of the county. Map of the state, United States and world. Patrons directory, reference business directory and departments devoted to general information. Analysis of the system of U. S. land surveys, digest of the system of civil government . . . 2 p. l., 7–63, viii, x–xxiii pp. incl. 37 col. maps, illus. fol. Chicago, G. A. Ogle & co. 1916. 5063

TRIPP.

Ogle, G. A., & co.

Standard atlas of Tripp county, South Dakota, including a plat book of the villages, cities and townships of the county. Map of the state, United States and world. Patrons directory, reference business directory and departments devoted to general information. Analysis of the system of U. S. land surveys, digest of the system of civil government . . . 2 p. l., 7–77, viii, x–xxiii pp. incl. 58 col. maps, illus., ports., diagrs. fol. Chicago, G. A. Ogle & co. 1915. 5064

TENNESSEE.

Cities.

CHATTANOOGA.

Hopkins, G. M., co.

Plat book of the city of Chattanooga, Tenn., and vicinity. From official records, private plans and actual surveys . . . 1 p. l., index map, 41 plates, incl. 40 col. maps. fol. Philadelphia, G. M. Hopkins co. 1914. 5065

TEXAS.

Historical.

Ramsey, G. D.

Atlas of Texas history. 1 p. l., 33 pp. incl. 24 maps, illus. (part col.), ports. large fol. Chicago, Union school furnishing co. [1914] 5066

NOTE.—These are large sheets arranged on roller, and printed on both sides of sheet. On title-page: Historians consulted in preparation, Bancroft, Brooks, Brown, Clark, Kennedy, Garrison, Barker, Wooten, Yoakum.

Atlas of Texas history for Texas and United States histories . . . 39 pp. incl. 30 maps, illus. large fol. Chicago, Union school furnishing co. [1918?]. 5067

NOTE.—Wall atlas.

At head of title: Revised edition.

Noted on title-page: "Historians consulted, Bancroft, Brooks, Brown, Clark, Kennedy, Garrison, Barker, Wooten, Yoakum." Full page illustration entitled, "Texas under six flags."

Physical.

United States. *Geological survey.*

Topographic atlas of the United States. Physical geography of the Texas region, by Robert T. Hill . . . cover-title, 12 pp., 10 sheets incl. 33 maps, 22 views, 1 fold. map at end. fol. Washington, U. S. geological survey, 1900. 5068

NOTE.—At head of title: Department of the interior, United States geological survey, Charles D. Walcott, director.

VERMONT.

Counties.

LAMOILLE.

Beers, F. W., & co.

Atlas of the counties of Lamoille and Orleans, Vermont. 62, 64–99 pp. incl. 49 col. maps. fol. New York, F. W. Beers & co. 1878. 5069

NOTE.—Title-page ornamented with view of the state house, Montpelier, Vt.

ORLEANS.

Beers, F. W., & co.

Atlas of the counties of Lamoille and Orleans, Vermont. 62, 64–99 pp. incl. 49 co., maps. fol. New York, F. W. Beers & co. 1878. 5070

NOTE.—Title-page ornamented with view of the state house, Montpelier, Vt.

VIRGINIA.

Cities.

RICHMOND.

Baist, G. W.

Atlas of the city of Richmond, Virginia, and vicinity. From actual surveys, official records and private plans . . . 1 p. l., 20 (*i. e.* 21) col. maps. fol. Philadelphia, G. W. Baist, 1889. 5071

WASHINGTON.

Counties.

ASOTIN.

Ogle, G. A., & co.

Standard atlas of Asotin county, Washington, including a plat book of the villages, cities and townships of the county. Map of the state, United States and world. Patrons directory, reference business directory and departments devoted to general information . . . 2 p. l., 7–45, viii, x–xxiii pp. incl. 26 col. maps, illus., diagrs. fol. Chicago, G. A. Ogle & co. 1914. 5072

COLUMBIA.

Ogle, G. A., & co.

Standard atlas of Columbia county, Washington, including a plat book of the villages, cities and townships of the county. Map of the state, United States and world. Patrons directory, reference business directory and departments devoted to general information. Analysis of the system of U. S. land surveys, digest of the system of civil government . . . 2 p. l., 7–79, viii, x–xiii pp. incl. 39 col. maps, illus., diagrs. fol. Chicago, G. A. Ogle & co. 1913. 5073

DOUGLAS.

Ogle, G. A., & co.

Standard atlas of Douglas county, Washington, including a plat book of the villages, cities and townships of the county. Map of the state, United States and world. Patrons directory, reference business directory and departments devoted to general information. Analysis of the system of U. S. land surveys, digest of the system of civil government . . . 2 p. l., 101, viii, x–xxiii pp. incl. 65 col. maps, illus. fol. Chicago, G. A. Ogle & co. 1915. 5074

GARFIELD.

Ogle, G. A., & co.

Standard atlas of Garfield county, Washington, including a plat book of the villages, cities and townships of the county. Map of the state, United States and world. Patrons directory,

Ogle, G. A., & co.—Continued.

reference business directory and departments devoted to general information. Analysis of the system of U. S. land surveys, digest of the system of civil government . . . 2 p. l., 7–65, viii, x–xxiii pp. incl. 25 col. maps, illus., diagrs. fol. Chicago, G. A. Ogle & co. 1913. 5075

GRANT.

Standard atlas of Grant County, Washington, including a plat book of the villages, cities and townships of the county. Map of the state, United States and world. Patrons directory, reference business directory and departments devoted to general information. Analysis of the system of U. S. land surveys, digest of the system of civil government . . . 2 p. l., 7–111 [1] xxii pp. incl. 82 col. maps, illus. fol. Chicago, G. A. Ogle & co. 1917. 5076

KLICKITAT.

Ogle, G. A., & co.

Standard atlas of Klickitat county, Washington, including a plat book of the villages, cities and townships of the county. Map of the state, United States and world. Patrons directory, reference business directory and departments devoted to general information. Analysis of the system of U. S. land surveys, digest of the system of civil government . . . 2 p. l., [7]–99, viii, x–xxiii pp. incl. 89 col. maps, illus., diagrs. fol. Chicago, G. A. Ogle & co. 1913. 5077

Cities.

SEATTLE.

Kroll map co.

Kroll's ownership atlas of central Seattle. cover-title, 23 maps. fol. [Seattle] Kroll map co. 1917. 5078

Note.—Blue print.
"Co. 1917 Carl Kroll."

WISCONSIN.

State.

Page, H. R., & co.

Illustrated historical atlas of Wisconsin, containing maps of every county in the state, with many villages and city plats. Also maps of Michigan, Indiana, Ohio, Illinois, Wisconsin, Minnesota, Iowa, Missouri, Dakota, Nebraska, Kansas, Colorado, New Mexico and Texas, compiled from late and authentic sources . . . 221 [7] pp. incl. 104 col. maps, illus. fol. Chicago, H. R. Page & co. 1881. 5079

Note.—Beside maps of many towns and villages, contains maps of the following cities: Madison, Milwaukee, Sheboygan, Oshkosh, Fon du Lac, La Crosse, Eau Claire.

Counties.

ADAMS.

Ogle, G. A., & co.

Standard atlas of Adams county, Wisconsin, including a plat book of the villages, cities and townships of the county. Map of the state, United States and world. Patrons directory, reference business directory and departments devoted to general information. Analysis of U. S. land surveys, digest of the system of civil government . . . 2 p. l., 7–59, xxii pp. incl. 24 col. maps, illus. fol. Chicago, G. A. Ogle & co. 1919. 5080

BARRON.

Webb publishing co.

Atlas and farm directory with complete survey in township plats, Barron county, Wisconsin, containing plats of all townships with owners' names; also maps of the state, United States and world; also an outline map of the county showing location of townships, villages, roads, schools, churches, railroads, streams . . . Published by the Farmer . . . Drawn and engraved by the Kenyon co., Des Moines, Iowa. 70 (*i. e.* 72) pp. incl. 32 col. maps, illus. fol. St. Paul, Minn., Webb publishing co. ©1914. 5081

BUFFALO.

Webb publishing co.

Atlas and farm directory with complete survey in township plats of Buffalo county, Wisconsin, containing plats of all townships with owners' names; also maps of the state, United States and world; also an outline map of the county showing location of townships, villages, roads, schools, churches, railroads, streams, etc., etc. Compiled from latest data on record. Published by the Farmer. Drawn and engraved by the Anderson publishing co., Chicago, Ill. 45, [12] pp. incl. 22 col. maps, illus. fol. St. Paul, Minnesota, Webb publishing co. ©1914. 5082

BURNETT.

Ogle, G. A., & co.

Standard atlas of Burnett county, Wisconsin, including a plat book of the villages, cities and townships of the county. Map of the state, United States and world. Patrons directory, reference business directory and departments devoted to general information. Analysis of the system of U. S. land surveys, digest of the system of civil government . . . 2 p. l., 8–91, viii, x–xxiii pp. incl. 32 col. maps, illus. fol. Chicago, G. A. Ogle & co. 1915. 5083

114882°—19——26

CLARK.

Ogle, G. A., & co.

Standard atlas of Clark county, Wisconsin, including a plat book of the villages, cities and townships of the county. Map of the state, United States and world. Patrons directory, reference business directory and departments devoted to general information . . . 2 p. l., 7–67, viii, x–xxii pp. incl. 40 col. maps, illus. fol. Chicago, G. A. Ogle & co. 1906. 5084

CRAWFORD.

Webb publishing co.

Atlas and farm directory with complete surveys in township plats, Crawford county, Wisconsin, containing plats of all townships with owners' names; also maps of the state, United States and world; also an outline map of the county showing location of townships, villages, roads, schools, churches, railroads, streams . . . Published by the Farmer. 41, [12] pp. incl. 15 col. maps, illus. fol. St. Paul, Minn., Webb publishing co. ©1914. 5085

GRANT.

Ogle, G. A., & co.

Standard atlas of Grant county, Wisconsin, including a plat book of the villages, cities and townships of the county. Map of the state, United States and world. Patrons directory, reference business directory and departments devoted to general information. Analysis of the system of U. S. land surveys, digest of the system of civil government . . . 2 p. l., 7–111, xxii pp. incl. 56 col. maps, illus. fol. Chicago, G. A. Ogle & co. 1918. 5086

GREEN.

Ogle, G. A., & co.

Standard atlas of Green county, Wisconsin, including a plat book of the villages, cities and townships of the county. Map of the state, United States and world. Patrons directory, reference business directory and departments devoted to general information. Analysis of the system of U. S. land surveys, digest of the system of civil government . . . 2 p. l., 7–67, xxii pp. incl. 31 col. maps, illus. fol. Chicago, G. A. Ogle & co. 1918. 5087

GREEN LAKE.

Webb publishing co.

Atlas and farm directory with complete survey in township plats, Green Lake county, Wisconsin, containing plats of all townships with owners' names; also maps of the state, United States and world; also an outline map of the county . . . Compiled from latest data on record. Published by the Farmer . . .

Drawn and engraved by the Kenyon company, Des Moines, Ia. 31 [12] pp. incl. 19 col. maps, illus. fol. St. Paul, Minn., Webb publishing co. [1914] 5088

IOWA.

Ogle, G. A., & co.

Standard atlas of Iowa county, Wisconsin, including a plat book of the villages, cities and townships of the county. Map of the state, United States and world. Patrons directory, reference business directory and departments devoted to general information. Analysis of the system of U. S. land surveys, digest of the system of civil government . . . 2 p. l., 7–91, viii, xxiii pp. incl. 24 col. maps, illus. fol. Chicago, G. A. Ogle & co. 1915. 5089

JACKSON.

Webb publishing co.

Atlas and farm directory with complete survey in township plats of Jackson county, Wisconsin, containing plats of all townships with owners' names; also maps of the state, United States and world; also an outline map of the county . . . Compiled from latest data on record. Published by the Farmer . . . Drawn and engraved by the Anderson publishing co., Chicago, Ill. 61 [12] pp. incl. 33 col. maps, illus. fol. St. Paul, Minn., Webb publishing co. [1914] 5090

JEFFERSON.

Ogle, G. A., & co.

Standard atlas of Jefferson county, Wisconsin, including a plat book of the villages, cities and townships of the county. Map of the state, United States and world. Patrons directory, reference business directory and departments devoted to general information. Analysis of the system of U. S. land surveys, digest of the system of civil government . . . 2 p. l., 7–83, xxii pp. incl. 41 col. maps, illus. fol. Chicago, G. A. Ogle & co. 1919 5091

JUNEAU.

Webb publishing co.

Atlas and farm directory with complete survey in township plats, Juneau county, Wisconsin, containing plats of all townships with owners' names; also maps of the state, United States and world; also an outline map of the county showing location of townships, villages, roads, schools, churches, railroads, streams, etc., etc. Compiled from latest data on record. Published by the Farmer. Drawn and engraved by the Kenyon company, Des Moines, Ia. 56, [12] pp. incl. 25 col. maps, illus. fol. St. Paul, Minn., Webb publishing co. ©1914. 5092

KEWAUNEE.

Rooney, W. T., *and* **Schleis, A. M.**

Atlas of Kewaunee county, Wisconsin. 2 p. l., 10 col. maps. fol. Kewaunee, Wis., W. T. Rooney & A. M. Schleis, 1895. 5093

NOTE.—Maps by E. P. Noll & co., map publishers, Philadelphia.

LAFAYETTE.

Ogle, G. A., & co.

Standard atlas of Lafayette county, Wisconsin, including a plat book of the villages, cities and townships of the county. Map of the state, United States and world. Patrons directory, reference business directory and departments devoted to general information. Analysis of the system of the U. S. land surveys, digest of the system of civil government . . . 2 p. l., 7–101, xxiii pp. incl. 43 col. maps, illus. fol. Chicago, G. A. Ogle & co. 1916. 5094

LANGLADE.

Ogle, G. A., & co.

Standard atlas of Langlade county, Wisconsin, including a plat book of the villages, cities and townships of the county. Map of the state, United States and world. Patrons directory, reference business directory and departments devoted to general information. Analysis of the system of U. S. land surveys, digest of the system of civil government . . . 2 p. l., 7–93, viii, x–xxiii pp. incl. 49 col. maps, illus. diagrs. fol. Chicago, G. A. Ogle & co. 1913. 5095

LINCOLN.

Ogle, G. A., & co.

Standard atlas of Lincoln county, Wisconsin, including a plat book of the villages, cities and townships of the county. Map of the state, United States and world. Patrons directory, reference business directory and departments devoted to general information . . . 2 p. l., 7–109, viii, x–xxiii pp. incl. 35 col. maps, illus., diagrs. fol. Chicago, G. A. Ogle & co. 1914. 5096

MONROE.

Ogle, G. A., & co.

Standard atlas of Monroe county, Wisconsin, including a plat book of the villages, cities and townships of the county. Map of the state, United States and world. Patrons directory, reference business directory and departments devoted to general information. Analysis of the system of U. S. land surveys, digest of the system of civil government . . . 2 p. l., 7–113, viii, x–xxiii pp. incl. 36 col. maps, illus. fol. Chicago, G. A. Ogle & co. 1915. 5097

OUTAGAMIE.

Ogle, G. A., & co.

Standard atlas of Outagamie county, Wisconsin, including a plat book of the villages, cities and townships of the county. Map of the state, United States and world. Patrons directory, reference business directory and departments devoted to general information. Analysis of the system of U. S. land surveys, digest of the system of civil government . . . 2 p. l., 7–111, viii, x–xxiii pp. incl. 38 col. maps, illus. fol. Chicago, G. A. Ogle & co. 1917. 5098

POLK.

Ogle, G. A., & co.

Standard atlas of Polk county, Wisconsin, including a plat book of the villages, cities and townships of the county. Map of the state, United States and world. Patrons directory, reference business directory and departments devoted to general information. Analysis of the system of U. S. land surveys, digest of the system of civil government . . . 1 p. l., 7–113, viii, x–xxiii pp. incl. 35 col. maps, illus. fol. Chicago, G. A. Ogle & co. 1914. 5099

PORTAGE.

Ogle, G. A., & co.

Standard atlas of Portage county, Wisconsin, including a plat book of the villages, cities and townships of the county. Map of the state, United States and world. Patrons directory, reference business directory and departments devoted to general information. Analysis of the system of U. S. land surveys, digest of the system of civil government, etc., etc. Assisted in record work and platting by Robert K. McDonald . . . 2 p. l., 99, viii, x–xxiii pp. incl. 25 col. maps, illus. fol. Chicago, G. A. Ogle & co. 1915. 5100

RICHLAND.

Ogle, G. A., & co.

Standard atlas of Richland county, Wisconsin, including a plat book of the villages, cities and townships of the county. Patrons directory, reference business directory and departments devoted to general information. Analysis of the system of U. S. land surveys, digest of the system of civil government . . . 2 p. l., 7–61, xxii pp. incl. 27 col. maps. fol. Chicago, G. A. Ogle & co. 1919. 5100a

RUSK.

1914

Ogle, G. A., & co.

Standard atlas of Rusk county, Wisconsin, including a plat book of the villages, cities and townships of the county. Map of the state, United States and world. Patrons directory, reference

Ogle, G. A., & co.—Continued.

business directory and departments devoted to general information. Analysis of the system of U. S. land surveys, digest of the system of civil government . . . 2 p. l., 7–111, viii, x–xxiii pp. incl. 48 col. maps. 6 pl., 1 map in text. fol. Chicago, G. A. Ogle & co. 1914. 5101

1915

Rusk county abstract co.

Plat book of Rusk county, Wisconsin. 53 pp. incl. 52 maps. 16°. Ladysmith, Wis., Rusk county abstract co. 1915. 5102

NOTE.—Maps by Foust & Jungblut, map makers, Milwaukee, Wis.

ST. CROIX.

Webb publishing co.

Atlas and farmers' directory of St. Croix county, Wisconsin. Containing plats of all townships with owners' names: also maps of the state and United States, with an outline map of the county showing location of townships, villages, roads, schools, churches, railroads, streams . . . Published by the Farmer . . . [3]–47 (*i. e.*, 55) [8] pp. incl 23 col. maps. fol. St. Paul, Minn., Webb publishing co. ©1914. 5103

SHEBOYGAN.

Donohue, J.

Atlas of Sheboygan county, Wisconsin . . . 85 pp. incl. 42 maps (part col.). fol. Sheboygan, Wis., Dix printing co. [1916] 5104

NOTE.—"Printed by Dix printing co. Bound by the Bishop co. Plates made by the Commercial engraving co."

Contains large colored map of the state.

TAYLOR.

Ogle, G. A., & co.

Standard atlas of Taylor county, Wisconsin, including a plat book of the villages, cities and townships of the county. Map of the state, United States and world. Patrons directory, reference business directory and departments devoted to general information. Analysis of the system of U. S. land surveys, digest of the system of civil government . . . 2 p. l., 7–95, viii, x–xxiii pp. incl. 51 col. maps, illus. diagrs. fol. Chicago, G. A. Ogle & co. 1913. 5105

TREMPEALEAU.

Webb publishing co.

Atlas and farm directory with complete survey in township plats of Trempealeau county, Wisconsin, containing plats of all townships with owners' names; also maps of the state, United States and world; also an outline map of the county showing location of townships, villages, roads, schools, churches, railroads, streams, etc., etc. Compiled from latest data on record. Published by the Farmer . . . Drawn and engraved by the Anderson publishing co., Chicago, Ill. 50, [12] pp. incl. 24 col. maps, illus. fol. St. Paul, Minn. Webb publishing co. °1914. 5106

VERNON.

Webb publishing co.

Atlas and farm directory with complete survey in township plats of Vernon county, Wisconsin, containing plats of all townships with owners' names; also maps of the state, United States and world; also an outline map of the county . . . Compiled from latest data on record. Published by the Farmer . . . Drawn and engraved by the Anderson publishing co., Chicago, Ill. 58 [12] pp. incl. 26 col. maps, illus. fol. St. Paul, Minn., Webb publishing co. [1915] 5107

WASHBURN.

Ogle, G. A., & co.

Standard atlas of Washburn county, Wisconsin, including a plat book of the villages, cities and townships of the county. Map of the state, United States and world. Patrons directory, reference business directory and departments devoted to general information. Analysis of the system of U. S. land surveys, digest of the system of civil government . . . 2 p. l., 8–103, viii, x–xxiii pp. incl. 32 col. maps, illus. fol. Chicago, G. A. Ogle & co. 1915. 5108

WAUKESHA.

Ogle, G. A., & co.

Standard atlas of Waukesha county, Wisconsin, including a plat book of the villages, cities and townships of the county. Map of the state, United States and world. Patrons directory, reference business directory and departments devoted to general information. Analysis of the system of U. S. land surveys, digest of the system of civil government . . . 2 p. l., 7–133, viii, x–xxiii pp. incl. 33 col. maps, illus. fol. Chicago, G. A. Ogle & co. 1914. 5109

WAUSHARA.

Webb publishing co.

Atlas and farm directory with complete survey in township plats, Waushara county, Wisconsin, containing plats of all townships with owners' names; also maps of the state, United States and world; also an outline map of the county . . . Compiled from the latest data on record. Published by the Farmer . . . Drawn and engraved by the Kenyon company, Des Moines, Ia. 41, [12] pp. incl. 23 col. maps, illus. fol. St. Paul, Minn., Webb publishing co. [1914] 5110

Cities.

LA CROSSE.

Biddenback, H. J.

City atlas of La Crosse, Wisconsin. Compiled from actual surveys and the city and county records. 3 pp., 24 (*i. e.* 22) col. maps. fol. La Crosse, Wis., H. J. Biddenback, 1898. 5111

NOTE.—Engraved by Balliet & Volk, Phila.

MILWAUKEE.

1907

Caspar, C. N., co.

Official quarter-sectional atlas of the city of Milwaukee. According to records of the register of deeds at the court house and at the office of the city engineer, city hall. Drawn and compiled under direction and supervision of Charles J. Poetsch . . . by Edward F. Liedel . . . Embracing the entire territory within the present city limits, in 100 charts, a new complete map of the city with key to all plats and additional auxiliary maps, references, indices, footnotes . . . 7 p. l., 101 col. maps. fol. Milwaukee, C. N. Casper co. 1907. 5112

NOTE.—Scale of maps: 150 feet to the inch. Corrected from title 2677.
Index map on the reverse of front cover.

1914

Official quarter-sectional atlas of the city of Milwaukee. According to the records of the register of deeds at the court house and at the office of the city engineer, city hall. Drawn and compiled under the direction and supervision of Edward F. Leidel . . . George W. Cloos . . . and the cooperation of the Milwaukee abstract and title co., the Milwaukee county abstract co., Mathias J. Guenther . . . The official atlas supplement, 1906 to 1914. Comprising 23 additional new charts of quarter sections, adjoining the old city limits, north, west and south, including the village of East Milwaukee with diagrams of all additions and subdivisions of the official atlas published in 1906 . . . Including 54 new diagrams of subdivisions and additions . . . also a new key map . . . A situation diagram . . . 1 p. l., 3 l., 25 col. maps. fol. Milwaukee, C. N. Caspar co. 1914. 5113

NOTE.—Scale of maps: 150 feet to the inch.
Index map on the reverse of front cover.
At head of title: Supplementary volume 1906 to 1914.

1915

Official quarter-sectional atlas of the city of Milwaukee, according to the records of the register of deeds at the court house and at the office of the city engineer, city hall, drawn and compiled under the direct supervision of city engineers George H. Benzenberg and Charles J. Poetsch, city draughtsmen William Schmidt, Edward F. Leidel, and others. Thoroughly revised, brought up to date, and augmented by George W. Cloos . . . Embracing the entire territory within the present city limits and East Milwaukee, in 124 charts, a new complete map of the city with key to all plats and additional auxiliary maps, references, indices, footnotes . . . 8 p. l., 124 maps. fol. Milwaukee, Wis., C. N. Caspar co. 1915. 5114

NOTE.—On reverse of front cover, Map of the city of Milwaukee, 1912. On reverse of back cover map entitled, Location and elevations of bench marks of the city of Milwaukee, 1914.

WYOMING.

Miscellaneous.

Yellowstone National Park.

Hague, A.

Atlas to accompany monograph xxxii on the geology of the Yellowstone national park. 3 p. l., 24 maps. fol. Washington, J. Bien & co. 1904.
[United States. Department of the interior. Geological survey] 5115

NOTE.—House miscellaneous documents. 3d sess., 55th cong. 1898–99.

MEXICO.

CITIES.

Ward, E. E. S., *lady.*

Six views of the most important towns, and mining districts, upon the table land of Mexico. Drawn by mrs. H. G. Ward and engraved by mr. Pye. With a statistical account of each. 2 p. l., 6 l., 6 pl. obl. fol. London, H. Colburn, 1829. 5116

NOTE.—Views engraved by John Pye.

CONTENTS.

no. 1. Guadalaxara.
" 2. Zacatecas.
" 3. Sombrerete.
" 4. Catorce.
" 5. Valladolid.
" 6. Tlalpuxahua.

VIEWS.

Berlandier, L., *& others.*

Voyage au Mexique. Vues diverses. 52 views. fol. 1827-1831. ms. 5117

Note.—Sketches by Luis Berlandier, T. M. Losada and mr. Grases, in pencil and india ink, made on the expeditions of the "Comision de limites" of Mexico appointed by the government of the United States of Mexico in 1827 to settle the limits of the possessions of Mexico to the northeast.

A daily account of the expeditions was kept by Luis Berlandier and Rafael Chovel with the title, *Diario de viage de la Comision de limites que puso el gobierno de la republica, bajo la direccion del exmo. sr. general de division d. Manuel de Mier y Teran. Lo escribieron por su órden los individuos de la misma comision d. Luis Berlandier y d. Rafael Chovel. México, J. R. Navarro, 1850.* This account does not refer to the sketches, but in a number of cases the dates and localities in the *Diario.* A number of the views are marked, "Comision de limites."

CONTENTS.

no. [1] L'Atta Vela île des Antilles.
" [2-8] [Without title]
" [9] Mazatlan harbor.
" [10] Mont Casattique èlevé de 60 B. environ situé près l'hacienda de Vanegas . . . Mexico etat du Potois. m^r^. Grases pinx^t^. d^bre^. 1827. Comision de limites.
" [11] Vista del Creiton. Chico y Grande de Mazatlan. T. M. Losada.
" [12] Cabo de S. Lucas. Visto desde la plaza. Baja California.
" [13] Camino p^a^. la Par desde S. José, aspecto montanoso. Baja California.
" [14] Vista de la mision de S. José . . . Baja California.
" [15] P^to^ Mazatlan visto desde la Isla. T. M. Losada.
" [16] Valle de Santiago. Guanaxuato. T. Losada.
" [17] Tampico de Tamaulipas. Vue prise du S. S. E. à bord du brick l' Hannah Elisabeth mouillé dans le rio de Panuco. Voyage au Mexique.
" [18] Queretaro vue prise en venant de Mexico. T. M. Losada.
" [19] Valenciana cerca Guanaxuato.
" [20] Mellado cerca Guanaxuato.
" [21] Situo, porta entrada de Leon. T. M. Losada del.
" [22] Salvatierra, Guanaxuato. T. Losada.
" [23] Hacienda de la Olla vista de frente.
" [24] Vue de Zelaya prise du port de la Laja. T. M. Losada del.
" [25] Guanaxuato capital del departament. T. Losada.
" [26] Vue de la ville de Guadalaxara prise sur la route en venant de Mexico.
" [27] Portion de la Sierra et vue de la mesa de los Catujanos prise de l' hacienda du Carrizal.
" [28] Volcan del Cerro partido cerca Santa Barbara.
" [29] Cerro de la Silla vu de Cadereyta.
" [30] Plaza del Real de San Nicolas. (Tamaulipas)
" [31] Vue de quelques cases en terre situées au pied N. E. du mont Peñol de los Caños près de Mexico. (Las Salinas)
" [32] Vista del Cerro del Bernal d'Itorcasitas tomada desde el E. N. E.
" [33] Vista del Cerro del Bernal de' Itorcasitas tomade desde los ranchos del Carrizo.

no. [34] Vue du Cerro Colorado prise de l' hacienda du Carrizal.—Cerrito de la Caña vue prise de l' hacienda du Carrizal. Comision de limites. L. Berlandier. 1828.
" [35] Plaza y Bernal de Itorcasitas.
" [36] Vue prise des bords du Rio del Signe a San Fernando.
" [37] Vista del Cerro de la Peña, muralla oriental del valle de Matehuala; tomada desde el Campo Santo.
" [38] [Indistinct pencil sketch without title]
" [39] Mesa de la Malinche a l'ouest de l' hacienda de Tuna Mansa près de San Carlos de Tamaulipas. L. Berl^r^. 1831.
" [40] Matamoros de Tamaulipas vue prise de l'Est.
" [41] Montagnes du Nouveau Leon, chaîne au nord des ranchos de la Rinconada, entre le Saltillo et Monterrey.
" [42] Montagnes du Nouveau Leon, entre la Rinconada, et Sta. Catarina, chaine du Cerro de las Mitras. L. Berl^r^.
" [43] Vista de una parte del Cerro de las Mitras. Cerca Monterrey, estado de Nuevo Leon. L^s^. Berlandier 1828. Comision de limites.
" [44] Fabrica de hilados de D^n^. Çay^s^ Rubio a una legua de Queretaro camina de la Canada. T. M. Losada.
" [45] Salamanca, Guanaxuato. T. Losada.
" [46] Voyage au Mexique. Vue d'une partie de la Serra Madre prise du N. E. à la voile dans le lac de Tamiagua. Berlandier del.
" [47] Montañas estratificadas de Caliza y Pizarra de la Rinconada entre Monterrey y el Saltillo. L. Berlandier 1828. Comision de limites.
" [48] Cerro del Carrizal y Cerro de la Candela. L. Berlandier p^t^. 1828. Comision de limites.
" [49] Cerro del Carrizal. L. Berlandier cop. 1828.
" [50] Hacienda y Cerro del Carrizal. L. Berlandier 1828. Comision de limites.
" [51] Corte y vista principal del Castillo de S^n^ Diego de Acapulco.
" [52] Corte y vista principal del Castillo de San Diego de Acapulco.

GENERAL.

1811

Humboldt, F. W. H. A., *freiherr von.*

Atlas géographique et physique du royaume de la Nouvelle-Espagne, fondé sur des observations astronomiques, des mesures trigonométriques et des nivellemens barométriques . . . 2 p. l., 4 pp. 12 maps, plates, plans, tables. fol. Paris, F. Schoell, 1811. 5118

NOTE.—This atlas accompanies *Voyage de Humboldt et Bonpland.* Contents same as 1812 edition. See title 2682.

1913.

Rand, McNally & co.

Atlas of the Mexican conflict, containing detailed maps showing the territory involved; pertinent statistics of Mexico and the United States; summary of recent events in Mexico. [16] pp. incl. 8 col. maps. fol. Chicago-New York, Rand, McNally & co. 1913. 5119

1916

Rand, McNally & co.

Atlas of Mexico. cover-title, 14 col. maps. sm. fol. Chicago, New York, Rand, McNally & co. 1916. 5120

NOTE.—Index on cover.

STATES.

PUEBLA.

Mexico. *Comisión geográfico-exploradora.*

Carta geográfica general de la republica mexicana, comenzada en 1878 . . . Atlas topografico de los alrededores de Puebla. 3ª serie.—letra ap. 1ª. ed. Escala de 1: 50,000. 2 p. l., 13 maps. obl. 8°. [Mexico, imp. de la comisión geográfico-exploradora, 1879-1883] 5121

NOTE.—Dates on maps vary from 1879-1883.

CITIES.

MEXICO.

Gualdi, P.

[Views of the city of Mexico] 8 pp., 9 views. fol. [Mexico, J. M. Lara, 1850?] 5122

NOTE.—Views lithographed by Masse y Decaen.

View no. 9, Interior de Mexico, is colored and marked Ch. Nebel del., imp. par Bernard. Arnout lith.

CONTENTS.

no. 1. Alameda de Mejico.
" 2. Paseo de la Independencia.
" 3. Casa Municipal.
" 4. Plaza de Sto. Domingo y Aduana.
" 5. Catedral de Mejico.
" 6. Colegio Minería.
" 7. Interior de la Universidad de Mejico.
" 8. Camara de los Diputados
" 9. Interior de Mexico.

CENTRAL AMERICA.

GENERAL.

1912

Mendioroz, L.

Atlas de Centro-America. Tomado del Prontuario geográfico de Centro-America que va à ser publicado proximamente. 1 p. l., 78 maps. fol. [Berlin, B. Gisevius, 1912] 5123

COSTA RICA.

BOUNDARIES.

Costa Rica. *Costa Rica-Panama arbitration.*

Maps annexed to the answer of Costa Rica to the argument of Panama . . . 1 p. l. 7 maps. 8°. Washington, D. C., Gibson brothers inc., 1914. 5124

NOTE.—Two maps are called "no. 3;" the one at end, showing geological relations belongs to the geologist's report taken from the *Report of the commission of engineers.*

CONTENTS.

no. 1. Carte de la ligne frontière entre le Costa Rica et la Colombie.
" 2. Showing the position of the principal ridges between Piedra Grande and Chirripó Grande, extending from the north divide to the left banks of the rivers Sixaola and Tarire (or Telire)
" 3. Showing the "Area between the Sixaola river and Punta Mona which is enclosed by four lines."
" 4. Profile no. 1. The correct divide.—Profile no. 2. The so-called divides.
" 5. Showing the beginning of the boundary line requested by Panama in her argument.
" 6. Mapa grãl. del Nuevo Reyno de Granada formado de otros particulares de órden del exmõ. sõr. Virrey D. José espeleta año d. 1790. Copiado de Orden del exmõ. sõr. grãl. en gefe del exercito d. Pablo Morillo año de 1816.
" 7. Map showing geological relations, to accompany geological report to the commission of engineers, Costa Rica-Panama boundary arbitration.

WEST INDIES.

GENERAL.

1766

Rueda, M. de.

Atlas americano, desde la isla de Puerto-Rico, hasta el puerto de Vera-Cruz, para los navios de el rey, y de el comercio. Año de 1766. 1 p. l., 12 maps. fol. [Havana, 1766] 5125

NOTE.—Navarrete and Trelles give entries for an atlas composed of 12 maps of ports of Porto Rico, etc., by Rueda, engraved in 1765.

In this copy, map no. 4, *Mapa d[e] la ensen^{da}. de la aguada d[e] S^{n} Fran^{co}*, and map no. 10, *Plano y descripcion d[e] l^{s}. cayos del norte desde la costa de la Habana*, give date 1765. On several maps additional shipping has been sketched in with a pen.

CONTENTS.

no. [1] La isla de Puerto Rico, con la aguada del norte y del oeste.
" [2] Plaza de S^{n}. Juan de Puerto Rico y su puerto.
" [3] Aguada del norte de la ysla de Puerto Rico, donde van à hacerla las flotas.

Rueda, M. de—Continued.

no. [4] Mapa d[e] la ensen[da]. de la aguada d[e] S[n]. Fran[co]. 1765.
" [5] La Bahia de Ocoa en la isla de S[to]. Domingo.
" [6] Costa del Puerto de la Havana hasta el de Matanzas, con sus reconocimientos de las sierras de Iaruco, y plan de Matanzas para embocar la canal de Bahama.
" [7] Surgidero de Losada en el cabo de S[n]. Antonio al oeste de la ysla de Cvba.—Plano del puerto del Mariel en la ysla de Cvba. 1741.
" [8] Puerto de Cavaña situado en la costa septentrional de la isla de Cuba.
" [9] Bahia Honda en la costa septemtrion[l] de la ysla de Cuba.
" [10] Plano y descripcion d[e] l[s]. Cayos del norte desde la costa de la Habana. 1765.
" [11] La sonda de Campeche, y derrota de las flotas para Vera Cruz.
" [12] Costa dela Uera Cruz desde punta delgada hasta el rio de Medellin con sus yslas Yarezifes. Inset: Perspectiva del castillo de San Juan de Ulua.

1795

Jefferys, T.

The West-India islands; from actual surveys and observations: in eighteen correct maps: with plans of the most distinguished harbours. To which is added an historical description of the West-Indies. A new edition. 28 pp., 18 maps. fol. London, R. Laurie & J. Whittle, 1795. 5126

CONTENTS.

no. 1. A new and complete map of the West Indies. 1793.
" 2. Jamaica. Insets: The harbour of Bluefields.—The harbours of Kingston and Port Royal.
" 3. Ruatan, or Rattan. 1794. Insets: Old Providence and S[ta]. Catalina.—New Port-Royal harbour.
" 4. The windward passage, with the several passages from the east end of Cuba & from the north part of St. Domingo. 1794.
" 5. The Virgin Islands. 1794.
" 6. St. Christophers. 1794. Inset: Nevis.
" 7. Antigua. Inset: English harbour.
" 8. Guadaloupe. 1795.
" 9. Dominica. 1773.
" 10. Martinico. Inset: Cul de Sac Royal.
" 11. St. Lucia. 1794. Inset: Plan of the Carenage.
" 12. Barbadoes. 1794.
" 13. St. Vincent. 1794.
" 14. Bequia or Becouya. 1775.
" 15. Carte de l'Isle de la Grenade. 1794.
" 16. Tobago. 1794. Inset: A survey of Great & Little Courland bays.
" 17. Turks Islands. 1775.
" 18. Curaçao. 1794. Inset: Plan of Fort Amsterdam.

SEPARATE ISLANDS.

CUBA.

CITIES.

HABANA.

Garnerey, H. J. B.

[Vues de la Havane et des environs] 6 pl. obl. fol. [Paris, Madrid, etc., Bulla, 1830?] 5127

NOTE.—Views in aquatint.
Titles of views also in spanish.
All views marked, "Peint d'après nature et gravé par Hippolite Garnerey, déposé."

CONTENTS.

no. [1] Vue de la place vieille. Marché principal de la Havana.
" [2] Vue de la promenade de S[t]. F[ois]. de Paul à la Havana.
" [3] Vue de la baie et entrée du port de la Havane prise du chemin de Guanabacoa.
" [4] Vue de la promenade principale de la Havane hors les murs.
" [5] Vue de la place d' armes de la Havane.
" [6] Vue générale de la Havane, capitale de l' isle de Cuba.

GUADELOUPE.

1820?

[**Eight** original water-color sketches in Guadeloupe, made about 1820] 8 views. obl. fol. ms. 5128

NOTE.—Bound in half morocco. Typewritten title. No artist given.

CONTENTS.

no. [1] [View of Port Louis]
" [2] [View looking up Grand river from the waters edge—the mountain du Corps de Garde, civil hospital and convict barrack]
" [3] [View looking up grand river—mountain La Fayette on left and a bois noir tree on right]
" [4] [The Piton de la riviere Noire]
" [5] [View looking up the Grand river—mountain La Fayette]
" [6] [Colophane, ebony and other native wood]
" [7] [View of montagne du Reinpart]
" [8] [Mango tree]

JAMAICA.

1793

Leard, J., *& others.*

[Charts and plans of Jamaica from surveys and observations made by order of Philip Affleck, esq., rear admiral of the White, and commander-in-chief of his majesty's ships and vessels at

Leard, J., *& others*—Continued.

Jamaica in part of the years 1789, 1790, 1791, and part of 1792 . . .] 15 maps. fol. [London, J. Leard, 1793] 5129

NOTE.—Title-page wanting. Many of the maps are marked, "Sold by Mount & Davidson, & W. Faden."

Maps engraved by S. I. Neele.

CONTENTS.

no. [1] The island of Jamaica. 1793.

" [2] A plan of Port Morant. Surveyed by J. Leard in 1792. 1793.

" [3] A plan of the anchorage at Morant bay and the coast from Belvedere Point to Fisherman's bay. Surveyed by J. Leard, 1792. 1793.

" [4] A plan of Port Royal and Kingston harbors, with the sea coast & anchorage of Cow bay & Salt Pond bay, Jamaica. Surveyed by I. Leard in 1791 & 1792. 1793.

" [5] A plan of the anchoring places at Old Harbour, Long's wharf, Salt river, Peake bay and Walkers bay. Surveyed by order of Philip Affleck esq^{r}. Surveyed by I. Leard & W^{m}. Buller in 1791. 1793.

" [6] A plan of the anchorage at Blewfields, Jamaica. Surveyed by John Leard & W^{m}. Buller, 1791. [Inscribed with pen, "Publish'd 26 april 1793 by the author"]

" [7] A plan of the anchorage at Savanna La Mer, Jamaica; & the shoals between it & John's Point. Surveyed by Jno. Leard, 1791. 1792.

" [8] The harbour of Lucea, on the north side Jamaica. Surveyed by Jno. Leard and Stephen Seymour in 1790. 1793.

" [9] Montego bay, on the north side Jamaica. Surveyed by John Leard & Stephen Seymour, 1791. 1793.

" [10] Martha Brae, Jamaica. 1793.

" [11] S^{t}. Ann's bay, Jamaica, surveyed by Jno. Leard & Stephen Seymour, 1790. 1792.

" [12] Port Antonio, on the north side of Jamaica. Surveyed by John Leard & St^{n}. Seymour in 1790. 1792.

" [13] Plan of Port Royal & Kingston harbours, as surveyed, in 1788. Geo. Vancouver & Jos. Whidbey. 1792.

" [14] Musquito Cove on the north side Jamaica, surveyed by John Leard and Stephen Seymour, 1792. 1793.

" [15] A plan of the island of Jamaica, & the plans of the principal harbours & anchoring places about the island, as surveyed in part of the year 1789, 1790, 1791, & part of 1792. John Leard. 1792.

SOUTH AMERICA.

RIVERS.

Amazon River.

Brazil. *Commissão hydrographico.*

Primeiros traços geraes da carta particular do rio Amazonas no curso brazileiro. Levantada pelo sr. João Soares Pinto capitão-tenente d'A. N. I. coadjuvado de Belem a Teffe' pelo sr. Vincente

Pereira Dias, primeiro-tenente do corpo d'engenheiros. Nos annos de 1862 a 1864. 1 p. l., 1 map on 14 sheets. fol. [Rio de Janeiro, 1866?] 5130

Note.—At head of title: Trabalhos hydrographicos ao Norte do Brazil dirigidos pelo capitão de fragata d'A. N. I. José da Costa Azevedo.

GENERAL.

1814–1820

Humboldt, F. W. H. A., *freiherr von.*

Voyage de Humboldt et Bonpland. Première partie, relation historique. Atlas géographique et physique du nouveau continent. 2 p. l., 12 maps, 7 pl. fol. Paris, F. Schoell, 1814–[1820] 5131

Note.—Maps 3, 5, 7–14, 22, 25, 27 wanting.

CONTENTS.

no. [a] Humanitas. Literæ. Fruges. Engr by Roger. [Allegorical picture]
" 1. Limite inférieure des neiges perpétuelles à différentes latitudes. 1808.
" 2. Tableau physique des îles Canaries. 1817.
" 4. Chemin de La Guayra, par la Cumbre. 1817.
" 6. Profil du chemin de Carthagène des Indes au plateau de Santa Fé de Bogota. 1820.
" 15. Carte du cours de l'Orénoque depuis l'embouchure du rio Sinaruco jusqu'à l'Angostura. 1815.
" 16. Carte itinéraire du cours de l'Orénoque, d'Atabapo, du Casiquiare, et du Rio Negro offrant la bifurcation de l'Orénoque et sa communication avec la rivière des Amazones. 1814.
" 17. Carte du cours du rio Apure et d'une partie de la chaine des montagnes de la Nouvelle Grenade. 1813.
" 18. Carte de la partie orientale de la province de Varinas comprise entre l'Orénoque, l'Apure et le rio Meta. 1812.
" 19. Carte du cours de rio Meta et d'une partie de la chaine orientale des montagnes de la Nouvelle Grenade. 1817.
" 20. Carte du Rio Caura. 1816.
" 21. Carte spéciale de la partie du Rio Apure. 1800.—Cours du Rio Guaviara. 1814.
" 23. Carte de l'île de Cuba. 1820. Inset: Plan du port et de la ville de la Havane.
" 24. Carte du Rio Grande de la Magdalena. Insets: Plan topographique de l'Angostura de Carare. 1801.—Carte du Rio Grande de la Magdalena, par. F. J. de Caldas.
" 26. Carte géologique du Nevado de Antisana.
" 28. Tableau géologique du volcan de Jorullo. 1804.
" 29. Plan du volcan de Jorullo.
" 30. Esquisse géologique des environs de Guanaxuato. 1817.

1914

Philip, G., & son.

Philip's comparative wall atlas of South America. Edited by J. F. Umstead . . . & E. G. R. Taylor . . . 8 col. fold. maps, 41 x 33½ each. Scale 1: 9,000,000. fol. London, G. Philip & son [1914] 5132

NOTE.—Accompanied by *Explanatory handbook, South America. cover-title, 19 pp. 8°. London, G. Philip & son, 1914.*

CONTENTS.

no. [1] Climate, may 1–oct. 31.
" [2] Climate, nov. 1–april 30.
" [3] Density of population.
" [4] Economic.
" [5] Natural vegetation.
" [6] Political divisions.
" [7] Relief of land & communications.
" [8] Temperature.

ARGENTINA.

BOUNDARIES.

Argentine Republic. *Comision Argentina demarcadora de limites con el Brasil.*

[Planos topográficos. Islas del Rio Uruguay . . . Islas del Rio Iguazú] 34 maps. sm. fol. [Buenos Aires, Taller tip. de la Penitenciaría nacional, 1900–1904] 5133

NOTE.—Maps in portfolio without text. List of maps on reverse of front cover.

CONTENTS.

Rio Uruguay.

no. 1. Isla Pacú. 1901.
" 2. Isla Grande Superior. 1901.
" 3. Isla Grande Inferior. 1901.
" 4. Isla Chaparro. 1901.
" 5. Isla Aguapey. 1902.
" 6. Isla Murciélago. 1901.
" 7. Isla Tacuaras. 1901.
" 8. Isla del Vado. 1903.
" 9. Isolote del Tigre. 1902.
" 10. Isla del Cuay. 1902.
" 11. Iª. Stª. Ana. 1902.
" 12. Isla de Santa Lucia. 1902.
" 13. Isla Vargas. 1902.
" 14. Isla Sⁿ. Mateo. 1902.
" 15. Islotes Sarandi. 1902.
" 16. Isla Grande (de arriba). 1902.
" 17. Isla Sⁿ. Lucas Grande. 1902.
" 18. Isla Cerrito. 1902.
" 19. Isla Piratiny. 1902.
" 20. Islas de Sⁿ. Isidro. 1902.

no. 21. Isl^{otes}. del Iyuhy. 1902.
" 22. I^{a}. Itacaruaré Chica. 1902.
" 23. Islas é islotes abajo de San Javier. 1902.
" 24. Islas é Islotes de Chafariz. 1902.
" 25. Isla de Dino ó Nao. 1902.

Rio Iguazú.

" 26. Grupo dela Isla Grande. 1903.
" 27. I. S. Agustin.
" 28. Cataratas del Iguazú. 1903.
" 29. Limite oriental en misiones. 1903.
" 30. Rio Iguazú desde su desembocadura hasta el S^{n}. Antonio. 1903.
" 31. Rio Uruguay. Primera parte desde et Rio Miriñay hasta Garruchos. 1901-2.
" 32. Rio Uruguay. Secunda parte desde Garruchos hasta el Pepiri Guazú. 1902.
" 35. Limite entre las cabeseras de las rios San Antonio y Pepiri Guazú. 1903.
s/n Plano de la frontera entre la República Argentina y los Estados Unidos del Brasil. 1900–04.

SCHOOL.

Bavio, E. A.

Atlas escolar de la república Argentina para uso de las escuelas de aplicación anexas á las normales y escuelas comunes del país . . . Undécima edición . . . 2 p. l., [5]-43 pp., 26 col. maps. sm. 4°. Buenos Aires, A. Estrada & c^{ia}. [191-?] 5134

GENERAL.

1893

Beyer, C.

Atlas general de la república Argentina . . . Grabado y revisado por los s. s. W. & A. K. Johnston . . . Sexta edicion . . . 2 p. l., 33 l., iv pp., 1 l., 6 pp., incl. 30 col. maps. fol. Buenos Aires, A. Estrada & cia. 1893. 5135

NOTE.—Gives plan of the city and province of Buenos Aires.

1910

Estrada, A. & cia.

Atlas general de la república Argentina . . . Construidò segun los datos mas recientes. Grabado é impreso por los s. s. W. & A. K. Johnston, ltd. de Londres y Edimburgo. 9. ed. 1 p. l., lv [2] 7 [3] pp., 30 col. maps on 33 l. sm. fol. Buenos Aires, A. Estrada & cia, 1910. 5136

NOTE.—Contains two maps of the city of Buenos Aires.
Part of the list of the publications of Angel Estrada & cia. on inside of back cover.

PROVINCES.

CÓRDOBA.

Rio, M. E., *and* **Achával, L.**

Geografía de la provincia de Córdoba . . . Excrita por encargo del excmo. Gobierno de la provincia. Publicación oficial. Atlas. 1 p. l., 8 col. maps, 6 pl., 1 diagr. fol. Buenos Aires, Campania sud-americana de billetes de banco, 1905. 5137

NOTE.—To accompany their work of the same title in 2 v. 1904–1905. Corrected from v. 1, title 2737.

CONTENTS.

Maps.

no. [1] Mapa general. Dib. por J. W. Caldenty.
" [2] Mapa de las vias de comunicacion.
" [3] Mapa hidrografico. Cuenca superior de los rios. Primero, segendo, de Cruz del Eje, de los Sauces y Otros.
" [4] Mapa hidrografico. Cuenca superior de los rios. Tercero y cuarto. Dibujado por Javier W. Caldentey.
" [5] Mapa geologico. Construido según datos recogidos hasta 1890, por los doctores Stelzner, L. Brackebusch y G. Bodembender.
" [6] Mapa fitogeogafico, construido por el dr. Federico Kurtz.
" [7] Mapa hipsométrico.
" [8] Distribución del area cultivada.

BOLIVIA.

BOUNDARY.

Peru. Juicio de limites entre el Perú y Bolivia; prueba peruana presentada al gobierno de la república Argentina por Victor M. Maurtua . . . 12 v. 4°. Atlas. 3 v., v. 1. 4°; v. 2-3. fol. Barcelona, Henrich co. 1906–1907. 5138

NOTE.—For note see entry under Peru. Boundary, title 5149, and titles 2738, 2767.

GEOLOGICAL.

Bolivia. *Ministerio de justicia e industria.*

[Atlas of geological, mineralogical and industrial maps of Bolivia] "Anexos á la Memoria de 1912." cover-title, [2] pp., 11 col. maps (fold.) fol. [La Paz, H. Heitmann, 1913?] 5139

BRAZIL.

AGRICULTURE.

Brazil. *Ministerio da agricultura. Serviço de informaçoes e divulgação, secçao de expedição.*

[Atlas de Brazil] 39 col. maps, tabs. fol. São Paulo, Weiszflog irmãos, [1908] 5140

Note.—All maps headed "Sociedade naçional de agricultura. Secção de geographia agricola. Grande premio na exposição nacional de 1908." All these maps are signed "Visto, D. E. Wencytin Silk (?) Organisado, por M. Paulino. Cavalcanti."

Text in portuguese and french. Each map dated 1908.

GENERAL.

1911

Sampaio, T.

Atlas dos estados unidos do Brazil. 2 p. l., 24 col. maps. fol. Bahia, Reis & ca. 1911. 5141

1912

Homem de Mello, B., *and* **F. I. M.**

Geographia-atlas do Brazil e das cinco partes do mundo. Conforme o "Atlas do Brazil" do Barão Homem de Mello e F. Homem de Mello e os melhores auctores para a "parte geral." Com um prologo do Francisco Cabrita . . . 1ª ed. 2 p. l., xii, 99 [1] pp., front. (port.), 34 col. maps, illus., diagrs. 4°. Rio de Janeiro, F. Briquiet & cia. 1912. 5142

MISCELLANEOUS.

Araguari River.

Brazil. *Commissão de exploração do rio Araguary.*

Commission brésilienne d'exploration du haut Araguary. Sous la direction de Felinto Alcino Braga Cavalcante . . . 1896. 1 p. l., 3 maps (1 fold.) fol. [Paris, 1899] 5143

[Brazil. Frontières entre le Brésil et la Guyane française. Mémoires . . . Paris, A. Lahure, 1899–1900. v. 7]

Maps engraved and printed by A. Simon, Paris.

CHILI.

PHYSICAL.

Pissis, A., *i. e.* **P. J. A.**

Geografía física de la república de Chile. x pp., 1 l., 536 (*i. e.* 356) pp. 8°, *and* atlas of 14 pl. (3 col.) map, tab., 7 profiles. obl. fol. Paris, Instituto geográfico de Paris, C. Delagrave, 1875. 5144

RAILROADS.

Chile. *Inspección jeneral de ferrocarriles.*
Atlas de la monografia de lineas ferreas fiscales en estudio y construccion . . . 1 p. l., 34 maps, 7 diagrs. fol. [Santiago de Chile, impr. Cervantes?] 1910. 5145

NOTE.—Binder's title.

SCHOOL.

Chile. *Ministerio de instrucción pública.*
Mapa escolar de Chile mandado hacer por órden del ministro de instrucción pública . . . Construido segun los últimos datos jeográficos en la inspectión jral. de jeografía i minas de la dirección de obras públicas. Injeniero jefe José del G. Fuenzalida. 1 col. map on 9 sheets, illus. fol. Gotha, J. Perthes, 1911. 5146

CITIES.

VALPARAISO.

Scott, A.
República de Chile. Puerto de Valparaiso. Proyecto de mejoramiento. Planos generales y detalles de las obras proyectados. cover-title, 64 maps. obl. fol. [Londres, Vacher & sons] 1910. 5147

NOTE.—In portfolio.
Table of contents on inside of cover. Imprint taken from maps.

MISCELLANEOUS.

Yeso River.

Broekman, G. van M.
Lago del Yeso. xv, 87 pp. plates, tables, 14 diagrs. *and* atlas of 20 fold. pl. (incl. maps, diagrs.) fol. Valparaiso, lit. é impr. "Moderna" [1912] 5148

NOTE.—Atlas in portfolio, with title on cover: Lago del Yeso. Atlas del proyecto.

PERU.

BOUNDARY.

Peru. Juicio de límites entre el Perú y Bolivia; prueba peruana presentada al gobierno de la república Argentina por Victor M. Maurtua . . . 12 v. 4°. Atlas. 3 v., v. 1. 4°; v. 2–3. fol. Barcelona, Henrich co. 1906–1907. 5149

NOTE.—Collation: v. 1, portfolio, 34 fold. maps; v. 2, 1 p. l., [4] pp. 58 maps; v. 3, 12 maps.
Reproductions from various sources.
Atlas to accompany a collection of documents for the most part previously unpublished.

A few maps have accompanying text: v. 1, no. 25, text: *Plano general de las montañas orientales al reyno del Perú . . .* v. 1, no. 14; v. 2, nos. 18 and 57 have border text; v. 2, no. 35, has a full page of text entitled, *Los fundamentos de este trabajo geografico se indican . . . Notas al mapa.*
Most of the maps in v. 1–2 are colored.
For contents of v. 1–2, see v. 1, title 2767.

CONTENTS.

v. 3, no. 1. Del mapa de Cano y Olmedilla.
" " 2. Descripcion geografica de la frontera ĝ. corre desde la ribera occidental del rio Paranà, hasta mas abaxo de la union del rio Guaporè con el Mamoré. La linea de puntos de carmin denota la divisoria con arreglo al tratado preliminar de limites de 11 d[e] octubre del año de 1777.
" " 3. Plano delas provincias del Çuzco, y demas pana la direccion delas tropas del Rey contra del rebel de Joseph Gabri'l. Fupac Amano.
" " 4. Mapa fisico y politico del alto y bajo Peru. Año de 1826.
" " 5. El mapa de Paz Soldan rectificado por su autor.
" " 6. Mapa geografico de la provincia de Caupolican compilado por Eduardo Idiaquez.
" " 7. Mapa de las exploraciones y estudios verificados por el coronel de artilleria Juan L. Muñoz. 1896.
" " 8. Region del n. o. de Bolivia, conforme a varias informaciones de la oficina nacional de inmigracion estadistica y propaganda geográfica. 1902.
" " 9. Plan geográfico que me ha pasado el naturalista de s. m. don Tadeo Haenke.
" " 10. Mapa de las misiones de Apolobamba y sus reduccions del oñ de nño P. S. Fran^{co}.
" " 11. Mapa corografico de la república de Bolivia. Con la topografia de las fronteras limitrofes. Mandado levantar por el ex^{mo}. sor. presidente José Ballivian y formado por el coronel de ingenieros Felipe Bertres. 1843.
" " 12. Mapa general de la república de Bolivia. 1906.

GENERAL.

1865

Paz Soldan, M. F.

Atlas géographique de la république du Pérou . . . Édition française par P. Arsène Mouqueron . . . avec la collaboration de Manuel Rouaud y Paz Soldan . . . 1 p. l., 82 pp. 27 maps, 24 plates, 24 plans. fol. Paris, librairie de A. Durand, 1865. 5150

Note.—Bibliographie: pp. [77]–82.
Contents same as spanish edition. See title 2769.
The first geographical work of the author was the *Geografia del Peru,* 1861, of which the physical sections were written by his brother Mateo. Then followed this atlas of Peru, which involved immense labor and research, and called for great tact and perseverance in its execution. Señor Paz Soldan made a special journey to Paris to arrange for the engraving and publication. See *Royal geographical society. Proceedings. June, 1887. Obituary, by C. R. Markham. pp. 386–387.*

VENEZUELA.

1916

Lecuna, V.

Atlas de Venezuela . . . Dibujado y grabado por Luis Muñoz Tébar con los mejores datos y según los últimos trabajos hechos por el personal del mapa fisico y politico. Escala 1:500,000. 3 col. maps on 5 sheets. fol. [Caracas, lithografia de la Escuel nacional de artes y oficios] 1916. 5151

NOTE.—Title on each map.

CONTENTS.

no. [1-2] Estado Apure.
" [3-4] Estado Zulia.
" [5] Estados Cojedes y Portuguesa.

EUROPE.

CITIES AND FORTS.

Beek, A., Ballieu, C., *& others.*

[Collections of plans of fortifications and battles, by various authors and published at various places] 116 col. maps. fol. [1684-1709] 5152

NOTE.—Has a manuscript list of the maps headed, "Registre du plan et fortifications et des battalies."

Contents shows this to be a factitious atlas.

Maps are by the following cartographers: Sprecht, Morden, Lea, Browne, Lafeuille, Visscher, Baillieu, Beek, Blaeu, Mortier, Allard, Mee, Skynner, Fricx, Plouich, Wit, Cartier, Gutschoúen, Mosburger, Hooge, Gournay and Husson.

CONTENTS.

no. [1] Tafel in welke vertoont werden alle werk-tuygen behorende tot de krygs-kunde door Casper Sprecht. 1703.
" [2] This actuall survey of London, Westminster & Southwark is humbly dedicated to y[e] l[d]. mayor & court of aldermen by R[o]. Morden, Phil. Lea, Chr. Browne.
" [3] Lutetiæ Parisiorum universæ Galliæ metropolis novissima & accuratissima delineatio per Jacobum de la Feuille.
" [4] La ville et havre de Toulon avec ses forts. Amsteldam chez Nicolas Visscher. Insets: Plan de la ville de Toulon.—Pays ou environs de Toulon.
" [5] Plan géometral de la ville citadelles, port et arcenaux de Marseille. Par Razaud à Amsteldam chez Nicolas Visscher.
" [6] Plan de la ville et château de Nice. Paris chez le s[r]. Baillieu. 1708. Inset: Environs de la ville et chasteau de Nice.
" [7] Villa Francia apvd Niciam ad Varvm.
" [8] Porto di Villafranca.
" [9] Nicæa civitas.
" [10] Cvnevm vulgo Coni.
" [11] Cvnevm. Invenalis Boettus Fossanensis, delineavit.

no. [12] Veue de la ville de Turin et ses environs, dessinée par le soin de Pierre Mortier.

" [13] Plan de la ville et citadelle de Turin comme elles ont étez assiègez par les françois le 7 septemb. l' an 1706 à la Haye chez Anna Beek.

" [14] Exigua & celeberrima Verrvca, qvam Carolvs Emanvel I Sab. dvx immunitam fortissime defendit: Carolvs Carolvs Emanvel II ut ipsa sese deferenderet, communivit.

" [15] Ivrea. Formentus fecit. I. de Ram fecit aqua forti. Amstelodami apud Joannem Blaeu.

" [16] Veue de casal dit de S^t. Vas exactement dessinée sur lieu mis au jour par le soin de Pierre Mortier. Inset: Casal.

" [17] Crémone ville du duché de Milan, exactement dessinée sur le lieu mis au jour par le soin de Pierre Mortier.

" [18] Trévigny ou Trévise. Amsterdam par Pierre Mortier. Inset: Veue de Trevigny.

" [19] Novissima et accuratissima delineatio Romæ veteris et novæ auctore Iacobo de la Feuille.

" [20] De haven en straat van Gibraltar, door Carel Allard. Inset: Estrecho de Gibraltar.

" [21] Plan de la ville de Gibaltar. Amsterdam par Nicolas Visscher. Inset: Plan de la ville de Ceuta.—Veue de la ville de Gibaltar.

" [22] Caarte vande landingh inde baay van Vigos als meede het inneemen van twee casteels en het verooveren der spaansche silvre vloot ten ancker leggende inde baay voor Redondella den 23 en 24 october 1702, by Anna Beeck. Jan van Calle fecit. Gedeekendt. door L. du Meé.

" [23] Geteekent door L. du Mee. Plaan vande dissante of landing in Spangien voor Cadix met de campe menten en marse door den hertog van Orment en den generaal majoor en baron de Spar gedaan ceedert den 26 augustus tot den 27. septem^r anno 1702. J. van Call fec. In t'Hage bÿ Anna Beek.

" [24] Plan de la ville de Barcelone et château de Mont Iuy à la Haye chez Anna Beek. Alex^r Forbes.

" [25] A new and exact plan of ye towne and port of Dunkirk. M. Skynner f^t. 1706. Insets: A prospect of the castle of Risbanck at the entrance of Dunkirck harbour.—Dunkirk and its confines.

" [26] Neoportvs vulgo Nievport.

" [27] Plan de la ville d'Ostende fait par C. Hoppach. Harrewyn fecit aqua forti simul et sculpsit Brux. Bruxelles, chez Eugène Henry Fricx. 1707.

" [28] Plasschendaele.

" [29] Plan de l'action qui s'est passée à Wynendale le 28 sep^e., 1708. In 's Gravenhage, by Anna Beeck. 1708.

" [30] Dixmvda. [Dedicated by] Vedastvs dv Plovich geometra.

" [31] Plan de la ville d'Ipres. Paris, chez le sieur Baillieu.

" [32] Plan de la ville de Menin. P. van Kal fecit. A la Haye, chez Anna Beeck.

" [33] Afbeelding van de linien of retrenchementen door den koning van Vranckryr Louis de XIV in de jaren 1692 en 93 doen maken. Getekent door mons^r. Charles Desbordes t'Amsteldam by Nicolaus Visscher.

Beek, A., Ballieu, C., & others—Continued.

no. [34] Plan de la ville et citadelle de Lille. P. v. Call fec. A la Haye, chez Anna Beek . . .

" [35] Armentières. Vedastus du Plouich fecit. F. de Wit excudit Amstelodami.

" [36] Le véritable plan de la ville et citadelle de Tournay. P. v. Cal fecit. A la Haye, chez Anna Beek.

" [37] Introitus in urbem expugnatam. Huchtenburg fec. et ex.

" [38] Cortracvm vulgo Cortryck, Gallice Covrtray. F. de Wit excudit.

" [39] Plan de bataille d'Oudenaerde du 11 juillet 1708. Levé sur le lieu par G. L. Mosburger. A Bruxelles chez Eugène Henry Fricx. Harrewyn. fecit.

" [40] Plan d'Oudenarde. Paris, chez le sieur Baillieu. 1708.

" [41] Gerardimontivm vulgo Gheertsberghe.

" [42] Plan du siège et des attaques de la ville et citadelle de Gand assiègée par les armées des alliez le 22 décem^e. 1708. P. v. Cal f. à la Haye, chez Anna Beek.

" [43] Carte d'une partie de la Flandre. A la Haie chez Anna Beek. I. v. Call fec.

" [44] Plan van Hulst met zyn onderhorige forte mitgaders de attaque der France gedaan Anna Beek. Jan van Call fec.

" [45] Plan van de batailje der holland en franse armée voorgevallen tussen Muÿsbroeck Wilmerdonck en orderen op den 30. junÿ . . . 1703. Dessinée sur la lieux par mons^r. Ÿvoÿ Gartier. A la Haye, chez Pierre Husson.

" [46] Plan de la ville de Dendermonde. A la Haye Anna Beek. P. v. Cal fecit. Inset: Le prospect de la ville de Dendermonde.

" [47] Sylva dvcis Gallis Bojs le Dvc german s Hartogen Bos. F. de Wit excudit Amstelodami.

" [48] Breda. [Dedicated by] J. Blaeu. F. de Wit excudit Amstelodami.

" [49] Plan de la ville et citadelle d'Anvers. Paris, chez le sieur Baillieu. A. Coquart sculp. Inset: Marquisat du S^t. Empire d'Anvers.

" [50] Lier.

" [51] Mechlinia vulgo Malines. F. de Wit excudit Amstelodami.

" [52] Lovanivm. [Dedication by] Gerardus a Gutschoúen. And. Pauli fecit.

" [53] Plan du passage des lignes de Brabant forcées le 18 juillet 1705. A la Haye, Anna Beek. I. v. Call.

" [54] Plan de là situation du payx et ligne ennemis entre la rivière Mahangne et geete fait le 28me. décembre. 1703. A la Haie, chez Anna Beek.

" [55] Plan et attaque la ville de S^t. Leeuw. A la Haye, chez Anna Beek.

" [56] Thienen.

" [57] Praelium in Belgio. Huchstenburg fec. et ex.

" [58] Plan de la situation ou la bataille de Ramillis, le 23 may 1706. Dessiné sur les lieux par G. L. Mosburger. A la Haye, chez Anna Beek. Inset: [View of battle] I. v. Vianen fecit.

" [59] Middelbvrgvm. F. de Wit excudit Amstelodami.

" [60] Dordracvm vulgo Dortt. F. de Wit excudit Amstelodami.

" [61] Rotterdam. F. de Wit excudit.

" [62] Delfi Batavorum venacule Delft. F. de Wit excudit Amstelodami.

" [63] Hagæ comitis nuperrima delinaetio per Petrum Schenk. Inset: [View of city]

" [64] Harlemvm vulgo Haerlem. F. de Wit excudit. Amstelodami.

no. [65] Amstelædami novissima delineatio per Petrum Schenk. Inset: [View of water front]

" [66] Urbis Traiecti ad Rhenum novissima et accuratissima delineatio per C. Specht a° 1695. Jan v. Vianen fecit.

" [67] Nymegen sterck stadt in Gelderland met de nieuwe fortificatie door de heer Coehorn. T' Amsterdam by P. Mortier.

" [68] Gelder, a°. 1703, 20 april. s'Gravenhage by A. Beek. I. v. Call. Inset views: Attaque de Hartenfledt.—Attaque de Verth.

" [69] Rvræmvnda vulgo Roermond. F. de Wit excudit.

" [70] Plan de la ville de Keyserewert. Anna Beek ex.

" [71] Plan de Maestrich. Paris, chez Ballieux. 1708.

" [72] Plan du camp de l' armée des alliés le 14 de may 1703. G. L. Mosburger fecit. A la Haie, chez Anna Beek.

" [73] t'Plan van Antwerpe. Anna Beeck excudit.

" [74] Situatie van Limburgh. Anna Beek excudit.

" [75] Plan de la ville et citadelle de Liège. L. Loisel fecit. Paris, chez C. Gournay.

" [76] Plan de la ville, château et forte de Huy. Bernard de Roy. 1705.

" [77] Namurcum. 1695. Uyt gegeven by Pieter Persoy tot Amsterdam. [Dedication by] Romanus de Hooge.

" [78] Plan du siège de Namur. 1695. Paris, chez C. Gournay.

" [79] Urbs capta, dum arx adhuc obluctatur. Huchtenburg fecet ex.

" [80] Plan des lignes et campements des armées des alliéz commandées par le roy de la Grande Bretagne devant la ville et château de Namur 1695. Amsteldam, chez Nicolas Visscher. Ottomar Elliger inv. et pin.

" [81] Plan du camp, que prit l' armée des alliés le 30° du mois de iuin à Woutergem, comme aussi de celui qu' elle prit le 13 de iuillet à Arsele et sa retraite vers Gand à la veüé des ennemis, à 6 heures après-midi le 14° iuillet 1695. Ottomar Elliger inv. et pin., G. v. Gouwen sculp. Amsteldam, chez Nicholas Visscher.

" [82] Luxemburgum. 1684, ex conatibus Romani de Hooge et formis Nicolai Visscher.

" [83] Famosissimi fortalitu Charleroy vulgo dicti vera ichnographica effigies. Auctore et editore F. de Witt.

" [84] Plan de Mons, le 25. septemb. 1709. P. v. Cal. f. A la Haye, chez Anna Beek.

" [85] Plan de Condé. Paris, chez le s^r. Baillieu. 1708.

" [86] A la gloire immortelle des illustres princes et heros s. a. s. le prince Eugène de Savoye &c. s. a. le duc de Marlborough &c. s. e. le comte de Tilly &c. ce plan de l' importante et glorieuse bataille de Blangies, donnée le 11 septembre, 1709 est humblement offert et dédié par Anna Beek.

" [87] Plan et profil de la ville de Mauberge. P. v. Cal. fet. A la Haye, chez Pierre Husson.

" [88] Plan de la ville de Douay, à la Haye chez Anna Beek. Inset: Bout de plan de l' attaque de Douay.

" [89] Plan de la ville d'Aath, à la Haye, chez Anna Beek.

" [90] Plan de la ville et cittadelle de Valenciennes, le 17°. du mois de mars en 1677. A Paris, chez le s^r. Baillieu.

" [91] Plan de la ville et citadelle de Cambray le 5me avril 1677. A Paris, chez le s^r. Baillieu. 1709.

Beek, A., Ballieu, C., *& others*—Continued.

no. [92] Plan de Béthune. A Paris, chez la s^r^. Baillieu. 1708.

" [93] Plan de la ville et citadelle d' Arras. A Paris, chez la s^r^. Baillieu. 1709.

" [94] Plan de la ville d' Aire et du fort S^t^. François. A Paris, chez le s^r^. Baillieu. 1708.

" [95] Plan de la ville de S^t^. Omer. A Paris, le s^r^. Baillieu. 1708.

" [96] Plan de la ville et château de Traarbach, à la Haye, chez Anna Beek.

" [97] Plan de la ville et des nouveaux ouvrages de Trèves. I. v. Call fecit. A la Haye, chez Anna Beek.

" [98] Plan et attaque de la ville de Landaw. I. v. Call fecit. A la Haye, chez Anna Beek.

" [99] Le fort Louis du Rhin. A Paris, chez le s^r^. Baillieu. 1708.

" [100] Philipsbourg. 1708. A Paris chez G. Baillieu.

" [101] Sar-Louis. A Paris, chez le sieur Baillieu.

" [102] Plan de la ville de Strasbourg et du fort de Kell. A Paris, chez Baillieu. 1708. Inset: Carte particulière des environs de Strasbourg.

" [103] Plan du vieux et du Neuf Brisac. A Paris, chez le s^r^. Gaspar Baillieu. 1708. Inset: Environs de Fribourg et de Brisac.

" [104] Plan des villes et château de Fribourg. A Paris, chez Gaspar Baillieu. 1708. Gravé par Montulay. Inset: Environs de Fribourg et de Brisac.

" [105] Huningue. 1708. A Paris, chez le s^r^. Baillieu.

" [106] Plan de la ville impériale et fortresse de Ulm. I. v. Call fec^t^.

" [107] Ordre de battaille au camp de Burckheim de l'armée des allies en Allemagne le 15me. de juillet an 1704 by Anna Beek.

" [108] Accvrata delineatio praelii Hochstetensis. anno 1704 A. D. 13 avgvsti. G. Valk exc. Huchtenburgh fec.

" [109] Plan de la glorieuse bataille donnée le 13 aoust 1708 près de Hochstett sur le Danube entre les villages de Plintheim, Oberklaw et Lutzigen. Dessiné sur les lieux par mons^r^. d' Jvoy. A la Haye, chez Anna Beek.

" [110] Curieuse astekening van de glorieuse actie voorgevallen by Donawaart op den 2 july 1704. I. v. Cal f^t^. Anna Beek.

" [111] Plan de la ville de Vienne en Austriche et ses environs. A Amsterdam chez Pierre Mortier.—Plan de la ville de Vienne et ses environs. Par le s^r^. Sanson.

" [112] [Siege of Vienna. 1683] Amstelodami apud Nicolaum Visscher.

" [113] Hamburg. Pet. Schenk exc. Amstelod. Inset: [View of city]

" [114] Beleg en ontset van Nerva, 27. nov. 1700. [Dedicated by] Romanus de Hooghe, ex formis Petri Schenk.

" [115] Plan de la fameuse bataille donnée aux environs de Poltawa en Ucraine entre l'armée de sa majesté csarienne Pierre I. empereur de la Grande Russie et celle de s. m. le roy de Suède de Charles XII, le 27 juin-8 juillet 1709. P. v. Cal f. A la Haye, chez Pierre Husson.

" [116] Théâtre de la paix entre les chrestiens et les turcs. 26 jan. 1699.

Jansson, J.

Illvstriorvm principumque urbium septentrionalium Evropæ tabulæ. 3 p. l., 229 pp. incl. 52 pl. 1 fold. pl. fol. Amstelodami, ex officina J. Janssonii [1657?] 5153

NOTE.—Engraved half-title reads: "Theatrum præcipuarum urbium, positarum ad septentrionalem Europæ plagem."

Most of the plates are from those by Georg Hoefnagel in Braun's *Civitates orbis terrarvm.* A sonnet to the cities of northern Europe included in this atlas is by Marcus Zuerius Boxhorn.

Jansson published atlases of the cities of Italy, Spain, France, Germany and Belgium from ca. 1652–1657.

CONTENTS.

no. [1] Londinvm vulgo London.
" [2] Civitas Exoniæ (vulgo Excester)
" [3] Cantvarbvry.
" [4] Palativm regivm in Angliæ regno appellatvm Noncivtz. Effigiauit Georgius Houfnaglius anno 1582.
" [5] Brightstowe.
" [6] Oxonivm.—Vindesorivm. Depingebat Georgius Hoefnagle.
" [7] Nordovicvm.
" [8] Cantebrigia.
" [9] Cestria vvlgo Chester.
" [10] Yorke.—Shrowesbvry.—Lancaster.—Richmont.
" [11] Edenbvrgvm vulgo Edenbvrg.
" [12] Galwaye.—Dvbline.—Lymericke.—Corcke.
" [13] Hafnia vulgo Kopenhagen. 1587.
" [14] Elsenor.—Ripen.
" [15] Freti Danici or svndt accvratiss delineatio. Inset: Interior Arcis magnificentia.
" [16] Topographia insulæ Huenæ in celebri porthmo regni Daniæ. 1586. Inset: Vranibvrgvm Arx. [2 Views]
" [17] Helsheborch.—Lvnden.—Elbogen.—Landeskron.
" [18] Civitatis episcopalis Othenarvm sive Otthoniae, vt vvlgo dicitvr, Fioniae, insvlarvm Daniae regni. 1583.
" [19] Visbia Gothorvm.
" [20] Colding Schlos vnd stat.
" [21] Berga Noorwegiæ.
" [22] Schleiswygh.
" [23] Ekelenforda.
" [24] Flensbvrgvm.—Itzohoa Florentissimae Holsatiae op.
" [25] Hvsemvm dvcatvs Slesvicensis ad sinvm Herveram opp.—Haderslebia. 1585.
" [26] Toninga Eiderstadiae.—Hvsvm.
" [27] Oitinense oppidulum.—Delinaetio ciuitatis Tonderensis.
" [28] Chilonvm vulgo Kyell.
" [29] Segeberga olim Aelberga. Vrbs & arx in Holsatia.
" [30] Crempa.—Reinholdsbvrga.
" [31] Plona. 1593.
" [32] Heida.—Meldorpivm. Daniel Friese Dietmariensis pingabat.
" [33] Stockholm.—Stocholm. Donabat huic operi, Hieronymus Scholeus.
" [34] Riga.

Jansson, J.—Continued.

no. [35] Mons Regivs; Prvssiæ.—Riga . . . emporium celebre, & Liuoniæ metropolis.
" [36] Dantzigt.
" [37] Elbing.
" [38] Thorvnivm.—Thoren.
" [39] Cracovia metropolis regni Poloniae.
" [40] Cracovia minoris Poloniae metropolis. Depictum ab Egidio vander Rye, communic. Georgius Houfnaglius.
" [41] Tipvs civitatis Lvblinēsi in regno Poloniæ.
" [42] Mons Calvariae.
" [43] Posnania.—Crosno.
" [44] Leopolis Russiæ australis vrbs.
" [45] Premislia celebris Rvssiae civitas.
" [46] Varsovia.
" [47] Lovicensis civitas qvæ est archiepiscopa.
" [48] Vera designatio vrbis in Littavia Grodnae.
" [49] Sendomiria.—Biecz.
" [50] Zamoscivm, noua Poloniæ ciuitas.
" [51] Vilna Litvaniae metropolis.
" [52] Moscavw.
" [53] Moscovia vrbs metropolis totius Russiæ Albæ.

COAST.

Petit, Le, neptune français; or, french coasting pilot, for the coast of Flanders, channel, bay of Biscay, and Mediterranean. To which is added, the coast of Italy from the river Var to Orbitello; with the gulf of Naples, and the island of Corsica; illustrated with charts, plans, &c. xvi, 147 pp., 4 l. 42 maps. front. 4°. London, W. Faden, 1793. 5154

NOTE.—Frontispiece, east south east view of the tower of Cordouan, from an original, engraved by order of Louis XIII, in 1636.

ETHNOGRAPHICAL.

Istituto geografico de Agostini.

L'Europe ethnique et linguistique. Atlas descriptif en trois cartes spéciales à couleurs avec texte démonstratif. 42, [1] pp., 3 col. fold. maps. 4°. Novare, Institut géographique de Agostini, [1917] 5155

NOTE.—"A. Dardano, réd. et dessinateur."

CONTENTS.

no. 1. Carte ethnique et linguistique de l'Europe.
" 2. " " " " " " centrale.
" 3. " " " " " l'orient européen.

HISTORICAL.

Cram, G. F., & co.

Historical atlas of Europe, past and present. For the library, the home and the school. cover-title, 19 [1] pp., incl. 10 maps, illus. fol. New York, Chicago, G. F. Cram & co. ©1916. 5156

NOTE.—Table of contents on cover.
Portraits of the various european rulers on maps.

Johnston, W., & A. K.

W. & A. K. Johnston's wall atlas of european history. 24 col. maps. fol. Edinburgh, W. & A. K. Johnston, ltd. [1917] 5157

NOTE.—All maps are marked "Natural scale 1: 6,500,000."
These maps, from which the rods have been removed, have been placed in a portfolio.

CONTENTS.

no. 1. Formation of the roman empire.
" 2. Roman empire showing the barbarian inroads.
" 3. Roman empire showing the teutonic settlements. A. D. 476. Insets: Europe in the reign of Theodoric A. D. 500.—Europe at the death of Justinian A. D. 565.
" 4. Europe in the time of Charles the great, A. D. 768–814. Insets: The western empire as divided at Verdun, 843.
" 5. Europe in the time of Otto the great A. D. 962.
" 6. Europe in the time of the third crusade A. D. 1190. Inset: Syria showing the geographical results of the crusades.
" 7. Europe A. D. 1360. Inset: France A. D. 1429.
" 8. Europe at the accession of Charles V, A. D. 1519.
" 9. Europe after the peace of Westphalia A. D. 1648.
" 10. Central Europe in the time of the french revolution and empire 1789–1809.
" 11. Europe A. D. 1814–1863.
" 12. Europe A. D. 1863–1897.
" 13. The growth of Prussia A. D. 1415–1914. Insets: Principality of Neuchatel ceded 1857.—Gold coast acquired 1683-1687; ceded 1720.—Principality of Orange claimed 1702, claim abandoned 1713.
" 14. Formation of the modern German Empire A. D. 1914. Inset: German possessions in Africa and Oceania.
" 15. Europe in the time of Louis XIV. A. D. 1702. Inset: The partitions of Poland.
" 16. Europe under Napoleon A. D. 1810.
" 17. Commercial map of the British Isles in the time of the middle ages. Insets: England shortly after the time of domesday 1100–1200.—The British Isles at the present time showing the chief crops, live stock, industries and fisheries.
" 18. The world illustrating the age of the discoveries.
" 19. Switzerland showing the growth of the confederation. Insets: Switzerland showing the nineteen cantons under the act of mediation 1803–1815.—Switzerland showing the twenty-two cantons 1815.
" 20. The Russian empire. Inset: [Russia]
" 21. The Netherlands in the time of Charles V., A. D. 1543.—The Netherlands 1814–1839.—The Maaslands after the treaties of 1783 and 1785.—Siege of Antwerp, 1584–1585.

Johnston, W., & A. K.—Continued.

no. 22. Italy in A. D. 1859.—The House of Savoy in Italy 1418.—The growth of the House of Savoy in Italy between 1418 and 1748.
" 23. The Balkan Peninsula A. D. 1861–1878.—The Balkan States A. D. 1878–1914.
" 24. Europe A. D. 1914. Insets: Berlin and environs.—Paris and environs.

McKinley publishing co.

McKinley's outline atlases for history classes; containing 25 outline maps to be filled in by pupils with ink or colors. Atlas no. 6. European history. 2d. rev. ed. 2 p. l., 25 maps. obl. 12°. Philadelphia, Pa., McKinley publishing co. [©1915] 5158

Neubauer, F.

Geschichts-atlas insbesondere zu den lehrbüchern der geschichte . . . Für den geschichtsunterricht in quarta bis untersekunda. 13e auf. 12 col. maps. 8°. Halle, buchhandlung des waisenhauses, 1914. 5159

Philip, G., & son, *ltd.*

Philips' wall atlas of modern history. Edited by professor Ramsay Muir . . . and George Philip. 8 col. maps, 33 x 43 each. London, G. Philip & son, ltd.; New York, C. S. Hammond & co. [1916?] 5160

CONTENTS.

no. [1] Roman Britain.—Anglo-Saxon England in the heptarchic period.
" [2] Mediaeval England and Wales with part of Scotland.—England in France.
" [3] England in 1700, before the industrial revolution.—England in 1911, after the industrial revolution.
" [4] Europe about 800 A. D.
" [5] Europe in the age of the crusades.
" [6] Europe at the time of the reformation, 1555.
" [7] North western Europe, 1681. Inset: Waterloo campaign: 1815.
" [8] Europe under Napoleon, 1810.

Robertson, C. G., *and* **Bartholomew, J. G.**

An historical atlas of modern Europe from 1789 to 1914, with an historical explanatory text . . . 24 pp., 36 col. maps. fol. London, New York, Oxford university press, 1915. 5161

ITINERARIES.

Desnos, L. C.

Nouvel itinéraire général comprenant toutes les grandes routes et chemins de communication des provinces de France, des isles britanniques, de l'Espagne, du Portugal, de l'Italie, de la Suisse, de tous les Pays-bas, de l' Allemagne, d'une partie de la Hongrie, de la Pologne, de la Prusse et du Dannemarck &, &, avec les distances en lieuës ou milles d'usage dans ces différens pays. Ouvrage de la plus grande utilité pour le commerçant et le voyageur. Dressé par des auteurs connus qui ont beaucoup voyagé et dont les ouvrages sont aussi répandus qu' estimés . . . 2e. partie. 3 p.l., 23 maps on 76 l. 4°. Paris, Desnos, 1768. 5162

NOTE.—Elaborately illustrated title on two leaves engraved by Le Charpentier in 1766.

At foot of title-page "2e partie." Title-page contains notice of the third edition of Michel and Desnos, *L'Indicateur fidèle, 1766.*

Maps divided into five sections. Section 5, "Isles Britanniques," consisting of two maps, one on eight leaves, is wanting.

The large map *Carte d'Espagne et de Portugal,* on 12 l., and *Carte d'Italie* on 12 l. are by Brion de la Tour.

Other maps are by Michel, Rizzi Zannoni and Brion de la Tour. Several maps engraved by P. Starckman.

LINGUISTIC.

Istituto geografico de Agostini.

L'Europe ethnique et linguistique. Atlas descriptif en trois cartes spéciales à couleurs avec texte démonstratif. 42, [1] pp., 3 col. fold. maps. 4°. Novare, Institut géographique de Agostini, [1917] 5162a

NOTE.—"A. Dardano, réd. et dessinateur."

CONTENTS.

no. 1. Carte ethnique et linguistique de l'Europe.
" 2. " " " " " " centrale.
" 3. " " " " " l'orient européen.

MARITIME.

Bougard, R.

Le petit flambeau de la mer, ov le veritable guide des pilotes côtiers; où il est clairement enseigné la manière de naviger le long de toutes les côtes de France, d' Angleterre, d'Irlande, d'Espagne, de Portugal, d'Italie, de Sicile, de Malte, de Corse & Sardaigne, & autres isles du détroit, & des côtes de Barbarie, depuis le Cap Bon jusqu'au Cap de Verd . . . 4. éd. rev., cor. & augm. . . . 4 p.l., 413 [23] pp. incl. charts, diagrs. 12°. Havre de Grace, G. Gruchet, 1709. 5163

NOTE.—First published 1684.

The imprint is printed on a slip and pasted over the imprint of the edition of 1702, which reads, "Au Havre de Grâce, chez Jacque Hubault, marchand libraire, imprimeur du roy et de la ville, MDCCII. Avec privilège de sa majesté." An "Extrait du privilège du roy," at the end of the volume, is also dated 1702. For bibliographical information, see v. 1, title 2852.

Goos, P.

The lighting colomne or sea-mirrour, containing the sea-coasts of the northern, eastern and western navigation; setting forth in

Goos, P.—Continued.

divers necessarie sea-cards all the ports, rivers, bayes, roads, depths and sands; very curiously placed on its due polus-heighth furnished with the discoveries of the chief countries, and on what course and distance they lay one from another: never heretofore so clearly laid open, and here and there very diligently bettered and augmented, for the use of all sea-men. As also the situation of the northernly countries, as Island, the Strate Davids, the isle of Ian Mayen, Bear-island, Old-Greenland, Spitsbergen and Nova Zembla: adorned with many sea-cards and discoveries. Gathered out of experience and practice of divers pilots and lovers of the famous art of navigation. Whereunto is added a brief Instruction of the art of navigation, together with new tables of the suns' declination, also an Almanack extending to the year 1661. 2 v. in 1. eng. title [46] 103 (*i. e.* 115) 108 pp., 57 (*i. e.* 60) maps, 4 maps in text, diagrs. fol. Amsterdam, P. Goos, 1660-[1661] 5164

NOTE.—The first edition of the *Lichtende colomne, ofte zee-spiegel*, was issued in dutch in 1654 and was followed by two editions 1656–1657, and 1664. See v. 3, title 3984.

The same engraved plate which, with the center blank, precedes the title-page in the dutch edition of 1656–1657, is used in this edition with the english title printed on a slip and pasted over the blank center.

The maps are not all arranged in the right order according to number and index. They are numbered in arabic figures. One map is called for by the index following no. 23, and is numbered in roman letters xxiii. This map is entitled, *Caerte van Archangel*, and is wanting in this copy.

Map no. 9, *De custen van Noorwegen tusschen Neus en Schuitenes*, and no. 18, *De custen van Noorwegh tusschen Dronten en Tromsondt* are wanting. In place of the latter a map entitled, *De custen van Finmarken tusschen Dronten en Sanien*, has been inserted. Map no. 25, *De custen van Denemarcken en Sweden*, is the same map as the corresponding map in the dutch edition of 1656–1657 with a different cartouche and lettering in the title. All other maps in this english edition correspond with those in the dutch edition of 1656–1657, except that they are the second impression of the plate, and that on map no. 2, *Pascaarte van de Noortzee*, the date has been changed from 1656 to 1660, and map no. 24, *Pascaarte vande Oost-zee*, from 1656 to 1661.

Tiele, Bierens de Haan and Muller give a number of editions of the Goos atlases but do not give this english edition.

Waghenaer, L. J.

Spieghel der zeevaerdt, vande nauigatie der westersche zee, innehoudende alle de custē vā Vranckrijck Spaignen eñ t'principaelste deel van Engelandt, in diuersche zee caerte begrepē met den gebruijcke van dien, nu met grooter naersticheijt bij ee vergadert eñ ghepractizeert. Cum priuilegio ad decennium Reg. 1583 matis. et cancellarie Brabantie, 2 v. in 1. 3 p. l., 36 pp. incl. 23 maps; 2 p. l., 1 l., 7 pp., 21 maps. fol. Ghedruct tot

Leyden by Christoffel Plantijn, voor Lucas Janssz Waghenaer van Enckhuysen, anno 1585. 5165

NOTE.—Collation: v. 1, title-page engraved by Joannes a Doetecum headed, Teerste deel vande, recto p. l. [1]—Sonet op den spieghel der zeevaert, signed I. Dovza, on the reverse of p. l. [1]—Aen den doorluchtighen ende hoochgeboren vorst, Wilhelm by der gratien Gods, prince van Oraengien, dated october, 1583, signed Lucas Janss Waghenaer, p. l. [2]—Op den spieghel der zeevaert, recto p. l. [3]—Sommarisch begrijp ende inhout vam d'eerste deel deses caertboeck, verso p. l. [3]—23 maps on 46 l. with description on reverse of first leaf, reverse of second leaf begin blank except map no. 19, which carries text on the reverse of both leaves.—v. 2, Het tweede deel vanden spieghel der zeevaert: inhoudende de gheheele Noordtsche ende Oostersche schipvaert, beghinnende vande hoofden oft voorlant van Enghelant, tot Wyburch ende der Nerue in verscheyden caerten begrepen: Midtsgaders t'gebruyck van dien. Met grooter neersticheyt nu eerst by een vergadert, ende beschreuen door Luycas Janssz, Waghenaer, stierman, woonende inde vermaerde coopstadt van Enckhuysen. Cum priuilegio regiæ maiestatis, & cancellariæ Brabantiæ. Ghedruct tot Leyden, by Christoffel Plantijn, voor Luycas Janssz Waghenaer van Enckhuysen. anno 1585, recto l. [1]—Sommarisch begrijp ende inhout deses tweede deel der caertboeck, Tafel vande caerten des tweeden boeck, verso, l. [1]—Aen de . . . Heeren de staten t'slants van Hollant, ende West Vrieslant, dated, 17th of july 1585, signed Luycas Janss Waghenaer, l. [2]—21 maps on 42 l. with description on the reverse of first leaf, reverse of second leaf being blank except map no. 4, which carries text on the reverse of both leaves.—A l. mounted and numbered 20 is evidently inserted between maps 19 and 20, the number of map no. 20 being changed with pen to 21.—7 pp. at end contain: Alsoo . . . etlycke fransoysche, spaensche ende enghelsche namen van steden . . . —p. [1]—Totten leser, p. [2]— Omme die declinatie recht te ghebruycken, p. [3–5]—Privileges, one dated 20 dec., 1579, the other 7 may, 1580, p. [6]—Aen den boeckbinder, p. 7.

The plates included in the text are perfect, the first, Tamme drayende compasse oft instrumenten metten ghesternte, having intact the movable compass so often missing on plates of a like character in early works.

Nineteen of the 23 maps in v. 1 and all the 21 maps in v. 2 are signed by Joannes a Doetecum as engraver.

In v. 1, 2 maps are dated 158–, 1 map 1580, 1 map 1581, 12 maps 1583, and 7 maps are without date. In v. 2, 1 map is dated 158–, 4 maps 1583, 1 map 1584, 1 map 1585, and 14 maps are without date.

This copy of the atlas carries the Huth book plate.

The atlas is very rare and the few descriptions of its contents vary somewhat.

The entry in the Bibliotheca Hulthemiana agrees with this copy except that map no. 23, which is the first map in v. 2 of the Hulthem copy is the last map in v. 1, of this copy, which is the arrangement according to the index. The only other difference noticeable, from the Hulthem catalogue entry, is that of the inserted page in this copy. The inserted page is headed: *Beschryuinghe van Eyderste, Ditmaer ende zee-custen daer ontrent gheleghen ligghende op haer winden, mylen ende streckinghe.* The first edition consisting of the first volume only was published in 1584. This edition, 2 v. in 1, in 1585, and Tiele sites an example of an issue dated 1585 with the latin title, *Pars prima. Speculum nauticum super navigatione maris Occidentalis etc.* . . . and with 19 pages of text in v. 2.

Waghenaer, L. J.—Continued.

For extensive notes on the latin edition of 1586, see v. 3, title 3980, and on the english edition with additions by sir Anthony Ashley, title. 3981.

The maps are the same as those in the latin edition of 1586, the contents of which is given in v. 3, title 3980, except that the maps in the latin edition have many additional inscriptions; on map no. 21, v. 1, in this edition the title reads, "Beschrÿuinghe der zee custen van Englandt, tusschen Pleÿmouth eñ Porthlandt, met zÿne principale hauenen elex in heure gedaente," and in the latin editions 1586 on the corresponding map, a latin title has been inserted before the dutch, reading: "Angliae maritimæ inter Plemoutham et Portlandiam simul et praecipuorũ portium, vera effigies et delineatio"; map no. 19 of v. 2, in this edition, *Descriptio ditionum littoralium maris Germanici*, differs considerably from the corresponding map in the latin edition; map no. 22 of v. 2 in the latin edition not appearing at all in this copy of the 1585 edition. The descriptive text on the reverse is a translation into latin of the inserted page in this copy of the 1585 edition.

Atlas listed in G. D. Smith's sales catalogue and purchased in 1915.

MILITARY.

Boyer, A.

The draughts of the most remarkable fortified towns of Europe, in 44 copper plates. With a geographical description of the said places. And the history of the sieges they have sustain'd, and the revolutions they have undergon, for above these two hundred years last. To which is prefix'd an introduction to military architecture, or fortification. Containing the origin and progress of that noble art; with the explanation of all the terms belonging to the same. A work very useful to all gentlemen, and officers in the army. 2 p. l., 29 pp., 44 pl. sm. 4°. London, for I. Cleave & J. Hartley, 1701. 5166

CONTENTS.

no. 1. A general draught of all the parts of a regular fortification.
" 2. Oostend.
" 3. Newport with the haven and country about it.
" 4. Oudenarde.
" 5. Mastrick.
" 6. Tournai.
" 7. Berg St. Winox or Winoxberg.
" 8. An exact draught of Dunkirke as it is now fortified by the french king.
" 9. Liège.
" 10. Dinant.
" 11. Aeth.
" 12. Mons.
" 13. Namur.
" 14. Charleroy.
" 15. Luxemburgh.
" 16. Cambray.
" 17. Calais.
" 18. Particular chart of the road and adjacent coasts of St. Malo as also of the mouth of the river Dinan.

no. 19. S^{t}. Malo.
" 20. The marquisate and government of Bell-Isle divided into its four parishes of the Palace, Bangor, Lomaria and Sauzon.
" 21. A profil of the town & palace of Bell Isle.
" 22. A chart of ye road and adjacent coasts of Brest.
" 23. Brest.
" 24. The island city & port of Cadis.
" 25. Cologne.
" 26. Bonne.
" 27. Rheinberk.
" 28. Trier.
" 29. Coblentz.
" 30. Mayence.
" 31. Philisbourg.
" 32. Manheim.
" 33. Strasburg.
" 34. Fort Louis on the Rheine.
" 35. Landaw.
" 36. Huningen.
" 37. Brisach.
" 38. Freiburgh.
" 39. Basel.
" 40. Mont Royal.
" 41. Sarlouis.
" 42. Pignerol.
" 43. Coni in Piedmont.
" 44. Casel.

La Feuille, P. de.

The millitary [!] tablettes, containing a choice of mapps, for the use of officers and travellers: containing also the gennerall [!] mapps of the world, and with the particular ones of the places where the theatre of the warr is at present in Europe. With the plans of the fortresses the most exposed in the present revolutions. Enriched with the millitary [!] architecture of a new and abriged [!] methode very easy to learn geography, and to attain inso [!] a speedy knowledge of the globes. 4 p. l., 29 maps, 1 pl. sm. 4°. Amsterdam, D. de La Feuille, 1707. 5167

Note.—This atlas was taken from the *Atlas portatif ou le nouveau théâtre de la guerre en Europe*, published by Daniel de La Feuille in 1706.
Editions were brought out in 1711 and 1732 in dutch, in 1708 in french, and in 1717 in both french and dutch titles and text. For editions of 1708, 1717, 1732, and the Atlas portatif of 1706, see Index.
The same maps are used in all editions.
Many of the maps are ornamented with coats of arms or very small engravings of cities and towns.
The following maps relate to America:
no. [1] Mapemonde planisphère.
" [6] L'Amérique méridionale.
" [7] L'Amérique septentrionale.

La Feuille, P. de.—Continued.

Les tablettes guerrières, où cartes choisies pour la commodité des officiers et des voyageurs, contenant toutes les cartes générales du monde, avec les particulières des lieux où le théâtre de la guerre se fait sentir en Europe. Avec les plans des fortresses les plus exposées aux revolutions présentes. Enrichis de l'architecture militaire, & d'une nouvelle methode abrégée pour aprendre facilement la géographie, & pour avoir une prompte connoissance des globes. Augmenté dans cette edition des 102 articles des ordonnances militaires de L. H. P. pour maintenir le bon ordre dans l'armée. 16 pp., 32 maps, 1 pl. 12°. Amsterdam, D. de la Feuille, 1708. 5168

NOTE.—The statement in the title that this edition is augmented shows that an earlier edition had appeared. The Library of Congress has two later editions, one published in 1717 and the other in 1732. Both of these differ slightly and contain more maps. The only map in this edition which does not occur in the others is map no. [25] "La Livonie." It does not appear in the 1732 edition.

PHYSICAL.

Friederichsen, M.

Methodischer atlas zur länderkunde von Europa, entworfen, bearbeitet und herausgegeben . . . gezeichnet von K. Seick . . . lief. 1-2. fol. Hannover & Liepzig, Hahns, 1914-1915. 5169

CONTENTS.

Pt. 1. Ost-Europa und die Ostseeländer. 6 tafeln zu je 8 kärtchen.
" 2. Die Nordseeländer und Frankreich.

SCHOOL.

Agostini, G. de.

Atlante geografico muto fisico politico a colori ed albo di esercitazioni cartografiche in due fascicoli. Terza edizione: dal XXX al XLV migliaio. Fascicolo primo, secondo i programmi governativi per la 1ª e 2ª complementare, normale 1ª, 2ª, 4ª e 5ª ginnasiale, 1ª e 2ª tecnica e il 1° anno d' Istituto tecnico o nautico . . . 1 p. l., [35] pp. incl. 17 col. maps. obl. 8°. Novara, Istituto geografico de Agostini, [1914] 5170

SEAS.

ÆGEAN.

Bartolommeo da li sonetti.

[Isolario; ossia, Carte del mare Egeo; in versi. Venezia, Guglielmo detto Anima mia, 1485?] 5170a

Fo. 1a. Al Diuo Cinquecento cinque e diece/Tre cinq, a do Mil nulla tre é do vn cēto/nulla./questa opra dar piu cha altri lecce.
Fo. 3a, 1.17 Per aprobar questa opereta fata/per me bartolomeo da li sonetti.
Fo. 3b. S. per linsula di cerigo.

Fo. 55b S. per linsula di cipro.
Fo. 56 [Map of Cyprus; verso blank]
Without title page, place, date, printer's name, pagination, signatures, or catchwords. 56 leaves; in 12, 8, 6, 10, 6, 8 & 6 verso of last leaf blank; 14–42 lines to the page; paper measures 32.2 x 17 cm. Gothic type; 49 illustrated maps, engr. on wood. Original Venetian (?) binding; wood covered with stamped sheep, clasps on sides, top and bottom; mended. From the Libri collection: "Ex Bibliotheca Sobolewskiana."

MEDITERRANEAN SEA.

Reproductions.

Freducci, C. di O.

Portolan atlas, Conte de Ottomaño Freducci, MCCCCCXXX7:—facsimile, with introduction by Edward Luther Stevenson. 4 p. l., facsim. 5 col. charts. fol. New York, 1915. 5171

NOTE.—Publication of the Hispanic society of America, no. 95.
In portfolio.
"A numbered edition of one hundred copies." This copy is no. 24.

General.

Roux, J.

Recueil des principaux plans des ports, et rades de la mer Mediterranée, estraits, de ma carte en douze feüilles . . . 1 p. l., 2 pp., 121 (*i. e.* 122) maps. obl. 16°. Marseille, 1764. 5172

NOTE.—A copy of a later edition of this atlas published at Genoa in 1779 is also in the Library of Congress. See v. 1, title 196.
Engraved title inscribed, "Laurent inv. et sculp."
Map no. 35, Barbarie, is duplicated.
Roux' *Carte de la mer Méditerranée*, mentioned in the title, was published in 1764.

TRAVELS.

Taylor, T.

The gentlemans pocket companion, for travelling into foreign parts: being a most easy, plain and particular description of the roads from London to all the capital cities in Europe. With an account of the distances of leagues or miles from place to place, all reduced to the english standard. Illustrated with maps curiously engraven on copper plates. With three dialogues in six european languages. The first being to ask the way, with other familiar communications. The second is common talke in an inn. The third other necessary conversation. Printed and sold by Tho: Taylor at the Golden Lyon overagainst Serjeants inn in Fleetstreet, London, 1722. Where are to be had all sorts of the best maps, and french, dutch and italian prints. 1 p. l., 19, [14] l., 9 col. maps. 16°. London, 1722. 5173

NOTE.—Separate title-page for language guide reads: *Three dialogues in six european languages, viz. english, french, italian, german, spanish, and flemish.*

Taylor, T.—Continued.

The first being to ask the way, with other familiar discourse. The second being common talk in an inn. The third, other necessary conversation. London, printed for Thomas Taylor, at the Golden-Lyon in Fleet street. 1723.

The British Museum has note: "The date on the title page of pt. 1 has been altered in ms. to 1742."

CONTENTS.

no. [1] Europe in general.
" [2] England.
" [3] France.
" [4] Spain and Portugal.
" [5] Italy.
" [6] Flanders & Holland.
" [7] Germany.
" [8] Turky.
" [9] Denmarck & part of Sweden.

WARS.

Husson, P.

Variæ tabulæ geographicæ in quibus loca in orbe bello flagrantia conspiciuntur ut in Flandriâ, Brabantiâ, Leodiensi Tractu, Germaniâ, Hungariâ, Galliâ, Hispaniâ, Portugalia, Italia, Polonia, Moscovia, America, &c. . . .—Diverses cartes de géographie, où l'on peut voir le theatre de la guerre dans tout le monde. Comme dans les païs de Flandres, de Brabant, de Liége, d'Allemagnè, de Hongrie, de France, d'Espagne, de Portugal, d'Italie, de Pologne, de Moscovie, en Amérique, &c. . . .—Geographise land-kaarten, waar in kan nagesien worden de theater van den oorlog in de wereld, als in de landen van Vlaanderen, Brabant, Luykerlant, Duytslant, Hongarie, Vrankryk, Spangie, Portugaal, Italien, Poolen, Moscovien, West Indien, &c. . . . 1 p. l., 45 col. maps, 4 col. pl. fol. Gravenhage, P. Husson, [1709?] 5174

NOTE.—Gregorii in his, *Curieuse gedancken von den vornehmsten und accuratesten alt- und neuen land-charten*, speaks of Husson as an accountant at Amsterdam and commends his maps as containing many new names not noted by others.

A similar title-page was used by Visscher in his atlases issued 1700?–1709?

CONTENTS.

no. [1] Mappe-monde. Par m. de L'isle.
" [2] L'Europe. Par H. Iaillet.
" [3] L'Asie. Par G. de L'isle.
" [4] L'Africa. Par G. de l'Isle.
" [5] L'Amérique Septentrionale. Par G. de L'isle.
" [6] L'Amérique Méridionale. Par G. de L'isle.
" [7] L'Europe représentée par la géographie naturelle et historique et par le blazon.
" [8] Corona Portugalliæ et Algarbiæ. á Petro Schenck. 1703.
" [9] Lisbona.
" [10] Carte générale des royaumes d'Espagne & de Portugal. 1705.
" [11] Aftekening van Gibraltar.—Plan de la ville de Gibraltar.

no. [12] Principauté de Catalogne. Par G. Valck.
" [13] L'Italie. Par G. de l'Isle.
" [14] Continentis Italiæ pars media penes Petrum Schenk. 1703.
" [15] Les estats de Savoye, Piémont, et le comté Nice. Par le s^{r}. Sanson.
" [16] Plan de la ville et citadelle de Turin. Assiegées par l'armée de France. le 3e juin 1706.
" [17] Carte nouvelle du royaume de France. 1708.
" [18] Delphinatus præfectura. Per Gerardum Valk.
" [19] Plan de la ville et de la rade de Toulon. Assiégée par l'armée des alliés; le—août. 1707. Inset: Toulon.
" [20] Les Isles britanniques. Par G. De l'Isle.
" [21] Carte générale des provinces vnies des Pais-Bas. Inset: [Limbourg]
" [22] Tableau des XVII provinces des Pays-Bas. 1706.
" [23–28] Flandriæ comitatus.
" [29] Bruxellensis tetrarchia.
" [30] Plan du champ de bataille, près d' Oudenaerde l' 11 juillet 1708.—Plaen van de bataille, by Oudenaerde, den 11 july 1708.
" [31] Plan de la ville de Menin avec les attacques; de la manière comme elle a été faite par les troupes des alliez.
" [32] Plan du siège de Lille.
" [33] Plan de l'action entre le corps des troupes alliéz au près de Wÿnendale, le 28 sept. 1708.
" [34] Plan du siège et des attaques de la ville et cittadelle de Gand assiégée par l'armée des alliez le 25 décembre 1708. 1709.
" [35] Plan de la ville et citadelle de Tournay.
" [36] Tetrarchia Lovaniensis. M. van Medtman. 1706.—Carte contenant le duché de Limbourg. Par M. van Medtman.
" [37] Le royaume de Danemark. Par H. Iaillot.
" [38] Regionum Coloniense edita per Nicolaum Visscher.
" [39] Archiepiscopatus ac electoratus Trevirensis ditio. Per Nicolaum Visscher.
" [40] Extractissima tabula sedisbelli Palatinatus ad Rhenum per Nic. Visscher.
" [41] Totius Alsatiæ novissima tabula. Per Nicolaum Visscher.
" [42] S. R. I. Sueviae circulus atq[ue] ducatus. Per Nicolaum Visscher.
" [43] La battaille de Hoechstedt. Remporté par le hauté [!] alliez sur les Francois et Bavarois le 13 aout 1704.
" [44] Bavariæ circulus atq[ue] electoratus. Per Nicolaum Visscher.
" [45] Regnum Hungariæ. Per Nicolaum Visscher.
" [46] Sveciæ, Norwegiæ et Daniæ nova tabula.
" [47] Republicae et status generalis Poloniæ, nova tabula. Per F. de Witt.
" [48] Novissima Russiae tabula. Authore Isaaco Massa.

GENERAL.

1589

Mercator, G.

Italiae, Sclavoniæ, et Græciæ tabule geographice. Per Gerardum Mercatorum illustrissimi ducis Julie, Clinie &c. cosmographum. Duysburgi edita. Cum gratia & privilegio. 2 p. l., 11 pp. 22 maps, port. fol. [Duisburg, 1589] 5175

NOTE.—Collation: engraved title, verso blank, p. l. [1]—Dedication to Ferdinand de Medici, dated "13 martij anno 1589," recto p. l. [2]—Candido lectori, dated "13 martij anno 1589," verso p. l. [2]—portrait, Gerardi Mercatoris Rvpelmvndani effigiem annordvorvm et sex—Aginta, svi ipsvm stvdii cavsa depingi cvrabat Franc. [Hogenberg] 1574. 22 maps on 44 l. with text on first reverse, second reverse, blank; Index locorvm tabvlæ generalis Italiae, pp. [1-7]—Index locorvm in tabvlam generalem Graeciae, pp. [7-11]—Index tabvlarvm Italiae et Graeciae, p. [11]

The first part of Mercator's atlas entitled, *Galliae tabulae geographicae*, containing also *Belgii Inferioris geographicae tabulae*, and *Germaniae tabula geographicae*, was published in 1585 and the second part in 1589.

Raemdonck gives the date of the publication of the second part as 1590 and that date was given in the preceding volumes for entries under Mercator. Raemdonck took the date from *Vita Gerardi Mercatoris à Gualtero Ghymmio conscripta*, reading, *Hisce peractis, Italiæ generalem ac particulares tabulas æri insculpere aggressus est, prosperoque successu, anno nonagesimo, mense Aprili, easdem absolvit, et Potentissimo ac Serenissimo Ferdinando Medici, Duci Etruriæ dedicavit.* Anno nonagesimo, the ninetieth year, would however be 1589. A later publication, Ortroy's *Bibliographie sommaire de l' oeuvre mercatorienne*, gives the date as 1590, but Denuce's *Oud-Nederlandsche kaartmakers in betrekking met Plantijn*, gives 1589 and as his authority, an entry in the Plantin Archives which reads as follows, Plant. Arch. LXVI (Journal 1589) f° 149ᵛ. Adi 4° novembre: d° Abrahamo Ortelio: 1 Mercatoris Italia . . . fl. 8.

1592

Quad, M.

Evropae totivs orbis terrarvm partis praestantissimæ vniversalis et particvlaris descriptio. Aere potes paruo regiones visere multas quas liber hic tenuis, spectator candide, monstrat. 2 p. l. [222] pp. incl. 54 double maps. fol. Coloniae, ex officina typographica J. Bussemechers, 1592. 5176

1622

Blaeu, W. J.

The light of navigation wherein are declared and lively pourtrayed all the coasts and havens of the west, north and east seas. Collected partly out of the books of the principall authors which have written of navigation . . . partly also out of many other expert seafaring mens writings & verbal declarations . . . divided into tvvo bookes. Hereunto are added (beside an institution in the art of navigation) new tables of the declination of the sunne . . .

by William Iohnson. 3 pts. in 1 vol. obl. 4°. Amsterdam, W. Iohnson, 1622. 5177

NOTE.—Collation: eng. title, [2]–162 [*i. e.* 158] pp. 130, [1] pp. incl. 41 maps. Signatures: A–D^4, E–G^6, H^2, I^6, K^2, L^4, M–Q^2, R^8, S^2, T^4, V^2, X^8, Aa^1, Bb^4 Cc^6, Dd–Ff^2, Gg^6, Hh^2, Ii^2, Kk^4, Ll^2, Mm^6, Nn–Pp^2, Qq^4, Rr^2, Ss^6, (1 extra leaf) Tt^2, Vv^2, Xx^2.

The title page has view of Amsterdam in lower margin; reverse, blank. Title is pasted over dutch title bearing date of 1620. On second l. is an engraving representing a lesson in hydrography. On the verso: "To the reader." A 3 recto —E3 verso: A briff and short introdvction for the vnderstanding of the celestial sphere . . . ; E4 recto—[X8] verso: The first book of the light of navigation, wherein are described and drawn al the coasts and hauens of the west seas: as of Holland, Sealand, Flanders, France, Spain, and Barbarie . . . with the south and west coasts of Ireland and England . . . 1622; Aa [1] recto—[xx] verso: the second book of the light of navigation, wherein are described all the coasts hauens and ilands of the north and east seas: as of Freesland, Iutland, Denmarke, Pomerland, Prussia, Leefland, Sweathland, Norvvaie, Lapland and Moscovia, as also, all the north and east coasts of Scotland and England . . . 1622; [xx2] recto: A table of the light of navigation, contayning the arguments of every chapter; verso: blank.

According to P. Q. Tiele the first edition in dutch was published in 1608, and contains the same view of Amsterdam and same number of maps and plates. (*cf.* his article entitled: *De eerste uitgave van Blaeu's licht der zeevaert,* in *Bibliographische adversaria, v. 5. 1883–6. pp. 293–5*)

Maps have french and dutch titles, contained in ornamented cartouches. Although similar in construction to the maps in the L. C. copy of 1622, those of this edition have additional illustrations; the cartouches also have been changed.

On map no. 15 is a plan of "Angra."

Not mentioned in P. A. Tiele's *Nederlandsche bibliographie, 1884,* and no copy is listed as being in the British Museum or in the Bibliothèque nationale.

Inserted in the text are numerous views and aspects of the coasts.

The name William Iohnson appearing on the title-page is an english translation of the christian names of Blaeu, which are Willem Janszoon in dutch. On the french copy of this atlas, in the Library of Congress, the names are given as "Gvilliavme Ianszoon. According to P. J. H. Baudet, in his *Leven en werken van Willem Janz. Blaeu, 1871.* p. 118: "Blaeu signed very often "Willem Jansz." or Guil. Janssonius." The address given in the imprint of this atlas "upon the water . . . at the Signe of the golden sundyall," corresponds to the address of other works of Blaeu.

17—

Cleynhens, B,

Accuraat geographisch kaart-boekje of zak-atlas van het keyzerryk en geheel Duytsland, de oostenrykse Nederlanden, nevens een groot gedeelte van Vrankryk, het Canaal, de hoek van Engeland, en verder aangrenzende landschappen; alwaar den tegenwoordigen oorlog genvoerd word. Tot nut en gemak geschikt voor alle heeren officieren, reyzigers en andre liefhebbers der

Cleynhens, B.—Continued.

geographie, om in die zak gedragen te worden . . . 40, 23 pp., 51 l., incl. 25 maps. 16°. Te Haerlem, B. Cleynhens [17—]. 5178

NOTE.—Latest historical date in atlas, 1689.

1715

English, The, pilot.

Part I. Describing the sea coasts, capes, head-lands, bays, roads, harbours, rivers, and ports, together with the soundings, sands, rocks and dangers in the southern navigation upon the coasts of England, Scotland, Ireland, Holland, Flanders, Spain, Portugal, to the straights-mouth, with the coasts of Barbary, and off to the Canary, Madera, Cape de Verd, and Western islands. Shewing the courses and distances from one place to another. The setting of the tides and currents. The ebbing and flowing of the sea, &c. 1 p. l., 37 [1] 2, 4, 43–56, 65–88 pp., 31 maps, 1 map in text, illus. fol. London, for R. & W. Mount & T. Page, 1715. 5179

NOTE.—Pagination irregular.

For the 1718 edition of Part I of the English pilot, see v. 1, title 2837, and for the 1747 edition v. 3, title 3496.

The 12 unnumbered pages of illustrations show the coast line of the various countries, and are interspersed through the text.

A number of the maps show that John Seller's name has been erased from the title.

CONTENTS.

no. [1] A chart of the North sea.

" [2] A draught of the sands, shoals, buoys, beacons, & sea marks upon the coast of England from ye South Foreland to Orford Ness. F. Lamb sculp. Insets: The river of Thames.—The Gore.

" [3] A chart of part of North sea from ye South Foreland to Burnham Flatts, and from Callis to Schelling isle. F. Lamb sculp.

" [4] A draught of the new chanel of Wintertonness.

" [5] A chart for the Newcastle trade. Describeing the sea coasts of England from the South Foreland to Newcastle. Insets: A chart of Yarmouth sands.—The river Tyne and coast from Sunderland to Blythe.—Harwich and Hanford Water.

" [6] A description of the coast of Flanders from the island Walcheren to Calice. Ia. Clerk sculp.

" [7] A chart of the sea coast of Zealand.

" [8] The coast of Holland from the Maes to the Texel.

" [9] A new and correct draught of the channel between England and France. Engraved by C. Price. 1712. Insets: Portsmouth harbour.—The river of Thames from London to the Downes.

" [10] A new chart of England, Scotland and Ireland.

" [11] A new chart of the sea coast of Scotland with the islands thereof.

" [12] A chart of the coasts of Ireland and part of England.

" [13] [The county of Waterford.—Wexford county.—Wicklow county]

" [14] A chart of the sea coasts of Ireland from Dublin to London-Derry. Insets: Lough Foyle.

no. [15] A chart of the northwest coast of Ireland from Lough Swilly to Slyne Head.
" [16] A chart of the bay of Galloway and river Shannon.
" [17] The south west coast of Ireland from Dungarvan to the river Shannon.
" [18] The harbour of Corke.
" [19] The sea coast of France from Ushent to Olone. Insets: Brest harbour.—The river Loire from Saille to Nantes.
" [20] The sea coasts of France from Olone to Cape Machiacaca in Biscay.
" [21] A chart of the sea coasts Biscay and Gallicia between Cape Machiacaca and Cape de Pinas and from Cape de Pinas to Cape de Finisterre.
" [22] A sea chart of part of the coasts of Gallisia and Portugall from Cape de Finisterre to the Burlings and from the Burlings to Cape de S^t^. Vincent.
" [23] The coasts of Portugall and part of Spain from Cape Finisterre to Gibralter. Inset: The harbours of Lisbon and Setual.
" [24] A chart of the sea coasts of Algrave and Andalusia between Cape S^t^. Vincent and the Strait of Gibralter and C. Spartel.
" [25] A chart of the sea coast from England to the streights. H. Moll f. Inset: The harbour of Cadiz.
" [26] The city and harbour of Cadiz by an officer of the fleet 1695, with additions of the present fortifications &c. I. Harris sculp. Inset: A prospect of Cadiz.
" [27] A chart of the straits of Gibralter. Joel Gascoyne sculp.
" [28] A chart of the sea coastes of Barbary from the straits mouth to Cape de Verd.
" [29] The Western isles.
" [30] A chart of the Canarie & Madera islands.
" [31] A chart of the isles off Cape Verd.

1727?

Moll, H.

A set of thirty-two new and correct maps of the principal parts of Europe, &c., with the great or post-roads and principal cross-roads, done in the year 1725, 1726 and 1727. All, except four, viz., England, Scotland, Ireland, and a general map of Turky in Europe; which has been done and printed before . . . 2 p. l., 32 maps. 8°. [London, 1727?] 5180

NOTE.—For note and list of maps of America, see entry under "World." v. 4, title 4281.

1760?

[A collection of maps of various parts of Europe] 83 maps. 12°. n. p. [1760?] 5181

NOTE.—Title-page wanting.
Most of the maps give the form of the name of the country in several languages.
Contains an inserted view entitled, *Vuë des côtes de la Lothiane du côté de Stony.*

CONTENTS.

no. 1. Evropa.
" 2. Germania, Lamagna, Deutschlanndt, Almagne.
" 3. Belgivm, il Paese Basso, Niderlandt, le Pays Bas.
" 4. Gallia, Franza, Franckreich, France.
" 5. Hispania, Spagna, Spanien, Espagne.

[A collection of maps . . . of Europe]—Continued.

no. 6. Italia, Italien, Italie.
" 7. Bohemia, Beheym, Boheme.
" 8. Hvngaria, Ungaria, Hungeren, Hongrie.
" 9. Polonia, Polen, Polongne.
" 10. Dania, Danemarcha, Dennemarct, Danemarche.
" 11. Svedia, Schueden, Suède.
" 12. Scotia, Schotlandt, Escosse.
" 13. Anglia, Ingilaterra, Engellandt, Angleterre.
" 14. Helvetia, Svissa, Schweitz, Svisse.
" 15. Franconia, Franckenlandtt, Franconie.
" 16. Palatinatvs Svperior, Bavariae.
" 17. Clivia, Cleue, Cleues.
" 18. Ivlia, Julich, Iulliers.
" 19. Westphalia, Westphalen, Westphalie.
" 20. Comtatvs Waldeckensis, de grafschaft Waldeck, la conté de Waldeck.
" 21. Hassia, Hessen, Hesse.
" 22. Holsatia, Holstein, Holsatie.
" 23. Mansfeldia, Mansfeltt, Mansfelt.
" 24. Thvringia, Thvrungen, Thuringie.
" 25. Misnia, Meidden, Misne.
" 26. Silesia, Schlesien, Silesie.
" 27. Moravia, Mehern, Moraine.
" 28. Sweviae circulus, Schwabische Kraiss, Swabe.
" 29. Du Wirtenberg, herz Wirtmberg, la duché de Wirtemberg.
" 30. Bavaria, Baiern, Bauiere.
" 31. Episcopatvs Salczbvrgensis.
" 32. Tyrol.
" 33. Bistbumss Luttch, Leuesche, de Liege.
" 34. Trier.
" 35. Bvrgvndia, Burgund, Borgongne.
" 36. Carinthia, Karntn, Carinthie.
" 37. Stiria, Steyrmarch, Stiremarche.
" 38. Brabantiæ, Dvcatvs Brabant.
" 39. Geldriae dvcatvs, Gelleren hertzogthumb.
" 40. Lvtzenbyrgensis dvcatvs, Lutzenburg hertzogthumb.
" 41. Limbvrgensis dvcatvs et comitatvs Valkenbvrgensis et Dalememsis.
" 42. Flandria, Fiandra, Flaenderen, Flandren.
" 43. Nobilis comitatvs Hannoniæ, Henegau, Hainaultt.
" 44. Artesia.
" 45. Namvrcvm, Namur.
" 46. Hollandiæ comitatvs, Hollant.
" 47. Zelandia.
" 48. Zutphaniae comitatvs.
" 49. Vltraiectensis episcopatvs.
" 50. Transisvlana ditio.
" 51. Groningense territorivm.
" 52. Frisia occidētalis.
" 53. Frisia orientalis.
" 54. Lvsatiae marchionatvs.
" 55. Prvssia, Preussen, Prusse.
" 56. Basilense territorivm.
" 57. Vero mandvorvm comitatvs, le comté de Vermandois.
" 58. Andegavensis dvcatvs, Aññou herzogthumb.

no. 59. Tractvs Danvby pars.
" 60. Avstriæarchi dvcatvs.
" 61. Illyricvm.
" 62. Livonia, Lieflandt, Liuoniae.
" 63. Cambria, Cambry, Wales.
" 64. Cyprvs, Cipro Livren.
" 65. Grecia, Griechnlandt, Grece.
" 66. Hibernia, Irlandt, Irlande.
" 67. Regnvm Neapolitanvm.
" 68. Forvmlvly, Friuli.
" 69. Histria, Isterreich, Istrie.
" 70. Zaræ et Sebenici descripto.
" 71. Vrbis Romane territorivm.
" 72. Thvscia.
" 73. Senensisditio.
" 74. Marchia Anconitana olim Picenvm.
" 75. Territorivm Patavinvm.
" 76. Veronæ vrbis territorivm.
" 77. Agri Cremonensis typvs.
" 78. Parmensis Placentinio, dvcatvs descriptio.
" 79. Mediolanensis dvcatvs.
" 80. Pedemontanvs principatvs.
" 81. Pvglia, Terra di Otranto.
" 82. Picardia, Picardie.
" 83. Ponthiev comitatvs.

1912

Philip, G., & son, ***ltd.***

Philips' comparative wall atlas of Europe. Edited by J. F. Unstead . . . & E. G. R. Taylor . . . 8 col. maps. fol. London, G. Philip & son [1912] 5182

1915

Rand, McNally & co.

On the battle lines. cover-title, 9 maps. 12°. Chicago, New York, Rand, McNally & co. [1915] 5183

1916

Larousse, Librairie.

Atlas de poche du théâtre de la guerre . . . [2. éd.] 2 p. l., 59 pp., incl. 56 maps. 12°. Paris, Larousse [1916] 5184

BALKAN PENINSULA.

1881

Kiepert, H., ***i. e.*** **J. S. H.**

Cartes des nouvelles frontières entre la Serbie, la Roumanie, la Bulgarie, la Roumélie orientale et les provinces immédiates de la Turquie, selon des décisions du congrès de Berlin, juillet 1878. Réduction des levés originaux, exécutés en 1879 par la Commission européenne de délimitation et imprimés comme manuscrit en photozincographie, échelle de 1:42,000 . . . cover-title, 4 fold. maps. sm. fol. Berlin, D. Reimer, 1881. 5185

AUSTRIA-HUNGARY.

HISTORICAL.

K. Akademie der wissenschaften, *Vienna.*

Historischer atlas österreichen Alpenländer . . . 1. Abteilung: Die landgerichtskarte bearbeitet unter leitung von weil. Edward Richter. 1. Lieferung: Salzburg, von Edward Richter, Oberösterreich, von Julius Strnadt, Steiermark, von Anton Mell und Hans Pirchegger. cover-title, 12 col. maps. obl. fol. Wien, A. Holzhausen, 1906. 5186

NOTE.—Corrected from title 2858[a]. Accompanied by text entitled: *Erläuterungen zum historischen atlas der österreichen Alpenländer . . . 3 pts. [1906]-1910.*

PROVINCES.

DALMATIA.

Dainelli, G.

La Dalmazia, cenni geografici e statistici illustrati da 32 figure fuori testo con un atlante di 22 tavole a colori comprendenti 60 carte. 2 v.; 8° & fol. Novara, Istituto geografico de Agostini, 1918. 5186a

NOTE.—Contains maps showing the climate, geology, vegetation, forestry, agriculture, ethnology, population, history, etc. of the country.

Contains plans of the following cities:

Tav. XIV: Pianta della cittá di Zara.—Pianta della cittá di Ragusa—Pianta della cittá di Spalato.

BELGIUM.

CITIES.

Deventer, J. R., *known as* **J. de.**

Atlas des villes de la Belgique au XVIe siècle. Cent plans du géographe Jacques de Deventer executés sur les ordres de Charles-quint et de Philippe II reproduits en fac-similé chromographique par l'Institut de géographie, à Bruxelles. Text par m. m. Alvin . . . Bormans . . . sous la direction de Ch. Ruelens. pt. 1–20. fol. Bruxelles, institut national de géographie, [1884–1914] 5187

NOTE.—The first 15 pts. published 1884–1895. No more published until 1908. For extended note see v. 1, title 2870.

"Publication commencée par Ch. Ruelens . . . et continuée sous la direction de Ém. Ouverleaux . . . [et] J. van den Gheyn."

STATISTICAL.

Belgium. *Office du travail.*

Atlas statistique du recensement général des industries et des métiers (31 octobre 1896) 56 pp., 23 maps. fol. Bruxelles, 1903. 5188

BRITISH ISLES.

CONTOUR-RELIEF.

McDougall's educational co. *ltd.*

McDougall's contour atlas of the British Isles . . . cover-title, 16 pp. incl. 19 col. maps. 4°. London, Edinburgh, McDougall's educational co. *ltd.* [1919?] 5189

GEOLOGICAL.

Woodward, H. B.

Stanford's geological atlas of Great Britain and Ireland with plates of characteristic fossils preceded by descriptions of the geological structure of Great Britain and Ireland and their counties; of the channel islands; and of the features observable along the principal lines of railway . . . 3d ed. xii, 214 pp., front., 36 col. maps, 33 pl. 12°. London, E. Stanford, 1914. 5190

Photographic supplement to Stanford's geological atlas of Great Britain and Ireland. Arranged and edited by Horace B. Woodward . . . with the co-operation of miss Hilda Sharpe. 3 p. l., 113 pp. incl. illus. 12°. London, E. Stanford, 1913. 5191

HISTORICAL.

Johnston, A. K.

The half-crown atlas of british history. 1 p., 24 pp. 31 (*i. e.* 29) col. maps. 12°. Edinburgh & London, W. & A. K. Johnston [1871] 5192

NOTE.—Table of contents on title-page.
Date attached to prefatory note, at end of book.

POSSESSIONS.

ST. HELENA.

Bellasis, G. H.

Views of Saint Helena . . . 16 l., incl. 6 col. plates. obl. fol. London, J. Tyler, 1815. 5193

NOTE.—Each plate followed by a descriptive text.

CYPRUS ISLAND.

Kitchener, H. H.

A trigonometrical survey of the island of Cyprus. Executed & published by command of h. e. major general sir R. Biddulph, high commissioner . . . 1882. Scale of one inch to one statute mile=1:63,360. 2 p. l., 15 (*i. e.* 16) col. maps. fol. London, E. Stanford, 1885. 5194

NOTE.—In lower left-hand corner of title-page: Sergeant A. Sutherland R. E. in charge of survey party.
Index map given first.

114882°—19——29

VIEWS.

Finden, W.

The ports, harbours, watering-places, and coast scenery of Great Britain. Illustrated by views taken on the spot, by W. H. Bartlett; with descriptions by William Beattie. 2 v. eng. title, 2 p. l., [162] pp. 50 views, front.; engr. title, 2 pl., 190 pp., 72 views, front. sm 4°. London, G. Virtue, 1842. 5195

NOTE.—Added t.-p., engr.: v. 1. *Finden's views of the ports, harbours & watering places of Great Britain, continued by W. H. Bartlett;* v. 2. *Finden's ports, harbours and watering places.*

A revised ed., much enlarged, of William and Edward Finden's *Views of ports and harbours . . . on the english coast (London, 1838)* the letter-press of which was written by W. A. Chatto.

CONTENTS.

v. 1, no. front. General view of London. (From the Southwark side)
" " [1] Tynemouth castle.
" " [2] Cullercoats.
" " [3] Entrance to Shields harbour.
" " [4] Berwick bridge.
" " [5] Berwick. From the south east.
" " [6] Newcastle-upon-Tyne.
" " [7] Bamborough. From the south east.
" " [8] " . From the south west.
" " [9] Holy island castle.
" " [10] Castle of Holy island.
" " [11] Dunstanborough castle. From the eastward.
" [12] "
" " [13] Blyth.
" " [14] Sunderland. The light house on the south pier.
" " [15] " . The bridge from the westward.
" " [16] Robin Hood's bay.
" " [17] Whitby.
" " [18] " . From the north west.
" " [19] Scarborough.
" " [20] Flamborough head.
" " [21] Burlington quay.
" " [22] Hull.
" " [23] Hartlepool.
" " [24] Entrance to Portsmouth harbour.
" " [25] Rigging hulk and frigate, Portsmouth.
" " [26] Men of war at Spithead.
" " [27] View from the saluting platform, Portsmouth.
" " [28] Gosport, flag ship saluting.
" " [29] Tintagel castle.
" " [30] Brixham.
" " [31] View from the beach at Sidmouth.
" " [32] Exmouth.
" " [33] Budleigh Salerton.
" " [34] Ramsgate.
" " [35] Chatham.
" " [36] Hastings.
" " [37] "

v. 1, no. [38] Folkston. Kent.
" " [39] Weymouth.
" " [40] Caves at Ladram bay.
" " [41] Plymouth. Devon.
" " [42] Mount edgecumbe. Devon.
" " [43] Cowes. Hampshire.
" " [44] Southampton. Hants.
" " [45] Brighton. Sussex.
" " [46] Dover. Kent.
" " [47] " . From the Ramsgate road.
" " [48] Harwich. Essex.
" " [49] Yarmouth. Norfolk.
" " [50] Cromer.
v. 2, front. Mary-port pier.
" " [1] Entrance to the port of Berwick.
" " [2] Dunottar castle, near Stonehaven.
" " [3] Abbey of Arbroath.
" " [4] Banff.
" " [5] Greenock.
" " [6] Slaines castle,—near Peterhead.
" " [7] Peterhead.
" " [8] Aberdeen.
" " [9] " . From above the chain bridge.
" " [10] The light house, Aberdeen.
" " [11] The Buller of Buchan near Peterhead.
" " [12] Stonehaven.
" " [13] Entrance to the port of Dundee.
" " [14] Dundee, from the opposite side of the Tay.
" " [15] Macduff, near Banff.
" " [16] Montrose.
" " [17] Port Glasgow.
" " [18] Leith pier and harbour.
" " [19] New Bridge and Bromielaw, Glasgow.
" " [20] Newhaven pier. Firth of Forth.
" " [21] Maryport.
" " [22] Bath.
" " [23] Allonby.
" " [24] Harlech castle.
" " [25] The Solway from Harrington harbour.
" " [26] Conway castle.
" " [27] Conway quay.
" " [28] Suspension bridge at Clifton near Bristol.
" " [29] Barmouth.
" " [30] Port Penryn and Bangor.
" " [31] Blackpool.
" " [32] Blackpool sands.
" " [33] Beaumaris.
" " [34] Hurst castle.
" " [35] Gloucester.
" " [36] The Menai bridge, Bangor. North Wales.
" " [37] The eagle tower, Carnarvon castle.
" " [38] Carnarvon.
" " [39] Holyhead.
" " [40] Bridge to the South stack lighthouse near Holyhead.

Finden, W.—Continued.

v. 2, no. [41] Redcliffe church and basin, Bristol.
" " [42] Bristol. From Rawnham ferry.
" " [43] Canning dock and custom house, Liverpool.
" " [44] St. Nicholas' church, Liverpool From St. George's basin.
" " [45] The Mersey at Liverpool.
" " [46] New Brighton.
" " [47] Cardiff.
" " [48] Swansea bay.
" " [49] Oystermouth, Swansea bay.
" " [50] The Mumbles rocks and lighthouse, Swansea bay
" " [51] The walls of Southampton.
" " [52] Scene at Fleetwood, on Wyre.
" " [53] Broadstairs. Kent.
" " [54] Wreck in Kingsgate bay. Isle of Thanet.
" " [55] "The Westminster" and "Claudine," ashore near Margate.
" " [56] Sandwich. Kent.
" " [57] Yarmouth, with Nelson's monument. From the Lowestoft road.
" " [58] The quay, Yarmouth.
" " [59] Rye. Sussex.
" " [60] London from Greenwich park.
" " [61] Whitehaven with St. Bees-head.
" " [62] Whitehaven harbour.
" " [63] Matlock bath.
" " [64] Workington. Cumberland.
" " [65] The sands at Southport.
" " [66] Ness sands lighthouses. Near Bristol.
" " [67] St. Bees college.
" " [68] St. Bees head.
" " [69] Lytham.
" " [70] The port of London.
" " [71] The tower of London.
" " [72] Gravesend.

WATERING PLACES.

Watering, The, places of Great Britain and fashionable directory, illustrated with views. 1 p. l., 200, 40 pp., 30 pl. 4°. London, published for the proprietors, by I. T. Hinton, 1831.
[With Fay, S. Views in New York. New York, 1831] 5196

NOTE.—Illustrations made by W. H. Bartlett, D. Cox, etc. Bound at end are pp. 21–24 and 2 plates, relating to Paris, evidently belonging to some other work.

CONTENTS.

no. 1. Chain pier, and Albion hotel. Brighton.
" 2. Pavilion, statute of Geo. IV, and new church. Brighton.
" 3. Worthing.
" 4. Little Hampton.
" 5. Bognor. Sussex.
" 6. Rottingdean.
" 7. Eastbourne.
" 8. Lt. Leonard's hotel. New town Hastings.
" 9. Hastings. Sussex.

no. 10. Hastings. From the interior.
" 11. Hythe.
" 12. Sandgate. Kent.
" 13. Folkstone. Kent.
" 14. Dover.
" 15. Dover.
" 16. Ramsgate.
" 17. Torquay.
" 18. Deal.
" 19. Rye.
" 20. Southampton.
" 21. Penzance, Cornwall.
" 22. Swanage, Dorsetshire.
" 23. The Tor, Devonshire.
" 24. Sherborne Spa, Cheltenham.
" 25. Broadstairs.
" 26. Royal hotel, Margate. Kent.
" 27. Margate pier, and harbour. Kent.
" 28. Gravesend. Kent.
" 29. Cowes. Isle of Wight.
" 30. Rhyde. Isle of Wight.

GENERAL.

1723

Collins, G.

Great Britain's coasting pilot. In two parts. Being a new and exact survey of the sea-coast of England and Scotland, from the river of Thames to the westward and northward. With the islands of Scilly, and from thence to Carlisle. Likewise the islands of Orkney and Shetland. Describing all the harbours, rivers, bays, roads, rocks, sands, buoys, beacons, sea-marks, depth of water, latitude, bearings and distances from place to place; the setting and flowing of tides, with directions for the knowing of any place; and how to harbour a ship in the same with safety. With directions for coming into the channel between England and France. 3 p. l., 26 pp., 49 maps. fol. London, for T. Page, & W. & F. Mount, 1723. 5197

NOTE.—The engraved title contains a small map of the British Isles.

Maps engraved by I. Harris, E. Bowen, F. Lamb, Ia. Clerk, J. Moxon, H. Moll, F. W. Oetjes.

The following views on the maps:

no. [6] King William landing novembr. 5, 1688.
" [15] At Sherehampton near King Road, landed his majtie. on the 6t. of septr. 1690.
" [23] Peel castel.
" [24] A prospect of Carreck-Fergus. Being the place where king William landed in Ireland.
" [42] Prospect of Leith from the east.

1738

Collins, G.

Great Britain's coasting pilot. In two parts. Being a new and exact survey of the sea-coast of England and Scotland from the river of Thames to the westward and northward. With the islands of Scilly, and from thence to Carlisle. Likewise the islands of Orkney and Shetland: describing all the harbours, rivers, bays, roads, rocks, sands, buoys, beacons, sea marks, depths of water, latitude, bearings and distances from place to place; the setting and flowing of tides, with directions for the knowing of any place; and how to harbour a ship in the same with safety. With directions for coming into the channel between England and France. eng. title, 2 p. l., 26 pp., 49 maps. fol. London, for W. Mount & T. Page, 1738. 5198

NOTE.—Maps engraved by H. Moll, F. W. Oetjes, I. Harris, Ia. Clerk, N. Yeates and F. Lamb. For other editions consult v. 1.

Corrected from v. 3, title 4003.

1744

Collins, G.

Great Britain's coasting pilot. In two parts. Being a new and exact survey of the sea-coast of England and Scotland from the river of Thames to the westward and northward. With the islands of Scilly, and from thence to Carlisle. Likewise the islands of Orkney and Shetland: describing all the harbours, rivers, bays, roads, rocks, sands, buoys, beacons, sea marks, depths of water, latitude, bearings and distances from place to place; the setting and flowing of tides; with directions for the knowing of any place, and how to harbour a ship in the same with safety: with directions for coming into the channel between England and France. 3 p. l., 26 pp., 49 maps. fol. London, for W. Mount & T. Page, 1744. 5199

NOTE.—Engraved title contains small map of British Isles.

Maps engraved by I. Harris, F. Lamb, Ia. Clerk, J. Moxon, H. Moll and N. Yeates.

The following views appear on various maps:

no. [6] King William landing novemb^{r}. 5, 1688.

" [14] At Sherehampton near King road, landed his maj^{tie}. on the 6^{t}. of sept^{r}. 1690.

" [23] Peel castel.

" [24] A prospect of Carreck-fergus. Being the place where king William landed in Ireland.

" [42] Prospect of Leith from the east.

Library of Congress has also editions of 1723, 1738, 1756, 1767, and 1785. Consult "Author list."

1804

Smith, C.

Smith's new english atlas: being a complete set of county maps, divided into hundreds, on which are delineated all the direct and cross roads . . . cities, towns, and most considerable villages, parks, gentlemen's seats, rivers, and navigable canals: preceded by a general map of England and Wales, on which the principal roads are carefully described, for the purpose of facilitating the connection of the respective maps. The whole accompanied by an index villaris, containing upwards of forty thousand names of places mentioned in the work, with reference to their situation. 2 v., 2 p. l., 54 pp; 45 col. maps. fol. & obl. fol. London, for C. Smith, 1804. 5200

NOTE.—Each map is separately dated, jan. 6, 1804.

1912

Philip, G. & son, *ltd.*

Philips' comparative wall atlas of the British Isles. Edited by J. F. Umstead . . . & E. G. R. Taylor . . . 8 maps. fol. London, G. Philip & son [1912] 5201

NOTE.—Accompanied by *Explanatory handbook, British Isles. cover-title, 16 pp. 8°. London, G. Philip & son, 1912.*

ENGLAND.

Roads.

Cary, J.

Cary's survey of the high roads from London to Hampton Court, Bagshot, Oakingham, Binfield, Windsor, Maidenhead, High Wycombe, Amersham, Rickmansworth, Tring, St. Albans, Welwyn, Hertford, Ware, Bishops Strotford, Chipping Ongar, Chelmsford, Gravesend, Rochester, Maidstone, Tunbridge Wells, East Grinsted, Ryegate, Dorking, Guildford, Richmond. On a scale of one inch to a mile; wherein every gentleman's seat situate on, or seen from the road, <however distant> are laid down, with the name of the possessor; to which is added the number of inns on each separate route; also, the different turnpike gates, shewing the connection which one trust has with another. 2 p. l., 82 maps. sm. 4°. London, for J. Cary, 1790. 5202

Ogilby, J.

Britannia depicta or Ogilby improv'd; being a correct coppy of mr. Ogilby's actual survey of all ye direct & principal cross roads in England and Wales: wherein are exactly delineated & engraven, all ye cities, towns, villages, churches, seats &c. scituate on or near the roads, with their respective distances in measured and computed miles . . . By In°. Owen . . . Lastly particular & correct maps of all ye counties of South Britain . . . By Eman: Bowen engraver. 3 p. l., 273 pp., incl. 253 maps. 12°. London, T. Bowles, 1720. 5203

NOTE.—Border text to maps.

GENERAL.

1643

Langeren, J. van.

A direction for the english traviller [!] by which he shal be inabled to coast about all England and Wales; and also to know how farre any market or noteable towne in any shire lyeth one from an other . . . and also the distance betweene London and any other shire or great towne . . . 3 l. [40] fold. maps, 1 tab. 16°. [London] T. Jenner, 1643. 5203a

NOTE.—In lower left corner of title-page: "Jacob van Langeren sculp."
Each map is accompanied by a table of distances.

1724

Moll, H.

A new description of England and Wales, with the adjacent islands. Wherein are contained, diverse useful observations and discoveries in respect to natural history, antiquities, customs, honours, privileges, &c. with a particular account of the products, trade, and manufactures of the respective places in every county, and their improvemants or decays. Together with many uncommon observations concerning mines of several sorts. Also, several errors of different kinds are rectified. The whole illustrated with many historical and critical remarks. To which is added, a new and correct set of maps of each county, their roads and distances; and, to render 'em the more acceptable to the curious, their margins are adorn'd with great variety of very remarkable antiquities . . . 1 p. l., xi [1] 343, x pp., 50 maps. fol. London, for H. Moll; T. Bowles, [etc.] 1724. 5204

1764

Rocque, J.

The small british atlas; being a new set of maps of all the counties of England and Wales; to which is added a general map, with tables of length, breadth, areas, cities, boroughs and parishes in each county, likewise a parlimentary map of England, with tables of the produce of the land-tax; also a scheme of the proportion the several counties paid to the three shilling aid, 1699, compared with the number of members they sent to parliament.—Le petit atlas britannique: ou recueil des provinces d'Angleterre et de la principaute de Galles, avec une carte general, et tables contenant la longueur, largeur, superficie, les villes, bourgs, lieux de marché, paroisses, & le nombre de membres que chaque province envoie . . . 2 p. l., 2 maps, 54 (*i. e.* 51) maps. 8°. London, J. Rocque, 1764. 5205

1784–1789

Rapin-Thoyras, P. de.

[Atlas to accompany Rapin's History of England . . . Translated by J. Kelly] 65 maps. fol. [London, J. Harrison, 1784–1789] 5206

NOTE.—Maps engraved by G. Allen, T. Bowen, G. Terry, Simpkins and E. Sudlow.

Maps relating to England delineated by J. Haywood and engraved by E. Sudlow.

Title-page wanting.

Contains many ancient maps of other parts of the world as well as those relating to England.

The following maps relate to America:

no. [18] Attack of the rebels upon Fort Penobscot in the province of New England in which their fleet was totally destroyed and their army dispersed the 14th. augst. 1779, by an officer present. 1785.

" [20] The river St. Lawrence accurately drawn from d'Anville's map. Simpkins sc.

" [26] Map of Louisiana, from d'Anville's atlas. Haywood del. Bowen sculp. Inset: Upper Louisiana.

1793

Cary, J.

Cary's new and correct english atlas: being a new set of county maps from actual surveys. Exhibiting all the direct & principal cross roads, cities, towns, and most considerable villages, parks, rivers, navigable canals &c. Preceded by a general map of South Britain, shewing the connexion of one map with another, also a general description of each county, and directions for the junction of the roads from one county to another. [96] l., 17 pp. incl. 47 maps. 4°. London, for J. Cary, 1793. 5207

1805–1820

Great Britain. *Ordnance survey.*

[Maps of counties of England and Wales] 9 l., 37 maps. fol. [London, 1805–1820] 5208

NOTE.—These maps are taken from the collection of ordnance survey maps of Great Britain.

Plates are not numbered consecutively.

Index of each part is pasted on the cover-title of each part.

CONTENTS.

pt. 1, nos. 1–2, 47–48. Essex with portions of Suffolk, Cambridgeshire, Hertfordshire, Surrey, Kent and Middlesex.

" 2, " 20–27. Devonshire, part of Somersetshire, part of Dorsetshire, part of Glamorganshire, and the eastern part of Cornwall.

" 3, " 29–33. Cornwall, and part of Devonshire.

" 4, " 15–18. Dorsetshire, with portions of the adjoining counties.

" 5, " 4–5, 9–11. Sussex, with portions of Kent and Hampshire, including the Isle of Wight.

Great Britain. *Ordnance Survey*—Continued.

pt. 6, nos. 8, 12. Surrey with portions of Hampshire, Wiltshire, Berkshire, Middlesex and Sussex.
" 7, " 14, 19. Wiltshire, a portion of Somersetshire, and the remaining part of Hampshire.
" 8, " 3, 6. Kent with portions of Surrey and Sussex.
" 9. " 28, 38–40, 58. Pembrokeshire, with portions of Cardiganshire and Caermarthenshire, and the Island of Lundy.

1810

Randle, C.

83 drawings in manuscript. 37 maps, 46 col. pl. sm. fol. [1810] 5208a

NOTE.—A series of manuscript maps and water color views many of which are dated 1810 and are signed C. Randle.
For note and contents, see entry under North America.

Cities.

LONDON.

1905?

Bacon, G. W.

Bacon's pocket atlas of London . . . 3 p. l., 17, 24 [4] pp., front., 20 (*i. e.* 22) col. maps, 7 pl. 12°. London, G. W. Bacon & co. [1905?] 5209

NOTE.—Contains portraits of king Edward VII and queen Alexandria.
Also contains the following views: Trafalgar square—Buckingham palace.—Houses of parliament—from the river.—St. Paul's cathedral.—Westminster Abbey.—Tower and Tower bridge.—Windsor castle—from the river Thames.

1916

Bacon, G. W., & co., *ltd.*

Bacon's large scale atlas of London and suburbs (revised edition) with an alphabetical index of over 20,000 names. New enlarged and improved edition, with additional road maps of the home counties and a series of seventeen special maps showing the different areas controlled by government departments, local authorities, and supply companies having statutory powers in and around the city and county of London. Edited by William Stanford. 2 p. l., [46] pp. 61 col. maps. sm. fol. London, G. W. Bacon & co. [1916] 5210

NOTE.—Maps variously numbered.

1916?

Bacon's pocket atlas of London. 2 p. l., 42 pp. 30 col. maps, 7 pl. 12°. London, G. W. Bacon & co. ltd. [1916?] 5211

NOTE.—Cover-title: *Bacon's up to date atlas and guide to London.*

1917?

Philip, G., & son, *ltd*.

Philip's A. B. C. pocket atlas-guide to London with new postal areas. 8th revised edition. 1 p. l., xii, 80 pp. 25 col. maps, illus. 16°. London, G. Philip & son, ltd.; Liverpool, Philip, son & nephew, ltd. [1917?] 5212

OXFORD.

Oxford historical society.

Old plans of Oxford. 4 facsim. (maps) on 15 sheets. fol. [Oxford, 1899].

[Oxford historical society. Publications. vol. 38] 5212a

NOTE.—In portfolio.
Title and sketch map of Oxford mounted on inside of cover.

CONTENTS.

no. [1] Agas's map of Oxford. Made 1578, engraved 1588.
" [2] Agas's map of Oxford with Bereblock's views. Engraved by Robert Whittlesey, 1728.
" [3] Hollar's map of Oxford, A. D. 1643.
" [4] Loggan's map of Oxford. From "Oxonia illustrata," 1675.

SCOTLAND.

Historical.

Lothian, J.

Lothian's historical atlas of Scotland, consisting of five general maps, exhibiting the geography of the country in the 1st, 5th, 10th, 15th & 19th centuries with a map of the Highlands, A. D. 1715–45, shewing the territories of the clans, and tracing the route of the unfortunate prince Charles, accompanied by a journal of his successes & disasters. Containing also facsimiles of two curious maps of Scotland constructed by Ptolemy, A. D. 46[!] and by Richard, monk of Cirencester, 1336. 2 p. l., 2 pp. 8 col. maps. sm. fol. Edinburgh, J. Lothian, 1829. 5213

GENERAL.

1725

Moll, H.

A set of thirty-six new and correct maps of Scotland divided into its shires, &c. Reprinted from the first edition of 1725. 3 p. l., 36 maps. obl. 4°. Stirling, R. S. Shearer & son, 1896. 5214

NOTE.—Contains facsimiles of the original title-page with notes concerning the maps on the verso, and 1 p. of text entitled, *Of Scotland in general. By John Adair.*
On the verso of the modern title-page the imprint of the second edition of 1745 is also given.

1770?

Kitchin, T.

[Minature atlas of Scotland from latest surveys] 33 maps. 12°. [1770?] 5215

NOTE.—Title-page wanting.

Contains map of the whole of Scotland and separate maps of each of the shires.

FRANCE.

CITIES.

Tassin, N.

Les plans et profils de tovtes les principales villes et liovx considérables de France. Ensemble les cartes générales de chacune prouince: & les particulières de chaque gouuernement d'icelles. 2 v., 39 pp., 16 l., 156 maps, 48 pl.; 44 pp., 20 l., 181 maps, 31 pl. obl. 12°. Paris, M. Tavernier, 1638. 5216

NOTE.—Vol. 1 contains 2 half titles of sections not in the 1636 edition. In several places the maps and leaves have been bound in wrong order.

Vol. 2 lacks map no. 2 of the section, *Plans et profilz des principales villes de la prouince de Beavlce*, which is a view entitled, *Bovrges.*

With the exceptions noted this edition is a reprint of the 1636 edition published by I. Messager.

The 1636 edition has added Tassin's *Description des tovs les cantons, villes, bovrgs, villages, et avtres particvlaritez dv pays des Svsses . . . Paris, S. Cramoisy, 1635,* which is not included in the other editions. See v. 1, no. 3145.

COLONIES.

Pelet, P.

Atlas des colonies françaises dressé par ordre du ministère des colonies . . . 1 p. l., iv, 74 [2] 27 [1] pp., 27 col. maps. fol. Paris, A. Colin [1914?] 5217

NOTE.—Maps dated from 1898–1914.

First edition issued in parts from 1898–1902. See v. 1, no. 2954.

The following maps relate to America:

no. 1. [Planisphère] Colonies françaises. 1901.

" 23. Guyane. 1899.

" 24. Guadeloupe, Martinique, St. Pierre et Miquelon. 1898.

" 27. Points d'appui de la flotte. Fort de France. 1901.

HYDROGRAPHICAL.

France. *Dépôt des cartes et plans de la marine.*

Recherches hydrographiques sur le régime des côtes. Neuvième cahier reconnaisance de l'embouchure de la Gironde en 1874 par m. L. Mauen . . . et mon. E. Larousse, E. Caspari et I. Hanusse . . . Atlas cartes, planches et tableaux. 2 p. l., iv pp., 1 l. 24 maps (partly fold.) xviii tables, 23 diagrs. obl. fol. Paris, imprimerie nationale, 1878. 5218

NOTE.—At head of title: N° 598.

PORTS.

Miger, P. A. M.

Les ports de France, peints par Joseph Vernet et Huë; dont les tableaux enrichissent la galerie du sénat conservateur, au Luxembourg; accompagnés de notes historiques et statistiques sur chacune des villes où ils se trouvent situés. On y a joint les portraits des auteurs, et l'ouvrage et précédé de la vie de J. Vernet. 2 p. l., xv, 126, [2] pp. 24 pl., 2 port. (incl. front.) 4°. Paris, chez l'éditeur [etc.] 1812. 5219

NOTE.—All views marked, "Dése et gravé par Legrand le Lorrain."
The frontispiece contains portrait of C. J. Vernet.

CONTENTS.

Views.

no. [1] Vue de l'entrée du port de Marseille.
" [2] Vue de l'intérieur du port de Marseille.
" [3] Vue de port de Cette.
" [4] Vue du vieux port de Toulon.
" [5] Vue de la rade de Toulon.
" [6] Vue du port neuf de Toulon.
" [7] Vue de la rade d' Antibes.
" [8] Vue de la ville et du port de Dieppe.
" [9] Vue du port de la Rochelle.
" [10] Vue du port de Rochefort.
" [11] Vue de la ville et du port de Bordeaux prise du château Trompette.
" [12] Vue de la ville et du port de Bordeaux prise de côté des Salinières.
" [13] Vue de la ville et du port Baïonne prise de l'Allée de Boufflers.
" [14] Vue de la ville et du port de Baïonne prise de la mi- côté des Salinières.
" [15] Vue du golfe de Gandol.
" [16] J. F. Huë. [port.]
" [17] 1re Vue de la rade de Brest.
" [18] 11e. Vue de l'intérieur du port de Brest.
" [19] 111e. Vue de l'intérieur du port de Brest.
" [20] Vue de la ville et de la rade du port St. Malo.
" [21] Vue du port de Lorient.
" [22] Vue du port et de la ville de Granville.
" [23] Vue et prise de l'isle de Grenade.
" [24] Combat de la Baïonnaise et de l'Embuscade.
" 25] Vue du port de Boulogne.

TOPOGRAPHICAL.

France. *Dépôt de la guerre.*

Carte de la France à l'échelle de 1 pour 320,000, dressée au dépôt de la guerre d'après la carte topographique au 80,000e. Levée par les officiers du corps d'état-major. 32 maps. fol. Paris, dépôt de la guerre, 1852. 5220

NOTE.—Map no. 5 contains title and is placed first.

WARS.

Duvotenay, T.

Atlas pour servir à l'intelligence des campagnes de la révolution française de m. Thiers. Gravé par Ch. Dyonnet. 2 p. l., 32 maps. obl. 4°. Paris, Furne & cie. [1846?] 5221

Note.—First issued in 1839?

For 1880? edition, see v. 1, title 2965.

GENERAL.

1638

Tavernier, M.

Théâtre géographiqve dv royavme de France, contenant les cartes et descriptions particulières des prouinces d'iceluy, auec celles des frontières & païs adjacents; le tout suiuant la table contenüe en l'autre part. title, 1 l., 101 (*i. e.* 90) maps. fol. Paris, M. Tavernier, 1638. 5222

Note.—Imperfect, maps no. 7, La France de Strabon, no. 29, l'Orléannois, no. 42 Le païs de Messin, no. 82 Lorraine générale, are wanting.

On the leaf following the title is a printed "Table de tovtes les cartes des provinces de France."

Maps are by various cartographers including I. Hondius, P. Bertius, Cornelis Danckertz, H. Hondius, Nicolas Sanson, Jan Jansonius, Petit Bourbon, Hardy, Jean Jubrien, I. van Damme, d'Armendale, Beins, Tassin, Evert Symons, Joannes Tardo, J. Le Clerc, de Classun, I. Fayanus, I. Surhonius, J. C. Visscher, de Chattillon, Gaspar Baudoin.

Maps variously dated 1623-1640.

The three following maps by P. Bertius are dated 1640:

no. [2] Carte de l' Evrope.

" [3] Carte de l' Asie.

" [4] Carte de l' Afriqve.

The first edition of this atlas, issued in 1634, is fully described by sir Herbert George Fordham, in the *Proceedings of the Cambridge antiquarian society 1908-9. v. 13, p. 106*, in an article entitled:

Cartography of the provinces of France, 1570-1757, from which the following is quoted:

"Although his (Tavernier's) work in the engraving and publication of maps was, undoubtedly, very considerable, as an engraver he cannot be said to have had much artistic merit, and as a publisher of maps very little originality can be claimed for him . . . It may be assumed that he assisted in laying a good foundation, by the collection and re-engraving of maps of various cartographers and engravers—principally, following Le Clerc, with additions from the Dutch and Flemish schools—for the work of Nicolas Sanson, who succeeded him, particularly as regards the maps of the Provinces of France, to which subject it appears from his title pages that he mainly devoted himself . . .

The collation of the maps in the various volumes containing some at least engraved by Tavernier is, however, exceedingly difficult, as the maps attributed to him and those associated with them are largely from foreign sources bearing frequently the names of the Hondiuses, Janssons, Blaeus, and others of the same period. As regards the total number of maps which Tavernier copied, and, so far, assimilated as a part of his cartographic publications I do not like even to make a guess—it may run to as much as a couple of hundred. Indeed nearly a hundred such titles of maps connected with France itself can be collected—but it is, of course, doubtful whether anything like this number came from Tavernier's press. He does not seem to have published a general atlas of the world, although his atlases of France and the surrounding and frontier countries are prefaced by maps of the world and of the several continents . . . If Tavernier had any distinctive style of his own, it must be sought for in the maps he seems actually to have engraved in connection with the military movements during the reign of Louis XIII, maps coarsely drawn, but clear, and without superfluous ornament. These maps of the 'seat of war' deal with the famous siege of La Rochelle, with the campaign of a few years later in Italy, with the war in the Grisons, over the question of the possession of the Valteline, and with some naval operations for the conquest from the spaniards of islands on the Mediterranean coasts. The earliest of this series of maps were engraved in 1625. They present a certain interest as probably the first systematic work of this kind, especially if they are studied with the military and political memoirs of the period, as, for instance, the Mémoires du mareschal de Bassompierre (1579–1646), who played a leading part in the wars of the period."

Of these "war maps" (listed in the above-mentioned article), this atlas contains the following:

no. [66] Carte du pais d'Aunis et gouvernement de La Rochelle.
" [67] Carte de la coste de La Rochelle à Brouaigs et de l'isle d'Oléron. 1627. Observée par de lesr Chattillon, ingénieur du roy.
" [88] Charte de la Suisse, de la Rhétie, ou des Grisons, de la Valteline, du Valay par Gaspar Baudoin, ingénieur militaire. 1625.
" [89] Carte générale de la Valtoline. 1625.

"Tavernier's cartographic activity extends from at least as early as 1625 till his death, at an advanced age, in 1641. He thus filled the period between Jean Le Clerc (who died in 1621 or 1622) and Sanson, whose greatest activity in map production culminated in the early fifties of the century." (Fordham Op. cit.)

Besides maps of France, this atlas also contains maps of the world, the continents, and various maps of the Netherlands, Germany, the Rhine & Danube rivers, Italy.

Contains plans of the following cities:

no. [72] Plan de la ville de Lymoges [Ant. Jo. Fayano]
" [75] [Views of] Ghendt—Brugge—Oostende—Sluys—Yperen—Duynkercke. By Claes. Janss. Visscher. 1633.

The following maps relate to America:

no. [1] Nova totius terrarum geographica tabula. Auct. Ind. Hondio. 1638.
" [2] Carte de l'Evrope. P. Bertius. 1640. [Shows part of Greenland.]
" [3] Carte de l'Asie. P. Bertius. 1640. [Shows Partie de l'Amériqve.]
" [5] Carte de l'Amériqve. P. Bertius.

1667

Boom, H., *and* **Boom, T.**

Atlas françois ou description générale de tout le royaume de France. Contenant non seulement une description géographique avec les cartes de chacune province, mais aussi généalogique des illustres familles et historiques . . . 2 v. fol. Amsterdam, H. & T. Boom [1667] 5223

NOTE.—These two volumes are volumes 7, and 8, of Blaeu's *Le grand atlas, ov Cosmographie Blaviane,* in 12 v., published in 1667, v. 1, no. 479. The general title-page has been omitted and a slip containing the above title pasted over the blank space of the engraved title-page of v. 7, of Blaeu's work. Vol. 1 of this copy corresponding with v. 7, of Blaeu, lacks the general title-page of Blaeu's large work, the index, and a map entitled, *Dioecesis Eborcensis, vulgo l'évesché d' Evreux.*

Volume 2, corresponding with v. 8, of Blaeu, lacks title-page and map entitled, *Comitatvs Rvscinonis vulgo Rovssillon,* and the part devoted to Switzerland.

1719

Chiquet, J.

Nouveau atlas françois contenant la France ses 12 gouvernements generaux, les archevêchez, é vêchez, le nombre des paroisses en chaque diocèse; leurs revenus, leurs distances de Paris, l'étandüe des parlements, les généralitez et vniversités du royaume. Ouvrage très vtile pour ceux qui veulent finstruire dans la géographie . . . 18, [1] l. incl. 15 maps. obl. 8°. [Paris, Cheveanau, 1719]
[With his Le nouveau et curieux atlas géographique et historique . . . obl. 8°. Paris, Cheveanau, 1719] 5224

NOTE.—Date, 1719, found on maps. Engraved title-page. The Library of Congress has another copy in separate form.

1763-1766

Desnos, L. C.

Atlas chorographique, historique, et portatif des élections du royaume. Généralité de Paris, divisée en ses vingt deux élections, et représentée dans toutes ses parties par autant de cartes particulières, d'une manière chorographique et complette, avec le nombre des paroisses et des feux, la position des villes, des bourgs, des villages, des hameaux, des abbayes, des bois, des prairies, des montagnes, des étangs, des marais, des rivières, des routes, de tous les lieux enfin qui la composent, levées sur le terrein; par une société d'ingénieurs. Accompagnées d'une description dans laquelle on explique l'histoire particulière de chaque ville . . . par m. l'abbé Regley . . . viii, xxxiv [2] 122, xi pp. 25 maps, 1 pl. sm. fol. Paris, Savoye; Despilly, [etc] 1763-[1766] 5225

NOTE.—Page numbering from 97 to 100 repeated and from 105 to 108 omitted. Three maps are dated 1766.

Contains map of Paris entitled, *Plan général de la ville et faubourgs de Paris, divisé en ses ving quartiers . . . 1766.*

1833?

Woerl, I. E.

Carte de la France, composée de vingt-cinq feuilles, à l' échelle de 1:500,000 de la grandeur naturelle construite sur le principe de la projection de Flamsteed par J. H. Weiss . . . exécutée d' après les meilleurs matériaux. Gravée sur pierre et imprimée avec une nouvelle méthode d' employer l'encre rouge pour l' indication des routes, des positions et des limites. 2 p. l., 1 map on 24 sheets. obl. fol. Fribourg en Brisgau, B. Herder [1833?] 5226

NOTE.—Contains small inset maps of the following cities: Paris, Nantes, Orléans, Strasbourg, Lyon, Bordeaux and Rouen.

1860?

Dufour, A. H., *and* **Duvotenay, T.**

La France. Atlas des 86 départements et des colonies françaises, divisés en arrondissements et cantons, avec un tracé des routes royales et départementes, des chemin de fer, canaux, rivières et cours d' eau; indiquant les relais de postes aux chevaux, aux lettres, les sources d'eaux minérales . . . Avec une notice historique sur chaque départment, par m. Albert-Montemont . . . 1 p. l., [2] 88 pp., 88 (*i. e.* 89) col maps. fol. Paris, A. Aubrée, G. Harvard, successeur [1860?] 5227

NOTE.—The latest historical date in the atlas is 1842.

1910–1912

Reclus, O.

Atlas pittoresque de la France; recueil de vues géographiques et pittoresques de tous les départements, accompagnées de notices géographiques et de légendes explicatives. 3 v. fol. Paris, Attinger frères [1910–1912] 5228

NOTE.—Issued also in parts (1st fasc., 1909)
At head of title: Publié sous les auspices de la *Société de géographie* de Paris.

CONTENTS.

v. 1. Ain–Eure-et-Loir.
" 2. Finistère–Nord.
" 3. Oise–Yonne.

1913

Atlas de la plus grande France. Géographique, économique, politique, departemental, colonial . . . Ouvrage formant le complément naturel de l'Atlas pittoresque de la France publié sous les auspices de la Société de géographie. 2 p. l., 160 pp. 160 col. maps. sm. fol. Paris, Attinger frères [1913] 5229

NOTE.—Maps are shown to illustrate population, industries, production, commerce, transportation, wealth, vegetation, geology, colonies and many other subjects.
Many small maps in text.
Contains two maps of Paris.

1914

Larousse, Librarie.

Atlas départemental Larousse. 2 p. l., [10, 184] pp. 100 maps, 10 maps in text. fol. Paris, librairie Larousse [1914] 5230

NOTE.—"Copyright 1914".

Besides maps of the departments, the atlas contains maps showing the geology, relief, railroads, commerce, agriculture, industry, mineral, railroads, population, universities, judicial, ecclesiastical, ancient provinces, and the military. The text is by Georges Treffel, and is illustrated by numerous small views of castles, cathedrals, public buildings and portraits of prominent men, with statistical and historical data. Under each department is also given a list of the principal cities.

Contains plans of the following cities:

no. 9. Bourg.
" 10. Laon.
" 11. Moulins.
" 12. Digne.
" 13. Gap.
" 14. Nice.
" 15. Privas.
" 16. Mézières et Charleville.
" 17. Foix.
" 18. Troyes.
" 19. Carcassonne.
" 20. Rodez.
" 22. Marseille.
" 23. Caen.
" 24. Aurillac.
" 25. Angoulême.
" 26. La Rochelle.
" 27. Bourges.
" 28. Tulle.
" 29. Bastia-Ajaccio.
" 30. Dijon.
" 31. Saint-Brieuc.
" 32. Guéret.
" 33. Niort.
" 34. Périgueux.
" 35. Besançon.
" 36. Valence.
" 37. Evreux.
" 38. Chartres.
" 39. Quimper.
" 40. Nîmes.
" 41. Toulouse.
" 42. Auch.
" 43. Bordeaux.
" 44. Montpellier.
" 45. Rennes.
" 46. Châteauroux.
" 47. Tours.
" 48. Grenoble.
" 49. Lons-le-Saunier.

no. 50. Mont-de-Marsan.
" 51. Blois.
" 52. St. Etienne.
" 53. Le Puy.
" 54. Nantes.
" 55. Orléans.
" 56. Cahors.
" 57. Agen.
" 58. Mende.
" 59. Angers.
" 60. Saint-Lô.
" 61. Châlons-sur-Marne.
" 62. Chaumont.
" 63. Laval.
" 64. Nancy.
" 65. Bar-le-Duc.
" 66. Vannes.
" 67. Nevers.
" 68. Lille.
" 69. Beauvais.
" 70. Alençon.
" 71. Arras.
" 72. Clermont-Ferrand.
" 73. Pau.
" 74. Tarbes.
" 75. Perpignan.
" 76. Lyon.
" 77. Vesoul.
" 78. Macon.
" 79. Le Mans.
" 80. Chambéry.
" 81. Annecy.
" 82. Paris.
" 83. "
" 84. "
" 85. Versailles.
" 86. Melun.
" 87. Rouen.
" 88. Amiens.
" 89. Albi.
" 90. Montauban.
" 91. Draguignan.
" 92. Avignon.
" 93. La Roche-sur-Yon.
" 94. Poitiers.
" 95. Limoges.
" 96. Epinal.
" 97. Auxerre.
" 98. Alger.
" 99. Constantine.
" 100. Oran.

CITIES.

PARIS.

Views.

Arnout, J.

Paris, vues et monuments; dessinés et lithographiés en couleur. eng. title, 1 p. l., 35 col. pl. obl. 4°. Paris, Goupil & comp. [1855?] 5231

General.

1760

Robert de Vaugondy, G.

Tablettes parisiennes qui contiennent le plan de la ville & des fauxbourgs de Paris divisé en vingt quartiers, avec une dissertation sur ses aggrandissemens, et une table alphabétique pour trouver les rues, quais, ports, places publiques, collèges, &c. de cette ville . . . 3 p. l., 3–64 pp., 3 maps on 22 l. 8°. Paris, chés l'auteur, 1760. 5232

NOTE.—Engraved title-page signed, "Arrivet inv. & sculpsit."

1830?

Plan de Paris, avec détails historiques de ses agrandissemens et de ses embellissemens, depuis Jules César jusqu'à ce jour, joint à la banlieue côté de l'ouest jusqu'à Saint-Cloud, gravé sur cuivre, et réduit géométriquement, suivant les dessins de Giroux, et données de m. B. A. H. Devert, géomètres, d'après mm. Verniquet, architecte; Lagrive et Rousseau, ingénieurs. Sur ce même plan est cotée et désignée la position des diverses communes et hameaux des environs de cette capitale, de même que les embranchemens et bassins des canaux de l'Ourcq et de l'Yvette, tant projectés qu'exécutés, qui y sont figurés; avec l'indice de ses principaux monumens et établissemens publics y existans, ainsi que plusieurs autres nouvellement proposés et partis confectionnés; suivis de quelques notes véridiques des événemens extraordinaires qui ont eu lieu successivement depuis plusieurs siècles; accompagnés: 1°. Du premier et second plan de cette vaste cité . . . 2°. D'un tableau récapitulatif des principales productions et consommations . . . 3°. Le plan de Saint-Denis . . . 4°. Du plan ou carte générale du canal de l'Ourcq à Paris . . . 5°. D'un plan et description de la scie mécanique . . . 6°. Enfin d'un tableau mathématique des 130 départemens . . . Par une société d' artistes, en 1803, 1807, 1820 et années suivantes. 2 p. l., [80] pp. 2 maps, 2 diagrs., 1 tab. 4°. Paris, Baradelle [1830?] 5233

NOTE.—Various pagination.

1855

Leynadier, C.

Nouveau plan de Paris illustré, dédié au commerce et à l' industrie, contenant, 1°, Une revue chronologique sur Paris; 2°, Une notice historique des principaux monuments de la capitale; 3°, Un guide indicateur des acheteurs, donnant aux étrangers les noms, professions et adresses des principaux commerçants de Paris . . . 1 p. l., 112 [24] pp. 12 maps. 8°. Paris, H. Morel, 1855. 5234

NOTE.—Maps illustrated with views of the important buildings in the different parts of the city.

Contains 12 maps showing the 12 arrondissements of Paris which all carry the following title: *Paris industriel et commercial. Nouveau plan illustré. Ernest Lebrun. Saunier sculp.*

1868

Seine. (*Department*) *Direction des travaux de Paris.*

Atlas administratif des 20 arrondissements de la ville de Paris. Publié d'après les ordres de m. le baron G. E. Haussmann . . . 1 p. l., 2 maps, 1 map on 16 sheets. fol. [Paris] 1868. 5235

NOTE.—"Ce plan est une reproduction du plan général à l' échelle de $\frac{1}{5000}$ dressé par les géomètres du Service municipal du plan de Paris." See title 5236

The names of different publishers appear on various sections of the map, *i. e.* V. Janson, Hangard-Maugé, Becquet and Lemercier & cie.

1878

Atlas municipal des vingt arrondissements de la ville de Paris, dressé sous l'administration de m. Ferdinand Duval, préfet, sous la direction de m. Alphand, insp^{r}. g^{al}. des ponts et chaussées, directeur des travaux de Paris par les soins de m. L. Fauve, géomètre en chef, avec le concours des géomètres du plan du Paris. 1 p. l., 1 map on 16 sheets, 1 map. fol. [Paris] 1878. 5236

NOTE.—The name "B. de Sevray, Rue Michel-Ange, 23 Paris (Auteui)" is stamped on the title-page and is evidently that of a book seller.

An earlier edition was published in 1868, under the direction of G. E. Haussmann. See title 5235.

1912–1913

Blondel la Rougery, E.

Plan de Paris-atlas, comprenant, 1°.—Un indicateur des rues, stations du métropolitain autobus, omnibus, tramways tous renseignements utiles, monuments. Musées adresses, etc. 2°—Un plan de Paris a l' échelle du 1:18,000^{e} divisé en 9 feuilles . . . 112 pp. 10 col. maps. 12°. Paris, E. Blondel la Rougery [1912–1913]

[Cartes-guides Campbell publiées sous le patronage de la Fédération des automobile-clubs régionaux de France] 5237

MISCELLANEOUS.

CORSICA.

Linguistic.

Gilliéron, J., *and* **Edmont, E.**

Atlas linguistique de la France . . . Corse. pts. 1–4, 200 maps each. fol. Paris, H. Champion, 1914–1915. 5238

NOTE.—"L'atlas linguistique de la Corse est la suite et le complément nécessaire de l'Atlas linguistique de la France . . . A [la Corse] seront consacrés 10 fascules de 200 cartes chacune qui paraîtront, à raison de 4 fascicules par an, de 1914 à 1915." [Advertisement of publisher]

For their *Atlas linguistic de la France* in 17 port-folios, see v. 3, title 4020.

France. *Ministère de la marine.*

Pilote de l'isle de Corse. Levé dans les années 1820, 1821, 1822 et 1824 par m. de Hell . . . Secondé par m. M. T. Deloffre et Aé. Mathieu . . . T. Allègre, E. Lapierre, F. Brait et E. Long . . . Publié par ordre du roi sous le ministère de m. le vice-admiral comte de Rigny. 2 p. l., 95 maps. fol. [Paris] 1831–[1855] 5239

NOTE.—The date on the title-page is 1831, but most of the maps have been published after that date, the latest in 1855.

CONTENTS.

no. 1. Carte générale de l'ile de Corse. 1831.
" 2. Carte des bouches de Bonifacio. 1823.
" 3. Plan des passages de la Piantarella et du golfe de Santa Manza. 1827.
" 4. Plan des portes de Porto Liscia. 1823.
" 5. Plan de porto Palma.—Plan de la rade d'Agincourt. 1823.
" 6. Plan de la rade d'Arsacheria.—Plan de porto Cervo.—Plan de Longo Sardo. 1824.
" 7. Carte de la côte occidentale de l'ile de Corse. 1825.
" 8. Plan du port de Figari.—Plan de la calanque de Conca.—Plan du port de Bonifacio. 1825.
" 9. Plan des Moines ou Monachi. 1825.
" 10. Plan du mouillage de Propriano.—Plan du mouillage de Porto-Pollo.—Plan du mouillage de Campo-Moro. 1825.
" 11. Plan des mouillages situés au fond du golfe d' Ajaccio. 1825.
" 12. Plan des iles Sanguinaires. 1826.
" 13. Carte de la côte occidentale de l'ile de Corse. 1829.
" 14. Plan du mouillage de Sagone. 1829.
" 15. Plan du golfe de Lava.—Plan du golfe et du port de Girolata. 1830.
" 16. Plan du golfe et du port de Galéria. 1829.
" 17. Carte de la côte N. O. de l'ile de Corse. 1829.
" 18. Plan des golfes de Calvi et de Revellata. 1829.
" 19. Plan du danger de l'Algajola.—Plan du port de Malfalco.—Plan du port et de la côte de Centuri. 1829.
" 20. Plan du mouillage de l'ile Rousse. 1829.
" 21. Carte de la côte septentrionale de l'ile de Corse. 1828.
" 22. Plan du golfe de St. Florent. 1828.

no. 23. Plan des mouillages situés à la côte septentrionale de l'île de Corse. 1828.
" 24. Plan de la côte de Bastia. 1830.
" 25. Plan du port de Bastia. 1831.
" 26. Carte de la côte orientale de l'ile de Corse depuis l'embouchure du Fium-Orbo jusques à Bastia. 1831.
" 27. Carte de la côte orientale de l'ile de Corse depuis l'entrée des bouches de Bonifacio jusqu'à l'embouchure du Fium-Orbo. 1827.
" 28. Plan du golfe de Pinarello.—Plan du port de Favone.—Plan de Porto Nuovo. 1828.
" 29. Plan du golfe de porto Vecchio. 1828.
" 30. Plan des iles Cerbicale. 1827.
" 31–32. Vue de la côte de Corse.
" 33. Plan des mouillages de Siddi-Ferruch. 1831.
" 34. Plan des mouillages de Mers-el-Kibir. (Baie d'Oran) 1831.
" 35. Carte des golfes de Stora et de Collo. 1833.
" 36. Carte particulière du golfe de Bougie. 1833.
" 37. Plan particulier de l'ile de la Galite. 1834.
" 38. Plan particulier des iles Zafarines. 1834.
" 39. Plan particulier du mouillage d'Arzeu. 1834.
" 40. Carte particulière des mouillages de Bone. 1834.
" 41. Carte des attérages d'Oran et d'Arzeu. 1835.
" 42. Carte particulière des attérages de Bone. 1835.
" 43. Carte de la côte septentrionale d'Afrique (partie comprise entre Alger et l'ile de la Galite) 1836.
" 44. Carte de la côte septentrionale d'Afrique (partie comprise entre Alger et les iles Zafarines) 1836.
" 45. Plan particulier du mouillage d'Alger. 1836.
" 46. Carte particulière des attérages d'Alger. 1837.
" 47. Carte particulière des attérages de Cherchell. 1849.
" 48. Croquis de l'anse de Djemma-el-Ğazaouet.—Plan du port d'Oran.—Plan du mouillage de Tenez.—Plan du port de Cherchell. 1847.
" 49. Plan du port d'Alger. 1847.
" 50. Plan du mouillage de Bougie. 1847.
" 51. Plan du port de Gigelly.—Croquis du port de Collo.—Plan du port de Bone.—Plan du port de la Calle. 1847.
" 52. Plan particulier du mouillage de Djidjéli. 1849.
" 53. Plan particulier du mouillage de Dellys. 1849.
" 54. Carte particulière du mouillage de Mostaganem et de l'embouchure du Chélif. 1849.
" 55. Plan des mouillages de Stora et de Philippeville. 1851.
" 56. Plan du mouillage de Collo. 1852.
" 57. Plan des mouillages de Tabarque. 1855.
" 58. Plan du port de Tipaza et de la bai de Schenouah. 1855.
" 59. Plan du port de la Calle et de ses atterrages. 1855.
" 60. Plan de l'ile de Rachgoun et de l'embouchure de la Tafna. 1855.
" 61. Plan de la rade de Livourne (Livorno) 1849.
" 62. Plan de porto-Ferrajo. 1849.
" 63. Plan du Golfe de la Spezia, côtes d'Italie. 1849.
" 64. Plan du mouillage de Vado. 1850.
" 65. Plan de Porto-Longone. 1850.
" 66. Carte particulière des côtes d'Italie, partie comprise entre le golfe de la Spezia et l'embouchure de l'Arno. 1852.

France. *Ministère de la marine*—Continued.

no. 67. Carte particulière des côtes d'Italie. Partie comprise entre l'embouchure de l'Arno et le cap Castiglioncello. 1852.

" 68. Carte particulière des côtes d'Italie. Partie comprise entre le cap Castiglioncello et la tour Popolonia. 1852.

" 69. Plan de l'ile de la Gorgone. 1852.

" 70. Plan de Porto-Ercole. 1853.

" 71. Plan du port de Civita-Vecchia. 1853.

" 72. Carte particulière des côtes d'Italie. Partie comprise entre la tour Troja et Talamone. 1853.

" 73. Plan de la baie de Talamone. 1855.

" 74. Plan du port de San Stefano. 1853.

" 75. Carte particulière des côtes d'Italie. Partie comprenant les iles Pianosa et Monte-Christo. 1854.

" 76. Plan de l'ile Pianosa. 1854.

" 77. Plan de l'ile Monte-Christo. 1854.

" 78. Carte particulière des côtes d'Italie. Partie comprenant le mont Argentaro et les iles Giglio et Giannutri. 1854.

" 79. Carte particulière des côtes d'Italie. Partie occidentale de l'ile d'Elbe et ile Pianosa. 1854.

" 80. Carte particulière des côtes d'Italie. Canal de Piombino. 1854.

" 81. Carte particulière des côtes d'Italie, comprenant le mont Argentaro, l'ile de Giannutri et la partie occidentale des états Romains. 1854.

" 82. Carte particulière des côtes d'Italie. Partie comprise entre Montalto et la tour Linaro. 1854.

" 83. Plan de l'ile Capraja. 1854.

" 84. Plan de l'ile de Giglio. 1854.

" 85. Plan de l'ile de Giannutri. 1854.

" 86. Plan de l'ile St. Pierre. 1843.

" 87. Carte des iles St. Pierre et Miquelon. 1843.

" 88. Plan de l'anse de Miquelon. 1843.

" 89. Carte particulière du canal de San Pietro. 1844.

" 90. Carte particuliére de la baie de Palmas. 1845.

" 91. Carte particulière de la côte orientale de Sardaigne. 1845.

" 92. Carte générale de la côte méridionale de l'ile de Sardaigne. 1846.

" 93. Carte particulière de la côte méridionale de Sardaigne, depuis la cap Teulada jusqu'à la tour de Pula. 1846.

" 94. Carte particulière de la côte méridionale de Sardaigne, depuis la tour de Pula jusqu'au cap Saint-Elie. 1846.

" 95. Carte particulière de la côte méridionale de Sardaigne depuis le cap St. Elie jusqu'à la tour de Capo Boï. 1846.

GERMANY.

CITIES.

Krauss, P., *and* **Uetrecht, E.**

Meyers deutscher städteatlas. 50 stadtpläne mit 34 umgebungskarten, vielen nebenplänen und vollständigen strassenverzeichnissen . . . [382] pp. incl. 63 col. maps. 4°. Leipzig und Wien, bibliographisches institut, 1913. 5240

Note.—Various paging.

COLONIAL.

Eckert, M.

Wirtschaftsatlas der deutschen kolonien: auf veranlassung der deutschen kolonialgesellschaft . . . topographische grundlage von P. Sprigade und M. Moisel. viii pp., 52 l. incl. 53 col. maps, 65 tab. fol. Berlin, D. Reimer (E. Vohsen) [1912] 5241

NOTE.—Preface dated january, 1912.
This atlas shows routes of navigation, numerous statistical tables.
The following maps relate to cities:
no. 14. Plan von Lome.
" 20. Plan von Duala.
" 28. Plan von Swakopmund.—Plan von Lüderitzbucht.—Plan von Windhuk.
" 36. Plan von Daressalam.
" 52. Plan von Tsingtau.

Germany. *Kolonialamt.*

Grosser deutscher kolonial-atlas. Bearb. von Paul Sprigade und Max Moisel. Hrsg. von der kolonial-abtheilung des auswärtigen amts. pt. 1–8. 26 maps. fol. Berlin, D. Reimer, 1901–1912. 5242

NOTE.—For note see v. 1, title 3020.

Langhans, P.

Deutscher kolonial-atlas. 30 karten mit 300 nebenkarten. 3 p. l. [18] pp., 30 col. maps. fol. Gotha, J. Perthes, 1897. 5243

MILITARY.

Weimar geographisches institut.

Topographisch-militairische charte von Teutschland in 204 sectionen. Maasstab von zwey deutschen geogr. meilen, 1=51 grad. 4 v. obl. fol. [Weimar, Geographisches institut, 1807–1813] 5244

NOTE.—An index map on the verso of the front covers of v. 1–2, and 4.
Date 1813 found on index map of v. 4.
In v. 2, sections 92–93 are wanting.
Besides the sections of the map, v. 1 contains a map on 1 sheet entitled, *Orographische uebersicht von Teutschland* . . . and a map on 4 sheets entitled, *General-charte von Teuschland in vier blättern* . . . Nach den vorzüglichsten quellen bearbeitet und gezeichnet von Friedrich Wilhelm Streit . . . 1810."

WARS.

Fer, N. de.

Le théâtre de la guerre dessus et aux environs du Rhein, oû se trouvent l'Alsace, le Palatinat, les electorats de Mayence, de Trèves, et de Cologne, les duchez de Iuliers, de Clèves et de Berg, les états de Lorraine, les XVII provinces des Pays Bas. eng. title, 26 maps, 2 pl. 4°. Paris, 1705. 5245

NOTE.—On eng. title is found the following: "Guerard. Invenit et fecit.
Maps engraved by H. van Loon, C. Insclin, A. Coquart, P. Starck-man, & L. G. Begule.

Fer, N. de.—Continued.

Maps are dated 1702 to 1705.

The following map no. [18] is inserted: *Les environs de Vienne en Autriche. 1705.*

CONTENTS.

no. [1] L'Allemagne, divisée par cercles. H. van Loon, sculpc. 1705.
" [2] Les XIII cantons des Suisses. 1705.
" [3] Les armes des XIII cantons des Suisses. 1705.
" [4] Plan de la bataille de Fredelingue. 1702.
" [5] Les quatre villes foréstières, situées sur le Rhein. 1705.
" [6] Le cours du Rhein depuis Mayence jusques à Coblens.
" [7] Les environs de Landau. 1705.
" [8] Le cours du Rhein depuis Coblens jusques à Cologne. 1705.
" [9] Le cours du Rhein depuis Cologne jusques à Rheinberg. 1702.
" [10] Cologne. 1705.
" [11] Le cours du Rhein depuis Rheinberg jusque à Arnhem. 1705.
" [12] Le cours de la Moselle depuis l'embouchure de la Saare jusques à Cocheim. 1705.
" [13] Le cercle de Souabe. P. Starck-man, sc[t]. 1705.
" [14] Cercle de Bavière. P. Starck-man, sculp[t]. 1705.
" [15] La grande salle de Ratisbonne. 1705.
" [16] Plan de la ville d' Ulm. 1705.
" [17] Munich. A. Coquart, sculp. 1705.
" [18] Les environs de Vienne. 1705.
" [19] Vienne. 1705.
" [20] Veuë septentrionale de Vienne. 1705.
" [21] Haute et basse Alsaçe. P. Starck-man, scul[t].
" [22] Les environs des deux Brisachs. C. Inselin, sculpsit.
" [23–24] Les environs des deux Brisachs et de Fribourg. A. Coquart, sculp. 1705.
" [25] Les eveschés de Trente, et de Brixen, le comté de Tirol. 1705.
" [26] Le cours de la Sare. Gravé par P. Starck-man. 1705.
" [27] Les duchez de Lorraine, et de Bar. Gravé par P. Starck-man. 1705.
" [28] Souveraineté de Neuchatel et de Vallangin. C. Inselin, sculps[t]. 1705.

Jomini, A. H. de, *baron.*

[Collection of maps showing the war in Germany, 1796] 10 maps.

NOTE.—Maps in portfolio. 5246

CONTENTS.

no. 1. Plan pour l'intelligence des operations militaires entre la Lahn & la Siège du 14 au 21 juin 1796. Marked Gr. v. Sanktjomanser.
" 2. Affaire de Malsch le 9 juillet, 1796.
" 3. Bataille de Heresheim le 11 aust 1796.
" 4. Carte pour la bataille d'Amberg et les combats de Temingen & de Neumarck en 1796.
" 5. Bataille de Wurzbourg livrée le 3 septembre 1796. Marked. Die berge schraffirt von F. v. Harscher, K. B. Lieutenant.
" 6. Bataille de Biberach le 2 octobre 1796. Marked, Ant. Fulger gravient A. Tevini die Berge.

no. 7. Bataille près d'Emmendingen le 19me octobre 1796.
" 8. Affaire de Schliengen livrée le 24 octobre 1796.
" 9. Plan du siège de Kehl en 1796. Marked, Aus bearbeitet von F. Fluischmann.
" [10] Theâtre de la guerre de 1796 en Allemagne.

Roesch, J. F.

Collection de quarante deux plans de batailles, sièges et affaires les plus mémorables de la guerre de sept ans, tirés des sources les plus respectables, et soigneusement collationnés avec les ouvrages les plus célèbres et les plus estimés qui aient paru sur cette matière. Dédiée à son altesse royale monseigneur le prince royal Frédéric Guillaume de Prusse par . . . J. C. Jaeger. A Frankfort sur le Mayn, J. C. Jaeger, 1796.—Plans von zwey und vierzig haupt-schlachten, treffen und belagerungen des siebenjaehringen kriegs. Aus den seltesten und geprüftesten quellen gezogen, mit den besten werken über diesen krieg sorgfaeltigst verglichen. Unterthaenigst zu geiegnet von Johann Christian Jaeger . . . 8 p. l., [84] pp., 42 maps. sm. fol. Frankfurt, Jaegerischen buchhandlung, 1796. 5247

NOTE.—The french title preceeds the german. Both engraved title-pages ornamented with flags, swords and shields, and signed Abel sc. Dedication, list of subscribers, and note in german. Explanatory lists preceeding each map in both german and french. Titles of maps in french.

Zannoni, G. A. R-.

Atlas géographique et militare ou théâtre de la guerre présente en Allemagne où sont marqués les marches campemens des armées, depuis l'entrée des trouppes prussiennes en Saxe en aoust 1756, jusqu'au commencement de 1762 . . . 4 p. l., [4] 72 [2] pp., 1 map. 1 map on 16 sheets. 24°. Paris, Lattré, [1763] 5248

NOTE.—Text entitled, *Journal de la guerre, en Allemagne, depuis l'invasion des troupes prussiennes en Saxe (26 août 1756) jusqu'à la signature des préliminaires de la Paix à Fontainebleau (3 novembre 1762) En France, 1763.*
Appended, *Catalogue du fonds du sieur Lattré.*
Engraved, hand colored title-page signed P. P. Choffard fecit.
Engraved map on 16 sheets entitled, *Carte général des expéditions militaires en Allemagne . . . 1756* . . . 1762, signed L. Legrand jnv. et scul.

GENERAL.

1635

Tavernier, M.

Carte d' Alemagne, où en cinq feüilles l'on peut voir comme elle est distinguée en . . . dix cercles, ou prouinces. La situation des villes archiepiscopales & episcopales, & de celles qui ont des vniuersitéz ou académies. Les villes impériales, les demeures des princes. Et ce qui est . . . tenu par la maison d' Austriche, & la Ligue catholique . . . & la roine de Suéde & les princes & estats protes-

Tavernier, M.—Continued.

tans d'autre part. title, 5 p. l., 5 maps. fol. Paris, M. Tavernier, 1635. 5249

NOTE.—Contains a "*Description très exacte et particvlière de l' Allemagne povr l'intelligence des cartes; dans lesquelles se verront plusieurs belles remarques . . . qui n'ont ınsques à prèsent encores esté nottées à toutes les autres cartes cy deuant imprimées.*" (Dated 1633)

On the first p. l. is an "Indice dv contenv en chascvne des cinq cartes d' Alemagne":

I. Carte d'Alemagne diuisée par prouinces.
II. " " " " cercles.
III. " " " " diocèses, ou éueschez.
IV. " " " " estats, & seigneuries particulières.
V. " " " " ligues, & partis.

On verso of last map are ms. notes: "Il y a eu de grands changements depuis que ceste carte est faicte. Et faut corriger comme il s'ensuit."

These notes were evidently written after 1657, as in one of them it is stated: "L'électeur de Saxe . . . & autres princes & estats d' Alemagne se sont séparez de l' Union & alliance de la reine de Suède & accommodez auec l'empereur."

A notice of the life and work of Tavernier is given in H. G. Fordham's article: *Cartography of the provinces of France 1570–1757*, in the *Proceedings of the Cambridge Antiquarian society. 8°. Cambridge, 1909. v. 13. pp. 96–97, 106.*

Quoted in part in title 5222.

1677

Bodenehr, H. G.

Sac. imperii Romano Germanici geographica descriptio. Teutschland mit angrenzenden königreich- und provinzien . . . zu sonderbahr bequemen gebauch in 32 auffeinander zutreffende tabellen vorgestellet . . . 19 p. l., [53] pp. 3 maps on 68 l., 1 pl. nar. 16°. Augspurg, [Augsburg] H. G. Bodennehr, 1677. 5250

NOTE.—Engraved half title-page reads: S. Imperii Romano Germanici geographica descriptio. Teutschland zu bequemen gebrauch in 32 geographische tabellen vorgestelt.

Library of Congress has an edition of 1682. See v. 1, title 3033.

BAVARIA.

Topographical.

Bavaria. *Topographisches bureau des K. B. generalstabes.*

[Topographischer atlas vom königreich Bayern. Maassverhältniss 1:800,000] 113 maps. fol. [Munich, 1812–1867] 5251

NOTE.—Title-page wanting.

Dates taken from maps.

Date on cover and on index map, 1843.

In 1796 a revision of the map of Bavaria was ordered by the Austrian general staff. A topographical office was established in 1800 under the leadership of colonels Bonne and Henry in Munich. These two men with the aid of von Riedl laid the foundation and plans for a topographical atlas of Bavaria. The first map completed was a plan of Munich. This with Munich and vicinity and Wolfrathausen was published in 1812. The work was continued under the directorship of von Riedl, Seiffer, and others. In 1867 the atlas was completed.

GENERAL.

1838

Spruner von Merz, K.

Atlas zur geschichte von Bayern. 1 p. l., 7 maps. obl. fol. Gotha, J. Perthes, 1838. 5252

NOTE.—Table of contents on cover.

Between cover and title-page are 8 pp. of text entitled, *Vorbemerkungen zum atlas der geschichte von Bayern.*

PRUSSIA.

Cities.

Zeiller, M.

Topographia electorate Brandenburgici et ducatus Pomeraniæ, rc. das ist beschreibung der vornembsten vnd bekantisten stätte vnd plätz in dem hochlöblichsten churfürstenthum vnd march Brandenburg; vnd dem hertzogtum Pomeren. Zusampt einem doppelten anhang, 1, vom lande Preussen . . . 2, von Lifflande . . . 3 pts. in 1 vol.; 4 p. l. [226] pp. [57] pl. incl. maps, plans & views. 4°. [Frankfurt am Mayn] M. Merian seel:erben [1652 ?] 5253

NOTE.—The 13th part of Merian's *Topographiæ.* Preface is dated 1652.

Matthaeus Merian (1593–1650) began the compilation of his "Topographiæ" in 1642, but died before the completion of the work, which was continued by his sons Matthaeus and Caspar and finished in 30 volumes in 1688.

The text of the *Topographiæ* was compiled by Martin Zeiller for Merian, excepting that for the part relating to Alsace, which was compiled by Merian himself.

Many of the plates which greatly contributed to the fame of the work were engraved by Merian.

Map no. [73] bears the date 1703 and must have been inserted later; the descriptive text does not correspond to that date.

Detailed bio-bibliographical information relating to Merian is found in H. Eckardt's *Matthaeus Merian, eine Kultur historische studie. 8°. Kiel, 1892.*

The title-page of the above work was designed by "Mathæus Merian iunior" . . . and engraved by Melchior Kusell . . ."

Bound with it is the *Topographia Heluetiæ, Rhætiæ et Valesiæ . . . 1642.*

The following are all views unless otherwise specified.

CONTENTS.

no. [1] Brandebvrgvm marchionatvs. [Map]
" [2] Dramburg.
" [3] Ambt Himmelstädt.
" [4] Ambt Cartzig.
" [5] Schönfliess.
" [6] Wulffshagen.
" [7] Pomeraniæ dvcatvs tabvla. [Map]
" [8] Anklam.
" [9] Tangermünd.
" [10] Arnsswalde.

Zeiller, M.—Continued

no. [11] Klein Berlin.
" [12] Statt Bardt.
" [13] Grundriss des lusthauses zu Cöln an der Spree. [Map]
" [14] Statt Peitz.
" [15] Bärwalde.
" [16] Bärnstein.
" [17] Bötzenburg.
" [18] Bärnaw.
" [19] Colbergh, an der Ost see..
" [20] Cüstrin, zur andern seiten.
" [21] Haus Badingen.
" [22] Damm in Pommern. [Map]
" [23] Statt und vestung Demmin.
" [24] Prospect des passes Damgarten.
" [25] Vestung Driesen. I. H. O. W. delineavit. [Map]
" [26] New stadt Eberswalde.
" [27] Franckfurt an der Oder. [Map]
" [28] Statt Garleben.
" [29] Statt Gransee.
" [30] Grieffs Waldtt.
" [31] Greiffswaldt. [Map]
" [32] Grimmen.
" [33] Grÿphiswaldia.
" [34] Fürstenwalde.
" [35] Statt Havelberck.
" [36] Landsbergk. An der Wahrte.
" [37] Lippehn.
" [38] Loitz.
" [39] Bötzau. Oranien Burgk. Johan Gregor Memhard delineav.
" [40] Penkun.
" [41] Prentzlow.
" [42] Perleberck.
" [43] Pyritz in Pommern.
" [44] Pritzwalck.
" [45] Stadt Retz.
" [46] Soldim.
" [47] Stadt Schiefelbein.
" [48] Schweet.
" [49] Seehausen.
" [50] Sonnenburch.
" [51] Spandaw.
" [52] Rattenaw.
" [53] Stendalia.—Stendel.
" [54] Strasborck in der Vcker Marckt.
" [55] Stetinum.
" [56] Stetinum. [Map]
" [57] Schloss zu alten Stettin. Carl Henr. a' Osteningen delineav.
" [58] Stralsvndia. Jo. Staud delineauit.
" [59] Templin.
" [60] Stättl. Zedenick.
" [61] Abriss der einfarth auss der Ost see in die Oder die Swine genandt.
" [62] Prospect des passes und newfehr Schantz. Erict. Jönson: deli.
" [63] Ykermÿnde.

no. [64] Ysedomb.
" [65] Werben.
" [66] Wrietzen an der Oder.
" [67] Wittstock.
" [68] Ambt Zechlin. Casp. Merian fecit.
" [69] Wollgast.
" [70] "
" [71] Brandenbvrga.
" [72] Dantiscvm. Dantzig.
" [73] Elbing. 1703. M. Merian fecit.
" [74] Pillaw.
" [75] Thorvnivm.—Thoren.
" [76] Livonia . . . [Map]
" [77] Revalia.—Reueln.
" [78] Nerva.
" [79] Riga.

Coast.

Prussia. *Ministerium für handel, gewerbe und öffentliche arbeiten.*
Preussen's see-atlas. Geschichte; übersichtskarte; leuchtthürme; küstenansichten. 2 p. l., 10 pp., front., 1 map, 14 pl. obl. 4°. Berlin, ministerium des handels, 1841. 5254

ITALY.

COAST.

Italy. *Ufficio idrografico.*
Vedute delle coste d' Italia disegnate dal vero da Porro Alberto. Pubblicate dall' ufficio idrografico della regia marina sotto la direzione del capitano di vascello G. Cassanello. Parte prima da porto Buso al promontorio d'Ancona. 1 p. l., 1 map, 26 pl. nar. fol. [Roma] 1897. 5255

NOTE.—Engraved title-page. Plates engraved by G. Bernasconi, V. Colombo, A. Garbotti, E. Parmianie.

MILITARY.

Italy. *Ministero della guerra.*
Il genio nella campagna d'Ancona e della bassa Italia. Atlante . . . 3 p. l., 3 l., 6 maps, 25 pl. fol. Torino [Favale? 1864] 5256

NOTE.—To accompany: *Il genio nella campagna d'Ancona e della bassa Italia con un proemio del gen. Menebrea. Torino, Favale, 1804.*

TRAVELS.

Dury, A.
Le porte-feuille nécessaire à tous les seigneurs qui font le tour d'Italie, oú l'on trouve une description exacte des villes, bourgs, villages & rivières, l'explication des vues, qui se présentent sur la droite et sur la gauche . . .—Il portafoglio necessario a tutti quelli

Dury, A.—Continued.

che fanno il giro d'Italia, nel quale si trova un' esatta descrizione delle città, borghi, ville e fiumi: la speigazione delle più belle vedute che occorrono per la strada, si a destra che a sinistra . . . 36 pp., 26 col. maps. 12°. Londres, A. Dury, 1774. 5257

NOTE.—Contains detailed maps of the roads between the principal cities of Italy in 1774.

WAR.

1718

Nolin, J. B.

Nouvelle édition du théâtre de la guerre en Italie contenant les cartes particulières de tous les estats d'Italie et plusieurs provinces des dits estats . . . 1 p. l., 15 maps. sm. fol. Paris, chez la veuve de J. B. Nolin, 1718. 5258

GENERAL.

1688

Zeiller, M.

Topographia Italiæ, das ist: warhaffte und curiôse beschreibung von gantz Italien, darinnen nach historischer warheit, die berûhmtesten stådte, vestungen, marckflecken und andere oerter, sampt ihren antiquitåten; auch was sich sonsten merck und denckwûrdiges sowol in geistlichem als politischem stande, biss auff diese unsere zeit zugetragen, oder durch die natur und kunst denenselben mitgetheilet worden: auff das fleissigste angemercket wird. Deme beygefûgt, eine kurtze und auszfûhrliche beschreibung derer im kônigreich Morea befindenden vornehmsten stådte und plåtze, darinn derer alterthum, erlittene schwere kriege, und was an ein und andern orten merckwûrdiges zubesehen, imgleichen was die durchl. republic Venedig, durch dero siegreiche waffen zeithero darinn erobert und eingenommen. Alles auss denen bewåhrtesten, alten und neuen scribenten, mit netten kupffer abbildungen aller hauptsåchlichsten stådte, fûrstl. und anderer pallåste, wie auch accuraten und kûnstlichen land-karten aussgefertiget, und zum ersten mal herauss gegeben. Nebst einem vollståndigen register. 2 p. l., 160, [11] 29, [3] pp., 29 maps, 24 pl. fol. Franckfurt, M. Merians seel. erben, 1688. 5259

NOTE.—The last volume of the *Topographia* with text by Zeiller and maps and plates by Mathias Merian published in 30 parts from 1642 to 1688. After the elder Mathias Merian's death the work was carried on by his two sons Mathias and Caspar. The half title page which is elaborately engraved by Jacob Sandrart reads: *Topographia Italiæ das ist warhaffte und curiöse beschreibung Italien. Sambt einen anhang von königreich Morea. Franckfurt ben Matthæi Merians seel: erben, 1688.*

CONTENTS.

no. [1] Italia antiqva. Philippo Cluvero designatore.
" [2] Nova Italiæ delineatio.
" [3] Nova et accvrata dvcatvs Venetiani, Mediolani, Genvæ, Mantvæque et finitimorvm principatvum delineatio.
" [4] Ancona.
" [5] Bononia vetvstissima mvsarvm sedes. [View]
" [6] Ferraria.
" [7] Florentia. [View]
" [8] Gallipoli.
" [9] Genva. [View]
" [10] Prospect des berümpten seeports und hafens zu Lerice.
" [11] Lavretvm. [View]
" [12] Lvca.
" [13] Valletta. Inset: [Islands of Malta, Comeno, Gozzo]
" [14] Mantova.
" [15] Mantva dvcatvs.
" [16] Messina.
" [17] Sicilia regnvm.
" [18] Castell zu Meÿlandt.—Castellvm Mediolanense.
" [19] Mediolanvm.
" [20] Gaeta, Mola. [View]
" [21] Regno di Napoli.
" [22] Neapolis.
" [23] Scÿlla et Charÿbtis. [View]
" [24] [Sinus Pvteolanus]
" [25] Forvm Vulcani vocavit antiquitas qvem hodie vulgo la Solfatara appellant. Per Ioach. Sandrart del: [View]
" [26] Vesuvivs mons neapoleos. [View]
" [27] Ostia. [View]
" [28] Padova.
" [29] Panormo.
" [30] Nova Palma.
" [31] Parma.
" [32] Ticinvm.—Pavia.
" [33] Pervsia. [View]
" [34] Piacenza.
" [35] Pisa.
" [36] Roma.
" [37] Castell S^t. Angeli.—Zwei marmorsteinerne pferdt auff dem berg Quirinalis.—S^t. Bartolomei insul.—Arcus Septimii Seueri. [Views]
" [38] Capitolivm. [View]
" [39] Campo Vacchina. Ioach. Sandrard delin. [View]
" [40] Stato della Chiesa con la Toscana.
" [41] Siena.
" [42] Tivoli.—Templum Sibilla.—Lapsus Tiueronis fluuy. [View]
" [43] Tvrino.
" [44] Venetia.
" [45] Piazza S. Marco di Venetia. [View]
" [46] L'altra parte della Piazza di s. Marco in Venetia. [View]
" [47] [Confessus Senat. Venet.] [View]

Zeiller, M—Continued.

no. [48] Candia, cum insulis alÿs proxime ei adiacentibus. Insets: Corfu.—Cefalonia.—Zante.
" [49] Candia.—Corphv. [Views]
" [50] Verona. [View]
" [51] Die stadt und vestung Coron. 1685.
" [52] Ragusa.—Negroponte. [Views]
" [53] Die stadt Prevesa und die vestung S. Maura.

1704–1705

Blaeu, J.

Het nieuw stede boek van Italie, ofte naauwkeurige beschryving van alle deszelfs steden, paleyzen, kerken, &c. Nevens de landkaarten van alle deszelfs provincien . . . Alles naar de orgineelen, op de plaatsen afgeteekend, nevens de plaaten die hy in zyn leeven daar van heeft laaten snyden, waar van eenige om naauwkeuriger te weezen, binnen Rome gemaakt zyn. Waar by gevoegt zyn veele steden, havens, kerken en andere gebouwen naar de Roomsche voorbeelden &c. . . . 4 v. in 3. fol. Amsterdam, P. Mortier, 1704–1705. 5260

NOTE.—The same as the french edition of this date. See v. 1, title 3053.
This copy of the dutch edition wants many maps which are called for by the index, and which appear in the french edition. Volume 1, wants 25 maps, v. 2, 8 maps, v. 3–4, 10 maps and the index of v. 4.

CONTENTS.

v. 1. Lombardye te weeten, de republyk van Genua.—De hertogdommen van Milane, Parma, Modena, en Mantua.—De republyk van Venetie, Luka, en het groot hertogdom van Toskane.
" 2. Den Kerkelylen staat.
" 3–4. Het koninkryk van Napels en van Sicilie. 1704.—De amphiteaters, theaters, schouwburge, zegenboogen, tempels, piramide, graafstede, obeliscus, kerken, paleizen, &c. 1705.

1854–1875

Sardinia. *Corpo reale dello stato maggiore.*

Carta topografica degli stati in terraferma di s. m. il re di Sardegna. Alla scala di 1. a 50,000 . . . 1 map on 89 sheets. fol. [Turin, 1854–1875] 5261

NOTE.—Title on foglio no. 1.
Index sheet wanting.
Pubblicato nell' anno 1854—Riveduto nell' anno 187[5].

1876–1884

Italy. *Ufficio idrografico.*

[Carte delle provincie meridionali, alla scala dell' 1:50,000] 2 v. 160 maps, 1 pl.; 128 maps. fol. [Genova, 1876–1884] 5262

NOTE.—Sections of the map drawn from 1868–1875. Reproduced from 1876–1877. One pl., *Segni convenzionali,* dated 1884.
No title-page.
Contains index sheet.

PROVINCES.

LIGURIA.

Italy. *Ministero della marina.*

Portolano della Liguria. 26 l. incl. 24 maps. obl. fol. Genova, Armanino, 1855. 5263

NOTE.—Corrected title. See v. 1, title 3066.
Contains the following plans of cities:
no. 3. Rada e porto di Nizza.
" 4. Porto di Nizza.
" 5. Piano di Villa Francà.
" 6. Golfo di San Gioan.
" 7. Porto di Monaco.
" 8. Rada e porto di San Remo.
" 9. Rada e Porto Maurizio.—Rada di Oneglia.
" 10. Rada di Diano il Cervo e Andora.
" 11. Rada di Languaglia ed Alassio.
" 12. Rada del Borghetto e Ceriale.—Rada di Borsio, la Pietra e Loano.
" 13. Golfo di Genova.
" 14. Rada di Vado e porto di Savona.
" 15. Porto di Savona.
" 16. Rada e porto di Genova. 1854
" 17. Porto di Camogli.
" 18. Golfo di Rapallo.
" 19. Porto Fino.
" 20. Porto di Rapallo.
" 21. Rada di Sestri di Levante.
" 22. Rada del Mesco.
" 23. Golfo della Spezia.
" 24. Piano dell' isola di Capraia. 1854.
" 25. Porto di Capraja.
" 26. Carta del littorale della Liguria e Contado di Nizza . . . Sotto la direzione del v[ce]ammiraglio C[re]. G[pe]. Albini. 1854. 1855.

NAPLES.

Italy. *Istituto topografico militare.*

Carta delle province Napolitane in fogli 25 fotoincisa col procedimento del generale. Avet alla scala di 1: 250,000 . . . 1874 . . . 1 p. l., 1 map on 25 sheets. obl. fol. [Naples, 1874] 5264

SICILY.

Italy. *Ufficio tecnico del corpo di stato maggiore.*

Quadro d'unione della carta della Sicilia al 100,000 riduzione foto-incisa da quella rilevata alla scala di 1:50,000. 1 map on 48 sheets, index map. obl. fol. [Turin] 1872. 5265

CATANIA.

Public health.

Fischera, F.

Progretti di massima pel risanamento di Catania . . . [Atlante] cover-title, 10 maps. sm. fol. [Catania, tipografia C. Galatola, 1887] 5266

NOTE.—To accompany his work of the same title.

MISCELLANEOUS.

Pontine Marshes.

Prony, G. C. F. M. R., *baron* de.

Atlas des marais Pontins. viii pp. 6 maps (2 fold.) 32 diagrs. Paris, Firmin Didot, 1823. 5267

NOTE.—To accompany his *Description hydrographique et historique des marais Pontins.*

NETHERLANDS.

CITIES.

Coronelli, M. V.

[Collection des vues des villes et des plans dans les Pays-Bas] 8 t. p., 13 maps, 65 pl. obl. 8°. [Venetia, 1697?] 5268

NOTE.—This collection of maps and views has no general title page, but has eight illuminated half titles to the different parts as follows: *Ducato di Gueldria del p. Coronelli.—Il ducato de Gueldria.—Contado d' Olanda.—Roterdam, rappresentatio in differenti vedute.—Signoria d'Utrecht.—Contea di Zutphen.—Signoria d' Overissel õ Transisselana.—Brabante.*

Many of the plates are taken from Coronelli's *Viaggi. Venetia, G. B. Tramontino, 1697.*

Among the views is one in four parts showing Rotterdam.

REPRODUCTIONS.

Deventer, J. R.

Nederlandsche steden in de 16e eeuw . . . Facsimile-uitgave met eene inleiding van R. Fruin . . . cover-title, 62 col. maps. fol. s'Gravenhage, M. Nijhoff, 1916. 5269

NOTE.—In portfolio.

Published in ten incomplete parts.

Pts. 5-6 wanting.

In a note, dated august 1918, at the foot of a list giving the contents of the parts as far as published, the publisher states that all the maps selected for this series which are in the Netherlands have been issued and that owing to unsettled conditions due to the war, the reproduction of those maps which have been selected from collections in Brussels and Madrid will be supplied at a later date, and the set completed.

HISTORICAL.

Netherlands. *Commissie van den geschiedkundigen atlas van Nederland.*

Geschiedkundige atlas van Nederland. De Bourgondische tijd. pt. 1, 94 pp. 8°. 's-Gravenhage, M. Nijhoff, 1915. 5270

NOTE.—Text to accompany map no. 7 of atlas. See title 5271.

CONTENTS.

pt. 1. De Noordelijke Nederlanden in 1476, door dr. P. J. Blok.—Het Bourgondische rijk in 1476, door dr. P. J. Blok.—De St. Elizabethsvloed, 1424, door dr. A. A. Beekman.

Geschiedkundige atlas van Nederland. Uitgegeven door de Commissie voor den geschiedkundigen atlas van Nederland en geteekend door het lid der Commissie dr. A. A. Beekman. 3 v. 4°. and Atlas in portfolios. fol. 's-Gravenhage, M. Nijhoff [1911]-1916. 5271

NOTE.—All published to date.
To be published in 89 sheets, six or eight to appear yearly.
Each map accompanied by text bound separately. See titles 5270, 5272, 5273.
A new edition has been issued of sheet no. 15 of map no. 12, De republiek in 1795.

CONTENTS.

Maps.

no. 5. Holland, Zeeland en Westfriesland in 1300. 5 sheets, no. 1. 1916.
" 7. De Bourgondische tijd. 6 (i. e. 4) sheets. nos 1–4. 1915.
" 12. De republiek in 1795. 19 (*i. e.* 20) sheets. [1911-1914]
" 12a. De rijnverdeeling in de 17e en 18e eeuw, door J. W. Welcker. 5 sheets. 1914.
" 15. De rechterlijke indeeling na 1795, door mr. dr. J. C. Overvoorde. 3 sheets. 1915.

Geschiedkundige atlas van Nederland. Holland, Zeeland en Westfriesland in 1300, door dr. A. A. Beekman. 54 pp. 8°. 's-Gravenhage, M. Nijhoff, 1916. 5272

NOTE.—Text to accompany map no. 5 of atlas. See title 5271

CONTENTS.

pt. 1. Holland's Noorderkwartier.

Geschiedkundige atlas van Nederland. De rechterlijke indeeling na 1795, door mr. dr. J. C. Overvoorde . . . 32 pp. 8°. 's-Gravenhage, M. Nijhoff, 1915. 5273

NOTE.—Text to accompany map no. 15 of atlas. See title 5271.

GENERAL.

1588

Guicciardini, L.

Descrittione di M. Lodovico Gvicciardini, gentilhvomo fiorentino, di tvtti i paesi bassi, altrimenti detti Germania inferiore. Con tutti le carte di geographia del paese, & col ritratto naturale di molte terre principali; riueduta di nuouo, & ampliata per tutto la terza volta dal medesimo autore. Al gran' re cattolico, Don Filippo d'avstria. Con amplissimo indice di tutte le cose piu memorabili. 12 p. l., 432 [18] pp. 78 maps. fol. Anversa, C. Plantin, 1588. 5274

NOTE.—Map no. 5: pp. [82–83].

NORWAY.

PROVINCES.

TRONDHJEM.

Historical.

Koren, K. B.

Karter og topografiske tegninger vedkommende Trondhjem og Trøndelagen. Udgivne af Trondhjems historiske forening ved Kristian Koren. pt. 1, 1 p. l., [6] pp., 5 maps, 3 pl. fol. Trondhjem, 1899. 5275

POLAND.

HISTORICAL.

Bansemer, J. M., *and* **Zaleski Falkenhagen, P.**

Atlas, containing ten maps of Poland, exhibiting the political changes that country has experienced during the last sixty years, from 1772 to the present time . . . preceded by a geographical, historical, political, chronological, statistical, literary, and commercial table; compiled from the works of Malte-Brun, Stanislas Plater, Lelewel, Swiencki, Rulhiere, Ferrand, Balbi, Schnitzler, Hassel, L. Chodzko, and other eminent writers . . . 4 p. l., 10 maps. fol. London, J. Wyld; J. Ridgway & sons, 1837. 5276

CONTENTS.

no. [1] Poland in 1772 with its principal geographical divisions.
" [2] Poland in 1772 after the first partition.
" [3] Poland in 1793 after the second partition.
" [4] Poland in 1795 after the third partition.
" [5] Poland in 1807 after the Treaty of Tilsit.
" [6] Poland in 1809 after the Treaty of Schönbrunn.
" [7] Poland in 1815 after the Congress of Vienna.

no. [8] Poland in 1831 after the war of independence.
" [9] Poland and the neighbouring countries according to the religion of the majority.
" [10] Poland and the neighbouring countries according to the languages of the inhabitants.

PORTUGAL.

GENERAL.

1830–1835

Lopez, T., *i. e.,* **T. L. de V. M.**

Atlas geográfico de España, que comprende el mapa general de la península, todos los particulares de nuestras provincias, y el del reino de Portugal . . . 2d ed. corregida por sus hijos. 2 p. l., 38 maps on 204 l. fol. Madrid, 1830–[1835] 5277

NOTE.—For notes consult card under Spain, title 5286.

RUSSIA.

RAILROADS.

Koch, W., *and* **Opitz, C.**

Eisenbahn und verkehrsatlas von Russland. 3. verb. aufl. 64 pp., 33 col. maps. 12°. Leipzig, J. J. Arnd, 1912. 5278

WARS.

1855–1856

Simpson, W.

The seat of war in the east . . . Dedicated by permission to her most gracious majesty, the queen. 2 v., cover-title, 1 p. l., 40 (*i. e.* 30) views; cover-title, 1 p. l., [14] pp., 41 (*i. e.* 40) views. fol. London, P. & D. Colnaghi, 1855–1856. 5279

NOTE.—Many views are accompanied by small outline sketches which serve as indexes to points in the views.

Two views called for by the index are on the covers.

In v. 1, ten views are wanting. The small outline sketches for nos. 18 and 19 appear, while the views are wanting.

There is no letterpress to the first volume. A volume containing descriptions of the views in v. 1, and the small outline sketches which have been inserted in v. 1, was published separately in 1855 by George Brackenbury and entitled, *Descriptive sketches illustrating Mr. William Simpson's drawings of the seat of the war in the east. First series.* A copy of this work is in the Library of Congress.

CONTENTS.

v. 1, no. 1. The Malakoff tower. (On title-page)
" " 2. The cavalry affair on the heights of Bulganak, 19th sept. 1854. [Wanting]
" " 3. Balaklava, looking toward the sea. [Wanting]
" " 4. The gale off the port of Balaklava. 14th. nov. 1854.

Simpson, W.—Continued.

v. 1, no. 5. Sebastopol from the rear of the english batteries.
" " 6. The heavy cavalry charge of 25th october, 1854. [Wanting]
" " 7. The second charge of the guards at the battle of Inkermann. [Wanting]
" " 8. Lord Raglan's head quarters at Khutor-Karagatch.
" " 9. Distant view of lord Raglan's head quarters before Sebastopol.
" " 10. A quiet day in the Diamond battery, with portraits of capt. William Peel, com. Burnet, &c. [Wanting]
" " 11. The field of Inkermann.
" " 12. Sentinel of the Zouaves, before Sevastopol.
" " 13. Commissariat difficulties. The road from Balaklava to Sevastopol at Kadikoi, during the wet weather.
" " 14. The graves in the fort on Cathcart's hill.
" " 15. The light cavalry charge of the 25th october, 1854. [Wanting]
" " 16. Huts and warm clothing for the army.
" " 17. Camp of the naval brigade, before Sebastopol.
" " 18. Camp of the first division. [Wanting]
" " 19. Sebastopol from the 26-gun battery on the extreme right of the french attack. [Wanting]
" " 20. Head of the harbour, Sebastopol.
" " 21. Graves at the head of the harbour of Balaklava.
" " 22. Sebastopol from the sea. Sketched from the deck of h. m. s. Sidon.
" " 23. Embarkation of the sick at Balaklava.
" " 24. A quiet night in the Greenhill battery.
" " 25. The camp of the second division, looking east. January, 1855.
" " 26. The ruins of Inkermann and the city of caverns.
" " 27. Highland brigade camp, looking south.
" " 28. The railway at Balaklava, looking south.
" " 29. The new works at the siege of Sebastopol on the right attack. From the mortar battery on the right to Gardon's battery.
" " 30. A Christmas dinner on the heights before Sebastopol.
" " 31. Sebastopol from the east or extreme right of english attack.
" " 32. View from the heights above Balaklava, looking toward Sebastopol.
" " 33. Excavated church in the caverns at Inkermann, looking west.
" " 34. A hot day in the batteries.
" " 35. A hot night in the batteries.
" " 36. The valley of the shadow of death. Caves in the Woronzoff road behind the 21-gun battery.
" " 37. Russian rifle pit. Now part of the british advance trenches, on the left of the right attack, or Gordon's battery.
" " 38. Prince Woronzoff's palace near Yalta on the south coast of the Crimea.
" " 39. The monastery of St. George and cape Fiolente.
" " 40. The light-house at cape Cheronese.

v. 2, no. 1. Disembarkation of the expedition to Kertch at Kamish Bournou.
" " 2. Fortress of Yenikle, looking toward the sea of Azoff.
" " 3. Kertch from the north.
" " 4. Straits of Yenikale with the bay and town of Kertch. From the old fortress of Yenikale.
" " 5. Funeral cortege of lord Raglan leaving head quarters.

v. 2, no. 6. The town batteries or interior fortifications of Sebastopol, from the advance parallel of Chapman's attack, 23 june, 1855.
" " 7. Burning of the government buildings at Kertch, 9th. june, 1855.
" " 8. Interior of lord Raglan's head quarters.
" " 9. Camp of the 4th. division. July 15th. 1855.
" " 10. Cavalry camp, july 9th. 1855.
" " 11. Camp of the light division.
" " 12. Camp of the 3rd. division.
" " 13. Sketch of the interior of the Mamelon Vert, looking south.
" " 14. Battle of the Tchernaya, 16th. August 1855.
" " 15. Valley of the Tchernaya. Looking north.
" " 16. Balaklava shewing the state of the quays & the shipping in may, 1855.
" " 17. Cape Aliya. Looking north, toward Balaklava.
" " 18. The valley of Baidar. From near Petroski's villa, looking east.
" " 19. The attack on the Malakoff.
" " 20. The interior of the Redan.
" " 21. Church in the rear of the Redan . . . showing the effects of shot and shell.
" " 22. Sebastopol from the rear of fort Nicholas, looking south
" " 23. The investiture of the order of the Bath. At the head quarters of the british army before Sebastopol.
" " 24. The north side of the harbour of Sebastopol. 22nd. june 1855.
" " 25. Ditch of the bastion Du Mât.
" " 26. Docks at Sebastopol with ruins of fort S. Paul.
" " 27. Interior of the Malakoff with the remains of the round tower.
" " 28. Kamiesch.
" " 29. Interior of fort Nicholas.
" " 30. Public library & Temple of the winds.
" " 31. Quarantine cemetery and church, with french battery no. 50.
" " 32. The Admiralty, Sebastopol.
" " 33. Hospital and cemetery at Scutari.
" " 34. One of the wards of the hospital at Scutari.
" " 35. Church of S^{t}. Peter & S^{t}. Paul.
" " 36. Sebastopol from old Chersonese, and ancient church of S^{t}. Valdimir.
" " 37. A bomb proof chamber in the Malakoff. (On title-page)
" " 38. Redan and advance trenches of british right attack.
" " 39. Ditch of the Malakoff, battery Gervais and rear of the Redan.
" " 40. Mine of the bastion Du Mat.
" " 41. Bastion Du Mat, from the central bastion.

PROVINCES.

CAUCASIA.

I. Russkoe geograficheskoe obshchestvo, St. Petersburg. Kavkazskiĭ otdi͡el, Tiflis.

Атласъ кв X книжкѣ записокъ кавказскаго отдѣла императорскаго русскаго географическаго общества. title, 1 p. l., [2], 7 fold. maps. 8°. **Тифлисъ**, 1879. 5280

NOTE.—"Atlas to accompany the 10th volume of Zapinski's works on the Caucasian region."

FINLAND.

Sällskapet för Finlands geografi.

Suomen kartasto, 1910. [Atlas de Finlande, 1910.—Atlas öfver Finlande, 1910] 2 p. l. iii, 7 pp., 63 col. maps, tab. fol. [Helsingfors, J. Simelii arfvingars boktryckeriaktiebolag, 1911] 5281

NOTE.—At head of title: Suomen Maatieteellinen Seura.
To be accompanied by 2 v. of text, 8°.
The atlas is published in one edition only, the descriptions being in finnish, swedish and french on each map. Copies are issued with the title and preliminary matter in one or another of the three languages, while the text is published separately in each of the three languages. The Library of Congress has a copy with the french title (see v. 3, title 4063) and the two volumes of text in french, also the two volumes of text in swedish.
For the 1st edition of the publication, see v. 1, title 3121.

CITIES.

PETROGRAD.

Akademiía nauk. *Petrograd.*

Plan de la ville de St. Petersbourg avec ses principales vües dessiné & gravé sous la direction de l'Académie impériale des sciences & des arts. 1 p. l., 6 pp. 2 maps, 13 pl. (5 fold.) fol. St. Petersbourg, 1753. 5282

NOTE.—Title in russian and french.

MISCELLANEOUS.

Neva River.

Russia. *Gidrograficheskiĭ departament.*

Атласъ рѣки Невы отъ С. Петербурга до Ладожскаго озера, составленный по новѣйшимъ изслѣдованіямъ при Гидрографическомъ департаментѣ. cover-title, index map, 12 maps. obl. fol. [Petrograd] 1863 5283

NOTE.—"Atlas of the river Neva from St. Petersburg to Ladoga lake."

SPAIN.

WARS.

Spain. *Cuerpo de estado mayor del ejército.*

Atlas topográfico de la Narración militar de la guerra carlista de 1869 á 1876. Pub. por el depósito de la guerra á cargo del Cuerpo de e. m. del ejército. 2 p. l., 58 pl. (maps, part double). fol. [Madrid] lit. del depósito de la guerra [1890?] 5284

NOTE.—To accompany the following work: *Narración militar de la guerra carlista de 1869 á 1876, por el Cuerpo de estado mayor del ejército. Pub. por el depósito de la guerra . . . Madrid, impr. del depósito de la guerra, 1883–89. 14 v.*

GENERAL.

1787

Tofiño de San Miguel, V.

[Atlas maritimo de España] 11 maps, 4 pl. fol. [Madrid, por la viuda de Ibarra, hijos y compañia, 1787] 5285

NOTE.—An official letter in the files of the Central archivo del ministerio de marina notes the sudden death of jefe de escuadra Tofiño in Isla de Leon (San Fernando) the morning of jan. 15, 1795, of a palsy fit.

For notice of Tofiño, see Navarrete, *Biblioteca espanola, v. 2, pp. 772–777.*

CONTENTS.

no. [1] Carta esférica de la costa de Espana en el Mediterraneo, y de su correspondiente de Africa. 1786.
" [2] Carta esférica del estrecho de Gibraltar. 1786.
" [3] Plano geométrico de la bahia de Algeciras y Gibraltar. 1786.
" [4] Carta esférica desde punta de Europa á cabo de Gata en la costa de Europa, y desde ceuta hasta cabo Hone en la de Africa.
" [5] Carta esférica de la costa de España, desde cabo de Gata, hasta cabo de Oropesa. 1786.
" [6] Carta esférica desde cabo Oropesa a cabo de Creux. 1786.
" [7] Carta esferica de las yslas Baleares y Pithyusas. 1786.
" [8] Carta esférica de las islas de Iuizay formentera. 1786. Inset: Plano del puerto de la isla de Iuiza.
" [9] Carta esférica de la isla de Mallorca y sus adyacentes. 1786. Insets Plano del puerto de Andraix ó Andrache.—Plano del puerto de Soller.—Plano de puerto Pi.—Plano del puerto de la isla de Cabrera.—Plano de puerto Petra.—Plano de Cala Longa.
" [10] Carta esférica de la isla de Menorca. 1786. Insets: Plano del puerto de Fornells.—Plano del Pto. de Ciudadela.
" [11] El puerto de Mahon.

1830–1835

Lopez, T., *i. e.*, T. L. de V. M.

Atlas geográfico de España, que comprende el mapa general de la península, todos los particulares de nuestras provincias, y el del reino de Portugal . . . 2d ed. corregida por sus hijos. 2 p. l., 38 maps on 204 l. fol. Madrid, 1830–[1835] 5286

NOTE.—Dates on maps vary from 1765 to 1835.

For note consult v. 3, title 4065.

Map no. 2, *Mapa de la provincia de Toledo,* is dated 1834; map no. 74–77, *Mapa geografia del principado de Cataluña,* dated 1835.

The map of Portugal in eight parts is dated 1778. Another edition appeared in 1811.

Contains also a plan of the city of Oviedo. no. 33.

1864

Ferreiro, M.

Atlas geográfico de España. Islas adyacentes y posesiones Españolas de ultramar. Coleccion de mapas grabados en acèro . . . 1 p. l., 8 [1] pp. 58 maps. 8°. Madrid, Gaspar & Roig, 1864. 5287

NOTE.—At head of title: Gaspar y Roig, editores.

Maps engraved by R. Alabern.

The following maps relate to America:

no. [1] [World]
" [54] Isla de Cuba.
" [55] Isla Española.
" [56] Isla de Puerto-Rico.

1900–1903

Escudé y Bartolí, M.

Atlas geográfico ibero-americano. España. Descripción geográfica y estadística de las provincias españolas, con el número de habitantes, edificios y viviendas de cada ayuntamiento, según resulta de los datos provisionales del censo de 1897. Índice alfabético de los ayuntamientos con la población de 1901. 2 v. 52 double maps. sm. fol. Barcelona, A. Martín [1900–1903] 5288

NOTE.—[Vol. 2] Cartas corográficas, cuidadosamente rectificadas por personal facultativo bajo la dirección del capitán de ingenieros D. Benito Chías y Carbó.

SWITZERLAND.

CITIES.

Zeiller, M.

Topographia Helvetiæ, Rhætiæ, te [!] Valesiæ: das ist, beschreibung und eigentliche abbildung der vornehmsten städte und plätze in der hochlöblichen eydgenossenschaff, Graubündten, Wallis . . . 90, [7] pp., 78 pl. incl. maps, plans & views. 4°. Franckfurt am Mayn, zum truck verlegt von denen Merianischen erben, 1654. 5289

NOTE.—Bound with his . . . *Topographia . . . Brandenburgici et ducatus Pomeraniæ. 1652?*

Added engraved title: Topographia Heluetiæ, Rhætiæ et Valesiæ . . . 1642.

For note regarding Merian, see title 5253 *Zeiller's Topographia electoratū Brandenburgici . . . [1652?]*

CONTENTS.

Unless otherwise specified the following are views.

no. [1] Nova totius Germaniæ descriptio. [Map]
" [2] Die eÿdtgnoschafft Pünten vnd Wallis Helvetia cum confinijs. [Map]
" [3] Vicus Elggeuw.
" [4] Mure monasterium.
" [5] Tigurvm.—Zürych.
" [6] " Zurich. " I. Casp. Nüscheler delineauit. [Map]
" [7] Forsteck. I. Arteuser ingen. delin.

no. [8] Eglisaw.
" [9] Grifensee. I. C. Gÿger inuent.
" [10] Grüningen. H. T. inu.
" [11] Regensperg. I. Ziegler inu.
" [12] Stein am Rhein.
" [13] Winterthur.
" [14] Andelfingen.
" [15] Kÿburg.
" [16] Statt Wilisaw.
" [17] Schloss Wedeschwÿl.
" [18] Bern. Ioseph Plep figur: M. Merian sculp.
" [19] Oron. Casp. Merian fec.
" [20] Araw.
" [21] Arberg.
" [22] Arburg.
" [23] Lentzburg. Io. Plep fig.
" [24] Brugg. Ios. Zechender delin.
" [25] Habspurg.
" [26] Burgdorf. Jos. Zehender fig.
" [27] Lavsanna. [Plan]
" [28] Thvna.
" [29] Vevey. Casp. Merian.
" [30] Gletchers im Grünwalt. Ioh. Plepp figurau.
" [31] Murten.
" [32] Neuis.—Niow.
" [33] Aventicum.
" [34] Lvcern.
" [35] Abbildung der 4. Waldstätten see.
" [36] Sempach.
" [37] Sursee.
" [38] Munster im Argaw.
" [39] Altorff.
" [40] Svitia. [Schwytz]
" [41] Prospect des haupt fleckens Schwytz.
" [42] Einsideln.
" [43] Underwaldia.
" [44] Engelberg.
" [45] Zug.
" [46] Glaris.
" [47] Basilea—Basel. [Map]
" [48] " "
" [49] Prospectvs Templi cathedralis qvod est Basileæ.
" [50] Münchenstein.
" [51] Liechstall. M. I. I. Ringle deline.
" [52] Wallenburg.
" [53] Pierre Pertuise. Ios. Plep figurau. M. Merian fecit.
" [54] Romanostier. Casp. Merian fecit.
" [55] Freyburg.
" [56] Soloturvm.
" [57] Schaffhausen. I. Caspar Lang inv. M. Merian sculp.
" [58] Lauffen. [Rhine falls]
" [59] Nünkirch.

Zeiller, M.—Continued.

no. [60] Appenzell. Inset: Herissaw.
" [61] Baden im Argow.
" [62] Klingnaw.
" [63] Leüggeren.
" [64] Wettingen.
" [65] Der mittlere fall des Rheins.
" [66] Zurzach.
" [67] Brenngarten.
" [68] Lvgano.
" [69] Bellinzona.
" [70] Diessenhofen.
" [71] Frauenfeld.
" [72] Mellingen.
" [73] Rapperswyl.
" [74] Pfefers. [Plan]
" [75] Pfefers. M. Merian fecit.
" [76] Mühlhausen.—[Plan] Sculp. M. Merian.
" [77] Bienna—Biel. Ioh. Heinrich Laubscher delinea.
" [78] S. Gallen. [Plan]
" [79] Genève. [Plan]
" [80] Genèue.
" [81] Nüwenburg am see.
" [82] Weÿerhaus. Casp. Merian fecit.
" [83] Chur.
" [84] Plursivm.
" [85] Plursivm terræ.
" [86] Ursprung des hinderen vndt vorderen Rheins.
" [87] S. Lutzisstein in Pünten. [Plan]
" [88] Leug.
" [89] S. Maurise in Wallis.
" [90] Sitten. Hudolff delin.
" [91] Breiten Landenberg.
" [92] Bryg naters.
" [93] Fischbach.
" [94] Werdenstein.—Monasteriû S. Urbani.
" [95] Sandeck.
" [96] Movister. Casp. Marian fec.
" [97] Schloss Chastillard.
" [98] " de Blonaÿ.

ASIA.

LITERARY AND HISTORICAL.

Bartholomew, J. G.

A literary & historical atlas of Asia . . . xi, 226 pp. incl. 90 col. maps, 10 pl. 16°. London, J. M. Dent & sons ltd.; New York, E. P. Dutton & co. [1918]

[Everyman's library. Edited by E. Rhys. Reference] 5290

NOTE.—Contains maps of the following cities: Dehli.—Lucknow.—Cawnpore.—Lahore.—Rangoon.—Lhasa.

Contains a brief survey of the coinage of Asia, maps of the notable battles connected with the history of Asia, and a gazatteer of towns and places.

GENERAL.

1803

Laurie, R., *and* **Whittle, J.**

The country trade East-India pilot; for the navigation of the East-Indies and oriental seas, within the limits of the East India company, extending from the cape of Good Hope, to China, New Holland, and New Zeeland, with the Red sea, gulf of Persia, bay of Bengal, and China seas: chiefly composed from actual surveys and draughts communicated by experienced officers of the East-India company, and from the Neptune oriental, by m. d'Après de Mannevillette . . . A new edition with many additions and improvements. 3 p. l., 87 (*i. e.* 84) maps. fol. London, R. Laurie & J. Whittle, 1803. 5291

NOTE.—The following noted at foot of title-page: "An entire new . . . book of sailing directions for this work is published as above, the second edition" . . .
Maps dated from 1762–1803.
Maps no. 56–57, 87 wanting.
The following maps relate to the Philippine islands:
no. 1. Laurie and Whittle's new chart of the Indian and Pacific oceans. 1800.
" 65. The southern part of the Philippine islands. 1794.
" 67. A new chart of the China sea. 1802.
" 77. The Philippine islands. 1794.
" 79. Plan of the port of Lubec in the isle of Luconia. 1794.
" 80. Plan of the bay of Manila. Surveyed by Señor Alexandro Malaspina and communicated by Captn. G. G. Richardson. 1798.
" 81. Plan of Solsogon harbour on the south coast of Luconia.—Chart on the eastern coast of Bongo bay in the island of Mindanao. 1794.

1810

The complete East-India pilot; or, oriental navigator: being an extensive collection of charts, both general and particular, with plans of bays, roads, and harbours, with appearances of land . . . for the navigation not only of the Indian and Chinese seas with those of New Holland, but also of the seas between the British isles and the cape of Good Hope. Chiefly composed from actual surveys and draughts, communicated by experienced officers of the honorable East-India company, and from the french Neptune oriental, by mons. d'Après de Mannevillette. Improved ed. . . . v. 1, 2 p. l., 61 maps. fol. London, R. Laurie & J. Whittle, 1810. 5292

1912

Philip, G., & son, *ltd.*

Philip's comparative wall atlas of Asia. Edited by J. F. Umstead . . . & E. G. R. Taylor . . . 8 maps. fol. London, G. Philip & son, [1912]. 5293

NOTE.—Accompanied by *Explanatory handbook, Asia. cover-title, 16 pp. 8°. London, G. Philip & son, 1912.*

CHINA.

GENERAL.

1655

Martini, M.

Novvs atlas Sinensis . . . serenmo. archidvci Leopoldo Gvilielmo Avstriaco dedicatvs. [French edition] 5 p. l., 232, xvi, 44 pp., 17 maps. fol. [Amsterdami, J. Blaeu, 1655] 5294

NOTE.—Collation: colored, engraved title, verso blank, p. l. [1]; dedication, recto p. l. [2]—recto p. l. [4]; Privilegium Caesareum, dated Viennæ 7 Januarii, 1655, verso p. l. [4] verso p. l. [5]; Svmma privilegii, dated Hagæ Comitis, 20 Martii 1655, verso p. l. [5]; Text: Atlas de la Haute Asia, ou description géographique de l'empire de la Chine.—La table des degrez de longitude et de latitvde, 232 pp.; 17 maps; Addition dv royavme de Catay, par Jacqves Gool, xvj pp.; Histoire de la guerre de Tartarie, 44 pp. This atlas was published in two latin editions and in french, dutch, german and spanish. As part of the Blaeu atlases appears in many languages.

Backer mentions an english edition and states that the text without maps appears in the collection of Thevenot.

The 17 maps are the same in all editions.

Martin Martini, a jesuit missionary, was the superior of the mission at Hangtcheon, China, where he arrived in 1643, dying there in 1661.

For list of maps see v. 3, title 3430.

1917

Far eastern geographical establishment.

The new atlas and commercial gazetteer of China, a work devoted to its geography & resources and economic & commercial development. Edited by Edwin John Dingle. Containing 25 bi-lingual maps with complete indexes and many coloured graphs. Compiled and translated from the latest and most authoritative surveys and records . . . 6 p. l., xi, 88 [4] 187, xxxiii [61] pp. incl. 18 col. diagrs. 22 (*i. e.* 28) col. maps. fol. Shanghai, North-China daily news & herald, [1917] 5295

NOTE.—Largest and most comprehensive atlas of China in english so far published.

Contains a detailed survey of China, geographical, commercial, economic and educational, a trade research section, others on China's productions, railways, afforestation, geology, fauna and flora. The commercial section gives detailed information on China's imports and exports, the opium, silk, tea and treasure trades. Under "Communications in China," besides the railroads are found the main roads, water communications, telegraphs, telephones and the chinese post. Manufacturies and industries are dealt with, and the chinese maritime customs. There is also a list of the "Principal commodities of the world's commerce compiled with special reference to the economic and commercial development of China."

"List of changed place-names in China," pp. 30–33.

"List of open ports in China," p. 60.

CONTENTS.

no. 1. Chihli.
" 2. Shantung.
" 3. Honan.
" 4. Shansi.
" 5. Shensi.
" 6. Kansu.
" 7. Szechwan.
" 8. Hupeh.
" 9. Hunan.
" 10. Kiangsi.
" 11. Anhwei.
" 12. Kiangsu.
" 13. Chekiang.
" 14. Yunnan.
" 15. Kweichow.
" 16. Kwangsi.
" 17. Kwangtung.
" 18. Fukien.
" 19. Manchuria.
" 20. Sinkiang.
" 21. Mongolia.
" 22. Tibet.
" [23] Forestry map of China.
" [24-25] New production map of China.
" [26] The Kaiping coalfields.
" [27] Forestry map of Manchuria.
" [28] Railway map of China. Inset: Sketch map of Manchuria.

1917

Stanford, E.

Complete atlas of China, containing separate maps of the eighteen provinces of China proper . . . and of the four great dependencies . . . together with an index to all the names on the maps with the latitude and longitude of each place, all railways, telegraph stations, ports, & protestant mission stations marked . . . Specially prepared . . . for the China inland mission. 2. ed. v [3] 16 pp., 22 col. maps. sm. fol. London, Philadelphia, China inland mission; E. Stanford [1917] 5296

NOTE.—First edition published 1907, entitled: *Atlas of the Chinese empire.*

"Following closely upon the publication in 1908 of the first edition of this Atlas, a large wall map of China was issued based upon the same surveys and on the same scale. Four editions of this map have already appeared, in 1909, 1911, 1913 and 1916 respectively, each edition being thoroughly revised and brought up to date. The present work, therefore, though only the second edition of the Atlas, represents the fifth revision of this joint work on China." See Preface to new edition, signed Marshall Broomhall, editorial secretary.

For note on 1st ed. see v. 1, title 3195.

114882°—19——32

MISCELLANEOUS.

HONGKONG ISLAND.

View.

Great Britain. *Ordnance survey.*

Ten outline sketches of the island of Hong Kong. To accompany the ordnance map of Hong Kong. Royal engineers office, Hong Kong, 27th august, 1846. Printed by order of the honourable board of ordnance. 1 p. l., 10 pl., diagr. obl. fol. [London, 1846] 5297

Note.—Drawn by lt. Thomas Bernard Collinson, r. e., and lithographed by Dickinson & co., New Bond st.

YANGTZE AND YALONG RIVERS.

France. *Service hydrographique de la marine.*

Chine. Haut Yang-Tseu et Yalong, levé exécuté en 1910 par m. [L] Audemard, capitaine de frégate. Atlas de 37 feuilles à l'échelle de 1:37,500 et d'une feuille d'assemblage . . . cover-title, 29 (*i. e.* 35) maps, 4 pl. fol. Paris, imprimerie Gentil, 1914.

Note.—At head of title: Mission Audemard. 5298

INDIA.

HISTORICAL.

Joppen, C.

Historical atlas of India, for the use of high schools, colleges, and private students. 3d rev. & enl. ed. 20 pp., 33 col. maps. 4°. London, New York [etc.] Longmans, Green & co. 1914. 5299

STATISTICAL.

Saunders, T.

An atlas of twelve maps of India illustrating the mountain and river systems; the irrigation; civil divisions, population, and languages; railways, roads, telegraphs, post offices, ports, etc. Military commands and posts; famines; meteorology; crops; forests; and one-inch surveys. Accompanied with tables and notes . . . 4 p. l., 37 pp., 12 maps. fol. London, E. Stanford, 1889. 5300

GENERAL.

1827–1862

Great Britain. *India office.*

[The Indian atlas. 2 v., 30 maps; 38 maps. fol. London, J. Walker, 1827–1862] 5301

NOTE.—Volume 1 contains the northern part of India and V. 2, the southern part.

Contains the early sheets of the Indian atlas published up to 1862, which have been superseded by later editions from time to time. The editions of the sheets published between the years 1827–1836 were published by James Horsburgh, who preceded John Walker, in the Geographical department of the India office.

Sheet no. 27 wanting.

Index sheets are pasted in the reverse of front covers.

Sir Clement Markham, in his *Memoir on the Indian surveys*, gives the following comprehensive statement concerning the Indian atlas: "The labours of the topographical surveyors of the Madras military institute, based on the triangulation of colonel Lambton, began to attract attention as soon as their results arrived in England, and the necessity for the publication of more accurate and detailed maps of India than had hitherto been produced was soon acknowledged. Aaron Arrowsmith was of course consulted. He constructed a projection for a new atlas of India, on the scale of four miles to an inch, and the Madras survey maps were placed in his hands. The result was the publication of his atlas of South India, . . . which appeared in July, 1822.

"The question of the publication of the results of the great trigonometrical and topographical surveys, which had now been in progress for upwards of 20 years, was carefully and anxiously considered by the Court of directors, and colonel Salmond, then military secretary, was, for some years, in consultation with colonel Mackenzie, the surveyor general at Calcutta, on the subject. Colonel Hodgson, Mackenzie's successor, returned to England, in the hope and expectation that the great work would be entrusted to him. It, however, would no doubt have been given to Aaron Arrowsmith, who had already made the projection, and indeed published several sheets in the best style of the day; but, just at that time, the veteran cartographer died. The East Indian directors then appointed mr. John Walker to compile and engrave the sheets of the great atlas of India.

"Mr. Walker came of a family of map engravers. His father had worked for Dalrymple . . . The son was thoroughly trained and the amount of judgment and ability he brought to the great task he undertook is shown by the often disputed but ever approved excellence of his work.

"The Indian atlas was designed to occupy 177 sheets, 40 inches by 27, and the globular projection and scale (4 miles to the inch), originally proposed by mr. Aaron Arrowsmith, were adopted. The scheme embraces the region from Karáchi to Singapore, and includes Ceylon. From 1825 mr. Walker combined the various documents sent home by the surveyor in India, prepared the sheets for publication, engraved them on copper, and issued them to the surveyor general in India and to the London agent.

"The first sheets of the atlas were of course those for which the Madras topographical surveys furnished the materials. The first was published in 1827. Then followed one of Bandalkhand from captain Franklin's work, and the Himalayan region from Hodgson's and Herbert's surveys. These, however,

Great Britain. *India office*—Continued.

have since undergone complete revision. In 1860, and again in 1863, remonstrances were received from India at the delay in the execution of the sheets after the materials for them had been sent home. With a view to obviating this delay, a proposal was made by the surveyor general in july, 1864, that the sheets of the atlas should henceforth be brought out in quarter sheets. Mr. Walker concurred that this arrangement would expedite the work, and it was accordingly adopted. There has always been the highest testimony to the accuracy and excellent style in which mr. Walker has produced the atlas sheets.

"Mr. John Walker died, in his 86th year on april 19th, 1873, having been in the employment of the East India company and of the India Office for 48 years.

"In 1868 the question was raised whether the time had not come when the remaining sheets of the Atlas might with advantage be taken up by the surveyor general himself, and engraved at Calcutta. Hitherto the difficulties in the way of such a course had consisted in the want of means and the absence of an efficient staff. These difficulties had to a great extent been surmounted during the time that colonel Thuillier had been in charge.

"The change was accordingly sanctioned, and colonel Thuillier was deputed to make the necessary arrangements in England during the year 1868. He arranged with mr. Walker that all plates of sheets of the atlas actually in progress or for which materials had been sent to England, should be finished by mr. Walker; and that the rest should be undertaken by the surveyor general in India. Thus time was given for colonel Thuillier to organize his increased staff at Calcutta. Up to that time mr. Walker had completed the engraving of 84 of the atlas sheets.

"Colonel Thuillier returned to India with a staff of carefully selected english engravers, in January, 1869 . . .

"In 1870 the first quarter sheets of the Indian Atlas engraved in India . . . were issued."

Markham's *Memoir*, 1878, contains a reduced index map to the whole atlas at that date.

PALESTINE.

HISTORICAL.

Smith, G. A.

Atlas of the historical geography of the Holy Land. Prepared under the direction of J. G. Bartholomew . . . xxxvi, 12 pp., 57 col. maps on 60 l. fol. London, Hodder & Stoughton, 1915. 5302

PHILIPPINE ISLANDS.

SCHOOL.

Spain.

[An atlas of the Philippine Islands. Published in the year 1897 at Manila, for use in the public schools; edited by two army officers under the authority of the spanish government] 1 p. l., 33 maps. obl. 4°. [Manila, C. Chofrè & cª. 1897] 5303

NOTE.—Title-page wanting.

GENERAL.

1777

[Descripcion de plazas, prendos y fuertes de las Filipinas, &c.] 1 p. l. 92 numb. l. incl. 24 maps. fol. [1777?] 5304

NOTE.—In manuscript.

On the p. l. is the coat of arms of Spain with the inscription: "Asolis ortv vsqve ad occasvm Carolvs III Dei gratiæ rex."

Charles III reigned from 1759 to 1788.

The latest date found is 1777 (p. 51)

Contains detailed description of various towns, villages, forts, etc., followed by a "Data de la real taxa en dicho año de 1757."—Bookplate reads: "N°. . . . de la biblioteca de d. Lucas Alaman."

CONTENTS.

no. [1] Manila.
" [2] Pverto de Cavite.
" [3] Fverza de Zamb[a].
" [4] " " Zebv.
" [5] Fverte del presidio de Yligan.
" [6] " " " " Dapitan.
" [7] " " " " Cagaian el Chico.
" [8] Fverza del presidio de Oton.
" [9] Fverza de Capis en la provincia de Panay.
" [10] Fverte del pveblo de Romblon.
" [11] Fverza del presidio de Caraga.
" [12] Fverte del presidio de Castel.
" [13] " " " " Linao.
" [14] Fverza del presidio de Calamianes.
" [15] Fverte del pveblo de Cvio.
" [16] " " " de Agvtaya.
" [17] " " " " Cvlion.
" [18] " " " " Linacapan.
" [19] Fverza del pres°. de Cagaian Grande.
" [20] Fverte del pveblo de Capinatan.
" [21] Fverte del pres°. de Cabicvngan.
" [22] Fverte del presidio de Bagabag.
" [23] " " " "
" [24] Fverza del pres°. de Plaia Honda.

1845

Blanco, M.

Mapa general de las almas que administran los pp. Augustinos calzados en estas islas Filipinas, con espresion de los religiosos, conventos, situacion topógrafica de los pueblos, industria de sus habitantes, y años de su fundacion. Formado en 1845. 80 pp., incl. 11 maps. 2 tables. 8°. Manila, M. Sanchez, 1845. 5305

NOTE.—"En 4° de 80 pp., 11 cartas, de las provincias administradas levantadas por el p. fr. Manuel Blanco, el autor de la concocida Flora de Filipinal grabadas por Jacobo de Arquiza y Alexandro Sánchez. Es un libro raro que debo á la ambilidad del r. p. fr. Baldomero Real, augustino." See Pardo de Tavera, T. H. *Biblioteca Filipina. 4°. Washington, D. C., 1903. p. 247.*

Blanco, M.—Continued.

CONTENTS.

no. 1. Mapa del territorio de Tondo. 1832.
" 2. " Batangas. 1832.
" 3. " Bulacan. 1832.
" 4. la Pampanga. 1832.
" 5. " Pangasinan. 1832.
" 6. " Ylocus. 1832.
" 7. Mapa de la prov[a]. de Cebu. 1834.
" 8. " YloYlo. 1834.
" 9. " Capis. 1834.
" 10. " Antique. 1834.
" 11. Mapa de la isla de Panay. 1834.

SIBERIA.

1914.

Russia. *Glavnoe upravlenīe zemleustroĭstva i zemledi͡eli͡ia. Pereselencheskoe upravlenīe.*

Азіатская Россія . . . Изданіе Переселенческаго управленія Главнаго управленія землеустройства и земледѣлія. 2 v. illus., plates (1 col., part fold., part double) ports., maps (part double) plans, diagrs. 4°. *and* atlas of 71 (*i. e.* 60) pl. (part col., incl. maps, plans, diagrs., coats of arms) fol. С.-Петербургъ [Т-во "А. Ф. Марксъ"] 1914. 5306

NOTE.—Descriptive letterpress on verso of each plate.

"Йздано подъ ближайшимъ общимъ руководстомъ Г. В. Глинки. Текстъ редактированъ И. И. Тхоржевскимъ. Подборъ рисунковъ исполненъ проф. А. В. Праховымъ. Подборъ картъ и всѣхъ матеріаловъ по изданію—М. А. Цвѣтковымъ."

"Исторія изученія Азіатской Россіи": v. 2, pp. [617]-638.

CONTENTS.

v. I. Люди и порядки за Ураломъ. v. II. Земля и хозяйство.

TURKEY IN ASIA.

ASIA MINOR.

1902–1906

Kiepert, R.

Karte von Kleinasien, meist nach noch nicht oder in kleinstem massstabe veröffentlichten aufnahmen in 24 blatt bearbeitet von Richard Kiepert. Gestochen von R. Serbeck, terrain von F. Klimesch. Massstab 1:400,000. 24 (*i. e.* 25) sheets, each 19 x 24½. Berlin, D. Reimer (E. Vohsen) 1902–1906. 5307

NOTE.—The 1st and 2d editions of sheet A iv. Sinob are bound herein. Changes in that portion made it necessary to correct the 1st edition of the sheet by a 2d edition, which, according to a note, belongs to the 1st edition of the map. Explanatory text found on both sides of the index sheet.

AFRICA.

COLONIES.

French.

France. *Gouvernement général de l' Afrique occidentale française. Service géographique.*

Atlas des cartes ethnographiques et administratives des différentes colonies du gouvernement général. Année 1911. 2 p. l., 7 col. maps. fol. Paris, E. Larose, 1911. 5308

Note.—Maps dated 1910-1911, bear name "Gugelmann." Scale varies, 1: 2.000.000 and 1: 4.000.000.

CONTENTS.

no. [1] Sénégal.
" [2] Mauritanie.
" [3] Haut Sénégal & Niger & territoire militaire (Partie ouest)
" [4] Territoire militaire (Partie est)
" [5] Guinée frçaise.
" [6] Côte d' ivoire.
" [7] Dahomey.

HISTORICAL.

Bartholomew, J. G.

A literary & historical atlas of Africa and Australasia . . . xi, 218 pp. incl. 98 maps, 10 pl. 12°. London, J. M. Dent; New York, E. P. Dutton [1918].

[Everyman's library. Edited by Ernest Rhys. Reference] 5309

Note.—Contains maps of the following cities:

Africa.

p. 124. Cairo.
" 125. Cape Town.
" 126. Durban.
" 127. Pretoria.
" 128. Johannesburg.
" 129. Port Elizabeth.

Australasia.

" 130. Canberra.
" 131. Melbourne.
" 132. Sydney.
" 133. Auckland.—Wellington.
" 134. Dunebin.—Christchurch.

GENERAL.

1656

Sanson, N., *d'Abbeville.*

L'Afriqve en plvsievrs cartes novvelles, et exactes; & en divers traicté's de géographie, et d'histoire. Là où sont descripts succinctement, & auec vne belle méthode, & facile ses empires, ses monarchies, ses estats, &c. Les moevrs, les langves, les religions, le négoce, et la richesse de ses pevples, &c. Et ce qu'il y a de plus beau, & de plus rare dans toutes ses parties, & dans ses isles. Dediée à messire Nicolas Fovcqvet, vicomte de Melvn, et de Vavx; ministre d'estat. 2 p. l., [49] l., 18 maps. 8°. Paris, chez l'avthevr, 1656. 5310

NOTE.—"Avec privilège pour vingt ans."

Published separately 1656, 1660.

"L'Europe, l'Asie, l'Afrique & l'Amérique par les sieurs Nicolas Sanson père et fils, in 4. Paris, 1656, 1657, & 1658. 4 volumes qui se relient quelquefois en deux ou en un. L'Europe est de m. Sanson fils: le père a fait les trois autres parties. Les cartes en sont proprement gravées: on l'a contrefait en Hollande; mais la géographie a changé de face depuis que messieurs Sanson ont publié cet ouvrage."—Nicolas Lenglet Dufresnoy, *Méthode pour étudier la géographie. v 1, p. 339.*

1913

Philip, G. & son, *ltd.*

Philip's comparative wall atlas of Africa. Edited by J. F. Umstead . . . & E. G. R. Taylor . . . 8 maps. fol. London, G. Philip & son, *ltd.* [1913] 5311

NOTE.—Accompanied by *Explanatory handbook, Africa. cover-title, 16 pp. fol. London, G. Philip & son, ltd. [1913]*

STATES.

CONGO FREE STATE.

De Boeck, A.

Petit atlas du Congo belge. 32 (*i. e.* 68) pp. incl. 26 maps, xvi col. illus. 12°. Bruxelles, A. de Boeck, [1911?] 5312

NOTE.—Corrected from v. 3, title 4083a.

Reviewed by C. Knapp in *Société neuchâteloise de géographie. Bulletin. v. 21, pp. 238–239.*

GERMAN EAST AFRICA.

Sprigade, P. *and* **Lotz, H.**

Karte des sperrgebiets in deutsch-Südwestafrika in 10 blättern. Im auftrage der deutschen diamanten-gesellschaft m. b. h., bearb. von P. Sprigade und H. Lotz. Maszstab 1:100000 . . . cover-title, 10 fold. maps. fol. Berlin, D. Reimer (E. Vohsen) [1913] 5313

TUNIS.

Archælogical.

France. *Ministère de l'instruction publique et des beaux-arts.*

Atlas archéologique de la Tunisie. Édition spéciale des cartes topographiques publiées par le ministère de la guerre. Accompagnée d'un texte explicatif par E. Babelon, R. Cagnat, S. Reinach. pt. 1–15. fol. Paris, E. Leroux, 1892–1913. 5314

NOTE.—In progress.
For note see v. 3, title 4086.

—— —— Deuxiéme sér. liv. 1– fol. Paris, E. Leroux, 1914. 5315

NOTE.—On cover: Description de l'Afrique du Nord, entreprise par ordre de m. de ministre de l'instruction publique et des beaux-arts.
For first series see v. 3, title 4086.

OCEANICA.

HISTORICAL.

Bartholomew, J. G.

A literary & historical atlas of Africa and Australasia . . . xi, 218 pp. incl. 98 maps, 10 pl. 12°. London, J. M. Dent; New York, E. P. Dutton [1918]
[Everyman's library. Edited by Ernest Rhys. Reference] 5316

NOTE.—Contains maps of the following cities:

Africa.

p. 124. Cairo.
" 125. Cape Town.
" 126. Durban.
" 127. Pretoria.
" 128. Johannesburg.
" 129. Port Elizabeth.

Australasia.

" 130. Canberra.
" 131. Melbourne.
" 132. Sydney.
" 133. Auckland.—Wellington.
" 134. Dunebin.—Christchurch.

SCHOOL.

Bartholomew, J. G., *and* **Cramp, K. R.**

Australasian school atlas, physical, political economic and historical. xvi, 64, [4] pp. incl. 58 col. maps, 3 pl., 2 diagrs. 4°. Melbourne, H. Milford, 1915. 5317

NOTE.—Contains an "Introduction, a guide to the historical maps."

"The maps in the historical section of this atlas have been carefully compared with originals and copies in the Mitchell library, Sidney."

On pp. XIV & XV: "Map projections" with diagrams contain maps of the following cities: Sidney.—Melbourne.—Adelaide.—Constantinople.—Venice.—Naples.

Also reproductions of early maps showing the gradual development of the cartography of Australia, including the "Dauphin chart 1530 circa, supposed to be the first map of Australia."—Maps showing interior explorations from 1788–1901.—Maps illustrating the "Constitutional history" of Australia, from 1786 to 1914.—General index.

The following maps relate to America:

no. [1] Time chart of the world.
" [2] The world.
" [3] Physical chart of the world.
" [4] Political divisions of the world.
" [33] North America. Physical & political.
" [34] Dominion of Canada. Physical & political.
" [35] United States & Alaska. Physical & political.
" [36] Mexico, Central America & West Indies on a uniform scale.
" [37] South America. Physical.
" [38] " " Political.
" [39] Arctic regions.—Antarctic regions.

GENERAL.

1791–1793

Beautemps-Beaupré, C. F.

Atlas du voyage de Bruny-Dentrecasteaux, contre-amiral de France, commandant les frégates la Recherche et l'Espérance, fait par ordre du governement en 1791, 1792 et 1793. Publié par ordre de sa majesté l'empereur et roi, sous le ministère de son excellence le vice-amiral Decrès. 2 p. l. 37 maps, 2 plates. fol. Paris, dépôt général des cartes et plans de la marine et des colonies, 1807. 5318

1886

Garran, A.

Picturesque atlas of Australasia, edited by hon. Andrew Garran . . . Illustrated under the supervision of Frederic B. Schell, assisted by leading colonial and american artists. With over eight hundred engravings on wood . . . 3 v. fol. Sydney, Melbourne, London, and Springfield, Mass., Picturesque atlas publishing company, ltd., 1886. 5319

NOTE.—Vol. 1 has added title-page engr.
Published in 1892 under title: *Australasia illustrated.*

1892

Garran, A.

Australasia illustrated; ed. by hon. Andrew Garran . . . illustrated by leading australian and american artists under the supervision of Frederic B. Schell. With over eight hundred engravings on wood. 3 v. fol. Sydney, New York [etc.] Picturesque atlas pub. co. 1892. 5320

1915

Philip, G., & son.

Philips' comparative wall atlas of Australasia. Edited by J. F. Umstead . . . & E. G. R. Taylor . . . Scale 1:6,000,000. 8 col. fold. maps. fol. London, G. Philip & son, [1915] 5321

NOTE.—Accompanied by *Explanatory handbook, Australasia. cover-title, 24 pp. 8°. London, G. Philip & son, 1915.*

CONTENTS.

no. [1] Climate, summer conditions, nov. 1–april 30.
" [2] Climate, winter conditions, may 1–oct. 31.
" [3] Density of population & exploration.
" [4] Economic.
" [5] Natural vegetation.
" [6] Pacific ocean.
" [7] Relief of land & communications.
" [8] Temperature.

AUSTRALIA.

1875

Stieler, A.

Adolf Stieler's hand-atlas über alle theile der erde und über das weltgebäude. Neu bearbeitet von d[r]. Aug. Petermann, d[r]. Herm. Berghaus und Carl Vogel . . . Ergänzungsheft iv . . . Inhalt: A. Petermann: Specialkarte von Australien in 9 blättern. 1: 3,500,000 . . . cover-title, 1 map on 11 sheets. obl. fol. Gotha, J. Perthes. 1875. 5322

STATE.

QUEENSLAND.

GYMPIE GOLDFIELD.

Queensland. *Geological survey.*

Geological and topographical atlas of the Gympie goldfield and environs . . . By B. Dunstan . . . cover-title, 36 col. maps. fol. [Brisbane] 1910–1911.

[Publications nos. 221A, 221B] 5323

NOTE.—At head of title, Department of mines.

ANTARCTIC REGION.

Charcot, J. B. A. E.

Deuxième expédition antarctique française (1908–1910) commandée par Jean Charcot. Sciences physiques: documents scientifiques. cover-title, 11 fold. maps. 4°. Paris, Masson & cie. 1912. 5324

INDEX

Numbers refer to main entries.
Letters t, n, c refer to titles, notes, and contents.
The number following the letter c refers to the number in the contents.

A.

B.

C.

D.

E.

F.

G.

H.

K.

L.

P.

Q.

S.

U.

V.

W.

o

Lightning Source UK Ltd.
Milton Keynes UK
UKHW020103310119
336364UK00006BA/309/P